CONTRIBUTIONS OF AGRICULTURAL ECONOMICS TO CRITICAL POLICY ISSUES

PROCEEDINGS OF
THE TWENTY-SIXTH CONFERENCE
OF THE INTERNATIONAL
ASSOCIATION OF AGRICULTURAL ECONOMISTS

Held at Gold Coast, Australia
12–18 August, 2006

Edited by
Keijiro Otsuka and Kaliappa Kalirajan
National Graduate Research Institute for Policy Studies
and
Foundation for Advanced Studies on International Development
Japan

2008

Blackwell
Synergy

350 Main Street, Malden, MA 02148-5020, USA
108 Cowley Road, Oxford OX4 1JF, UK
550 Swanston Street, Carlton, Victoria 3053, Australia

First published 2007 by Blackwell Publishing Ltd.

Library of Congress Cataloging-in-Publication Data

International Conference of Agricultural Economists (26th : 2006 : Gold Coast, Qld.)
Contributions of agricultural economics to critical policy issues : proceedings of the twenty-sixth International Conference of Agricultural Economists held at Gold Coast, Australia, 12-18 August, 2006 / edited by Keijiro Otsuka and Kaliappa Kalirajan.
        p. cm.
Includes index.
ISBN-13: 978-1-4051-8100-6 (pbk.)
1. Agriculture–Economic aspects–Congresses. I. Title: Proceedings of the twenty-sixth International Conference of Agricultural Economists. II. Otsuka, Keijiro. III. Kalirajan, K. P. IV. Title.

HD1405.I58 2008
338.1–dc22

2007033948

For further information on
Blackwell Publishing, visit our website:
http://www.blackwellpublishing.com

CONTENTS

Invited Panels

IAAE Synopsis: contributions of agricultural economics to critical policy issues

Introduction: the 26th conference of the IAAE

Keijiro Otsuka, Kaliappa Kalirajan

1. Preamble

The contribution of the agricultural sector to the growth process of any nation cannot be underestimated. This directly reflects on the contributions of agricultural economics through research and development of appropriate policy measures towards creating and maintaining the growth momentum in any country. Thus, there is a strong relationship between agricultural economics and the general welfare. This relationship gets stronger and stronger with the tremendous transformation of the agricultural sector in the last five decades across the world. The pace of transformation has been influenced differently in different countries by both "behind the border" and "beyond the border" factors, which have implications for initiating various policy measures. In the course of the transformation of agriculture, traditional subsistence farming has given way slowly and steadily to commercial farming in few countries, though subsistence farming is still predominant in several countries. The introduction of the Green Revolution in the mid 1960s has lifted agricultural productivity significantly mainly through the contribution of national and international research institutions. However, it is widely known that the impact of the Green Revolution varies widely across different countries and across regions within a country. The reasons mainly are the existing differences between farmers' potential and actual yields at the field level, which are due to differences mainly in "behind the border" factors such as natural and physical resource endowments, infrastructure facilities including market opportunities and institutional set up within which the farming communities operate. Some agricultural experts expressed a view that due to environmental degradation and other factors, the marginal productivities of the modern inputs have been falling. New avenues of growth are being researched, particularly for promoting sustainable agriculture and rainfed agriculture by eliminating the negative effects of "behind the border" factors such as lack of proper institutions that prevail within each country.

The "beyond the border" external environment factors have also changed. The World Trade Organization (WTO), a multilateral, transparent, and rule-based international organization came into existence on 1, January 1995. For the first time, agriculture, textiles, and clothing have been included under the multilateral trade discipline. Even though the Agreement on Agriculture under the Uruguay Round permits only a small reduction in subsidies and limited market access and permits many exemptions, there is a hope that in the next round of negotiations further liberalization of agricultural trade will take place to help developing countries in terms of globalizing their agriculture.

It is apparent that globalizing any country's agriculture basically has three major components: convergence of potential and realized outputs, increase in agricultural exports and value addition activities using agricultural produce, and access to domestic and international markets that are overly protected. Concerning international market access to agricultural exports, the findings of an earlier study of the OECD countries plus Korea by Kym Anderson and Yujiro Hayami (*The Political Economy of Agricultural Protection*, Allen and Unwin, London, 1986) clearly point out that protection for the agricultural sector was generally positive and that it increased between 1950 and 1980. A later OECD publication (*Agricultural Policies, Markets and Trade, Monitoring and Outlook*, OECD, Paris, 1994) estimates the producer subsidy equivalent (PSE) in the OECD countries in 1993 at 42% of the total value of agricultural output. It also estimates the average nominal assistance coefficient (ratio of border plus PSE to border price) at 1.69 for OECD as a whole, the figure varying from 1.10 in Australia to 2.93 in Japan. The implication is that food exports from developing countries may not make a quantum jump given the "beyond the border" factors and the still existing restrictions on exports based on the food self-sufficiency argument. Thus, to make developing countries' agricultural exports profitable, they should be in the form of value addition to basic agricultural produce. Exports of processed vegetables, fruits, fish, and meat products must meet environmental standards of the developed countries. In this context, it becomes imperative to disseminate information about possible export markets to farmers, so that market access is achieved with minimum cost. Given the information about market and profitability, the possibility of farmers investing and developing appropriate local infrastructures is very high.

In the context of making agriculture profitable to farmers, recently, Hayami (2005) in his Presidential Lecture at the Fifth Conference of the Asian Society of Agricultural Economists held in Iran argued that governments in middle-income countries are confronted with two competing issues of securing low-cost food to urban consumers and supporting the income of farmers in rural areas, which force them to tinker with agricultural policies widening the income gap between farm and nonfarm workforce. He further called for more research in this area to prevent such a widening of income gap between farm and nonfarm workers, which has the potential to lead to several unwanted socioeconomic problems derailing the growth momentum.

Therefore, a critical policy question that has occupied the minds of many researchers and policymakers in recent times is what type of policy reforms should be implemented toward eliminating the negative effects of "behind the border" and "beyond the border" factors to make agriculture and allied activities provide a decent livelihood to rural dwellers in general and to the farmers in particular. It is in this context; the theme of the 26th conference, *Contribution of Agricultural Economics to Critical Policy Issues* sets in. The President of the IAAE, Prabhu Pingali, himself took up the issue of the impact of "behind the border" and "beyond the border" factors on agricultural and overall economic development by addressing *Agricultural Growth and Economic Development: A View through the Globalization Lens*. He argues that there has been strong empirical evidence that agriculture growth has significantly led to overall economic development in several countries with the exception of a few. The central focus of his address is to identify the "behind the border" and "beyond the border" factors "that contribute to or constrain the process of agricultural transformation." The important question that he has raised is: Will the opportunities created due to the process of globalization be utilized by developing countries without further marginalizing lower income developing countries? He has prescribed the type of policy interventions that are needed "to reduce the costs of transition to a globalized agricultural system" without neglecting those who are left behind the process of globalization. Finally, he concludes with a thought-provoking question: "For low income countries with a high share of rural populations and few opportunities outside the agriculture sector, if agriculture cannot be the 'engine of growth,' then what can?"

Hans Binswanger, who delivered the prestigious Elmhirst Lecture at the conference, in a way provided answers to some of the questions raised in the presidential address. In his address, *Empowering Rural People for their Own Development*, Binswanger discussed "the features of the institutional environment which allow rural people in low income countries to design, plan and implement their own rural development." For analytical purposes, he classified the institutional environment into two broad categories of "behind the border" and "beyond the border" factors, which he calls "the institutional environment for rural development (the private sector, communities, civil society, local government, and sector institutions) and the factors governing profitability of investment in agriculture." Though he supports the view that there has been improvement in the institutional environment in several low-income countries over the last two decades, he points out that, "the most poorly performing countries still have by far the poorest environment for local government in the world." He elaborates by arguing that "within an empowering institutional environment, the rate of agricultural and rural development is determined by investments of many different types that in turn depend primarily on the profitability of agriculture. Among the many factors that determine profitability few are under the direct control of farmers or agricultural sector institutions, but depend on governance and investments in other sectors such as trade and transport. In many of the poorest countries there has been considerable improvement in macro-economic management and sector policies over the past 20 years, but progress in international and intra-regional trade policies, in agricultural trade policies, in transport infrastructure, and in agricultural research and extension has been limited."

When both "nature-made" and "human-made" obstacles disturb the potentially positive equilibrium relationship between agricultural growth and the general welfare, what the policy prescriptions to correct the disequilibrium should be are discussed in the conference under the following four major headings: (1) Economics of Natural Disasters; (2) Trade and Marketing of Agricultural Commodities in a Globalizing World; (3) Risk, Food Safety, and Health; and (4) Transformations of Unfavorable Areas: Technologies, Institutions, and Market Access.

2. Economics of natural disasters

It is very much saddening to learn that the December 2004 tsunamis destroyed and devastated the lives of several thousands of people in South and Southeast Asia and before that in January 2004, Cyclone *Heta* destroyed most crops and plantations in South Pacific islands leaving many families with no regular flow of income. Discussions about what policy measures need to be taken to escape from such natural disasters that mostly affect the poor and the vulnerable were organized as the first plenary session. Hartwig de Haen and Günter Hemrich analyzed the impact of natural disasters on food security in their article *The Economics of Natural Disasters: Implications and Challenges for Food Security*. The authors argue for the need for mutually supportive development policy and disaster management to alleviate disaster impact on poor and vulnerable groups. They further argue that "... in disaster-prone locations measures to improve disaster resilience should be an integral part of food security policies and strategies." The authors extended their analysis from the "twin-track approach to hunger reduction to a 'triple track approach,' giving due attention to crosscutting disaster risk management measures." Their policy prescription to reduce disaster risk vulnerability in agriculture is that the strategies for protecting agricultural lands, water, and other assets should be given high priorities in the formulation of development and food securities policies by the governments. The authors point out that an important contribution of agricultural economists in disaster risk management programs is to measure the benefits, costs, and trade-offs involved.

The next article, by Stephen Devereux, also concerns food security. However, this article considers the impact of two contrasting disasters of droughts and floods on food security. As the title *The Impact of Droughts and Floods on Food Security and Policy Options to Alleviate Negative Effects* suggests, the article also discusses different policy options to mitigate the problems. Drawing on Amartya Sen's "entitlement approach," this article develops an analytical procedure to examine the impacts of droughts and floods on rural livelihoods with a special focus on Malawi. The author cautions that weather shocks may induce a sequence of "entitlement failures" and if there were no government policy interventions to alleviate such failures, the result would be famine. "Policy responses can compensate for failures of production-based entitlement (free or subsidized input distribution); labor-based entitlement (public works programmes or 'employment-based safety nets'); trade-based entitlement (grain reserve management or food pricing policies); and transfer-based entitlement (food aid or cash transfers)."

The third article, by Yasuyuki Sawada, analyzes *The Impact of Natural and Manmade Disasters on Household Welfare*. As a first step in the analysis, he considers "*ex ante* risk management and *ex post* risk-coping behaviors separately, showing evidence from the Asian economic crisis, earthquakes, and tsunami disasters." In the next step, he differentiates "idiosyncratic risks from nondiversifiable aggregate risks which characterize a disaster." He further discusses "the difficulties of designing index-type insurance against natural disasters, which are often rare, unforeseen events." Finally, he investigates "the role of self-insurance against large-scale disasters under which formal or informal mutual insurance mechanisms are largely ineffective." An important result of his analysis is: "Credit accessibility is identified as one of the key factors facilitating risk-coping strategies."

3. Trade and marketing of agricultural commodities in a globalizing world

While the first plenary session discussed the impact of mostly "nature-made" disasters on food security and general welfare of households, the next plenary session discussed the impact of mitigating mostly "human-made" constraints on agricultural trade. The first article, *The Doha Agenda and Agricultural Trade Reform: the Role of Economic Analysis* by Will Martin and Kym Anderson, discusses the contribution of economics towards improving our understanding and measuring of the welfare gains from liberalizing agricultural trade. "This paper shows that research on international agricultural trade reform can make much greater contributions to understanding than was feasible in earlier trade negotiations. While current models typically estimate gains of less than one percent of GDP, new developments in theory and methodology provide the potential for quantitative analysis to be improved in at least six areas: measurement of protection for goods; incorporation of barriers to foreign trade and investment in services; representation of the counterfactual; disaggregation of products and regions; incorporation of new products; and inclusion of the productivity enhancement associated with trade reform."

The second article, *Globalization, Privatization, and Vertical Coordination in Food Value Chains in Developing and Transition Countries* by Johan F. M. Swinnen and Miet Maertens, discusses how the transformation in food and agricultural commodity value chains in developing and transition economies took place over the years. The authors argue that liberalization and privatization policies made the state-controlled vertical coordination disintegrate gradually over time. "More recently, private vertical coordination systems have emerged and are growing rapidly as a response to consumer demand for food quality and safety on the one hand and the farms' production constraints caused by factor market imperfections." The objectives of this article are to "(a) demonstrate the importance of these changes, (b) discuss the implications for efficiency and equity, and (c) provide empirical evidence on the effects in several developing and transition countries." In the next article, *Food Regulation and Trade under the WTO: Ten Years in Perspective,* David Orden and Donna Roberts provide a review of the performance of the World Trade Organization with particular reference to national regulatory policies affecting agricultural and food trade. This article highlights how important it is to eliminate the negative effects of "beyond the border" constraints to agricultural trade. "A picture emerges of modest international disciplines on the regulatory decisions of sovereign nations and the need for ongoing improvements. A road map to regulations is presented and empirical assessments of the effects

of technical regulation on trade are reviewed. Conflicts over sanitary and phytosanitary barriers raised in the relevant WTO committee are summarized and formal dispute settlement cases involving technical trade barriers are evaluated. Drawing on these reviews, suggestions are made for improving international food regulation."

4. Risk, food safety, and health

The third plenary session is highly correlated with the first two plenary sessions in the sense that "nature-made" and "human-made" disasters and food security were discussed in the first two sessions, while food safety and health risks occupied the attention in the third session. Matin Qaim, Alexander Stein, and J. V. Meenakshi through their article *Economics of Biofortification* discuss the existence of malnutrition and remedies to overcome this serious public heath problem in developing countries. Their analysis concentrates on biofortification, which is a breeding program for staple food crops fortified with micronutrient contents. Though not much about its negative implications, if any, are discussed, they highlight "the main factors influencing success" along with discussion of "a methodology for economic impact assessment." They point out that the possibility of biofortified crops reducing the shortage of micronutrients present in food consumption in India and other countries in a cost-effective way is high. They argue that more empirical research is required with data from several countries to consolidate the impact of biofortification on human health and to examine some of the unresolved questions concerning this modern agriculture-based method of biofortification.

Dina Umali-Deininger and Mona Sur, in their presentation *Food Safety in a Globalizing World: Opportunities and Challenges for India*, argue for partnership of government and private sector to promote food safety citing their empirical research with data from India. "Rising incomes and urbanization, increasing consumer awareness prompted by widely publicized food safety crises and an expansion in agricultural exports have been important drivers for the increased attention to food safety in India. But the development of effective food safety systems is hampered by a number of factors, including: restrictive government marketing regulations, a weak policy and regulatory framework for food safety, inadequate enforcement of existing standards, poor market infrastructure and agricultural support services, and the predominance of small farms. Addressing food safety concerns in India is likely to require adoption of appropriate legislation, strengthening capacity to enforce rules, promoting adoption of good agricultural, manufacturing and hygiene practices, greater collective action, and some targeted investments." An important question concerning food safety is whether it is a global public good. If so, is there sufficient investment in food safety globally? These are the questions raised and analyzed by Laurian J. Unnevehr in her presentation *Food Safety as a Global Public Good*. She argues, "Globalization of the food system increases the shared risks from food safety, making it a global public good. Food safety is addressed as a global public good through improved private sector information, institutional innovations such as the Sanitary and Phytosanitary Standards (SPS) Agreement under the World Trade Organization, and trade capacity building to improve food safety in developing country exports. Although meeting standards for high income consumers motivates trade facilitation, there could be large positive spillovers for developing country consumers from such investments." However, as discussed in the Elmhirst lecture by Binswanger, several developing countries may find it difficult to adjust their method of production to satisfy SPS requirements of developed countries with minimal adjustment cost and collaboration and integration among countries will be a feasible choice to comply with SPS regulations at an affordable cost.

5. Transformation of unfavorable areas: technologies, institutions, and market access

In the presidential address Pingali has emphasized that scientific research and technological development can facilitate farmers operating in unfavorable areas to improve their productivity by reducing production variablility. While research and development has contributed to agricultural growth in unfavorable areas to some extent, Mahabub Hossain argues in his article *Technological Progress for Sustaining Food-Population Balance: Achievement and Challenges* that there is an urgent need to increase funding for more

research and technological development towards improving agricultural growth in unfavorable areas in order to meet the food-population balance. Hossain cautions about the status of agricultural technological progress, which contributed to growth until the early 1990s, by saying that there are simply not appropriate technologies at the field level for unfavorable rainfed production environments. He rings the warning bell by pointing out that lack of suitable technologies for unfavorable production environments would lead to a consequence of the world's inability to meet the food-population balance in near future. What are his suggestions to improve the research and technology situation concerning agriculture? "Rice research must deal with a number of difficult problems to meet the challenge: raising the yield ceilings of the current available rice varieties; protecting the past yield gains in the irrigated ecosystem; and using biotechnology tools to develop high yielding varieties for the rainfed systems that are tolerant to drought, submergence, and problem soils."

Thomas Reardon, Kostas Stamoulis, and Prabhu Pingali offer an additional method of improving the livelihoods of rural poor besides engaging in agricultural production in their article *Rural Nonfarm Employment in Developing Countries in an Era of Globalization*. Citing the empirical evidence that about 35% of rural income in Africa and 50% in both Asia and Latin America originated from rural nonfarm employment (RNFE), the authors highlight the surging importance of rural nonfarm income, which was once identified with "a sleepy hinterland activity cut off from changes in the national, let alone the global economy," to the livelihoods of rural poor. The authors offer "emerging evidence that the strongest and most positive effects on RNFE of globalization come in the zones that are rur-urbanized, with a tradables growth-motor induced RNFE sector with clusters of small/medium enterprises for manufactures, and a preponderance of services." The article shows that trade effects on RNFE are relatively lower than that of domestic market transformation effects. "The most challenges are posed for zones that are rur-urbanized and dense zone RNFE with low-moderate local growth motors. The least effects are on hinterland zones." The policy suggestions offered by the authors are "to promote tradables growth motors (key to creating RNFE in services, the major component of RNFE), and to incorporate 'competitiveness'—in a changing urban and global economy—into RNFE promotion."

6. Invited panels

Unlike the last publication of the proceedings of IAAE conferences, some selected articles (10 articles) from the Invited Panel are included in this volume. There were 13 Invited Panel sessions with 52 articles under the following sub-themes related to the main theme of the conference: (1) Food Safety Standards and Agri-Food Exports from Developing Countries; (2) Advances in Spatial Economic Analysis for Agricultural Economists: Tools and Topics; (3) Agriculture, Nutrition, and Health in High and Low-Income Countries: Policy Issues; (4) Drought: Economic Consequences and Policies for Mitigation; (5) Rural Industrial Clusters in Developing Countries; (6) Land Productivity, Land Markets and Poverty Reduction in Africa; (7) Access of African Farmers to Domestic and International Markets: Opportunities and Constraints; (8) The Role of Economic Statistics in Agricultural Policy Shifts; (9) Market-Based Instruments: Policy and Information Issues; (10) Economics of Biofuels; (11) Agricultural Trade Liberalization and Developing Countries: What Do We Really Know?; (12) WTO and Asian Agriculture; and (13) Using both Partial and General Equilibrium Analyses to Gain Insights into the Agricultural Trade Impacts of the Doha Development Agenda.

Per Pinstrup-Anderson examines the existing two-way causal relationship between global food system and health nutrition in his article *Agricultural Research and Policy for Better Health and Nutrition in Developing Countries: A Food Systems Approach.* He argues that development policies should be integrated rather than sector based and recommends that health policy should be integrated with food policy. He suggests that research and policies need to be tailored to bring maximum positive two-way relationship between health and nutrition and the food system. Barry Popkin and Shu Wen Ng in their article *The Nutrition Transition in High- and Low-Income Countries: What Are the Policy Lessons?* examine "the speed of changes in diets, activity patterns and body composition" in lower- and middle-income countries, which is supplemented with some examples from higher-income countries too.

They point out that the problem of obesity is "shifting from the rich to the poor globally." The authors review some of the policy options to increase the awareness among consumers about the importance of having nutritionally balanced diets.

Sushil Pandey, Humnath Bhandari, Shijun Ding, Preeda Prapertchob, Ramesh Sharan, Dibakar Naik, Sudhir K. Taunk, and Asras Sastri in their article *Coping with Drought in Rice Farming in Asia: Insights from a Cross-Country Comparative Study* argue that rice production in rainfed Asian agriculture is very much influenced by drought. In spite of the fact that drought management is crucial to increase rice production in rainfed areas, the authors drawing on a cross-country analysis of rainfed rice production in southern China, eastern India, and northeast Thailand show that the dissemination about drought coping mechanisms among farmers is very weak. The article also indicates the huge loss in income to farmers due to drought in these countries. Based on their empirical findings, the authors advocate for improved technology design and effective policy implementations to alleviate the overall welfare loss created by drought. In their article *Productivity in Malagasy Rice Systems: Wealth-Differentiated Constraints and Priorities*, Bart Minten, Jean-Claude Randrianarisoa, and Christopher B. Barrett attempt to identify the factors that are constraining rice productivity in Madagascar "using a range of different data sets and analytical methods, integrating qualitative assessments by farmers and quantitative evidence from panel data production function analysis and willingness-to-pay estimates for chemical fertilizer." They have suggested ways to improve fertilizer application at farm level to increase productivity.

Bruce Gardner, Barry Goodwin, and Mary Ahearn in their article *Economic Statistics and U.S. Agricultural Policy* brings out the relationship between statistics and agricultural policy making in the United States. Using historical data, the authors show the diversity that exists in the interplay between economic statistics and agricultural policy. This situation points to an important issue that economic data collection should be tailored in such a way as to satisfy the needs of not only academicians, but also policy makers. Siwa Msangi and Richard E. Howitt in their article *Income Distributional Effects of Using Market-based Instruments for Managing Common Property Resources* show "the trade-offs between efficiency and equity that arise from the application of market-based instruments to a heterogenous population of agents drawing from a natural resource pool." Using the case study of groundwater, the authors highlight the importance of striking an amicable balance between efficiency and equity in designing development policies.

Mark Eigenraam, Loris Strappazzon, Nicola Lansdell, Craig Beverly, and Gary Stoneham in their article *Designing Frameworks to Deliver Unknown Information to Support Market-Based Instruments* show how a "market-based instrument has been fully integrated from desk to field with a biophysical model for the purchase of multiple outcomes" using data from Australia. The results also show the gain in procuring the environmental goods using the suggested approach. Through their article *Tariff Line Analysis of U.S. and International Dairy Protection*, Jason H. Grant, Thomas W. Hertel, and Thomas F. Rutherford illustrate a methodology that combines a partial equilibrium model with a standard general equilibrium model for the analysis of tariff line. The suggested methodology facilitates drawing policy implications both at micro and macro levels.

Another study that combines aggregated and disaggregated analytical frameworks for trade analysis is by Sebastian Hess and Stephan von Cramon-Taubadel. Their article, *Meta-Analysis of General and Partial Equilibrium Simulations of Doha Round Outcomes*, shows that though simple regression results may be feasible, nonexperts may not easily understand interpretations of the results due to various interactions of model characteristics. Hence, the authors argue for the importance of meta-analysis, which considers the interactions of model characteristics facilitating direct interpretation of results. Mohamed Hedi Bchir, Stephen N. Karingi, Andrew Mold, Patrick N. Osakwe, and Mustapha Sadni Jallab in their article *The Doha Development Round and Africa: Partial and General Equilibrium Analyses of Tariff Preference Erosion* examine "the importance of preference erosion question due to MFN liberalization on agriculture." How the ranking of preference erosion is influenced by the selected methodology is analyzed using general and partial equilibrium analyses. The authors conclude that preference erosion affects both welfare and incomes for preference-receiving countries.

We are sure this brief introduction will motivate the readers to explore the full contents of these articles presented in this volume.

Acknowledgment

On behalf of IAAE, we would like to express our sincere gratitude to the Australian Government and the Queensland Government for their support in hosting the 26th Conference of the International Association of the Agricultural Economists in such a magnificent site on earth as Gold Coast. We are extremely pleased to report that well more than one thousand participants attended the conference, which is the record in the 77-year history of the IAAE. Moreover, we have had extremely serious, thought-provoking, and useful debates throughout the conference. Without generous support of the national and state governments of Australia, such a successful conference could not have been organized.

We would like to acknowledge great contributions to the extremely successful conference by the Local Organizing Committee (LOC), the Conference Program Committee consisting of members of the IAAE, and a large number of sponsors. The LOC led by Julian Alston, Philip Pardey, and Malcolm Wagener, tirelessly organized the conference by setting up conference venues and program structure, undertaking fund raising, and coordinating conference details in collaboration with the Hoteliers led by Rhonda Hendicott and her team. Their generous support is much appreciated. We are grateful to generous sponsorship for the LOC by the Convening Sponsors (AusAID, ACIAR, ABARE, and AARES), the Premier Sponsors (Australian Government Department of Agriculture, Fisheries, and Forestry, The ATSE Crawford Fund, Queensland Government Department of Primary Industries and Fisheries, Victorian Government Department of Primary Industries, Victorian Government Department of Sustainability and Environment, and Grains Research & Development Corporation), Major Sponsors (Australian Government Rural Industries Research and Development Corporation and Murray-Darling Basin Commission), Other Conference Sponsors (Department of Agriculture and Food, AgEcon Search, URS, Yalumba, Australian Government Grape and Wine Research Corporation, Winemakers' Federation of Australia, Buller, and John Duval Wines), and the Pre-Conference Workshop Sponsors (The ATSE Crawford Fund, An Australian Government Initiative Biotechnology Australia, Monsanto, INSTEPP, Cargill, World Bank, UC Davis, IFPRI, Canola Canada, Ford Foundation, USDA, Stanford University, JATRC, Australian Government National Water Commission,

FAO, and Ministry of Agriculture, Forestry, University of California Agricultural Issues Center, the Ministry of Agriculture, Forestry, and Fisheries of Japan).

Ruerd Ruben and Kees Burger of the Wageningen University managed the administration of selecting contributed articles. They conducted review of a record high 865 articles in the most efficient manner and splendidly organized a large number of contributed article sessions. In collaboration with Ruerd Ruben and Kees Burger, William Meyers of the University of Missouri and Vince Smith of the Montana State University engaged in the selection of the poster papers. Jikun Huang and Linxiu Zhang of the Chinese Academy of Science were responsible for the selection and organization of symposia, whereas Oscar Cacho of the University of New England organized computer presentations. The invited panel sessions were organized by Kei Otsuka. These conference program committee members made every effort to select through careful reviews the best contributed and poster papers, invited panels, and symposia, while adding the space of a nearby hotel to accommodate an unexpectedly large number of sessions. We would also like to mention the contribution made by Philip Pardey and Julian Alston for the wonderful organization of the Pre-Conference Workshops on Biotechnology, China, Water, and Trade Policy, and Learning Workshop. The daily newssheet, Cowbell, was nicely edited by Wally Tyner of Purdue University.

IAAE received generous financial supports from a large number of organizations, including African Economic Research Consortium (AERC), Agricultural Economics Society of Japan, American Agricultural Economics Association Foundation (AAEA), Department for Environment, Food and Rural Affairs of UK (DEFRA), FAO, International Agricultural Trade Research Consortium (IATRC), IFPRI, Jimmye and Helen Hillman Foundation, Richard Keenan & Co. Ltd., and European Commission—African, Caribbean, and Pacific (EC-ACP). In addition, DEFRA, IFAD, IRRI, National Graduate Institute for Policy Studies of Japan (GRIPS), Sasakawa Africa Association, United Kingdom Agricultural Economics Society, and USAID supported symposia. In total we received nearly US$280 thousand and supported the participation of almost 110 researchers from developing countries.

We would like to congratulate seven selected Honorary Life Members: Douglas Hedley, Roley Piggott, Jimmye Hillman, Michele Veeman, Robert Evenson, Wilfred Mwangi, and Arie Kuyvenhoven.

Finally, we would like to thank President Prabhu Pingali, the Elmhurst Lecture presenter, Hans Binswanger, and the authors of the plenary, and invited panel articles who have contributed to this volume. Because of the space limitation, a limited number of invited panel articles were selected and included in this volume. Needless to say, all the participants in the IAAE Conference, including discussants of the plenary articles, made truly invaluable contribution to this volume. We would like to thank all of them. Thanks are also due to Mayuko Tanaka for her excellent editorial assistance.

Agricultural growth and economic development:
a view through the globalization lens

Prabhu Pingali*

Abstract

This article re-visits the age-old proposition that agriculture growth contributes to overall economic development, and asks whether the relationship still holds in an increasingly globalized world. There is overwhelming empirical support for the above proposition, indeed, it is hard to find exceptions, barring a few city states, where sustained economic development has not been preceded by robust agricultural growth. However, there are a large number of countries that have witnessed neither agricultural growth nor economic development. Even in countries where agricultural growth has been significant, dramatic inter-regional differences persist. This article examines the factors that contribute to or constrain the process of agricultural transformation. Does the process of globalization, and the resultant changes in agrifood systems, offer new opportunities for agriculture-led growth, or will it further marginalize excluded countries, regions, and groups? The factors that cause exclusion are examined both in terms of globalization forces and in terms of domestic shortcomings in policies and governance. Policy interventions that attempt to reduce the costs of transition to a globalized agricultural system are explored, including safety nets for those left behind.

JEL classification: N50, O13, O38, Q13, Q18

Keywords: agricultural growth; economic development; globalization; food imports; agricultural transformation; sustainable resource use

1. Agricultural growth and economic development

Development economists in general and agricultural economists in particular have long focused on how agriculture can best contribute to overall economic growth and modernization. Many early analysts (Rosenstein-Rodan, 1943; Lewis, 1954; Scitovsky, 1954; Hirschman, 1958; Jorgenson, 1961; Fei and Ranis, 1961) highlighted agriculture because of its abundance of resources and its ability to transfer surpluses to the more important industrial sector. The conventional approach to the roles of agriculture in development concentrated on agriculture's important market-mediated linkages: (i) providing labor for an urbanized industrial work force; (ii) producing food for expanding populations with higher incomes; (iii) supplying savings for investment in industry;

(iv) enlarging markets for industrial output; (v) providing export earnings to pay for imported capital goods; and (vi) producing primary materials for agroprocessing industries (Johnston and Mellor, 1961; Ranis et al., 1990; Delgado et al., 1994; Timmer, 2002).

There are good reasons for why these early approaches focused on agriculture's economic roles as a one-way path involving the flow of resources towards the industrial sector and urban centers. In agrarian societies with few trading opportunities, most resources are devoted to the provision of food. As national incomes rise, the demand for food increases much more slowly than other goods and services. As a result, value added from the farm household's own labor, land, and capital as a share of the gross value of agricultural output falls over time. Farmers' increasing use of purchased intermediate inputs and off-farm services adds to the relative decline of the producing agriculture sector, *per se*, in terms of overall GDP and employment (Timmer, 1988; 1997; Pingali, 1997).

Agricultural and Development Economics Division, FAO, United Nations, Rome, Italy.

Rapid agricultural productivity growth is a prerequisite for the market-mediated linkages to be mutually beneficial. Productivity growth that resulted from agricultural R&D has had an enormous impact on food supplies and food prices, and consequent beneficial impacts on food security and poverty reduction (Hayami and Herdt, 1977; Pinstrup-Andersen et al., 1976; Binswanger, 1980; Hazell and Haggblade, 1993).

Because a relatively high proportion of any income gain made by the poor is spent on food, the income effects of research-induced supply shifts can have major nutritional implications, particularly if those shifts result from technologies aimed at the poorest producers. (Alston et al., 1995, p. 85)

Agricultural productivity growth also triggers the generation of nonmarket mediated linkages between the agricultural sector and the rest of the economy. These include the indirect contributions of a vibrant agricultural sector to: food security and poverty alleviation; safety net and buffer role; and the supply of environmental services (FAO, 2004a). While agriculture's direct, private contributions to farm households are tangible, easy to understand, and simple to quantify, its numerous indirect benefits tend to be overlooked in assessing rates of returns. Ignoring the whole range of economic and social contributions of agriculture underestimates the returns to investment in the sector (Valdes and Foster, 2005).

Substantial empirical evidence exists on the positive relationship between agricultural growth and economic development (Valdes and Foster, 2005). The transformation of agriculture from its traditional subsistence roots, induced by technical change, to a modernizing and eventually industrialized agriculture sector is a phenomenon observed across the developing world. However, there are also a large number of countries that have stalled in the transformation process or have yet to "get agriculture moving." These are almost always countries that are classified as the "least developed." Even within countries that are well on the pathway towards agricultural transformation there are significant inter-regional differences (Eastern India, for example). Some of the reasons for the poor performance of their agriculture are as follows:

(i) low and inelastic demand for agricultural output due to low population density and poor market access conditions;

(ii) poor provision of public good investments in rural areas;

(iii) lack of technology R&D on commodities and environments important to the poor;

(iv) high share of agro-climatically constrained land resources; and

(v) institutional barriers to enhancing productivity growth.

Will globalization make a difference? Will trade integration and increased global inter-connectedness enhance or impede the process of agricultural transformation for countries that have successfully used agriculture as an "engine of growth." What about countries at the low end of the transformation pathway? These questions are addressed in the rest of the article.

2. Globalization and the transformation of food systems

Globalization has resulted in the rapid growth of world trade, internationalization of production by multinational corporations, and declining information and communications costs. The potential trade benefits for agriculture arise from three aspects. The first stems from the possibility of directly increased exposure of agriculture to international competition. The ability to access global markets and specialize in areas of comparative advantage could yield high gains for this sector. The second stems from the indirect effects of increased international trade on the growth of non-agricultural sectors changing the domestic demand for agricultural goods both quantitatively and qualitatively (Pingali and Khwaja, 2004).

Third, an often-unrecognized consequence of globalization is lifestyle changes including diets, particularly among the urban middle class, as a result of increased global inter-connectedness through travel and communications. The diet transition is characterized by diversity, convenience, and a break from tradition. Consumers in large, urban centers are more exposed to nontraditional foods as a result of their access to food retail outlets and marketing campaigns (Reardon et al., 2003). Large urban markets create the scope for the establishment of large supermarket chains, and they attract foreign investments and advertising from global corporations. Nontraditional foods are more accessible as a result of trade liberalization and declining costs of transportation and communication (Chopra et al., 2002). Moreover as more women enter the labor force, we expect to see an increase in the consumption of processed food, ready-made meals, or meals that cut the long preparation time of traditional dishes (Regmi and Dyck, 2001).

Food markets in developing countries are undergoing profound changes that are fuelled by rapid urbanization, diet diversification, trade integration, and the liberalization of foreign direct investment in the food sector. The most commonly observed changes are: (i) rising food imports; (ii) vertical integration of the food supply chain; and (iii) commercialization and diversification of domestic production systems.

2.1. Rising food imports

FAO's study on agriculture towards the year 2015/2030 indicates that the trends in international trade of foodstuffs, which have seen developing countries turn from net exporters to net importers of food commodities, are expected to continue in the future (FAO, 2002). In 1961/1963 developing countries as a whole had an overall agricultural trade surplus of US$6.7 billion, but this gradually disappeared so that by the end of the 1990s trade was broadly in balance, with periodic minor surpluses and deficits. In the case of the least developed countries (LDCs) the deficit is much more pronounced; by end of the 1990s, agricultural imports were more than double their exports (FAO, 2004b). The outlook to 2030 suggests that the agricultural trade deficit of developing countries will widen markedly, reaching an overall net import level of US$31 billion (FAO, 2002).

The net imports of the main commodities in which the developing countries as a group are deficient (mainly cereals and livestock products) will continue their rapid rise. At the same time, the net trade surplus in traditional agricultural exports (for example, tropical beverages, bananas, sugar, vegetable oils, and oilseeds) is expected to rise less rapidly or to decline (FAO, 2002). Over the past three decades the share of gross food imports in GDP more than doubled for an average developing country. The increase was most pronounced for the LDCs, where the value of food imports rose from 1% of GDP to over 4% (FAO, 2004b).

Over the past 30 years the countries most vulnerable to food insecurity (the LDCs) have spent, on average, an increasing share of their limited foreign exchange earnings on commercial food imports (FAO, 2004b).

Increased developing country imports of cereals and livestock products are due to increased demand combined with the low competitiveness of their domestic agriculture, though the relative weight of these factors varies across countries. Low competitiveness is often the result of insufficient resource mobilization for the enhanced competitiveness of poor rural communities, the sustainable use of natural resources, the provision of market infrastructure, and research. Growing food imports are also the result of inflows of lower-priced food from subsidized agriculture in developed countries. Rapid urbanization, especially the growth of mega-cities on the coast, has added to the competitiveness of food imports relative to transporting it from the hinterlands.

With regard to agricultural exports, markets for traditional exports are generally saturated, but there is potential for significant gains by developing countries if the processing and marketing of value-added tropical products is moved from consumer to producer countries (FAO, 2004b). However, lack of capacity on the part of the exporters and the presence of tariff escalation in the importing countries both contribute to the loss of potential export revenue. Capacity limitations are particularly felt in markets where access depends on increasingly strict sanitary and phytosanitary standards. Much is said about the developing countries responding to niche markets, but they will always be just that—niche markets, small, highly variable and subject to the vagaries of changing consumer demand.

2.2. The vertical integration of the food supply chain

The change in urban food demand is almost simultaneously accompanied by consolidation in the retail sector. The result is an impressive increase in the volume of food marketing handled by supermarkets, but also substantial organizational and institutional changes throughout the food marketing chain (Dolan and Humphrey, 2001). Such changes include the setting of private grades and standards for food quality and safety, and the adoption of contracts between buyers and sellers at various points along the food marketing chain.[1]

Subcontracting for products of specified quality and traits is likely to proliferate as a form of interaction between retail food chains and producers. If regions where supermarket retailing is more developed (for example, Latin America) are a precursor of what will follow elsewhere, then supermarkets and large-scale distribution will progressively dominate the food marketing chain in urban areas. Vertically integrated supply chains have also been focusing on the export market. There are numerous examples of successfully integrated food supply systems that are managed from the farm to the consumer's plate (Reardon and Berdegué, 2002a; Reardon et al., 2002, 2003).

However, concentration of food trade in the hands of a few retailers and large market intermediaries threatens the existence of small traders and small business, central "spot" food markets and neighborhood stores. On the production side, these trends may mean the gradual disappearance of those smallholders who are unable to meet the private standards on health and safety set by large retailers and wholesale buyers as well as neighborhood stores and spot wholesale markets (Dolan and Humphrey, 2001; Reardon and Berdegué, 2002b). The prospects for small holder agriculture are discussed in the next section.

2.3. Changing agricultural production systems

There are five issues at stake in this area. First, an increasing commercial orientation of production systems is expected due, *inter alia*, to rapidly rising urban food demand, changing consumption patterns, and the increasing integration of domestic and international markets for agricultural products. Some of the resulting changes include: larger operational holdings; reduced reliance on nontraded inputs; and increased specialization of farming systems. While the speed of these transformations differs substantially across countries, they are all moving in the same direction (Pingali, 1997).

As economies grow, the returns to intensive production systems that require high levels of family labor are

---

[1] See Reardon and Berdegué (2002a) and Reardon et al. (2002, 2003) for a more comprehensive coverage of the issues related to the proliferation of supermarkets.

generally lower than those from exclusive reliance on purchased inputs. With the expected rise in operational holding size, the ability of the household to supply adequate quantities of nontraded inputs declines. Power, soil fertility maintenance, and crop care are the primary activities for which nontraded inputs are used in subsistence societies. With the increased opportunity costs, family labor will be used less as a source of power and more as a source of knowledge (technical expertise), management, and supervision.

Farm decisions become increasingly responsive to market signals, domestic as well as international, and less driven by traditional practice. While at a regional or subregional level, trends towards diversification out of cereal monoculture systems are being observed, at the individual farm level the trend is towards product specialization. In China, for example, while livestock production was traditionally a sideline activity for farm households, more farms are now specializing in livestock production. Chinese households that specialize in livestock production accounted for 15% of national livestock production in 2000 (Fuller et al., 2001).

Second, in the process of commercialization, rapidly increasing scales of production are being observed particularly in the livestock sector, trying to supply rapidly growing markets for meat, milk, and eggs. Both global analyses and country case studies (conducted by FAO in Brazil, India, Thailand, and the Philippines) confirm that advanced technology embodied in breeds and feeds appears to be critical to the success stories for poultry around the world, and the same is likely to become true for hogs over time. Much of this technology appears to be transferable, but only at relatively large scales of operation, at least for poultry. Thus there is strong reason to believe that technology itself is a prime driver of the displacement of smallholders from the livestock sector. Small-scale producers obtain lower financial profits per unit of output than large-scale producers, other things equal. This suggests that, in the absence of deliberate action, small-scale producers will eventually be put out of business by competition from large-scale producers, especially since the better-off producers will scale up (De Haen et al., 2003).

Third, the observed negative relationship between the farm size and productivity may not hold as agricultural systems become more vertically integrated. There is a considerable literature that testifies to the productive efficiency of small farms (see Eastwood et al. (2005) for an extensive review of the literature). On the basis of this, it is argued that small farms, if they can overcome some constraints, tend to be more productive than large farms. The major reason cited for higher levels of efficiency is the higher productivity of farm family labor and lower supervision costs compared to large farms. However, this efficiency is often rooted in traditional labor-intensive cereal crop production where the opportunity cost of family labor is low. It is unlikely that small farms sustain this advantage in a vertically integrated food supply system because of the transactions costs involved in participation. Also, rising wages and the decreasing relevance of traditional knowledge systems further reduce the advantage for small farms.

Fourth, declining competitiveness of marginal lands could be expected with increased integration of global food markets. Marginality could be a consequence of remoteness to sources of demand, such as mega cities, or because of poor agro-climatic conditions, such as drought-prone environments. Global integration of food markets makes availability of food through imports, particularly for cities on the coast, cheaper than bringing food from the hinterlands. Moreover, low productivity and lack of technology for marginal lands make them harder to compete against better-endowed environments.

Fifth, preserving the natural resource base will be a formidable challenge. Policies for enhancing food security through the promotion of intensive agriculture production systems, such as irrigated rice systems in Asia, have had significant environmental costs, which in turn limit productivity. The problem was not intensification, *per se*, but rather the limited incentives at the farm level for efficient and judicious use of inputs such as fertilizers, pesticides, and water (Pingali, 1998). Also, the costs associated with the loss of environmental goods and services were not reflected in agricultural input and output prices. Further intensification and yield growth are subject to limits for reasons of plant physiology, but also because of environmental stresses associated with crop choice, improper input use, and poor management practices (Pingali et al., 1997; Murgai et al., 2001). Examples of intensification-induced degradation of the land resource base can also be found in Sub-Saharan Africa, particularly in intensive maize systems (Dixon et al., 2001). Rising

opportunity cost of labor could lead to increasing herbicide use as a substitute for hand weeding in commercializing staple crop systems. Also, where property rights are not clearly established, high-value crop production in upland environments could lead to higher risks of soil erosion and land degradation.

Will increased trade liberalization result in improved incentives for sustainable resource use? Yes, to the extent that integration into international markets increases the pressure and capacity to consider environmental values in managing natural resources, and where domestic policy reform, especially the removal of input subsidies, encourages more efficient input use. Moreover, the need to reduce unit costs of production in order to enhance the competitiveness of domestic agriculture contributes to the drive towards input use efficiency. The quest for sustaining competitiveness could contribute to environmental sustainability. However, efficiency-enhancing technologies are knowledge and time intensive, and in rapidly growing economies, rising opportunity cost of labor could work against their adoption. Finally, where rapid overall economic growth draws populations out of the agricultural sector the release of marginal lands from low productivity agriculture can contribute to increased supply of eco-system services, such as carbon sequestration and biodiversity conservation (Lipper et al., 2006).

3. Globalization impacts on the agriculture sector

Whether particular countries, regions within countries, and particular societies gain or lose in the process of globalization depends on where they are in the process of agricultural transformation and the extent to which they can adjust. Consider three categories of countries: (i) those at the low end of the agricultural transformation process; (ii) those in the process of agricultural modernization; and (iii) those at the high end of the transformation process.

3.1. Countries at the low end of the agricultural transformation process

Countries in this category are invariably low-income, least developed countries; a vast majority of them are in Sub-Saharan Africa. Most of them are in the bottom half of the UNDP's Human Development Index.

They face low prospects for meeting the Millennium Development Goals of hunger and poverty reduction. These countries essentially lose out in the process of globalization because their low productivity agricultural systems are uncompetitive in an increasingly integrated global food market. While some may benefit from exports to niche markets, the volumes tend to be small and variable and the long-term prospects are for increasingly negative terms of trade in the primary food staples (FAO, 2004b). The prospects for "getting agriculture moving" are limited by perennial obstacles such as low demand conditions, unfavorable agro-climatic environments, and poor institutions.

Moreover, a history of urban bias in macroeconomic policies and public good investments tends to dampen incentives for enhancing agricultural productivity growth. Structural adjustment policies of the late 1980s and 1990s have to some extent corrected the macroeconomic disincentives, including overvalued exchange rates; however, the bias against the rural sector created by a historical discrimination in public good investments has generally not been corrected. The easy availability of lower priced food on the global market makes it unlikely that massive rural investments will be forthcoming, especially where urban centers are located on the coast.

3.2. Countries in the process of agricultural modernization

Countries in this category have successfully used agriculture as an engine of overall growth and are experiencing a steady decline in the share of agriculture in GDP and the share of agriculture in total labor force. Rapidly growing Asian and Latin American economies, mostly in the middle-income level, are examples of countries that fall into this category. Small farm led staple food productivity growth, such as for rice and wheat, drove the process of agricultural transformation. Rising productivity in the agricultural sector has also stimulated growth in the nonagricultural sectors through forward and backward linkages. These countries witness widespread impacts of globalization, both positive and negative.

Past investments in rural infrastructure, productivity-enhancing technologies, as well as market institutions, makes these societies more responsive to global market signals. Globalization and trade integration lead to both an improvement in the competitiveness of the staple food sector as well as a move towards diversification out of staples. Reducing unit production cost through efficiency improvements is the primary means by which the staple food systems sustain their competitiveness. For instance, the switch to conservation tillage reduced production costs by as much as 30% per ton of wheat and soybean in Argentina and Brazil (Ekboir, 2003). At the same time, the staple food sector is reorientated towards supplying the diversified urban diets and towards high-value exports. The returns to diversification are, however, conditional on investments in post-harvest technologies for processing, quality, and food safety. The benefits from a global orientation of the agricultural sector can be pro-poor where the production and post-harvest activities continue to be labor intensive.

On the negative side, it ought to be noted that there can be significant inter-regional differences, even within countries well on the path towards agricultural transformation, in terms of agricultural productivity and responsiveness to urban and global market signals. Eastern India, Western China, and Northeast Brazil are examples of regions that get left behind even as these countries are making rapid economic progress. Relatively higher levels of poverty and food insecurity persist in these regions. As discussed earlier, marginal production environments face declining competitiveness. Migration to urban areas or to regions of higher agricultural productivity (such as the Indian Punjab) is one of the few viable options for small farm and landless labor populations in these areas.

The prospects for smallholders depend on the extent to which staple food production can remain competitive and the extent to which they can participate in the market for high-value products. Smallholders, even in high-potential environments, may lose out in the process of integration into the supply chains for high-value products that serve domestic or export markets.

Small farmers find an increasingly skewed structure in the food system, facing on the one hand a small and reducing number of large food companies and food retailers. On the other hand, at the point of input supply to farmers, large chemical and seed companies are creating patented input supply systems controlled by a small number of companies (e.g., Monsanto and Dekalb Genetics Corporation/Delta & Pine Land, DuPont and

Pioneer HiBred) (Napier, 2001). Facing this structure, small agricultural producers will find it increasingly difficult to negotiate favorable terms of the contract.

Thus, entering the food system on a competitive basis is problematic for small farmers because of physical investments needed to enter but also because of the transactions costs associated with the new agricultural market (Pingali et al., 2006). The increasing disconnects between the modern food system and the established social networks and traditional institutions tends to aggravate the costs of market participation. Farmers will not enter markets when the value of participating is outweighed by the costs of undertaking the transaction (Sadoulet and de Janvry, 1995).

3.3. Countries at the high end of the transformation process

These are mainly high-income countries with relatively small rural populations. Their agriculture sectors are highly commercialized, vertically integrated and globalized. For these countries the big challenge will be to create new opportunities for rural incomes while liberalizing trade. In this context the noncommodity roles of agriculture, such as biodiversity conservation, agro-tourism, carbon sequestration, provide opportunities for the emergence of markets. Preserving rural societies and landscapes becomes important not only for political and nostalgic reasons, but also as a matter of economics. This could become an increasingly important trend in middle-income countries as they reach the end of the transformation process. Public policy needs to create an enabling environment for the emergence of markets for environmental services. Direct public support for sustaining the noncommodity roles of agriculture would only be necessary under market failure conditions. Fortunately the OECD countries have the income to pay for this support, if necessary.

4. Public policy for managing agricultural transition

Designing food and agriculture policy is substantially more complex in a globalized world than it was in a world of relatively closed food economies. While chronic hunger and poverty continue to be daunting problems in much of the developing world, globalization brings about new policy challenges both for countries well into the process of agricultural transformation and for countries at the low end of the transformation process. The traditional policy agenda for promoting agricultural growth and economic development needs to be redesigned and adapted to the new realities of an increasingly inter-connected global economy. The following are some of the areas of policy focus and redirection.

4.1. Continued emphasis on promoting agriculture as an "engine of growth"

For countries at the low end of the transformation process, concerted action towards enhancing food security especially through agricultural productivity growth is crucial in the quest for income growth and economic development. The same is true for low productivity regions in countries that are well into the process of agricultural modernization. While "trickle down" from globalization-induced income growth can to some extent help alleviate poverty and food insecurity it will not be adequate without concerted efforts targeted at the neediest populations.

Some argue that the benefits of low food prices are as easily accessed by trade as by investing in domestic agriculture (Sachs, 1997). This argument ignores the strong historical connection between domestic food production and consumption because of the difficulty and expense of transporting and marketing food staples in rural areas, far from ports and efficient transport links (Timmer, 2002). "For both microeconomic and macroeconomic reasons, no country has ever sustained the process of rapid economic growth without first solving the problem of food security" (Timmer, 2002).

Enhancing food security in the rural areas entails improvements in the productivity of smallholder agriculture. In the first instance, enhancing local food supplies contributes to improved household nutrition and thereby contributes to labor performance improvements. In the long-term it broadens participation in market-led growth. Promoting sustainable use of natural resources; improving rural infrastructure, research, and communications; facilitating the functioning of markets; and enhancing rural institutions are integral parts of the strategy. Productivity-induced agricultural growth has a wider impact on rural areas through the strengthening of off-farm activities, rural employment, and wages thus moving the society, region, and country onto the agricultural transformation trajectory.

4.2. Reorienting agricultural research and development priorities

Harnessing the best of scientific knowledge and technological breakthroughs is crucial as we attempt to "retool" agriculture to face the challenges of an increasingly commercialized and globalized agriculture sector. The primary objective of the research system remains to generate new technologies that sustainably improve productivity and farmers' income. Governments have a difficult task to perform: on one hand, continued food security needs to be assured for populations that are growing in absolute terms; on the other hand, research and infrastructural investments need to be made for diversification out of the primary staples. In responding to diversification trends, the research should not abruptly shift from an exclusive focus on one set of commodities to another set of commodities. The focus of research should be to provide farmers the flexibility to make crop choice decisions and to move relatively freely between crops and other agricultural enterprises (Pingali and Rosegrant, 1995).

For countries at the early stages of the transformation process, modern science and technology can help provide new impetus for addressing the age-old problems of yield improvement, production variability, and food insecurity especially for rural populations living in marginal production environments. Whilst the real and potential gains from science and technology are apparent, it is also necessary to take into consideration the fact that research and technology development are more and more in the private domain: biotechnology is a prime example.

For commercial crops in favorable production environments private sector generated transgenic crops have reduced yield variability, and reduced unit production costs, the latter due to the diminished need for insecticides. An enabling policy environment that includes intellectual property protection, reduced trade barriers, and a transparent bio-safety procedure will lead to further private sector research investments for commercial production systems in the countries that are

well into the transformation process. However, large areas of the developing world, especially Sub-Saharan Africa, remain outside the orbit of private sector interest. The private sector is also unlikely to invest in research for difficult growing environments, such as drought-prone or high-temperature environments. Public sector research investments ought to complement the rapid progress being made by the private sector in order to meet the needs of the poor (FAO, 2004c).

4.3. Creating an enabling environment for smallholder transformation

The challenges faced by smallholder agriculture should be seen in the context of the general trends that will influence the structure of agricultural production. Namely, the transformation of diets and rising import competition will contribute to the increasing commercialization of the small farm sector. Governments ought to help create an enabling environment for smallholder commercialization through infrastructure investments and institutional reform.

Rural infrastructure investments play a crucial role in inducing farmers to move toward a commercial agricultural system. The emphasis for public investments should be on improving general transport, communications, and market infrastructure, while allowing the private sector to invest in commodity-specific processing, storage, and marketing facilities. Accessible and cost-effective communication systems such as mobile telephones can help generate information and other market-related services. The Internet explosion and related technologies have drastically reduced exchange and search costs in many Organisation for Economic Co-operation and Development countries and may be highly indicative of the potential benefits to developing countries (Bussolo and Whalley, 2002).

Efficient land markets and secure property rights are essential to capture agricultural growth (Binswanger et al., 1993). Where land rights are secure, farmers have the greater incentive needed to invest in land improvements. Moreover, land ownership is an important source of collateral that can improve the credit status of farmers, leading to easier access to funding for inputs and so forth (Feder et al., 1988). Individual farmers and households need to be assured "stable engagement" with other resources, such as water, and water use rights that are flexible enough to promote comparative advantage in food staples and cash crops. Those rights must be matched by access to rural credit and finance and the dissemination of technology and good practices in water use (De Haen et al., 2003).

4.4. Reducing small farm transaction costs

Smallholder participation in commercial and vertically integrated markets is becoming an issue of major concern, especially in countries with rapidly modernizing agricultural systems. Because transaction costs vary over households and enterprises, commodities and regions, there is no single innovation or intervention, public or private, which can reduce them. However, there are a number of ways in which market entry by small farmers can be developed. These include contract farming, the development of farmer organizations for marketing, development of the supply chain for high-value exports produced by smallholders through an appropriate mix of *private* and *public* sector initiatives, and facilitating private sector provision of market information via improved telecommunications (Kydd et al., 2000). The role of government is crucial in specifying property rights and enforcing contracts in order to promote specialization and reduce the costs of market exchange (North, 2000). Moreover, government policy needs to create incentives and send signals that encourage private sector participation in developing rural economies. The bottom line is that public sector interventions are best left for public good provision and institutional reforms to correct incomplete or absent markets. The reduction of transaction costs associated with particular production systems is best left in the hands of the private sector.

4.5. Seeking complementarity between trade and domestic policy

Trade liberalization can be a powerful tool to promote economic growth. However, low-income countries, in order to benefit from trade reform, will need to enhance domestic competitiveness through policy and institutional reform (FAO, 2005). Liberalization of domestic markets, through removal of quantitative restrictions on trade, and opening up of economies to internal trade opportunities is often a key step in starting or accelerating the process of commercialization. Trade can also have adverse effects, especially in the short run as productive sectors and labor markets adjust.

Opening national agricultural markets to international competition—especially from subsidized competitors—before basic market institutions and infrastructure are in place can undermine the agricultural sector with long-term negative consequences for poverty and food security. Some households may lose, even in the long run. To minimize the adverse effects and to take better advantage of emerging opportunities, such as those arising from agriculture diversification to bio-energy and other nonfood products, governments need to understand better how trade policy fits into the national strategy to promote poverty reduction and food security. Trade liberalization should go hand in hand with public support for improving agriculture productivity and competitiveness.

4.6. Establishing safety standards and regulations

Globalization increases the "effective demand" for safe and healthy food. Government schemes to certify quality and safe food according to public regulations are required. This is important for domestic consumption and food safety, and even more so if a country wants to access foreign markets. If a country wants to export, it is necessary that an independent body will guarantee that the produce adheres to the required quality and safety standards[2] (De Haen et al., 2003). However, public systems to ensure food quality and safety suffer from lack of organization and adequate funding. To the extent that developing country governments do not impose international-level standards, private standards are being implemented by the leading players in retail and food processing (Reardon and Farina, 2001).

---

[2] The Codex Alimentarius Commission, jointly serviced by FAO and WHO, is charged with the responsibility of developing a food code. Its recommendations are based on the principle of sound scientific analysis and evidence, involving a thorough review of all relevant information. Codex international food standards are developed to protect the health of the consumers and ensure fair practices in the food trade. The SPS Agreement of the WTO cites Codex standards, guidelines, and recommendations as the preferred international measures for facilitating international trade in food. The focus of the Codex is shifting to take account of the changing global food system.

4.7. Enhancing incentives for sustainable resource use

Public policy can play an important role in encouraging the sustainable use of natural resources. First, by correcting incentive-distorting policies that encourage unsustainable use of the resource base (Pingali and Rosengrant, 2001). Second, by identifying market-based instruments for promoting the supply of environmental services through appropriate changes in agricultural production systems and land use.

Governments have a role to play in stimulating desirable land use change as well. In the process of economic development, as agricultural populations shrink and nonagricultural sectors grow, the potential for setting aside land for nonagricultural uses is high. Conversion of marginal agricultural lands to forests contributes to carbon sequestration, watershed protection, and biodiversity conservation. OECD countries are going through this process of land use change supported by public policies such as the Conservation Reserve Program in the United States. For developing countries with similar conditions in the agricultural sector, national and international public sector support for land use changes that generate global environmental goods and services can be an important means of attaining sustainable resource use. However, the successful incorporation of environmental services into the livelihoods of the poor via changes in either agricultural production systems or land use is dependent on the presence of enabling conditions such as property rights, food security, and low transactions costs, as well as local and global recognition and willingness to pay for environmental goods and services.

4.8. Enabling income and livelihood diversification

It is important to start by recognizing that rural households, at all stages of development, rely on a diverse set of nonfarm opportunities for earning incomes and sustaining food security and livelihoods. Higher agricultural productivity has contributed to the growth in rural nonfarm and off-farm income earning opportunities through backward and forward linkages. Surveys of the rural nonfarm literature indicate rural nonfarm income represents on average 42% of rural income in Africa, 32% in Asia, 40% in Latin America,

and 44% in Eastern Europe and CIS countries (Davis, 2004; FAO 1998). The diversity of income-generating activities in the rural areas calls for policies with wider impact as opposed to sector-specific policies: education and rural infrastructure such as communications, roads, and electrification will have beneficial effects to a wide spectrum of rural activities (Winters et al., 2006). Public investments ought to be accompanied by policies that induce complementary flows of private investment. Finally, public investments made to create an enabling environment for nonfarm employment will also be useful in preparing populations for exits from rural areas as economic development proceeds.

5. Conclusions

Agricultural growth has played a historically important role in the process of economic development. Evidence from industrialized countries as well as countries that are rapidly developing today indicate that agriculture was the engine that contributed to growth in the nonagricultural sectors and to overall economic well-being. Economic growth originating in agriculture can have a particularly strong impact in reducing poverty and hunger. Increasing employment and incomes in agriculture stimulates demand for nonagricultural goods and services, providing a boost to nonfarm rural incomes as well.

Trade liberalization and global inter-connectedness pose new opportunities and challenges for developing countries. Countries that are well into the process of agricultural transformation and modernization will find themselves benefiting from exposure to globalization trends. Past investments in rural infrastructure and productivity-enhancing technologies, as well as market institutions, makes them more responsive to global market signals. The transition will be pro-poor to the extent that production and post-harvest activities continue to be labor intensive and to the extent that there is an expansion in employment opportunities outside agriculture.

The transition process is by no means frictionless. Public policy needs to pay attention to inter-regional and intra-societal differences, particularly the prospects for small farm participation in commercialized markets. Also, the absorption of the rural poor in the industrial and service sectors has significant costs in terms of learning new skills and family dislocations that need to be addressed.

Countries at the low end of the transformation process tend to lose out because their low-productivity agricultural systems are uncompetitive in an increasingly integrated global food system. These societies, most of them food insecure, face daunting physical, infrastructural, and institutional obstacles to "getting agriculture moving." Increasing and stabilizing local food supplies continues to be the primary avenue for enhancing food security and thereby contributing to labor productivity and eventual market participation. For low-income countries with a high share of rural populations and few opportunities outside the agriculture sector, if agriculture cannot be the "engine of growth," then what can?

References

Alston, J. M., G. W. Norton, and P. G. Pardey, *Science Under Scarcity: Principles and Practices for Agricultural Research Evaluation and Priority Setting* (Cornell University: Ithaca, NY, 1995).

Binswanger, H. P., "Income Distribution Effects of Technical Change: Some Analytical Issues," *South East Asian Economic Review* 1 (1980), 179–218.

Binswanger, H. P., K. Deininger, and G. Feder, "Agricultural Land Relations in the Developing World," *American Journal of Agricultural Economics* 75 (1993), 1242–1248.

Bussolo, M., and J. Whalley, "Globalization in Developing Countries: The Role of Transaction Costs in Explaining Economic Performance in India," *Development Centre Working Papers* (OECD Development Centre: Paris, 2003).

Chopra, M., S. Galbraith, and I. Darnton-Hill, "A Global Response to a Global Problem: The Epidemic of Overnutrition," *Bulletin of the World Health Organization* 80 (2002), 952–958.

Davis, J., *The Rural Non-Farm Economy, Livelihoods and their Diversification: Issues and Options* (Natural Resource Institute: Chatham, UK, 2004).

De Haen, H., K. Stamoulis, P. Shetty, and P. Pingali, "The World Food Economy in the Twenty-First Century: Challenges for International Co-operation," *Development Policy Review* 21 (2003), 683–696.

Delgado, C. L., J. Hopkins, V. A. Kelly, P. Hazell, A. A. McKenna, P. Gruhn, B. Hojjati, H. Sil, and C. Courbois, *Agricultural Growth Linkages in Sub-Saharan Africa* (US Agency for International Development: Washington, DC, 1994).

Dixon, J., A. Gulliver, and D. Gibbon, *Farming Systems and Poverty: Improving Farmers' Livelihoods in a Changing World* (FAO and World Bank: Rome, 2001).

Dolan, C., and J. Humphrey, "Governance and Trade in Fresh Vegetables: The Impact of UK Supermarkets on the African Horticultural Industry," *Journal of Development Studies* 37 (2001), 147–176.

Eastwood, R., M. Lipton, and A. Newell, "Farm Size," in R. Evenson, and P. L. Pingali, eds., *Handbook of Agricultural Economics* (North Holland Press: Amsterdam, 2005).

Ekboir, J. M., "Adoption of No-till by Small Farmers: Understanding the Generation of Complex Technologies," in L. Garcia-Torres, J. Benites, A. Martinez-Vilela, and A. Holgado-Cabrera, eds., *Conservation Agriculture: Environment, Farmers Experiences, Innovations, Socio-Economy, Policy* (Kluwer Academic Publishers: The Netherlands, 2003), pp. 749–756.

FAO, *The State of Food and Agriculture 1998: Rural Non-farm Income in Developing Countries* (Food and Agriculture Organization: Rome, 1998).

FAO, *World Agriculture: Towards 2015/2030* (FAO: Rome, 2002).

FAO, "Socio-economic Analysis and Policy Implications of the Roles of Agriculture in Developing Countries," *Research Programme Summary Report. Roles of Agriculture Project* (FAO: Rome, 2004a).

FAO, *The state of Agricultural Commodity Markets* (FAO: Rome, 2004b).

FAO, *The State of Food and Agriculture 2003–2004: Agricultural Biotechnology, Meeting the Needs of the Poor?* (FAO: Rome, 2004c).

FAO, *The State of Food and Agriculture 2005: Making Trade Work for the Poor* (FAO: Rome, 2005).

Feder, G., Y. Onchan, Y. Chalamwong, and C. Hongladarom, *Land Policies and Farm Productivity in Thailand* (Johns Hopkins University Press: London, 1988).

Fei, J. C., and G. Ranis, "A Theory of Economic Development," *American Economic Review* 514 (1961), 533–565.

Fuller, F., F. Tuan, and E. Wailes, "Rising Demand for Meat: Who Will Feed China's Hogs?" in USDA, ed., *China's Food and Agriculture: Issues for the 21st Century*. AIB-775, (Economic Research Service, United States Department of Agriculture: Washington, DC, 2001).

Hayami, Y., and R. W. Herdt, "Market Price Effects of Technological Change on Income Distribution in Semi-Subsistence Agriculture," *American Journal of Agricultural Economics* 59 (1977), 245–256.

Hazell, P., and S. Haggblade, "Farm-nonfarm Growth Linkages and the Welfare of the Poor," in Lipton, and M. J. van de Gaag, eds., *Including the Poor* (World Bank: Washington, DC, 1993).

Hirschman, A. O., *The Strategy of Economic Development in Developing Countries* (Yale University Press: New Haven, CT, 1958).

Johnston, B. F., and J. W. Mellor, "The Role of Agriculture in Economic Development," *American Economic Review* 51 (1961), 566–593.

Jorgenson, D. G., "The Development of a Dual Economy," *Economic Journal* 71 (1961), 309–334.

Kydd, J., C. Poulton, et al. *Globalisation, Agricultural Liberalisation, and Market Access for the Rural Poor* (Wye College: Kent, UK, 2000).

Lewis, W. A., "Economic Development with Unlimited Supplies of Labour," *Manchester School of Economics* 20 (1954), 139–191.

Lipper, L., P. Pingali, and M. Zurek, "Less-Favoured Areas: Looking Beyond Agriculture Towards Ecosystem Services," *ESA Working Paper* 06-07 (Food and Agricultural Organization of the United Nations: Rome, 2006).

Murgai, R., M. Ali, and D. Byerlee, "Productivity Growth and Sustainability in Post-Green Revolution Agriculture: The Case of the Indian and Pakistan Punjabs," *World Bank Research Observer* 16.2 (2001), 199–218.

Napier, R., "Global Trends Impacting Farmers: Implications for Family Farm Management," Paper presented at Pulse Days, 2001, Saskatoon (New South Wales: Australia, 2001).

North, D. C., "Revolution in Economics," in C. Menard, ed., *Institutions, Contracts, and Organisations: Perspectives from New Institutional Economics* (Edward Elgar: Cheltenham, UK, 2000).

Pingali, P. L., "From Subsistence to Commercial Production Systems: The Transformation of Asian Agriculture," *American Journal of Agricultural Economics* 79 (1997), 628–634.

Pingali, P. L., "Confronting the Ecological Consequences of the Rice Green Revolution in Tropical Asia," in C. K. Eicher and J. M. Staatz, eds., *International Agricultural Development* (Johns Hopkins University Press: Baltimore, MD, 1998).

Pingali, P. L., and M. Rosegrant, "Intensive Food Systems in Asia: Can the Degradation Problems be Reversed?" in D. R. Lee and C. B. Barrett, eds., *Tradeoffs or Synergies? Agricultural Intensification, Economic Development and the Environment* (CABI: Wallingford, UK, 2001).

Pingali, P. L., and Y. Khwaja, "Globalisation of Indian Diets and the Transformation of Food Supply Systems," ESA Working Paper No. 04-05. (FAO: Rome, Italy, 2004).

Pingali, P. L., M. Hossain, and R. V. Gerpacio, *Asian Rice Bowls: The Returning Crisis?* (CAB International: Wallingford, UK, 1997).

Pingali, P. L., Y. Khwaja, and M. Meijer, "The Role of the Public and Private Sector in Commercializing Small Farms and Reducing Transaction Costs," in J. Swinnen, ed., *Global Supply Chains, Standards, and the Poor* (CABI: Oxfordshire, UK, 2006).

Pinstrup-Andersen, P., N. Ruiz de Londaño, and E. Hoover, "The Impact of Increasing Food Supply on Human Nutrition: Implications for Commodity Priorities in Agricultural Research," *American Journal of Agricultural Economics* 58 (1976), 131–142.

Ranis, G., F. Stewart, and E. Angeles-Reyes, *Linkages in Developing Economies: A Philippine Study* (ICS Press: San Francisco, 1990).

Reardon, T., and E. M. Farina, "The Rise of Private Food Quality and Safety Standards: Illustrations from Brazil," *International Food and Agribusiness Management Review* 4 (2001), 413–421.

Reardon, T., and J. Berdegue, "The Rapid Rise of Supermarkets in Latin America: Challenges and Opportunities for Development," *Development Policy Review* 20 (2002a), 371–388.

Reardon, T., and J. Berdegue, "Supermarkets and Agrifood Systems: Latin American Challenges," *Development Policy Review* 20, (2002b).

Reardon, T., J. Berdegue, and J. Farrington, "Supermarkets and Farming in Latin America: Pointing Directions for Elsewhere?" *Natural Resource Perspectives*, no. 81 (Overseas Development Institute: London, 2002).

Reardon, T., C. P. Timmer, C. Barrett, and J. Berdegue, "The Rise of Supermarkets in Africa, Asia, and Latin America," *American Journal of Agricultural Economics* 85 (2003), 1140–1146.

Regmi, A., and J. Dyck, "Effects of Urbanization on Global Food Demand," in A. Regmi, ed., *Changing Structures of Global Food Consumption and Trade.* ERS WRS 01-1 (Economic Research Service, United States Department of Agriculture: Washington, DC, 2001).

Rosenstein-Rodan, P. N., "Problems of Industrialization of Eastern and South-Eastern Europe," *Economic Journal* 53 (1943), 202–211.

Sachs, J., "Nature, Nurture, and Growth," *Economist* June 14 (1997), 9–27.

Sadoulet, E., and A. de Janvry, *Quantitative Development Policy Analysis* (Johns Hopkins University Press: Baltimore, MD, 1995).

Scitovsky, T., "Two Concepts of External Economies," *Journal of Political Economy* 62 (1954), 143–151.

Timmer, C. P., "The Agricultural Transformation," in H. Chenery and T. N. Srinivasan, eds., *Handbook of Development Economics* (North Holland Press, Amsterdam, 1988).

Timmer, C. P., "Farmers and Markets: The Political Economy of New Paradigms," *American Journal of Agricultural Economics* 79 (1997), 621–627.

Timmer, C. P., "Agriculture and Economic Development," in B. Gardner, and G. Rausser, eds., *Handbook of Agricultural Economics* (Elsevier Science: Amsterdam, 2002).

Valdes, A. and W. Foster, *Reflections on the Role of Agriculture in Pro-Poor Growth,* paper prepared for the Research Workshop: The Future of Small Farms, Kent., Wye College, 2005.

Winters, P., G. Carletto, B. Davis, K. Stamoulis, and A. Zezza, "Rural Income-Generating Activities in Developing Countries: A Multi-Country Analysis," paper prepared for the Conference beyond Agriculture: The Promise of the Rural Economy for Growth and Poverty Reduction, January 16–18, 2006.

Empowering rural people for their own development

Hans P. Binswanger*

Abstract

This Elmhirst lecture first discusses the factors that allow rural people in low-income countries to design, plan, and implement their own rural development. These are divided into two broad groups: the institutional environment for rural development (the private sector, communities, civil society, local government, and sector institutions) and the factors governing profitability of investment in agriculture. While in many poor countries the institutional environment has improved over the last 20 years, the most poorly performing countries still have by far the poorest environment for local government in the world. Within an empowering institutional environment, the rate of agricultural and rural development is determined by investments of many different types that in turn depend primarily on the profitability of agriculture. Among the many factors that determine profitability few are under the direct control of farmers or agricultural sector institutions, but depend on governance and investments in other sectors such as trade and transport. In many of the poorest countries there has been considerable improvement in macro-economic management and sector policies over the past 20 years, but progress in international and intra-regional trade policies, in agricultural trade policies, in transport infrastructure, and in agricultural research and extension has been limited.

JEL classification: I30, O12, O13, O18, Q10, Q18

Keywords: empowerment; rural development; communities; civil society; social capital; local and central governments; agricultural profitability

1. Introduction

Between 1981 and 2001 the number of poor people living with incomes of less than a dollar a day in East and South Asia declined from 1,234 million to 702 million, or a decline of 532 million, of which the decline in China alone was 422 million. At the same time the number of people living with less than a dollar a day in Sub-Saharan Africa rose from 164 million to 316 million, or by 152 million (Chen and Ravallion, 2004). Much of these enormous differences in poverty outcomes were the consequences of sharply different performances in agricultural and rural development. For China, Ravallion and Chen (2004) show that "rural economic growth was far more important to national poverty reduction than urban economic growth; agriculture played a far more important role than

the secondary or tertiary sources of GDP. Rising inequality within the rural sector greatly slowed poverty reduction. . . . Taxation of farmers and inflation hurt the rural poor; external trade had little short term impact" (p. 1). In an earlier article, Ravallion and Datt (1995) had shown that in India rural growth was far more powerful in reducing both rural and urban poverty than urban growth, while urban growth only reduced urban poverty.

During the last four decades the agricultural performance of Sub-Saharan Africa has continuously been poor: From 1961–1964 to 1995–1998 per capita agricultural production has fallen by 13%, whereas in Asia it has grown by 69% (Gelb et al., 2000, Chapter 6). The recent poverty data and findings are perhaps the most powerful demonstration we have ever had that the fate of most of the world's extremely poor people depends on their countries' and regions' performance in agricultural and rural development. The question of which factors lead to rapid agricultural and rural development is therefore a central issue of development economics.

* *Tshwane University of Technology, Tshwane, South Africa, Community and Enterprise Development Against Stigma (CEDAS Trust), PO Box 295, Willow Acres, Tshwane 0095, South Africa.*

In my article "Patterns of Rural Development: Painful Lessons," (1994), I discussed how the fields of Agricultural and Rural Development slowly overcame the ideological and scientific biases which ruled them until the 1960's. These biases fostered policies that inflicted untold damage on rural populations in the developing world. In "Painful Lessons" I discussed a range of patterns of under-performance in agriculture. In this lecture I will concentrate primarily on the pattern of "agricultural stagnation," which primarily includes the low-income countries in Africa but also countries such as Haiti, Nepal, North Korea, or Myanmar. I will also comment on countries in Latin America, which have had reasonable agricultural growth rates, but have "prematurely expulsed agricultural labor" and therefore failed to reduce rural poverty. These countries will be contrasted with the recent high performers in Asia that benefited from the green revolution and improving policies and institutions.

The growing knowledge has led to revisions of development policies of countries and of donor institutions. The growing consensus on what needs to be done has been summarized in the World Bank agricultural and rural development strategy of (World Bank, 2003a). The objective of this lecture is not to question these consensus views. Nor will this lecture add significant new knowledge developed over the past few years. Instead the objective is to summarize once again what is known about how to foster agricultural and rural development in an easily understandable analytical framework. In addition, I will discuss how some of the ideas have evolved in the World Bank, and how well they are applied by that institution for which I have worked for 25 years.[1]

The basic premise of this article is that rural people are the key actors in planning and implementing their own agricultural and rural development (World Bank, 2002).[2] Despite our knowledge, rural people in Africa and other parts of the developing world are still blocked or hindered in doing this by poor institutions, policies, technology, and insufficient human and physical capital. The resulting under-performance is not caused by lack of knowledge, but usually by deliberate policies and institutions which tend to reduce agricultural profitability and disempower rural people, especially the poor and women (Binswanger and Deininger, 1997).

The factors that empower rural people and determine performance in agricultural and rural development fall into two broad groups: (i) the institutional environment for agricultural and rural development; and (ii) the policies and other factors that determine farm profits, agricultural investment, and rural growth. The institutional environment and policies not only determine rural growth, but also determine who can participate in development, and the distribution of the benefits. This lecture will focus mostly on growth. Of course the distribution of the benefits is equally important, not only for its own sake, but also because of the mounting evidence that more equal income and asset distributions are good for growth and poverty reduction.

2. The institutional pillars of rural development

In 1980, in a typical country in Africa, a young rural women (or man) who wanted to help develop her community found herself almost completely disempowered. Three of the five pillars of the institutional environment for rural development discussed below were poorly developed: The first pillar, the private sector, was largely confined to small-scale farming and the informal sector. Much of the marketing input supply and agro-processing was in the hands of parastatal enterprises. The second pillar, independent civil society, community organizations, and traditional authorities were highly constrained or suppressed. In the wake of decolonization, central governments had suppressed the third pillar, local government, or starved it of fiscal authority and resources. Since none of these three pillars were providing much opportunity for the young woman or man, she/he had to join the central government if she/he wanted to contribute to her community. But the central institutions failed the rural sector miserably (World Bank, 1982).

Well-structured institutions can tackle all the components of rural development, from health and education to infrastructure, agricultural services, social

---

[1] The lecture covers a very large area, and many topics are only briefly touched upon. A first place to look for more in depth discussion would be the rural development strategy of (World Bank, 2003a), as well as other references cited.

[2] In "From Many Lands: Voices of the Poor" (Narayan and Pettesch, 2002) poor people were particularly clear about being allowed to create their own institutions and organizations, and manage their own development. The Sourcebook on Empowerment and Poverty Reduction of the World Bank (2002) also stresses this view.

protection, resource management, and more. Not only does the institutional environment determine who can contribute to development and how successful it will be, it also is the most important determinant of the distribution of the benefits. More specifically, where institutions are disempowering, they can be used by strong individuals and groups to direct the benefits of development to themselves, via elite capture.

Local development is a core component of rural development, although the latter also involves nonlocal components such as transport, processing, and marketing activities. No institution by itself can carry the burden of local development. Instead the paradigm that has emerged gives equal weight to the private sector, communities and civil society, local government, and the sector institutions such as health, education, and agriculture (World Bank, 2004b). This is a departure from the past when different disciplines and sectors single mindedly advocated approaches involving only one of the four sets of actors. A broad consensus has been reached that local development (and therefore rural developments) has to be viewed as a co-production by all these four groups of actors. They need to take account their comparative advantage, delegate functions to the other partners in co-production, and reform themselves to be able to function under this new paradigm. How such an integrated approach would be fostered in a particular country should depend on past history, what currently exists and can be built on, the prevailing traditions and cultures, and past history, and a diagnosis of the existing capacities and dis-functionalities. Figure 1 illustrates this emerging consensus. One can think of the capacities of each of the sectors by the size of the circles in a country-specific variant of Figure 1. Different countries would have different diagrams with some having small circles for local governments while others would have small circles for their communities. Only country-specific analysis can reveal where the greatest weaknesses are and the best opportunities for improvements in the institutional environment. There are no universal magic bullets.

2.1. The private sector

The World Bank's structural adjustment programs identified the suppression of the private sector, the underperformance of parastatal enterprises, and the fiscal black holes they created as the root cause of the underperformance problem. While this view was par-

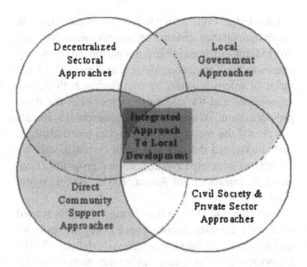

Figure 1. An integrated approach to local development.

tially correct, it was too narrow. The withdrawal of the parastatals did not lead to spontaneous growth of private replacements. Too many other problems existed in the "business environment," including corruption, overregulation, poor infrastructure and services. Only in the last few years have cross-sector analytical work and programs addressed the business environment in a systematic way (Economic Commission for Africa, 2004, 2005a; World Bank, 2005b, 2005c).

2.2. Communities, civil society, and social capital

In the early 1990s the World Bank woke up to the important role of communities, civil society, and social capital, which activists and academics had emphasized much before them. In the World Bank the focus on communities came from two sources: Sector specialists in water supply and natural resource management had started in the 1980s to involve communities systematically, and found this to enhance project performance significantly (World Bank, 1996b). The other source was social funds, which quickly discovered the power of communities to assist in project design and implementation. In some of the early Social Funds, NGOs were used as intermediaries to substitute for the presumed lack of capacity at the community level. But this approach proved to be costly and has increasingly been abandoned in favor of direct empowerment of communities with knowledge and resources, while NGOs remain important facilitators and sources of knowledge. From letting communities participate in the design, finance, and maintenance of micro-projects, World Bank-financed programs have moved on to truly empower them to choose, design, and execute a large range of micro-projects, by transferring both the responsibility and the co-financing resources for these project to them. At about the same time social scientists discovered the merits of social capital and traditional institutions, and they are now often systematically assessed and integrated into policies and programs (Economic Commission for Africa, 2005a, 2005b; World Bank, 2003b).

Since the mid 1980s a broad range of NGOs started to sharply criticize donor financed projects, policies and structural adjustment programs (Mallaby, 2004). Democratization in Africa and in other parts of the developing world created space for national and local advocacy and service NGOs (Economic Commission for Africa 2005a, 2005b). For agricultural development, a particularly important development is the formation and progressive development of independent farmers' organizations, and micro-finance institutions (World Bank, 1991a). They are increasingly replacing or complementing cooperatives that were often created by the state, and did not really lead to empowerment. The growth and development of communities, NGOs, and social capital is not only important for the implementation of development programs, diversity, and strength of these organizations but is also a defense against elite capture of programs and project benefits.

2.3. Local government

During the late 1980s democratization in Latin America, and later in other parts of the world, led to the restoration or strengthening of local governments. Nevertheless, most World Bank and IMF economists could only talk about the fiscal dangers of decentralization (Tanzi, 1991). They ignored the fact that it was usually provincial and state governments, as well as major cities, not the local governments, which were building costly institutions, and draining the coffers of central governments. Indeed, in countries as far apart as Mexico and India, states or provinces were themselves highly centralized, and a major factor in disempowering local rural populations. Fortunately by the mid 1990s, the negative views on decentralization had

given way to a more balanced assessment, recognizing both successes and failures (World Bank, 1995; Faguet, 1997; Piriou-Sall, 1997). Equal emphasis on political, administrative, and fiscal decentralization is needed. Unsuccessful decentralization programs are almost always characterized by inadequate allocation of fiscal resources to the local level (Shah, 1994; Manor, 1999). Successful decentralization is often pursued by strong leaders in relatively strong states, and puts a lot of emphasis on accountability at all levels (Manor, 1999).

Local governments can of course become an instrument for elite capture and corruption. To prevent that, they must be democratic institutions, but that in itself is not enough. Without strong communities and civil society, and a strong private sector, local governments will not be subject to the scrutiny and the bargaining processes that are needed to make local development inclusive and efficient. A bargaining equilibrium along the lines of the Becker theorem is needed as much at the local as at the national level to lead to efficient development (Becker, 1983, 1985).[3]

In the early 1990s the World Bank first discovered the power of local governments in its Community-Driven Development Programs in Mexico (World Bank, 1991b), and later in North East Brazil. The innovation spread from there to Indonesia and East Asia, then to Africa and the rest of the world. Social funds started to build the capacity of local governments, and entrust them with coordination and some implementation functions, and eventually the distinction between community-driven development and social funds

---

[3] The Becker Theorem states that bargaining will lead to decisions that will benefit all stakeholders or pressure groups (Pareto/welfare-improving choices) if the following conditions hold. (1) All pressure groups have correct and equal information about the consequences of each option. (2) All pressure groups have equal lobbying power or technology. (3) All decision and expenditures have to be evaluated against a single aggregate budget constraint. (4) Redistribution is costly. (5) The usual convexity properties that ensure a unique maximum for the model. The logic of this theorem is simple. If all groups have full information and equal bargaining power, no group can secure unanimity on proposals that benefit it alone. So the bargaining process will drive participants towards proposals that benefit all stakeholders. The common budget constraint connects the decisions to each other and ensures that decisions improve welfare for all groups. Of course the Becker Theorem portrays an ideal which human institutions can at best approximate, but institutional design and development must seek such increasing approximation.

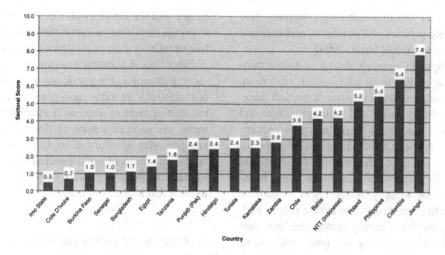

Figure 2. Index of sector decentralization in 19 countries, in the 1990s.

disappeared. A research program on Decentralization, Fiscal Systems, and Rural Development in the mid 1990s strengthened our understanding of this nexus of issues (Piriou-Sall, 1997; McLean et al., 1998). It analyzed the level of decentralization of rural service delivery in 19 countries (or provinces thereof) across the World (Figure 2). Four African countries had the lowest decentralization scores, while Jianxi province in China had the highest one. Latin American countries scored in the upper half, while Karnataka state of India ranked ninth and Punjab, Pakistan thirteenth. The recent Governance Report of the Economic Commission for Africa (2005a) shows that not much progress has been made in the past decade and a half: Decentralization, along with corruption, still receives one of the lowest scores of a whole series of governance indicators studied in 28 countries of Africa.

There are powerful reasons for using the lowest level of local government for coordination and execution of rural development. At the local level people have direct knowledge of the local conditions. Transparency is relatively easy to achieve, since people can often verify the result of expenditures, or lack thereof, with their own eyes. Given the heterogeneity of rural space, coordination of the sectors involved in rural development at the central level is almost impossible. Empowered and properly resourced local governments can mobilize latent capacities in communities and at the local level more easily than centralized systems. And finally, local governments do exist in remote areas where neither NGOs nor the private sector tend to operate.

In most OECD countries and in the high performing China, local governments perform functions in education, health, social protection, environment, agriculture, land, local and community infrastructure, and promotion of private sector development. They are a multi-sector coordination tool, even though their coordination capacity is always imperfect.

2.4. Sector institutions

In 1980, sector institutions were the main focus of donor financed programs, even though they again and again were unable to effectively implement programs in widely dispersed rural areas. There has been a growing realization that the sector institutions should delegate implementation to the private sector, communities, civil society organizations, and local governments, using the principles of subsidiarity[4] and comparative advantage. The other pillars of the institutional environment will not reach their full potential without fundamental change in the sector institutions. Instead of

---

[4] The principle of subsidiarity states that functions should be allocated to the lowest level capable of effectively performing them while at the same time minimizing adverse spillover effects to neighboring units at the same or higher levels.

providing services and implementing programs they should formulate policies, set standards, and enhance and control quality (World Bank, 2004b).

Rural development involves almost all sector ministries, from the police, local government, education, and health to land, environment, agriculture, and more. The ones specifically associated with agriculture and natural resources have often been a particularly sorry and corrupt lot. Agricultural credit institutions and insurance systems not only achieved little for small and poor farmers, they also were fiscal black holes, benefiting primarily the wealthy. Ministries of lands have lacked an effective constituency to ensure proper budgets for them, are often highly centralized, and corrupt. Ministries of agriculture are notoriously weak and politicized. In addition they are notoriously poor at collecting the necessary data, monitoring sector developments, analyzing sector policy issues, and designing and implementing appropriate agricultural policy regimes and programs. Worst of all, they are often captured by large farmer elites and function more like pressure groups for them. Efforts to reform individual sectors one by one have had little success. Transformation and de-concentration of the sector institutions is probably better done via cross-sector governance and public sector reforms.

2.5. The central government and other central institutions

Today the functions of central governments considered important for development are very different from the roles they saw for themselves in the 1960s and 1970s. Today the central government still has the ultimate design, oversight, and coordination role of national development programs, including those for rural development. But central government is less and less in a direct service delivery and executing role, except in defense, taxation, management of expenditures and of the intergovernmental fiscal system, and the electoral processes. However, the central government has a particularly important role to play in bringing about the changes needed for successful co-production among the four institutional pillars discussed above. It has to drive forward the process of decentralization of functions, resources and accountability mechanisms to local governments and to the end users, and to ensure that the sector institutions transform themselves. It has to

ensure that the business climate for the private sector improves, and that communities and civil society are free to take on their co-production functions.

Other specific central institutions, such as the judiciary, parliament, the press, and national civil society organizations are today recognized as important for rural development as well, such as for contract enforcement, resource allocation to development programs, and provision of information. In addition, they should be the guardians of good governance. They also need to press for further devolution of power and resources to local levels and communities.

3. Agricultural profits and rural investment

Once a well-developed institutional environment is in place, and except for marginal agricultural areas, rural development can be viewed as primarily a multi-faceted agricultural investment issue. Few of the needed investments will occur if agriculture is not profitable. This is obvious for the on-farm investments; but none of the other institutional pillars are in a position to invest unless agriculture and agro-industry are profitable: Unless they can save, communities will not have the means to finance or co-finance their investments. Independent civil society organizations (rather than creations from the outside) must finance a share of their costs from local sources, and these again depend directly or indirectly on profits from agriculture and other natural resources. Local governments, which do not mobilize part of their own resources tend not to be accountable to their constituencies (Manor, 1999), and instead they will be vulnerable to elite capture. The local tax base in turn depends on agricultural and natural resource profits.

It is often assumed that rural nonfarm activities can be an independent engine of growth for rural development. But most rural nonfarm activities produce goods and services that are linked to agriculture via forward, backwards, and consumer demand linkages (World Bank, 1983; Hazell and Hagbladde, 1993). Some industrial activities producing for the economy at large sometimes locate in rural areas because of low wages (Foster and Rosenzweig, 2003). But the advantage of lower rural wages is frequently offset by other disadvantages of a rural location. Therefore the potential for rural industrialization is usually overestimated. Agricultural growth, therefore, remains the single most important driver of the rural nonfarm sector.

In areas with limited agricultural potential, investment opportunities also exist, but will be limited (Fan and Hazell, 2001) even if the institutional environment is properly developed and agriculture in general is profitable. While these favorable conditions will enable the limited potential to be fully developed, that is not enough to provide for income growth of the populations of these areas. A development approach to these areas has to empower the local populations with the authority and sufficient fiscal resources to provide the necessary human development and social services, so that the new generations have the human capital needed if they choose to migrate. Those who choose to stay behind can then combine remittances and social assistance with locally earned income for a decent living standard. As Foster and Rosenzweig (2003) have shown, such areas may also be able to attract some industrialization based on their lower labor costs.[5]

3.1. Margins of profitability: from the world market to the farm gate

3.1.1. Distorted world prices

Evidence has accumulated since the 1980s that OECD agricultural policies have a significant depressive effect on world prices. Poor developing countries tend to be net gainers from these depressed world prices because their poor agricultural performance has made them into net importers of food (Anderson and Tyers, 1990). But their agriculture cannot grow without increased agricultural profits. While the major beneficiaries of reduced OECD protection would be the high agricultural performers in Asia and Latin America, as well as Canada and Australia, as the low performers

---

[5] Foster and Rosenzweig showed that in India, rural industries have located preferably in areas which benefited relatively little from the green revolution and the subsequent agricultural development and where rural wages were generally lower. Rural industrialization has therefore reduced rural poverty and inequality among and within rural areas. Rapid growth of rural industries in the 1990s followed an increase in the overall growth rate of the economy, which was itself partly a consequence of improved agricultural development, and may have been aided by restrictive labor laws whose impact and enforcement may be less in rural areas than urban areas. It is not clear how much these lessons apply to the under-performing countries, which are suffering from low overall and low agricultural growth.

address their problems, they too would benefit greatly from freer agricultural markets. Eliminating the restrictive OECD policies has therefore become a central issue for them. The Uruguay round had made some progress in bringing agriculture into the normal international trade regime. But most countries imposed such high tariff bindings that the impact of the Uruguay Round on reducing OECD protection has been minimal (World Bank, 2005a). Unfortunately the Doha round of negotiations has now collapsed.

3.1.2. Overvalued exchange rates and export taxes

In the 1970s and 1980s, domestic distortions were more important depressors of agricultural profits in low-income countries than OECD subsidies. Krueger et al. (1991) demonstrated that indirect taxation via exchange rate overvaluation and industrial protection was significantly more important than direct agricultural export taxes. Overvalued exchange rates not only depress export prices but also import prices of food such as rice, which have displaced traditional staple crops in urban markets, thereby depriving local farmers of markets. The increasing recognition of the importance of macro-economic stability and relatively low import taxation, reinforced by adjustment lending, has significantly reduced the indirect effects, while the direct export taxes have largely disappeared (Binswanger and Townsend, 2000). Of course there are still a number of countries in which import protection of manufacturing imposes an indirect tax on agricultural exports. Nigeria has only recently started to implement policies to combat Dutch disease and other sources of overvaluation. South African agriculture is suffering from the high value of the Rand, and Zimbabwe continues to massively overvalue its currency. After some progress in reducing export taxation in the Ivory Coast, the sharks have had a field day since the eruption of the conflict, and direct taxation measures and monopoly systems have re-emerged to reduce farm gate prices for cocoa and other export crops to a small fraction of the border price. Nevertheless, progress in developing countries' macro-economic, trade and agricultural policies has been far more important than in OECD subsidies.

3.1.3. Phytosanitary rules and regulation

These are steadily emerging as more important barriers for developing country agricultural and agro-industrial exports. (The latter are also a victim of tariff escalation.) Their increasing stringency is driven by consumer demand factors, as well as by their potential to replace tariff barriers as a protection against imports (World Bank, 2005a). Developing countries have little choice but to insert themselves into the standard-setting processes and bodies, and to build up their capacity to comply with these regulations (Ingco and Nash, 2004). Small countries are at a particular disadvantage, as they will have difficulties providing the necessary services. Regional collaboration and integration will be necessary to enable compliance at an affordable cost.

3.1.4. Barriers to intra-regional trade

The other margin of profitability of agriculture is an increase in intra-regional trade. Domestic demand for most agricultural commodities is price and income inelastic, and therefore rapid gains in production will inevitably lead to lower prices and quickly reduce gains in farm profits. Moreover, high production volatility translates into high price variability and risk. Opening sub-regional trade can reduce the impacts of these factors and increase regional food security.

Nevertheless, regional integration in agriculture has been slow in Latin America and South and South-East Asia. The Economic Commission for Africa has shown that "there have been some strides in trade, communications, macroeconomic policy and transport. Some regional economic communities have made significant strides in trade liberalization and facilitation, . . . in free movement of people, . . . in infrastructure, . . . and in peace and security, . . . Overall, however, there are substantial gaps between the goals and achievements of most regional economic communities, particularly in greater internal trade, macroeconomic convergence, production and physical connectivity" (Economic Commission for Africa, 2004, p. 1).

3.1.5. Transport and handling costs

High transport and handling costs have as detrimental an impact on producer incomes as low output and high input prices. They not only affect export commodities, but also the imports of fertilizers, as well as the opportunities and costs of rural nonfarm enterprises. Sub-Saharan Africa contains a large share of the world's landlocked countries and is poorly endowed with transport infrastructure. At 6.48 kilometers of roads per 100 square kilometers, road density is well below that in Latin America or Asia (12 km and 18 km per 100 square kilometers, respectively). Transport costs are among the highest in the world, and can reach as high as 77% of the value of exports (Economic Commission for Africa, 2004). And African farmers have to pay up to three times the price for fertilizer than farmers in Thailand, India, or Brazil.

But it is not just the state of infrastructure, which counts. Before the 1980s most transport businesses in Africa, including railways, bus and trucking companies, airports, seaports, and civil aviation, were publicly owned and managed, and heavily regulated. These enterprises charged low tariffs, and their reduced viability imposed heavy costs on both users and the national economies. Since the 1990s the transport businesses have mostly been deregulated and privatized. Concessions for operating railways, ports, and airports, have become common. Remaining public enterprises have been given more autonomy, and arbitrary regulation has been replaced by regulation through consensual performance contracts. In the highway sector, setting up of more sustainable institutions—autonomous road agencies and dedicated road funds—has become the norm, and has started to show positive results (World Bank, 2003a; and Africa Transport Unit website).

A serious problem in Africa is the extractions and bribes imposed by the police and others at border posts and roadblocks. "Along the West African road corridors linking the ports of Abidjan, Accra, Cotonu, Dakar and Lomé to Burkina Faso, Mali, and Niger, truckers paid $322 million in undue costs at police customs and gendarmerie checkpoints in 1997, partly because the Inter-State Road Transport Convention had not been implemented" (Economic Commission for Africa, 2004). Since these extractions respond to the profitability of the commodities transported, there is therefore a real danger that if other margins of profitability improve, these extractions will go up and prevent the transmission of improvements to the farm. Well-organized producer organizations are needed to ensure that governments crack down on these practices (World Bank, 1991a).

3.1.6. Financial services and interest rates

Many poorly performing countries have suffered from macro-economic instability and as a result had high real interests. Agriculture is rarely so profitable that it can compete with urban investments in such environments. In addition, rural areas in general, and small farmers in particular face enormous disadvantages in financial markets. Clients are usually small and widely dispersed, and seasonality and covariant risk make financial intermediation difficult (Binswanger and Rosenzweig, 1986). While cooperative institutions have been a success for larger farmers in middle income countries such as Brazil, specialized agricultural financial institutions have been a failure all over the world (World Bank, 1996a). The micro-finance movement can make a modest contribution, but it has found it difficult to overcome the rural disadvantages and emerge as an important agricultural lender (Gine, 2004). Successful approaches to improving rural financial intermediation have been focused on savings mobilization, postal systems, and improving access to finance by the rural nonfarm sector, input suppliers, marketing systems, and contract farming (Yaron et al., 1998).

The government of India has forced commercial banks to open rural branches and reserve a proportion of their lending to agriculture and agro-industry. Two separate studies have shown significant impact on agricultural growth and the rural wage (Binswanger and Khandker, 1995).

To conclude this subsection, the six off-farm margins that influence agricultural profitability have been the subject of studies for a number of years. However, they are rarely studied together, and it is therefore often difficult to decide on which ones to focus intensive policy dialogue. Commodity or value chain studies involving colleagues from other sectors are a way to integrate the knowledge of all these margins in a more systematic way.

3.2. Farm-level efficiency and profitability

3.2.1. Irrigation and drainage

The green revolution has shown how important water control is to make high levels of input use profitable. In India the new varieties and higher input use spread first to those areas with the best water control in the Northwest and South, and moved East and to the Center later, partly as a consequence of farmer investment in irrigation and drainage, and partly because research made high yielding varieties available for dry-land crops. Sub-Saharan Africa is lagging badly

in irrigation and drainage: Less than 7% of crop area in Africa is irrigated, compared to 33% in Asia (Gelb et al., 2000). Large-scale irrigation has suffered from unaffordable costs and centralized bureaucratic institutions. While models for changing these institutions into autonomous entities partially or fully controlled by the farmers have been successful in some countries such as Mexico, or the Office du Niger, this approach has not yet been replicated in many countries, and therefore even rehabilitation is often not yet a viable option. Small-scale irrigation is a more promising option, but investments are constrained by low profitability of agriculture and therefore low investment capacities of the farmers.

3.2.2. Land rights

Farmers will rarely invest in fixed assets unless they have secure land rights. While traditional tenure systems have often provided secure inheritable usufruct rights, in many parts of Africa they have come under pressure from rising population density and increased market access (World Bank, 2004c; Economic Commission for Africa, 2005c). They also often failed to provide secure tenure rights to women, and to manage the potential conflicts, which arise when immigrants need to be accommodated and enclosure of pasture threatens the livelihood of herders. Assisting these systems to evolve is therefore an important priority.

Excessive inequality of land ownership tends to reduce access to land and efficiency of its use (Binswanger et al., 1995). Large-scale farms from Brazil to the Philippines, Zimbabwe, and Namibia have under-utilized their land, and have depended on subsidies to reduce their dependence on hired labor via mechanization. Small farms on the other hand have inadequate access to capital to make their operations more efficient and improve their profits. As a consequence, both farm sectors suffer an efficiency loss. For these reasons, the World Bank has become a major player in land reform programs in the countries that still have an important land reform agenda (Binswanger and Deininger, 1999).

3.2.3. Soil erosion

Neither higher population nor poverty necessarily leads to land degradation.[6] In the transition from long

_____

[6] The CGIAR has summarized the literature on this topic in an easily accessible website (CGIAR, 2005).

fallow systems to permanent agriculture soil fertility declines and farmers eventually have to introduce new techniques to stem and reverse this decline. This they tend to do during the evolution of the farming system to higher land use intensity, as discussed so well by Ester Boserup (1965) and Hans Ruthernberg (1976), Their theories are consistent with an increasing number of studies which have shown that the normal processes of land improvement associated with agricultural intensification are taking place in many countries (Pingali et al., 1987; Tiffen et al., 1994). Significant cases of soil degradation, on the other hand, are usually associated with open access regimes, insecurity of tenure, and other policy failure, which imply that the normal investment responses of individuals are impeded, and the necessary soil investments are not made (Heath and Binswanger, 1996).

Clearly, the alarmist view that in many parts of the developing world land is being rapidly and irreversibly degraded is exaggerated. When I started at the World Bank, a sector report estimated that land losses in Burkina Faso amounted to something like 2% of GDP per year. Today the land supports nearly twice the population than in 1980 and Kaboré and Reij (2004) have documented how this was achieved. The change is visible to the naked eye: on a recent visit crops looked greener and healthier than I had ever seen them before, crop livestock integration had happened in many parts, degraded arid lands were being recuperated via traditional and new techniques, a number of new crop varieties had been introduced and there were more trees on the land. This does not mean that desertification and soil erosion are not a problem worthy of attention, only that we can be more optimistic than the usual rhetoric implies.

3.2.4. Gender relations

In many parts of the developing world women are a majority of the agricultural labor force, and in Sub-Saharan Africa, they are the majority of the farmers. Yet their rights over land are often poorly developed, and they face disadvantages in education and health care, markets and capital. These restrictions have a negative impact on the efficiency of both men and women, and of agriculture as a whole (Economic Commission for Africa, 2005c). Over the last decades, OECD countries have become major advocates for women's rights in the developing world, but entrenched social attitudes constrain the progress which has been achieved.

3.2.5. Human capital

A large literature confirms the importance of human capital for agriculture (Schultz, 1988). Rural areas suffer disadvantages in access to education, health care, and nutritional knowledge. The paradox is that nutrition is often worst where food is grown! Nevertheless, even the lagging countries have made significant strides in improving access to education, although with important variations among them. UNESCO Data Center (2007) uses the concept of school life expectancy to measure changes in education in a consistent way across countries and over time. The measure is the total number of years a child can expect to stay in school at the primary, secondary, and tertiary level. In the period from 1990 to 2001 the greatest increase in schooling participation took place in Africa and South America, where the median school life expectancy increased by 1.5 years. Yet by 2005 the school life expectancy in Sub-Saharan Africa was 8.1 years while in Asia it was 11.5 years.

Many health and education systems remain centralized, focus on direct service provision by the state, and fail to empower the users (World Bank, 2004a). It is hard to see how these systems will ever serve rural people without the radical change discussed in part two of this lecture.

Over the past two decades, HIV/AIDS has emerged as the single most important threat to human capital in Sub-Saharan Africa. Life expectancy in the hard hit countries has reverted to the levels prevalent at the time when I was born. Human capital is lost through the death of people in the prime of their lives, including agricultural extension staff, researchers, teachers, and medical personnel. Moreover, the transmission of human capital from generation to generation may be hampered because of higher dependency ratios and the huge number of orphans. As shown by Bell et al. (2003), the dynamic losses can be catastrophic. It is hard to see how agricultural and rural development will thrive in the hard hit countries of Africa unless the epidemic is stopped in its track. This can come about through more systematic prevention, and through free and universal access to HIV/AIDS treatment. In addition the impacts on the orphans must be mitigated by much better social protection programs. I have argued elsewhere that all these programs will need to be highly decentralized and community driven, involve the private sector, and be coordinated at the local level (Binswanger et al., 2005).[7]

3.2.6. Technology: the ultimate source of agricultural growth

Despite the enormous growth in human population and incomes, for more than 150 years agricultural commodity prices have followed a declining trend. This astonishing phenomenon has been caused by the combination of increasing international trade and sustained technical change in agriculture (Mundlak, 2001). Adaptation of the stock of scientific and technical knowledge to local conditions and implementation of new technology are most impressive in OECD countries, where the necessary investments have benefited from the distortions in favor of agriculture. Asia and parts of Latin America have also done well. In particular India and China have had some of the most impressive agricultural performances and therefore over a third of humanity has escaped from the threat of famine during the past 30 to 40 years.

In the low performing countries of Africa agricultural yields are half or less than half those in other regions of the world (Gelb et al., 2000). While there have been some notable advances in agricultural technology over the past 30 years, investment in agricultural research, whether measured per unit of output or per cropped area, has been much lower there than in any other region of the world (Pardey et al., 1991). This problem was already an issue in the mid 1970s, when I was attending my first international conference at Airlie House (Arndt et al., 1977). Unfortunately over the past decade and a half, international support for agricultural technology development has declined in real terms. I cannot see how African agriculture can prosper without bringing agricultural research spending to comparable levels as in the rest of the developing world.

Eventually most, if not all, benefits from technical change in agriculture elude the farmers and are transferred to consumers in the form of lower commodity prices, the famous agricultural treadmill. Evenson and Collin (2003) show this once again for the Green Revolution from 1996 to 2000. It is therefore not sufficient to improve the institutional environment and eliminate the barriers to profitability in the low-income countries so that they may adopt the already available technology. In a global agricultural system, agricultural profits will go to those who are ahead of the curve in terms of implemented technology, human capital, and institutions. The under-performing countries will need to produce a steady stream of new technology by strengthening and re-building their agricultural research and technology adoption systems.

4. Some conclusions

4.1. What are the key priorities for the low performers?

As emphasized in the introduction, priority setting in any given country must depend on an analysis of the strengths and weaknesses of the country's policies, institutions, and infrastructure, and on the opportunities of the country as determined by these, as well as its location and agro-climatic conditions. There are enormous variations in all of these factors and there are only a few general recommendations that can be made. The few, which I dare to make, are as follows:

I regard further improvements in the institutional environment as critical for empowering rural people. No comprehensive reviews of the state of the institutional environment for rural and agricultural development have yet been produced. The tools to do so already exist, including a toolkit for the review of the institutional environment for community and local development, of the business environment, and of the social environment (World Bank, 2003b, 2004a, 2004b, 2005d). In Africa governments are still the most centralized and progress in decentralization, especially in the administrative and fiscal area, deserves priority attention. It is also clear that the business environment in most of Africa still needs a lot of improvement. In particular corruption ranks with decentralization as the lowest among more than a dozen governance indicators studied in 29 countries by the Economic Commission for Africa (2005b).

Even though the Copenhagen Consensus (Lomborg, 2004) did not focus specifically on agricultural and

---

[7] The large-scale World Bank HIV-AIDS programs in Africa emerged late (Mallaby, 2004). They now apply Community-Driven Development to the field of HIV/AIDS, and have developed the most decentralized and empowering approaches to fight the epidemic with the best chances for a truly scaled up response.

rural development of the lagging countries, I agree with three of their top priorities: Combating HIV/AIDS, further trade liberalization, in particular in agriculture, and the development of new agricultural technology.

4.2. Most margins of profitability are beyond the control of farmers

Of the 12 margins or profitability, farmers only have partial or full control over three of them: the adoption and implementation of available technology, soil erosion, and irrigation and drainage. They can influence several other margins by organizing to manage some of the services they need themselves, and put other service providers under competitive pressures. These include marketing, quality control, processing, agricultural credit, agricultural extension, and management of irrigation infrastructure. To influence all the other margins, they need to organize politically at the local, national, and now even the international level.

4.2.1. The growing need of multi-sectoral approaches

Improvements in four of the five institutional pillars involve a holistic, multi-sectoral approach and intensive collaboration across sectors in analytical work, policy dialogue, and institutional reform. Such approaches are now common in work focusing on the central government pillar, the private sector, and involvement of civil society. But work on the investment climate still does not systematically involve agricultural economists. Local and community-driven development, and the associated decentralization and sector reforms cannot be pushed by an individual sector and should bring together specialists from all the relevant sectors. Of the 12 "margins of profitability" only agricultural technology, soil erosion, irrigation and drainage, and phytosanitary restrictions fall into the realm of agricultural specialists. In all other areas progress depends on the work of, and/or collaboration with specialists in infrastructure, macro- and fiscal economics, human development, social development and social protection, gender, and more. While some progress has been made in moving towards multi-sectoral operations, many systems and incentives in the countries, donor organizations, and the World Bank are tilted in favor of specific analytical work and operations in single sectors.

Research on the institutional environment and on the margins of profitability remains scattered in many different reports, disseminated to specialized audiences, and poorly used for policy dialogue. In addition there are often serious gaps. For example I am not aware of any recent comparative studies across low-income countries that decompose the difference between world prices and farm gate prices of outputs and inputs such as fertilizers into the many margins of profitability. Such work is essential for a coherent policy dialogue and for politically mobilizing farmers' organizations to fight for their interests, and equip them with the knowledge to do so effectively. What is needed here are a series of value chain studies across high-performing and low-performing countries for different commodities, in order to have standards against which the low performers can be compared.

4.3. Outlook

Since I first became interested in development about 40 years ago, our understanding of what it takes to develop agriculture and rural areas has steadily improved. And progress has been huge for rural populations in most of Asia. In Latin America progress has been significant in terms of agricultural growth, but rural poverty has declined little. But sub-Saharan Africa and a number of other low performing countries have made little progress, rural poverty has increased, and chances for progress are viewed with pessimism. I want to conclude by focusing on some positive trends, and changes in some underlying factors which may give reasons for hope.

4.3.1. The success of the high performers

Forty years ago, the profession was deeply pessimistic about China, South Asia, and South East Asia. It seemed impossible that these regions would become food self sufficient, and major exporters in a number of products. But it has happened, thanks to the Green Revolution, and improving rural development policies and institutions. More recently the strong urban growth performance of many of these economies has fueled the demand for their agricultural sectors, and increasingly provides remunerative employment, and therefore also drives up rural wages. Sub-Saharan Africa has not yet been able to break out of its vicious cycle of poor governance, poor investment climate, central-ized states, under-funding of agriculture, technological backwardness, and aid dependence. But the continent is enormous, and does have a huge agricultural po-tential. It would be wrong to assume that it cannot or will not develop as other of the "hopeless cases" have. Finding locally adapted solutions is a challenge, not an impossibility.

4.3.2. The rise of democracy

Over the past 20 years many of the former military regimes and other authoritarian states have moved to-wards democracy, greater space for communities, civil society organizations, and farmers' organizations. Un-fortunately the gains are not irreversible, and in many countries the depth of change leaves a lot to be desired (Economic Commission for Africa, 2005a). Neverthe-less I am hopeful that what we have seen is only a beginning. Working systematically on the institutional underpinnings of rural development will assist these forward movements.

4.3.3. Agricultural policy reform in the low-income countries

Compared to agricultural policy changes in OECD countries, macro-economic, trade, and agricultural pol-icy reforms in Africa and other poorly performing countries over the past 20 years has been very signif-icant. These changes have started to positively affect agricultural growth rates (Binswanger and Townsend, 2000). The international community and our profes-sion need to keep up the pressure for more progress, especially on the investment climate and those margins of agricultural profitability which are still to be tackled systematically.

4.3.4. International agricultural trade

NEPAD and the African Union have initiated re-gional integration, and the international community is supportive. Agricultural subsidies of OECD countries have become *the issue over which WTO negotiations collapsed*. Hopefully progress can resume soon. As the example of textiles has shown, the dismantling of the adverse agricultural policies may take 20 to 30 years.

4.3.5. Political determinants

As Klaus Deininger and I showed in the article on "Determinants of Agricultural and Agrarian Policies in the Developing World" (1997), poor performance and exploitation of rural populations have their roots in material conditions of rural areas—spatial dispersion, seasonality, and covariant risk—which make it diffi-cult for the rural poor to organize politically and resist elite domination and the associated adverse institutions and policies. Of course these material conditions have not changed since we wrote this article. Nevertheless many poorly performing countries have become more democratic, given more space to civil society, and in-vested at least modestly in education. In addition, the rise of the internet and the spread of cell phones mean that rural populations can no longer be kept in the dark, and special dispersion has become less of a barrier for social mobilization and political organization. Farm-ers' organizations and organizations of landless work-ers have become stronger, and started to make a real difference in some countries, such as Brazil, which has finally started to tackle its enormous land reform prob-lem. They are also becoming an important interlocutor in the process of policy formulation in a number of African countries. At the same time donor organiza-tions are fostering greater participation in policy for-mulation and program implementation via PRSPs, anti-corruption programs, social and gender assessments, programs to assist civil society organizations, support to universal primary education programs, and last but not the least, community-driven development.

References

Anderson, K., and R. Tyers, "More on Welfare Gains to Develop-ing Countries from Liberalizing World Food Trade," *Journal of Agricultural Economics* 44 (1990), 189–204.

Arndt, T. M., D. G. Dalrymple, and V. W. Ruttan, eds., *Resource Allocation and Productivity in National and International Agri-cultural Research* (University of Minnesota Press: Minneapolis, MN, 1977).

Becker, G. S., "A Theory of Competition among Pressure Groups for Political Influence," *Quarterly Journal of Economics* 98 (1983), 371–400.

Becker, G. S., "Public Policies, Pressure Groups, and Dead Weight Costs," *Journal of Public Economics* 28 (1985), 329–347.

Bell, C., S. Devarajan, and H. Gersbach, *The Long Run Economic Cost of AIDS: Theory and Application to South Africa* (World Bank, mimeo: Washington, DC, 2003).

Binswanger, H. P., "Patterns of Rural Development: Painful Lessons." *Agrecon* 4, (1994), 165–74.

Binswanger, H. P., and M. R. Rosenzweig, "Behavioral and Material Determinants of Production Relations in Agriculture," *Journal of Development Studies* 22 (1986), 503–539.

Binswanger, H. P., and S. R. Khandker, "The Impact of Formal Finance on the Rural Economy of India," *Journal of Development Studies* 32 (1995), 234–262.

Binswanger, H. P., and K. Deininger, "Explaining Agricultural and Agrarian Policies in Developing Countries," *Journal of Economic Literature* 35 (1997), 1958–2005.

Binswanger, H. P., and K. Deininger, "The Evolution of the World Bank's Land Policy: Principles, Experience, and Future Challenges," *World Bank Research Observer* 14 (1999), 247–276.

Binswanger, H. P., and R. F. Townsend, "The Growth Performance of Agriculture in Subsaharan Africa," *American Journal of Agricultural Economics* 82 (2000), 1075–1086.

Binswanger, H. P., K. Deininger, and G. Feder, "Power Distortions Revolt and Reform in Agricultural Land Relations," in J. Behrman, and T. N. Srinivasan, eds., *Handbook of Development Economics Vol. III* (Elsevier Science B.V.: Amsterdam, 1995).

Binswanger, H. P., S. Gillespie, and S. Kadiyala, "Scaling up Multi-Sector Approaches to Combating HIV/AIDS," Presented at International Conference on HIV/AIDS and Food and Nutrition Security, Durban, South Africa, April 14–16, 2005.

Boserup, E., *Conditions of Agricultural Growth: The Economics of Agrarian Change under Population Pressure* (Aldine Publishing Co.: New York, 1965).

Chen, S., and M. Ravallion, "How Have the World's Poorest Fared since the Early 1980?" *World Bank Research Observer* 19 (2004), 141–170.

CGIAR, "What Causes Desertification," *Desertification, Drought, Poverty and Agriculture (DDPA) Challenge Program* (2005), available at: http://www.ddpa.net/what-causes.htm.

Economic Commission for Africa, "Assessing Regional Integration in Africa," *A Policy Research Report* (ECA: Addis Ababa, 2004).

Economic Commission for Africa, "Striving for Good Governance in Africa: Synopsis of the 2005" African Governance Report" (ECA: Addis Ababa, 2005a).

Economic Commission for Africa, "Governance for a Progressing Africa," *Fourth African Development Forum* (ECA: Addis Ababa, 2005b).

Economic Commission for Africa, "Land Tenure Systems and Their Impact on Food Security and Sustainable Development in Africa," (ECA: Addis Ababa, 2005c).

Evenson, R. E., and D. Collin, "Assessing the Green Revolution, 1960 to 2000," *Science* 300 (2003), 758–762.

Fan, S., and P. Hazell, "Returns to Public Investments in the Less-Favored Areas of India and China," *American Journal of Agricultural Economics* 83 (2001), 1217–1223.

Faguet, J. P., *Decentralization and Local Government Performance, Technical Consultation on Decentralization* (FAO: Rome, 1997).

Foster, A. D., and M. R. Rosenzweig, *Agricultural Development, Industrialization and Rural Inequality* (Harvard University, Mimeo: Kenbridge, 2003).

Gelb, A. H., A. G. Ali, T. Dinka, I. Elbadawi, C. Soludo, and G. Tidrick, *Can Africa Claim the 21st Century* (World Bank: Washington, DC, 2000).

Gine, X., *Literature Review on Access to Finance for SME and Low-income Households* (World Bank, Mimeo: Washington, DC, 2004).

Hazell, P., and S. Hagbladde, "Farm-Nonfarm Growth Linkages and the Welfare of the Poor," in M. Lipton, and J. van der Gaag, eds., *Including the Poor* (World Bank: Washington, DC, 1993, pp. 190–204.

Heath, J., and H. P. Binswanger, "Natural Resource Degradation Effects of Poverty Are Largely Policy-Induced: The Case of Colombia," *Environment and Development Economics* 1 (1996), 65–84.

Ingco, M., and J. Nash, *Agriculture and the WTO: Creating a Trading System for Development* (World Bank: Washington, DC, 2004).

Kaboré, D., and C. Reij, "The Emergence and Spreading of an Improved Traditional Soil and Water Conservation Practice in Burkina Faso," EPTD Discussion Paper No. 114 (IFPRI: Washington, DC, 2004).

Krueger, A., M. Schiff, and A. Valdés, *Political Economy of Agricultural Pricing Policy*, Vol. I, *Latin America*; Vol. II, *Asia*; Vol. III, *Africa and the Mediterranean* (Johns Hopkins University Press: Baltimore, MD, 1991).

Lomborg, B., ed., *Global Crises, Global Solutions* (Cambridge University Press: Cambridge, UK, 2004).

Mallaby, S., *The World's Banker: A Story of Failed States, Financial Crises, and the Wealth and Poverty of Nations* (Council on Foreign Relations and Penguin Press: Washington, DC, 2004).

Manor, J., *The Political Economy of Democratic Decentralization* (World Bank: Washington, DC, 1999).

McLean, K., G. Kerr, and M. Williams, "Decentralization and Rural Development: Characterizing Efforts of 19 Countries," *World Bank Working Paper* (World Bank: Washington, DC, 1998).

Mundlak, Y., "Explaining Economic Growth," *American Journal of Agricultural Economics* 83 (2001), 1154–1167.

Narayan, D., and P. Pettesch, eds., *From Many Lands: Voices of the Poor* (World Bank and Oxford University Press: Washington, DC, 2002).

Pardey, P. G., J. Roseboom, and J. Anderson, eds., *Agricultural Research Policy: International Quantitative Perspectives* (Cambridge University Press: Cambridge, UK, 1991).

Pingali, P., Y. Bigot, and H. P. Binswanger, *Agricultural Mechanization and the Evolution of Farming Systems in Sub-Saharan Africa* (Johns Hopkins University Press: Baltimore, MD, 1987).

Piriou-Sall, S., *Decentralization and Rural Development: A Review of Evidence* (World Bank: Washington, DC, 1997).

Ravallion, M., and G. Datt, "Growth and Poverty in Rural India," *World Bank Policy Research Working Paper* No. 1405 (World Bank: Washington, DC, 1995).

Ravallion, M., and S. Chen, *China's (Uneven) Progress against Poverty* (World Bank: Washington, DC, 2004).

Ruthenberg, H., *Farming Systems in the Tropics*, Second Edition (Clarendon Press: Oxford, 1976).

Schultz, T. P., "Education Investments and Returns," *Handbook of Development Economics* Vol. I (North-Holland: Amsterdam, 1988).

Shah, A., "The Reform of Intergovernmental Fiscal Relations in Developing and Emerging Market Economies," *Policy and Research Series* No. 23 (World Bank: Washington, DC, 1994).

Tanzi, V., *Public Finance in Developing Countries* (Edward Elgar: Cheltenham, UK, 1991).

Tiffen, M., M. Mortimore and F. Gichuki, *More People Less Erosion: Environmental Recovery in Kenya* (John Wiley & Sons: Chichester, UK, 1994).

UNESCO Data Center, Table 8, "School life expectancy" (2007), http:// stats.uis.unesco.ogy, accessed August 19, 2007.

World Bank, "Agriculture and Economic Development," *World Development Report* (World Bank: Washington, DC, 1982).

World Bank, "Growth and Employment in Rural Thailand," Report No. 3906-TH. (World Bank: Washington, DC, 1983).

World Bank, *Investing in Rural Producer's Organizations*. Note 28 (Rural Development Department, Agricultural Technology, World Bank: Washington, DC, 1991a).

World Bank, "Decentralization and Regional Development," *Staff Appraisal Report* No. 8786-ME (World Bank: Washington, DC, 1991b).

World Bank, "Decentralization: Rethinking Government," *World Development Report Chapter 5* (World Bank: Washington, DC, 1995).

World Bank, "A Review of World Bank Lending for Agricultural Credit and Rural Finance (1948–1992): A Follow Up," Report no. 15221 (Oper. Eval. Department: Washington, DC, 1996a).

World Bank, *Participation Source Book* (World Bank: Washington, DC, 1996b).

World Bank, *Empowerment and Poverty Reduction: A Sourcebook* (World Bank: Washington, DC, 2002).

World Bank, "Reaching the Rural Poor—A Renewed Strategy for Rural Development," *Sector Strategy Paper* (World Bank: Washington, DC, 2003a).

World Bank, *A User's Guide to Poverty and Social Impact Analysis* (World Bank: Washington, DC, 2003b).

World Bank, "Making Services Work for the Poor," *World Development Report* (World Bank: Washington, DC, 2004a).

World Bank, *Local Development Discussion Paper*. June 16–18 (International Conference on Local Development, World Bank: Washington, DC, 2004b).

World Bank, "Land Policies for Growth and Poverty Reduction," *Policy Research Report* (World Bank: Washington, DC, 2004c).

World Bank, *Global Agricultural Trade and the Developing Countries* (World Bank: Washington, DC, 2005a).

World Bank, *Agricultural Investment Sourcebook* (World Bank: Washington, DC, 2005b).

World Bank, "A Better Investment Climate for Everyone," *World Development Report* (World Bank: Washington, DC, 2005c).

World Bank, *CDD toolkit for PRSP*. 2005d, forthcoming.

Yaron, J., B. McDonald, and S. Charitonenko, "Promoting Efficient Rural Financial Intermediation," *World Bank Research Observer* 13 (1998), 147–170.

Plenary 1

The economics of natural disasters: implications and challenges for food security

Hartwig de Haen* and Günter Hemrich**

Abstract

A large and growing share of the world's poor lives under conditions in which high risk of natural hazards coincides with high vulnerability. As a result natural disasters hit the poor disproportionately. In the last decade, natural disasters claimed 79,000 lives each year and affected more than 200 million people, with damages amounting to almost US$70 billion annually. Experts predict that disasters will become even more frequent and their impact more severe, expecting a 5-fold global cost increase over the next 50 years, mainly due to climate change and a further concentration of the world's population in vulnerable habitats. The article argues that in order to mitigate disaster impact on poor population groups, development policy and disaster management need to become mutually supportive. Focusing on challenges disasters pose to food security, it proposes that in disaster-prone locations measures to improve disaster resilience should be an integral part of food security policies and strategies. It expands the twin-track approach to hunger reduction to a "triple-track approach," giving due attention to cross-cutting disaster risk-management measures. Practical areas requiring more attention include risk information and analysis; land use planning; upgrading physical infrastructures; diversification and risk transfer mechanisms. Investments in reducing disaster risk will be most needed where both hazard risk and vulnerability are high. As agriculture is particularly vulnerable to disaster risk, measures to reduce this vulnerability, i.e., protecting agricultural lands and water and other assets, should get greater weight in development strategies and food security policies. Investing in disaster resilience involves trade-offs. Identifying the costs, benefits, and trade-offs involved will be a prominent task of agricultural economists.

JEL classification: E61, Q18, Q54

Keywords: food security; natural disasters; economic impact; resilience

Reducing disaster vulnerability in developing countries may very well be the most critical challenge facing development in the new millennium.
(Mechler, 2003, p. 1)

1. Introduction

Natural disasters have been affecting people and their livelihoods throughout the history of humankind, causing enormous losses of human lives and material destruction. The tsunami of December 2004, though extreme in terms of numbers of lives lost, was only one of many types of natural hazards, which continue to occur in various parts of the world, often without sufficient early warning. Besides earthquakes, the list includes cyclones, floods, hurricanes, droughts, fires, volcanic eruptions, and land slides.

Particularly worrisome is the fact that during the last decades, natural disasters have become more frequent, more intense and more costly (Freeman et al., 2003a). In the past decade alone, 79,000 people died and 200 million people were directly affected by natural disasters on average per year. Damages are estimated at US$67 billion per annum. Both the number of natural hazard events and the number of affected people has been growing rapidly. The costs associated with natural disasters are difficult to quantify and most likely underestimated. However, there is sufficient evidence that they have increased several-fold since the 1950s

Agricultural Economist, former Assistant Director-General of FAO and Professor (retired), Department of Agricultural Economics and Rural Development, University of Göttingen.

**Food Systems Economist, Agricultural and Development Economics Division, FAO.*

and there are strong indications that this trend will continue. Scientific predictions point to a further increase in the frequency and intensity of hazards, with a 5-fold global cost increase over the next 50 years, mainly due to climate change and to further concentration of the world's population in vulnerable habitats.

Equally important is the fact that natural disasters hit the poor disproportionately. Not only do most disasters affect almost systematically the tropics and hence mostly developing countries—the exception being geological disasters, which are more equally shared between tropical and temperate zone regions. Within developing countries, poor communities, households, and individuals carry the greatest burden. It is not simply by chance that more than 95% of the death toll of natural disasters in recent years was in developing countries and that the cost of the physical damages as a share of GDP was far higher in developing countries than in industrialized countries.

The combination of rising costs and disproportionate losses and damages amongst the poor makes it urgent to integrate disaster preparedness, mitigation, and prevention into development strategies. A paradigm shift is needed. For too long, disaster management and development policy have been pursued in parallel. Building resilience in the broadest sense—physical, social, and institutional—needs to become a component of investment in development.

This article seeks to identify key principles and measures of natural disaster risk management, which need to become part of development strategies. As natural disasters hit the poor more than the better-off, the impact on food security, both short and long-term, is often detrimental. The focus of the article is therefore on related economic choices regarding food security in developing countries.

2. Natural disasters: a product of hazard and vulnerability

To better understand the underlying forces of natural disasters, it is important to recall that these are the product of natural hazard and vulnerability (see Figure 1). The extent of a disaster depends on both the intensity of the hazardous event and on the degree of vulnerability of the society it affects. In recent decades, both probabilities are showing a rising trend in many parts of the world.

As regards the intensity of natural hazards, there are strong indications that climate change will continue to have an increasing impact in the decades to come (Intergovernmental Panel on Climate Change, 2001). Average surface temperatures continue to rise, leading to higher water absorption in the atmosphere. In turn, this results in more frequent and more intense windstorms, rains, and floods in some regions and droughts in others, or even alternations of both in the same locations. Increased vulnerability is mainly due to two factors: firstly, a growing share of the world's population lives in hazard-prone locations; and secondly many of these people have little chance of escaping the impacts of hazards, especially as structures built in those areas are often without proper protection. As a result the number of disasters shows a rising trend (Figure 2).[1]

The number of recorded fatalities also shows an increasing trend over the period 1975–2005, although only a few major deadly disaster events strongly influence the overall picture (Figure 3).[2]

A large and growing share of the world's population lives under conditions in which high hazard risk coincides with high vulnerability. They live in hazard prone areas and have no or little chance to prevent the impact of hazards (such as floods or droughts), access risk insurance, or benefit from investments in mitigation. Vulnerability is particularly high in urban areas, where an event of a given intensity affects many more people than in areas with lower population density. The exposure of urban people to risk is further accentuated by the fact that a high share of them (13 of the world's 19 megacities) is located in coastal areas, which are particularly exposed to floods, and in future, potentially to sea-level rises. Since most of the future global population growth is expected in the urban areas of developing countries, the proportion of people who will be particularly vulnerable to natural disasters is likely to rise further.

---

[1] Natural disasters are defined as catastrophic events caused by natural hazards by which at least 10 people have been killed and more than 100 persons affected and for which a state of emergency has been declared.

[2] The disasters with exceptionally high casualties include the 1976 earthquake in Tangshan, China (estimates range from 240,000 to 650,000) people killed, the 1984 famine in Ethiopia where drought and economic collapse combined killed more than one million people, the 1991 cyclone in Bangladesh claiming the lives of more than 138,000 people and the 2004 Indian Ocean tsunami with a death toll exceeding 217,000 people.

Hazard risk		Vulnerability		Disaster risk
Probability of an event with sufficient intensity to cause damage	**X**	Degree of exposure and fragility – Probability of damage in case of a hazard occurring	**=**	Combined probability of hazard and damage.

Figure 1. Hazard risk, vulnerability and disaster risk. *Source:* Adapted from CEPAL, BID, 2000 p. 6.

3. Impacts and costs of natural disasters

The combined effect of more frequent and more intense hazards and the ongoing population concentration in vulnerable zones results in enormous costs of global damages caused by natural disasters. The economic impacts of disasters can be grouped into direct and indirect impacts (Benson and Clay, 2004).

3.1. Direct and indirect impacts

Direct losses comprise human injuries and loss of lives and the physical damages of infrastructure, buildings, machinery, and agricultural assets. They can be considered roughly as equal to stock impacts.

The direct impact of natural disasters, especially floods and storms, has risen steeply since the early 1960s. Figure 4 shows estimated damages in the past 50 years. In addition, disasters may change the flow of goods and services, thereby leading to indirect losses of incomes, reduced consumption and savings, or interruption of trade flows. Exact and complete cost estimates and comparisons over longer periods are, however, particularly difficult to obtain (Guha-Sapir et al., 2004; Riebeek, 2005). According to some estimates, total economic costs associated with natural disasters have risen 14-fold since the 1950s and amounted to US$70 billion a year during the last decade (IFRC, 2001; Yates et al., 2002; OECD, 2003; Guha-Sapir et al., 2004, p. 13;). Experts of the Munich Reinsurance Company have estimated that the cost of natural disasters may rise 4-fold to US$300 billion by the year 2050 (Freeman et al., 2003a, p. 8).

Indirect effects of disasters may occur with a considerable time delay and are difficult to distinguish from other trends. These indirect disaster impacts are often not fully accounted for in damage assessments. This introduces a systematic bias and underestimation of total disaster costs in official statistics. Drought in particular tends to be underrepresented in damage statistics as it causes significant indirect cost without damaging physical infrastructure. This may also explain why the African region appears as rather little affected by natural disasters although the region

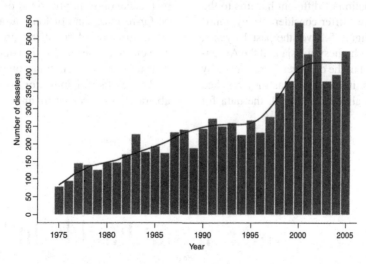

Figure 2. Number of natural disasters, long-term trend 1975–2005. *Source:* EM-DAT: The OFDA/CRED International Disaster Database—www.em-dat.net—Université de Louvain, Brussels, Belgium.

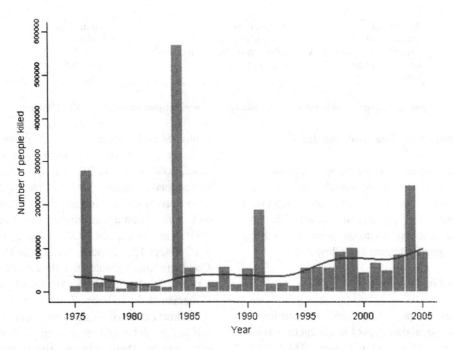

Figure 3. Fatalities in natural disasters, 1975–2005. *Source:* EM-DAT: The OFDA/CRED International Disaster Database—www.em-dat.net—Université de Louvain, Brussels, Belgium.

suffers rather frequently from droughts. Also, as a consequence of disasters, a number of infectious diseases, some of which were long thought to have been conquered, are staging a comeback, and new ones are emerging with devastating effects in some parts of the world (Kirch et al., 2005).

The relative contribution of different hazards to the average annual damages differ considerably by continent, as is shown in Figure 5. Over the past 15 years, absolute damages were highest in Asia and the Americas. While in Asia most of the damages were caused by flood and earthquakes, in the Americas they resulted from windstorms. As already indicated, the data for

Africa could be particularly biased due to the under representation of drought in the damage statistics.

3.2. Macroeconomic impacts

Depending on the scale and type of disaster, the macroeconomic implications of natural disasters can be far-reaching and of long duration, not only due to the destruction of countries' production capacity, but also due to the destabilization of public finance and the deterioration of their trade position (Mechler, 2003, p. 11). Statistical indicators can only give a rather abstract and incomplete impression of the scale of

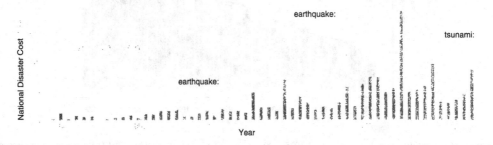

Figure 4. Estimated damage, 1950–2005*. *Source:* Riebeek (2005). *In constant 2004 US$.

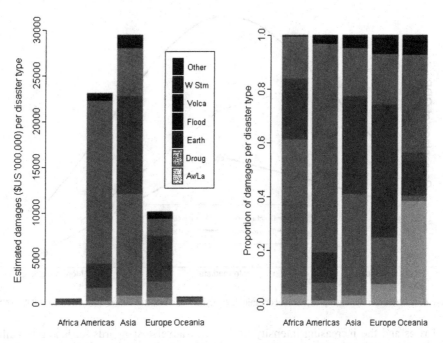

Figure 5. Average annual damages of natural disasters, 1990 to 2005. *Source:* EM-DAT: The OFDA/CRED International Disaster Database—www.em-dat.net—Université de Louvain, Brussels, Belgium.

destruction. Nevertheless, the dimensions of the damage can be approximated by recording the costs in percent of GDP that resulted from some major disasters during the last decade. These costs have in many cases had orders of magnitude that amounted to several percent of GDP. For example, during the 1990s Nicaragua suffered average damages of 15.6% of GDP, and even for China the damage has been estimated at 2.5% in that period. Individual events can be even more devastating: In Honduras, Hurricane Mitch caused losses equal to 41% of GDP (World Bank, 2004).

3.3. Impact on the poor

The effects of natural disasters are particularly adverse for the poor. This is primarily the result of three factors. Firstly, most low-income countries are located in regions that happen to be at far higher risk of natural hazard than those in the Northern hemisphere, including the impact of climate change. Many countries in Latin America and parts of Asia are at particularly high risk of hazards. Secondly, within countries, as Blaikie et al. (2004) have shown, the poor are normally affected much more than others due to economic and

social factors, including race, class, gender, and ethnicity. The majority of the poor cannot afford to live in locations with lower risk of disaster. Typically, they live in houses that are ill-protected against destruction by earthquakes or wind storms, or they live in lowlands that are the first to be covered by floods or else they farm on dry lands without sufficient water storage and irrigation to sustain periods of drought. Women and children are often hit the hardest, bearing the brunt of economic, food security, and nutrition impacts. Thirdly, there may be a perpetuation or even worsening of initial inequities, if the public sector (due to other needs for public funds) discontinues previously existing social programs or discriminates against the poor (especially the homeless, tenants, and women) in the targeting of compensation programs. The owners of smaller property will typically also have inadequate insurance coverage.

The statistics speak for themselves. During the 1990s, more than 90% of all major natural disasters occurred in developing countries. Half of the 49 Least Developed Countries (LDCs) are classified as being at "high-level disaster risk." More than half of the 25 countries most prone to disasters are Small Island Developing States (SIDS), which are at particular risk,

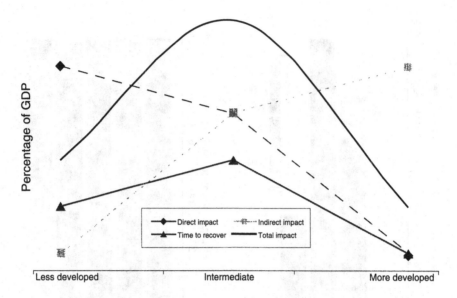

Figure 6. Inverted U relationship between economic development and disaster vulnerability. *Source:* ODI (2005).

due to sea-level rises and the increasing intensity of cyclones (Freeman et al., 2003a). During the 1990s, 96% of all deaths from natural disasters were in developing countries.[3]

3.4. Countries at intermediate development level are particularly vulnerable

There are indications that countries at intermediate level of economic development (middle-income countries) are particularly vulnerable to natural disasters (see Figure 6). This may be because the relationship between the level of development and the relative impact of natural disasters in percent of GDP has the form of an inverted U, implying the shape of a "Kuznets curve." While the underlying hypothesis needs further empirical research, it follows the argument that, typically, the physical, institutional, and social changes that accompany economic development may render economies initially more vulnerable. Possible reasons for this include the breakdown of traditional mechanisms of risk aversion and coping, movements of people into new, mostly urban, and often more hazard-prone settlements, and low priority on setting adequate

risk-adverse standards for land use, buildings, and infrastructure. If returns to national investments and to external development assistance are not to be lost, mainstreaming disaster risk management into development policy and strategy is thus particularly important for this group of countries. At higher levels of economic development, the costs of the damages caused by disasters, though high in absolute terms, are mostly lower relative to the overall GDP. Typically, higher-income developing countries and developed countries, if situated in disaster-prone regions, have established more rigorous rules and have invested more in early warning and awareness, preparedness, and mitigation (ODI, 2005).

3.5. Environmental degradation increases natural hazard risk

History provides many examples that show that there is a close positive link between the state of degradation of natural resources and the risk from natural hazards. Over thousands of years, humans have accumulated vast experience in protecting the natural resource base in order to achieve adequate resilience against the risk of damage from extreme weather events, earthquakes, hurricanes, floods, droughts, or influx of transboundary pests and diseases. These experiences have allowed local people to be good caretakers of a well-balanced ecosystem, e.g., by maintaining a sufficient

---

[3] Between 1992 and 2001, 96% of deaths from natural disasters were in countries classified by the UN Development Programme (UNDP) as medium and low human development. See also Twigg (2004).

forest cover, especially on slopes and in semi-arid or arid zones, or by protecting the water systems of rivers and lakes and the surrounding lands against floods, over-use, and pollution. With increasing population density and rising demand for land and energy that accompany economic development, these traditional mechanisms have either been replaced by new technologies and practices which are less environment-friendly or elsewhere people continue with sustainable practices but are affected by the negative externalities caused elsewhere. Global warming is only one, though a most worrisome, example of such developments.

3.6. Long-term implications

The implications of natural disasters can be long lasting. People who lose their houses, personal effects, and livelihood are bound to change their patterns of behavior, communication, and income earning, all of which takes years of adaptation. Investments in rehabilitation and reconstruction are made at the cost of abandoning or postponing previous plans for investment in productive or social capital and thus result in a slowdown of economic growth. Finally, there may be longer-term effects on some sectors due to the lengthy duration of rehabilitation. Examples are to be found in particular in agriculture, forestry, and fisheries, where the reforestation, replanting of perennials, and repopulation of fish stocks can take decades. In the meantime, affected people are forced to seek alternative sources of income, to migrate or, lacking such opportunities, are driven into deeper poverty.

4. Building resilience to disasters into food security strategies—a triple-track approach

The aim of disaster risk management measures is to reduce the natural disaster risk and build resilience. Resilience is the ability of a system, community, or society to adapt to shocks in order to maintain an acceptable level in functioning (Institute for Catastrophic Loss Reduction, 2004). The key economic question is whether to take disaster risk as a given, invest in normal development and repair eventual damage only *ex post*, or to anticipate disaster risks in development investments by enhancing resilience *ex ante*. In most cases, prevention is out of reach and the possibilities of mitigation

are limited. In any case, investing in resilience needs to be seriously considered and the benefits and costs assessed. Resilience requires social, institutional, and informational resources that enable a community to respond effectively to a hazard impact. It also entails early warning systems and institutions for enhanced coping and adaptation (DFID, 2004).

Food security strategies are a particularly appropriate framework for measures to build resilience against risks of natural disasters.[4] There are essentially five reasons for this proposition:

1. Given the range and intensity of the impact of natural disasters, it is evident that these can greatly affect all dimensions of food security: economic and physical access to food, availability and stability of supplies, and utilization. The specific implications for food security depend mainly on whether a disaster affects primarily people's physical and economic access to food or the availability of food or, in the worst cases, both. The extent to which shortfalls in local food production results in reduced food availability depends on people's access to local food reserves, imports, or food aid. Experience has shown that under most circumstances, international emergency aid arrives rather promptly. Nevertheless, people in remote areas and those for whom physical access has been interrupted through a disaster event often suffer significant shortfalls in food intake.

2. Success stories in poverty reduction show clearly that, as a prerequisite, people must have immediate and direct access to food. Hungry people cannot make use of the opportunities, which pro-poor investments offer. Hunger compromises their health, learning ability, and productivity. Therefore, disaster risk management should aim to ensure that access to food (e.g., school feeding, food for work) is maintained as one of the essential basic social services, even under disaster conditions.

3. Agricultural growth is critical for reducing poverty in developing countries. About two-thirds of the poor in developing countries live in rural areas and depend directly or indirectly on agriculture for their livelihood. As agriculture is also particularly

---

[4] For example, the key role of food security is explicitly recognized in the Hyogo Framework for Action 2005–2015. See ISDR (2005).

vulnerable to disaster risk, measures to reduce this vulnerability, i.e., protecting agricultural lands, water, and other assets, are vital for maintaining food security.

4. Appropriate agricultural technologies can play a key role in poverty reduction. Therefore, practices of land use for agriculture, livestock, and forestry, including the management of related natural resources (such as water and biodiversity), need to be adapted to make them less vulnerable to extreme weather events.

5. Finally, the past decade has shown that public investments (national as well as international), have increasingly neglected agriculture and rural areas of developing countries, in spite of the sector's key importance for the poor and for the entire economies of most of these countries (de Haen, 2005; Pingali et al., 2006). Given the current nascent political will to step up such investment, the occasion should be seized to explicitly include investments in greater disaster resilience in development plans.

To integrate natural disaster risk management into food security strategies, a triple-track approach is suggested. Such an approach would expand the so-called "twin-track approach" first presented jointly by FAO, IFAD, and WFP in 2002 (FAO, IFAD and WFP, 2002) and later elaborated in FAO's proposal of an Anti-Hunger Programme (FAO, 2003a). The twin-track approach builds on the fact that hunger is both the result and a cause of poverty. Consequently it proposes to combine investment in productivity growth for the poor, focusing especially on smallholder agriculture and rural infrastructure (track 1), with the creation of social safety nets to ensure direct and immediate access to food for the neediest (track 2). Most countries that are successful in reducing poverty have indeed followed such twin-track strategies.

Depending on the specific circumstances, the measures foreseen under the two tracks must be focused on the particular needs and constraints of the food-insecure people concerned. For countries that are vulnerable to natural disasters, it is proposed that the twin-track approach be expanded to include a third track of longer-term measures that address the disaster vulnerability of people and their assets so as to build greater resilience against the vagaries of natural factors that cause disasters. Such resilience measures would in

principle need to be applied to all four elements of food security: availability, access, stability, and utilization, Table 1 provides a schematic overview of the triple-track approach.

5. Some practical entry points

There are various concrete entry points for interventions to build resilience against natural disasters for countries, communities, or households as a third track of food security policies. These include: risk information and analysis, settlement and land use planning, upgrading physical infrastructures, diversification of economic activities away from disaster risk, and risk transfer mechanisms. Some entry points are not necessarily distinct from those of the second track (agricultural and rural development). However, as they are being designed to reduce disaster risk, related investments are likely to be more costly.

5.1. Risk information and analysis

A prerequisite for enhanced resilience and effective disaster risk management is improved risk awareness. It is only when people know about the possible risks inherent in their particular environment and are informed about how they can protect themselves against these risks that they may be able to avert, or at least reduce, the effects of natural disasters when these strike. A recent, noteworthy case of the need for greater awareness is Hurricane Katrina in 2005. It caused the death of more than 1,300 people and billions of dollars in damages in spite of the fact that it occurred in a country with highly sophisticated early warning systems.

Risk analysis encompasses hazard as well as vulnerability and resilience analysis that identify potential protective and adaptive capabilities (see Figure 7). Its objective is to assess the probability of occurrence and the potential adverse effects of natural disasters.

The "Disaster Risk Hotspots" project, initiated by the World Bank and Columbia University, constitutes an example of a global disaster risk assessment. It evaluates global risks of disaster-related mortality and economic losses associated with cyclones, drought, earthquakes, floods, landslides, and volcanoes. Such

Table 1
A triple-track approach to food security in disaster-prone countries

Track	Availability	Access	Stability	Utilization
One Rural development and productivity enhancement	Improving productivity and production capacity, esp. of low-income farmers Investing in infrastructure Improving the functioning of input and output markets	Promoting income earning opportunities Enhancing access to assets Facilitating the creation of rural enterprises Improving the functioning of rural financial systems and labor markets	Facilitating diversification Reducing production variability (irrigation, water harvesting, pest control, etc.) Monitoring production and consumption shortfalls Improving access to credit and saving services Protecting natural resources	Food handling and storage infrastructure Food safety regulation and institutions Safe drinking water and sanitation
Two Direct and immediate access to food	Food aid Market information Transport and communication	Cash transfers School meals Food for work programs Community and extended family structures	Safety nets	Nutrition intervention, health and education programs
Three Building greater resilience against natural disasters	Risk information, analysis, and early warning Legislation; Settlement and land use planning Upgrading physical infrastructures Diversification Risk transfer mechanisms (insurance and capital markets) Improving transition and sequencing of emergency rehabilitation-development efforts			

Source: Adapted from FAO (2003b).

initiatives may help identify and support global early warning and disaster mitigation efforts (see Dilley et al., 2005).

Risk analysis can also contribute to strategic mitigation measures at regional, national, and local levels. It can further support regional watershed management initiatives, help integrate disaster mitigation in national sector policies, and identify vulnerable areas and population groups at sub-national levels.[5]

There is also a need to analyze concrete examples of effective resilience. For example, in the case of the tsunami, some indigenous ethnic groups, such as the Moken of Thailand, abandoned their villages before the tsunami hit, thanks to traditional lore which prompted them to head to the hills when sea levels receded, in anticipation of a natural disaster ("How a tribe of Thai animists listened to the sea, and survived," International Herald Tribune, 24 January 2005). This

points to the significance of the contribution of indigenous knowledge to resilience as a factor in reducing risk and vulnerability.

5.2. Settlement and land use planning

Disaster risk is commonly being associated with geographic location: Sub-Saharan Africa with drought, Central America with earthquakes, and the Pacific and Caribbean islands with tropical cyclones (UNDP, 2004 p. 25). However, it is not location alone that generates disaster risk. Human settlement and land use patterns are important determinants of vulnerability and resilience. It is therefore critical that measures to reduce food insecurity and enhance resilience become an integral part of settlement and land use planning strategies.

Settlements along seismic fault lines, in coastal regions subject to storm damage, and along rivers subject to frequent floods, are highly prone to disaster impact. Urban expansion may generate and create new

---

[5] For a detailed list of mitigation measures enhancing the resilience of farming systems to storm-related disasters see FAO (2001).

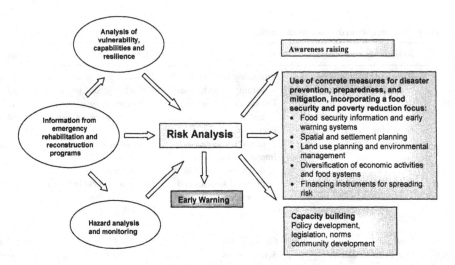

Figure 7. Inputs and outputs of risk analysis. *Source:* Adapted from GTZ (2004).

hazard patterns. Today, some 50 to 60% of residents in Bogota, Bombay, Delhi, Buenos Aires, and Lusaka live in informal settlements; 60 to 70% in Dar-es-Salaam and Kinshasa, and more than 70% in Addis Ababa, Cairo, and Luanda (UNDP, 2004 p. 59). The size and vulnerability of informal settlements, generally built in unstable areas such as coastal zones, flood-prone planes and ravines, and geologically unstable slopes, greatly increase their susceptibility to risk (Bigio, 2003).

Hazard mapping, land-use planning, building codes, and other disaster management standards, as well as training of rural and urban developers are critical to ensuring that settlements are made more disaster-resilient. National policies, programs, and the interplay of institutions may make a big difference as to whether a hazard will cause a disaster. Given the magnitude of the risk in some locations, remedial measures must not only include safeguards to protect the poor (and in particular environmental refugees) from risk of food insecurity and loss of livelihood. More serious consideration must also be given to banning construction in larger high-risk locations (along seismic fault lines, in vulnerable coastal regions, and on river shorelines).

For women and men living in poor and informal settlements, the opportunities of vacating disaster-vulnerable areas in exchange for safer ones will, to a large extent, depend on the degree to which they are able to meet their food security and livelihood

needs. Where there is a need to relocate populations and economic activities to less vulnerable areas, it will be important to examine how measures and investments to reduce poverty and improve food security and resettlement, and land use policies can reinforce one another.

5.3. Upgrading physical infrastructure

Three categories of investments in physical infrastructure are classic examples of disaster risk reduction measures:

- adoption of standards and building codes that ensure adequate levels of robustness of houses and bridges as protection against earthquakes and hurricanes;
- large-scale engineering investments in dams, dikes to control floods, seawalls to break storm surges; rerouting rivers and building canals; and
- irrigation, water harvesting, and water storage to prepare for drought.

The implications of investments in such activities for the various components of food systems need to be examined as part of a triple-track food security strategy. It has been estimated that investments of US$40 billion in disaster preparedness, prevention, and mitigation would have reduced global economic losses in the 1990s by US$280 billion (Freeman et al., 2003b). The net benefits of investments in greater resilience may even justify public funding in cases where the incentives for private investment are insufficient.

5.4. *Diversification away from disaster risk*

Diversification of production and sources of livelihood is another well-established strategy of risk aversion and a typical response to risk and uncertainty in market economies. Livelihood diversification in the form of multiple sources of income is central to poor people's coping strategies. The long-term implications of economic structure are, however, frequently overlooked in disaster mitigation programs. Diversification for disaster reduction can take many forms and measures can be devised at different levels of aggregation.

At a macro level, trade liberalization and the promotion of market links can be seen as diversifying the risk of a national hazard's impact on food supplies. For example, Del Ninno et al. argue that the liberalization of trade between Bangladesh and India prior to the 1998 floods prevented a steep hike in prices. Massive rice imports, in particular from India, helped to stabilize domestic prices. If they had risen by 50%, as was the case during the 1974 famine, severe food insecurity for millions of people might have ensued (Del Ninno et al., 2003).

Diversifying agricultural systems is another key entry point to reducing vulnerability. There are a number of measures through which cropping systems can be made more resistant to extreme weather-related hazards, be it wind, water, or drought. For example, Bangladesh's long-term agricultural and investment policies in the 1980s fostered the development of winter—or "boro"—rice, which contributed to limiting the food security impacts of the 1998 floods. The substantial increase in the proportion of winter rice over the years meant that the devastating impact of the 1998 floods on the monsoon "aman" crop did not lead to disastrous food security effects. This is only one example of lessons learnt from the effects of frequent floods, which Bangladesh has been using to invest in greater resilience for the future.

Water efficiency and drought resistance need to be improved in drought-prone areas and salt resistance in areas susceptible to the risk of sea-water intrusion. Perennials at high risk of destruction by winds and hurricanes, e.g., bananas, may need to be replaced by other perennials or else be better protected. Investment in water storage and expanded irrigation systems is advisable in areas likely to be affected by more frequent droughts (FAO, 1992, 2001). An example from the Pacific Islands illustrates how short-term profit considerations can result in cropping systems, which are not resilient against natural disasters. In response to unprecedented high prices for *kava* in 1998, farmers in some of the four-*kava* exporting countries (Vanuatu, Fiji, Tonga, and Samoa) increased by a factor of ten the planting density of this crop. Given the high frequency of cyclones in these countries, there is now a reasonable probability that one will affect an intensive *kava* plantation once in a 5-year production cycle (McGregor, 1999, pp. 21–23). To ensure resilience, consideration may need to be given to appropriate extension or even regulatory measures.

There are numerous other mechanisms through which diversification of economic activities can reduce vulnerability to disaster risk. One example is the category of so-called social funds, which support measures to enhance human capital as a way of spreading risk. The rationale is that households with higher levels of education and better health status are more likely to cope with shocks, heed warnings, and find alternative means of generating income. The most-studied case is perhaps Mexico's PROGRESA program.[6] Another example is micro-finance institutions addressing the consequences of disasters. They have the potential to help reduce vulnerability and support recovery through rescheduling of loans or stimulating pre-disaster measures through emergency funds and lending for specific disaster preparedness activities (Twigg, 2004, p. 227).

5.5. *Strengthening risk transfer mechanisms*

No matter how much is invested into disaster prevention and mitigation, a significant risk of damage from natural disasters will remain in many hazard-prone areas. It is therefore appropriate that modern forms of risk transfer mechanisms have recently been created. The two basic tools for transferring the risk of disasters

---

[6] Skoufias and others argue that social funds, if in place before a disaster strikes, reduce significantly the start-up cost of disaster relief. See Skoufias et al. (2003), cited in: Dayton-Johnson (2004).

are insurance and instruments for spreading the risk directly to the capital market.

Insurance against certain forms of natural disasters play an important role in developed countries. However, a number of specific characteristics of natural disaster risk pose challenges to insurability, particularly in developing countries (Mechler, 2003, pp. 58–59):

1. Natural disasters are low-frequency events with potentially large consequences. This type of risk requires a high amount of risk capital to back the underwritten policies, which is often not available in developing countries.
2. Natural hazards like earthquakes, floods, and windstorms often impact entire developing regions. Thus, the risk portfolio is highly correlated, thereby limiting the economic feasibility at national or regional level, unless globally operating reinsurance companies are available.
3. Due to the low frequency of many types of natural disasters, the willingness of the private sector to take out insurances tends to be low. The reluctance to pay for insurance is further limited by the perception that governments and aid agencies will anyway provide assistance in the recovery effort.
4. Additional difficulties in adopting insurance arise from traditional or ill-defined property rights, with individuals and even companies lacking formal titles to their holdings.

As a result of the above constraints, commercial insurance has been largely confined to richer countries and people. While in the United States more than 50% of the loss of catastrophes is insured, in countries with per capita income below US$10,000 insurance cover is less than 10%, and in countries with per capita income under US$760 it is about 1% (Freeman et al., 2003a, p. 20).

New forms of insurance are needed in developing countries. To give just one example, a consortium of research institutions, including, *inter alia*, IFPRI and the World Bank, has developed the concept of a weather-based index insurance, which does not depend on costly individual verification of damages, but uses location-specific trigger indicators (IFPRI, 2001). A similar pilot initiative by the World Food Programme (WFP)

has just been initiated. WFP has taken out a contract that will pay the agency should rainfall measures at 26 weather stations in Ethiopia fall below a certain level (see *International Herald Tribune*, 7 March 2006). The rationale is that response to a potential drought would not have to wait for the mobilization of donor funds, but could commence promptly. In addition, the pilot aims also at exploring whether it would make sense for governments to take out their own insurance, and whether that would lead to a reduced impact of drought on the government's budget and the country's population.

Capital markets as mechanisms for risk transfer have emerged rapidly in recent years as new financial instruments for hedging against weather and natural disaster risks. These include the following:[7]

- *catastrophe bonds*, which charge a high interest rate premium, but are subject to default if a defined catastrophe occurs during the life of the bond;
- *catastrophe swaps*, which allow insurance portfolios with potential payment liability to be swapped for a security and its associated cash flow payment obligations;
- *weather derivatives*, which protect companies from climate variability under contracts that provide payouts in the event of a specified number of days with temperatures or rainfall above or below a specified trigger point;
- *contingent surplus notes*, which give insurers as notes owners the option to use pre-specified investors' trust funds as standby source of cash in periods of exceptionally high losses caused by obligations from natural disasters;
- *exchange-traded catastrophe options*, which provide options for payments if an index of property claims exceeds a threshold level; and
- *catastrophe equity puts*, which provide that the insurer can sell equity shares against an up-front fee after a disaster has occurred.

The development of these new promising tools is partly a response to dramatic increases in the cost of insurance.

The alternative to insurance and capital market instruments is contingent financing in the form of public calamity funds, which is still the main financial

---

[7] See Freeman et al., 2003a.

tool used in developing countries. The source of those funds can be national budgets as well as international grants or concessional loans. While contingent financing can be released relatively quickly, especially when the source is an earmarked fund, it has a number of disadvantages, which need to be addressed by appropriate institutional provisions. One is the limited availability of public funds. The other issue is the moral hazard problem, sometimes referred to as the "Samaritan's dilemma" (Freeman et al., 2003a, p.17). Being aware and indeed expecting public assistance in the aftermath of a disaster, individuals, communities, and the private sector in general have a limited incentive to take appropriate preventive and precautionary *ex ante* action.

6. Policy implications

This article has reviewed evidence of rising damages caused by natural disasters, affecting the poor disproportionately and arresting development efforts in an increasing number of countries. Development policy and disaster management strategies would benefit from mutual integration of basic principles with a view to building resilience against disasters into all development efforts in hazard-prone locations, focusing especially on the poor. In particular, it is evident that while natural hazards are mostly natural geo-dynamic and hydro-meteorological processes, the impact of the resulting disasters can often be reduced considerably, as, in many cases, these are manifestations of "unresolved problems of development."[8]

Natural disasters can affect all dimensions of food security. To date, investment in disaster preparedness and resilience has too often fallen into the cracks between traditional food security policies on the one hand and humanitarian assistance on the other. The first, even if adequately focused on rural poverty and undernourishment, has normally not been associated with the paradigm of "direct life saving." The latter, i.e., humanitarian assistance and disaster risk management, have not sought to promote an "escape from poverty" as part of their strategy.[9] It is therefore critical to integrate disaster risk management into food security strategies as part of overall poverty reduction and development policies. For countries with high disaster risk, the proposed

triple-track food security strategy could make a difference in reducing the vulnerability of the poor and in protecting development gains in agricultural and rural areas.

The challenge is how to translate the proposed paradigm shift into practice. This will require political will as well as difficult choices in allocating scarce resources to investments for immediate benefit versus those for reduced longer-term vulnerability and disaster resilience. In this context, identifying and drawing lessons from more practical examples of successful reduction of vulnerability, such as the case of Bangladesh, is an important task for the research community.

Political commitment: Following recent disasters, political leaders have confirmed at the highest level that they are ready to mainstream disaster risk reduction in development strategies. The most prominent example is the 2005 Kobe Conference, which called for a more effective integration of disaster risk considerations into sustainable development policies, planning, and programming at all levels. If followed by action, the returns are likely to be high in terms of reduced disaster risk, better environmental protection and socioeconomic benefit for the poor.

Political will is particularly needed to address the causes of climate change and the resulting greater risk of landslides, floods, and droughts. Awareness and knowledge of the causes and implications of climate change are now clearly more widespread than they were one or two decades ago. This should be a motivation for industrialized countries to reduce their own contribution to the causes of climate change and, recognizing their responsibility as main originator, to grant disaster risk management higher priority in international development assistance. Action is in the interest of all, because in a globalized world, the adverse effects of disasters may indirectly affect the geo-political, economic, and security interests of poor and rich countries alike.

Policy choices: Decisions regarding the level of investment in longer-term disaster resilience will depend on the value attached to the discounted benefit of investing in prevention or reduction of a probable future damage, as compared to investment in short- and medium-term development. In the context of food security strategies, the choice relates to the allocation of scarce resources to productivity enhancement for

---

[8] See Yodmani (no year).

[9] Twigg (2004); Christoplos et al. (2001).

the poor (track 1) and to the provision of food and safety nets with immediate benefits for the poor and needy (track 2) as compared to investments in disaster resilience (track 3). In terms of trade-offs between investments under tracks 1 and 2 versus those under track 3, decisions should be the more in favor of investments in disaster resilience the higher the probability of the natural hazard concerned and the higher the likely loss it can create. As shown above, the frequency of extreme weather events as well as the vulnerability of developing countries, and in particular of the poor within these countries, is continuously rising. Therefore, building resilience should be given greater weight in development strategies, including food security policies. This would also contribute to the achievement of several Millennium Development Goals.

Public versus private responsibility: Even with more investment in early warning, mitigation, and prevention, the nature, time, and intensity of most types of natural disasters will remain unpredictable. Therefore, the public sector will face the continuing challenge of investing in preparedness and proceed with rehabilitation when a disaster occurs. However, as has been pointed out, this can create moral hazard problems, which need to be addressed through appropriate institutional provisions. Governments need to share the burden of investing in resilience widely with the private sector. While the public sector definitely needs contingency plans and to accept liabilities, state obligations must be kept to realistic levels. There are various ways to reduce a potential moral hazard through appropriate legislation, such as obligatory community-level contingency funds or mandatory insurance coverage.

The chances of arriving at a political consensus for mainstreaming disaster risk management into food security policies and protecting agricultural lands, water, and other assets of the poor are particularly good at this point in time. Not only does the political will exist on the part of the disaster management community. There is also a nascent awareness at highest levels of government that efforts to achieve food security and hunger reduction must be key elements of any poverty reduction strategy and that the sustainability of poverty reduction strategies depends on increased investments in agriculture and rural areas. The moment should therefore be seized to bridge the two policy domains and include investments in greater disaster resilience in poverty and food security strategies in all disaster-prone locations.

To facilitate decision-making, agricultural economists have a prominent task in identifying and flagging the costs, benefits, and trade-offs involved.

References

Benson, C., and E. Clay, *Understanding the Economic and Financial Impacts of Natural Disasters* (World Bank: Washington, DC, 2004).

Bigio, A. G., "Cities and Climate Change," in A. Kreimer, M. Arnold, and A. Carlin, eds., *Building Safer Cities: The Future of Disaster Risk* (World Bank Disaster Management Facility: Washington, DC, 2003).

Blaikie, P., T. Cannon, I. Davis, and B. Wisner, *At Risk: Natural Hazards, People's Vulnerability and Disasters*, second edition (Routledge: New York, 2004).

CEPAL, BID, *A Matter of Development: How to Reduce Vulnerability in the Face of Natural Disasters* (Economic Commission for Latin America and the Caribbean (CEPAL) and Inter-American Development Bank (BID: Washington, DC, 2000).

Christoplos, I., J. Mitchell, and A. Liljelund, "Re-forming Risk: The Changing Context of Disaster Mitigation and Preparedness," *Disasters* 25 (2001), 185–198.

Dayton-Johnson, J., "Natural Disasters and Adaptive Capacity," *Working Paper* 237 (OECD Development Centre: Paris, 2004).

de Haen, H., "Promoting Agriculture for Poverty Reduction—Building on the New Political Commitments," *Quarterly Journal of International Agriculture* 44 (2005), 327–334.

Del Ninno, C., P. A. Dorsch, and L. C. Smith, "Public Policy Markets and Household Coping Strategies in Bangladesh: Avoiding a Food Security Crisis Following the 1998 Floods," *World Development* 31 (2003), 1211–1238.

DFID, *Disaster Risk Reduction: A Development Concern: A Scoping Study on Links between Disaster Risk Reduction, Poverty and Development* (DFID: London, 2004).

Dilley, M., R. S. Chen, U. Deichmann, A. Lerner-Lam, and M. Arnold, "Natural Disaster Hotspots: A Global Risk Analysis," *Synthesis Report* (World Bank and Columbia University: Washington, DC and New York, 2005).

FAO, "The Role of Agro-Meteorology in the Alleviation of Natural Disasters," *FAO Agrometeorology Series Working Paper* No. 2 (1992).

FAO, "Reducing Agricultural Vulnerability to Storms," Paper presented by Günter Hemrich at the Asia-Pacific Conference on Early Warning, Prevention, Preparedness and Management of Disasters in Food and Agriculture (FAO: Chiang Mai, Thailand, 2001).

FAO, *Anti-Hunger Programme—A Twin-Track Approach to Hunger Reduction: Priorities for National and International Action* (FAO: Rome, 2003a).

FAO, "Strengthening Coherence in FAO Initiatives to Fight Hunger," Conference Document C 2003/16 (FAO: 2003b).

Freeman, P. K., M. Keen, and M. Mani, "Dealing with Increased Risk of Natural Disasters. Challenges and Options," *IMF Working Paper 03/97* (2003a).

Freeman, P. K., M. Keen, and M. Mani, "Being Prepared," in *Finance & Development*, 40(3) (2003b), 42–45.

GTZ, "Risk Analysis—A Basis for Disaster Risk Management," *Deutsche Gesellschaft für Technische Zusammenarbeit* (GTZ) GmbH, Eschborn (2004).

Guha-Sapir, D., D. Hargitt, and P. Hoyois, *Thirty Years of Natural Disasters 1974–2003: The Numbers* (UCL Presses Universitaires De Louvain: Brussels, 2004).

Institute for Catastrophic Loss Reduction, *Background paper on Disaster Resilient Cities*. (Infrastructure Canada, Ottawa, 2004).

Intergovernmental Panel on Climate Change, *Climate Change 2001: Impacts, Adaptation, and Vulnerability*. Technical Summary, 2001.

International Federation of Red Cross and Red Crescent Societies (IFRC), *World Disasters Report 2000* (IFRC: Geneva, 2001).

International Food Policy Research Institute (IFPRI), "Can World Financial Markets Work for the Poor?" Issue Briefs for Journalists, November (2001).

ISDR, "Hyogo Framework for Action 2005–2015. Building the Resilience of Nations and Communities to Disasters," Presented at World Conference on Disaster Reduction, 18–22 January 2005 Kobe, Hyogo, Japan.

Kirch, W., B. Menne, and R. Bertollini, eds., *Extreme Weather Events and Public Health Effects* (Springer: Berlin, 2005).

McGregor, A., *Linking Market Development to Farming Systems in the Pacific Islands* (FAO-SAPA Publication: Apia, Samona, 1999).

Mechler, R., "Natural Disaster Risk Management and Financing Disaster Losses in Developing Countries," Dissertation. Fakultät für Wirtschaftswissenschaften der Universität Fridericiana zu Karlsruhe (2003).

ODI, "Aftershock: Natural Disaster Shock and Economic Development Policy," *Briefing Paper* (Overseas Development Institute: London, 2005).

OECD, Emerging Risks in the 21st Century: An Agenda for Action (Organization for Economic Co-operation and Development: Paris, 2003).

Pingali, P., K. Stamoulis, and R. Stringer, "Eradicating Extreme Poverty and Hunger: Towards a Coherent Policy Agenda," *ESA Working paper* No. 06-01 (FAO: Rome, 2006)

Riebeek, H., *The Rising Cost of Natural Hazards* (NASA Earth Observatory, 2005), http://earthobservatory.nasa.gov/Study/RisingCost.

Twigg, J., *Disaster Risk Reduction: Mitigation and Preparedness in Development and Emergency Programming* (Overseas Development Institute: London, 2004).

United Nations Development Programme (UNDP), *Reducing Disaster Risk: A Challenge for Development* (United Nations: New York and Geneva, 2004).

Yates, R., J. Twigg, D. Guha-Sapir, and P. Hoyois, *Development at Risk*, The brief for The World Summit on Sustainable Development, Johannesburg, South Africa, 26 August–4 September, 2002.

Yodmani, S., "Disaster Risk Management and Vulnerability: Protecting the Poor," Paper Presented at the Asia and Pacific Forum on Poverty, organized by the Asian Development Bank, no year specified.

World Bank, *Natural Disasters: Counting the Cost* (World Bank: Washington, DC, 2004).

The impact of droughts and floods on food security and policy options to alleviate negative effects

Stephen Devereux*

Abstract

This article introduces an analytical framework for understanding the impacts of droughts and floods on rural livelihoods, based on Sen's "entitlement approach," and applies the framework to the recent food crises in Malawi. Weather shocks trigger a sequence of "entitlement failures," which can result in a famine unless public action intervenes to mitigate these impacts. Policy responses can compensate for failures of production-based entitlement (free or subsidized input distribution); labor-based entitlement (public works programs or "employment-based safety nets"); trade-based entitlement (grain reserve management or food pricing policies); and transfer-based entitlement (food aid or cash transfers).

JEL classification: Q18, Q54, Q58, R2

Keywords: agriculture; cash transfers; entitlement; food security; Malawi; vulnerability

1. Introduction

In rainfed agricultural systems, erratic rainfall can have comprehensive and devastating impacts on affected livelihoods and local economies. This article makes the argument that food crises triggered by droughts or floods can be modeled as a sequence of "entitlement failures," and that effective intervention to address any one of these entitlement failures can prevent the drought or flood event from evolving into a food crisis. Conversely, contemporary food crises or famines can be attributed to failures of public action (or to successful public action, in cases where the food crisis is a product of malevolent intent).

The first part of this article sets out the "food crises as entitlement failures" framework, while the second part examines remedial interventions for each of these entitlement failures. Empirical support for both the argument and the policy responses comes from the author's work on the recent food crises in Malawi. The framework for the argument is summarized in Figure 1.

In Figure 1, entitlement failures are depicted as occurring sequentially—first production fails, then labor markets fail, then commodity markets (trade-based entitlements) fail, and finally transfers fail. This is schematic: in reality, entitlements collapse during food crises in complex, iterative, and interacting ways. But Figure 1 does illustrate two important points: first, weather shocks (droughts and floods) trigger not only harvest failures but a sequence of knock-on shocks to local economies and societies, and second, there are several points in this sequence where effective intervention could mitigate the shock and prevent a production shock from evolving into a full-blown famine. With sophisticated early-warning systems and humanitarian response capabilities, and given that most droughts and floods are slow-onset disasters (allowing lengthy lead times for external intervention), what needs to be explained in contemporary food crises is not what triggered the production shock (this is "old famine" thinking) but why there was no response. "New famine" thinking shifts the burden of explanation from analysis of production failures and entitlement failures to understanding response failures (Devereux, 2007). This article considers both sides of the story.

Institute of Development Studies, University of Sussex, Brighton, BN1 9RE, UK.

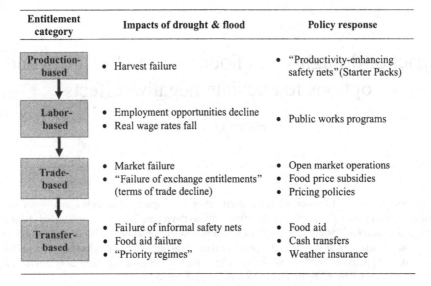

Entitlement category	Impacts of drought & flood	Policy response
Production-based	• Harvest failure	• "Productivity-enhancing safety nets"(Starter Packs)
Labor-based	• Employment opportunities decline • Real wage rates fall	• Public works programs
Trade-based	• Market failure • "Failure of exchange entitlements" (terms of trade decline)	• Open market operations • Food price subsidies • Pricing policies
Transfer-based	• Failure of informal safety nets • Food aid failure • "Priority regimes"	• Food aid • Cash transfers • Weather insurance

Figure 1. Droughts, floods, and entitlement failures.

2. Impacts of droughts and floods

Following Sen's categorization of four sources of entitlement to food, this section considers the impacts of weather shocks on production, labor, trade, and transfers, both in a general sense and in the particular context of Malawi.

2.1. Failures of production-based entitlement

The most immediate impact of erratic rainfall on rural livelihoods is on crop production. Droughts and floods undermine farm yields and the national harvest, reducing household and national food availability, and agricultural income derived from crop sales. Poor harvests threaten food security and livelihoods from household to national level, to varying degrees according to the extent that the family or nation depends on agriculture for its food and income. Households and economies that are more diversified are less vulnerable to these direct impacts of droughts and floods, provided that their alternative income sources are neither correlated with rainfall nor directly or indirectly dependent on agriculture (i.e., vulnerability falls to the extent that complementary sources of income and food are non-covariate).

In the longer term, Dorward and Kydd (2002) note that the presence of risk lowers the productivity of rural economies in three ways: (1) reducing returns to investment, (2) distorting investments away from income-maximizing toward risk-reducing activities, and (3) discouraging investment altogether, because returns are low and investors are risk averse. In these ways, weather risks contribute to underinvestment and hence to long-run agricultural stagnation and rural poverty in countries that are dependent on rainfed agriculture.

Livelihoods in Malawi are dominated by agriculture. Less than 15% of the national population is urbanized, 89% of the labor force works on smallholder farms or commercial estates (tobacco, tea, sugar), and 72% of Malawi's exports are agricultural (Wobst et al., 2004). Agriculture in Malawi is predominantly rainfed, but rainfall is variable and unpredictable. This combination of high dependence on rainfed agriculture, while rainfall is highly—possibly increasingly—erratic, leaves household livelihoods and the national economy highly vulnerable to weather shocks.

Figure 2 tracks the national maize harvest in Malawi in the 20 years preceding the 2001/2002 food crisis. The high interannual variability in maize production is mainly attributable to erratic rainfall. Although the trend is generally rising, maize production per capita has been falling since the 1970s (Wobst et al., 2004). Moreover, the coefficient of variation has visibly increased since the early 1990s. The food crisis

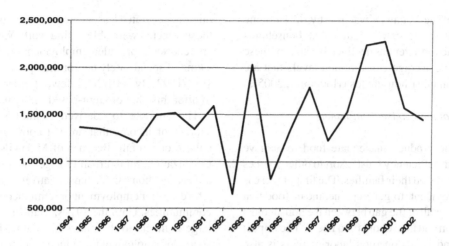

Figure 2. Maize production in Malawi, 1984–2002 (metric tonnes). *Source:* Phiri (2005).

of 2001/2002 followed two bumper harvests, and the "failed harvest" of 2001 was actually 6% above the 10-year average (Devereux and Tiba, 2007).

Following the food crisis of 2001/2002 in Malawi, a survey of 1,200 households and 99 focus group discussions were conducted in 11 rural districts (Devereux et al., 2003). Survey respondents were asked to recall the month in which their granaries were depleted for the previous three years: 2000/2001 (the year before the crisis, a bumper season), 2001/2002 (the famine year), and 2002/2003 (another poor harvest, which instigated a second emergency appeal). Given the self-sufficiency ambitions of most Malawian farmers, the responses largely reflect the impact of rainfall variability on household food security outcomes. In cumulative terms, 19% of households surveyed harvested less than three months of maize in 2000/2001, while 37% had less than six months, 63% had less than nine months, 77% had less than 12 months of maize, and 23% were self-sufficient or had a surplus. Since this was a bumper year for maize production in Malawi, the implication is that less than one rural Malawian in four is self-sufficient even in a good year, while three in four are chronically food insecure—they never achieve self-sufficiency in maize.

In the food crisis year of 2001/2002, by contrast, only 2.6% of households in our survey were self-sufficient in maize, while 37% had less than three months, 70% had less than six months, and 92% had emptied their granaries after nine months. The impact of drought and flooding on agriculture in Malawi was dramatic: not

only was the national harvest cut by 32%, at household level the food gap lengthened by several months. Instead of looking for alternative sources of food for 3–4 months, affected households had to find food from off-farm sources for 6–8 months, or even longer.

The impacts of transitory weather shocks are compounded by longer-term processes such as falling landholdings and declining access to inputs. Between 1977 and 1998, population growth rates above 2% per annum resulted in a doubling of the Malawi population and of population density, from 59 to 112 people/km^2, and a halving of cropland per capita, from 0.42 to 0.23 hectares (Government of Malawi, 2000). Declining farm sizes have not been offset by agricultural intensification or livelihood diversification. Instead, yields of staple crops have remained low, soil fertility has declined, cultivation of high-yielding varieties of maize remains limited, and per capita food availability declined throughout the 1980s and 1990s.

Under the Banda regime, smallholders accessed input credit through the Smallholder Agricultural Credit Association (SACA), while fertilizer was sold at subsidized prices by ADMARC, the agricultural marketing parastatal. But SACA collapsed in 1992 and fertilizer subsidies were phased out under structural adjustment conditionalities between 1987 and 1995, which resulted in access to inputs being confined to wealthier farmers who could afford to pay commercial interest rates for credit and full market prices for fertilizer. Since 1995, fertilizer prices have risen rapidly to unaffordable levels for most Malawian farmers, fuelled by repeated devaluations of the Malawi Kwacha—by 62% on one occasion in 1998. A survey found that households whose access to fertilizer has declined because of these price hikes have average consumption levels that are 13% lower than other households (Hoddinott, 2005).

2.2. Failures of labor-based entitlement

Farmers who produce inadequate food to achieve production self-sufficiency must resort to other sources of entitlement to feed their families. The first of these is off-farm employment, to generate income or food that will cover part or all of the gap between the household's crop production and household food needs. The impact of droughts and floods on rural labor markets is also likely to be negative, however, because weather shocks undermine not just agricultural production but the entire rural economy. Sen (1981) introduced the concept of "derived destitution" to explain how a shock such as drought reduces the demand for goods and services in affected communities, threatening the livelihoods of those whose incomes depend indirectly on agriculture, such as traders and rural barbers.

Because most smallholders in Malawi are no longer self-sufficient in maize, and with limited nonagricultural employment options, rural Malawians depend heavily on casual employment (*ganyu*) for cash or food to fill their annual production deficit. In the past, *ganyu* was readily available and provided the main source of off-farm income for smallholder households. In recent years, though, *ganyu* has become increasingly scarce, and real wage rates are stagnant or falling. Many households that previously hired labor are now looking for work themselves, and there is a surplus of labor in most rural communities in most years.

Weather shocks compound the imbalance between labor supply and demand in rural Malawi. Following a poor harvest, the proportion of production deficit households rises, and the length of the food gap in each farming household increases. As a consequence, the supply of labor rises sharply, while the number of households offering work on their farms falls. By the time of the 2001/2002 food crisis, the number of people looking for work far exceeded the availability of casual work, and this is one reason why the rural economy was unable to absorb the impact of the weather shock that reduced the harvest that year. A comparable harvest shock in 1991/1992, also triggered by erratic

rainfall, generated less severe outcomes, partly because those affected were able to find work. Wealthier farmers reportedly provided employment on their farms as a kind of social safety net for their poorer neighbors in 1991/1992. By 2001/2002, fewer farmers could afford to offer this kind of labor-based safety net.

The antidote to "derived destitution" is to find sources of income that are not correlated with agriculture or rainfall. Because of Malawi's low level of urbanization, rural–urban linkages are limited and relatively few households have relatives working in town who can offer employment or remit income to the rural communities. Until the 1970s, Malawians migrated in large numbers to the mines in South Africa, but this source of employment and income ceased in the early 1980s and migration no longer provides employment and income on the same scale as before.

2.3. Failures of trade-based entitlement

People who do not produce enough food and cannot raise income through employment are forced onto the market to buy food, where their access to food is determined by the price of food and the value of assets that they can exchange or sell for food. Droughts and floods have a strongly negative effect on commodity markets. First, as noted, weather shocks that reduce harvests cause food availability decline (FAD). Since the demand for food is highly price inelastic (food being a basic necessity), a relatively small shortfall in marketed supplies can cause a major increase in food prices. Second, as people come to the market with assets to exchange for cash or food, excess supply of these commodities causes their prices to collapse, so the terms of trade of assets to grain falls dramatically. This effect has been described as a terms of trade scissors movement—rising grain prices and falling asset prices result in a collapse in trade-based entitlement to food. Pastoralists are particularly badly affected by such effects: livestock that they sell or exchange for grain are worth only a fraction of their pre-crisis value after a weather shock disrupts demand and supply patterns on local commodity markets (Swift and Hamilton, 2001).

In Malawi, erratic weather events have had the predicted effects on both food and asset prices. Figure 3 graphs the price trajectory of two staple foods—white maize, and dried cassava—in the year before the famine of 2001/2002, and during the crisis period itself.

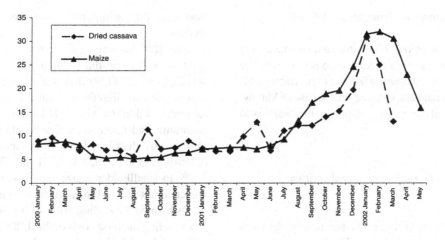

Figure 3. Average maize and cassava prices in Malawi, 2000–2002 (MK/kg). *Source:* Tiba (2005).

Every year, food prices follow a predictable seasonal pattern: starting off low after the main annual harvest in April–May, rising steadily through the calendar year and peaking during the "hungry season" months of January–March. In 2001/2002, retail prices of maize and cassava started rising rapidly soon after the poor harvest and reached unprecedented heights in January 2002, more than 300% above the average post-harvest prices. It is clear from Figure 3 that private trade and public interventions failed to stabilize food supplies and prices, and it was high prices that undermined access to food and converted a relatively minor production decline into a famine. One expert witness to the UK Parliamentary Inquiry into the humanitarian crisis in Southern Africa argued that "if you had stabilized the price of maize in 2001 in Malawi, no crisis would have occurred" (IDC, 2003: EV67).

According to Dorward and Kydd (2002), failures of agricultural markets in Malawi are explained by high transactions costs—low volumes, small margins, weak transport and communications infrastructure—and co-ordination failures, because high-risk premiums and margins are needed to make trade profitable in this context. Even unusually high food prices (as in early 2002) send insufficient signals of demand to attract traders, because these markets are thin and temporary.

2.4. Failures of transfer-based entitlement

The coping-strategies literature has shown that informal transfers—assistance from relatives and neighbors—is more reliable following idiosyncratic shocks (e.g., illness or death of a family member) than following a covariate shock such as a drought or flood, which undermines food production and livelihoods at the community or regional level. The more severe or protracted the resulting food crisis, the more informal transfers are likely to contract, as the ability of affected households to respond to requests for assistance from others steadily erodes.

In Malawi and other African countries, several factors have combined in recent years to reduce the capacity of communities to support their members through livelihood crises. First among these is social change. Malawians characterize each other as more individualistic and less community-oriented now than in the past, and the famine of 2001/2002 was accompanied by a breakdown of law and order and a rise in vigilante justice unparalleled in Malawi's history (Devereux, 2002). A second factor is the high prevalence of HIV/AIDS, which has raised vulnerability levels and undermined coping capacity within communities. A third factor, unique to Malawi, is an unusually low level of urbanization (under 20%), which means that rural–urban linkages are more restricted than in other countries, so that fewer rural families have relatives employed in towns who can be called on to remit income or food in times of crisis. Taken together, these factors mean that informal transfers in Malawi are low and probably declining as an insurance mechanism against livelihood shocks triggered by erratic weather.

3. Policy responses to droughts and floods

The discussion below follows the same format as the previous section, and considers responses to weather shocks in terms of addressing failures of production, labor, trade, and transfers. Once again, the case of Malawi is used to ground these policy responses in a real-world context.

3.1. Responses to production-based entitlement failure

Some efforts to mitigate the potentially devastating impacts of droughts and floods on agriculture are pre-emptive rather than reactive, and involve enhancing farmers' access to inputs (improved seeds, chemical fertilizers, tools) that will boost production and/or minimize crop losses following a weather shock. In Malawi a range of interventions has been implemented since smallholder access to inputs was undermined in the early 1990s, under the generic heading of "productivity-enhancing safety nets" (Devereux, 1999). The most significant of these is the free distribution of agricultural inputs.

Seeds and fertilizers have been given out free of charge to farmers in Malawi almost every year since 1992, first as a rehabilitation intervention following the 1992 southern African drought, but later as a response to rapid fertilizer price inflation in the mid 1990s. In 1998 the Government of Malawi launched the "Starter Pack" program, which gave all 2.8 million farmers a package comprising enough fertilizer and maize and legume seeds to plant 0.1 hectares. The rationale for the Starter Pack initiative was that subsidizing food production is more cost-effective and sustainable than subsidizing food consumption with food aid. Levy (2005) estimates that the universal Starter Pack cost approximately the same as general fertilizer subsidies (US\$20 million per annum), but considerably less than equivalent volumes of food aid (US\$100 million per annum), commercial food imports (US\$70–100 million per annum) or unconditional cash transfers (US\$107 million per annum). Starter Packs added 100–150 kg of maize to each farmer's harvest and up to 400,000 tonnes to the national harvest (Levy, 2005). At a time when the national maize deficit often exceeded 500,000 tonnes per annum, the Starter Pack substantially narrowed the

food gap, reducing import requirements and emergency appeals.

After 2000 the universal Starter Pack program was scaled down by two-thirds, becoming the Targeted Inputs Programme (TIP) that was delivered to about 1 million poor smallholders—though mistargeting, elite capture, and dilution within communities who resisted community selection meant that beneficiaries were almost evenly distributed across the income quantiles (Chinsinga et al., 2002). In 2001, the TIP added only 3–4% to smallholder maize production, whereas the universal Starter Pack had added 16% in 1999. Many critics blamed the scaling down of the Starter Pack for exacerbating the food crisis of 2001/2002, though it remains unclear whether the Starter Pack would have protected the national harvest against the weather shocks of the 2001 agricultural season.

Other observers argue that the significance of the Starter Pack was more in terms of its impacts on food prices, and hence on access to food, than on food production. As noted above, the price of maize is a crucial determinant of food (in)security in Malawi, and Levy (2005) argues that the Starter Pack contributed to keeping maize prices relatively low, by reducing the market demand for maize from smallholders in the hungry season months, after their granaries are depleted. In 2001/2002, however, the reduced food availability following weather shocks and the scaled-down TIP precipitated sharp rises in maize prices—from MK10/kg in October 2001 to MK44/kg five months later—and it was this that triggered the food crisis in early 2002.

3.2. Responses to labor-based entitlement failure

Public works programs are labor market interventions that are often introduced to provide alternative employment opportunities, in contexts of widespread poverty where labor markets are thin. As an employment-based safety net, public works serve the purpose of offering farmers an additional source of food (food-for-work) or income (cash-for-work) for consumption-smoothing purposes when their harvests have failed. Public works are popular with policy makers because they are self-targeting (the heavy work requirement and payment of subsistence food rations or submarket wages discourages the nonneedy from applying), and they offer the potential of creating useful assets (e.g., community infrastructure) while simultaneously transferring food or income to the poor.

The best known employment-based safety net is Maharashtra's Employment Guarantee Scheme (EGS), which was recently expanded to all of rural India, under the National Rural Employment Guarantee Act (NREGA) of 2005, which extends the right to 100 days of employment at the local average agricultural wage to every rural Indian household. A key principle is the guarantee of employment, which assures any household affected by a livelihood shock, such as drought, of access to an alternative source of income. This has the immediate effect of smoothing food consumption through the period of shortage, and the long-run effect of increasing risk-taking behavior by farmers. The countercyclical benefits are highly significant—one study found that income variability halved in villages where EGS employment was available compared with villages without guaranteed employment (Ravallion, 1990). Even more strikingly, a famine was prevented following flooding in Bangladesh in 1988, to a significant extent because the Rural Works Programme and the Food-For-Work Programme increased their employment by 90% and 20%, respectively (Ravallion, 1990).

Apart from transferring food or income directly, the works undertaken on employment-based safety nets or labor-intensive public works are also intended to ameliorate the impacts of future weather shocks, for instance by drought-proofing the local economy through soil and water conservation activities such as terracing, earth dams, and microirrigation. This approach has been followed for decades in Ethiopia, although the returns in terms of reduced food insecurity have been limited, owing to poor quality of construction and inadequate maintenance.

Some design features of public works undermine their effectiveness in terms of achieving certain objectives. First, setting the wage rate below local market rates, or paying workers subsistence rations, encourages self-targeting but reduces the value of the transfer to such an extent that the consumption-smoothing objective is compromised—especially if manual labor is involved that requires high energy expenditure, reducing the net calorie transfer to the worker. Second, the heavy work requirement disqualifies many of the most vulnerable individuals from participating, espe-

cially the labor-constrained—people with physical disabilities, older people, the chronically ill.

Finally, public works often have gender-equity objectives. In Malawi, the World Food Programme (WFP) selects food-for-work projects that either attract women workers or create assets that benefit women directly—such as community woodlots and water-points that reduce women's firewood- and water-collection time—while the Malawi Social Action Fund (MASAF) targets women and female-headed households on its public works projects, "since female-headed households make up a disproportionate share of the poorest" (MASAF, 2006:16). Critics have questioned the implications for women's workloads of requiring them to undertake heavy manual labor, given their double burden of domestic duties and income-generating responsibilities. Instead of labor market interventions, other forms of emergency relief might be preferable for the labor-constrained and the time-poor.

3.3. Responses to trade-based entitlement failure

Numerous interventions and instruments are available to policy makers concerned to mitigate the effects of food price inflation following a disruption to food supplies, or to protect consumers against regular food price seasonality. These include open market operations such as buffer stock management, and pricing policies such as food price subsidies or legislated price banding. Many governments have used parastatal marketing agencies to intervene in weak markets—buying grain after harvest when prices are low and supplies are high, storing for 6–8 months until prices start rising and market supplies are dwindling, then releasing this onto local markets at cost, to boost supplies and dampen prices.

Malawi has operated a Strategic Grain Reserve (SGR) for decades. In early 2001, the SGR was fully stocked with maize that was rotting following two bumper harvests. The IMF advised the Government of Malawi to sell off this stock (preferably by exporting it to avoid disincentive effects on local producers) and to replenish it to a lower level—reducing the SGR from 180,000 tonnes to 60,000 tonnes. Unfortunately, this advice was abused by powerful individuals in government, who purchased SGR grain cheaply and stored it, realizing that the harvest was inadequate in 2001 and that prices could rise to record levels, then selling it locally and making large profits. Also, because the harvest was poor in 2001, the parastatal marketing agency (ADMARC) was unable to purchase maize locally, and the national grain reserve was depleted precisely when it was most needed. If the SGR had been properly managed as intended, it could have prevented the unprecedented maize price rises that were blamed for magnifying the food crisis in 2001/2002 (Devereux, 2002).

Another mechanism for controlling food prices is through legislated floor and ceiling prices, or by implementing food price subsidies. Until the 1980s, many African governments implemented pan-seasonal and pan-territorial pricing policies—farmers received the same payment for their produce from marketing parastatals wherever they lived in the country, and consumers paid the same price for food at all times of year. These policies protected farmers from isolated regions against high transport costs (taking their produce to market), and protected consumers against the price seasonality that is characteristic of tropical countries with one or two harvests each year. Typically these policies required heavy subsidies to be paid by governments, but by the 1980s these subsidies were considered to be unaffordable, and were phased out under agricultural sector reform processes that aimed to remove the interventionist state and stimulate private traders to fulfil the roles that had been monopolized by marketing parastatals.

In Malawi the abolition of producer and consumer price subsidies was achieved over a period of time by gradually expanding the price band between a floor price (below which food would not be purchased from farmers) and a ceiling price (above which consumers would not have to pay for food). Since these are often the same people—deficit producers are forced to sell some of their produce at low post-harvest prices to meet nonfood expenses, and buy food back in the hungry season at high pre-harvest prices—the abolition of subsidies reintroduced this source of household food insecurity, which was magnified in years when weather shocks reduced harvests, lengthening the hungry season and raising food prices to unaffordable levels. While parastatal operations might have been inefficient and price subsidies might have been unsustainable, the removal of these pillars of food security in Malawi exposed the rural poor to the most severe consequences of predictable seasonality and unpredictable weather shocks. More than a decade after the phasing out of price subsidies, traders have yet to fill the gap left by ADMARC in grain marketing and deficit farmers and consumers are more food insecure than ever before.

3.4. Responses to transfer-based entitlement failure

Once informal social support systems fail, the case for external transfers becomes compelling. Humanitarian responses to droughts and floods have been dominated by food aid, on the assumption that affected households (especially farmers) have lost their access to food and need consumption support at least until the next harvest. Recently, however, cash transfers have been piloted as an alternative intervention in many emergencies (Harvey, 2005; Creti and Jaspars, 2006). This section considers the case for and against both food aid and cash aid.

3.4.1. Emergency food aid

Several arguments are made in support of food aid. Apart from saving lives during emergencies, food aid can help to address underlying vulnerability. Dercon and Krishnan (2004) and Quisumbing (2003) find that food aid has been effective in reducing household vulnerability in Ethiopia, and Hoddinott et al. (2003) note the importance of food aid in smoothing consumption and protecting assets among households facing food stress. One more general point often made in favor of food aid is that it can achieve improved nutrition better than cash because more food is consumed for equivalent values of transfer (Edirisinghe, 1998), which may partly be a consequence of women controlling food in the household (Haddad et al., 1997).

One limitation of food transfers is their high transaction costs. Barrett and Maxwell (2005) estimate that more than half (53%) the value of U.S. food aid in 2000 was spent on shipping and handling costs. Clay et al. (1998) claim that whenever it is systematically analyzed, financial aid is more cost-effective than food aid. Both reviews conclude that food is preferable to cash transfers only where local markets are functioning extremely poorly and inelastic food supply means that cash injections would merely inflate commodity prices and harm the poorest.

Interestingly, popular perceptions that food aid causes disincentives and dependency have been challenged by recent empirical studies. A regression analysis of food aid in Ethiopia finds that disincentive effects are insignificant among the poor but increase with household wealth, which suggests that most observed disincentives are the result of mistargeting wealthier households (Dayton-Johnson and Hoddinott, 2004). Barrett and Maxwell's (2005) review of food aid concludes that (1) food aid rarely induces dependency because the amounts transferred are usually small; (2) the evidence of food crowding out other transfers is mixed; (3) well-targeted and well-timed food aid has minimal negative price effects in local markets, because it reaches households who are already priced out of the market; but (4) food aid can affect local production, labor markets, and consumption patterns; and so (5) food aid should be locally sourced wherever possible.

Following the 2001/2002 food crisis in Malawi, the Joint Emergency Food Aid Programme (JEFAP) distributed 240,000 MT of food to over 3 million Malawians between July 2002 and June 2003, in the form of general food distribution (2.9 million beneficiaries each month), therapeutic and supplementary feeding, and school feeding. Available evidence suggests that the general food distribution was weakly targeted on the poorest and most drought-affected households, but well targeted by observable indicators of vulnerability such as households with orphans or chronically ill members and female-headed households (Sharma, 2005b). Impacts of food distribution were limited by the low levels of participation (only 38% of rural households), infrequent rather than monthly receipt of food, and transfers of less than full rations. In terms of food consumption levels and adoption of coping strategies like selling assets, no statistically significant differences in outcomes were recorded between food aid beneficiaries and non-beneficiaries (Sharma, 2005a).

3.4.2. Emergency cash transfers

The case for cash transfers is often made by contrasting cash aid with food aid. Cash transfers are seen as preferable because they are cheaper to administer and avoid the risks associated with commodity transfers (such as dependency and disincentives); they are less paternalistic because they enable individual choice; and they contribute to pro-poor growth by

being invested as well as consumed, and generating income- and employment-multiplier effects (Schubert et al., 2005). Cash transfers are also expected to stimulate markets by boosting purchasing power in contexts of demand failure, and there is some evidence of this positive effect from cash transfer programs in nonemergency contexts, such as social pensions in southern Africa (Devereux et al., 2005). Evaluations of cash-for-work and unconditional cash grants have found that cash transfers are invariably cheaper and more cost-effective to deliver than commodities (food-for-work or food aid) (Creti and Jaspars, 2006).

Many NGOs, including Oxfam GB, Novib, the Red Cross, and Save the Children, have used cash transfers in emergency contexts, including recent droughts in Ethiopia, Kenya, and Somalia; floods in Bangladesh, Haiti, and Mozambique; Hurricane Mitch in Guatemala and Nicaragua; and the Indian Ocean tsunami of 2004. In 2005/2006, the World Food Programme successfully piloted a cash transfer scheme in Sri Lanka as a post-tsunami recovery measure.

In 2005/2006, Concern Worldwide and Oxfam GB implemented unconditional cash transfers in Malawi as a complementary intervention to humanitarian food aid, following a combination of drought and flooding that reduced the national maize harvest by 25%. Oxfam delivered US$26/month to 6,000 households in one district for five months. Monitoring reports found that most of this money (80–85%) was spent on food (Oxfam, 2006).

Concern's Food And Cash Transfers (FACT) project differed from the Oxfam project in three innovative respects: (1) it provided a package of food (maize, beans, and oil) plus cash (enough to buy the same food basket); (2) transfers were adjusted by household size; (3) the cash transfer was adjusted each month to reflect food price movements in local markets. This last point was the most crucial advance on previous cash-based interventions in emergencies, as it ensured that beneficiaries maintained a constant entitlement to adequate food throughout the crisis period. Maize prices far exceeded predictions in late 2005 and early 2006, rising to unprecedented levels and undermining the purchasing power of Oxfam's cash transfer, which was fixed in nominal terms but fell in real terms during the food crisis. By contrast, Concern effectively underwrote the price risk facing market-dependent consumers. The budgetary implications of this decision were extremely onerous—Concern paid out almost twice as much cash to beneficiaries in March 2006 as in January—but the benefits to vulnerable households were substantial.

Baseline and post-distribution monitoring surveys were conducted in several hundred FACT beneficiary and nonbeneficiary households. Before FACT started, households throughout rural Malawi were rationing their food consumption in response to the livelihood shock precipitated by the poor harvest of April 2005. After FACT was introduced in January 2006, meals per day in beneficiary households stabilized while this indicator continued to fall in nonbeneficiary households. As the new harvest started coming in (March–April), food consumption improved and meals per day recovered to pre-crisis levels, but at a faster rate in beneficiary households. Differences in average meals per day between beneficiary and nonbeneficiary households were statistically nonsignificant in the pre-project period, but significant (at the 0.01 level) in February and March 2006 (Devereux et al., 2006).

A comparison of beneficiary use of Concern's food packages and cash transfers reveals that the cash was used for a more diverse range of purposes than the food, which was mostly consumed at home, with relatively small amounts being shared with poorer relatives and neighbors who were excluded from the FACT project. Over the four months of the intervention, just under 60% of cash transfers were spent on buying food, while the remaining 40% was spent on grocery items (including costs of milling maize), health and education costs, debt repayment, and investment or asset accumulation (purchasing small stock, renting land, buying fertilizer, petty trading). Clearly, the cash transfer enabled beneficiaries to meet a wide range of nonfood needs, and they exercised choice in allocating this cash, which suggests some tradeoff between immediate consumption smoothing and longer-term accumulation objectives. In this sense it appears that the FACT project achieved both "livelihood protection" and "livelihood promotion" outcomes.

4. Conclusions

This article has adapted Sen's entitlement approach to the analysis of impacts of droughts and floods, and has characterized these impacts as a sequence of inter-

acting "entitlement failures": weather shocks first disrupt production, then labor and commodity markets, so that labor-based entitlements and trade-based entitlements to food are undermined. Being covariate shocks, droughts and floods also constrain the capacity of community members to support each other through the livelihoods crisis that they induce in affected populations. The corollary of this analysis of impacts is that public intervention can address any or all of these entitlement failures—and, in fact, effective intervention at any point in the sequence should be sufficient to prevent the initial shock escalating toward a famine.

Despite endorsing a well-designed food and cash transfer program as an effective response to the humanitarian emergency precipitated by droughts and floods in Malawi in 2005/2006, this article concludes by arguing that unconditional cash transfers are little better than a "fourth best" solution to the risks to lives and livelihoods that droughts and floods bring in their wake.

The "first best" solution is to prevent subsistence crises from occurring at all, even after a drought or flood event—through strengthening production systems (e.g., introducing irrigation to reduce dependence on unreliable rainfall), strengthening markets (to minimize supply failures), and reducing chronic poverty (to minimize demand failures). This requires a range of pre-emptive measures, including investing in agricultural technology, building transport infrastructure to integrate markets, and building asset buffers at the household level to reduce their vulnerability.

A "second best" solution would be to strengthen insurance mechanisms against the impacts of weather shocks. India's Employment Guarantee Programme is one form of insurance. Another is weather-based insurance, whereby payouts to countries or individual farmers are triggered by rainfall below a specific volume or index value. Pilot projects using weather-based insurance are already underway in India, Mongolia, Mexico, Ethiopia, Kenya, and Malawi. One challenge these innovative projects face is high premiums required to cover the likelihood of heavy payouts, given that a drought strikes these countries every few years. A second challenge arises from the reality that agricultural droughts can be very localized in time and space—in many cases, total rainfall across a farming season appears adequate, but poor distribution means that crops are first "burned" and later flooded, resulting in harvest failure. This happened in Malawi in 2005.

A "third best" solution is to intervene in commodity markets to correct for market failures, through open market operations. This need not imply a return to the days of government agencies buying food crops after harvest, storing and selling this food later at cost to stabilize supplies and prices interseasonally. Though interventions of this kind are less fashionable now than cash transfers, the case for some kind of interventionism is strong in contexts where markets are weak and liberalization has failed to engender a class of entrepreneurial traders who adequately meet the food security mandate that agricultural marketing parastatals in Africa once tried (and usually failed) to fulfill. Alternative models are to look to new institutional forms—such as new-generation producer cooperatives—to undertake this intertemporal arbitrage function, or to use call options on commodity exchanges to ensure access to imports and reduce price uncertainty. Malawi used a call option on the South African commodity exchange in 2005/2006, saving US$60–90 on each ton of maize imported, at a cost of US$25 per ton (Alderman and Haque, 2006: 18).

Handing out food or cash to people affected by droughts and floods is a "fourth best" solution. The purpose is to compensate individuals who have lost their access to food, but as a compensation mechanism this has a number of limitations. First, targeted transfers are always subject to numerous targeting errors, notably exclusion (failing to identify and reach some people who need assistance) and inclusion (giving transfers to some people who do not need assistance).

Second, compensating selected individuals for a structural problem—market failure—does little to address the structural problem. Food aid has long been criticized for causing dependency and disincentives to both farmers and traders. The case for providing cash transfers rather than food aid to cover a food gap is Sen's argument that droughts and floods cause collapses in purchasing power, and that this is best addressed by restoring purchasing power. This argument challenged previous conceptualizations of food crises as caused by collapses in food availability. It is also argued that predictable cash transfers might stimulate trade and contribute to strengthening markets, but the risk is that food supplies might indeed be constrained and injecting cash might not produce the desired supply response.

Cash transfer programs are currently fashionable in Africa, especially among international NGOs and donors, as a mechanism for reducing dependency on food aid and strengthening household and local economies. But decisions about optimal responses to mitigate the impacts of droughts and floods must be based on context-specific analysis. Cash transfers have many advantages over food aid, but they should not be promoted as a panacea, to the neglect of policies that strengthen agricultural production, build input and output markets and rural infrastructure, and provide effective insurance against livelihood shocks.

References

Alderman, H., and T. Haque, *Insurance Against Covariate Shocks: The Role of Index-Based Insurance in Social Protection in Low-Income Countries of Africa (draft)* (World Bank: Washington, DC, 2006).

Barrett, C., and D. Maxwell, *Food Aid after Fifty Years: Recasting its Role* (Routledge: London, 2005).

Chinsinga, B., C. Dzimadzi, M. Magalasi, and L. Mpekansambo, *TIP Evaluation Module No. 2: TIP Messages: Beneficiary Selection and Community Targeting, Agricultural Extension and Health (TB and HIV/AIDS)* (Statistical Services Centre, University of Reading: Reading, 2002).

Clay, E., N. Pillai, and C. Benson, "Food Aid and Food Security in the 1990s: Performance and Effectiveness," *ODI Working Paper* 113 (Overseas Development Institute: London, 1998).

Creti, P., and S. Jaspars, *Cash-Transfer Programming in Emergencies* (Oxfam: Oxford, 2006).

Dayton-Johnson, J., and J. Hoddinott, *Examining the Incentive Effects of Food Aid on Household Behavior in Rural Ethiopia*, mimeo (International Food Policy Research Institute: Washington, DC, 2004).

Dercon, S., and P. Krishnan, "Food Aid and Informal Insurance," in S. Dercon, ed., *Insurance against Poverty* (Oxford University Press: Oxford, 2004), pp. 305–330.

Devereux, S., "Making Less Last Longer: Informal Safety Nets in Malawi," *IDS Discussion Paper* 373 (Institute of Development Studies, University of Sussex: Brighton, 1999).

Devereux, S., *State of Disaster: Causes, Consequences and Policy Lessons from Malawi* (Action Aid Malawi: Lilongwe, 2002).

Devereux, S., "Introduction: From 'Old Famines' to 'New Famines',"in S. Devereux, ed., *The 'New Famines': Why Famines Persist in an Era of Globalisation* (Routledge: London, 2007).

Devereux, S., W. Chilowa, J. Kadzandira, P. Mvula, and M. Tsoka, *Malawi Food Crisis Impact Survey: A Research Report on the Impacts, Coping Behaviours and Formal Responses to the Food Crisis in Malawi of 2001/02* (Institute of Development Studies and Centre for Social Research: Brighton, UK and Lilongwe, Malawi, 2003).

Devereux, S., J. Marshall, J. MacAskill, and L. Pelham, *Making Cash Count: Lessons from Cash Transfer Schemes in East and Southern Africa for Supporting the Most Vulnerable Children and Households* (Save the Children UK, Help Age International and Institute of Development Studies: London and Brighton, 2005).

Devereux, S., P. Mvula, and C. Solomon, *After the FACT: An Evaluation of Concern Worldwide's Food and Cash Transfers Project in Three Districts of Malawi 2006* (Institute of Development Studies, University of Sussex: Brighton, 2006).

Devereux, S., and Z. Tiba, "Malawi's First Famine: 2001–2002," in S. Devereux, ed., *The 'New Famines': Why Famines Persist in an Era of Globalisation* (Routledge: London, 2007), pp. 143–177.

Dorward, A., and J. Kydd, *The Malawi 2002 Food Crisis: The Rural Development Challenge* (Imperial College at Wye: Wye, 2002).

Edirisinghe, N., "The Food Factor," paper presented at *Time for Change: Food Aid and Development Conference, Rome*, October 1998 (World Food Programme: Rome, 1998).

Government of Malawi, *Profile of Poverty in Malawi: Poverty Analysis of the Integrated Household Survey 1998* (National Economic Council: Lilongwe, 2000).

Haddad, L., J. Hoddinott, and H. Alderman, *Intrahousehold Resource Allocation in Developing Countries* (International Food Policy Research Institute: Washington, DC, 1997).

Harvey, P., "Cash and Vouchers in Emergencies," *HPG Discussion Paper* (Overseas Development Institute: London, 2005).

Hoddinott, J. *Vulnerability, Shocks, and Impacts in Ethiopia and Malawi: Implications for Public Action* (International Food Policy Research Institute: Washington, DC, 2005) .

Hoddinott, J., M. Cohen, and M. Bos, *Redefining the Role of Food Aid* (International Food Policy Research Institute: Washington, DC, 2003).

International Development Committee (IDC), "The Humanitarian Crisis in Southern Africa," *Third Report of Session 2002–2003* (House of Commons: London, 2003).

Levy, S., ed., *Starter Packs: A Strategy to Fight Hunger in Developing Countries? Lessons from the Malawi Experience 1998–2003* (CABI Publishing: Wallingford, 2005).

Malawi Social Action Fund (MASAF), *The Evaluation of the 'Improving Livelihoods through Public Works Programme', ILTPWP* (MASAF: Lilongwe, 2006).

Oxfam, G. B., *Unconditional Cash Transfers as a Response to Acute Food Insecurity: Principles and Lesson's from Oxfam-GB's Projects in Malawi and Zambia*, November 2005–March 2006 (Oxfam: Oxford, 2006).

Phiri, A., *Regional Vulnerability Analysis for Malawi: Poverty, Agriculture and Nutrition Security* (Bunda College of Agriculture: Lilongwe, 2005).

Quisumbing, A., "Food Aid and Child Nutrition in Rural Ethiopia," *World Development* 31 (2003), 1309–1324.

Ravallion, M., "Reaching the Poor through Rural Public Employment: A Survey of Theory and Evidence," *World Bank Discussion Paper 94* (World Bank: Washington, DC, 1990).

Schubert, B., B. Schramm, N. Wiebe, M. Baak, B. Wolter, and H. Wegener, *Social Cash Transfer in Development Cooperation: Kalomo District, Zambia* (GTZ: Eichborn, 2005).

Sen, A., *Poverty and Famines* (Clarendon Press: Oxford, 1981).

Sharma, M., *The Impact of Food Aid on Consumption and Assets Levels in Rural Malawi* (International Food Policy Research Institute: Washington, DC, 2005a).

Sharma, M., *Targeting of Emergency Free Food Distribution Program in Malawi: An Assessment* (International Food Policy Research Institute: Washington, DC, 2005b).

Swift, J., and K. Hamilton, "Household Food and Livelihood Security," in S. Devereux and S. Maxwell, eds., *Food Security in Sub–Saharan Africa* (ITDG Publishing: London, 2001), pp. 67–92.

Tiba, Z., "A New Type of Famine with Traditional Response: The Case of Malawi, 2001–2003," PhD thesis (School of Oriental and African Studies, University of London: London, 2005).

Wobst, P., H. Lofgren, H. Tchale, and J. Morrison, *Pro-poor Development Strategies for Malawi: An Economy-wide Analysis of Alternative Policy Scenarios* (Imperial College at Wye, University of London: Wye, 2004).

The impact of natural and manmade disasters on household welfare

Abstract

In this article, we provide selective evidence on the impact of natural and manmade disasters on household welfare. First, we consider *ex ante* risk management and *ex post* risk-coping behaviors separately, showing evidence from the Asian economic crisis, earthquakes, and tsunami disasters. Second, we differentiate idiosyncratic risks from nondiversifiable aggregate risks that characterize a disaster. We also discuss the difficulties of designing index-type insurance against natural disasters, which are often rare, unforeseen events. Then, we investigate the role of self-insurance against large-scale disasters under which formal or informal mutual insurance mechanisms are largely ineffective. Credit accessibility is identified as one of the key factors facilitating risk-coping strategies.

JEL classification: D80, G22, I3, O1

Keywords: natural disaster; manmade disaster; risk management; risk coping; risk sharing; insurance

1. Introduction

In developed as well as developing countries, people are at a wide variety of risks to their livelihood. Accidents, sickness, or sudden death can disable the head of a household or even an entire family. Agricultural production involves a variety of price and yield risks that appear to be prevalent especially for small-scale, poor farmers in the semiarid tropical areas in developing countries. Even for households in urban, industrial, or commercial sectors, income fluctuates over time due to contractual and physical risks in the handling of products, intermediate goods, and employees in LDCs. Macroeconomic instability or recessions, which tend to generate harsh inflation/deflation and widespread unemployment, can also significantly reduce the real value of household resources. However, natural disasters can generate the most serious consequences ever known. Recently, a number of natural disasters hit both developed and developing countries alike. We still remember vividly how a huge number of lives were lost in the Indian Ocean tsunami, Pakistan earthquake, Great Hanshin–Awaji (Kobe) earthquake, and Hurricane Katrina. In addition to disasters caused by natural events, manmade disasters such as economic crisis, terrorism, and wars also create serious damage.

In this article, we will provide selective evidence of the impact of natural and manmade disasters on household welfare. Three aspects differentiate this study from earlier related studies. First, while there has been a remarkable progress in the theoretical and empirical literature on risk and household behavior (Fafchamps, 2003; Dercon, 2005), shocks generated by a disaster, which potentially gives a clean experimental situation, have rarely been investigated or utilized. Second, unlike previous studies on household behavior against general idiosyncratic shocks, we explore quantitatively the role of savings, borrowing, and other risk-coping devices against disasters as a covariate shock. Finally, by using preliminary results based on a unique data set collected in the earthquake- and Tsunami-affected areas, we discuss the role of public policy to facilitate households' risk-coping behavior against disasters.

In general, a *disaster* is defined as an unforeseen event that causes great damage, destruction, and human suffering that overwhelms local capacity, necessitating a request at a national or international level for external assistance (Centre for Research on the

* *Faculty of Economics, University of Tokyo, 7-3-1 Hongo, Bunkyo-ku, Tokyo 113-0033, Japan.*

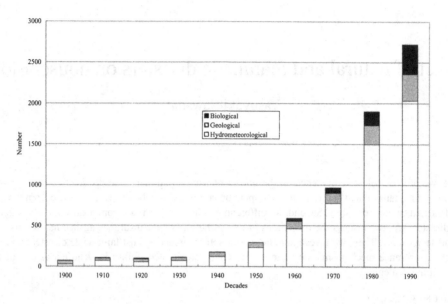

Figure 1. Number of natural disasters, 1900s–1990s. *Source:* EM-DAT: The OFDA/CRED international disaster database. <http://www.em-dat.net> UCL-Brussels, Belgium.

Epidemiology of Disasters, 2006).[1] Disasters in this definition include warfare, civil strife, economic crisis such as hyperinflation and financial crisis, hazardous material or transportation incident (such as a chemical spill), explosion, nuclear incident, building collapse, blizzard, hurricane, drought, epidemic and pandemic, earthquake, fire, flood, or volcanic eruption.

Augmenting the classification system of United Nations International Strategies for Disaster Reduction (UNISDR; 2005), these disasters can be classified into three broad categories: natural disasters, technological disasters, and manmade disasters. First, natural disasters can be divided into three subgroups: (1) hydrometeorological disasters including floods, storms, and droughts; (2) geophysical disasters including earthquakes, tsunamis, and volcanic eruptions; and (3) biological disasters such as epidemics and insect infestations. Second, the technological disasters are mainly composed of two subgroups: (1) industrial accidents such as chemical spills, collapses of industrial infrastructures, fires, and radiation, and (2) transport accidents by air, rail, road, or water. Finally, manmade dis-

asters are also composed of two subcategories: (1) economic crises including growth collapse, hyperinflation, and financial and/or currency crisis, and (2) violence such as terrorism, civil strife, riots, and war.

Figure 1 shows the number of natural disasters registered in EM-DAT: the OFDA/CRED International Disaster Database for 1900–2004. We can see the apparent increasing trend of natural disasters, especially of hydrometeorological disasters. A closer look at the data for 1995–2004 by type of triggering hazards reveals that floods are the most commonly occurring natural disaster, followed by droughts and related disasters, epidemics, and earthquakes and tsunamis (Table 1). Table 1 also reveals that epidemics are serious in Africa, while Asia was hit by a large number of earthquakes and tsunamis.

The number of people affected and killed by natural disasters has also been increasing in the last 30 years. Yet, the estimated damage from natural disasters does not necessarily increase with that of the numbers of disasters and victims. The amount of damage seems to depend on the location of the disaster. According to Table 2, the level of damages from natural disasters is much higher in developed countries than that in developing countries, while the impact of disasters to a national economy may be higher in developing countries. The Great-Hanshin (Kobe) earthquake and

---

[1] The Centre for Research on the Epidemiology of Disasters (2006) recorded a disaster that fulfills at least one of the following criteria: 10 or more people reported killed, 100 people reported affected, declaration of a state of emergency, and call for international assistance.

Table 1
Number of natural disasters by type of triggering hazards: regional distribution 1995–2004

Region	Hydrometeorological disasters						Geological disasters		Biological disasters	
	Floods	Wind storms	Droughts and related disasters	Landslides	Avalanches	Waves and surges	Earthquakes and tsunamis	Volcanic eruptions	Epidemics	Insect infestations
Africa	277	70	123	11	0	0	18	4	346	14
America	269	298	205	43	1	1	51	23	48	2
Asia	444	326	229	97	16	6	193	13	154	3
Europe	180	86	156	7	10	0	28	2	37	1
Oceania	35	68	37	8	0	0	9	6	10	3
World	1205	848	750	166	27	7	299	48	595	23

Source: EM-DAT: The OFDA/CRED International Disaster Database. Available at <http://www.em-dat.net> UCL-Brussels, Belgium.

Hurricane Katrina recorded the two largest economic damages in history (see Table 2 and also Horwich [2000]). These changes in natural and manmade disasters suggest the increasing importance of research on disasters.

As for manmade disasters, the number of complex economic crises also seems to be increasing. A seminal work by Kaminsky and Reinhart (1999) reveals that the number of currency crises per year did not increase much during the 1980s and 1990s, while the number of banking crises and simultaneous banking and currency crises, that is, *twin crises*, increased sharply in the 1980s and 1990s (Table 3).

In response to the wide variety of shocks caused by natural and manmade disasters, households have developed formal and informal mechanisms to weather the shocks. We classify such insurance mechanisms by two dimensions. First, we consider *ex ante* risk management and *ex post* risk-coping behaviors separately. Second, we divide insurance mechanisms into mutual and self-insurance through market and nonmarket mechanisms (Hayashi et al., 1996). The rest of this article is organized as follows. In Section 2, we discuss risk management and coping behaviors. Some evidence from the Asian economic crisis, earthquakes, and tsunamis is shown. In Section 3, we differentiate idiosyncratic risks that can be diversified away through mutual insurance from nondiversifiable aggregate risks that characterize a disaster. Then, we investigate the role of self-insurance against large-scale disasters under which formal or informal mutual insurance mechanisms are weak. In the final section, we will discuss public policy issues of disasters, which will be followed by the concluding remarks.

2. Risk management and coping against disasters

While people in developing countries, especially the poor, face many risks in their daily lives, maintaining a stable consumption level above subsistence is essential for maintaining households' standard of living over time. Poverty occurs when a household's per capita consumption level falls below a properly defined poverty line. Hence, the central behavioral problem of LDC households becomes a reconciliation of income fluctuation and consumption smoothing. This problem can be theoretically captured as the problem of intertemporal consumption smoothing under a stochastic income process. Following Morduch (1995), we can capture the negative welfare costs of risks by calculating how much money households would be willing to pay to completely eliminate income variability. Mathematically, such an amount of money is represented by m which satisfies the following relationship:[2] $u(\bar{y} - m) = E[u(\tilde{y})]$, where $u(\cdot)$ is a well-behaved utility function, $\tilde{y}$ is a stochastic income, and $\bar{y}$ is its mean value. Taking a first-order Taylor expansion of the left-hand side around $m = 0$ and a second-order Taylor expansion of the right-hand side around the mean income gives:[3]

$$\frac{m}{\bar{y}} = \frac{1}{2} \underbrace{\left(-\frac{u''(\bar{y})\bar{y}}{u'(\bar{y})} \right)}_{\text{Coefficient of RRA}} \times \underbrace{\left(\frac{\sqrt{\text{Var}(\tilde{y})}}{\bar{y}} \right)^2}_{\text{Coefficient of variation}}. \tag{1}$$

Equation (1) indicates that, approximately, the fraction of average income that a household would be willing

---

[2] The variable m represents a standard risk premium.

[3] This is the so-called Arrow–Pratt risk premium.

Table 2
Direct damages from natural disasters

Event (Year)	Damages (US$, billion)	Loss as percentage of GDP
Hurricane Katrina (2005)	125[h]	1.7[j]
Tsunami in India (2004)	1.02[a]	0.17[e]
Tsunami in Indonesia (2004)	4.45[b]	2.14[e]
Tsunami in Maldives (2004)	0.47[c]	2.58[e]
Tsunami in Sri Lanka (2004)	0.97–1.00[d]	4.4–4.6[e]
Chuetsu earthquake in Japan (2004)	28.3[f]	0.6[g]
Earthquakes in Turkey (1999)	22[i]	5[i]
Hurricane Mitch in the United States (1998)	1.96[i]	0.03[i]
Great Hanshin–Awaji earthquake in Japan (1995)	95–147[i]	2.5[i]
Hurricane Andrew in the United States (1992)	26.5[i]	0.5[i]
Cyclone/floods in Bangladesh (1991)	1[i]	5[i]
Great Kanto earthquake (1923)	32.6[g] (in 2003 price)	43.6[g]

[a] Asian Development Bank, United Nations, and World Bank (2005) "India Post Tsunami Recovery Program—Preliminary Damage and Needs Assessment."

[b] BAPPENAS and the International Donor Community (2005), "Indonesia: Preliminary Damage and Loss Assessment: The December 26, 2004 Natural Disaster."

[c] World Bank, Asian Development Bank, and UN System (2005), "Tsunami: Impact and Recovery."

[d] Asian Development Bank, Japan Bank for International Cooperation, and World Bank (2005), "Sri Lanka 2005 Post-Tsunami Recovery Program-Preliminary Damage and Needs Assessment."

[e] The author's calculation based on World Bank's World Development Indicators.

[f] Niigata Prefecture, Japan.

[g] The author's estimates using information from the Cabinet Office and the Ministry of Finance of the Government of Japan.

[h] The author's calculation based on the information from Risk Management Solutions (RMS).

[i] Table 1 in Freeman et al. (2003).

[j] United Nations International Strategy for Disaster Reduction.

to give up can be calculated as half of the coefficient of relative risk aversion multiplied by the square of the coefficient of variation of income. Table 4 shows the estimated welfare costs of risks in India and Pakistan. These results indicate that the welfare cost of risks is at least 10% and can be 30–50% of household income. Since natural and manmade disasters generate larger income volatilities than these income fluctuations, the welfare costs estimated here may be regarded as lower-

Table 3
Frequency of economic crises over time

Type of crisis	1970–1979		1980–1995	
	Total	Average per year	Total	Average per year
Balance of payments	26	2.6	50	3.13
Twin	1	0.10	18	1.13
Single	25	2.50	32	2.00
Banking	3	0.30	23	1.44

Source: Table 1 of Kaminsky and Reinhart (1999).

bound estimates of the negative welfare impacts of natural or manmade disasters.

Based on the framework of the Life-Cycle Permanent Income Hypothesis (LC-PIH), the recent microdevelopment literature examines the role of risks in determining the nature of poverty. These studies address the effectiveness of formal and informal risk management or coping mechanisms of households (Alderman and Paxson, 1992; Townsend, 1994, 1995; Udry, 1994; Besley, 1995; Morduch, 1995; Deaton, 1997; Fafchamps, 2003; Dercon, 2005).

2.1. Risk management and risk-coping strategies

Risk management strategies can be defined as activities for mitigating risk and reducing income instability before the resolution of uncertainties in order to smooth income (Walker and Jodha, 1986; Alderman and Paxson, 1992). Farmers have traditionally managed agricultural production risks by crop diversification, inter-cropping, flexible production investments, the use of low-risk technologies, and special contracts such as sharecropping. Even in commercial and industrial sectors, ethnicity- or kinship-based longterm business relationships are often formed in order to

Table 4
Quantifying the seriousness of risks

	Coefficient of relative risk aversion	Coefficient of variation	Estimated m as a percentage of income (%)
Pakistan	1.12–3.34[a]	42.1–54.3[b]	9.93–49.24
India	1.39[c], 1.77–3.10[c]	47.0[d]	15.35–34.24

[a] Table 5–3, 5–4, and 6–3 of Kurosaki (1998).

[b] Morduch (1990).

[c] Fafchamps (2003), p. 184.

[d] Table 10.6 of Walker and Ryan (1990).

alleviate various contractual risks beforehand. It has been argued that *ex ante* investments in mitigating the risk of natural disasters are very cost-effective in providing *ex post* compensations for losses from disasters (World Bank, 2001, ch. 9). However, it is often difficult by nature to set proper risk management strategies against natural disasters because they are typically rare events and sometimes, even worse, they are unforeseen.

Accordingly, even if households adopted a variety of risk management strategies, a disaster can happen unexpectedly, causing serious negative impacts on household welfare. For example, crops and livestock may be destroyed by a natural disaster on an unprecedented scale. Sudden accidents, sickness, or death can disable the household head or family unexpectedly. Against these unexpected natural disasters, *ex post* risk coping will be indispensable where risk-coping strategies are defined as *ex post* strategies to reduce consumption fluctuations (Alderman and Paxson, 1992). In general, the existing literature identified the following different risk-coping mechanisms. First, households can reduce consumption expenditure while maintaining total caloric intakes. Second, households can use credit to smooth consumption by reallocating future resources to today's consumption. Third, households can accumulate financial and physical assets as a precautionary device against unexpected income shortfalls. Finally, locating household members and/or receiving remittances in emergency is a form of risk coping.

2.2. The Asian crisis in the late 1990s

First, a household can maintain total nutritional intake while it reduces food purchases and other expenditures. This is accomplished by changing the quality and composition of food expenditures or by reducing nonfood expenditures, such as those for luxuries. As revealed in recent studies on the aftermath of the currency crisis in Indonesia, Korea, Thailand, and Mexico, consumption reallocation is indeed an important coping strategy (Frankenberg et al., 1999, 2003; Townsend, 1999; McKenzie, 2003, 2004; Strauss et al., 2004; Kang and Sawada, 2007a). According to Table 5, Indonesian households seem to have weathered the crisis by cutting back meat consumption, medical and education expenses, and leisure expenditure by approximately 40–60% while maintaining stable food consumption.

Table 5

Changes in per capita consumption in Indonesia (unit: 1,000 Rupiah, per month value at December 1997 price)

	1997 (Rp)	1998 (Rp)	Change rate (%)
Urban households			
Per capita consumption	319	184	−42
Staple	41.4	37.9	−8
Meat	40.5	19.1	−53
Medical	5.5	2.7	−50
Education	15.7	8.3	−47
Leisure	8.2	3.8	−54
Rural households			
Per capita consumption	194	128	−34
Staple	59.3	50.4	−15
Meat	24.2	12.5	−48
Medical	2.3	0.9	−61
Education	4.6	2.3	−50
Leisure	3.6	2.2	−39

Source: Frankenberg et al. (1999).

In Korea under the financial crisis, a decrease in leisure expenditure would be an important coping behavior as well (Table 6). Yet, unlike Indonesian households, Korean households did not cut back medical and education expenses significantly. This difference between Indonesia and Korea may cause a different long-term impact of the manmade disaster because human capital accumulation might be disrupted seriously in Indonesia.

Second, facing a disaster, households can use credit to smooth consumption by reallocating future resources to current consumption. The lack of consumption insurance can be compensated for by having access to a credit market (Eswaran and Kotwal, 1989; Besley, 1995; Glewwe and Hall, 1998). However, poor households usually have only limited access to credit markets and are constrained from borrowing for a variety of reasons such as the lack of collateral assets. In any case, the existence of credit constraints has important negative impacts on the risk-coping ability of poor households. According to Table 6, the average amount of Korean household debt increased by 28% during the financial crisis, but the nature of the financial crisis worked negatively on the role of credit as a risk-coping behavior (Goh et al., 2005). Kang and Sawada (2007a) revealed that between 1997 and 1998, the likelihood of facing credit constraints increased significantly. The expected welfare loss from binding credit constraints is

Table 6
Changes in per capita consumption in Korea (unit: 10,000 Won, per year value at 1995 price)

	Mean (standard error)		
	Aug 1996–July 1997	Aug 1997–July 1998	Change rate (%)
Consumption expenditure			
Food expenditure	351.54 (216.26)	297.99 (177.63)	−15.2
Education and medical expenditure	304.17 (371.30)	242.21 (336.21)	−20.4
Expenditures for luxuries (cultural activities, entertainment, dining out, and durable goods)	147.25 (333.75)	53.98 (86.36)	−63.3
Income, Assets, and Debts			
Wage income or earnings from work	2064.81 (1734.66)	1523.41 (1264.16)	−26.2
Private transfers received	51.38 (214.14)	54.90 (209.45)	6.9
Public transfers received	19.18 (116.35)	20.99 (134.08)	9.4
Sales of assets (land, real estate, securities, and withdrawal of time deposits)	195.01 (1305.44)	203.62 (1089.94)	4.4
Total assets (savings account, shares, bonds, insurance, loan clubs, current value of house)	7681.19 (9403.04)	7533.37 (11895.05)	−1.9
Outstanding debt (formal banks, informal banks, and personal)	842.02 (2177.78)	1074.34 (5252.27)	27.6

Source: Kang and Sawada (2007a).

estimated to increase at least by 29% during the crisis, suggesting the seriousness of the credit crunch at the household level.

Third, households can accumulate precautionary financial and physical assets *ex ante* against unexpected shocks caused by a disaster.[4] Forms of precautionary savings in developing countries include grain storage (Townsend, 1995; Park, 2006), cash holdings (Townsend, 1995), liquidation of bullocks (Rosenzweig and Wolpin, 1993), and sales of goats and sheep (Fafchamps et al., 1998). However, according to Kang and Sawada (2003b), during the Korean crisis, sales of assets did not increase significantly, and assets declined by a mere 2%, implying that such sales did not serve as an important coping device (Table 6). This may indicate that households were reluctant to sell their assets to cope with the negative shock since land and stock prices declined sharply (Goh et al., 2005).

On the other hand, private and public transfers rose by 8% and 11%, respectively. Yet transfers constituted only 4% of total income, and merely 22% of total

households received transfers. Particularly, the amount of private transfers was still not sufficient to support households living in urban areas (Kang and Sawada, 2003; Kang and Sawada, 2007b). Public transfers consisted predominantly of pensions, which take 82% of public transfers on average, since most of the social safety net programs were not yet in place during the initial phase of the crisis.

2.3. Hanshin–Awaji (Kobe) earthquake

In the early hours of January 17, 1995, the Hanshin (Kobe) area in Japan was hit by a major earthquake. The area is densely populated, comprising more than 4 million people and is a part of the second largest industrial cluster in Japan. The earthquake induced a human loss of more than 6,400, a housing property loss greater than US$60 billion, and a capital stock loss of more than US$100 billion, making it the largest economic damage recorded in history (Table 2; Horwich, 2000; Sawada and Shimizutani, 2005). Given the fact that only 3% of the property in Hyogo Prefecture, where Kobe is located, was covered by earthquake insurance, it is reasonable to assume that the earthquake was entirely unexpected in this area.

---

[4] This is also called "self-insurance." To quantify the degree of precautionary saving, the existing studies estimate the prudence parameter. See, e.g., Lee and Sawada (2007).

Sawada and Shimizutani (2005; 2007b) utilize an unique household-level data that was collected from the earthquake-affected households in October 1996, 22 months after the earthquake. With this data set, Sawada and Shimizutani (2005) employ binary-dependent variables of the three risk-coping strategies, that is, borrowing, receiving public and private transfers, and dissaving. According to their analysis, among the respondents who faced a negative impact due to the earthquake, more than half utilized their dissavings (Table 7). Borrowing and receiving transfers were also considered as significant risk-coping strategies for approximately 10% and 12% of valid responses, respectively.

The survey was also carried out in order to record the details of the damage caused to the respondents by the earthquake, such as damages to the house, household assets, and the health of the family members.[5] In Table 7, it should be noted that 85.6% and 86.7% of the respondents suffered from damages to their house and household assets, respectively. These figures are indicative of the seriousness of the economic loss caused by the unexpected earthquake.

Sawada and Shimizutani (2005) investigated further the relationship between the damages and coping strategies. They found that transfers may be particularly ineffective as insurance against losses for coresident households. Households borrow extensively against housing damages, whereas dissavings are utilized for smaller asset damages, implying a hierarchy of risk-coping measures, from dissaving to borrowing.

The Kobe earthquake caused historically large damages to the economy and the people. To identify the peculiarity of the large-scale disaster, we can compare it with a smaller natural disaster. Ichimura et al. (2006) collected data of about 600 victims of the Chuetsu earthquake of October 2004. The total economic losses caused by the Chuetsu earthquake were around one fifth of that caused by the Kobe earthquake (Table 2). According to the data set, about 32.3% managed to cope with the damages by dissavings and about 9% utilized borrowings from banks, relatives, friends, and government schemes. More importantly, receiving public and

---

[5] It should be noted that, shortly after the earthquake, the local governments conducted metrical surveys and issued formal certificates for housing damages which the households could later use to obtain government compensations. Therefore, we believe that the information obtained on housing damages is fairly objective and accurate.

Table 7
Damages and coping strategies under the Great Hanshin–Awaji (Kobe) earthquake

Variable description	Mean
Shock variables	
Dummy = 1 if major housing damage was caused by the earthquake	0.174
Dummy = 1 if moderate housing damage was caused by the earthquake	0.251
Dummy = 1 if minor housing damage was caused by the earthquake	0.431
Dummy = 1 if major household asset damage was caused by the earthquake	0.094
Dummy = 1 if minor household asset damage was caused by the earthquake	0.773
Dummy = 1 if the family suffered health-related shocks caused by the earthquake	0.213
Coping variables	
Dummy = 1 if reallocations of the constituents of the consumption were the most significant means of coping	0.250
Dummy = 1 if dissaving was the most significant means of coping	0.537
Dummy = 1 if borrowing was the most significant means of coping	0.096
Dummy = 1 if receiving transfers was the most significant means of coping	0.117

Source: Sawada and Shimizutani (2005).

private transfers were considered as a significant risk-coping strategy for approximately 47% of respondents. This high proportion suggests that government support and an informal social safety net can be quite effective if the scale of the disaster is not too large.

2.4. Indian tsunami disaster

In the morning of December 26, 2004, a tsunami caused by the Sumatra earthquake hit the eastern and southern coastal areas of India. Estimated damages were highest in Tamil Nadu State (US$815.0 million) and the fishery sector was affected most (Sawada, 2007). The number of deaths caused by the tsunami was also the highest in Tamil Nadu State, especially in the Nagapattinum district, where 6,065 people perished (Sawada, 2007). The majority of the victims were women and children.

In January–April 2006, we conducted a survey of 400 households from eight villages in the Nagapattinum district that were affected by the tsunami

Table 8
Damages and coping strategies under the tsunami in India

Variable description	Mean
Shock variables	
Dummy = 1 if lost house	0.040
Dummy = 1 if house seriously damaged	0.160
Dummy = 1 if lost utensils	0.150
Dummy = 1 if lost productive assets such as boats	0.785
Dummy = 1 if lost job	0.240
Dummy = 1 if income declined	0.603
Dummy = 1 if lost members	0.053
Dummy = 1 if members got injured or sick	0.013
Coping variables during the relief phase (Dec 26, 2004–April 30, 2005)	
Dummy = 1 if sales of assets was an important means of coping	0.088
Dummy = 1 if borrowing was an important means of coping	0.405
Dummy = 1 if receiving transfers was an important means of coping	0.905

Source: Sawada (2007).

(Sawada, 2007). A stratified random sampling scheme was adopted to obtain representative information of the damaged villages. Table 8 summarizes the damages caused by the tsunami and households' risk-coping means adopted against the damages. As for the damages, the majority of households lost productive assets such as boats and faced income losses. It is notable that receiving aid from government, relatives and neighbors, self-help groups, and NGOs were important means of coping for more than 90% of households, followed by borrowing for around 41% of households (Table 8).

3. The role of market and nonmarket institutions

The next issue we will discuss in this article is the role of market and nonmarket institutions against disasters. For this, it is useful to classify different types of risks by the level at which they occur. Idiosyncratic shocks affect specific individuals while aggregate shocks affect groups of households, an entire community and region, or a country as a whole. This distinction is important because the geographic level at which risks arise determines the effectiveness of market and nonmarket institutions against risk. On the one hand, a risk that affects a specific individual can be traded with other people in the same insurance network through informal

mutual insurance as well as a well-functioning formal insurance or credit market. Such risks include illness, injury, death, unemployment, crime, and domestic violence. On the other hand, a risk that affects an entire region cannot be insured within the region and necessitates a formal market in which region-specific risks are diversified away across regions. Examples of aggregate or covariate risks are earthquake, flood, drought, epidemic, terrorism, war, and economic crises. In fact, the extent to which a risk is idiosyncratic or correlated depends considerably on the underlying causes.

Households have developed formal and informal risk-coping mechanisms against these wide variety of shocks (Cochrane, 1991; Mace, 1991; Townsend, 1994; Besley, 1995; Fafchamps, 2003; Dercon, 2005). Largely, we classify such insurance opportunities as mutual and self-insurance opportunities. Mutual insurance provides consumption insurance opportunities across households through a variety of either market or nonmarket mechanisms such as formal insurance markets, credit market transactions that reallocate future resources to current consumption (Eswaran and Kotwal, 1989), and informal reciprocal transfers and credit among relatives, friends, and neighbors.[6] The government can also complement the household risk-coping behavior by direct public transfers, such as unemployment insurance. Regarding self-insurance, in the event of unexpected negative shocks, households can utilize their own financial and physical assets that have been accumulated beforehand (Lee and Sawada, 2007).

3.1. Full insurance through market or nonmarket mechanisms

To investigate the implications of the full consumption insurance, we can solve a benevolent social planner's problem by maximizing the weighted sum of people's lifetime utilities given intertemporal resource constraints (Mace, 1991).[7] A solution to this problem is that under full insurance, idiosyncratic household in-

---

[6] The self-enforcement mechanisms of this self-interested mutual insurance scheme could be sustained as subgame perfect Nash equilibria in a repeated game (Coate and Ravallion, 1993; Kocherlakota, 1996).

[7] This condition is also derived from solving the household optimization problem with complete contingent markets.

come changes should be absorbed by all other members in the same insurance network. As a result, after controlling for aggregate shocks, idiosyncratic income shocks should not affect consumption when risk sharing is efficient. The theoretical implications for the existence of full risk-sharing arrangements within an insurance network are widely tested in the literature (Townsend, 1994, 1995; Udry, 1994).

The theoretical model employed here is based on Mace (1991), Cochrane (1991), Udry (1994), and Townsend's (1994) full insurance model in a pure exchange economy. In the model, an economy with an insurance network, which can be a village or a district, is composed of N infinitely lived households, each facing serially independent income draws. A hypothetical social planner will allocate endowments so as to equalize households' weighted marginal utility. Therefore, the full consumption insurance hypothesis implies that a household's consumption allocation should be independent of idiosyncratic variables. In other words, under full insurance, idiosyncratic household income changes should be absorbed by all other members in the same insurance network. As a result, idiosyncratic income shocks should not affect consumption.

The very strict full-insurance hypothesis does seem to be rejected statistically in most data sets, especially for the poorest farmers (Townsend, 1994, 1995). Yet, the empirical consensus tells us that, in general, the degree of missing markets is somewhat smaller than many had assumed and many better-off households seem to face almost complete insurance and credit markets against idiosyncratic shocks (Morduch, 1995; Townsend, 1995).

However, natural disasters are often rare, unexpected events by which people become burdened by abrupt damages. Hence, it is even harder to design mutual insurance for natural disasters. In fact, Sawada and Shimizutani (2007a) investigate whether people were insured against unexpected losses caused by the Great Hanshin–Awaji (Kobe) earthquake in 1995. They found that the full consumption insurance hypothesis is rejected overwhelmingly, suggesting the ineffectiveness of formal/informal insurance mechanisms against the earthquake.

3.2. Market versus nonmarket insurance

These tests of the complete consumption insurance hypothesis can examine the validity of a wide variety

of formal and informal insurance mechanisms such as borrowing and receiving private and/or public transfers *as a whole* (Mace, 1991). Yet it is not easy to disaggregate the effectiveness of formal and informal insurance mechanisms. In fact, there is very little research on formal insurance consumption (Outreville, 1990; Enz, 2000; Galabova and Lester, 2001). To capture the relative importance of market (formal) and nonmarket (informal) mechanisms, we can utilize cross-country data on life- and nonlife-insurance penetration, the *Sigma* database, complied by Swiss Re. This data set is supposed to capture formal insurance traded in markets.

According to Figure 2, there is a positive relationship between volume of life and nonlife premiums per capita and GDP per capita. Moreover, it is evident that the fitted slope will be larger than unity. This suggests that formal insurance appears to be a luxury, especially in low- and middle-income countries, and that people's preferences are characterized by increasing risk aversion. Yet, provided that the poor should have higher potential demand for insurance because their marginal utility loss from a downside risk is higher than the rich, more informal insurance devices should be demanded in developing countries.[8] In response to the macro–micro paradox in demand for insurance, Nakata and Sawada (2007) employed wealth data rather than income data to estimate insurance demand elasticity more precisely.

3.3. Idiosyncratic versus aggregate shocks

Having discussed the role of mutual insurance to diversify idiosyncratic risks, we should note that full insurance schemes against aggregate shocks such as regionwide weather shocks, droughts, and natural or manmade disasters cannot be constructed within a village because these sources of risk are village, region, or even nation specific. Yet, even across a village or region, households can build informal insurance networks that are not necessarily complete. For example, Lucas and Stark's (1985) evidence from Botswana shows that remittances from urban family members are particularly large when the drought is severe, which implies that there is a concern for preserving assets; households buy insurance by placing members in markets whose outcomes are not highly positively

---

[8] Galabova and Lester (2001) found that micro-data from several countries support the notion of insurance as a necessary item.

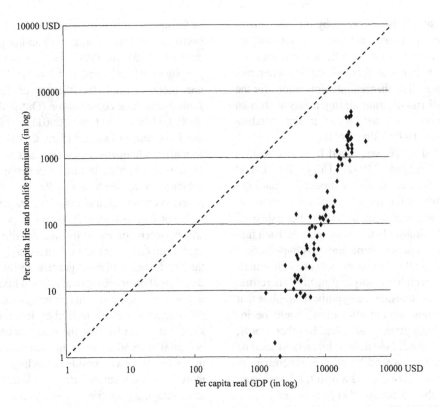

Figure 2. Cross-country income elasticity for life and nonlife formal insurance demand in 2000. *Source:* Penn World Tables Version 6.1, and Sigma, Swiss Re.

correlated. By analyzing Indian data, Rosenzweig and Stark (1989) found that marriage cum migration contributes significantly to a reduction in the variability of household food consumption and that farm households afflicted with more variable profits tend to engage in longer-distance marriage cum migration. Thus, the marriage of daughters aims at mitigating income risks and facilitating consumption smoothing.

Yet, a formal analysis of the validity of intervillage full risk sharing using IFPRI's rural Pakistan data over three years reveals that district- or nationwide full risk sharing hypotheses are rejected strongly (Kurosaki and Sawada, 1999). Their result suggests that a larger-scale formal or informal insurance network is far from complete. Natural disasters and manmade disasters are characterized by the correlated nature of their shocks, affecting many people at the same time. This implies that it may be difficult for existing social safety networks to insure people from natural or manmade disasters effectively.

3.4. Index insurance

As an effective insurance instrument against covariate shocks, index insurance contracts have been attracting wide attention (Hazell, 2003; Morduch, 2004; Lilleor et al., 2005; Skees et al., 2005). Index insurance contracts are written against specific events such as drought or flood defined and recorded at a regional level. As such, index insurance involves a number of positive aspects: they can cover aggregate events; they are affordable and accessible even to the poor; they are easy to implement and privately managed; and they are free from moral hazard, adverse selection, and high transaction costs that have plagued traditional agricultural insurance contracts such as crop insurance schemes. The World Bank and other institutions have been piloting weather-based index insurance contracts in Morocco, Mongolia, Peru, Vietnam, Ethiopia, Guatemala, India, Mexico, Nicaragua, Romania, and Tunisia (Skees et al., 2005).

Since natural disasters are typically an aggregate event, index insurance is thought to be an appropriate instrument to combat them. Yet there are three major constraints to design index-type insurance against natural disasters. First, natural disasters are often characterized by a rare event that makes it difficult to design actuarially fair insurance. Since obtaining historical data on the pattern of natural disasters is hard, it is almost impossible to set appropriate premiums for insurance (Morduch, 2004).

Second, related to the first issue, even if appropriate premiums are set, the poor, who potentially should demand insurance against natural disasters, may find it difficult to recognize the value of index-type insurance against natural disasters. This may be an inevitable consequence because natural disasters are often characterized by unforeseen contingencies by nature and because the poor are often myopic, with high time discount rates (Pender, 1996). Moreover, the existence of the "basis risk" with which an individual could incur damage but cannot be compensated enough, will also deter demand for index insurance. This problem has been identified as an inevitable drawback of index insurance because index contracts essentially trade off basis risk for transaction costs (Hazell, 2003; Morduch, 2004).

Finally, natural disasters are highly covariate risks that often cannot be diversified within a country. Accordingly, the insurers have a potential need to secure their financial position by utilizing international reinsurance markets. However, it is known that reinsurance markets and trades of catastrophe (CAT) bonds are still thin, with limited capacity. Also, as an overall effectiveness of mutual insurance across national borders, existing studies show that the extent of international risk sharing remains surprisingly small (Lewis, 1996; Obstfeld and Rogoff, 2001).[9] However, using data on hurricane exposure, Yang (2006) found that the poor's hurricane exposure leads to substantial increase in migrants' remittances, so that total financial inflows from all sources in the three years following hurricane exposure amount to roughly three-fourths of estimated damages. This suggests that aggregated shock arising from natural disasters can be insured at least partially, depending on the income level and the situation.

3.5. Self-insurance

As we have seen, efficient risk sharing is likely to be absent especially for natural disasters as a rare, covariate event. However, even for such risks, households are able to insure themselves against unexpected shocks by using self-insurance measures. For example, Shoji (2006) examines the effective coping strategy against the huge historical flood in Bangladesh in 1998, finding that under severe aggregate shocks, a group of people surrendered livestock assets when quasi-credit was available only for idiosyncratic shocks. Yet, one's own assets may be ineffective for disaster risk management or coping because these assets are often destroyed in a disaster. This leads us to think that effective disaster risk management and insurance should come from outside a region or even country.

To elaborate on these discussions, following Zeldes (1989) and Ljungqvist and Sargent (2000, ch. 13), we derive a self-insurance model by assuming a household chooses a path to maximize the conditional expectation of discounted lifetime utility subject to a nonnegativity constraint for assets and the usual intertemporal budget constraints. As a solution to this household problem, we obtain an augmented consumption Euler equation with the possibility of a liquidity constraint (Zeldes, 1989):

$$u'(c_{it}) = E_t \left[u'(c_{it+1}) \left(\frac{1+r}{1+\delta} \right) \right] + \mu_{it}, \qquad (2)$$

where $u(c_{it})$ is a utility function of the ith household's consumption, c_{it}, at time t, r is an exogenous interest rate, and δ is a household's subjective discount factor. The variable μ represents the Lagrange multiplier associated with liquidity constraints, indicating negative welfare effects generated by binding liquidity constraints.[10] Note that the self-insurance model represented by Eq. (2) involves weaker restrictions than the full risk sharing model (Saito, 1999, p. 53). From the intertemporal budget constraints, we obtain:

---

[9] Another approach to secure insurers is that the government provide reinsurances. This means that the aggregate shocks are diversified intertemporally rather than spatially. An example of this kind of reinsurance policy is the Japanese earthquake insurance, in which the government provides a reinsurance scheme.

---

[10] Since the household is constrained from further borrowing but not from further saving, μ has a positive sign.

$y_t^{PRT} + y_t^{PUT} + y_t^N - n_t = s_t + c_t$, where y_t^{PRT}, y_t^{PUT}, y_t^N, n_t, and s_t are private transfer income, public transfer income, nontransfer income, a negative shock to assets, and net savings, respectively. Combining this intertemporal budget constraint and Eq. (2), if the utility function is supposed to take the form of a constant absolute risk aversion (CARA) function, then we have the following optimal self-insurance equation (Flavin, 1999; Kochar, 2003; Sawada and Shimizutani, 2005):

$$\Delta b_{it} + \Delta y_{it}^{PRT} + \Delta y_{it}^{PUT} + \Delta d_{it}$$
$$= -\Delta y_{it}^N + \Delta n_{it} + \frac{1}{\alpha}\left[\ln\left(\frac{1+r}{1+\delta}\right)\right] + \mu_{it-1}' + \eta_{it},$$

$$(3)$$

where b and d are borrowings and dissavings, respectively. The last two terms on the right-hand side represent the effects of liquidity constraints and mean zero independent expectation error. Equation (3) formally shows that there are four possible risk-coping strategies, namely, borrowing additional amounts, receiving additional private transfer income, receiving additional public transfer income, and increased dissaving, against realized negative shocks, whose absolute values are represented by $-\Delta y_t^N + \Delta n_t$. Equation (3) indicates that when a household is under a borrowing constraint, i.e., when μ is positive, the sum of the right-hand variables become larger, suggesting that the sensitivity of different coping strategies against the same shock is forced to increase. When these coping strategies are not effective enough, the household is forced to reduce its consumption level.

By analyzing a 1998 survey of areas affected by Hurricane Mitch, Morduch (2004) found that for 21% of households, the main response to the hurricane was not to use savings, nor to borrow money; the main response was a drastic reduction in consumption. This suggests that these households are constrained from borrowing against the shocks. By investigating how victims of the Great Hanshin–Awaji (Kobe) earthquake in 1995 coped with their unexpected losses, Sawada and Shimizutani (2005) found that households without borrowing constraints can borrow and/or dissave to respond to damages caused by the earthquake, while those under a constraint are unable to either borrow or dissave against the losses. However, private transfers are used for both types of households, depending on the magnitude of the damages.

These findings suggest that credit market accessibility seriously affects the effectiveness of self-insurance possibilities. As we have seen in Table 6, facing lower accessibility of credit market due to the credit crunch during the financial crisis, Korean households did not liquidate assets significantly. The effectiveness of risk-coping strategies against natural and manmade disasters was weakened by increased seriousness of credit constraints.

4. Policy implications and concluding remarks

Our selective evidence confirms a serious lack of insurance markets for damages arising from natural and manmade disasters. Without effective *ex ante* measures, the actual economic losses caused by a disaster can be enormous. For example, the Great Hanshin–Awaji (Kobe) earthquake proved to be extremely large for the government to support effectively. In fact, after the Kobe earthquake, the central and local governments provided the largest financial support in the history of Japan to reconstruct the affected areas and to facilitate economic recovery of the victims. Despite the extensive support provided by the government, direct transfers to victims who lost their houses were merely US$1,000–1,500 per household.

In the process of preparing well-designed social safety nets against future natural disasters, there are several policy implications according to our analyses. First, in its attempt to provide *ex post* public support in the event of a natural disaster, the government may create a moral hazard problem by encouraging people to expose themselves to greater risks than required (Horwich, 2000). Theoretically, index-type insurance should be free from moral hazard problems but, as we have discussed, such an insurance contract would be difficult to design and sell in the case of rare, unexpected events. Since our empirical results from the Korean financial crisis, the Hanshin–Awaji and Chuetsu earthquakes, and the tsunami in India indicate that credit played an important role as a coping device and often the poor are excluded from credit transactions, providing subsidized loans rather than direct transfers to victims can be a good example of facilitating *ex post* risk-coping behavior; such interventions are less likely to create serious moral hazard problems.

Second, having discussed the difficulty of designing index insurance, it would be imperative to design *ex ante* risk-management policies against the disasters if at all possible. For example, development of markets for earthquake insurance would lead to the efficient pricing of insurance premiums and efficient land market prices reflective of the level of risk. This development would generate proper incentives to invest in mitigations such as investments in earthquake-proof constructions against future earthquakes. These *ex ante* measures would significantly reduce the overall social loss caused by the earthquake. Issues such as these will be important research topics in the future.

Third, under the initial "emergency rescue" phase of the recovery actions against a disaster, matching of emergency demands and massive proliferations of aid supply under imperfect information and uncertainties will be a major problem that should be solved properly. This phase is plagued by standard failures of traditional targeting programs, e.g., the first problem can be called a problem of "targeting failure" in which the wrong people are targeted (inclusion error) or the right targets are excluded (exclusion error).

Finally, even if the government can identify the proper target group without problems, the stakeholders of public aid or subsidies might act inappropriately *ex post*. Considering the lack of income information and the moral hazard problems of the means-test targeting, benefit eligibility in developing countries tends to be conditioned on personal or household characteristics or Akerof's (1975) "tags," which are thought to be manipulation-free (Conning and Kevane, 2002). Tags may be based on employment status, age, gender, number of dependents, location, and ethnicity. In the case of disaster relief, damage status can be used to tag households. Yet, tagging may not be entirely free from moral hazard problems. Even under "tagged" targeting interventions, which are thought to be better than the means-test targeting, there are perverse incentives for people to change their characteristics to gain eligibility.

As a future task, researchers should investigate the effectiveness and efficiency of matching supply and demand of emergency aid by gathering and analyzing data from areas after disasters. As a potential scheme, researchers can explore how the government can make use of the role of community to design community-based aid allocation schemes through which imperfect information and pervasive incentive problems of the traditional programs are effectively mitigated (Bardhan, 2002).

Acknowledgments

This paper was prepared for a plenary session, "Economics of Natural Disaster," of the International Association of Agricultural Economists (IAAE) triennial Conference in Brisbane on August 12–18, 2006. I would like to thank my research collaborators, Hidehiko Ichimura, Sung Jin Kang, Takashi Kurosaki, Hiroyuki Nakata, and Satoshi Shimizutani, for helpful comments and guidance and Sarath Sanga and Masahiro Shoji for excellent research assistance.

References

Akerof, G., "The Economics of "Tagging" as Applied to the Optimal Income Tax, Welfare Programs, and Manpower Planning," *American Economic Review* 68 (1975), 9–19.

Alderman, H., and C. H. Paxson, "Do the Poor Insure? A Synthesis of the Literature on Risk and Consumption in Developing Countries," *Policy Research Working Paper* 1008 (World Bank: Washington, DC, 1992).

Bardhan, P., "Decentralization of Governance and Development," *Journal of Economic Perspectives* 16 (2002), 185–205.

Besley, T., "Savings, Credit and Insurance" in J. Behrman and T. N. Srinivasan, eds., *Handbook of Development Economics*, IIIA (1995), 2125–2207.

Centre for Research on the Epidemiology of Disasters, *Disasters in Numbers* (CRED: Brussels, Belgium, 2006).

Coate, S., and M. Ravallion, "Reciprocity without Commitment: Characterization and Performance of Informal Insurance Arrangements," *Journal of Development Economics* 40 (1993), 1–24.

Cochrane, J. H., "A Simple Test of Consumption Insurance," *Journal of Political Economy* 99 (1991), 957–976.

Conning, J., and M. Kevane, "Community-Based Targeting Mechanisms for Social Safety Nets: A Critical Review," *World Development* 30 (2002), 375–394.

Deaton, A., *The Analysis of Household Surveys: A Microeconometric Approach to Development Policy* (Oxford University Press: Oxford, 1997).

Dercon, S., ed., *Insurance against Poverty* (Oxford University Press: Oxford, 2005).

Enz, R., "The S-Curve Relation between Per-Capita Income and Insurance Penetration," *Geneva Papers on Risk and Insurance* 25 (2000), 396–406.

Eswaran, M., and A. Kotwal, "Credit as Insurance in Agrarian Economies," *Journal of Development Economics* 31 (1989), 37–53.

Fafchamps, M., *Rural Poverty, Risk and Development* (Edward Elgar: Cheltenham, UK, 2003).

Fafchamps, M., C. Udry, and K. Czukas, "Drought and Saving in West Africa: Are Livestock a Buffer Stock?" *Journal of Development Economics* 55 (1998), 273–305.

Flavin, M., "Robust Estimation of the Joint Consumption/Asset Demand Decision," *NBER Working Paper* 7011 (1999).

Frankenberg, E., D. Thomas, and K. Beegle, *The Real Costs of Indonesia's Crisis: Preliminary Findings from the Indonesian Family Life Surveys*, mimeo (Rand Corporation, 1999).

Frankenberg, E., J. P. Smith, and D. Thomas, "Economic Shocks, Wealth, and Welfare," *Journal of Human Resources* 38 (2003), 280–321.

Freeman, P. K., M. Keen, and M. Mani, "Dealing with Increased Risk of Natural Disasters: Challenges and Options," *IMF Working Paper* WP/03/197 (2003).

Galabova, T., and R. Lester, "Is Insurance Luxury?" *The Actuary*, December (2001), 32–34.

Glewwe, P., and G. Hall, "Are Some Groups More Vulnerable to Macroeconomic Shocks than Others? Hypothesis Tests Based on Panel Data from Peru," *Journal of Development Economics* 56 (1998), 181–206.

Goh, C., S. J. Kang, and Y. Sawada, "How Did Korean Households Cope with Negative Shocks from the Financial Crisis?" *Journal of Asian Economics* 16 (2005), 239–254.

Hayashi, F., J. Altonji, and L. Kotlikoff, "Risk-Sharing Between and Within Families," *Econometrica* 64 (1996), 261–294.

Hazell, P., "Potential Role for Insurance in Managing Catastrophic Risk in Developing Countries," *Proceedings of the World Bank Conference on Financing the Risks of Natural Disasters*, June 2–3, (2003).

Horwich, G., "Economic Lessons from Kobe Earthquake," *Economic Development and Cultural Change* 48 (2000), 521–542.

Ichimura, H., Y. Sawada, and S. Shimizutani, "Risk-Sharing against an Earthquake: The Case of Yamakoshi Village," a paper presented at the Japan Statistical Society 75th Anniversary Symposium, "Recent Advances in Applied Econometrics," on September 24, 2006 at University of Tokyo.

Kaminsky, G. L., and C. M. Reinhart, "The Twin Crisis: The Causes of Banking and Balance-of-Payments Problems," *American Economic Review* 89 (1999), 473–500.

Kang, S. J., and Y. Sawada, "Are Private Transfers Altruistically Motivated? The Case of the Republic of Korea before and during the Financial Crisis," *Developing Economies* 41 (2003), 484–501.

Kang, S. J., and Y. Sawada, "Credit Crunch and Household Welfare: The Korean Financial Crisis," *Japanese Economic Review*, forthcoming (2007a).

Kang, S. J., and Y. Sawada, "Did Public Transfers Crowd Out Private Transfers in Korea during the Financial Crisis?" *Journal of Development Studies*, forthcoming, (2007b).

Kochar, A., "Ill-Health, Savings and Portfolio Choices in Developing Economies," *Journal of Development Economics* 73 (2003), 257–285.

Kocherlakota, N. R. "Implications of Efficient Risk Sharing Without Commitment," *Review of Economic Studies* 63 (1996), 595–609.

Kurosaki, T. R., *Household Behavior in Pakistan's Agriculture, Occasional Papers Series* (Institute of Developing Economies, JETRO: Tokyo, 1998).

Kurosaki, T., and Y. Sawada, "Consumption Insurance in Village Economies–Evidence from Pakistan and Other Developing Countries (in Japanese with English summary)," *Economic Review* 50 (1999), 155–68.

Lee, J.-J., and Y. Sawada, "Precautionary Saving: A Re-examination," *Economics Letters* 96 (2007), 196–201.

Lewis, K., "What Can Explain the Apparent Lack of International Consumption Risk-Sharing?" *Journal of Political Economy* 104 (1996), 267–297.

Lilleor, H. B., X. Gene, R. M. Townsend, and J. Vickery, "Weather Insurance in Semi-Arid India," mimeo (2005).

Ljungqvist, L., and T. J. Sargent, *Recursive Macroeconomic Theory* (MIT Press: Cambridge, MA, 2000).

Lucas, R. E. B., and O. Stark, "Motivations to Remit: Evidence from Botswana," *Journal of Political Economy* 97 (1985), 905–926.

Mace, B. J., "Full Insurance in the Presence of Aggregate Uncertainty," *Journal of Political Economy* 99 (1991), 928–996.

McKenzie, D., "How Do Households Cope with Aggregate Shocks? Evidence from the Mexican Peso Crisis," *World Development* 31 (2003), 1179–1199.

McKenzie, D., "Aggregate Shocks and Urban Labor Market Responses: Evidence from Argentina's Financial Crisis," *Economic Development and Cultural Change* 52 (2004), 719–758.

Morduch, J., "Risk, Production and Saving: Theory and Evidence from Indian Households," mimeo (Harvard University Press: Cambridge, MA, 1990).

Morduch, J., "Income Smoothing and Consumption Smoothing," *Journal of Economic Perspectives* 9 (1995), 103–114.

Morduch, J. "Micro-Insurance: The Next Revolution?," forthcoming in A. Banerjee, R. Benabou, and D. Mookherjee, eds., *What Have We Learned About Poverty?* (Oxford University Press: Oxford, 2004).

Nakata, H., and Y. Sawada, "Demand for Non-Life Insurance: A Cross-Country Analysis," *CIRJE Discussion Paper* F-461 (University of Tokyo: Tokyo, 2007).

Obstfeld, M., and K. Rogoff, "The Six Major Puzzles in International Finance: Is There a Common Cause?" *NBER Macroeconomics Annual* (2000), 339–390.

Outreville, J. F., "The Economic Significance of Insurance Markets in Developing Countries," *Journal of Risk and Insurance* 62 (1990), 487–498.

Park, A., "Risk and Household Grain Management in Developing Countries," *Economic Journal* 116 (2006), 1088–1115.

Pender, J. L., "Discount Rates and Credit Markets: Theory and Evidence from Rural India," *Journal of Development Economics* 50 (1996), 257–296.

Rosenzweig, M. R., and O. Stark, "Consumption Smoothing, Migration, and Marriage: Evidence from Rural India," *Journal of Political Economy* 97 (1989), 905–926.

Rosenzweig, M. R., and K. I. Wolpin, "Credit Constraints, Consumption Smoothing, and the Accumulation of Durable Production Assets in Low-Income Countries: Investments in Bullocks in India," *Journal of Political Economy* 101 (1993), 223–244.

Saito, M., "Dynamic Allocation and Pricing in Incomplete Markets: A Survey," *Monetary and Economic Studies* 17 (1999), 45–75.

Sawada, Y., "Insurance against Tsunami: Evidence Based on the Joint University of Tokyo and Tamil Nadu Agricultural University Survey," in progress (2007).

Sawada, Y., and S. Shimizutani, "Are People Insured against Natural Disasters? Evidence from the Great Hashin-Awaji (Kobe)

Earthquake," *CIRJE Discussion Paper* F-314 (Faculty of Economics, University of Tokyo: Tokyo, 2005).

Sawada, Y., and S. Shimizutani, "Consumption Insurance against Natural Disasters: Evidence from the Great Hanshin-Awaji (Kobe) Earthquake," *Applied Economics Letters* 14 (2007a), 303–306.

Sawada, Y., and S. Shimizutani, "How Do People Cope with Natural Disasters? Evidence from the Great Hanshin-Awaji (Kobe) Earthquake in 1995," *Journal of Money, Credit and Banking*, forthcoming (2007b).

Shoji, M., "Limitation of Quasi-Credit as Mutual Insurance: Coping Strategies for Covariate Shocks in Bangladesh," *COE Discussion Paper* F-138 (Faculty of Economics, University of Tokyo: Tokyo, 2006), available at http://www.e.u-tokyo.ac.jp/cemano/research/DP/documents/coe-f-138.pdf.

Skees, V., D. Larson, and P. Siegel, "Can Financial Markets be Tapped to Help Poor People Cope with Weather Risks?" in S. Dercon ed., *Insurance against Poverty* (Oxford University Press: Oxford, 2005), pp. 422–436.

Strauss, J., K. Beegle, A. Dwiyanto, Y. Herawati, D. Pattinasarany, E. Satriawan, B. Sikoki Sukamdi, and F. Witoelar, "Indonesian Living Standards Before and After the Financial Crisis: Evidence from the Indonesia Family Life Survey," *Rand Corporation and ISEAS* (2004).

Townsend, R. M., "Risk and Insurance in Village India," *Econometrica* 62 (1994), 539–591.

Townsend, R. M., "Consumption Insurance: An Evaluation of Risk-Bearing Systems in Low-Income Economies," *Journal of Economic Perspectives* 9 (1995), 83–102.

Townsend, R. M., "Removing Financial Bottlenecks to Labor Productivity in Thailand," in W. C. Hunter, G. G. Kaufman, and T. H. Krueger, eds., *The Asian Financial Crisis: Origins, Implications, Solutions* (Kluwer Academic Publishers, Norwell, MA, (1999).

Udry, C., "Risk and Insurance in a Rural Credit Market: An Empirical Investigation in Northern Nigeria," *Review of Economic Studies* 61 (1994), 495–526.

Walker, T. S., and N. S. Jodha, "How Small Farm Households Adapt to Risk," in P. Hazell, C. Pomareda, and V. Alberto, eds., *Crop Insurance for Agricultural Development: Issues and Experience* (Johns Hopkins University Press for the International Food Policy Research Institute: Baltimore, MD, 1986).

Walker, T. S., and J. D. Ryan, *Village and Household Economies in India's Semi-Arid Tropics* (Johns Hopkins University Press, Baltimore, MD, 1990).

World Bank, *World Development Report 2000/2001, Attacking Poverty* (World Bank: Washington, DC, 2001).

Yang, D., "Coping with Disaster: The Impact of Hurricanes on International Financial Flows, 1970–2002," mimeo (University of Michigan: Ann Arbor, MI, 2006).

Zeldes, S. P., "Consumption and Liquidity Constraints: An Empirical Investigation," *Journal of Political Economy* 97 (1989), 305–346.

Plenary 2

Plenary 2

The Doha agenda and agricultural trade reform: the role of economic analysis

Will Martin* and Kym Anderson**

Abstract

This article shows that research on international agricultural trade reform can make much greater contributions to understanding than was feasible in earlier trade negotiations. While current models typically estimate gains of less than 1% of GDP, new developments in theory and methodology provide the potential for quantitative analysis to be improved in at least six areas: measurement of protection for goods; incorporation of barriers to foreign trade and investment in services; representation of the counterfactual; disaggregation of products and regions; incorporation of new products; and inclusion of the productivity enhancement associated with trade reform.

JEL classification: F11, F12, F13

Keywords: multilateral trade negotiations; agricultural trade; welfare evaluation; WTO

1. Introduction

The negotiations under the WTO's Doha Development Agenda have followed a path reminiscent of the negotiations on nonagricultural trade during the GATT's Kennedy and Tokyo Rounds of the 1960s and 1970s: an ambitious formula approach to tariff reduction is agreed upon and then the focus of negotiations turns to dealing with the exceptions. The approach to agricultural trade during the Uruguay Round was a little different in that the agreed approach to liberalization—an agreed average cut in tariffs—was inherently flexible while maintaining consistency with the "formula." In all of these cases, the consequences of reforms were heavily influenced by the details, that is, by what was actually done by policy makers with the flexibility available for specific products.

In the Uruguay Round, and before, the challenges posed by the availability of data on protection made it difficult for analysts to assess, *ex ante*, the consequences of choices about the details of the negotiations. Even in the Uruguay Round, information about

*MSN 3-303, World Bank, 1818 H St NW, Washington, DC 20433, U.S.A.

**University of Adelaide and CEPR, SA 5005, Australia.

the protective effects of agricultural trade barriers had to be generated (Hathaway and Ingco, 1996), and information about the actual tariff cuts undertaken was available in electronic form only on a restricted basis even after the completion of the negotiations. Information about the structure of production, consumption, and global trade needed to make assessments of the consequences of reform was also extremely difficult to obtain before the Global Trade Analysis Project (GTAP) made these data widely available in 1992 (at www.gtap.org).

The contrast with the current negotiations is striking. The GTAP database makes available the needed information on production, consumption, and trade as well as applied tariffs and agricultural subsidies. In addition, detailed information about the *ad valorem* equivalents of not only applied but also bound agricultural and nonagricultural tariffs is available at the six-digit level of the Harmonized System, thanks to the excellent work of CEPII in Paris and the ITC in Geneva (at www.cepii.org). These data are used to build up estimates of the effects of protection at the level of aggregation used in the GTAP database. Because of those developments, informed assessments of the consequences of particular formulas, and of agreed flexibilities relative to these formulas, can now be used to make *ex ante* assessments of the consequences of reform (see, e.g., Anderson and Martin, 2006). These impacts can even be traced through to the household level to assess the impacts for poverty (as in Hertel and Winters, 2006). Evidently, there is a significant audience for these results, as they are widely cited by policy makers and in the media.

There are, however, some important remaining challenges for quantitative analysts. Many critics have raised concerns about or offered lukewarm defenses of the quantitative estimates that economists provide of trade agreements (see, e.g., Ackerman [2005] and Stiglitz and Charlton [2005], respectively). Liberal traders also worry that our greater capability to generate informed estimates of the costs of exceptions may create an impression that there are no worthwhile benefits from a prospective agreement—weakening the ability of negotiators to reach agreements that constitute feasible, incremental, and tangible (even if small) moves forward. In light of these concerns, it seems timely to take stock of what it is that analysts currently do successfully, and what we might be able to do better in the future.

2. What we can do

Today's global general equilibrium modelers are able to estimate the impact of commitments to reduce bound trade barriers that are negotiated in the WTO on the welfare or real income of the household or households represented in their model. These welfare measures are conceptually well grounded in the new welfare economics, and can be shown to relate closely to the Harberger Triangles that appear in simple, graphical treatments of the impacts of trade policy (Just et al., 2004, Ch. 9; Martin, 1997). A global trade reform will affect welfare through changes in consumer surplus, producer surplus, government revenues, and the terms of trade.

A key feature of these welfare estimates is that they are quite small as a share of GDP. The 0.7% of global GDP that Anderson and Martin (2006) conclude would be the average benefit from complete, global trade reform corresponding with roughly one month's growth in China or India. Part of the reason for this is that trade liberalization has already come a long way—average tariffs in developing countries have fallen from roughly 30% in developing countries in the early 1980s to not much over 10% today, other trade barriers such as quantitative restrictions and exchange rate overvaluation have been dramatically pared back (World Bank, 2001), and the accession of China to the WTO generated substantial global welfare gains (Bhattasali et al., 2004). However, the small size of these gains is more deeply rooted in the static nature of the benefit measures used. Bernhofen and Brown (2005) conclude that the static gains from Japan's move from near-complete autarky to near-free trade were roughly 8% of GDP, or more than 10 times what standard CGE models suggest.

The value of these welfare measures is also highly influenced by the values of parameters about which there is no consensus. A critical parameter is the Armington (1969) elasticity, which defines the extent to which domestic and imported goods are imperfect substitutes and allows for the widely observed phenomenon of simultaneous imports and exports of the same commodity. Even among studies using the same database, there are sharp differences in the chosen values of these parameters, based on differences in the interpretation of the econometric literature, and of the experience of economic growth. Many, if not most, econometric estimates of these parameters are sufficiently low that they generate implausibly large, adverse terms-of-trade impacts when countries grow rapidly. Ruhl (2005) points out that the relevant values of these parameters should be much larger than those that match short-term quantity adjustments to price changes, but there is, as yet, no consensus on the correct values for analysis of trade reform.

Most of the latest widely cited studies of agricultural trade reform (see, e.g., Anderson et al., 2006; Bouët, 2006; Hertel and Keeney, 2006; OECD, 2006) focus on models using the simplest of assumptions: perfect competition; tariff revenues redistributed costlessly to households; and a constant level of employment. This is not because these assumptions are totally realistic, but rather because the data and theory for the analysis of trade reform under these circumstances are well developed, and because alternative formulations are either not supported by consistent theory, data, and parameters, or can generate estimated impacts that are heavily dependent on the particular assumptions made.[1]

---

[1] Adding estimates of productivity gains from liberalization based on atheoretical models is one common alternative. Introducing a

Table 1
The share of estimated global gains from full goods trade liberalization that would come from agricultural policy reform, %

Anderson and Martin (2006)	63
OECD (2006)	59
Hertel and Keeney (2006)	67
Francois et al. (2005)	66

Table 2
Distribution of gains from full global agricultural trade liberalization due to each of the three agricultural pillars, %

Welfare effects from: (%)	Market access	Domestic support	Export subsidies	All agricultural policies
Developing countries	106	2	−8	100
High-income countries	89	6	5	100
World	93	5	2	100

Source: Hertel and Keeney (2006).

Standard CGE models can be extremely useful in answering a number of questions. One type of question involves the potential for reforms in particular regions or product markets to generate benefits. Another involves the sensitivity of the benefits of reforms to particular parameters of the negotiations, such as the share of products that are allowed more "flexible" treatment in the negotiations. The first type of question can be addressed using the basic data provided in an aggregate database of the type used for modeling, such as the GTAP database (www.gtap.org). The second type of question is much more demanding in its information requirements. It needs information about protection at a fine level of disaggregation, not just on applied protection but also on the tariff bindings that are the actual legal policy instruments changed as a consequence of WTO negotiations.

One key result emerging from standard CGE models is the continuing importance of agricultural trade distortions. As is evident from Table 1, elimination of all agricultural trade distortions is consistently found to generate around two-thirds of the global gains from abolition of all merchandise trade barriers. That these gains are so large from a sector that contributes only 6% or 7% of world trade and world GDP reflects the high levels and variability of protection in this sector both in industrial and in developing countries. This result is, however, not robust to alternative modeling specifications—models that include increasing returns to scale and a preference for variety in nonagricultural sectors or that lower producer real wages and expand employment following liberalization (e.g., Polaski, 2006) tend to obtain larger gains from nonagricultural liberalization.

Another example of this type of insight arises when considering the different "pillars" of assistance within agriculture—domestic support, export competition, and market access. From the attention showered on the issue of domestic support in the negotiations, one might have thought that it was at least equal in importance to market access, a view partly supported by the OECD's estimate that subsidies contributed 39% of the total support to OECD agriculture (Anderson et al., 2006; Table 1). However, the GTAP database, and the results of models based on it, gives a completely different perspective. As is clear from Table 2, abolishing domestic subsidies is expected to generate only around 5% of the global gains from agricultural trade reform and 2% of the gains to developing countries. Furthermore, careful investigation of the reasons underlying these results shows that the main cause of this result is the predominance of support provided through market access barriers (Anderson et al., 2006). Once the coverage of barriers is extended to include agricultural processing in the OECD countries, and assistance to agriculture in non-OECD countries, market access is estimated to provide 75% of the total support. Once allowance is made for the much greater variability of market access barriers relative to domestic support, and for the fact that export subsidies have a welfare-enhancing positive impact on trade, even a simple back-of-the-envelope calculation is able to replicate the model-based finding that domestic support contributes only a very small share of the total costs of agricultural support.

The availability of disaggregated information on applied and bound tariffs from the CEPII/ITC work on trade barriers (Bouët et al., 2004; Bchir et al., 2005) has allowed quantitative analysis to provide *ex ante* insights into the effects of specific tariff-cutting formulas

---

labor market in which consumer real wages are fixed and hence producer real wages fall and employment rises following trade reform tends to produce results in which the welfare effects are dominated by changes in employment (see, e.g., Polaski, 2006).

Table 3
Bound and applied agricultural tariff rates by region, %

	Bound	MFN	Applied
Developed	27	22	14
Developing (excl. LDCs)	48	27	21
LDCs	78	14	13
WORLD	37	24	17

Source: Jean et al. (2006).

Table 4
Proposed cuts in protection and the scenarios examined

	Top tariff cut, %	Sensitive products, %	EU/US AMS cut, %	Tariff cap
US proposal	90	1	83/60	75
EU proposal	60	8	70/60	100
G-20 proposal	75		80/70	100
Authors' reform scenario	75	0–5	75/75	200

Source: Jean et al. (2006).

on market access, and even to make informed assessments of the likely consequences of particular types of flexibility.

In the current negotiations, this has highlighted the extent of the gaps between bound and applied rates, and hence the need for much larger cuts in bound rates to achieve any given reduction in applied rates. It has also allowed analysis of the consequences of nonproportional cuts in tariffs, which must be based on information at the most disaggregated level available. Table 3 highlights the extent of the gaps between bound and applied rates, including the very large contribution of tariff preferences (unilateral and regional) to this overall gap in the industrial countries.

With this information, we can make assessments about the effects of nonproportional tariff-cutting formulas. In Anderson et al. (2006), we did this using a tiered formula with income-tax–style marginal rates of tax cutting increasing with the tariff rate to a peak of 75%. As shown in Table 4, these rates fitted within the range of tariff cuts under discussion up to the failed June 2006 Ministerial meeting. In addition, we considered the impact of several other key attributes of the proposals under discussion—sensitive products, special products, and a tariff cap.

Simulations of this type allow us to provide estimates of the consequences of trade reform that take account of the detailed features of these agreements. The first column of Figure 1 shows the impact of this tiered formula in agriculture on overall economic welfare. In making this assessment presented in the first column, we applied the tiered formula on agricultural tariffs to all agricultural tariffs, abolished agricultural export subsidies, and made the modest cuts in applied agricultural subsidies implied by the proposed cuts in domestic support. In the second column, we consider the impact of allowing developed countries to subject 2% of their tariff lines to much smaller cuts (15% in our case), rather than the tiered formula. In the third column, we consider the impact of incorporating a tariff cap of 200%. In the fourth column, we return to the original tiered formula in agriculture, and add a modest agreement consisting of 50% cuts in bound tariffs on nonagricultural (NAMA) products. Finally, in the fifth column, we consider the impact of removing the special and differential treatment that allowed the developing countries to make smaller cuts (by a factor of roughly two-thirds) in their tariffs under the previous scenarios.

The results presented in Figure 1 provide important insights into the consequences of potential trade reforms. The first point to note is that the first scenario—the tiered formula in agriculture—generates a little over a quarter of the estimated total potential gains from trade reform, of $287 billion per year or 0.7% of world GDP in 2015. This is a substantial share given that the cuts are in the middle of the range of possibilities being considered, and that they are based on bound rates in a situation where there is a large degree of binding overhang. The second point to notice is that a simple proportional cut[2] represented by the second pair of columns in Figure 1, which side-steps many of the problems associated with a complex tiered formula, generates gains that are almost as large as the tiered formula. The third point to note is that allowing even 2% of products[3] to be treated as sensitive and subject only to a 15% cut results in much smaller gains. The

---

[2] Calibrated to produce the same reduction in average bound tariffs in industrial and developing countries.

[3] Developing countries were allowed to treat an additional 2% of tariffs as "special" and to subject them to the same (lack of) disciplines.

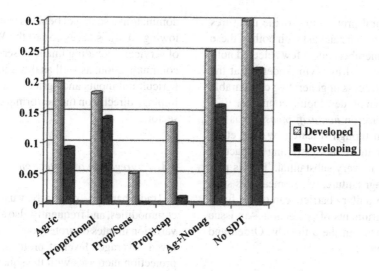

Figure 1. Impacts of tariff scenarios on welfare in developed and developing countries. *Source:* Anderson and Martin (2006, Ch. 12).

gains to developed countries fall by more than two-thirds, and the gains to developing countries disappear. When a tariff cap of 200% is introduced on all products, the gains to the high-income countries rebound substantially, reflecting the fact that these are the countries with mega-peak tariffs. Japan and the Republic of Korea benefit particularly strongly because this cap requires them to reduce their extremely costly tariffs on products such as rice.

The fifth pair of bars in Figure 1 shows the benefits when 50% cuts in nonagricultural tariff bindings are combined with the tiered formula for agriculture shown in the first pair of bars. The final pair of bars shows the effects if developing countries were to forgo the traditional type of special and differential treatment under which they make smaller cuts in their tariff bindings than the industrial countries. This, unsurprisingly, shows that the benefits to developing countries would increase if they made larger reductions in their own protection.

All of these simulations highlight important features of the menu of choices faced by trade negotiators and hence are potentially very useful. Note that it is the differences between the scenarios that provide the insights into the effects of the different alternatives—as noted above, the levels of the gains are extremely small in all cases.

Fortunately, there are a number of areas in which new research is creating the potential for us to obtain

better measures of the welfare benefits of reform, or at least pointing out the scope and approximate depth of our ignorance. It is in these areas that further work may allow us to make estimates of the effects of policies that are even more accurate and more useful in providing guidance for policy makers.

3. What we still need to do

While, as we have seen, there has been an enormous expansion in the contribution that quantitative economic analysis can make to trade policy debates, there is scope to improve on this in at least six areas: (i) the quality of our protection measures; (ii) the omission of trade reform in services; (iii) the aggregation of our information on trade barriers; (iv) the nature of the counterfactual; (v) the emergence of new products; and (vi) the potential productivity-enhancing impacts of trade reform.

3.1. Quality of protection measures

While we have detailed information on *tariffs*, this is insufficient. In agriculture, there is a particular problem in that the support provided to producers may differ considerably from the nominal tariffs. If, for instance, the commodity is an exportable, then tariffs are unlikely to provide significant support to producers. The OECD measures of agricultural protection provide measures based on price comparisons that deal with both of these problems for OECD members and a few selected non-members, and research led by Kym Anderson at the World Bank is in the process of generating comparable measures for more than 50 developing countries.

Our information base on *nontariff measures* is extremely limited, even though research by Kee et al. (2006) suggests that the trade-restricting impact of these measures remains very substantial. This is particularly the case in agriculture, where measures such as sanitary and phytosanitary barriers can easily function as disguised instruments of protection—an issue discussed in more detail in the article by Orden and Roberts in this session.

3.2. Trade barriers and reform in services

A key concern is that we are continuing to analyze the less rapidly growing part of global trade, and the part in which trade liberalization has been under way for the longest time—merchandise trade. For lack of good data and methods, however, the potential gains from trade liberalization in services are rarely considered. This is an extremely serious omission since there are indications that the costs of barriers to trade in services may be very substantial, and potentially larger than the barriers presented by conventional trade measures such as tariffs and subsidies (Department of Foreign Affairs and Trade, 1999; Dee et al., 2000). This omission is increasingly important for agriculture in an environment where input markets are becoming more important in developing country agriculture, and where efficient marketing channels such as those through supermarkets will have profound implications for the performance of the agricultural sector and its access to export markets.

Konan and Maskus (2004) point out that the costs of services protection are likely to be larger than those on merchandise trade because they typically involve restrictions not only on cross-border trade (Mode 1 of GATS) but also on supply by establishing enterprises in the country or by the movement of service suppliers (Modes 3 and 4 of GATS). When barriers to trade in services are represented as reducing productivity in producing sectors, the measured benefits of reforming trade in services are even larger. Jensen et al. (2007) find that the benefits of reform in services trade completely dominate as a source of benefits from likely reforms following Russia's accession to the WTO. A wide range of services, including financial services, transport, and communication, as well as those involved in supply of agricultural inputs and agricultural marketing services impinge directly on the performance of the agricultural sector.

3.3. Aggregation of protection

Trade barriers frequently vary enormously across commodities, and frequently also across suppliers. This variation in rates of protection increases the cost of any given "average" level of protection, since the cost of protection increases with the square of the rate of protection. Unfortunately, some degree of aggregation is essential if only because the available information on the structure of production and consumption is at a higher level of aggregation than information on tariffs and trade. Further aggregation is typically employed for computational reasons. Further problems are introduced by the typical approach to aggregation of trade barriers—the use of averages weighted by external trade. As protection rates rise, the weights associated with these measures decline, so that a tariff that completely blocks trade has the same measured impact as a zero tariff.

The modern approach to tariff aggregation pioneered by Anderson and Neary (1992) provides an indication of a possible means of dealing with the aggregation problem. Anderson and Neary develop a single tariff aggregator that captures the welfare impacts of a nonuniform tariff. Building on this approach, Bach and Martin (2001) used a tariff aggregator to capture the impacts of changes in the tariff regime on the expenditure required to achieve a given level of utility, and another to capture the impact on tariff revenues. Manole and Martin (2005) provide closed-form measures of these aggregators for the widely used Constant Elasticity of Substitution functional form. Applying these procedures to a sample of seven developing countries, they find that appropriate aggregation increases the estimated cost of protection on average 20-fold relative to the cost estimated using a weighted average tariff.

The problems of aggregation are particularly intense in agriculture because of the enormous variation in rates of protection across countries and commodities, especially among the industrial countries. Simple solutions, such as the representative-weighting approach used in some versions of the MAcMAP database, deal with the weighting problem without addressing the aggregation bias problem associated with nonlinearity in the costs of individual tariffs. In a recent article Anderson (2006) proposes a new aggregation method that deals with both the aggregation bias and weighting problems, and maintains global payment balances, allowing it to be applied in global models.

3.4. The protection counterfactual

The standard approach used in evaluating the consequences of WTO agreements is to compare the agreed tariff binding with the previously applied tariff rate, and to treat the post-agreement tariff rate as the lesser of the two rates. This essentially involves treating the current applied rate as a deterministic forecast of future protection rates in the absence of the agreement.

There are two potentially serious problems with this specification of the counterfactual. One is that the trend rate of protection responds systematically to underlying determinants that evolve over time. The second is that annual protection rates fluctuate substantially around that trend. Taking account of either or both of these counterfactuals can have very large impacts on the estimated benefits of international trade liberalization agreements.

Anderson and Hayami (1986) and Lindert (1991) provide insights into the likely evolution of agricultural trade policies in the absence of international agreements. Key findings include a strong tendency for agricultural protection to rise with economic development because of fundamental changes in the structure of the economy. In particular, there is a tendency for agricultural protection to be low or negative in very poor countries because the number of farmers is large and it is difficult for them to organize to apply pressure on governments. Because farmers are mainly subsisting at that stage, their real incomes are not greatly affected by increases in farm output prices. By contrast, the urban population in a poor country is far smaller and easier to organize, and food is an important part of consumer budgets.

As economies develop, however, all of these economic factors change in ways that shift the politics–economy balance more toward agricultural protection.

Farmers become fewer in number and easier to organize. They also become more commercial in orientation, so that their real incomes are more strongly influenced by agricultural output prices. At the same time, the urban population becomes larger and hence harder to organize, and the importance of food in consumer budgets declines. The end result can be a very rapid increase in agricultural protection rates in high-growth economies, as is evident from Figure 2 showing the nominal rate of border protection provided to rice in Japan during the twentieth century. A standard *ex ante* welfare evaluation of a hypothetical 1955 agreement constraining protection on rice in Japan to no more than its 1955 level of 46% would have concluded that no liberalization was achieved by this agreement. And yet, it is clear that such an agreement would have had a profound liberalizing effect, obviating the descent into costly protectionism that was to unfold in the subsequent decades.

Also evident from Figure 2 is the large variation in rates of protection over time. Variation of this type is very common in agriculture because trade policies are frequently used also to stabilize domestic agricultural prices in the face of variations in world prices.[4] These variations in protection have important implications for the value of trade agreements. As Francois and Martin (2004) show, even tariff bindings that are set well above average rates of protection may greatly diminish the costs of protection. Such bindings rule out the highest—and most costly—incidents of protection. They estimate, for example, that the European tariff binding on wheat, at 82%, reduced the cost of protection to this commodity by almost a third, despite being substantially above the average rate of protection prevailing during the preceding 15 years for which data were available.

3.5. The emergence of new products

Standard models used to assess the implications of trade reforms are based on the Armington (1969) assumption that expansion of exports following liberalization involves increasing the volume of the products initially being exported, but not of any other products.

---

[4] Tyers and Anderson (1992) point out that the variation in world prices is, in large measure, a consequence of these policies of insulating domestic markets.

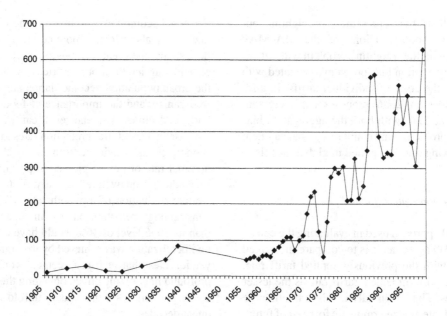

Figure 2. Nominal rate of border protection provided to rice, Japan, %. *Source:* Anderson and Hayami (1986), Martin (2002).

The Armington assumption also rules out expanding the markets to which goods are being supplied—if exports to a particular market are initially zero, they remain zero.

Recent research, however, highlights the key role of the "extensive" margin, where export expansion involves increases in the range of products exported (Hummels and Klenow, 2005) and expansion in the range of markets supplied (Evenett and Venables, 2002). Hummels and Klenow conclude that only about one-third of the export expansion associated with economic growth comes from the "intensive margin" where greater quantities of the same products are exported. Evenett and Venables found that about one-third of the expansion of exports from developing countries was obtained by exporting products to new markets.

In a world where importers exhibit a preference for variety in the goods they purchase, these observations on the importance of extensive margin growth have important implications. Increasing the volumes of the same products, as under the Armington assumption, has the inevitable consequence of driving down the price of exports and causing income losses to the exporter from deterioration in the terms of trade. Where exports are characterized by an expansion in the range of products supplied, the preference for variety exerts

a counteracting force—helping to increase the demand for exports. In simulations introducing the Hummels–Klenow preference for variety in exports from China and India, Dimaranan et al. (2006) found that the terms of trade for these exporters need not deteriorate significantly, despite very high projected rates of export growth.

Some traditional treatments of new varieties, such as those based on monopolistic competition and a love of variety inspired by Krugman (1980), are typically implemented with agriculture and services as perfectly competitive sectors and the rest of the economy characterized as monopolistically competitive. However, as Rodrik (2004) notes, the process of discovering efficient new exports is just as important and difficult in agriculture and services as in manufacturing. Models developed by Melitz (2003), with a fixed cost of entry into export markets, provide a basis for modeling the endogenous emergence of new products.

3.6. *Productivity-enhancing impacts of reform*

Economists have long suspected that participation in international trade provides a bonus through improvements in productivity. Most of the investigation of these gains has been empirical, based loosely on

Arrow's (1962) concept of learning by doing. Major contributions to this literature include Feder (1983), Dollar (1992) and Sachs and Warner (1995), all of which find strong links between export performance and economic growth. Rodriguez and Rodrik (2001) raise concerns about the robustness of the estimated relationship between aggregate exports and productivity. During the same period, Clerides et al. (1998) questioned the learning-by-doing framework on the basis of firm-level findings that exporting firms were more efficient before entering export markets, rather than because of learning by doing after entering these markets.

More recent research on the aggregate links between exports and productivity has more carefully examined the potential endogeneity of the relationship, and continues to find an aggregate relationship (Frankel and Romer, 1999). A number of subsequent firm-level studies have reexamined the relationship between exporting and growth, and have found evidence of productivity growth associated with learning by doing after firms enter exporting. Blalock and Gertler (2004) find evidence of an increase in firm productivity of between 2% and 5% after Indonesian firms enter export markets. Fernandes and Isgut (2007) find evidence of an increase in productivity from learning by exporting when Colombian firms entered export markets. Van Biesebrock (2005) finds that African exporting firms had higher productivity before entering export markets, and that their productivity levels, and their subsequent rates of productivity growth, grew after entering export markets. Girma et al. (2004) find both higher initial levels of productivity and higher productivity growth rates after entry into exporting.

In addition to the improvements in process efficiency that have been the focus of the literature on exports and growth, the recent literature has pointed to potentially important gains from improvements in the quality of exports. Hummels and Klenow (2005) suggest that these improvements in quality are sufficiently rapid that the prices received by countries for the products that they continue to export—as distinct from their new exports—actually rise by 0.09% for each increase of 1% in national income. This result is strikingly at variance with traditional Armington models, which generate a reduction in export prices when economies grow and exports expand.

4. Conclusions

A key piece of good news in this article is that recent advances in data and techniques have greatly expanded our ability to make informed assessments of the consequences of trade reform. We can now provide insights into the areas in which trade policy reforms might generate the largest gains, and about the implications of the details in which the true battle is fought and the true benefits of trade reforms are gained or lost. The bad news is that we are left making interesting and insightful comments about reforms that might, possibly, garner estimated benefits of 0.7% of GDP—less than a month's growth for fast-growing economies such as China or India.

Fortunately, however, there is more good news about improvements in our ability to say useful things about the gains from trade reform. Our measures of tariff barriers have improved enormously, and now is the time for us to make corresponding improvements in our measures of nontariff barriers and barriers to trade and investment in services.[5] Once we have these measures—or even before we have them—we need to improve the approaches to aggregation that are currently not using an enormous amount of the information we currently have in our hands.

We also need to pay much more attention to the counterfactual against which to compare the liberalization scenarios. We currently treat the counterfactual as the applied rate prior to the reform, and yet we have strong evidence that the average applied rate varies systematically with the determinants of economic development, and that reform can reduce the costly annual variations in protection around these underlying trend rates. Furthermore, we need to begin to take account of the fact that trade expansion takes place more by expanding the range of products exported, and their quality, than by increasing the volumes of traditional exports. Finally, we need to take advantage of new theoretical developments that are improving our ability to incorporate the implications of trade reform for productivity and that improve process efficiency and product quality.

---

[5] Financial markets also could be integrated into CGE models, to capture the gains from liberalizing them also. On those markets' importance, see Rajan and Zingales (2004).

References

Ackerman, F., *The Shrinking Gains from Trade: A Critical Assessment of Doha Round Projections* (Global Development and Environment Institute, Tufts University: Medford, MA, 2005).

Anderson, J., *Consistent Policy Aggregation* manuscript (Boston College: Cambridge, MA, 2006).

Anderson, J., and J. P. Neary, "Trade Reform with Quotas, Partial Rent Retention, and Tariffs," *Econometrica* 60 (1992), 57–76.

Anderson, K., and Y. Hayami, *The Political Economy of Agricultural Protection: East Asia in International Perspective* (Allen and Unwin: London, 1986).

Anderson, K., and W. Martin, eds., *Agricultural Trade Reform and the Doha Development Agenda* (Palgrave Macmillan: Basingstoke and Washington DC: World Bank, 2006).

Anderson, K., W. Martin, and E. Valenzuela, "The Relative Importance of Global Agricultural Subsidies and Market Access," *World Trade Review* 5 (2006), 357–376.

Anderson, K., W. Martin, and D. Van Der Mensbrugghe, "Doha Merchandise Trade Reform: What's at Stake for Developing Countries?" *World Bank Economic Review* 20 (2006), 169–195.

Armington, P., "A Theory of Demand for Products Distinguished by Place of Production," *IMF Staff Papers* 16 (1969), 159–178.

Arrow, K., "The Economic Implications of Learning by Doing," *Review of Economic Studies* 29 (1962), 155–173.

Bach, C., and W. Martin, "Would the Right Tariff Aggregator for Policy Analysis Please Stand up?" *Journal of Policy Modeling* 23 (2001), 621–635.

Bchir, H., S. Jean, and D. Laborde, "Binding Overhang and Tariff-Cutting Formulas," *CEPII Working Paper* 2005-18, October (2005).

Bernhofen, D., and J. Brown, "An Empirical Assessment of the Comparative Advantage Gains from Trade: Evidence from Japan," *American Economic Review* 95 (2005), 208–225.

Bhattasali, D., S. Li, and W. Martin, eds., *China and the WTO: Accession, Policy Reform and Poverty Reduction Strategies* (Oxford University Press: New York and Washington, DC: World Bank, 2004).

Blalock, G., and P. Gertler, "Learning from Exporting Revisited in a Less Developed Setting," *Journal of Development Economics* 75 (2004), 397–416.

Bouët, A., "What Can the Poor Expect from Trade Liberalization? Opening the "Black Box" of Trade Modeling," *MTID Discussion Paper* No. 93 (International Food Policy Research Institute: Washington, DC, 2006).

Bouët, A., Y. Decreux, L. Fontagné, S. Jean, and D. Laborde, "A Consistent, *ad Valorem* Equivalent Measure of Applied Protection across the World: the MAcMaps-HS6 database," *CEPII Working Paper* 2004-22 (CEPII: Paris, 2004).

Clerides, S., S. Lach, and J. Tybout, "Is Learning by Exporting Important? Micro-dynamic Evidence from Colombia, Mexico and Morocco," *Quarterly Journal of Economics* 113 (1998), 903–947.

Dee, P., K. Hanslow, and T. Phamduc, "Measuring the Cost of Barriers to Trade in Services," paper presented to the Eleventh Annual NBER East Asian Seminar, 22–24 June, Seoul (2000).

Department of Foreign Affairs and Trade, *Global Trade Reform: Maintaining Momentum. Australian Department of Foreign Affairs and Trade*, Canberra, www.thecie.com.au (1999).

Dimaranan, B., E. Ianchovichina, and W. Martin, "Trade Impacts of Accelerated Growth in China and India," processed (World Bank: Washington, DC, 2006).

Dollar, D. "Outward-Oriented Developing Economies Really Do Grow More Rapidly: Evidence from 95 LDCs, 1976–1985," *Economic Development and Cultural Change* 40 (1992), 523–544.

Evenett, S., and A. Venables, *Export Growth in Developing Countries: Market Entry and Bilateral Trade Flows.* Available at www.alexandria.unisg.ch/Publikationen/22177 (2002).

Feder, G., "On Exports and Economic Growth," *Journal of Development Economics* 12 (1983), 59–73.

Fernandes, A., and A. Isgut, *Learning-by-Exporting Effects: Are They for Real?* Mimeo (World Bank: Washington, DC, 2007).

Francois, J., and W. Martin, "Commercial Policy, Bindings and Market Access," *European Economic Review* 48 (2004), 665–679.

Francois, J. F., H. vanMeijl, and F. van Tongeren, "Trade Liberalization in the Doha Development Round," *Economic Policy* 42 (2005), 349–391.

Frankel, J. A., and D. Romer, "Does Trade Cause Growth?" *American Economic Review* 89 (1999), 379–399.

Girma, S., D. Greenaway, and R. Kneller, "Does Exporting Increase Productivity? A Microeconometric Analysis of Matched Firms," *Review of International Economics* 12 (2004), 855–866.

Hathaway, D., and M. Ingco, "Agricultural Liberalization and the Uruguay Round," in W. Martin and L. A. Winters, eds., *The Uruguay Round and the Developing Countries* (Cambridge University Press: Cambridge, U.K., 1996), pp. 30–58.

Hertel, T., and R. Keeney, "What is at Stake: The Relative Importance of Import Barriers, Export Subsidies and Domestic Support," in K. Anderson and W. Martin, eds., *Agricultural Trade Reform and the Doha Development Agenda* (Palgrave Macmillan: Basingstoke and Washington, DC: World Bank, 2006), pp. 37–62.

Hertel, T., and L. A. Winters, eds., *Poverty and the WTO: Impacts of the Doha Development Agenda* (Palgrave Macmillan: Basingstoke and Washington, DC: World Bank, 2006).

Hummels, D., and P. Klenow, "The Variety and Quality of a Nation's Exports," *American Economic Review* 95 (2005), 704–723.

Jean, S., D. Laborde, and W. Martin, "Consequences of Alternative Formulas for Agricultural Tariff Cuts," in K. Anderson and W. Martin, eds., *Agricultural Trade Reform and the Doha Development Agenda* (Palgrave Macmillan: Basingstoke and Washington, DC: World Bank, 2006), pp. 81–116.

Jensen, J., T. Rutherford, and D. Tarr, "The Impact of Liberalizing Barriers to Foreign Direct Investment in Services: The Case of Russian Accession to the World Trade Organization," *Review of Development Economics* 11 (2007), 482–506.

Just, R. E., D. L. Hueth, and A. Schmitz, *The Welfare Economics of Public Policy* (Edward Elgar: Cheltenham, UK, 2004).

Kee, H. L., A. Nicita, and M. Olarreaga, "Estimating Trade Restrictiveness Indices," *Policy Research Working Paper* No. 3840 (World Bank: Washington, DC, 2006).

Konan, D., and K. Maskus, "Quantifying the Impact of Services Liberalization in a Developing Country," *World Bank Policy Research Working Paper* 3193 (2004).

Krugman, P., "Scale Economies, Product Differentiation, and the Pattern of Trade," *American Economic Review* 70 (1980), 950–959.

Lindert, P. "Historical Patterns of Agricultural Protection," in P. Timmer, ed., *Agriculture and the State* (Cornell University Press: Ithaca, NY, 1991), pp. 29–83.

Manole, V., and W. Martin, "Keeping the Devil in the Details: A Feasible Approach to Aggregating Trade Distortions," paper presented to the European Trade Study Group meetings, Dublin, September (2005).

Martin, W. "Measuring Welfare Changes with Distortions," in J. Francois and K. Reinert, eds., *Applied Methods for Trade Policy Analysis* (Cambridge University Press: New York, 1997), pp. 76–93.

Martin, W. "Reforming Japan's Rice Policies: Comment" in R. Stern, ed. *Issues and Options for Japan-US Trade Policies* (University of Michigan Press: Ann Arbor, 2002), pp. 99–103.

Melitz, M. "The Impact of Trade on Intra-Industry Reallocations and Aggregate Industry Productivity," *Econometrica* 71 (2003), 1695–1725.

OECD. *Agricultural Policy and Trade Reform: Potential Effects at Global, National and Household Levels* (Organization for Economic Cooperation and Development: Paris, 2006).

Polaski, S., *Winners and Losers: Impact of the Doha Round on Developing Countries* (Carnegie Endowment for International Peace: Washington, DC, 2006).

Rajan, R., and Zingales, L., *Saving Capitalism from the Capitalists: Unleashing the Power of Financial Markets to Create Wealth and Spread Opportunity* (Princeton University Press: Princeton, NJ, 2004).

Rodriguez, F., and D. Rodrik, "Trade Policy and Economic Growth: A Skeptic's Guide to the Cross-National Evidence," in B. Bernanke and K. Rogoff, eds., *Macroeconomics Annual 2000* (MIT Press for the National Bureau of Economic Research: Cambridge, MA, 2001), pp. 261–318.

Rodrik, D., "Industrial Policy for the Twenty-First Century," processed (Harvard University: Cambridge, MA, 2004). http://ksghome.harvard.edu/ďrodrik/UNIDOSep.pdf

Ruhl, K. "Solving the Elasticity Puzzle in International Economics" (University of Texas: Austin, 2005).

Sachs, J. D., and A. Warner, "Economic Convergence and Economic Policies," *Brookings Papers on Economic Activity* 1 (1995), 1–95.

Stiglitz, J., and A. Charlton, *Fair Trade for All: How Trade Can Promote Development* (Oxford University Press: New York, 2005).

Tyers, R., and K. Anderson, *Disarray in World Food Markets: A Quantitative Assessment* (Cambridge University Press: Cambridge and New York, 1992).

van Biesebrock, J., "Exporting Raises Productivity in Sub-Saharan African Manufacturing Firms," *Journal of International Economics* 67 (2005), 373–391.

World Bank, "Trade Policies in the 1990s and the Poorest Countries," Chapter 2 in *Global Economic Prospects 2001* (World Bank: Washington, DC, 2001).

Globalization, privatization, and vertical coordination in food value chains in developing and transition countries

Johan F. M. Swinnen* and Miet Maertens*

Abstract

Food and agricultural commodity value chains in developing and transition countries have undergone tremendous changes in the past decades. Companies and property rights have been privatized, markets liberalized, and economies integrated into global food systems. The liberalization and privatization initially caused the collapse of state-controlled vertical coordination. More recently, private vertical coordination systems have emerged and are growing rapidly as a response to consumer demand for food quality and safety on the one hand and the farms' production constraints caused by factor market imperfections. In this article we (1) demonstrate the importance of these changes, (2) discuss the implications for efficiency and equity, and (3) provide empirical evidence on the effects in several developing and transition countries.

JEL classification: L14, O12, Q13, Q17

Keywords: vertical coordination; contract farming; agri-food supply chains

1. Privatization

Twenty-five years ago, a vast share of the poor and middle-income countries, covering a large share of the world's agricultural areas and farmers, were characterized by state-controlled supply chains for agricultural and food commodities. This was most extreme in the Communist world, spreading from Central Europe to East Asia, where the entire agri-food system was under strict control of the state. However, in many African, Latin American, and South Asian countries also, the state played a very important role in the agri-food chains. For example, in Brazil and Mexico, wholesale markets were run by the state; in South Asia, the state heavily regulated food markets and many African commodity markets and trade regimes were controlled by (para-) state organizations. In many of these countries, the state played an important role in agricultural production and marketing in the decades after independence from colonial power. Governments in Sub-Saharan Africa and South Asia were heavily involved in agricultural marketing and food processing through the creation of marketing boards, government-controlled cooperatives, and parastatal processing units. These government institutions were often monopoly buyers of agricultural products, especially for basic food crops and important export crops.[1]

---

[1] For example, in Indonesia marketing of rice was completely controlled by the state through the marketing board National Logistical Supply Organization (BULOG). Similarly, marketing of grain and other basic food crops was controlled and organized by government marketing boards, e.g., in Malawi, through Agricultural Development and Marketing Corporation (ADMARC); in Zambia, through National Agricultural Marketing Board (NAMBOARD), and in Kenya through National Cereals and Produce Board (NCPB). In many developing countries marketing and processing of major export crops was state-controlled through state-owned processing and exporting companies and organizations; e.g., for cotton in Malawi, through Malawi Textile Development Company (CMDT), in Cameroon, through SODECOTON, in Ghana, through the Ghana Cotton Development Board and in Kenya through Cotton Lint and Seed Marketing Board (CLSMB); for tea in Kenya, through the Kenyan Tea Development Cooperation (KTDA); for coffee through coffee marketing boards in Uganda, Kenya, Zimbabwe, and Ethiopia. In other countries marketing of agricultural products was realized through a government-controlled system of cooperatives, e.g., in Tanzania. In some cases government involvement was not limited

LICOS Center for Institutions and Economic Performance, K.U. Leuven, Debériotstraat 34 - bus 3511, B-3000 Leuven - Belgium.

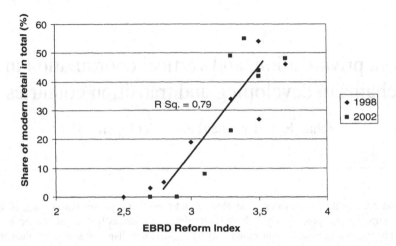

Figure 1. Impact of economic reforms on the growth of the modern retail sector in transition countries. Data include Bulgaria, Croatia, Czech Republic, Hungary, Poland, Romania, Russia, Slovakia, and Ukraine. *Source:* Dries et al., 2004.

This system of state intervention and control has undergone tremendous changes in the 1980s and 1990s as a global process of liberalization induced dramatic changes in many of these regions.[2] In the transition world, the liberalization of prices, trade, and exchanges, the privatization of the state enterprises, etc., removed much of the state control over the commodity chains as well as the vertical coordination (VC) in the chains. Similar processes of privatization and liberalization of domestic and international commodity and financial markets reduced the control of the state over the food and agricultural chains in many developing and emerging economies.

2. Globalization

Globalization of the food chains in transition and developing countries has been driven by several factors. Some factors are not specific to these countries,

such as the global process of increased international trade and investment and the structural changes in the global food markets. Specific factors are the liberalization of the trade and investment regimes in transition and developing countries—policy reforms that often accompanied the privatization and domestic price reforms. Here we focus on four factors that are of special importance.

First, trade liberalization caused major changes in agri-food trade. For example, in Central and Eastern Europe, it caused a major reorientation of the agri-food trade from "east to west," that is, from trade with the former Soviet countries to trade with western Europe, and a shift of the agri-food trade position from net exporters to net importers. Also the participation of developing countries in world agricultural trade has increased.

Second, the liberalization of the investment regimes induced foreign investments in agribusiness, food industry, and further down the chain, with major implications for farmers (Dries and Swinnen, 2004). Several food sectors in Eastern Europe, such as the sugar, dairy, and retail sector, have received massive amounts of foreign investment, which now holds dominant market shares. A well-advertised example of these investments is the rapid growth of modern retail chains ("supermarkets") in transition and (some) developing countries (Reardon and Swinnen, 2004). According to Dries et al. (2004), this was triggered by the reform process in former state-controlled economies (Figure 1).

---

to marketing and processing but extended into primary production as well; e.g., the *Plan Palmier* for the production of Oil Palm in Ivory Coast.

[2] In the Berg report of 1980, the World Bank argued that government marketing organizations should be reformed to operate on a commercial basis and allow the private sector to enter agricultural marketing to provide competition and encourage efficiency. This report laid the basis for economic reforms, including privatization and market liberalization, which started in the late 1980s—actually in 1978 in China and after 1989 Europe—and continued throughout the 1990s in many developing countries.

Third, in addition to an increasing volume of global agricultural trade, the structure of this trade also changed considerably during the past decades. There has been an increase in the share of high-value products—mainly fish and fishery products, and fruits and vegetables—in world agricultural trade. Developing countries, in particular, experienced a sharp increase in such high-value exports—from 21% in 1980 to 41% in 2000—while the importance of their traditional tropical export commodities—such as coffee, cocoa, and tea—has decreased sharply (Aksoy, 2005).

Fourth, associated with these changes is the spread of (private and public) food standards. Consumers are increasingly demanding specific quality attributes of processed and fresh food products and are increasingly aware of food safety issues. Food standards are increasingly stringent, especially for fresh food products such as fruits, vegetables, meat, dairy products, fish, and seafood products, which are prone to food safety risks. These food quality and safety demands are most pronounced in Western markets (and increasingly in urban markets of low-income countries) and affect traders and producers in transition and developing countries through international trade.

3. The fall and rise of VC

VC can take various forms, which can be thought of as institutional arrangements varying between the two extremes of spot market exchanges (0) and full ownership integration (1). Within this 0–1 interval, there is a large variety of different forms of coordination and an equally vast literature trying to classify these various forms, and to explain them. An often-made distinction, which is useful for our purposes, is between marketing contracts and production contracts. *Marketing contracts* are agreements between a contractor and a grower that specify some form of a price (system) and outlet *ex ante*. *Production contracts* are more extensive forms of coordination, vary widely, and additionally include some form of farm insistence such as extension and management services, inputs or credit supplied by the contractor, etc.

3.1. State-controlled VC

VC was widespread in state-controlled food supply chains. Again, this was most extreme in the communist

system, where production at various stages and the exchange of inputs and outputs along the chain was coordinated and determined by the central command system. The agricultural supply system was fully integrated and completely state-controlled (Rozelle and Swinnen, 2004). Production, processing, marketing, the provision of inputs and credit, retailing, etc., were all directed by the central planning authorities. Although there were some variations among countries in the extent and scope of control, this was the basic system extending from Central Europe and the Soviet Union to China and Vietnam.

However, in other regions where the state played an important role in food chains, VC was widespread also. For example, many of the African parastatal organizations provided both inputs to farmers and purchased their outputs. Government marketing organizations and parastatal processing companies used VC systems with upstream suppliers. The dominant form of state-controlled VC was that of seasonal input and credit provisions to small farmers in return for supplies of primary produce.[3] In fact, state-controlled VC was often the only source of input and credit provision for peasant farmers (International Fund for Agricultural Development [IFAD], 2003).

State-controlled VC in centralized agricultural marketing systems in developing and communist countries was often motivated by political motives and by objectives to provide cheap food for urban markets, the maximization of foreign exchange earnings, the creation of rural employment, ascertaining the viability of certain businesses, etc. State-controlled VC was often viewed as a way to protect peasant farmers and stimulate rural development.

Most analyses point at the deficiencies and inefficiencies of these systems. For example, the inefficiency in the processing, agribusiness, and marketing systems and in the central allocation of production factors are considered one of the primary causes of the inefficiency of the Soviet farming complex (Johnson and Brooks, 1983; Swinnen and Rozelle, 2006). In addition,

---

[3] For example, the government marketing boards ADMARC in Malawi and NAMBOARD in Zambia provided seasonal inputs to peasant farmers deducting the value of the inputs from the payment made for marketed output at harvest time. Also parastatal cotton companies such as CMDT in Mali, SODECOTON in Cameroon, and the Ghana Cotton Development Board in Ghana provided credit and inputs to cotton farmers (Poulton et al., 1998).

several studies conclude that state-controlled out-grower schemes in Africa were inefficient and poorly managed, which manifested itself in, among other things, low credit repayment rates (Warning and Key, 2002).[4]

3.2. Liberalization, privatization, and the breakdown of VC

This system of VC has undergone tremendous changes in the 1980s and 1990s. In the transition world, the liberalization of exchange and prices, and the privatization of farms and enterprises caused the collapse of VC and caused major disruptions in the food chain. These effects occurred most dramatically in the collapse of the state-controlled system in Central and Eastern European countries and the former Soviet Union.[5] Widespread forms of contract problems occurred, such as long payment delays, nonpayments for delivered products, or nondelivery. Payment delays were a major problem for companies in Eastern European countries and caused major drains on much needed cash flow for farmers. Food companies in Eastern Europe in the late 1990s considered late payments one of their most important obstacles to growth (Gorton et al., 2000).

The disruptions in relationships of farms with input suppliers and food companies also resulted in many farms' facing serious constraints in accessing essential inputs (feed, fertilizer, seeds, capital, etc.). Furthermore, in many developing countries, privatization and market liberalization led to the decline of input and credit supply to farms as it disrupted the working of various government-controlled agricultural institutions, cooperative unions, and parastatal processing

companies.[6] As government marketing boards and co-operatives have ceased to play a major role in the procurement of agricultural produce, so has the provision of credit and agricultural inputs through state-controlled VC. In addition, market liberalization led to the removal of price supports and input subsidies, a reduction in government research and extension services, and a decline in government (subsidized) credit to the agricultural sector.

3.3. The emergence of private VC

However, following privatization and liberalization, new forms of VC have emerged and are growing (IFAD, 2003; Swinnen, 2006a, 2006b; World Bank, 2006). New forms of VC are no longer state-controlled but are introduced by private companies. Private traders, retailers, agribusinesses, and food processing companies increasingly contract with farms and rural households to whom they provide inputs and services in return for guaranteed and quality supplies. This process of inter-linked contracts is growing rapidly in the transition and developing world.

The emergence and spread of private VC is caused by the combination of, on the one hand, an increasing demand for products of high quality and safety standards with private sector investments and increasing consumer incomes and demands (both domestically and through trade) and, on the other hand, the problems farms face to supply such products reliably, consistently, and in a timely manner to processors and traders due to a variety of market imperfections and poor public institutions.

Farmers in developing and transition countries face major constraints in realizing high-quality, consistent supplies. These include financial constraints as well as difficulties in input markets, lack of technical and managerial capacity, etc. Specifically for high-standards products, farmers might lack the expertise and have no access to crucial inputs such as improved seeds. To guarantee consistent and quality supplies, traders and processors engage in VC to overcome farmers' constraints.

---

[4] Some studies also point at successful state-controlled VC. For example, Poulton et al. (1998) argue that some large government outgrower schemes in Malawi were successful in achieving very high repayment rates. Also the outgrower schemes of the Kenyan Tea Development Authority are referred to as a success story, which is attributed to its extensive form of VC (Bauman, 2000).

[5] Interesting, the early Chinese liberalization of the marketing and input supply system also led to major exchange problems, which caused the Chinese government to make a U-turn on the reforms and reimpose state control on the marketing and fertilizer supply systems, which was then gradually liberalized much later (see Rozelle [1996] for an extensive discussion, and Rozelle and Swinnen [2004] for a summary).

[6] For example, in Kenya, the economic reforms have led to the collapse of the National Cereals and Produce Marketing Board, the Cotton Lint and Seed Marketing Board, the Kenya Grain Growers Cooperative Union, etc. (IFAD, 2003).

Table 1
Share of farms selling on contract in Central Europe (as percentage of total)

Type of contract	Czech		Slovak	Hungary	Bulgaria
	NRIF*	RIF*			
Individual farms					
Contract for crop products	4	37	29	8	5
Contract for livestock products	1	13	4	10	3
Contract for animals	2	7	6	na	Na
Contract for any product	5	46	35	17	7
Corporate farms					
Contract for crop products		79	82	86	42
Contract for livestock products		73	83	59	23
Contract for animals		49	77	na	Na
Contract for any product		96	98	94	43

*RIF = registered individual farms; NRIF = nonregistered individual farms.
Source: Swinnen (2005).

The importance of VC in developing and transition countries is further explained by the lack of efficient institutions and infrastructure to assure consistent, reliable, quality, and timely supply through spot market arrangements. VC is in fact a private institutional response to the above-described market constraints. To overcome problems of enforcement and constraints on quality supplies, private VC systems are set up by processors, traders, retailers, and input suppliers.

Increasing consumer demand for quality and food safety is another driving force behind private VC in transition and developing countries. Investment by modern processors and retailers (supermarket chains) reinforces the need for supplying large and consistent volumes by their use of private standards and requirements of extensive supervision and control of production processes. Emerging empirical evidence suggests that these new forms of private VC can be an engine of economic growth, rural development, and poverty reduction. The next section presents evidence on its effects in transition and developing countries.

4. The importance of private sector contracting and VC[7]

The importance of private VC is increasing in developing and transition countries. At the end of the 1990s,

in the Czech Republic, Slovakia, and Hungary, 80% of the corporate farms, which dominated farm production in these countries, sold crops on contract, and 60–85% sold animal products on contract; numbers that are considerably higher than the shares of farms in the United States and the European Union (Table 1). White and Gorton (2004), using a survey of agri-food processors in five CIS countries (Armenia, Georgia, Moldova, Ukraine, and Russia), found that food companies which used contracts with suppliers grew from slightly more than one-third in 1997 to almost three-quarters by 2003.

There is also significant growth of supplier support measures as part of the contracts and more farms are getting access to these. Credit, inputs, prompt payments, transportation, and quality control are the most commonly offered forms of support. Over 40% of processors in the CIS sample offer credit to at least some of the farms that supply them; and 36% offered inputs in 2003. In several sectors, including the dairy sector in Poland, Bulgaria, Slovakia, and Romania, the farm assistance programs offered by private dairy companies are quite extensive and include credit provisions, input supply, extension services, and veterinary services and, in some cases, bank loan guarantee (Table 2). Figure 2 shows how the growth of VC is closely and positively related to the reform process in transition countries.

In developing countries, private VC is emerging and growing in many sectors. Traditional tropical export products (coffee, tea, cocoa, rubber, and oil palm) were traditionally grown on fully integrated large-scale plantations because of large economies of scale in both production and marketing of these crops. However, these perennial crops are increasingly being grown by

[7] Not surprisingly, there are important variations among commodities—reflecting the specific production and processing characteristics—as well as variations among companies in the institutional design of VC, reflecting local conditions and company preferences, among other things. See Gow and Swinnen (2001), Maertens and Swinnen (2006), Swinnen (2006a, 2006b), and World Bank (2006) for details on this.

Table 2
Farm assistance programs offered by dairy companies in Central Europe

Company name	Credit	Input supply*	Extension service	Veterinary service	Bank loan guarantee
Poland**					
Mlekpol	Y	Y	Y	N	Y
Mleczarnia	N	Y	N	N	Y
Kurpie	Y	Y	Y	N	Y
Mazowsze	Y	Y	Y	N	N
ICC Paslek	Y	Y	Y	N	Y
Warmia Dairy	Y	Y	Y	Y	Y
Bulgaria					
Merone	Y (2000)	Y (???)	Y (1992)	N	N
Fama	Y (1994)	Y (1994)	N	N	Y (once)
Mlekimex	Y (1997)	Y (1997)	Y (1999)	Y (1997	Y (1998)
Danone	Y (1997)	Y (1998)	Y (2000)	Y (1995)	Y (1999)
Iotovi	N	Y (1995)	N	N	Y (1995)
Milky World	Y (1999)	Y (1999)	Y (1999)	N	Y (1999)
Markelli	Y (1999)	Y (1998)	N	N	N
Mandra Obnova	Y (1998)	Y (2000)	Y (2000)	N	N
Meggle	Y (2001)	Y (2001)	Y (2001)	N	N
PRL	N	N	Y (2002)	N	N
Serdika 90	Y (1997)	Y (1997)	Y (1997)	N	N
Slovakia					
Liptovska	Y (2000)	N	Y (1994)	N	N
Mliekospol	Y (1999)	N	Y (1992)	Y (1992)	Y (1992)
Rajo	Y (2001)	Y/N	Y (1992)	N	N
Levicka	Y (1998)	Y (1998)	Y (0000)	N	Y (1998)
Tatranska	Y (2001)	Y (2000)	Y (0000)	N	N
Nutricia Dairy	Y (2000)	N	N	N	Y (2000)
Romania					
Danone	Y	Y	Y		Y
Friesland	Y	Y	Y		Y
Promilch	Y	Y	Y		Y
Raraul	N	Y	Y		N

*Either the company provides inputs and the farmer pays back later, or the company offers forward credit, which the farmer uses to buy inputs.

**In Poland, no distinction is made between credit for dairy-specific investments and general investments. Farm-level evidence shows that the dairy companies mainly support dairy-specific investments.

Source: Swinnen (2005).

smallholders under contract farming arrangements and outgrower schemes, often with the provision of inputs, new technologies, credit, and extension services to farmers. For example, cocoa in Ghana and Nigeria; rubber in Malaysia, Nigeria, and Sri Lanka; coffee in Ivory Coast, Kenya, and Madagascar; oil-palm in West Africa; and tea in Kenya and Malawi. In Kenya, half of the coffee is produced by contracted smallholders (Bauman, 2000).

In South and Southeast Asia (SSA), there has been a sharp increase in the VC of primary production with input suppliers and processing/exporting firms during the past 20 years (Gulati et al., 2005). Especially in an-

imal production and dairy farming, VC is widespread. In SSA, private VC has become a dominant system of rural financing. For example, in Mozambique and Zambia it is virtually the only source of finance for agricultural households (IFAD, 2003). In Mozambique, an estimated 400,000 rural households, representing 12% of the rural population, are included in contract farming. Also in Kenya and Zambia, a high number of rural households are producing agricultural commodities on contract with agroindustrial firms (Table 3). The main crops that are grown under contractual arrangements in SSA include cotton, tobacco, and horticulture crops. Also in Latin America, VC is widespread over many

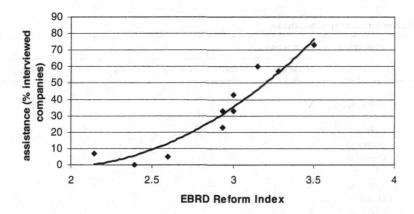

Figure 2. Impact of economic reforms on vertical coordination (*) in the dairy sector of transition countries (**). *Share of dairy companies providing substantive assistance to farms as part of production contracts. **Data based on surveys in Albania, Bulgaria, Poland, Slovakia (between 1994 and 2004). *Source:* Swinnen et al. (2006).

Table 3
Contract farming in Sub-Saharan Africa

Country	Commodity	Number of contracted smallholders
Kenya	Tea	406,000
	Sugar	200,000
	Horticulture	15,000–20,000
	Tobacco	>10,000
Zambia	Cotton	150,000
	Tobacco	570
	Horticulture	13,500
Mozambique	Cotton	270,000
	Tobacco	100,000

Source: IFAD (2003).

different agricultural commodities and includes various contractual arrangements, ranging from purely marketing contracts to production contracts with provision of inputs, credit, technical assistance, and marketing assistance (Table 4).

Finally, while private sector involvement has grown and the role of the government in agricultural production and marketing diminished, in several countries, especially in SSA, the government is still involved in agricultural supply chains, for example, through minority or majority shares in privatized food processing companies, through state-owned banks and government credit schemes (sometimes as part of multipartite VC), and provision of extension services. Zambia is one of the only countries in SSA with almost complete absence of the government in production, marketing,

regulation, or direct financial contributions to the agricultural sector, although the government continues to play a major role in the distribution of fertilizers (IFAD, 2003).

5. Effects of private VC

The emergence of private VC is often mentioned as a new engine for economic growth, rural development, and poverty reduction. In this section, we review the empirical evidence on the impact of VC in transition and developing countries. We distinguish between efficiency and equity effects.

5.1. Efficiency effects

The impact of private VC systems on productivity is difficult to quantify as several other factors affect output simultaneously and as company-level information is difficult to obtain. Still, the evidence suggests that successful private VC has important positive effects, both direct and indirect.

The *direct impact* is on the output and productivity of the processing company that initiates vertical contracting and of its suppliers involved in VC schemes. Supplying farmers have experienced beneficial effects on output, productivity, and product quality—and ultimately on incomes—through better access to inputs, timely payments, and improved productivity with new investments. Case studies indicate

Table 4
Vertical coordination in Latin American agri-food chains

| Product | Destination | Contracting | | | | | Vertical integration |
		Marketing	Technical assistance	Credit	Inputs	Management	
Tomato							
Nicaragua	Domestic	X					
Paraguay	Domestic						
Ecuador	Domestic						X
Mexico	Domestic	X					X
Peru	Domestic						X
F&V							
Guyana	Domestic	X					
Ecuador	Domestic	X					
Trinidad & Tobago	Domestic	X					
Mexico	Export	X	X	X	X	X	X
Guatemala	Export	X	X	X	X	X	X
El Salvador	Export	X	X	X	X		
Peru	Export	X					X
Chicken							
Trinidad & Tobago	Domestic	X	X	X	X		X
Jamaica	Domestic	X		X			
Tobacco							
Chile	na	X	X	X	X		
Guatemala	na	X	X	X	X		
Sugarcane							
Nicaragua	Exp&Dom	X	X		X		X
Guatemala	Exp&Dom						X
Sesame Seed							
Nicaragua	Export	X		X			
Guatemala	Export	X					
El Salvador	Export						
Malt, Barley							
Chile	Domestic	X	X		X		
Peru	Domestic	X		X	X		
Rice							
Trinidad & Tobago	Domestic	X	X		X		
Paraguay	na	X		X			
Dominican Republic	na	X					
Dairy							
Trinidad & Tobago	Domestic	X	X	X			
Jamaica	Domestic	X					
Ecuador	Domestic	X					

Source: Dirven (1996).

that private VC programs can lead to double-digit annual growth in output and productivity. For example, case studies of the sugar and dairy sectors in Eastern Europe show how new private contracts and farm assistance programs caused output, yields, and investments to grow dramatically (Gow et al., 2000; Dries and Swinnen, 2004; Swinnen, 2006a, 2006b). A major IFPRI-FAO study found that contract broiler farmers are significantly more efficient and produce higher profits than independent farms in the Philippines and Thailand (Gulati et al., 2005). Moreover, farm profits were found to be significantly higher through lower production and marketing costs for contract farms compared to independent smallholders in VC schemes for milk, broilers, and vegetables in India (Birthal et al., 2005). Maertens et al. (2007) find that the benefits from contract farming in horticulture production in Senegal in terms of higher rural incomes are substantial.

In their survey of CIS agri-business enterprise executives, White and Gorton (2004) concluded that various contract support measures had caused (separately) an average increase in yields of around 10%. The measures with the greatest impact on yields were specialist storage (especially cooling equipment in the dairy sector), veterinary support, and physical inputs. Specialist storage in the form of on-farm cooling tanks has been particularly important in raising yields and quality in the dairy sector, an effect also found in other countries (Swinnen et al., 2006). Market measures such as prompt payments, guaranteed prices, and market access also had large positive effects.

Quality of output also improved due to these measures. In the case of Polish dairy farms, milk quality rose rapidly following contract innovations by dairy processors in the mid 1990s. The share of the market held by highest-quality milk increased from less than 30% on average in 1996 to around 80% on average in 2001 (Dries and Swinnen, 2004). VC loans and loan guarantee programs contributed strongly to this by encouraging farm investments. In the Polish study, more than three-quarters (76%) of all farmers in the survey made investments in the past years, including many small farmers of less than 10 cows (Dries and Swinnen, 2004). Dairy loans are used for investments in enlarging and upgrading the livestock herd (30%) and cooling tanks (56%). Moreover, dairy assistance in the form of guarantees for bank loans helped farm investments. Also, programs that assist farms in accessing inputs (mainly feed) enhance investment indirectly by lowering input costs, or reducing transaction costs in accessing inputs and, consequently, through improved profitability.

Successful state-controlled VC programs exist. However, some case studies point out that state-controlled VC is generally less effective in realizing farm productivity growth than private VC. For example, in Ghana, liberalization of the cotton market and privatization of the Ghana Cotton Company induced more extensive VC programs, including timely plowing services, reliable fertilizer and pesticide supplies, prompt payment after harvest, and even plowing for farmers' food crops (Poulton, 1998). As a result of improved farm assistance programs, cotton production and yields increased dramatically (Poulton, 1998). Another example from the peanut industry in Senegal by Warning and Key (2002) illustrates this further.

After independence in 1960, the state began the confectionary peanut program (Arachide de Bouche Programme [ABP]), which grew into an outgrower scheme with 32,000 farmers providing peanuts destined for direct consumption. The ABP was completely privatized in 1990 and VC was extended from marketing contracts under state-controlled VC to production contracts in which the company handles all aspects of production, including selection and training of contracting farmers, provision of inputs, close monitoring of production, collection, and processing of the harvest and export of the produce, mainly to the EU. Comparing the private ABP VC program with the state-controlled VC program of the majority state-owned company SONACAS for oil-peanut processing, reveals that this state-controlled VC program has much lower yields than the private VC program of ABP (800 kg/ha vs. 1,300 kg/ha) and that they have much lower credit repayment rates (58% compared to 98%). In addition, participation in the ABP program was found to significantly increase the income of farmers and improve their living conditions.

Indirect effects emerge through (1) cross-company spillover effects (see next section) and (2) household and farm spillover effects. Household and farm spillovers occur as households' risk reduces; their access to capital increases, and the productivity of non-contracted activities increases. First, VC does not only imply the provision of inputs, working capital, and technical assistance to farmers, it also implies guaranteed sales, often at guaranteed prices. This comes down to decreased marketing risk for farmers. In addition, coordinating firms share in the production risk of farmers through *ex ante* provision of inputs and credit. Reduced production and marketing risks improve stability of farmers' income, which is an important benefit for farmers operating in high-risk environments and in the absence of insurance markets.[8] Second, VC credit arrangements and prompt payments after harvest improve farmers' cash flow and access to capital. This might ease farmers' financial constraints and benefit investment in other farm and nonfarm activities. This

---

[8] Guaranteed prices can also be counterproductive for farmers. For example, Gulati et al. (2005) point out that profits for contracted swine producers in the Philippines and Thailand were much lower than for independent producers in 2002. This was in part due to the strengthening of pork prices during the year, which did not benefit contracted farmers producing at guaranteed fixed prices.

Johan F. M. Swinnen and Miet Maertens

Table 5

Contract motivations for farms in Central Europe, former Soviet Union, and Sub-Saharan Africa

Reasons for contracting 1999 (% of farmers)	Most important reason				One of the reasons	
	Czech 1999	Slovak 1999	Hungary 1997	Kazakhstan	Madagascar 2004	Senegal 2005
Higher prices	9	8	10			11
Stable prices	7	22	33		19	45
Guaranteed sales	64	50	43	8		66
Guaranteed price				3		
Pre-financing	7	13	3	75		
Access to inputs/credit	7	6	11	10	60	63
Access to technical assistance				0	55	17
Stable income					66	30
Higher income					17	15
Income during the lean period					72	37
Other	6	2	0	3		

Source: Swinnen (2005), Minten et al. (2006), Maertens et al. (2007).

effect is particularly important in the case of capital market imperfections. Third, contract farming can lead to productivity spillovers on other crops, resulting from management advice, access to improved technologies, better input use, etc.

A number of empirical studies provide evidence for these household spillover effects. In a study on VC in South and Southeast Asia, Gulati et al. (2005) show that there is significantly less variation in yields and prices during the year for contract broiler farmers in India because they share risk with the contracted firm. A study on contracted vegetables in Uganda by Henson (2004) shows that there are important benefits for rural households from reduced risk and improved access to credit from vegetables production under contract in Uganda. Govereh and Jayne (2003) find important spillover benefits from VC in contracted cotton production on increased productivity on noncontracted activities.

Another illustrative example comes from Minten et al. (2006) on the FFV sector in Madagascar, one of the poorest countries in the world. The vast majority of FFV export from Madagascar goes through one company that has regular contracts with five supermarket chains in Europe. The company buys vegetables from more than 9,000 small farmers based on contracts. The firm provides seeds, fertilizer, and pesticides and engages in intensive monitoring and extension advice. Farmers largely benefit from this contract production through a combination of effects. The firm teaches farmers better technologies and management practices,

such as the use of compost, and this results in productivity spillovers on rice, with yields being 64% higher on plots under contract. In addition, smallholders who participate in contract farming have higher welfare, more stable incomes, and shorter lean periods.

There are a number of studies specifically examining the motivations of farmers to engage in contract production. These show that guaranteed sales and prices, access to inputs and credit are the most important motivations rather than direct income effects, which further proves the importance of household spillover effects from contract farming. For example, Table 5 shows that the dominant motivation for farms in Central Europe at the end of the 1990s was guaranteed access to markets (52% of the farms listed this as their primary motive) and to a lesser extent guaranteed prices (21%). The motivations for small cotton farmers in southern Kazakhstan to enter into contracts with gins are mainly the improved access to credit. For horticulture farmers in Senegal, guaranteed market access and access to inputs are the most important motivations for farmers to sign contracts while in Madagascar this is income stability and shorting of the lean period.

5.2. Equity effects

There are two potential equity issues with VC processes. The first concerns the distribution of rents in vertically coordinated food supply chains. The second concerns the participation and exclusion of smallholders and poorer farmers in contract farming.

First, VC implies sharing risks, costs, and benefits between coordinating firms—mostly food processors, exporters, and retail chains—and farmers/suppliers. By introducing an interlinked contract, farms can access credit, inputs, etc. that were unavailable before and processing companies can have access to higher-quality and timely supplies. Productivity and therefore income increases for the supply chain as a whole. However, a key question is who benefits from this increase in efficiency and total income? If the supplier and the processor benefit, both parties share in the gains from the institutional innovation, and everybody is better off. However, if the processing firm can set the terms of the contract such that it captures most or all of the rents, the productivity growth may not benefit the farms, and interlinking may even bestow additional monopoly power upon the processing company. Contract farming has often been criticized as being a tool for agroindustrial firms and food multinationals to exploit unequal power relationships with farmers and extract rents from the chain (Warning and Key, 2002). However, our review of empirical evidence on the effects of VC presented earlier indicates that farmers do share importantly in the benefits of contract farming and VC.

Second, the capacity of emerging VC in agri-food supply chains to serve as an engine of pro-poor economic growth critically depends on the types of farmers that are included in contract schemes. VC has the potential to affect the way income is distributed within a rural economy and can exacerbate existing patterns of economic stratification (Warning and Key, 2002). If agroindustrial firms prefer to contract with wealthier farmers, then poorer households will be excluded from direct benefits. There are three important reasons why this might be so. First, transaction costs favor larger farms in supply chains. Second, when some amount of investment is needed in order to contract with or supply to the company, small farms are often more constrained in their financial means for making necessary investments. Third, small farms typically require more assistance from the company per unit of output.

However, there are also reasons why agroindustrial firms do contract with smallholders and poorer farmers. First, the most straightforward reason is that companies have no choice. In some cases, small farmers represent the vast majority of the potential supply base. This is, for example, the case in the dairy sector in Poland and Romania, and in many other sectors in East-

ern European countries (Swinnen, 2006a, 2006b). Second, case studies from transition countries suggest that company preferences for contracting with large farms are not as obvious as one may think. While processors may prefer to deal with large farms because of lower transaction costs in collection and administration, contract enforcement may be more problematic and, hence, costly with larger farms. Processors repeatedly emphasized that farms' "willingness to learn, take on board advice, and a professional attitude were more important than size in establishing fruitful farm-processor relationships" (Swinnen, 2005, p. 46). Third, in some cases small farms may have substantive cost advantages. This is particularly the case in labor-intensive, high-maintenance production activities with relatively small economies of scale. Fourth, processors may prefer a mix of suppliers in order not to become too dependent on a few large suppliers.

Empirical studies and interviews with companies in Central and Eastern Europe and Sub-Saharan Africa generally confirm the main hypotheses coming out of global observations: transaction costs and investment constraints are a serious consideration and companies express a preference for working with relatively fewer, larger, and modern suppliers (Maertens et al., 2007; Swinnen, 2006a, 2006b). However, empirical observations show a very mixed picture of actual contracting, with many more small farms being contracted than predicted according to the arguments above. In fact, surveys in Poland, Romania, and CIS find no evidence that small farmers have been excluded over the past 6 years in developing supply chains. In the CIS, the vast majority of companies have the same or more small suppliers in 2003 than in 1997 (Swinnen, 2006a, 2006b; World Bank, 2006). Also for the peanut sector in Senegal, no evidence was found for a bias in the participation of farmers in contract schemes toward better-off households (Warning and Key, 2002).

A study on horticulture exports from Senegal by Maertens et al. (2007) finds that there are important effects on poverty reduction from high-value supply chains. The export of FFV from Senegal to the EU has increased considerably during the past decade. Initially export was based mostly on contracts with farming households. However, owing to increasingly stringent food standards, the VC system is changing in the past couple of years toward fully integrated production on agroindustrial holdings. This has decreased contract farming and increased employment on agroindustrial farms. The study shows that contract farming is highly beneficial for households, but biased to households with more land, livestock, and other assets. Employment in the agroindustry is not biased—the poorest households participate equally—and there are also important income effects, albeit less than those of contract farming. In combination, the effects on income from both contract farming and agroindustrial employment are significantly positive. This suggests that, as smallholder contract farming and large-scale industrial farming reach different groups of the poor, mixed VC systems can have major poverty reduction effects.

6. The role of competition

Liberalization has increased competition in agricultural markets. Competition will affect both equity and efficiency in supply chains. This issue is dealt with more explicitly in Swinnen and Vandeplas (2006).

First, competition induces VC spillover effects across the sector as other processors are forced to introduce similar supplier assistance programs since suppliers may not want to deliver unless they get similar conditions. Cross-company spillovers occur as firms competing for the same suppliers, and their fixed inputs, are forced to offer similar contractual arrangements. For example, in the case of the Slovak sugar sector, competition induced other sugar processors to introduce similar contracts. With some delay, this resulted in increases in productivity in the rest of the sugar sector. Other studies confirm the importance of this competition effect. Noev et al. (2004) and Dries et al. (2004) find that, respectively, in the case of the Bulgarian dairy sector and in contracting by modern retail companies in Croatia, competition for suppliers forces other companies to replicate farm assistance programs in order to secure supplies. Another example is from Ghana, where increased competition in the cotton market and the privatization of the Ghana Cotton Development Board (who provided production inputs, extension services, and guaranteed purchase of the supply to farmers under state-controlled VC) into the Ghana Cotton Company induced more extensive VC. Competing private companies have increased their services to farmers, including timely plowing services, reliable

fertilizer and pesticide supplies, prompt payment after harvest, and even plowing for farmers' food crops (Poulton, 1998). This finding is a specific case of more general conclusions that competition is a key factor for encouraging innovation and productivity growth and that technological development is primarily encouraged through the presence of competition.

Second, farmers benefit from competition between processing firms. More competition leads to more equal rent sharing, reflected in higher producer prices and more services to farmers. A comparative analysis of VC in the cotton sector in Central Asia confirms the importance of competition as an important factor to protect small farms against rent extraction by large processors (Sadler, 2006). The only places where we find clear evidence that farmers are consistently exploited is in government-controlled monopolized systems, such as the cotton system in Uzbekistan and Tajikistan (and Turkmenistan). In contrast, in Kazakhstan, the cotton chain is characterized by strong competition among private gins buying cotton seeds from small farms for processing. Competition among gins results in better contracts for small suppliers: in investment by gins in local cotton seed collection centers, reducing transport costs, and in better prices. In 2003, prices for Kazakh cotton farmers were two to three times higher than those in Uzbekistan or Tajikistan where competition does not exist.

However, there was also another effect of competition. If competition becomes too vigorous in the interlinked input and credit market, coordination may break down. Farmers may undermine their own long-run productivity through strategic defaulting in the short run. Several case studies report input programs that collapsed because of competition. In other cases, input programs remained sustainable under competition as a result of special institutional arrangements like frequent monitoring, buyer coordination, or local information networks. An important area for further research is to analyze the conditions under which competition leads to beneficial outcomes while avoiding VC failure.

7. Conclusion

Food and agricultural commodity value chains in developing and transition countries have undergone tremendous changes in the past decades—many of these unimaginable 25 years ago. The most important changes are the shift from domestically oriented to globally integrated food supply chains and from state-controlled systems to private governance in the agrifood system. Companies and property rights have been privatized, markets liberalized, and food supply chains integrated into the global economy. An important aspect of these changes is that liberalization and privatization initially caused the collapse of state-controlled VC. However, more recently, privately governed VC systems have emerged and are growing rapidly. This is a response to consumer demand for food quality and safety on the one hand and the farms' production constraints caused by factor market imperfections on the other hand. In this article, we have shown that these changes have major effects on the quality, equity, and efficiency of the agri-food systems and, more generally, have major implications for economic performance and development in these countries (and beyond). It is also clear that we do not yet sufficiently understand all the changes that are taking place and their implications and that this should be an important field for future research.

References

Aksoy, M. A., "The Evolution of Agricultural Trade Flows," in M. A. Aksoy and J. C. Beghin, eds., *Global Agricultural Trade and Developing Countries* (World Bank: Washington, DC, 2005), pp. 17–35.

Bauman, P., "Equity and Efficiency in Contract Farming Schemes: The Experience of Agricultural Tree Crops," *Paper* 139 (Overseas Development Institute: London, 2000).

Birthal, P. S., P. K. Joshi, and A. Gulati, "Vertical Coordination in High-Value Food Commodities: Implications for Smallholders," *MTID Discussion Paper* No. 85 (International Food Policy Research Institute: Washington, DC, 2005).

Dirven, M., *Agroindustria y Pequea Agricultura. Sintesis Comparative de Distintas Experiencies*. (LC/R.1663) (DEPAL: Santioga de Chile, 1996).

Dries, L., and J. F. M. Swinnen, "Foreign Direct Investment, Vertical Integration and Local Suppliers: Evidence from the Polish Dairy Sector," *World Development* 32 (2004), 1525–1544.

Dries, L., T. Reardon, and J. F. M. Swinnen, "The Rapid Rise of Supermarkets in Central and Eastern Europe: Implications for the Agrifood Sector and Rural Development," *Development Policy Review* 22 (2004), 525–556.

Gorton, M., A. Buckwell, and S. Davidova, "Transfers and Distortions along CEEC Food Supply Chains," in S. Tangermann and M. Banse, eds., *Central and Eastern European Agriculture in an Expanding European Union* (CABI Publishing: Wallingford, UK, 2000), pp. 89–112.

Govereh, J., and T. S. Jayne, "Cash Cropping and Food Crop Productivity: Synergies or Trade-Offs?" *Agricultural Economics* 28 (2003), 39–50.

Gow, H., and J. F. M. Swinnen, "Private Enforcement Capital and Contract Enforcement in Transition Countries," *American Journal of Agricultural Economics* 83 (2001), 686–690.

Gow, H., D. H. Streeter, and J. F. M. Swinnen, "How Private Contract Enforcement Mechanisms can Succeed where Public Institutions Fail: The Case of Juhocukor a.s.," *Agricultural Economics* 23 (2000), 253–265.

Gulati, A., N. Minot, C. Delgado, and S. Bora, "Growth in High-Value Agriculture in Asia and the Emergence of Vertical Links with Farmers," Paper presented at the workshop Linking Small-scale Producers to Markets: Old and New Challenges (World Bank: Washington, DC, 2005).

Henson, S. J., "National Laws, Regulations, and Institutional Capabilities for Standards Development," paper prepared for World Bank training seminar on Standards and Trade (World Bank: Washington, DC, 2004).

International Fund for Agricultural Development, *Agricultural Marketing Companies as Sources of Smallholder Credit in Eastern and Southern Africa. Experiences, Insights and Potential Donor Role* (IFAD: Rome, 2003).

Johnson, D.G., and K. M. Brooks, *Prospects for Soviet Agriculture in the 1980s* (Indiana University Press: Bloomington, 1983).

Maertens, M., and J. F. M. Swinnen, "Trade, Standards and Poverty: Empirical Evidence from Senegal," *LICOS Discussion Paper* 177 (2006). (http://www.econ.kuleuven.be/LICOS/DP/dp.htm)

Maertens, M., L. Dries, F. A. Dedehouanou, and J. F. M. Swinnen, "High-value Global Supply Chains, EU Food Safety Policy and Smallholders in Developing Countries: A Case-study from the Green Bean Sector in Senegal," in J. F. M. Swinnen, ed., *Global Supply Chains, Standards and the Poor* (CABI Publishing: Oxon, UK, 2007), pp. 159–172.

Minten, B., L. Randrianarison, and J. F. M. Swinnen, "Global Retail Chains and Poor Farmers: Evidence from Madagascar," *LICOS Discussion Papers* 164 (2006). Leuven, (http://www.econ.kuleuven.be/LICOS/DP/dp.htm).

Noev, N., L. Dries, and J. F. M. Swinnen, "Foreign Investment and the Restructuring of the Dairy Supply Chains in Bulgaria," LICOS, mimeo (2004).

Poulton, C., "Cotton Production and Marketing in Northern Ghana: The Dynamics of Competition in a System of Interlocking Transactions," in A. Dorward, J. Kydd, and C. Poulton, eds., *Smallholder Cash Crop Production under Market Liberalisation: A New Institutional Economics Perspective* (CABI Publishing: Oxon, UK, 1998), Chapter 4.

Poulton, C., A. Dorward, J. Kydd, N. Poole, and L. Smith, "A New Institutional Economics Perspective on Current Policy Debates," in A. Dorward, J. Kydd, and C. Poulton, eds., *Smallholder Cash Crop Production under Market Liberalisation: A New Institutional Economics Perspective* (CABI Publishing: Oxon, UK, 1998), Chapter 1.

Reardon, T., and J. F. M. Swinnen, "Agrifood Sector Liberalization and the Rise of Supermarkets in Former State-Controlled Economies: Comparison with Other Developing Countries," *Development Policy Review* 22 (2004), 317–334.

Rozelle, S., "Gradual Reform and Institutional Development: The Keys to Success of China's Agricultural Reforms," in J. McMillan and B. Naughton, eds., *Reforming Asian Socialism: The Growth of Market Institutions* (University of Michigan Press: Ann Arbor, 1996), pp. 197–220.

Rozelle, S., and J. F. M. Swinnen, "Success and Failure of Reforms: Insights from Transition Agriculture," *Journal of Economic Literature* 42 (2004), 404–456.

Sadler, M., "Comparative Analysis of Cotton Supply Chains in Central Asia," in J. F. M. Swinnen, ed., *The Dynamics of Vertical Coordination in Agrifood Chains in Eastern Europe and Central Asia: Case Studies* (World Bank: Washington, DC, 2006), pp. 73–114.

Swinnen, J. F. M., *When the Market Comes to You—Or Not. The Dynamics of Vertical Co-ordination in Agro-Food Chains in Europe and Central Asia* (World Bank: Washington, DC, 2005).

Swinnen, J. F. M., *Global Supply Chains, Standards and the Poor* (CABI Publishing: Oxon, UK, 2006a).

Swinnen, J. F. M., *The Dynamics of Vertical Coordination in Agrifood Chains in Eastern Europe and Central Asia: Case Studies* (World Bank: Washington, DC, 2006b).

Swinnen, J., and S. Rozelle, *From Marx and Mao to the Market:*

The Economics and Politics of Agricultural Transition (Oxford University Press: Oxford, 2006).

Swinnen, J. F. M., and A. Vandeplas, "Contracting, Competition, and Rent Distribution in Supply Chains: Theory and Empirical Evidence," LICOS, mimeo (2006).

Swinnen, J. F. M., L. Dries, N. Noev, and E. Germenji, "Foreign Investment, Supermarkets, and the Restructuring of Supply Chains: Evidence from Eastern European Dairy Sectors," *LICOS Discussion Paper* 165 (2006) (http://www.econ.kuleuven.be/LICOS/DP/dp.htm).

Warning, M., and N. Key, "The Social Performance and Distributional Impact of Contract Farming: An Equilibrium Analysis of the Arachide de Bouche Program in Senegal," *World Development* 30 (2002), 255–263.

White, J., and M. Gorton, *Vertical Coordination in TC Agrifood Chains as an Engine of Private Sector Development: Implications for Policy and Bank Operations* (World Bank: Washington, DC, 2004).

World Bank, *The Dynamics of Vertical Coordination in Agrifood Chains in Eastern Europe and Central Asia. Implications for Policy Making and World Bank Operations* (World Bank: Washington, DC, 2006).

Food regulation and trade under the WTO: ten years in perspective

David Orden[*] and Donna Roberts[**]

Abstract

This article reviews the performance of the World Trade Organization in the oversight of national regulatory decisions affecting agricultural and food trade. A picture emerges of modest international disciplines on the regulatory decisions of sovereign nations and the need for ongoing improvements. A road map to regulations is presented and empirical assessments of the effects of technical regulation on trade are reviewed. Conflicts over sanitary and phytosanitary barriers raised in the relevant World Trade Organization committee are summarized and formal dispute settlement cases involving technical trade barriers are evaluated. Drawing on these reviews, suggestions are made for improving international food regulation.

JEL classification: F13, F18, Q17, Q18, Q27

Keywords: World Trade Organization; technical barriers; sanitary and phytosanitary regulations

1. Introduction

Just over 10 years ago, the World Trade Organization (WTO) strengthened international rules designed to discipline the regulatory measures that countries adopt to achieve legitimate agricultural and food safety and quality goals. In the case of sanitary and phytosanitary (SPS) measures, the disciplines require a scientific risk assessment and that measures be formulated to achieve their technical objective in a least trade-distorting manner. In the case of quality goals, the agreement on technical barriers to trade (TBT) again requires that measures be appropriate to the objective and least trade distorting. The new disciplines were backed up by a more binding dispute settlement process.

How well these new multilateral agreements have worked is important for several reasons. First, when sovereign countries adopt regulations to address health, safety, and quality goals, they often fail to take into account the international implications of imposing a measure. International accountability is a major goal

of the SPS and TBT agreements. Second, the international agreements impose administrative costs on poor countries. In exchange, poor countries ought to benefit from the agreements by gaining market access that enhances their ability to participate in world trade. Third, agricultural trade is growing fastest in high-value products. These are products for which technical standards and regulations are prevalent. Fourth, acceptable standards for agriculture and food are evolving worldwide under various forces. New challenges thus arise for the multilateral agreements as a framework in which national rules are embedded.

This article provides a review in broad terms of the performance of the WTO in the international oversight of national regulatory decisions affecting agricultural and food trade since its launch in 1995. What emerges is a picture of modest international disciplines on the regulatory decisions of sovereign nations and the need for ongoing improvements.

National food markets are highly integrated through global trade and investment, yet nations retain the principal authority over almost all dimensions of their food regulation and standards. Increasingly, private-sector–promulgated standards, together with private supply chains of international scope, are determining food market access (see Henson, 2006, for a review). But optimal management of national food supplies

---

[*] *Department of Agricultural and Applied Economics, Virginia Polytechnic Institute and State University, Blacksburg, Virginia, USA and Markets, Trade and Institutions Division, International Food Policy Research Institute (IFPRI), Washington D.C., USA.*

[**] *Economic Research Service, USDA, 1800 M Street NW, Washington, DC, 20036-5831 USA.*

involves various forms of government intervention. Without exception, governments regulate their food sectors.

The justifications for regulatory coordination among countries and international oversight of national regulation stem from both the public goods aspects of disease and pest control and the opportunities to reduce market transactions costs for firms and consumers. By striving for more coherent decision making among themselves, countries can influence the conditions under which international trade is conducted and thereby address trade-related risks, improve product information, and foster welfare-enhancing transactions.

These justifications for effective coordination and disciplines internationally do not prevent controversy and conflict over regulations in the global food system. Regulation is often the subject of international disputes because national institutions are subject to domestic political pressures. It is easy even for countries with similarity of income levels and other characteristics to deviate in their regulatory decisions.

Appraisal of the net benefits of trade against any costs that arise from risks or market information failures linked to an open food system is a useful counterweight to the pressures for trade-related regulation, but is itself a difficult task. Such an appraisal entails an analysis of the expected benefits and costs of regulatory measures that includes a gains-from-trade calculation. Underprotection—that is, when too much trade is allowed by the regulations and standards in place or by their inadequate enforcement—is likely to be a problem at times. But overprotection—when relaxation of regulation would yield net welfare gains—is also evident in the food system.

Overall, two broad challenges are faced to improve existing food regulation. The first is to achieve the appropriate balance within countries between reliance on domestically determined and internationally agreed-on product specifications. Common risk-reducing measures can facilitate trade in low-cost, safe products, and the benefits of trade can be enhanced by lowering transaction costs through international harmonization. Conversely, adoption of the appropriate risk-reduction measures may depend on countries' specific circumstances, making harmonization inappropriate. Undue harmonization might also impose limits on consumer choice. Finding the right degree of international coordination is the dilemma.

The second broad challenge facing food regulation is to maintain both the confidence of consumers and the cooperation of producers in implementing regulations and standards, while avoiding political-economy regulatory capture by either group. The resolution of this dilemma is found in improving national regulatory capacities and developing the competence and authority of international institutions to define and enforce disciplines on national regulators, despite the known limitations of regulatory processes and institutions at even the national level.

2. A road map of food regulation

Food regulations can be classified as either risk reducing or related to nonrisk product quality. The measures used can also be categorized by whether they focus on content or process attributes of products and by their breadth, scope, and instrumentation.[1] The requirements for verifying compliance or equivalence with a measure are also important in assessments of food regulations. These classificatory variables allow some generalizations to be made about the appropriateness of regulations in achieving their objectives.

One argument that emerges in our judgment is that regulations are most often the appropriate instrument for risk-related goals. By contrast, measures undertaken voluntarily by the private sector—albeit with varying and sometimes significant degrees of government involvement, including prosecution of deceptive claims—are the preferred approach for food quality goals. This argument is not to deny that risk-related regulations are sometimes distorted for protectionist purposes, nor to reject the claim that market failures occur in the provision of product quality information. The former warrants international disciplines and the latter some degree of government intervention. Yet the global food system is best served when regulations are used predominantly for risk reduction and sparingly to govern food quality. The governance of food quality is more diffuse than that for risk because a greater proportion of food quality measures are both established and enforced by the private sector. It is the market, rather than the government, that is likely to be the more agile

---

[1] For elaboration on this and other ideas presented in this article see *Food Regulation and Trade: Toward a Safe and Open Global System* (Sasling et al., 2004).

institution for accommodating a wide range of continually evolving consumer preferences.

The importance in the modern global food supply of private sector standards and tightly controlled marketing chains reflects this reality. Nonetheless, some of the most serious tests facing the global food system arise from emerging national regulation about quality issues. Increased consumer demand for quality-related product differentiation is a positive, income-driven phenomenon, attainable at declining cost as information technology advances. Acting on this demand, interest groups that feel strongly about specific food attributes have an incentive to seek greater government regulation of product quality. In international discussions, some governments have argued that increased regulation reflects a new era in the food sector in which policy makers must be attuned to the demands of consumers as well as producer advocates. But the new focus on consumer-driven quality regulations can lead to regulatory overprotection. Producer groups also favor stronger regulations on quality in those instances in which they gain market advantage. This situation can also lead to overprotection and distort trade.

Regulatory measures that address risk in agricultural production and food consumption underpin the structure of market transactions within countries and influence competitive advantage among trade partners. For animal and plant pests and diseases, the basic standards for controls are often broadly accepted internationally. The costs of new infestations or epidemics can be high, such as when foot-and-mouth disease (FMD) breaks out in a country previously considered FMD-free. New zoonotic diseases, such as BSE (likely related to modern agricultural production practices) or deadly avian influenza (protection from which may require modern practices) also bear high costs. Given these costs, international borders sometimes become a convenient surrogate for risk differentiation, leading to inappropriate regulatory discrimination among products by country of origin. WTO rules disciplining SPS barriers to trade, together with dissemination of relevant scientific research by the multilateral standards organizations—L'Office International des Epizooties (OIE), the International Plant Protection Convention (IPPC), and the Codex Alimentarius Commission (CODEX)—are therefore critical to sustaining an open global food system.

The regulation of food safety (including zoonotic diseases) poses challenges for somewhat different reasons than the pests and diseases affecting only animals and plants. Risk perceptions can affect estimates of the benefits of food regulation, which authorities weigh against the costs to industry of reducing food-borne hazards. It has long been recognized that unnatural and unfamiliar risks such as those that might be associated with new food production technologies are more alarming to consumers than natural and familiar risks. Even when a natural contaminant is identified as the source of food-borne illness, broad consumer avoidance of the implicated product can trigger a dramatic fall in consumption out of proportion to the actual risk involved. Thus the global food system has much to gain from well-designed and rigorously enforced food safety regulations that target hazards to consumer health and maintain confidence in the food supply. Under the right conditions, consumers trust their regulatory institutions to ensure their food safety and to respond rapidly to any breakdown in risk management. Problems occur when such trust is lacking, and both domestic and foreign suppliers, as well as consumers, suffer from the ensuing loss of confidence.

The governance of food safety regulation from a global perspective is also challenging because demands for protection among countries from food-borne hazards depend on income differences and other determinants of consumers' risk aversion. Likewise, the capacity to regulate effectively varies with levels of national income and development. Poorer countries will typically have less comprehensive programs in place for the assurance of food safety. The export of high-value and processed foods from some developing countries suggests that consumers in developed countries are prepared to trust imported food if it meets the standards set in their domestic markets. But it follows that the impact on developing-country exports can be severe if those countries are unable to meet high standards. An evaluative literature has emerged on these issues and public capacity strengthening projects and private investments aimed at meeting food and agricultural standards have proliferated in developing countries over the past decade.

Food safety regulations that address the use of production-enhancing technologies, including pesticides and other agrochemicals, hormones, veterinary drugs, and product-enhancing food additives, remain controversial. For these technologies, the scientific basis for the regulation may itself be unknown or in dispute. Just as often, disputes arise when differences in public perceptions of risk persist among countries despite scientific consensus, or when countries have made different political choices about the desirability of adopting new technologies for reasons unrelated to safety. When strong differences in public perceptions are in play, or when risk-related and other goals become intertwined, international conflicts over regulations are often exacerbated. The duration and intensity of the long-unresolved beef hormones dispute between the United States and the European Union, for example, seem out of proportion to the economic stakes. But the highly politicized interests on both sides have allowed little room for the respective governments to find a satisfactory resolution.

The reform of food safety regulation, particularly in the wealthy countries, has placed emphasis on process standards, including those of Hazard Analysis and Critical Control Point (HACCP) programs, to achieve desired content attributes. Process standards are more difficult to implement internationally than product standards because they involve complex verification and enforcement procedures by private firms or regulatory institutions in two or more countries. Trade problems can arise from lack of trust in the regulatory processes across borders, inadequate public-sector enforcement capacity in some countries, and differences in accountability imposed on domestic and foreign products. Firms in developing countries are likely to have difficulty meeting food regulatory and traceability requirements imposed by the process standards of developed countries. Yet disagreements over process standards also arise between high-income countries with high regulatory standards and enforcement capacity. It is difficult to avoid the conclusion that in some instances, differences over process standards among developed countries are attributable to regulatory protectionism.

Regulations related to quality cover a wide range of characteristics both of products and how they are produced and handled. Governments intervene by creating public standards for unbranded products, such as identity standards for fish and seafood or quality standards for organic produce. Or a government may take another type of approach by setting disclosure requirements, such as country-of-origin labeling. Still other measures support the creation of brand identity

through geographical indications (GIs) that may have reputational connotations for consumers and thus are of value to firms in specific localities. Governments can also remedy informational failures related to branded products. Examples include setting identity standards for processed foods to prevent consumer deception, or requiring nutritional labeling so that consumers have information that private firms do not have an incentive to disclose.

Of these various regulatory measures that governments might adopt, some can be readily verified through product testing. But the proliferation of demands for government regulators to distinguish among products based on process attributes that are unrelated to detectable product characteristics is one of the critical new challenges in food regulation. Regulation of trade in biotech (GM) products based on their production process is perhaps the paramount controversy, but process attribute regulation is also essential to such emerging consumer-driven demands as organic certification and protection of animal welfare.

3. Effects of regulation on trade

Ten years ago it was difficult to find published articles that combined such phrases as "sanitary and phytosanitary measures" and "cost–benefit analysis." The body of literature that has emerged since then, including presentations of new papers at sessions of the 2006 IAAE conference, reflects the importance of food regulation issues since the WTO was created. This literature has several main strands. A set of partial equilibrium simulation studies have been completed that measure the price, trade, and welfare impacts of specific existing regulations and their potential modification. A few studies have evaluated trade-related agricultural and food regulation options within general equilibrium country models (e.g., Perry et al., 2003). Other studies of specific barriers have utilized gravity models to provide econometric estimates of the impacts of regulatory decisions (Wilson [2006] reviews one set of these studies). Complementing these academic papers are the economic assessments provided in the context of national regulatory decision-making processes and the adjudication of disputes in the WTO. From all of this, a rich body of evidence has developed highlighting the costs and benefits of specific measures.

A body of literature has also emerged that investigates the aggregate effects of regulatory measures. Initial efforts were simple tabulations of perceptions of barriers potentially subject to challenge. Roberts and DeRemer's (1997) systematic survey of these perceptions through field offices of the USDA Foreign Agricultural Service found that one tenth ($5.7 billion) of U.S. agricultural exports faced questionable technical barriers affecting market access, expansion, or retention. This study provided a template that has been replicated elsewhere. It has been institutionalized in several countries into annual reports tabulating technical trade disputes from unilateral national perspectives. Within the WTO, the SPS and TBT committees have become forums for discussion of such disputes, as discussed further later.

More recently, efforts have been made to quantify the aggregate effects of technical regulations and various other nontariff trade barriers (NTBs). These analyses estimate the effects of the barriers on traded quantities of agricultural and food products or the gap between domestic and world market prices. The latter approach is familiar from past assessments of Producer Support Estimates (PSEs) by the OECD and others, in which market support has been measured deterministically by calculating such a price gap at the farmgate level, after making adjustments for domestic and international transportation and marketing costs, processing costs, and product quality differences.

The recent empirical analyses of aggregate effects of NTBs take a nondeterministic approach. They utilize multiproduct gravity models to provide econometric estimates of the effects of regulations on trade quantities and price gaps while controlling for other determinants. Four papers presented at the May 2006 workshop on Food Regulation and Trade organized by the International Agricultural Trade Research Consortium (IATRC) are illustrative. Dean et al. (2006) assess the effects of NTBs on price gaps for 47 agricultural products among 67 developed and developing countries. They find that NTBs raise retail prices of fruits/vegetables and meats as much as 141% and 93%, respectively, when they control for endogeneity of the incidence of the trade-restrictive measures. Olper and Raimondi (2006) evaluate border effects (i.e., the extent to which trade across a border is less than trade within borders) on food products among the Quad countries (EU,

US, Canada, and Japan). They find that NTB effects (measured by their tariff equivalence) are generally larger than tariff effects, and again are larger when they account for endogeneity of the trade restrictions.

In the third IATRC conference paper, de Frahan and Vancauteren (2006) find that harmonization has increased intra-EU imports for 10 categories of agricultural and food products between 1990 and 2001. Utilizing their quantity estimates and category-specific elasticities of substitution between the domestic and imported goods estimated from an earlier study, they derive tariff equivalents of not harmonizing that range from low (about 10%) for meat and dairy to very high (above 200%) for fruits/vegetables. Finally, Moenius (2006) estimates the effects on 471 four-digit SITC industries of standards set by importers, exporters, and shared by the trade partners. He finds that importer standards provide protection against foreign products, exporter standards increase their foreign market access, and shared standards (that result in lower transaction costs but also reduce product variety) have a net negative effect on trade. This emerging body of econometric analysis reinforces the perception that technical barriers have a substantial influence on agricultural trade, but is still in its infancy and fraught with measurement, endogeneity, and other econometric difficulties.

A third focus of empirical analysis has been on the effects of technical barriers on the export opportunities of developing countries. Two themes have arisen. The first theme is that high standards, especially unjustifiably high standards, discriminate against developing countries, and particularly against poor farmers in these countries for two reasons: because they are difficult for exporters to meet and because the developing countries lack the resources to participate actively in the standard-setting process through either bilateral or multilateral mechanisms. The second theme is that the increasingly differentiated markets for agricultural and food products in developed and middle-income countries open opportunities for poor countries. Both themes have some merit. Specific cases consistent with each have been identified (e.g., Australian Centre for International Agricultural Research [ACIAR], 2005; Mehta and George, 2005; World Bank, 2005) and net assessment of the effects is still ongoing. The first theme puts an onus of responsibility on developed countries and their regulatory decisions. The latter theme highlights the important role of multinational supply chains and private sector investment, placing more emphasis on investment climate determinants and other public sector decisions of the developing countries.

By way of an illustration of several of these points, consider the long dispute between the United States and Mexico concerning importation of Hass avocados. Over the 15-year period 1991–2006, a complete trade ban has been replaced by U.S. imports from approved orchards in the state of Michoacan under a systems approach of risk management for fruit flies and avocado-specific pests. We have argued (Roberts and Orden, 1996; Orden and Peterson, 2007) that science (evidence of limited risk), opportunity (substantially higher prices in the U.S. market), traceability (of every box to an approved orchard), persistence (of the Mexican exporting association), and joint political will (first

under the NAFTA umbrella and later related to discussions of cross-border openness after discovery of a U.S. case of BSE) has each been a necessary condition for progress in opening of the U.S. avocado market.

A recent paper (Peterson and Orden, 2006) simulates the trade and welfare implications of the 2004 decision to open the entire U.S. market to imports year round, and considers further regulatory options. This study takes into account the systems approach compliance costs in Mexico, USDA's estimates of pest risks, and the costs of control for trade-related pest outbreaks within the United States. A synopsis of the results is presented in Table 1. The first column gives the benchmark data for the period October 2001–2003, when Mexico's market access was limited geographically (31 states and the District of Columbia) and seasonally (six winter months only). Column 2 gives the simulation

Table 1
Market equilibrium and welfare effects under alternative regulation of U.S. imports of Mexican Hass avocados

	Base values	Unlimited seasonal and geographic access with compliance measures	Unlimited access without fruit fly compliance measures	Unlimited access without compliance measures for fruit flies and avocado pests	
				Average risk	High risk
Producer prices			Dollars per pound		
Season 1 (winter)					
California	0.871	0.587	0.584	0.577	0.624
Chile	0.577	0.400	0.398	0.390	0.396
Mexico	0.540	0.508	0.502	0.470	0.469
Season 2 (summer)					
California	1.101	0.748	0.746	0.743	0.799
Chile	0.599	0.478	0.476	0.471	0.485
Mexico	0.540	0.537	0.532	0.505	0.510
Mexican compliance costs	0.107	0.056	0.045	0.000	0.000
Quantities (annual totals)			Million pounds		
California	346.011	306.943	306.606	303.433	290.008
Chile	176.813	146.621	146.257	145.000	146.680
Mexico	58.247	206.956	209.678	221.688	226.785
Pest-related costs			Million dollars		
Mexican compliance	6.267	11.644	9.414	0.000	0.000
U.S. expected control	0.000	0.020	0.021	3.091	25.257
Welfare effects			Million dollars		
Producer surplus					
California		−107.651	−108.483	−112.851	−119.989
Chile		−25.069	−25.341	−26.268	−24.959
Mexico		3.108	3.198	3.607	3.788
U.S. equivalent variation		179.443	182.029	193.308	175.675
Net U.S. welfare		71.791	73.547	80.442	55.562

Notes: Synopsis of analysis from Peterson and Orden (2006). Mexican compliance costs reported above include those incurred by producers and exporters. The U.S. expected pest control costs reported exclude small expenditures for fruit fly control by producers of crops other than avocados; net U.S. welfare differs from U.S. equivalent variation plus change in U.S. producer surplus by this expenditure.

results for the 2004 rule under the average pest risks estimated by USDA with the systems approach in place. Mexican exports more than triple, U.S. consumers are beneficiaries, and there is little pest risk to U.S. producers. Total Mexican compliance costs rise but the compliance cost per pound of exports drops by nearly half with the larger trade volume.

Column 3 gives results if the risk management measures related to fruit flies are eliminated in Mexico. This yields a small additional increase in trade volume and U.S. welfare with lower Mexican compliance costs. Finally, columns 4 and 5 show the effects of removing all of the systems approach risk management measures under USDA's average and high estimated risk probabilities in the absence of such measures. There are additional net U.S. welfare gains under average pest risks, but U.S. producers incur substantial pest-related costs. With the high estimated pest risks, expected pest control costs to U.S. producers rise to $25.3 million and net U.S. welfare is reduced compared to the 2004 rule. From these results, one can applaud the opening of the U.S. market in 2004, might argue for reconsideration of some components of the remaining requirements for pest risk management, and must be cautious about full elimination of the systems approach. Mexican producers and exporters credit improvements in their production and processing systems and emergence of a more cohesive industry to their need to comply with the U.S. requirements.

4. Role of the WTO in the food regulatory framework

National governments have paramount responsibility for food regulation, but the WTO has an important role in both enforcement of disciplines on national regulatory decisions and achieving international coordination of regulations and standards. The SPS and TBT agreements, supported by the technical expertise of the international standards organizations, offer the fundamental disciplines, which are backed up by recourse to the WTO's dispute settlement procedures. Other agreements—including the TRIPS agreement, the GATT, and some multilateral environmental agreements—also play a role in defining the latitude and limits to regulation within the food sector.

The SPS agreement contains principles to guide regulation, including transparency, science-based risk

management, harmonization, equivalence, and regionalization. The TBT agreement likewise encourages transparency and coordination of national regulations and standards through adoption of international norms. The WTO has had some success in each of the areas covered by these agreements, yet application of the basic principles has not progressed as far as it might have, and improvements can still be made.

The WTO has been successful in promoting symmetry of information about regulations and standards among its members through its notification process under the terms of the SPS and TBT agreements. Notification of new or modified measures has given firms a chance to change production methods to meet new import requirements. Notification also has provided WTO members with the opportunity to question, propose modification, or challenge new or existing measures in the committees that implement the two agreements. This increased regulatory transparency has led to far greater scrutiny of measures than occurred under the GATT.

Over the first 10 years of operation of the SPS agreement, WTO members submitted more than 5,350 SPS notifications. WTO members have taken advantage of this notification process, registering 330 complaints (or counter notifications) in the SPS Committee between 1995 and 2004 (Table 2).[2] These complaints provide some evidence of the extent to which new regulations have created barriers to trade. Developed countries were most often the source (58%) as well as the target (57%) of counter notifications that identified regulations as unjustified trade impediments. The number of counter notifications submitted by developed countries about the measures of other developed countries demonstrates that access to the same scientific information and technologies leaves ample scope for disagreement over SPS regulations. Developing countries have filed fewer counter notifications against

---

[2] Other WTO committees have formally adopted the term "counter notifications" to reference complaints recorded in the minutes or reports of committee meetings. The SPS Committee has not done so. Complaints are variously recorded under "information from members," "specific trade concerns," and "other business" in the committee minutes. The term *counter notification* is used here to help distinguish the complaints raised in the SPS Committee from the complaints that proceed to formal dispute settlement in the WTO. TBT counter notifications are more difficult to tabulate and we have not updated the results reported in Josling et al. (2004).

Table 2
Complaints (counter notifications) in the SPS committee against trade partners, 1995–2004*

Respondents	Complaints by developed countries				Complaints by developing countries				Total
	Human health	Plant and animal health	Other**	Subtotal	Human health	Plant and animal health	Other	Subtotal	
Developed country	56	30	4	90	57	32	9	98	188
Developing country	44	44	6	94	10	27	2	39	133
Multiple countries	2	4		6	–	3	–	3	9
Total complaints	102	77	17	190	67	62	11	140	330

*Entries exclude "repeat interventions" made by WTO members who registered complaints against the same measure more than once.
**Includes complaints related to horizontal regulations with multiple objectives (e.g., the regulation of genetically modified products); administrative requirements; or regulations with unknown objectives.
Source: Roberts and Unnevehr (2005).

other developing countries than against developed countries.

An examination of the counter notifications related to human health measures by commodity and hazard provides some insight into the sources of tensions over regulations in international agricultural and food markets (Table 3). Most notable are the number of counter notifications related to the regulation of transmissible spongiform encephalopathies (TSEs), which include BSE. The TSE measures alone accounted for 74 of the counter notifications related to food safety regulations between 1995 and 2004, indicating the significant disruption to international trade caused by the BSE outbreaks in Europe and North America over the

past 10 years. This impact is related to the fact that cattle, the source of BSE, provide so many food and industrial products, including meat and milk for human consumption, gelatin for pharmaceutical purposes, semen for breeding, and other byproducts used in cosmetics, commercial animal feed, and elsewhere. The EU and Switzerland together accounted for 30 of the TSE counter notifications, which were often directed at the initial emergency measures adopted by countries in 1996. The EU and individual member states later became the target of 23 complaints following implementation of their new, extensive BSE regulations. Examples include Chile and Peru's complaints against the EU's ban on the use of fish meal in ruminant feed,

Table 3
Distribution of complaints (counter notifications) in the SPS committee related to human health measures, 1995–2004*

Commodity	Complaints against measures regulating							
	TSEs**	Food additives	Foodborne pathogens	Toxins and heavy metals	Veterinary residues	Pesticide residues	Other***	Total
Multiple animal products	67		1	8	1		1	78
Meat, poultry, and fish	5		10	3	3			21
Multiple agricultural products		3		14		7	12	36
Dairy and eggs	–	–	6	1	–	–	2	9
Processed products				8		4	• 3	15
Feedstuffs	2			1	2			5
Horticultural products	–	1	1	–	–	1	–	3
Cereals	–		–	2	–	–	–	2
Total	74	4	18	37	6	12	18	169

*Entries exclude "repeat interventions" made by WTO members who registered complaints against the same measure more than once.
**Transmissable spongiform encephalopathies (TSEs) include bovine spongiform encephalopathy (BSE).
***Includes complaints related to horizontal regulations with multiple objectives (e.g., the regulation of genetically modified products); administrative requirements; or regulations with unknown objectives.
Source: Roberts and Unnevehr (2005).

and Australia's complaint against EU restrictions on selected cosmetics. More recently, China and Argentina have raised objections to U.S. measures, adopted following the identification of a BSE case in Washington State in 2003, which prohibited the use of selected cattle by-products in food, dietary supplements, and cosmetics and imposed new record-keeping requirements on all exporters, regardless of BSE status (WTO, 2005).

The obligation under the SPS agreement to base measures on scientific risk assessment has been crucial to reducing the disingenuous use of SPS regulations and to promoting convergence of SPS measures among countries. The impact of the risk management requirements of the SPS agreement has extended beyond WTO complaints and dispute settlement decisions to spur broad-based regulatory reviews by countries to determine whether they and their trading partners are complying with the obligation to base decisions on scientific risk assessments. In many cases, there is evidence that regulatory authorities are either unilaterally modifying regulations or voluntarily modifying regulations after technical exchanges. However, it is evident that some gaps remain in convergence around the principle of using science as a basis for regulation. In some circumstances, countries' reliance on the precautionary principle to guide risk management decisions has led to high-profile trade disputes, as in the hormones and GM food cases. In others, regulatory decisions impose large economic costs to achieve very minimal risk reduction. Such decisions are likely to be controversial.

The WTO's promotion of harmonization has been less successful than its attempts to increase transparency or require that measures be based on a risk assessment. The impact of harmonization on trade appears to have been constrained as much by the lack of international standards as by normative considerations since the SPS agreement came into force. The majority of early notifications (1995–1999) from WTO members stated that no international standard existed for the notified measure. Because international standards are a global public good, it is not surprising that national authorities have underinvested in such measures. Not only are there too few international standards in the food area, but too many of the current international standards are outmoded, contributing to the low adoption rate for those standards that do exist.

Equivalence is an alternative to harmonization. The SPS and TBT agreements require WTO members to allow imports from countries that have measures equivalent to their own. This provision endorses regulatory flexibility, which allows countries to allocate scarce resources efficiently rather than identically. Despite the conceptual appeal of equivalence, its use is constrained by various factors, both operational and political. The administrative burden of equivalence determinations is often significant even among countries with similar levels of capacity. Moreover, recognizing the equivalence of an alternative regulatory regime may require national regulators to offer the same alternative to domestic producers, requiring in turn new or revised domestic regulations before foreign producers can gain access to the market. Some progress has been made, but experience so far suggests that negotiating equivalence agreements is difficult and their use is not common. To encourage reporting of equivalence protocols, the WTO adopted specific notification procedures in 2001. However, since that time, no country has officially notified an equivalence arrangement to the SPS Committee.

Regionalization under the SPS agreement has also met so far with only limited success, and the successful cases have depended heavily on the efforts of the exporting countries. Argentina's numerous setbacks in its efforts to eradicate FMD underscores the fact that investments in public sector regulatory infrastructure are needed as an incentive to private sector eradication efforts and thus establishment of the pre-conditions for regionalization. But it is also evident that national regulation will not always work. Transborder pest or disease controls may be required where there are insufficient natural barriers or when animals (including wildlife) move freely across borders.

To summarize, the WTO agreements and committee procedures, together with the reviews that WTO rules have encouraged at national, bilateral, and regional levels, have provided useful channels through which countries can strengthen the framework for global food regulation. They may also challenge policies of their trade partners through these channels when they have doubts about whether regulations conform to international rules as they apply to food trade. The institutional innovations that emerged from the Uruguay Round have given the WTO an increased role in shaping regulation in the global food system. But the reach of the WTO disciplines and principles has been somewhat limited. National governments remain reluctant to cede too much authority over agricultural and food safety and quality to international decision making.

5. WTO dispute resolution

The compliance of countries with the WTO agreements is reinforced by the organization's formal dispute settlement procedures. Only a few conflicts over food regulations have led to the establishment of dispute panels, but these few cases have played a

critical role in defining the scope of WTO rules and obligations.

Of 41 formal requests for consultations about food regulations during 1995 to 2006, only 14 (related to 10 distinct cases) have advanced to dispute settlement proceedings (Table 4). There have been rulings by WTO panels in 8 of the 10 cases through 2006. The panels' findings in six cases were referred to the Appellate Body.

In the disputes related to the SPS Agreement heard by the Appellate Body—hormones, salmon, varietal

Table 4

Disputes over regulation of safety and quality of agricultural products advancing to WTO panels and appellate body, 1995–2006

Dispute settlement number	Petitioners(s)	Respondent	Issue	Agreement(s) referenced in dispute proceedings	Status
1995					
DS 18	Canada	Australia	Measures affecting importation of salmon	SPS, GATT	Panel and AB ruled against Australia
1996					
DS 26/48	United States/Canada	EC	Measures affecting meat and meat products (hormones)	SPS, TBT, GATT, AoA	Panel and AB ruled against EC; panel established in 2005 (DS320/321) to review U.S. and Canadian retaliatory tariffs
DS 58	India, Malaysia, Pakistan, Thailand	U.S.	Import prohibition on certain shrimp and shrimp products	GATT	Panel and AB ruled against the United States
1997					
DS 76	United States	Japan	Measures affecting agricultural products (varietal testing requirements)	SPS, GATT, AoA	Panel and AB ruled against Japan
1999					
DS 174/290	United States/Australia	EC	Protection of trademarks and GIs for agricultural products and foodstuffs	TRIPS, GATT, TBT, WTO Agreement	Panel ruled against EC
2001					
DS 231	Peru	EC	Trade description of sardines	GATT, TBT	Panel and AB ruled against EC
2002					
DS 245	United States	Japan	Measures affecting the importation of apples	SPS, GATT, AoA	Panel and AB ruled against Japan
DS 270	Philippines	Australia	Importation of fruits and vegetables	GATT, SPS, Import Licensing	Panel established in 2003; report not yet circulated
2003					
DS 287	EC	Australia	Quarantine regime for imports	SPS	Panel established in 2003; report not yet circulated
DS 291/292/293	United States/Canada/Argentina	EC	Measures affecting the approval and marketing of biotech products	SPS, GATT, AoA, TBT	Panel ruled against EC

Source: WTO (2006a).

testing, and apples—developed countries challenged the regulations of other developed countries, and in each case the panel and Appellate Body concurred that the regulation in question violated the requirement that it be based on a valid risk assessment. These outcomes demonstrate the importance accorded to the principle of science-based risk management in the SPS agreement and show that even the measures of countries with advanced scientific establishments are not immune to challenge.

The outcome in the hormones case demonstrates further that the WTO Appellate Body can rule against measures based on popular consumer misconceptions of risks, as well as more overtly discriminatory measures. The WTO rejected the EU's use of the precautionary principle in its legal defense, because no explicit reference to this principle appears in the SPS agreement. Article 5.7 of the agreement recognizes a conditional precautionary principle, which allows countries to provisionally adopt measures on the basis of "available pertinent information" while seeking additional information "necessary for a more objective assessment of risk." However, the EU could not defend its permanent ban by reference to this provision. This result removes a degree of national political sovereignty for regulations in cases in which evidence has not been marshaled to demonstrate any risk from trade. But the formal ruling has not resolved this dispute.[3]

The WTO dispute over EU measures regulating biotech products raised many of the same legal issues as the hormones case. Argentina, Canada, and the United States argued that the EU Commission's failure to complete the process set out in its own directives and regulations for the pre-marketing review of 27 biotech products between October 1998 and August 2003 constituted a *de facto* ban on these products which was not based on a risk assessment (United States, 2004). The complainants also argued that nine specific prohibitions by EU member states on biotech products that had been formally approved by the EU were likewise not based on a risk assessment. The EU argued that there have been no undue delays in its scientific approval processes which "are premised on the application of a prudent and precautionary approach" (European Communities, 2004). The WTO panel issued its report in this highly visible dispute in September 2006, concurring with the complainants that the EU had maintained a *de facto* ban on biotech products that violated its obligations under the SPS Agreement. Specifically, the panel noted that "it is clear that application of a prudent and precautionary approach is, and must be, subject to reasonable limits, lest the precautionary approach swallow the discipline" imposed by the SPS Agreement (WTO, 2006b). The panel likewise agreed with the complainants that the prohibitions maintained by EU member states were not based on a risk assessment.

In the two other cases of food regulation that advanced to rulings by the Appellate Body, developing countries lodged complaints against measures of developed countries. In the sardines case, brought by Peru, the Codex Alimentarius international standard was found to be effective and appropriate to achieve EU objectives of transparency, consumer protection, and fair competition. The importance of this case lies in demonstrating that international standards can take precedence over national regulatory decisions and can set bounds on the use of policies that, in effect, limit imports. In the second case, India, Malaysia, Pakistan, and Thailand challenged U.S. restrictions on importation of shrimp when countries failed to use turtle-excluder devices. The case established the precedent that process standards can be mandated in regulations to achieve an environmental goal. This precedent provides a small but significant exception to the product–process doctrine, which deems any regulation affecting trade based on how a product is produced to be out of compliance with the WTO rules. In the shrimp/turtle case, the WTO Appellate Body concluded instead that the objective of the U.S. law was legitimate under GATT Article XX and, ultimately, that U.S. implementation of its policy

---

[3] In 1999, the WTO authorized the United States and Canada to increase tariffs on $128 million of EU exports when the European Union failed to bring its measures into compliance with the SPS agreement following the Appellate Body ruling. Four years later, the EU notified the WTO that it had met its obligations under the SPS agreement with the adoption of Directive 2003/74/EC which left the ban in place but cited new studies to justify its measures. The United States and Canada disagreed with the EU's claim that the new Directive was based on science and that it reflected the WTO's recommendations and rulings, and left their retaliatory tariffs in place. In January, 2005, the EU requested that the legality of these tariffs be reviewed by a WTO panel under the terms of the Dispute Settlement Understanding (WTO, 2005). The panel expects to complete its final report to the parties in late 2006.

was justified because of its serious and ongoing efforts to minimize negative trade effects.

The greatest difficulties for WTO dispute resolution arise in cases such as beef hormones or biotechnology in which strongly held differences of views among countries have not been reconciled by other means. That the most contentious of these cases have involved issues of risk again demonstrates the practical limits of science in securing regulatory convergence. Unfortunately, too much reliance on the WTO's dispute resolution process to address these disagreements will create problems for the acceptance of its rulings, as may soon become evident for decisions related to biotech foods. When rulings for the complainant in such difficult cases lead to retaliatory tariffs because the respondent fails to change its policy or offer acceptable compensation, the trade system suffers, even if the validity of WTO procedures is upheld.

Overall, our review of technical trade barriers related to agricultural and food safety and quality suggests a trichotomy of cases. For a few dominant cases the economic stakes are high or issues of regulatory principles have been elevated to a high level of contestation. These cases include several involving consumer preferences and related political economy, such as beef hormones and biotech products. On these issues there have been WTO disputes in which appeals to science have proven insufficient to achieve a resolution.

The high-profile cases also include BSE, FMD, and, recently, avian influenza (Moore and Morgan, 2006). These cases have resulted in some restrictive trade regulations that have been challenged in bilateral deliberations and informal WTO committee discussions, but not in formal WTO disputes. The international standards organizations have offered some constructive evaluations in these cases. Yet, the reach of international disciplines is limited. For example, the OIE established that some traded products were not vectors for disease transmission after the announcement of a likely BSE link to human variant Creutzfeldt–Jakob disease disrupted world trade in beef and bovine products in 1996. This allowed certain initial prohibitions to be eased. Yet 9 years later, despite extensive IIE efforts and with BSE much better understood, Canada and the United States faced (and themselves imposed against others), costly embargos on meat trade without corresponding internal quarantines when single domestic incidences of BSE were discovered. The regulation of agricultural and food safety across versus within borders is often not as consistent as might be hoped, despite the disciplines attempted through the WTO.

Finally, there is widespread interest in many diverse food regulations affecting trade expressed among industry and consumer groups. A number of disagreements about trade are finding resolution. But the number of formal disputes, or even counter notifications, is relatively small. The current regime tolerates a large number of technical regulations without challenge.

6. Improving food regulation

Food regulation is likely to expand over the coming years in tandem with increased use of private standards, and the number of international disputes is likely to increase correspondingly. So far, the disciplinary mechanisms in place through the WTO—the negotiated agreements, implementation discussions and informal conflict resolution through the committees, and formal dispute resolution—have proven useful. There is no doubt at this point that the WTO rules remain necessary. Disingenuous use of regulatory measures is still evident in agricultural markets and these abuses need to be reined in. Contrary to the predictions of some consumer and environmental advocates, the WTO disciplines have not resulted in the "downward harmonization" of regulations. No credible evidence has emerged to indicate that WTO rules have prevented countries from achieving legitimate regulatory objectives, even when very trade-restrictive measures have been adopted.

The current global regulatory framework, in deference to national sovereignty, allows countries to adopt various measures for which global or even national costs outweigh their national benefits. Thus, there is scope for enhancing the efficiency and fairness of the global food system. The basic challenges, of achieving balance between harmonization and diversity and between political support and political capture, must be faced within the existing institutions.

Economic assessment of regulations is still an underdeveloped element of the food regulatory framework. The provisions of the SPS and TBT agreements provide only limited guidance on which measures are desirable to adopt. It remains a challenge for national regulators to build on the legal criteria of the SPS and TBT agreements to undertake the benefit-cost analysis that would give a more defensible basis for import protocols.

Toward this end, developed countries should adopt an "agreements plus" approach to both risk-reducing and quality regulations by balancing the benefits of regulation against all costs, including the costs of forgone trade. A change from the narrow risk-analysis perspective to the benefit-cost perspective for SPS measures would be a constructive move toward a desirable opening up of markets and would reduce the scope for trade disputes. Plant, animal, and human health and safety would not be sacrificed for trade, but trade would be taken into account as an integral part of the commercial environment that regulations affect. Countries should view trade as an activity that provides them with an expanded range of safe agricultural and food products at lowest cost, and regulations as a necessary way of ensuring the safety of food regardless of where it is produced.

Recognition of the benefits of imports also provides a rationalization for public investment in monitoring and inspection services at a time when the pressures to downsize public agencies are strong. It is not in the interests of importing or exporting countries to reduce the effectiveness of inspection services. This is all the more true since the September 2001 terrorist attacks in the United States—countries must now guard against biosecurity threats, but without creating prejudice against legitimate trade. The U.S. Bioterrorism Act (BTA) of December 2003, for example, was notified to the WTO under the SPS agreement. The U.S. Food and Drug Administration (FDA) estimated that 16% of firms exporting to the United States might cease doing so because of the tightened security measures for the agricultural and food products it covers, particularly smaller firms for which the new rules might be relatively most costly. Preliminary evidence comparing exports to the United States in 2003 and 2004 shows smaller firms more likely to have stopped or decreased volumes, perhaps due to the BTA (Wieck, 2006). The BTA has also been the subject of several WTO counter notifications by developed and developing countries due to the administrative requirements it imposes. Enhanced border security will have to be supported by increased public resources to minimize adverse effects on trade of such measures.

It also must be recognized that process standards are here to stay. HAACP is now well established and the regulation of some quality attributes of foods, such as organic, turtle-safe, or free-range, will always re-

quire process standards. Greater reliance on process standards places more responsibility on the regulatory infrastructure of the exporting country than on border inspection in the importing country. This trend in quality regulation is leading to increased use of private, third-party certification services in the food sector, especially within countries lacking satisfactory public certification infrastructure. These and other alternative certification options should be but one manifestation of a broader commitment by national food quality regulators to open and contestable markets that genuinely serve consumer interests.

We have noted the political-economy dimensions of food regulatory decisions and disputes in several ways. In closing, we note the broader political economy of agricultural support and protection policies in which food regulation is embedded. The high levels of tariff protection and domestic subsidies provided to agriculture by many countries taint the context in which food regulation decisions are made. Exporters are skeptical of new measures that add to the barriers their products face. Market signals in the developed countries are distorted by those countries' high levels of agricultural producer support and protection, which affects food regulatory decisions, particularly related to the adoption of cost-reducing and output-enhancing new technologies. The distortionary effects of agricultural support and protection policies on regulatory decisions are arguably just as significant an impediment to the efficiency of the world food system and to harmonious trade relations as the better-recognized direct effects of these policies. Lessening of these interventions, while it might risk inducing additional regulation as a substitute, would also provide more latitude for regulatory decisions to be considered on their merit.

Acknowledgment

Views expressed are those of the authors. We thank our oft-times coauthor Tim Josling for his contributions to the ideas we present.

References

Australian Centre for International Agricultural Research (ACIAR), "International Food Safety Standards and Processed Food Exports from Developing Countries: A Comparative Study of India and

Thailand," draft papers presented at a project workshop, Canberra, Australia, June (2005).

Dean, J. M., R. Feinberg, J. E. Signoret, M. Ferrantino, and R. Ludema, "Estimating the Price Effects of Non-Tariff Measures," presented at the International Agricultural Traded Research Consortium Symposium on Food Regulation and Trade, Bonn, Germany, May (2006).

de Frahan, B. H., and M. Vancauteren, "Harmonization of Food Regulations and Trade in the Single Market: Evidence from Disaggregated Data," presented at the International Agricultural Traded Research Consortium Symposium on Food Regulation and Trade, Bonn, Germany, May (2006).

European Communities, "Submissions: European Communities – Measures Affecting the Approval and Marketing of Biotech Products," (WT/DS291, 292, and 293), (2004). http://trade. ec.europa.eu/doclib/docs/2004/june/tradoc_117687.pdf

Henson, S., "The Role of Public and Private Standards in Regulating International Food Markets," presented at the International Agricultural Traded Research Consortium symposium on Food Regulation and Trade, Bonn, Germany, May (2006).

Josling, T., D. Roberts, and D. Orden, *Food Regulation and Trade: Toward a Safe and Open Global System* (Institute for International Economics: Washington, DC, 2004).

Mehta, R., and J. George, *Food Safety Regulations Concerns and Trade: The Developing Country Perspective* (Macmillan India Ltd.: New Delhi, 2005).

Moenius, J., "The Good, the Bad and the Ambiguous: Standards and Trade in Agricultural Products," presented at the International Agricultural Traded Research Consortium Symposium on Food Regulation and Trade, Bonn, Germany, May (2006).

Moore, T., and N. Morgan, "Avian Influenza: Trade Issues," *CAST Commentary* QTA2006-2, April (2006).

Olper, A., and V. Raimondi, "Explaining the Border Effects: The Role of Policy and Non-Policy Barriers in the Quad Food Trade," presented at the International Agricultural Traded Research Consortium Symposium on Food Regulation and Trade, Bonn, Germany, May (2006).

Orden, D., and E. Peterson, "Science, Opportunity, Traceability, Persistence and Political Will: Necessary Elements of Opening the U.S. Market to Avocados from Mexico," in U. Grote, A. K. Basu, and N. Chau, eds., *New Frontiers in Environmental and Social Labeling* (Springer: Heidelberg, 2007), pp.133–150.

Perry, B. D., T. F. Randolph, S. Ashley, T. Chimedza, Forman, J. Morrison, C. Poulton, L. Sibanda, C. Stevens, N. Tebele, and I. Yngstrom, *The Impact and Poverty Reduction Implications of Foot and Mouth Disease Control in Southern Africa, with Spe-*

cial Reference to Zimbabwe (International Livestock Research Institute (ILRI): Nairobi, Kenya, 2003).

Peterson, E., and D. Orden, "Linking Risk and Economic Assessments in the Analysis of Plant Pest Regulations: The Case of U.S. Imports of Mexican Avocados," *USDA/ERS Contractor and Cooperator Report* 25, November (2006).

Roberts, D., and D. Orden, "Determinants of Technical Barriers to Trade: The Case of U.S. Phytosanitary Restrictions on Mexican Avocados, 1972-1995," in D. Orden, and D. Roberts, eds., *Understanding Technical Barriers to Agricultural Trade* (International Agricultural Trade Research Consortium, Department of Applied Economics, University of Minnesota: St. Paul, MN, 1996), pp. 117–160.

Roberts, D., and K. DeRemer, "An Overview of Technical Barriers to U.S. Agricultural Exports," Economic Research Service, U.S., Department of Agriculture, Staff Paper AGEC-9705, 1997.

Roberts, D., and L. Unnevehr, "Resolving Trade Disputes Arising from Trends in Food Safety Regulation: The Role of the Multilateral Governance Framework," *World Trade Review* 4 (2005), 469–497.

United States, "Submissions: European Communities—Measures Affecting the Approval and Marketing of Biotech Products," (WT/DS291, 292, and 293), (2004). http://www.ustr.gov/Trade_Agreements/Monitoring_Enforcement/Dispute_Settlement/WTO/Dispute_Settlement_Index_-_Pending.html.

Wieck, C., "Trade Impacts of Administrative Food Import Regulations: Evaluating the U.S. Bioterrorism Act," presented at the International Agricultural Traded Research Consortium Symposium on Food Regulation and Trade, Bonn, Germany, May (2006).

Wilson, J. S., "Standards and Developing Country Exports," Presented at the International Agricultural Traded Research Consortium Symposium on Food Regulation and Trade, Bonn, Germany, May (2006).

World Bank, *Food Safety and Agricultural Health Standards: Challenges and Opportunities for Developing Country Exports* No. 31207 (Agriculture and Rural Development Department: Washington, DC, 2005).

World Trade Organization (WTO), "Specific Trade Concerns," G/SPS/GEN/204/Rev.5, February 25 (2005).

World Trade Organization (WTO), "Update of WTO Dispute Settlement Cases," WT/DS/OV28, October 11 (2006a).

World Trade Organization (WTO), "European Communities – Measures Affecting the Approval and Marketing of Biotech Products: Reports of the Panel," WT/DS/291R/292R/293R, September 29 (2006b).

Plenary 3

Economics of biofortification

Matin Qaim*, Alexander J. Stein* and J. V. Meenakshi***

Abstract

Micronutrient malnutrition is a serious public health problem in many developing countries. Different interventions are currently used, but their overall coverage is relatively limited. Biofortification—that is, breeding staple food crops for higher micronutrient contents—is a new agriculture-based approach, but relatively little is known about its ramifications. Here, the main factors influencing success are discussed and a methodology for economic impact assessment is presented. *Ex ante* studies from India and other countries suggest that biofortified crops can reduce the problem of micronutrient malnutrition in a cost-effective way, when targeted to specific situations. Further research is needed to corroborate these findings and address certain issues still unresolved.

JEL classification: I1, I3, O1, O3, Q1

Keywords: micronutrient malnutrition; public health; biofortification; agricultural technology; impact analysis; developing countries

1. Introduction

Micronutrient malnutrition is a widespread problem in many developing countries. An estimated 4 billion people are iron deficient, 2.7 billion are at risk of zinc deficiency, and hundreds of millions lack one or more essential vitamins (WHO, 2002; Hotz and Brown, 2004; UN-SCN, 2004). The prevalence is especially high among the poor, whose diets are usually predominated by relatively cheap staple crops, with insufficient quantities of higher-value nutritious foods. Micronutrient deficiencies are often the cause for increased mortality and morbidity, so that the resulting health burden can be immense. This health burden also entails significant economic costs in the developing world (Horton and Ross, 2003; FAO, 2004). Accordingly, controlling micronutrient malnutrition has been ranked as a top development priority by eminent international economists (Lomborg, 2004). Economic growth and poverty reduction will help reduce the problem in the long run. Yet there are also more targeted micronutrient interventions being implemented, including food supplementation, industrial fortification, and nutrition education programs (World Bank, 1994; Allen, 2003). Recently, an agriculture-based approach has been proposed as a supplementary strategy, namely breeding staple food crops for higher micronutrient contents. This breeding approach has been termed *biofortification* (Nestel et al., 2006). The potential positive effects of biofortification are obvious: if micronutrient-dense staple crops are widely grown and consumed by the poor, their nutritional status would improve, which could lead to significant health advantages and economic benefits. However, although plant breeders are working on the development of biofortified crop varieties, hardly any of these varieties has yet been released, so that the actual impacts are still uncertain.

In this article, we analyze the implications of biofortification from an economic perspective. In the next section, we provide some more background about the problem of micronutrient malnutrition, before describing the biofortification approach in greater detail and discussing important factors that will influence its future success. A methodological framework for assessing the impacts of biofortification is set out in Section 4.

*Department of Agricultural Economics and Rural Development, Georg-August-University of Goettingen, 37073 Goettingen, Germany.

**Department of Agricultural Economics and Social Sciences, University of Hohenheim (490b), 70593 Stuttgart, Germany.

**HarvestPlus, International Food Policy Research Institute, 2033 K Street NW, Washington, DC 20006, USA.

This methodology has been used for different empirical studies, results of which are presented in Section 5. The last section concludes and discusses research and policy implications.

2. Micronutrient malnutrition

For a long time, the food security debate had primarily focused on undernutrition in terms of calories. Calorie undernutrition is usually the result of an insufficient intake of macronutrients (carbohydrates, protein, and fat) and is associated with a feeling of hunger. Hunger is still a serious problem in large parts of the developing world. According to the FAO, 854 million people worldwide are currently undersupplied with calories (FAO, 2006). Micronutrient malnutrition is often less obvious for the people affected, which is also why the term *hidden hunger* is sometimes used. For certain micronutrients, deficiencies are even more widespread than calorie undernutrition (Figure 1). The major reason for the high prevalence of insufficient micronutrient intakes is the lack of dietary diversity among the poor. Typical diets in low-income households are dominated by staple crops, which are cheap sources of calories but only provide small amounts of vitamins and minerals. In addition to income constraints, lack of awareness and cultural factors also often limit the consumption of more nutritious foods, even where these are available and accessible. Women and children are the most vulnerable groups: pregnancies, breast-feeding, and menstruation as well as rapid body growth in children increase micronutrient requirements and make it even more difficult to achieve adequate intakes (WHO, 2002).

Even though deficient people are often not aware of their inadequate nutritional status, micronutrient malnutrition can have severe health consequences, including increased susceptibility to infectious diseases, physical and mental impairments, and increased mortality rates (Micronutrient Initiative, 2004). Apart from seriously affecting the well-being of the people directly concerned, micronutrient malnutrition negatively affects aggregate productivity and economic development (World Bank, 1994; Horton and Ross, 2003). Hence, efforts to control the problem are justified on humanitarian as well as efficiency grounds.

Several interventions are available to control micronutrient malnutrition. Common interventions include food supplementation, such as distributing vitamin capsules at regular intervals, and industrial fortification, that is, adding micronutrients to foodstuffs during processing. While existing micronutrient interventions have their particular strengths, they also have their weaknesses (Allen, 2003). For instance, large-scale distribution programs are resource-intensive, as they require continuous funding, infrastructure, trained

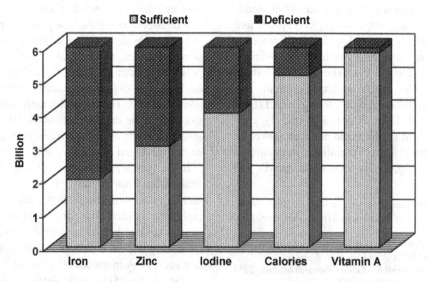

Figure 1. Number of people suffering from different forms of malnutrition worldwide. *Sources:* WHO (2002), Hotz and Brown (2004), UN-SCN (2004), FAO (2006).

personnel, reliable supplies, and monitoring. Moreover, information, education, and communication programs are necessary to ensure participation by the target groups. For industrial fortification, the main problem is reaching those in need, because the poor and malnourished often consume home-produced foods and only small amounts of processed products. Furthermore, fortified foods are often somewhat more expensive than their nonfortified counterparts, unless fortification is mandatory, which then, however, requires monitoring efforts to ensure compliance by food processors. While dietary diversification is considered the most sustainable approach to control micronutrient malnutrition, necessary behavior changes and income constraints are limiting factors in the short and medium run. In this context, the novel approach of biofortification may be a useful intervention to complement the existing set of strategies.

3. The biofortification approach

3.1. Ongoing research programs

For a long time, no particular role was seen for agricultural technology in the fight against micronutrient malnutrition; grain micronutrient content was simply not an important selection criterion for plant breeders. This has changed more recently, when nutritional quality started to receive higher priority, and breeders realized that increased micronutrient densities are not only compatible with superior agronomic traits, but may, in some cases, even enhance yields. Plant varieties that are more efficient in the uptake of trace minerals like iron and zinc can be higher yielding in low-quality soils, because these trace minerals are also required for plant vigor and growth (Graham et al., 1999; Welch, 2002).

A number of research and development (R&D) programs with the objective to increase micronutrient densities in staple crops through breeding have been launched in recent years. The term *biofortification* has been coined by the HarvestPlus Challenge Program of the Consultative Group on International Agricultural Research (CGIAR). This program concentrates on increasing iron, zinc, and beta-carotene (provitamin A) contents in six staple crop species, namely rice, wheat, maize, cassava, sweetpotato, and beans, and supports exploratory research in an additional 10 crops. At this

stage, research under HarvestPlus builds primarily on conventional breeding techniques, exploiting the variability of micronutrient contents found in available germplasm.

However, conventional techniques cannot be used when the micronutrient of interest is absent from a particular crop. A case in point is rice, which produces beta-carotene in leaves and in tiny amounts also in rice husks, but not in the endosperm. Hence, in the Golden Rice project, transgenic techniques have been used to introduce the beta-carotene biosynthetic pathway into the endosperm of grain (Ye et al., 2000; Paine et al., 2005). The Golden Rice project involves European research organizations, the International Rice Research Institute (IRRI), and local partners in developing countries. Another crop-specific project, funded as part of the Grand Challenges in Global Health Initiative, is the Africa Biofortified Sorghum Project, which seeks to develop a more nutritious and easily digestible sorghum that contains increased levels of beta-carotene, vitamin E, iron, zinc, and several amino acids. Furthermore, research has been conducted to genetically engineer iron-rich rice (Goto et al., 1999; Lucca et al., 2001; Murray-Kolb et al., 2002), rice that is rich both in iron and zinc (Vasconcelos et al., 2003), iron-rich maize (Drakakaki et al., 2005), and beta-carotene-rich potato (Ducreux et al., 2005). While this is not a complete list of all related research initiatives, the portfolio is indicative of the attention that biofortification is likely to receive in the future food and nutrition security debate.

3.2. Potential advantages

The major expected and intended impact of biofortification is to increase micronutrient intakes among the poor, thus improving their nutrition and health status. By focusing breeding efforts on staple crops, which are consumed by the poor in larger quantities, the approach is self-targeting. Tying micronutrients to staple crops also reduces people's nutritional vulnerability, because, when economic shocks occur, the poor tend to reduce their consumption of higher-value food commodities that are naturally rich in micronutrients. Furthermore, biofortification could be more sustainable than alternative micronutrient interventions. With a one-time R&D investment, biofortified germplasm can be shared

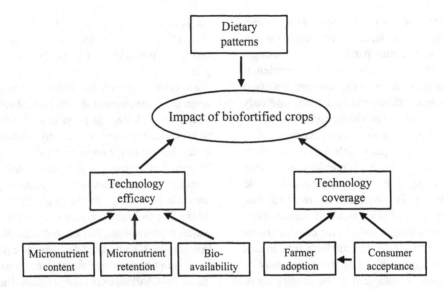

Figure 2. Factors influencing the impact of biofortified crops.

internationally, and the varieties could spread through existing seed distribution systems. Since biofortified seeds can easily be reproduced, poor farmers in remote rural areas, with limited access to formal seed markets, could also be reached. Thus, unlike other micronutrient interventions, which require large funds on an annual basis, biofortification could produce a continuous stream of benefits with minimal recurrent costs.

Biofortification promises to be a pro-poor and pro-rural approach, which could complement existing interventions. However, biofortified crops are still at the stage of R&D, so these potential advantages have not yet materialized. The only exception are beta-carotene-rich, orange-fleshed sweetpotatoes, which have been promoted in different countries (e.g., Low et al., 1997).

3.3. Factors influencing future impacts

Whether biofortified crops can really contribute to an improved nutrition and health situation in developing countries will depend on case-specific circumstances. Important factors influencing the impact in a given setting include local dietary patterns as well as technology efficacy and coverage (Figure 2). Local dietary patterns should determine the crop species to be targeted. Biofortification can only make a difference when the crop in question is an important local staple food, which is regularly consumed in relatively large quan-

tities. Therefore, the appropriate crop choice may vary regionally. Technology efficacy will be determined by the amount of the micronutrient in the crop, micronutrient retention after processing, and its bioavailability. Coverage, defined as the share of biofortified varieties in total quantities consumed of the crop, is mainly a function of farmer adoption and consumer acceptance.

3.3.1. Micronutrient content

Many varieties of staple food crops already contain certain amounts of micronutrients. For instance, high-yielding wheat varieties contain about 38 parts per million (ppm) of iron and 31 ppm of zinc.[1] Popular rice varieties contain 3 ppm of iron and 13 ppm of zinc in the milled grain. The potential to further increase these micronutrient contents by conventional breeding exists. Adequate genetic variations in concentrations of beta-carotene, other carotenoids, iron, zinc, and other minerals have been identified among cultivars, making selection of nutritionally appropriate breeding materials possible. For example, available orange-fleshed sweet-potato varieties contain over 100 ppm of beta-carotene. Nevertheless, with conventional breeding, achievable

---

[1] In the nutrition literature, micronutrient amounts in foods are often expressed in milligrams or micrograms per gram of food, but this may vary between vitamins and minerals. To have a uniform reference base, we use parts-per-million for all micronutrients. One ppm corresponds to one microgram per gram.

micronutrient contents are limited by the available genetic variation within each crop species. Transgenic techniques can help to further increase these levels, or to introduce micronutrients not naturally occurring in the crop. A case in point is Golden Rice: biotechnologists managed to produce a transgenic rice line containing up to 31 ppm of beta-carotene in the endosperm (Paine et al., 2005). Where exactly the micronutrient is located within the grain matters considerably. If it is found mainly in the aleurone layer of the grain, the nutritional impact can be small, since the outer layers are removed during the process of milling and polishing; the impact is greater when it is located in the endosperm. Micronutrient toxicities are not expected at levels achieved through biofortification. For beta-carotene, toxicity is not an issue at all, because the human body only absorbs as much beta-carotene as it needs.

3.3.2. Micronutrient retention

Micronutrient contents in the food actually consumed might be lower than those produced in the crop, because post-harvest and processing losses can occur. Beta-carotene in particular is sensitive to bright sunlight and extreme heat. For orange-fleshed sweetpotatoes, beta-carotene retention after boiling is around 80% (Nestel et al., 2006), but losses can be much higher with inappropriate storage and cooking techniques. Also for minerals, losses can occur, although they are usually less sensitive than vitamins and carotenoids.

3.3.3. Bioavailability

How much of particular micronutrients the human body can absorb and use for body functions depends on a number of factors. The exact chemical composition of the micronutrient matters, and also how the compound is stored within the plant cell. Furthermore, enhancing and inhibiting factors in people's diets can have an important influence. Beta-carotene absorption, for instance, depends on minimum fat intakes, while alcohol reduces bioavailability. Iron bioavailability is positively influenced by vitamin C intake, but phytates and tannins act as inhibiting factors. Haas et al. (2005) have shown that high-iron rice can indeed improve the iron status of women. Similarly, van Jaarsveld et al. (2005) have shown that the consumption of orange-fleshed sweetpotato improves the vitamin A status of children:

with 100 ppm of beta-carotene and 80% retention when consumed in boiled form, even a 50 g consumption of this crop is sufficient for meeting 75% of the recommended daily allowance of vitamin A for children. Also for Golden Rice, a relatively high bioavailability of the beta-carotene produced has been demonstrated in preliminary feeding trials (R. Russell, personal communication). While further research is needed to verify these findings in community settings, preliminary results from the dissemination of orange-fleshed sweetpotato in Mozambique are suggestive of substantial nutritional impacts among micronutrient-deficient target populations.

3.3.4. Farmer adoption

For farmers to adopt biofortified crops, micronutrient traits have to be bred into advanced lines, which are agronomically superior. Nutritional improvement at the cost of lower yields or other agronomic disadvantages is a nonstarter. For example, wheat breeders are attempting to biofortify varieties resistant to a rust that is expected to affect large areas in Pakistan and India. Thus, adoption of biofortified wheat there is expected to be driven by rust resistance. Also critical is local adaptation: varieties will have to be targeted to specific agroecological and socioeconomic conditions. The greater the number of locally adapted biofortified varieties, the higher the likely adoption. For wide coverage, plant breeders will need to focus first on biofortifying "mega" varieties, such as BR28 and BR29 of rice in Bangladesh, which together occupy almost 60% of the rice area in the Boro season, or BR11, which accounts for over a quarter of the Aman season rice area (IRRI, personal communication). Finally, the speed of adoption will depend on the efficiency of existing seed distribution channels and farmers' seed replacement rates. Although biofortified seeds can be reproduced on-farm, some initial public support might be needed for the new varieties to penetrate formal and informal seed markets.

3.3.5. Consumer acceptance

For reasons outlined earlier, awareness of micronutrient deficiencies is generally low, so that the nutritional advantages of biofortification might not be fully appreciated. But even if they are, the willingness and ability to pay higher prices for biofortified foods are likely to be limited among the poor, who bear the brunt of micronutrient malnutrition. Also, at equal prices, consumers will only purchase micronutrient-dense crops if they meet their personal preferences in terms of taste, texture, and visual appearance. Mineral biofortification at realistic levels is not expected to change consumer characteristics, that is, iron and zinc traits are invisible (Nestel et al., 2006). This is different for beta-carotene, which changes the color of the crop to deep yellow or orange, so that it will be necessary to invest more in demand creation for these varieties through communication and marketing efforts. Consumer acceptance also influences farmer adoption decisions, as low acceptance would translate into lower market prices.

4. Methodology for impact assessment

In agricultural economics, the usual approach to assess the impact of new crop technologies is to quantify the economic benefits arising from productivity increases as a result of technology adoption by farmers. Such productivity increases—either through yield gains or savings in production costs—cause a downward shift in the crop supply curve, based on which aggregate economic surplus and surplus distribution effects can be derived (Alston et al., 1995). However, the main focus of biofortification is on improving the nutritional status of consumers through quality enhancement. Quality improvements generally lead to a marginal benefit increase for consumers, which different authors have modeled as an upward shift in the crop's demand function (e.g., Unnevehr, 1986). Yet it is unlikely that biofortification would result in an upward shift in demand, because of awareness and purchasing power constraints among the poor. In this case, benefits of biofortification should rather be considered as positive nutrition and health outcomes for individuals suffering from micronutrient malnutrition and related externalities for society at large. Such effects are more complex to evaluate.

Dawe et al. (2002) looked at the potential nutritional effects of Golden Rice by analyzing likely improvements in vitamin A intakes in the Philippines. This approach implicitly builds on a measure of program success, which is commonly used also for other micronutrient interventions, namely the achieved reduc-

tion in the number of people with micronutrient intakes below a defined threshold (e.g., Fiedler et al., 2000). However, since micronutrient intake is not an end in itself but only a means to ensure healthy body functions, it is more appropriate to go further and quantify health outcomes directly. In a preliminary assessment of iron biofortification in India and Bangladesh, Bouis (2002) estimated the reduction in the number of anemia cases and attributed a monetary value to each case averted for a cost–benefit analysis. Zimmermann and Qaim (2004) suggested a more comprehensive approach in their analysis of the potential health benefits of Golden Rice in the Philippines: since micronutrient malnutrition causes significant health costs, which could be reduced through biofortification, they quantified the health cost of vitamin A deficiency with and without Golden Rice and interpreted the difference— that is, the health cost saved--as the technological benefit.

4.1. Quantification of health costs

There are different methodologies available for the quantification of health costs, including budgeting medical treatment costs, estimating productivity losses, and willingness-to-pay approaches (e.g., Brent, 2003). A framework that appears appropriate to quantify the health costs of micronutrient malnutrition in developing countries is the disability-adjusted life years (DALYs) approach. DALYs are used to establish the burden of a disease by measuring the health loss through mortality and morbidity in a single index (Murray and Lopez, 1996). The annual health costs of a disease are expressed in terms of the number of DALYs lost:

$$\text{Health costs} = \text{DALYs}_{\text{lost}} = \text{YLL} + \text{YLD}_{\text{weighted}}, \quad (1)$$

where YLL are years of life lost due to premature deaths, and YLD are years lived with disabilities resulting from the disease, which are weighted according to the severity of disabling conditions.

The DALYs approach has been used in very different contexts, such as quantifying the health costs of malaria or HIV/AIDS (e.g., Lomborg, 2004). The World Health Organization has used it to assess the global health costs of different risk factors, including undernutrition and micronutrient malnutrition (WHO,

Table 1
Adverse health outcomes of micronutrient deficiencies for different target groups

Target group	Iron deficiency	Zinc deficiency	Vitamin A deficiency
Children	Impaired physical activity	Diarrhea	Child mortality
	Impaired mental development	Pneumonia	Measles
	Child mortality (related to	Stunting	Night blindness
	maternal deaths)	Child mortality	Corneal scarring
			Blindness
Women	Impaired physical activity		Night blindness in pregnant
	Maternal mortality		and lactating women
Men	Impaired physical activity		

Source: Stein et al. (2005).

2002). In their Golden Rice study, Zimmermann and Qaim (2004) have refined the DALYs methodology to consider more explicitly different adverse health outcomes of vitamin A deficiency. Stein et al. (2005) have further developed the approach by incorporating new nutrition insights and extending it also to iron and zinc malnutrition. For each micronutrient, the number of DALYs lost can be calculated as:

$$
\text{DALYs}_{\text{lost}} = \underbrace{\sum_j T_j M_j \left(\frac{1 - e^{-rL_j}}{r} \right)}_{\text{YLL}}
$$
$$
+ \underbrace{\sum_i \sum_j T_j I_{ij} D_{ij} \left(\frac{1 - e^{-rd_{ij}}}{r} \right)}_{\text{YLD}}, \quad (2)
$$

where T_j is the total number of people in target group j, and M_j is the mortality rate associated with the particular deficiency. I_{ij} is the incidence rate of adverse health outcome i in target group j, D_{ij} is the corresponding disability weight, and d_{ij} is the duration of the outcome. For permanent health problems, d_{ij} equals the average remaining life expectancy L_j. Future life years lost are discounted at a discount rate of r. An overview of adverse health outcomes of iron, zinc, and vitamin A deficiency is shown in Table 1. Only those outcomes for which a definite causal relationship has been established in meta-analyses are included (Stein et al., 2005).

By inserting appropriate health and demographic statistics in Equation (2), the health costs of micronutrient malnutrition in a country or region can be calculated. Since biofortified crops are not yet consumed, this status quo situation is the benchmark without biofortification. Improved micronutrient intakes through consumption of biofortified crops will reduce mortality and incidence rates of adverse functional outcomes, so that the number of DALYs lost decreases.[2] The difference in micronutrient-related health costs—that is, the number of DALYs saved—is considered the benefit of biofortification.

4.2. Improved nutrition and health status through biofortification

Micronutrient intakes required for healthy body functions vary from individual to individual, based on age, sex, physical activity, and many other factors. Recommended dietary reference intake levels for each micronutrient are usually specified for particular target groups. If the actual intake of an individual is below the recommended one, the person is likely to be deficient. An illustrative distribution of micronutrient intakes is shown in the upper panel of Figure 3. In this example, a certain fraction of the population is deficient at current intake levels without biofortification.

Future consumption of a biofortified crop will shift the intake distribution to the right. The magnitude of the shift will depend on the actual improvement in bioavailable micronutrients, which is a function of dietary patterns as well as technology efficacy and coverage, as discussed above. Some individuals, who were deficient

---

[2] How the reduction in mortality and incidence rates can be derived is explained in the next subsection.

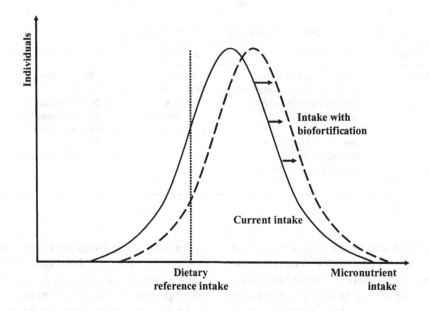

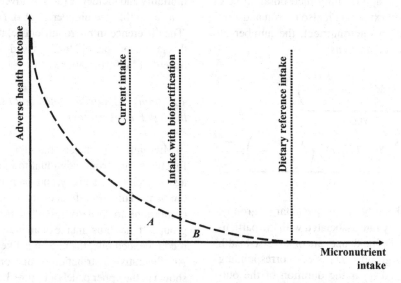

Figure 3. Improvement in micronutrient intakes and health outcomes through biofortification: (upper panel) Shift in the distribution of micronutrient intakes and (lower panel) Relationship between micronutrient intake and health outcome.

previously, will achieve sufficiency status; for them, possible adverse health outcomes will cease. However, individuals at the lower end of the intake distribution might still remain deficient, even after the shift. Also, for these individuals there will be an improvement in health status, though, because the prevalence and severity of adverse health outcomes is correlated with the degree of micronutrient deficiency. In fact, a convex relationship between micronutrient intake and adverse health outcomes can be assumed (Hallberg et al., 2000; Zimmermann and Qaim, 2004), as shown in the lower panel of Figure 3. The effectiveness of biofortification in improving health status can then be calculated as the ratio of the areas A and $(A + B)$. The mean effectiveness for a particular target group (E_j) can be used to derive new, reduced incidence rates of adverse health outcomes as $I_{ij}^{new} = (1 - E_j) \cdot I_{ij}$. For the reduction in mortality rates, the same formula can be used.[3]

4.3. Cost-effectiveness and returns on R&D investments

A comprehensive economic analysis of programs or policies requires that aggregate benefits be juxtaposed with aggregate costs. The major cost of biofortification is the investment in breeding, testing, and disseminating micronutrient-dense varieties. If the discounted biofortification investments are divided by the discounted number of DALYs saved, the average cost per DALY saved can be calculated, which is a common measure for the cost-effectiveness of health programs (e.g., World Bank, 1993). According to this per-DALY cost, it is possible to compare the cost-effectiveness of biofortification with that of alternative micronutrient interventions, other public health measures, or pre-defined thresholds for what is considered cost-effective.

One of the advantages of the DALYs approach is actually that health and life do not have to be expressed in monetary terms, since this is always associated with ethical concerns. Yet, since biofortification is an agricultural technology, which also competes with non–health-related, productivity-enhancing technologies in terms of funding, a comparison of the returns on R&D investments might be desirable in some cases. This requires that a monetary value be attributed to each DALY saved, in order to convert the health benefits into a dollar figure. What value to choose per DALY saved is not a straightforward decision. In developing country contexts, a standardized rate of $1,000 has sometimes been used (e.g., World Bank, 1994). Other authors have valued DALYs at the average per capita income in a country (e.g., Zimmermann and Qaim, 2004). These are certainly lower-bound values, and they should not be considered as an approach to quantify the intrinsic

value of life. But, since higher values translate into larger monetary benefits, the results are more cautious and convincing if favorable returns can already be shown at these lower-bound values.

5. Empirical analyses

5.1. Biofortification in India

Using the methodology outlined in the previous section, first comprehensive studies on the impacts of biofortification have been carried out in India (Stein, Qaim, et al., 2006; Stein, Sachdev et al., 2006; Stein et al., 2007), where micronutrient malnutrition is a widespread problem. About half of all women in India and three-quarters of all children are anemic (IIPS, 2000),[4] the risk of zinc deficiency is high (Hotz and Brown, 2004), and almost one-third of all preschool children are vitamin A–deficient (UN-SCN, 2004). In the framework of the HarvestPlus Challenge Program, crop scientists at IRRI and International Maize and Wheat Improvement Center (CIMMYT) are using conventional tools to breed higher amounts of iron and zinc into rice and wheat. The resulting breeding lines will be shared with the Indian public research system for backcrossing the micronutrient traits into local varieties. In addition, transgenic Golden Rice breeding lines, with high amounts of beta-carotene, will be transferred to India through the Golden Rice Humanitarian Board. Adaptive research, testing, and deregulating the technologies will still take some time; it is expected that the first biofortified varieties might be released in India in 2010. Both rice and wheat are important staple foods in India, so that significant positive nutrition and health benefits can be expected in the future.

Since much of the information needed for impact assessment is not observable at this stage, assumptions have to be made for *ex ante* analyses. According to expert interviews, two impact scenarios were constructed—one with optimistic and the other with more pessimistic assumptions. The major assumptions made on technology efficacy and coverage are shown in Table 2. Furthermore, estimated financial costs are

---

[3] While the approach described here can be used for all micronutrients, Stein et al. (2005) proposed an alternative method for iron, which derives the reduction in the prevalence of adverse health outcomes through biofortification by using the cumulative distribution function of iron intakes in a population. Where data availability permits, this alternative method is preferable for iron, but it is not suitable for zinc and vitamin A.

[4] Iron-deficiency anemia is only a subgroup of anemia. But, because it is the most important form, anemia is often used as a proxy for iron deficiency. It should be noted, however, that individuals can also suffer from iron deficiency without being anemic (Nestel and Davidsson, 2002).

Table 2
Assumptions used to simulate the impact of biofortification in India

	Iron-rich rice	Iron-rich wheat	Zinc-rich rice	Zinc-rich wheat	Golden rice
Baseline MN content	3 ppm Fe[a]	38 ppm Fe[b]	13 ppm Zn[a]	31 ppm Zn[b]	0 ppm βC[a]
		Optimistic scenario			
Improved MN content	8 ppm Fe[a]	61 ppm Fe[b]	35 ppm Zn[a]	68 ppm Zn[b]	31 ppm βC[a]
MN retention	100%	100%	100%	100%	65%
Coverage	50%	50%	50%	50%	50%
R&D cost (net present value)	US$3.6 m	US$4.5 m	US$3.6 m	US$4.5 m	US$27.9 m
		Pessimistic scenario			
Improved MN content	6 ppm Fe[a]	46 ppm Fe[b]	20 ppm Zn[a]	37 ppm Zn[b]	14 ppm βC[a]
MN retention	100%	100%	100%	100%	20%
Coverage	20%	30%	20%	30%	14%
R&D cost (net present value)	US$12.6 m	US$13.8 m	US$12.6 m	US$13.8 m	US$21.4 m

[a] Micronutrient contents shown are for milled rice.
[b] Micronutrient contents shown are for whole grain.
Notes: MN = micronutrient, ppm = parts per million, Fe = iron, Zn = zinc, βC = beta-carotene.
Sources: Stein, Qaim, et al., 2006; Stein, Sachdev, et al., 2006; Stein et al., 2007.

shown. These costs include only part of the international R&D investments, because the biofortified breeding lines will be shared also with other developing countries. In addition, national program costs for adaptive breeding, testing, and dissemination have been considered. For Golden Rice, the aggregate costs are higher than for iron and zinc biofortification for two reasons. First, since Golden Rice is a transgenic technology, more costly biosafety and food safety tests have to be carried out under the national regulatory requirements. Second, since the beta-carotene turns the color of the rice grain yellow, public marketing efforts will be necessary to promote farmer and consumer acceptance. More intensive marketing efforts are expected to increase technology coverage. Since the projected marketing expenditures account for a large part of the total cost, the cost estimates for Golden Rice are higher in the optimistic than in the pessimistic scenario.

On the basis of recent health and demographic statistics, the current health costs of micronutrient malnutrition in India were calculated. This was done separately for the three micronutrients iron, zinc, and vitamin A. The results are shown in Table 3. With an annual loss of 4 million DALYs, the aggregate costs of iron deficiency are higher than those of zinc and vitamin A deficiency. Although the latter two are associated with higher mortality, especially among children, they are less widespread than iron deficiency. For an *ad hoc* estimate of the total health costs of all three micronutrient deficiencies together, the individual results can

be added up, resulting in an annual loss of over 9 million DALYs. This indicates that hidden hunger is indeed a huge public health problem in India. The DALYs sum will underestimate the true costs, however, because—owing to micronutrient interactions—multiple deficiencies in individuals can lead to additional adverse health outcomes, which are not captured here. Only recently have nutritionists started to pay more attention to micronutrient interactions. At this stage, the knowledge available is not sufficient to incorporate these interactions into economic analyses. This is also the reason why iron, zinc, and provitamin A biofortification have been analyzed separately, although all three micronutrients might eventually be bred into the same crop varieties.

For the impact analyses, a nationally representative data set was used, which includes detailed food consumption data for 120,000 Indian households (NSSO, 2001). Using local food composition tables and consumer equivalence units, the consumption of different food commodities was translated into micronutrient intakes for individuals. The results on health cost reductions through biofortification for the two impact scenarios are shown in the lower part of Table 3. Under optimistic assumptions, biofortified rice and wheat varieties could more than halve the health costs associated with micronutrient malnutrition in India. Even under pessimistic assumptions, the reduction is still significant, ranging between 9% and 19%. These findings suggest that biofortification is an effective way to

Table 3
Impact of biofortification in India

	Iron biofortification[a]	Zinc biofortification[b]	Provitamin A biofortification[c]
Health cost of deficiency without biofortification (DALYs lost)	4.0 m	2.8 m	2.3 m
	Optimistic scenario		
DALYs saved through biofortification	2.3 m	1.6 m	1.4 m
Reduction in health cost (%)	58	55	59
Cost per DALY saved (US$/DALY)	0.46	0.68	3.06
IRR (%, DALY valued at US$620)	149	135	70
IRR (%, DALY valued at US$1,000)	168	153	77
	Pessimistic scenario		
DALYs saved through biofortification	0.8 m	0.5 m	0.2 m
Reduction in health cost (%)	19	16	9
Cost per DALY saved (US$/DALY)	5.39	8.80	19.40
IRR (%, DALY valued at US$620)	53	46	31
IRR (%, DALY valued at US$1,000)	61	53	35

[a] Iron biofortification of rice and wheat is considered.

[b] Zinc biofortification of rice and wheat is considered.

[c] Biofortification of rice with beta-carotene is considered (Golden Rice).

Sources: Stein , Qaim, et al., 2006; Stein, Sachdev, et al., 2006; Stein et al., 2007.

reduce hidden hunger, albeit unlikely to eliminate the problem completely. The differences in impacts between the two scenarios are mainly due to the underlying assumptions on micronutrient contents in the grain and coverage rates of biofortified varieties. Since these parameters can still be influenced through appropriate policies, the results also demonstrate that public support is important for increasing the positive impacts.

Results of cost-effectiveness analyses for the individual technologies are also shown in Table 3. The cost per DALY saved through biofortification is very low. The World Bank (1993) classifies health interventions as cost-effective, when the cost of saving one DALY is lower than US$200.[5] Thus, biofortification is highly cost-effective, even under pessimistic assumptions. Also, the cost-effectiveness of biofortification compares favorably with other micronutrient interventions. For instance, the cost per DALY saved through iron supplementation and industrial fortification efforts ranges between US$5.6 and 16.3 (Gillespie, 1998). For zinc supplementation and fortification programs, it ranges between US$5.0 and 18.0, and for vitamin A interventions between US$84 and 599 (Tan-Torres Edejer et al., 2005). The major reasons for the high

cost-effectiveness of biofortification are the enormous health gains it generates and the low recurrent cost that accrues once micronutrient-dense varieties have been developed and fed into existing seed distribution systems.[6] This was discussed in greater detail in Section 3.

In addition, internal rates of return (IRRs) for R&D investments in biofortification have been calculated using the lower-bound monetary values mentioned above for valuing each DALY saved, namely the international standard of US$1,000 and the average Indian per capita income of US$620. Under optimistic assumptions in particular, IRRs are very high (Table 3). Even under pessimistic assumptions, they are still comparable to the average returns on R&D investments in productivity-enhancing agricultural technologies (Alston et al., 2000). These are clear indications that biofortification can be a worthwhile investment from a social point of view.

5.2. Overview of other studies

Further *ex ante* studies on the impacts of biofortification have been carried out at different CGIAR centers

---

[5] The World Bank (1993) gives a threshold of US$150 (in 1990 dollars); in current terms this corresponds to more than US$200.

[6] Of course, where seed distribution systems are dysfunctional, coverage rates of biofortification will be lower or dissemination costs will be higher, both of which would result in a less-favorable cost-effectiveness.

Table 4

Impact of biofortification in selected crops and countries

	Reduction in health cost (%)		Cost per DALY saved (US$)	
	Optimistic	Pessimistic	Optimistic	Pessimistic
Iron				
Rice, Bangladesh	21	8	3	10
Rice, Philippines	11	4	49	197
Beans, Northeast Brazil	36	9	13	56
Beans, Honduras	22	4	20	114
Zinc				
Rice, Bangladesh	46	15	2	6
Rice, Philippines	39	11	7	46
Beans, Northeast Brazil	20	5	95	799
Beans, Honduras	15	3	48	423
Provitamin A				
Sweetpotato, Uganda	64	38	4	10
Maize, Kenya	32	8	10	44
Cassava, Nigeria	28	3	3	35
Cassava, Northeast Brazil	19	4	84	434

Source: Meenakshi et al. (2006).

for HarvestPlus target crops and countries. These studies were mainly conducted for research priority setting within the HarvestPlus Challenge Program. The methodological approach in these additional studies was largely the same as the one outlined here, although data constraints necessitated the use of average food consumption data instead of individual household observations. Therefore, projections of nutritional improvements are based on mean values for the individual target groups rather than the entire sample distribution of micronutrient intakes. Additional details on assumptions are provided in Meenakshi et al. (2006). Results in terms of health benefits and cost-effectiveness are shown in Table 4 for selected crops and countries. All the examples shown are based on micronutrient amounts that breeders reckon they can achieve using conventional breeding techniques.

These additional results confirm that biofortification can reduce the problem of micronutrient malnutrition in developing countries. Most of the examples also suggest that biofortification is a cost-effective approach, certainly in Asia and Africa, and also in certain contexts in Latin America. However, there are also striking differences between the individual results. Comparison of the studies for rice in Bangladesh and the Philippines, for instance, demonstrates the influence of local dietary patterns. While rice is the main food staple for the poor in Bangladesh, average rice quantities con-

sumed in the Philippines are lower, because maize is also an important staple in certain parts of the country. Similarly, cassava is only one staple crop among other important ones for poor households in the northeast of Brazil. More detailed assessments on appropriate approaches have to be case-specific. It is clear, however, that there is no single crop or technique that will work in every situation. Indeed, in certain situations, biofortification may not enjoy a cost advantage over other interventions.

6. Conclusions and research challenges ahead

Micronutrient malnutrition is a widespread problem in developing countries, especially among women and children in the poorer segments of the population. The social costs associated with adverse health outcomes are often sizeable. Biofortification is a new, agriculture-based intervention, which is likely to gain in importance in the future, as indicated by the large number of related international research programs recently launched. As biofortified crops are still under development, relatively little is known about their economic impacts and wider ramifications. In this article, we have discussed the main factors that will influence their future success and have illustrated a suitable methodology for economic impact assessment, which combines agricultural, nutrition, and health aspects.

Ex ante studies from India and other developing countries suggest that biofortified crops can reduce the problem of micronutrient malnutrition in a cost-effective way, when they are targeted to specific situations.

The approach presented here is only a first step to explicitly consider nutrition and health aspects in impact assessments of agricultural technology. More basic research could help to further improve and extend the methodology and develop welfare measures that include health and quality-of-life components. Moreover, additional empirical work is required to verify the preliminary results reported here, including *ex post* studies building on observable data once biofortified crops are disseminated. In the case of the deployment of orange-fleshed sweetpotato, HarvestPlus researchers are planning a randomized evaluation of impact, an approach not commonly used in agricultural economics. Such *ex post* analysis will pose new challenges, especially with respect to indicators of success, as impact on crop adoption, food and micronutrient intakes, and nutritional outcomes have rarely been assessed under a unifying paradigm. This interdisciplinary research—involving economists, other social scientists, agronomists, and nutritionists—is critical for a more comprehensive analysis of the multiplicity of impacts of biofortification.

Apart from impact analyses, there are also other open issues, which require further research. These include questions of bioavailability and micronutrient interactions in the human body. For instance, enhanced iron and zinc content go hand in hand for several crops, and their combined impact may be greater than what a single nutrient alone may achieve. Similarly, nutrient interactions are important in understanding the impact of biofortifying multiple crops. In many countries, diets often feature a primary and one or more secondary staple crops—cassava is commonly eaten with beans in many parts of Africa and Latin America, for example. The higher beta-carotene content of cassava may enhance the absorption of the iron in beans. Likewise, nutrient interactions in plants and linkages between high micronutrient concentrations and other crop characteristics are not yet fully understood. And finally, it is still unclear how stable the micronutrient traits will be when seeds are repeatedly reproduced by farmers. A rapid trait dilution would certainly put the assumed sustainability of the biofortification approach into question.

Where there are technical constraints in breeding, transgenic approaches could help to increase the amounts beyond what is possible through conventional breeding alone. Transgenic approaches are also needed when a particular micronutrient does not occur naturally in a crop. Cases in point are the lack of beta-carotene in the endosperm of rice and wheat. While transgenic approaches may further increase the impact of biofortification, they may also involve additional complications in terms of regulatory requirements and consumer acceptance.

In spite of further research challenges ahead, an important policy implication, which already emerges from the evidence so far, is that biofortification can play an important role in achieving nutrition security in particular situations. Apart from the high expected cost-effectiveness, preliminary cost–benefit analyses show that social returns on R&D investments into biofortification are favorable and highly competitive with productivity-enhancing agricultural technologies. Therefore, further pursuing the strategy of biofortification appears to be worthwhile. Related funding will have to come primarily from the public sector or humanitarian organizations. Although the projected social benefits are sizeable, neither farmers nor poor consumers are likely to have a higher willingness to pay for biofortified crops, so that incentives for the private sector to invest are rather limited.

To conclude, biofortification should not be seen as substitute for existing micronutrient interventions but as a complementary strategy. No single approach will eliminate the problem of micronutrient malnutrition, as our results also indicate. All interventions have their strengths and weaknesses in particular situations. While supplementation and industrial fortification might be more suitable for urban areas and feeding programs for well-defined target groups, biofortification is likely to achieve a wider coverage, including in remote rural areas, which are often underserved by other interventions. It is only in the long run that poverty reduction and economic growth may be expected to contribute to dietary diversification; in the interim, other interventions need to be implemented.

Acknowledgments

The financial support of the German Research Foundation (DFG) is gratefully acknowledged. We thank Penelope Nestel, H. P. S. Sachdev, and Zulfiqar A. Bhutta, who cooperated with us in this research and provided invaluable inputs on nutritional details.

References

Allen, L. H., "Interventions for Micronutrient Deficiency Control in Developing Countries: Past, Present and Future," *Journal of Nutrition* 133 (2003), 3875S–3878S.

Alston, J. M., C. Chan-Kang, M. C. Marra, P. G. Pardey, and T. J. Wyatt, "A Meta-Analysis of Rates of Return to Agricultural R&D – Ex Pede Herculem?" *IFPRI Research Report* 113 (International Food Policy Research Institute: Washington, DC,2000).

Alston, J. M., G. W. Norton, and P. G. Pardey, *Science Under Scarcity: Principles and Practice for Agricultural Research Evaluation and Priority Setting.* (Cornell University Press: Ithaca1995).

Bouis, H. E., "Plant Breeding: A New Tool for Fighting Micronutrient Malnutrition," *Journal of Nutrition* 132 (2002), 491S–494S.

Brent, R. J., *Cost-Benefit Analysis and Health Care Evaluations.* (Edward Elgar: Cheltenham, 2003).

Dawe, D., R. Robertson, and L. Unnevehr, "Golden Rice: What Role Could it Play in Alleviation of Vitamin A Deficiency?" *Food Policy* 27 (2002), 541–560.

Drakakaki, G., S. Marcel, R. P. Glahn, E. K. Lund, S. Pariagh, R. Fischer, P. Christou, and E. Stoger, "Endosperm-Specific Co-Expression of Recombinant Soybean Ferritin and Aspergillus Phytase in Maize Results in Significant Increases in the Levels of Bioavailable Iron," *Plant Molecular Biology* 59 (2005), 869–880.

Ducreux, L. J. M., W. L. Morris, P. E. Hedley, T. Shepherd, H. V. Davies, S. Millam, and M. A. Taylor, "Metabolic Engineering of High Carotenoid Potato Tubers Containing Enhanced Levels of β-Carotene and Lutein," *Journal of Experimental Botany* 56 (2005), 81–89.

FAO. *The State of Food Insecurit in the World* 2004 (FAO, Rome, 2004).

FAO. *The State of Food Insecurity in the World* 2006 (Food and Agriculture Organization of the United Nations: Rome, 2006).

Fiedler, J. L., D. Dado, H. Maglalang, N. R. Juban, M. Capistrano, and M. V. Magpantay, "Cost Analysis as a Vitamin A Program Design and Evaluation Tool: A Case Study of the Philippines," *Social Science & Medicine* 51 (2000), 223–242.

Gillespie, S., *Major Issues in the Control of Iron Deficiency.* (Micronutrient Initiative: Ottawa, 1998).

Goto, F., T. Yoshihara, N. Shigemoto, S. Toki, and F. Takaiwa, "Iron Fortification of Rice Seed by Soybean Ferritin Gene," *Nature Biotechnology* 17 (1999), 282–286.

Graham, R. D., D. Senadhira, S. E. Beebe, C. Iglesias, and I. Ortiz-Monasterio, "Breeding for Micronutrient Density in Edible Portions of Staple Food Crops: Conventional Approaches," *Field Crop Research* 60 (1999), 57–80.

Haas, J. D., J. L. Beard, L. E. Murray-Kolb, A. M. del Mundo, A. Felix, and G. B. Gregorio, "Iron-Biofortified Rice Improves the Iron Stores of Nonanemic Filipino Women," *Journal of Nutrition* 135 (2005), 2823–2830.

Hallberg, L., L. Hulthén, and L. Garby, "Iron Stores and Hemoglobin Iron Deficits in Menstruating Women; Calculations Based on Variations in Iron Requirements and Bioavailability of Dietary Iron," *European Journal of Clinical Nutrition* 54 (2000), 650–657.

Horton, S., and J. Ross, "The Economics of Iron Deficiency," *Food Policy* 28 (2003), 51–75.

Hotz, C., and K. H. Brown, eds., "Assessment of the Risk of Zinc Deficiency in Populations and Options for its Control," International Zinc Nutrition Consultative Group Technical Document No. 1, *Food and Nutrition Bulletin* 25 (2004), S91–S204.

IIPS, *National Family Health Survey (NFHS-2), 1998-99: India.* (International Institute for Population Sciences: Mumbai, 2000).

Lomborg, B., ed., *Global Crises, Global Solutions* (Cambridge: Cambridge University Press, 2004).

Low, J., P. Kinyae, S. Gichuki, M. A. Oyunga, V. Hagenimana, and J. Kabira, *Combating Vitamin A Deficiency through the Use of Sweetpotato.* (International Potato Center: Lima, 1997).

Lucca, P., R. Hurrell, and I. Potrykus, "Genetic Engineering Approaches to Improve the Bioavailability and the Level of Iron in Rice Grains," *Theoretical and Applied Genetics* 102 (2001), 392–397.

Meenakshi, J. V., N. Johnson, V. M. Manyong, H. De Groote, D. Yanggen, J. Javelosa, F. Naher, C. Gonzalez, J. Garcia, and E. Meng, "Analysing the Cost-Effectiveness of Biofortification: A Synthesis of the Evidence," paper presented at the Annual AAEA Meeting, July 23-26, 2006 Long Beach, CA.

Micronutrient Initiative, *Vitamin & Mineral Deficiency: A Global Progress Report* (Micronutrient Initiative, Ottawa and UNICEF: New York, 2004).

Murray, C. J. L., and A. D. Lopez, eds., *The Global Burden of Disease; Vol. I and II.* (Harvard University Press: Cambridge, MA, 1996).

Murray-Kolb, L. E., F. Takaiwa, F. Goto, T. Yoshihara, E. C. Theil, and J. L. Beard, "Transgenic Rice is a Source of Iron for Iron-Depleted Rats," *Journal of Nutrition* 132 (2002), 957–960.

Nestel, P., and L. Davidsson, *Anemia, Iron Deficiency, and Iron Deficiency Anemia* (International Nutritional Anemia Consultative Group ([NACG]: Washington, DC, 2002).

Nestel, P., H. E. Bouis, J. V. Meenakshi, and W. Pfeiffer, "Biofortification of Staple Food Crops," *Journal of Nutrition* 136 (2006), 1064–1067.

NSSO, "Level and Pattern of Consumer Expenditure in India 1999–2000," *NSS 55th Round, Report* No. 457 (National Sample Survey Organization: New Delhi, 2001).

Paine, J. A., C. A. Shipton, S. Chaggar, R. M. Howells, H. J. Kennedy, G. Vernon, S. Y. Wright, E. Hinchliffe, J. L. Adams, A. L. Silverstone, and R. Drake, "Improving the Nutritional Value of Golden Rice Through Increased Pro-vitamin A Content," *Nature Biotechnology* 23 (2005), 482–487.

Stein, A. J., J. V. Meenakshi, M. Qaim, P. Nestel, H. P. S. Sachdev, and Z. A. Bhutta, "Analyzing the Health Benefits of Biofortified Staple Crops by Means of the Disability-Adjusted Life Years Approach: A Handbook Focusing on Iron, Zinc and Vitamin A," *HarvestPlus Technical Monograph* 4 (International Food Policy Research Institute and International Center for Tropical Agriculture: Washington, D.C. and Cali, 2005).

Stein, A. J., M. Qaim, J. V. Meenakshi, P. Nestel, H. P. S. Sachdev, and Z. A. Bhutta, "Potential Impacts of Iron Biofortification in India," *Research in Development Economics and Policy Discussion Paper* No. 04/2006 (University of Hohenheim: Stuttgart, 2006).

Stein, A., H. P. S. Sachdev, and M. Qaim, "Potential Impact and Cost-Effectiveness of Golden Rice," *Nature Biotechnology* 24 (2006), 1200–1201.

Stein, A. J., P. Nestel, J. V. Meenakshi, M. Qaim, H. P. S. Sachdev, and Z. A. Bhutta, "Plant Breeding to Control Zinc Deficiency in India: How Cost-Effective is Biofortification?" *Public Health Nutrition* 10 (2007), 492–501.

Tan-Torres Edejer, T., M. Aikins, R. Black, L. Wolfson, R. Hutubessy, and D. B. Evans, "Cost Effectiveness Analysis of Strategies for Child Health in Developing Countries," *British Medical Journal* 331 (2005), e1177.

Unnevehr, L. J., "Consumer Demand for Rice Grain Quality and Returns to Research for Quality Improvement in Southeast Asia," *American Journal of Agricultural Economics* 68 (1986), 634–641.

UN-SCN, *5th Report on the World Nutrition Situation* (United Nations, Standing Committee on Nutrition: Geneva, 2004).

van Jaarsveld, P. J., M. Faber, S. A. Tanumihardjo, P. Nestel, C. J. Lomrad, and A. J. S. Benadé, "β-Carotene-Rich Orange Fleshed Sweetpotato Improves the Vitamin A Status of Primary School Children Assessed by the Modified-Relative-Dose-Response Test," *American Journal of Clinical Nutrition* 81 (2005), 1080–1087.

Vasconcelos, M., K. Datta, N. Oliva, M. Khalekuzzaman, L. Torrizo, S. Krishnan, M. Oliveira, F. Goto, and S. K. Datta, "Enhanced Iron and Zinc Accumulation in Transgenic Rice with the Ferritin Gene," *Plant Science* 164 (2003), 371–378.

Welch, R. M., "Breeding Strategies for Biofortified Staple Plant Foods to Reduce Micronutrient Malnutrition Globally," *Journal of Nutrition* 132 (2002), 495S–499S.

WHO, The World Health Report 2002 – Reducing Risks, Promoting Healthy Life (World Health Organization: Geneva, 2002).

World Bank, *World Development Report 1993; Investing in Health.* (Oxford University Press: New York, 1993).

World Bank, *Enriching Lives: Overcoming Vitamin and Mineral Malnutrition in Developing Countries* (World Bank: Washington, DC, 1994).

Ye, X., S. Al-Babili, A. Klöti, J. Zhang, P. Lucca, P. Beyer, and I. Potrykus, "Engineering the Provitamin A (β-Carotene) Biosynthetic Pathway into (Carotenoid-Free) Rice Endosperm," *Science* 287 (2000), 303–305.

Zimmermann, R., and M. Qaim, "Potential Health Benefits of Golden Rice: A Philippine Case Study," *Food Policy* 29 (2004), 147–168.

Food safety in a globalizing world: opportunities and challenges for India

Dina Umali-Deininger* and Mona Sur**

Abstract

Rising incomes and urbanization, increasing consumer awareness prompted by widely publicized food safety crises, and an expansion in agricultural exports have been important drivers for the increased attention to food safety in India. But the development of effective food safety systems is hampered by a number of factors: restrictive government marketing regulations, a weak policy and regulatory framework for food safety, inadequate enforcement of existing standards, poor market infrastructure and agricultural support services, and the predominance of small farms. Addressing food safety concerns in India is likely to require adoption of appropriate legislation; strengthening capacity to enforce rules; promoting adoption of good agricultural, manufacturing, and hygiene practices; greater collective action; and some targeted investments. Joint efforts by the government and the private sector are needed to implement these actions.

JEL classification: O130, Q170, Q180

Keywords: food safety; agricultural marketing; SPS, India; food policy; regulations

1. Introduction

Developing countries are paying increased attention to food safety because of growing recognition of its potential impact on public health, food security, and trade competitiveness. Increasing scientific understanding of the public health consequences of unsafe food, amplified by the rapid global transmission of information regarding the public health threats associated with foodborne and zoonotic diseases (e.g., *Escherichia coli* and H5N1 avian flu) through various forms of media and the internet has heightened consumer awareness about food safety risks to new levels globally (Buzby and Unnevehr, 2003; Unnevehr, 2003; Ewen et al., 2006). Increased understanding of the impact of mycotoxins, which can contaminate dietary staples such as wheat, maize, barley, and peanuts, has further raised

food security and public health concerns in many developing countries (Bhat and Vasanthi, 2003; Dohlman, 2003).

As developing countries seek to expand agricultural exports, especially to OECD countries, many are facing new challenges in meeting both government and private sanitary and phytosanitary (SPS) standards in export markets (Henson, 2003; Unnevehr, 2003; World Bank, 2005a). Private standards or supplier protocols are increasingly being adopted by modern supply chains as a means to ensure compliance with official regulations, fill perceived gaps in such regulations, and/or facilitate the differentiation of company or industry products from those of competitors. Trends in private standards increasingly tend to blend food safety and quality management concerns or have protocols that combine food safety, environmental, and social parameters (child labor, labor conditions, animal welfare) (Willems et al., 2005; World Bank, 2005a). Increasing globalization of trade also introduces greater risks of cross-border transfer of foodborne illnesses. Recent cases of disease episodes in the United States resulting from imported food produce, such as

---

*Lead Agricultural Economist, South Asia Sustainable Development Department, World Bank.

**Senior Economist, South Asia Sustainable Development Department, World Bank.

hepatitis A from strawberries and salmonella from cantaloupe (Calvin, 2003), illustrate the potential food safety challenges that can arise in a more globalized market.

Weaknesses in food safety systems can have a high cost to society and the global economy. In the United States, it is estimated that the annual costs of medical expenses, loss of productivity, and premature death due to five foodborne pathogens (*Campylobacter* [all serotypes], *Salmonella* [nontyphoidal], *Escherichia coli* O157, *E. coli* non-O157 STEC, and *Listeria monocytogenes*) was equivalent to US$6.9 billion in 2000 (Economic Research Service [ERS], 2006). The World Health Organization (2006) estimates that 20% of deaths among children under 5 in India are caused by diarrheal disease, frequently related to contamination of food and drinking water. Country reactions to protect their citizens from food safety risks can also significantly impact exporting countries. Otsuki et al. (2001) estimated that the European Union's new harmonized aflatoxin standard could reduce exports from nine African countries by 64% (US$670 million).

Food safety concerns are receiving widespread attention in India. The country's rural development strategy, for which a key element is the promotion of increased agricultural exports, is coming against tightening food safety and SPS standards in prospective markets (World Bank, 2007a, 2007b). From a domestic perspective, the large national market of 1.2 billion people is undergoing rapid change. Rising incomes, increased urbanization and literacy, and a population highly tuned to international trends fueled by the information technology boom are driving increased consumer priority to food quality and safety. However, a number of policy, regulatory, infrastructural, and institutional obstacles need to be overcome in order to improve food safety systems to meet domestic and export requirements.

This paper aims to (i) review the main drivers for the increased priority to addressing food safety risks in India in both the export and domestic markets, (ii) examine the nature and effectiveness of government and private responses to the food safety challenges, with special focus on high-value agriculture; (iii) identify the constraints to more effective responses; and (iv) examine the implications for policy.

2. Food safety and the Indian domestic market

Increasing incomes, urbanization, and literacy, as well as improved infrastructure and closer ties to global trends, especially during the last decade, are reshaping consumer demand and preferences in India. Sustained economic growth (6.0% per year in real terms from 1990/1991 to 2003/2004) resulted in GDP per capita increasing by about 70%, from about US$315 in 1990 to US$538 in 2004 (constant 2,000 dollars). The Indian food consumption basket is diversifying away from cereals toward higher-value and more perishable products, such as fruits and vegetables, dairy, meat, and fish. Increasing female participation in the work force and higher disposable incomes are driving growth in demand for prepared and semiprepared foods, and thus the growth of the processed food industries (Pingali and Khwaja, 2004).

These trends bring increased attention to safety concerns in the handling, processing, and marketing of foods. In addition, growing consumer preference for shopping convenience, increased exposure through television and the internet, and ownership of durables such as refrigerators and cars are fostering the growth of modern retailing (i.e., supermarkets and hypermarkets), which in turn demand greater efficiency and food quality and safety standards in the supply chain (Chenggapa, 2005; Mukherjee and Patel, 2005).

Increased vigilance by NGOs, consumer groups, and local research institutes is also raising awareness and spurring action among consumers and policy makers to address food safety risks. Findings of high levels of pesticides in bottled water and soft drinks in 2003 by the Centre for Science and Environment (CSE), a nongovernmental organization, shook the country. The CSE tested 30 bottled water brands from the major cities of Delhi and Mumbai and found that all except one contained pesticide residues (CSE, 2004). Mathur et al. (2003) tested 12 popular brands of soft drinks sold in Delhi for pesticide residues and found that all brands exceeded the EU maximum pesticide residue limit of 0.0005 ppm. The Government of India (GOI) established a special Joint Parliamentary Committee on "Pesticide Residues in and Safety Standards for Soft Drinks, Fruit Juice and Other Beverages" in August 2003 to investigate the allegations. Two GOI

Laboratories were instructed to conduct tests on the 12 brands (but using different samples) and their findings showed that 9 of the 12 samples exceeded the EU limits (Hindu Business Line, 2003).

Weak regulations and inadequate standards were major causes of these high-profile food safety crises. In response, the GOI issued a notification revising the standards for pesticide residues on bottled water, adopting the EU single residue limit of 0.0001 ppm and multiple residue limit of 0.0005 ppm (CSE, 2004). In the case of soft drinks, the Bureau of Indian Standards formulated the Indian Ready to Serve Non-Alcoholic Beverages Specifications, which established the limits for 16 pesticides in the finished product (0.0001 mg/L for individual pesticides and total pesticide residue limit of 0.0005 mg/L) (CSE, 2004).

Heavy-metal contamination in foods is becoming an increasing concern. Marshall et al. (2003) tested fresh cauliflower, okra, and spinach—common vegetables in the Indian diet—in five production sites around the Delhi region and in Delhi's Azadpur wholesale market from May 2001 to June 2003. They found that 72% of the 222 spinach samples exceeded the Indian MRLs for lead of 2.5 mg/kg, and 100% exceeded the Codex MRL of 0.3 mg/kg. They attributed the high lead content to a number of possible causes, including contamination of the irrigation water by sewage and industrial effluent and pollution. Contamination was exacerbated by their locations—the production sites and market were in periurban and urban areas. Currently, no regular testing for heavy metals in vegetables is undertaken by government agencies in India.

3. Food safety concerns in Indian exports

Increased globalization and liberalization of markets are opening new export markets for Indian agricultural products, both fresh and processed. Indian agricultural exports grew at an average annual rate of 7.2% from 1990/1991 to 2003/2004. In response to these new opportunities, India's agriculture exports diversified from traditional exports of tea, spices, and coffee to include horticultural, fish, and livestock products. Between the triennium ending (TE) 1991/1992 and TE 2003/2004, the value of fresh and processed fruit and vegetable exports rose from US$84 million to US$394 million in real terms (1993/1994 dollars) while marine product exports rose from US$516 million to US$1.5 billion during the same period.

As Indian agricultural exports diversify and the value of exports to high-income countries increases, India is facing new food safety challenges. Concerns over numerous rejections of Indian agro-food exports on food safety grounds have spilled over domestically, generating greater consumer attention to pervasive food safety problems in the supply chain, including high levels of pesticide residues, presence of heavy metals in food, and microbiological contamination.

3.1. Horticultural exports

In 2004, India exported US$575 million of fresh and processed fruits, vegetables, and flowers. Traditionally India's fresh fruit and vegetables exports were targeted to markets in neighboring South Asian countries, the Middle East, and East Asia. Since the early 1990s, India has achieved some success in exporting fresh horticultural produce to Western Europe. India has been quite proud of its penetration into the United Kingdom, Netherlands, and German fresh grape markets. Grapes are a highly seasonal crop and Indian exporters target a small market window in the European market between March and April, at the end of the main southern hemisphere production season (in South Africa and Chile) and before Egypt and Turkey enter the market.

In May 2003, Indian grape exporters catering to the European market received a pivotal wake-up call concerning the costs of failing to meet food safety standards. In the midst of a commercial dispute with an Indian grape exporter, a Dutch importer had samples of Indian grapes tested by a private laboratory. The tested samples contained residues of the insecticide methomyl in excess of the EU maximum residue limit (0.05 microgram/kg) (World Bank, 2007b). Dutch authorities, who were alerted about the finding, tested samples from the 28 containers of Indian grapes then in Rotterdam port and found that about 75% of the samples exceed the MRLs for methomyl and/or acephate. This triggered the EU Rapid Alert system, causing not only significant short-term economic losses but also considerable longer-term reputational damage. The price of Indian grapes dropped sharply, and the Indian grape shippers incurred losses, either in Dutch sales or by diverting the shipments to other markets (World Bank, 2007b).

3.2. Spice exports

India is the world's largest consumer and producer of spices and is also a significant exporter of spices (Jaffee, 2005). In 2004/2005, India's spice exports totaled US$399 million. India, however, has encountered a number of food safety problems with its spice exports, including high pesticide residues, aflatoxin contamination, and the use of prohibited food colorants. Between 1998 and 2000, Indian dry chili exports faced rejection in Germany, Italy, Spain, and the United Kingdom due to the presence of aflatoxin. In February 2005, a massive recall of some 600 food products took place in the United Kingdom because of the detection of Sudan 1 in Worcestershire sauce. The costs associated with the product recall were extremely high, estimated at around 200 million Euros (Jaffee, 2005). The source of the Sudan 1 dye in the Worcester sauce was traced to chili powder imported from India in 2002.

3.3. Fish and fish product exports

Fish and fish products are one of India's largest agricultural export earners, totaling US$1.3 billion in 2004/2005. Over the years, India has encountered several food safety problems with its fish and fish product exports. Most prominent, in 1997, the European Commission found the industry to be noncompliant in maintaining hygiene standards in fish-processing plants. Because of continued detection of salmonella, all exports of fish and fishery products to the EU from India were banned in 1997. While India has for the most part been able to address the hygiene-related problems plaguing its export of fish products in the late 1990s, Indian exports are now under scrutiny because of problems related to antibiotic residues and bacterial inhibitors (Henson et al., 2005). It is widely acknowledged that in the future, heavy metals and other contaminants could be an emerging issue for Indian exports of fish and fish products because of the increased attention to heavy metals in the EU.

4. Challenges to improving food safety in India

Improving food safety in India, whether for the domestic market or for export trade, is hampered by a number of structural, policy, institutional, technical, and cultural barriers.

4.1. Policy and regulatory environment

A number of policies and regulations governing agricultural marketing and food processing complicate the implementation of food safety measures by the government and by the private sector. Two critical marketing regulations are the State Level Agricultural Produce Marketing (Development and Regulation) Acts and the Small Scale Industry (SSI) Reservation Policy. Almost all states in India have an Agricultural Produce Marketing (APM) Act, which gives state governments the sole authority to establish and manage wholesale markets. The Act, adopted by most states in the 1960s and 1970s, prescribes the setting up of a network of state-controlled "regulated markets" or *mandis* and the establishment of Market Committees to operate each. All "notified" agricultural commodities grown in areas surrounding the market are required by law to be sold only through these markets, with the number of notified commodities varying by state and market. In 2005, there were nearly 8,000 regulated markets in the whole country. The requirement that all agricultural commodities be channeled through the regulated markets not only increases transactions costs, but it is also a major obstacle to preserving produce quality and traceability. In 2003, the GOI formulated a model Agricultural Produce Market Act for state governments to adopt, which removes the restrictions on farmer direct sales and permits entities outside of government to establish and operate wholesale markets. As of December 2006, only 10 of the 28 states and Union Territories have adopted the model Act (World Bank, 2007a).[1]

The SSI reservation restricts the processing of certain commodities to the small-scale sector. Currently, several processed agricultural products are still subject to SSI reservation, such as rapeseed, mustard, and groundnut oil,[2] bread, pastry, pickles and chutneys, and hard-boiled sugar candy (Department of Small Scale

---

[1] The states that adopted the model Act are Punjab, Madhya Pradesh, Andhra Pradesh, Orissa, Maharashtra, Rajasthan, Chhattisgarh, Himachal Pradesh, Sikkim, and Nagaland.

[2] Exceptions are rapeseed, mustard, and groundnut oil through solvent extraction and those processed by grower's cooperatives and state agro-cooperatives (Ministry of Small Scale Industries, 2006).

Industries, 2006). By limiting the size of enterprises, the SSI reservation limits the ability of firms to undertake the necessary investments (e.g., adopting Hazard Analysis Critical Control Point [HACCP] systems) and certifications required to meet domestic and international food safety and SPS requirements.

Prior to 2006, there was a complex web of laws governing the processed food sector, which complicated implementation of food safety measures. These laws, enforced by eight different ministries, authorized several agencies to lay down standards for food products: (1) Bureau of Indian Standards of the Ministry of Food, Consumer Affairs and Public Distribution; (2) Ministry of Food Processing Industry; (3) Ministry of Agriculture; (4) Ministry of Health and Family Welfare; (5) Export Inspection Council; and (6) the Defense Ministry for their own purchases. The laws and their associated regulations in some cases prescribed contradictory or differing standards. For example, while the Fruit Products Order allows the use of artificial sweeteners in fruit products, the Prevention of Food Adulteration Act bans it (Patnaik, 2005).

In September 2006, the parliament approved the new Food Safety and Standards Act, which aims to rationalize the various and often conflicting laws. The key provisions of the Act include the following: (i) the repeal of a number of Acts and Orders[3]; (ii) the establishment of a Food Safety and Standards Authority of India; (iii) definition of the standards for food additives, contaminants, genetically modified and organic foods, packaging and labeling, and food imports; (iv) accreditation of laboratories, research institutions, and food safety auditors; (v) licensing and registration of food business and setting penalties for offenses; and (vi) establishment of a Food Safety Adjudication Tribunal (Ministry of Food Processing Industries, 2005).

4.2. Smallholder agriculture

The current structure of the farm sector in India constrains farmer capacity to meet domestic and international food safety standards. Farming in India is dominated by small farmers—the average farm size in 1999/2000 was 1.8 ha. Most farmers face credit constraints (World Bank, 2004), and literacy rates are low.[4] These constraints impose limits on the number of farmers capable of adopting more sophisticated farm practices and undertaking necessary investments (e.g., obtaining certifications and investing in grading and cooling facilities) to meet more stringent food quality and safety requirements. They increase the cost of transacting business and monitoring compliance with food safety standards. Stringent land policies, such as land ceilings and restrictions on land rental, limit possibilities for greater land amalgamation (World Bank, 2007c). International experience indicates, however, that farm size constraints may be overcome through innovative interventions such as organizing farmers into producer groups, establishing collection centers (by supermarkets and exporters), using contract farming arrangements, and by creating public–private partnerships to assist farmers in a variety of ways, including accessing capital to make on-farm improvements and other investments, developing and improving farming skills through joint extension provision, and assistance in acquiring the required national and international certifications (Berdegué et al., 2003; Boselie et al., 2003; Dries et al., 2004; Reardon and Timmer, 2007).

To address various food safety concerns in both the spices and fresh and processed fruit and vegetable sectors, some exporters have initiated contract farming operations or "vendor screening" programs. For example in the pickled gherkin industry, about 50,000 smallholder farmers are engaged in outgrower schemes operated by the exporters. The companies provide intensive oversight and maintain extensive records of farmer practices, especially related to pesticide use. At least one company began the process of getting outgrowers certified under EurepGAP (World Bank, 2006b).

Until recently, contract farming was illegal in India as per the provisions of the APM Act. The only way entrepreneurs can legally enter into contract farming with farmers is to obtain a special waiver from the State Government. The new model APM Act provides the legal framework and guidelines for contract farming.

---

[3] The laws and orders repealed are the Prevention of Food Adulteration Act 1954 (37 of 1954), Fruit Products Order 1955, Meat Food Products Order 1973, Vegetable Oil Products (Control) Order 1947, The Edible Oils Packaging (Regulation Order) 1998, Solvent Extracted Oil, De-oiled Meal and Edible Flour (Control) Order 1967, Milk and Milk Products Order 1992, and other orders under the Essential Commodities Act 1955 (10 pf 1955) relating to food.

[4] The rural literacy rate in 1999/2000 was 50% (Indiastat, 2006).

Adoption of the model Act by state governments will therefore facilitate not only more efficient marketing, but also improved food safety and the adoption of improved agricultural practices.

4.3. Weak extension systems

The public agricultural extension systems at the state level are very weak and have not effectively caught up to the changing needs of farmers and the market (World Bank, 2005b). In view of the GOI's earlier concentration on food self-sufficiency, the state-level Department of Agriculture (DoA) extension systems generally focused on cereals, particularly rice and wheat, with an emphasis on the transfer of improved varieties and management practices. In many states, tight fiscal constraints have contributed to the breakdown of the state extension machinery (Rao, 2003). Private extension provision (fee for service) is emerging. There are an increasing number of input suppliers, traders, contract buyers, supermarkets, and exporters that provide extension services to farmers as an integral part of their trading arrangements (World Bank, 2005b). However in the national context, private extension remains limited.

The findings of a World Bank agricultural marketing survey, covering 1,579 farmers producing high-value crops (tomatoes, potatoes, mangoes, maize, and tumeric) in four states in India (Orissa, Tamil Nadu, Uttar Pradesh, and Maharashtra) conducted during February–May 2005 demonstrates the limited effectiveness of the national extension system. Farmers primarily depended on personal observation or on other farmers for information about crop prices, post-harvest practices, irrigation, and fertilizer and pesticide use (Table 1).

Although food safety concerns have not been a major focus in the extension program, it is partly addressed through the increased Ministry of Agriculture (MoA) priority to integrated pest management (IPM). MoA established the National Center for Integrated Pest Management in 1988 to develop and promote IPM technologies. Notably, there has been a decline in total pesticide consumption in India from 75,000 mt in 1990/1991 to 48,400 mt in 2002/2003 (Directorate of Plant Protection and Quarantine, 2006).

4.4. Poor infrastructure and services in the marketing system

Reducing food safety risks from the farm to domestic and export markets is constrained by inadequate infrastructure and facilities, particularly at the wholesale markets. The World Bank Agricultural Marketing Survey also collected information on the operations of 78 wholesale markets in the four states. The survey found that the infrastructure and facilities in these markets are limited and rudimentary. Overall, Maharashtra and Uttar Pradesh had slightly better infrastructure than the other two states. About 83% of markets had covered shops, but only 18% had paved roads within the market and 51% had public toilets (Table 2). Access to warehouses is limited, except in Maharashtra (85%). Less than 40% of markets had a drying area and no markets in Orissa or Uttar Pradesh had cold storage facilities (compared to 5% in Tamil Nadu and 20% in Maharashtra).

Waste management and pest control in the markets are very weak. Officials working in the wholesale markets were asked how the spoiled produce and waste products were disposed of. Fifty-four percent responded that market employees or contracted firms handled garbage disposal and waste management; 29% reported that they were just left to rot in the market, while 13% reported that they were left for the animals to eat. Market officials were also asked about the pest control measures they undertake. Fifty-nine percent indicated that no particular control measure for rats and insects are implemented in their market, and 32% indicated it was up to the individual shop owners to take care of their rat problems. Only 8% reported the market management or association or a subcontracted firm took care of rat problems. Reducing food safety risks will require significant public and private investments to upgrade the market infrastructure and services. For regulated markets, this will also require improving the operational and fiduciary management to ensure that more resources are reinvested back into the markets.

4.5. Cultural issues

Religious beliefs further constrain the kinds of food safety measures that could be adopted in India. The sacred value attached to cattle imposes limits on disease

Table 1
Farmer sources of information

Type of information/state	Farmers' source of information, %							
	Other farmers	Agric. traders	Personal observation	Agric. officers	Contract buyers	Input suppliers	Mass media	Other
Crop prices								
Tamil Nadu	34	45	0	6	0	1	13	1
Orissa	46	47	1	4	1	1	1	1
Maharashtra	78	6	1	11	0	1	2	1
Uttar Pradesh	67	25	0	3	2	0	1	0
Total	66	21	0	7	1	0	3	1
Sorting/grading of crops								
Tamil Nadu	30	4	50	8	2	4	2	0
Orissa	54	17	9	18	0	0	15	0
Maharashtra	79	1	4	11	0	0	0	4
Uttar Pradesh	76	13	0	2	8	0	2	0
Total	69	7	10	8	3	1	1	2
Post-harvest practices								
Tamil Nadu	31	1	52	7	0	3	6	0
Orissa	56	9	8	20	0	2	1	3
Maharashtra	77	0	3	11	0	2	0	5
Uttar Pradesh	77	13	0	2	7	0	2	0
Total	69	5	9	8	2	2	2	3
Irrigation use								
Tamil Nadu	26	1	53	14	0	4	2	0
Orissa	50	6	10	29	0	1	3	1
Maharashtra	81	0	4	10	0	0	0	4
Uttar Pradesh	86	6	0	3	0	1	2	2
Total	73	3	10	10	0	1	1	3
Fertilizer & pesticide use								
Tamil Nadu	14	6	27	21	1	27	3	1
Orissa	35	12	8	34	0	7	2	3
Maharashtra	74	1	2	11	0	10	2	1
Uttar Pradesh	60	13	0	8	0	14	3	1
Total	58	6	5	13	0	13	2	1

Source: World Bank (2007a).

control measures to address food safety and public health (BSE, foot and mouth disease), such as culling, to limit disease spread or to create disease-free zones.

4.6. Inadequate grades and standards for the domestic market and poor enforcement

The Directorate of Marketing & Inspection under the Department of Agriculture and Cooperation is responsible for enforcing and implementing the Agricultural Produce (Grading and Marking) Act. Its mandate includes promoting standardization and grading of agricultural products. Grades and standards have been prescribed for 164 commodities under the APM Act for domestic trade, for export trade, and for grading at the producer's level. The AGMARK grades are primarily voluntary grades covering aspects such as size, variety, weight, color, and moisture levels. Different grades and standards are laid out under AGMARK for domestic consumption versus exports (World Bank, 2007b).

The Directorate provides third-party certification under the AGMARK quality certification scheme. The "AGMARK" seal is supposed to ensure quality and safety. Any consumer, trader, or manufacturer can have products tested at one of the 23 regional AGMARK laboratories for designated commodities. Typically, testing is only carried out for adulteration-prone

Table 2
Market infrastructure and facilities in wholesale markets in Tamil Nadu, Orissa, Maharashtra, and Uttar Pradesh

Market infrastructure	Percentage of wholesale markets				
	Tamil Nadu	Orissa	Maharashtra	Uttar Pradesh	All
Covered shops	72	80	90	89	83
Paved road in market yard	30	5	15	22	18
Parking (all vehicles)	10	10	70	44	33
Drainage	75	35	70	83	65
Cold storage	5	0	20	0	6
Warehouse	5	50	85	33	44
Drying area	5	20	0	39	15
Public toilet	40	25	70	72	51
Fumigation equipment	10	5	0	6	5
Grading equipment	5	15	15	33	17
Drying machine	0	0	0	6	1
Mechanized crop handling	0	5	10	0	4

Source: World Bank (2007a).

commodities such as oils, ghee, whole and ground spices, honey, and whole and milled food grains. Blended edible vegetable oils and fat spreads are compulsorily required to be certified under AGMARK. As illustrated by the bottled water and soft drink pesticide residue incidents, inadequate standards and weak enforcement remain a problem.

4.7. Lack of proactivity in addressing food-safety issues

Domestic food safety scares and the more notable food-safety problems faced by Indian agro-exports suggest weak proactivity in addressing food safety concerns in India. Several factors contribute to this. In the case of exports, many if not most of the emerging SPS and international standards are widely viewed in India as not scientifically based and as representing unfair "barriers to trade" (World Bank, 2007b). These measures are viewed as efforts to protect foreign farmers or processors from competition, or are being fueled by unreasonable consumer fears in high-income countries and improved technologies for detecting hazards. Consequently, the approach of the government and private sector has been to try to negotiate away the problems with trading partners and, failing that, addressing the various measures in international standard-setting or dispute fora. As a consequence, insufficient attention is devoted to monitoring the requirements of official and private standards, interpreting their implications for Indian agriculture and using current and anticipated requirements as catalysts to upgrade existing operations and strengthen supply chain management (World Bank, 2007b).

This absence of proactivity has meant that India has either had to adopt a "defensive" strategy by avoiding markets with more stringent food safety and agricultural health standards or launch into a "fire-fighting" mode when it faces potential disruption or loss of trade due to noncompliance with standards. In the case of exports of fish and fishery products, despite problems dating from the 1980s, necessary monitoring and enforcement measures for ensuring that exports complied with food safety concerns were not put in place until the loss of European Union markets in 1997 (Henson et al., 2005).

A consequence of the lack of proactivity and the crisis management mode of operation has been the adoption of very rigorous and strict controls for commodities threatened with the loss or disruption of trade. This has led to extremely high costs of SPS compliance (World Bank, 2007b). In the case of grapes, the Government of India (GOI) Agricultural and Processed Food Products Export Development Authority (APEDA) formulated an integrated system of intensive grape supply chain oversight that included requirements that all farms growing grapes for export to Europe have to register with the Department of Agriculture; three mandatory field inspections (for registered exporters) during the crop cycle; inspection and registration of all grape export packinghouses by APEDA; mandatory pesticide residue testing from each registered field of export grapes; mandatory checking of every consignment by AGMARK to ensure conformity with EU quality specifications; and obtaining a phytosanitary certificate for every consignment.

In 2005, another procedure was added whereby National Research Center for Grapes would take a 5% sample of ex-packhouse grape consignments to retest for pesticide residues. The government also invested heavily in upgrading laboratory testing equipment, training field inspectors, subsidizing packhouse upgrades, and strengthening the National Research Centre for Grapes. Although grape exports to Europe were only about US$15 million in 2005, the cost of pesticide residue testing alone (excluding capital expenditures on laboratory equipment) is estimated at about US$680,000, equivalent to 5% of the FOB value of India's grape trade to Europe in 2005 (World Bank, 2007b).[5] If all other costs associated with the oversight of the grape supply chain including capital expenditures are added to the costs of pesticide residue testing, SPS compliance costs are estimated to account for at least 10% of the FOB value of grape exports to Europe.

While it is arguable that there are many spillovers and important lessons learned from the handling of the pesticide residue problem with grape exports and that these measures have been "successful" in that they have not resulted in further alerts or rejections, the heavy-handed approach with which the problems were addressed and the costs involved clearly suggest that it is not a strategy that is broadly replicable. Although India has not faced further rejections of exports to the EU, routine laboratory testing still reveals violative residues, indicative of the continuing need to focus on improving overall agricultural practices to ensure food safety.

4.8. Lack of good agricultural, manufacturing, and hygiene practices

The lack of good agricultural, manufacturing, and hygiene practices remains a major challenge for improving food safety both for the domestic and export market. It is only recently that efforts have been made to promote good practices. For example, the Marine Products Export Development Authority (MPEDA) promoted codes of good practice, particularly with regards to addressing antibiotic use. To this extent the organization was involved in monitoring antibiotic usage levels, providing training, and disseminating information (Henson et al., 2005). In the spices sector, the Spices Board (SB) undertook measures to address problems with regards to pesticide residues and aflatoxin. The SB, in conjunction with State Departments of Agriculture and various NGOs, supported measures to promote integrated pest management (IPM) and the production of organic spices (Jaffee, 2005). They helped address the aflatoxin concern by promoting better drying practices. The Ministry of Food Processing Industries and APEDA have both been promoting adoption of HACCP and ISO certification among processed food manufacturers through a range of training initiatives and private sector investment grants for upgrading processing plants to obtain HACCP/ISO certification.

However, the adoption of good practices remains limited. Much remains to be done in improving practices with regards to the manufacture and use of pesticides and improving post-harvest techniques. Although there have been some limited spillovers from the export sector into the domestic market in terms of improving production practices, for most commodities, farmers do not necessarily see any advantages or necessity for altering their practices since the vast majority of production is consumed in the domestic market. Until domestic consumer awareness and willingness to pay for improved food safety becomes more widespread, it is unlikely that addressing food safety concerns will become standard practice nationally.

Similarly, significant measures are needed to improve the safety of processed foods. In the food processing sector, there are a growing number of firms with modern factories and good quality assurance systems, but this segment coexists with large numbers of small firms and older factories that would need to make significant upgrades to implement HACCP and other quality assurance systems.

In the short term, developments in the food retail sector in India are likely to bring about improvements in food safety. International experience shows that modernization of the food retail sector is an important driver for change not only in the structure of production and

---

[5] Approximately 4,200 samples were tested at a cost of Rs 7,000 per sample.

wholesale marketing of produce, but also in fostering adoption of improved grades and food safety standards (Berdegué et al., 2003; Reardon and Timmer, 2005). Despite the ban on foreign direct investments in food retailing, the supermarket industry is growing rapidly, driven by investments from the Indian corporate sector.[6] Many of the modern retail outlets are beginning to undertake direct procurement from individual farmers or farmers associations. In some cases, farmers or associations supplying these outlets are required to follow a code of practice to meet quality and safety requirements of their buyers. The retail outlets are also involved in disseminating new agricultural techniques and information to their suppliers as well as providing training on quality control, produce handling, grading, and packaging.

There are also efforts by the public sector to promote good agricultural practices among producer groups and to help establish linkages with the organized food retail sector.[7] The Government of India and State governments are working closely with the supermarket industry (with support from USAID) to develop an India Good Agricultural Practice standard for agricultural produce (INDIA-GAP), which will in turn also provide the framework for government extension support to farmers.

4.9. Need for more collective action

International experience highlights the importance of collective action within the private sector to promote awareness of SPS matters, find solutions to emerging challenges, promote good agricultural and manufacturing practices, and otherwise provide a degree of self-regulation, which in turn reduces the need for government agencies to play enforcement roles. While there are some examples of successful collective action in both the spice and fishery export industries in India, it

has been lacking in many other sectors, notably in horticulture (World Bank, 2007b). For example, the Seafood Exporters Association of India (SEAI) has developed a model to provide a number of pre-processing units with common water, ice, and effluent infrastructure. SEAI in collaboration with MPEDA has also been involved in developing a system to ensure traceability for shrimp from aquaculture in order to address quality problems (Henson et al., 2005). In the spices sector, the All India Spice Exporters Forum has been an important player in trying to influence standards for pesticides in spices grown under tropical conditions and in finding solutions to address food safety concerns in its export markets (Jaffee, 2005).

5. Conclusion

The Indian experience illustrates the many challenges faced by developing countries in addressing food safety concerns in domestic and export markets. Despite a large number of food safety incidents in the past, it is only in the past 5 years or so that food safety issues have begun to receive greater attention.

Because of low consumer awareness and limited willingness to pay, the private sector engaged in agriculture, food processing, and the food retail industry in India, for the most part, has not taken the necessary steps to improve the quality and safety of food products. In most cases, the responsibility of ensuring food safety has fallen into the hands of government through enacting and enforcing legislation and setting standards. One of the positive results of globalization and the emergence of modern food retailing in India is the increased attention to quality and safety issues. As incomes are increasing, consumers are also more willing and able to pay for better-quality and safer food.

Addressing food safety issues in India will require the adoption of more appropriate legislation and better enforcement of this legislation (Table 3). Broad-based adoption of the model APM Act and the removal of the remaining agricultural commodities from the SSI reservation will foster both increased market efficiency and facilitate adoption by firms of appropriate food safety measures.

Joint efforts by the government and the private sector will be needed in a number of areas. These include better risk management, the promotion and adop-

---

[6] Corporate manufacturers such as Hindustan Lever Ltd, International Tobacco Company, Godrej, Bharti, Reliance, DCM Sriram Consolidated, RPG Group, and Pantaloon Group are setting up or have set up hypermarkets, supermarkets and retail outlets in rural areas (World Bank, 2007a).

[7] The Maharashtra Agricultural Marketing Board in collaboration with USAID is trying to promote good agricultural practices among mango farmers in the state and link these farmers with various supermarkets and other retail outlets that are interested in procuring better-quality and safer fruit.

Table 3
Role of public and private sector in enhancing food safety capacity

Role of public sector	Role of private sector
Policy and regulatory environment • Adopt domestic food safety legislation and standards suited to local risk conditions and preferences and consistent with WTO and other treaty obligations. **Risk assessment and management** • Strengthen national- or state-level systems of pest and animal disease surveillance and market surveillance programs. • Address animal health constraints that limit domestic (for imports) and foreign (for exports) market access (e.g., product inspection, development of disease-free areas). **Awareness building and promoting good practices** • Consumer awareness campaigns about food safety risk and improved hygiene at home. • Raise stakeholder awareness about and promote good agricultural, hygiene, and manufacturing practices and quality management. Incorporate into curricula of public agricultural/technical institutes and universities and extension program, including through public–private partnerships. • Accredit private laboratories and conduct reference/consistency testing. • Facilitate technical, administrative, and institutional change and innovation within the private sector, e.g., through public–private partnerships. **Public expenditures** • Invest in water supply and sanitation, marketing facilities, to reduce food safety hazards. • Support research to address food safety and agricultural health concerns. **International trade diplomacy** • Undertake continuous dialogue and periodic negotiations to address emerging constraints or opportunities.	**"Good" management practices** • Implement appropriate management practices to minimize food safety risks. Examples include "good" agricultural, hygiene, and manufacturing practices and HACCP principles. • Where commercially viable, gain formal certification for such adopted systems. • Develop incentives, advisory services, and oversight systems to induce the similar adoption of the above "good practices" by supply chain partners. **Traceability** • Develop systems and procedures to enable the traceability of raw materials and intermediate and final products in order to identify sources of hazards, manage product recalls or other emergencies, etc. **Develop Training, Advisory, and Conformity Assessment Services** • On a commercial basis, provide support services to agriculture, industry, and government related to quality and food safety management. • Invest in the needed human capital, physical infrastructure, and management systems to competitively supply such services. **Collective action and self-regulation** • Work through industry, farmer, and other organizations to share the costs of awareness raising and systems improvement, alert government to emerging issues, advocate for effective government services, and provide a measure of self-regulation through the adoption and oversight of industry "codes of practice."

Source: Adapted from World Bank (2007b).

tion of good agricultural, manufacturing, and hygiene practices, greater collective action, and some targeted public investments. Responsibilities for these functions need to be shared between the private and public sectors. While there are many critical regulatory, research, and management functions that are normally carried out by governments, the private sector also has an important role in the actual compliance with food safety requirements.

The challenges for ensuring food safety in the domestic market and in its food exports remain large. India has made some progress in the last decade to strengthen food safety measures at home and in meeting food safety and SPS standards abroad. The challenge for the future will be to adopt a more strategic, rather than crisis management, approach. This will be essential to ensuring the sustainability and cost-effectiveness of these efforts.

References

Berdegué, J., F. Balsevich, L. Flores, and T. Reardon, "Central American Supermarket's Private Standards of Quality and Safety in Procurement of Fresh Fruits and Vegetables," *Food Policy* 30 (2005), 254–269.

Bhat, R. V., and S. Vasanthi, "Mycotoxins Food Safety Risk in Developing Countries," in L. Unnevehr, ed., *Food Safety in Food Security and Trade, 2020 Vision for Food Agriculture and the*

Environment, Focus 20, Brief 3 (International Food Policy Research Institute: Washington, DC, 2003).

Boselie, D., S. Henson, and D. Weatherspoon, "Supermarket Procurement Practices in Developing Countries: Redefining the Roles of the Public and Private Sectors," *American Journal of Agricultural Economic* 85 (2003), 1155–1161.

Buzby, J. C., and L. Unnevehr, "Introduction and Overview," in Jean C. Buzby, ed., *International Trade and Food Safety, Economic Theory and Case Studies*. Agricultural Economic Report No. 828, Chapter 1, pp. 1-9 (USDA: Washington, DC, 2003).

Calvin, L., "Produce, Food Safety and International Trade, Response to US Foodborne Illness Outbreaks Associated with Imported Produce," in Jean C. Buzby, ed., *International Trade and Food Safety, Economic Theory and Case Studies*, Agricultural Economic Report No. 828, Chapter 5, 74-96 (USDA: Washington, DC, 2003).

Center for Science and Environment (CSE), *Poison vs Nutrition, A Briefing Paper on Pesticide Contamination and Food Safety*, mimeo (Center for Science and Environment: New Delhi, 2004).

Central Statistical Organization, *Socio Economic Statistics*. (Central Statistical Organization: New Delhi, 2002).

Chengappa, P. G, "Emergence of Organized Retail Chains in India During Post Liberalization Era," paper presented at the South Asia Regional Conference of International Association of Agricultural Economists Globalization of Agriculture in South Asia, Hyderabad, India, March 23-25, 2005.

Department of Small Scale Industries, "Name of the Items De-Reserved Vide Notification S.O. 420(E)," (2005) Accessed May 2006. http://www.laghu-udyog.com/publications/reserved items/dereserve03.htm.

Directorate of Plant Protection and Quarantine, "Pesticide Consumption in India," accessed May 2006 http://www.ncipm.org.in/asps/pesticides.asp.

Dohlman, E., "Mycotoxin Hazards and Regulations, Impacts on Food and Animal Feed Crop Trade," in Jean C. Buzby, ed., *International Trade and Food Safety, Economic Theory and Case Studies*, Agricultural Economic Report No. 828, Chapter 6, pp. 97-108 (USDA: Washington, DC, 2003).

Dries, L., T. Reardon, and J. Swinnen, "The Rapid Rise of Supermarkets in Central and Eastern Europe: Implications for the Agrifood Sector and Rural Development," *Development Policy Review* 22 (2004), 525–556.

Economic Research Service (ERS), "Economics of Foodborne Disease: Estimating the Benefits of Reducing Foodborne Disease," (2006), accessed January 2007 http://www.ers.usda.gov/briefing/FoodborneDisease/features.htm

Ewen, C., D. Todd, and C. Narrod, "Understanding the Links between Agriculture and Health, Agriculture, Food Safety, and Food Borne Diseases," *2020 Vision for Food, Agriculture and the Environment*, Focus 10, Brief 5 (International Food Policy Research Institute: Washington, DC, 2006).

Henson, S., "Food Safety Issues in International Trade", in L. Unnevehr, ed., *Food Safety in Food Security and Trade, 2020 Vision for Food Agriculture and the Environment*, Focus 20, Brief 10 (International Food Policy Research Institute: Washington, DC, 2003).

Henson, S., M. Saqib, and D. Rajasena, "Impact of Sanitary Measures on Exports of Fishery Products from India: The Case of Kerela," *Agriculture and Rural Development Discussion Paper* (World Bank: Washington, DC, 2005).

Hindu Business Line, "Pesticides in Soft Drinks—Industry May Present Views to JPC Today," accessed May 2006 http://www.thehindubusinessline.com/2003/10/21/stories/2003102101880500.htm.

Indian Council of Medical Research, "Pesticide Pollution: Trends and Perspectives," *ICMR Bulletin*, Vol. 31 (Indian Council of Medical Research: New Delhi, 2001).

Indiastat, accessed May 2006 http://www.indiastat.com/india/ShowData.asp?secid = 16611&ptid=367635&level=5

Jaffee, S., "Delivering and Taking the Heat: Indian Spices and Evolving Product and Process Standards," *Agriculture and Rural Development Discussion Paper* No.19 (World Bank: Washington, DC, 2005).

Marshall, F., R. Agarwal, D. te Lintelo, D. S. Bhupal, R. P. B. Singh, N. Mukherjee, C. Sen, N. Poole, M. Agrawal, and S. D. Singh, "Heavy Metal Contamination of Vegetables in Delhi," report prepared for the UK Department for International Development, mimeo, 2003.

Mathur, H. B., H. C. Agarwal, S. Johnson, and N. Saikia, "Analysis of Pesticide Residues in Blood Samples from Village of Punjab, mimeo, "CSE/PML/PR-21/2005 (Center for Science and Environment: New Delhi, 2005).

Mathur, H. B., S. Johnson, A. Kumar, *Analysis of Pesticide Residues in Soft Drinks*, mimeo (Center for Science and Environment: New Delhi, 2003).

Ministry of Commerce, *Annual Report* 2004/05 (Ministry of Commerce: New Delhi, 2005).

Ministry of Food Processing Industries, *Annual Report* 2004/05 (Ministry of Food Processing Industries: New Delhi, 2005).

Mukherjee, A., and H. Patel, *FDI in Retail Sector India* (Academic Foundation in association with ICRIER and Ministry of Consumer Affairs, Food and Public Distribution Government of India: New Delhi, 2005).

Otsuki, T., J. S. Wilson, and M. Sewadeh, "Saving Two in a Billion: Quantifying the Trade Effect of European Food Safety Standards on African Exports," *Food Policy* 26 (2001), 495–514.

Patnaik, G., *Review of Government of India Agricultural Marketing/Processing Policies and Programs*, mimeo (Global AgriSystems Pvt. Ltd:New Delhi, 2005).

Pingali, P., and Y. Khwaja, "Globalization of India Diets and the Transformation of Food Supply Systems," Keynote address XV11 annual Conference of The Indian Society of Agricultural Marketing, 5th February, 2004, in Acharya N.G. Ranga Agricultural University and Indian Society of Agricultural Marketing.

Rao, C. H., "Reform Agenda for Agriculture," *Economic and Political Weekly* 38 (2003), 615–620.

Reardon, T., and C. P. Timmer, "Transformation of Markets for Agricultural Output in Developing Countries since 1950: How Has Thinking Changed?" in R. E. Evenson, P. Pingali, and T. P. Schultz, eds., *Handbook of Agricultural Economics (Vol.3): Agricultural Development: Farmers, Farm Production and Farm Markets* (Amsterdam: North-Holland, 2007).

Unnevehr, L. J., "Overview," in L. Unnevehr, ed., *Food Safety in Food Security and Trade, 2020 Vision for Food Agriculture and the Environment*, Focus 20, Brief 1 (International Food Policy Research Institute: Washington, DC, 2003).

Willems, S., E. Roth, and E. van Roekel, "Changing Public and Private Food Safety and Quality Requirements in Europe—Challenges for Fresh Produce and Fish Exporters in Developing Countries," *Agriculture and Rural Development Discussion Paper* 15 (World Bank: Washington, DC, 2005).

World Health Organization, "Core Health Indicators," (2006), accessed May 2006 at ww3/who/int/whois/core/core'select'process.cfm

World Bank, *India: Scaling-up Access to Finance for India's Rural Poor*. Report No. 30740-IN (Finance and Private Sector Development Unit, South Asia Region, World Bank: Washington, DC, 2004).

World Bank, *Food Safety and Agricultural Health Standards: Challenges and Opportunities for Developing Country Exports*. Report No. 31207 (Poverty Reduction and Economic Management Sector Unit: Washington, DC, 2005a).

World Bank, *India Re-energizing the Agricultural Sector to Sustain Growth and Reduce Poverty* (Oxford University Press: New Delhi, 2005b).

World Bank, *India Taking Agriculture to the Market* Report No. 35953-1N. (South Asia Sustainable Development, Development Department, World Bank: Washington, DC, 2007a).

World Bank, *India's Emergent Horticultural Exports: Addressing Sanitary and Phyto-Sanitary Standards and Other Challenges* (South Asia Sustainable Development, Development Department, World Bank: Washington, DC, 2007b).

World Bank, *Land Policies for Growth* (Oxford University Press: New Delhi, 2007c).

Food safety as a global public good

Laurian J. Unnevehr*

Abstract

Globalization of the food system increases the shared risks from food safety, making it a global public good. Globally shared food safety risks include microbial pathogens, pesticide residues, or mycotoxins. Food safety is addressed as a global public good through improved private sector information, institutional innovations such as the Sanitary and Phytosanitary Standards Agreement under the World Trade Organization, and trade capacity building to improve food safety in developing country exports. Although meeting standards for high-income consumers motivates trade facilitation, there could be large positive spillovers for developing country consumers from such investments.

JEL classification: Q13, Q17, Q18, O19

Keywords: food safety; global public good; trade facilitation

1. Introduction

The links between food and health have received much attention in the last decade, with high-profile media coverage of food safety risks and of nutrition research findings. In part, this media coverage reflects the growing scientific understanding of food safety risks and ability to detect and track risks, as well as exciting advances in nutritional genomics and understanding of the functional characteristics of foods. The appearance of this information in the media, together with rising consumer incomes and aging populations in high-income countries, has spurred consumer food demand for health characteristics and for new food regulations.

At the same time, diets and food delivery systems are becoming more similar around the world, and trade in high-valued products is growing. The standards and delivery systems in high-income countries provide a model that is being adopted rapidly in middle-income countries. In this context, food–health linkages have become global public goods, because food–diet risks, benefits of risk control, and information, are increasingly interconnected across national boundaries.

Institutional innovations are emerging to address food safety as a global public good, such as widely recognized private standards for food safety assurance, the Agreement on Sanitary and Phytosanitary Measures (SPS Agreement) under the World Trade Organization (WTO), and foreign assistance aimed at improving food safety management for developing country exports, sometimes called trade capacity building. Previous studies have examined quality assurance in the private sector (Henson and Reardon, 2005), the role of standards in reducing trade (e.g., Otsuki et al., 2001), and the effect of the SPS Agreement in mitigating trade disputes over food safety (Josling et al., 2004; Unnevehr and Roberts, 2005). This article will contribute to the literature in three ways: First, the global public goods framework is used to recast approaches to addressing market failures, and to measuring costs and benefits from food safety improvement. Second, how the global public goods framework could be used to address recurring food safety failures in international trade is examined. Third, newly available data on trade capacity building provide a first look at this approach to sharing the costs of improvement.

This article begins with recent evidence on the "globalization" of food demand and food delivery, to demonstrate why demand for global public goods in the food system is growing. Next, the conceptual framework for

Department of Agricultural and Consumer Economics, University of Illinois, Urbana-Champaign, Chicago, Illinois.

food safety as a global public good is presented, including the implications for cost-benefit analysis. Then, the article turns to food safety failures in international trade, as revealed by United States (U.S.) import detentions and European Commission (E.C.) alerts, and how investments in global public goods might address these failures. Last, the trade capacity building investments by the U.S. and the European Union, as reported to the WTO, are examined to see how far these efforts address identified failures. Implications are drawn for future investments in food safety as a global public good.

2. Globalization in diets and food delivery

Income growth is a powerful force leading food expenditures towards certain universal patterns: reduced consumption of starchy staples, increased consumption of meat, fruits and vegetables, and processed high-value foods (Bennett, 1941; Regmi and Gelhar, 2005). These trends in demand are reshaping agricultural trade patterns. Trade in high-valued agricultural products is growing faster than trade in commodities since 1990, and trade is growing faster as a percent of world production for income-elastic commodities such as chicken and fruits (Unnevehr, 2004). Trade in perishable products such as seafood, meats, fruits, and vegetables, doubled from 1990 to 2004. Global food trade has become more specialized, with high-income countries exporting grains and processed products to low- and middle-income countries, who in turn export labor-intensive horticultural and fishery products (Aksoy, 2005). The growth in trade for perishable and high-value products of all kinds reflects expanding global demand as incomes rise and technical barriers to trade are reduced (Dyck and Nelson, 2003; Regmi and Gelhar, 2005). Even animal products, where emerging animal diseases have closed borders, have seen growth in trade (Blayney et al., 2006).

Changes in the composition of diets are not the only influence on the global food system. Food product and retail models from high-income countries have become increasingly common in middle-income countries through expansion of multinational retail and food service chains (Reardon et al., 2003; Coyle, 2006). Tastes and diets are being shaped by this global expansion of modern food retailing. Table 1 shows selected indicators of food system modernization, summarized for selected high-, upper-middle-, and lower-middle-income countries. Demand for packaged foods, soft drinks, food service, and fast food are all highly income elastic, and show the expected pattern of increase across country income categories. For example, packaged goods as a share of food sales increase from 26% for lower-middle-income countries to 52% for high-income countries; annual fast-food expenditures increase from $17 per capita to $191. The share of food purchased in standardized retail outlets (supermarkets, hypermarkets, discounters, and convenience stores) also increases across income categories, from 53% in lower-middle-income countries to 76% in high-income countries. The rates of growth in these indicators are strikingly higher in the upper-middle-income countries. Food service and fast-food service expenditures per capita are growing at 5% and 7% annually, which is faster than income growth in these countries. Change is occurring most quickly in China, Indonesia, South Africa, the Czech Republic, Hungary, and Brazil. As this list of countries indicates, the changes are not confined to a particular region, but are occurring in middle-income countries around the world.

The expansion of multinational retailing, food services, and high-value products is leading to what Birdsall and Lawrence (1999) call "deep integration" in how food is produced, delivered, and consumed around the world. This in turn leads to greater use of uniform standards of quality, content, and delivery (Caswell et al., 1998; Regmi and Gelhar, 2005). Deep integration inevitably brings increased sharing of food risks, including both acute and chronic risks. As trade integrates the food supply, food safety risks are increasingly shared across borders.

The demand for food safety improvements is increasing, driven by new science, greater consumer awareness, and the higher income needed to translate desire into effective demand. Changes in food production, marketing, and consumption have altered the incidence of risks and shifted responsibility from consumers to producers. Larger operations to produce meat or fish can introduce new hazards or speed the spread of existing ones. The increased purchase of prepared food or use of food service reduces consumer control over food preparation, shifting responsibility for safety to the food industry. New science and new detection methods have improved our understanding

Table 1
Selected indicators of food system modernization

	Lower middle income[a]		Upper middle income[b]		High income[c]	
	Level[d]	Growth[e]	Level[d]	Growth[e]	Level[d]	Growth[e]
Share of food sales in standardized retail outlets[f] (%)	52.76	1.03 China	61.10	1.66 Czech Republic	76.47	0.82
Share of packaged food in total food expenditures (%)	25.93	0.20 Brazil	39.83	−0.18 Czech Republic	52.25	−0.04
Per cap food service expenditures ($)	99.16	2.82 Indonesia	234.31	5.18 South Africa	854.54	4.78
Per cap fast-food expenditures ($)	17.08	4.50 Indonesia	38.73	6.58 South Africa	190.87	7.25
Per cap soft-drink expenditures ($)	32.90	3.26 China	42.47	6.81 Hungary	144.23	4.32

[a] Lower middle income includes Brazil, Colombia, Peru, China, Indonesia, Philippines, Thailand, Algeria, Egypt, Jordan, Morocco, Tunisia.

[b] Upper middle income includes Czech Republic, Hungary, Poland, Chile, Mexico, Malaysia, South Africa.

[c] High income includes Canada, USA, Australia, Japan, France, UK, Germany, Netherlands, Austria, Belgium, Finland, Greece, Italy, Spain, Sweden, Denmark, Ireland, Portugal.

[d] Level is average for latest year available which is 2005 for retail outlet share and 2004 for all other indicators.

[e] Growth is absolute change for percentage (share) indicators and percentage change for absolute variables. Change is over the years 1998–2005 for retail outlet share, 1998–2004 for packaged food, 1999–2004 for food service and fast-food expenditures, and 1990–2004 for soft-drink expenditures. The country with the fastest growth rate is indicated for each variable.

[f] Standardized retail outlets includes supermarkets, hypermarkets, discounters, and convenience stores.
Source: Euromonitor.

of risks and their consequences. Consumer awareness and incomes are both increasing, leading to greater demand for safety. Both the food industry and regulators have responded with new public and private standards.

In spite of this increased attention, food safety remains an important risk even in developed countries. In the U.S., the Centers for Disease Control estimate that there are 76 million cases of foodborne illness annually, and 5,200 deaths. The estimated U.S. cost of five common pathogens in 2000 was $6.9 billion in terms of medical expenses and lost productivity (U.S. Department of Agriculture, Economic Research Service, 2005). The negative consequences of poor food safety are even more important in the developing world, where the World Health Organization estimates that as much as 70% of the 1.8 million annual deaths from diarrhea are linked to contaminated food. Exposure to mycotoxins that pose chronic cancer risks is an important risk in parts of Africa. Pesticide exposure in the farm environment has also been implicated in farm household health in developing countries. Thus, food

safety risks are a global concern. The next section of the article considers how food safety improvements could be viewed as a global public good.

3. The global public good framework and food safety

Ferroni and Mody (2002) define a global public good as a "benefit providing utility that is, in principle, available on an international scale" (p. 6). Examples include property rights, predictability, and nomenclature, which can enable provision of final public goods, such as health or environmental quality (Kaul et al., 1999; Ferroni and Mody, 2002). The potential for global public goods arises whenever externalities (either positive or negative) cross borders (Kaul et al., 1999). To be truly global public goods, they must be nonrival and nonexcludable across international borders and global in scope. Of course, there are degrees to which goods are nonrival or nonexcludable in practice and there are variations in the international scope of global public goods.

Before considering why food safety is a global public good, it is useful to consider why it is often a local or national public good. Frequent public intervention at the national level to ensure food safety arises from several public goods characteristics. Individual producers or firms may not be able to adequately control a food safety hazard (externality) without cooperative effort, and the public sector may be needed to enforce controls, certify sanitary conditions (nonexcludability), or to make supporting infrastructure investments. Consumers may not be able to judge food safety or to avoid hazards (information asymmetry), or it may be desirable to protect vulnerable groups (equity), such as small children, by setting a minimum safety standard.

The changes in international trade, demand, and regulation discussed above have made food safety a global public good. With growth in food and animal trade, food safety risks, costs of hazard reduction, and benefits from improvement are all shared across borders. Food produced under one safety regime must pass standards under another, and standards are increasingly stringent. Risks vary across countries because there are differences in how food is produced and eaten. While trade can provide alternatives for consumers and potentially lower costs of safety, it can also introduce unfamiliar hazards or new hazards can disrupt trade. Incentives and information may be imperfect in international supply chains, many of which are relatively new.

Three potential "gaps" hinder provision of global public goods: a jurisdictional gap (when national borders become irrelevant); a participation gap (when new groups need to participate in governance); and an incentives gap (when international cooperation is not backstopped by incentives to change behavior) (Kaul et al., 1999). Food safety has all three gaps: There is a jurisdictional gap between the importing market and the exporting producer. There is an incentives gap when consumers in one country do not fully reward efforts for food safety improvement in another country, often because they cannot distinguish safety in the marketplace. Finally, there can be a participation gap in setting food safety standards; in other words, not all countries contribute equally to the process.

Three categories of approaches to internalizing global incentives have been identified (Ferroni and Mody, 2002). "Best shot" pushes or pulls private innovation using public funds, and for food safety would include investments in research for managing or assessing risks, such as development of new testing and tracking technologies. "Summation" is the development of global mechanisms to enforce individual behavior, so that the "sum" of individual actions leads to the desired outcome. An example is the use of mechanisms to enforce behavior along the supply chain or across borders through the private sector's use of third party certification or the application of internationally recognized principles to food safety regulation. "Weakest link" is the use of foreign aid to overcome the constraint imposed by those providing the smallest effort, for example when poor countries receive a subsidy to control animal or plant disease to prevent its spread elsewhere or foreign aid to help developing countries improve food safety in exports.

Using the global public good framework to assess food safety issues, there are at least three sets of questions. First, there are questions related to sharing risks, costs and benefits. For example, when would investments from one country in another country have benefits for the donor as well as the recipient? When would it yield overall welfare gains for one country to subsidize costs of control in another country? Such questions relate to the role of foreign aid in trade capacity building.

Second, there are questions related to the global consequences of individual countries' regulations. When would an adjustment of standards result in benefits from trade that more than offset consumer risk? Would harmonization of food safety standards increase or decrease consumer welfare? Would harmonization reduce the costs of coordinating control? These questions are currently addressed most often by the SPS Agreement under the WTO, and the related institutional framework for standards under the Codex Alimentarius.

Third, there are a set of questions about how best to enhance global welfare through capturing spillover benefits from investments in food safety. For example, if some global food safety czar could direct investments, where would they have the highest marginal net benefit? When would international coordination of management activities reduce the total costs of control? Could information in international markets be improved so as to internalize incentives for food safety improvement? Such questions are beyond the scope of most current institutional frameworks.

These questions set the stage for considering important food safety failures in international supply chains.

4. Food safety issues in international trade

One indicator of breakdowns in global food safety management is provided by public monitoring and rejection of food imports for failure to meet food safety standards. Product refusals and recalls have high private costs. When imports are refused or general alerts are raised about a product, it represents a failure in food safety management. When such refusals or alerts occur frequently for particular hazards or products, it is clear that management is challenging and imperfect. This may suggest areas for public intervention or investment.

The U.S. Food and Drug Administration reports information from import monitoring regarding import detentions and refusals. U.S. import detention data have been analyzed by several authors, including Allshouse et al. (2003), Caswell and Wang (2001), and Unnevehr (2000). The European Commission posts annual summary reports of similar problems, called rapid alerts, which reflect notifications of safety problems by member countries. Most of these alerts are for imports from third countries. Jaffee and Henson (2005) looked at both U.S. and E.C. data, and concluded that standards pose minimal barriers to trade overall. While that may be true, these two sources of data also reveal recurring food safety problems that point to failures in either private management or public policy.

Table 2 reports summary information from these two data sources. For the U.S., most detentions arise from microbial hazards in seafood, pesticides in vegetables, or contamination in fruits or nuts. (Meat and poultry are not prominent due to the separate import monitoring system that requires U.S. Department of Agriculture audits of foreign plants. This "preapproval" prevents most problems at the border.) The country sources of products most often detained include Vietnam, Thailand, and Indonesia for seafood; and China, Guatemala, and Mexico for vegetables. Middle-income countries are the most important sources of problems. Although they are important suppliers, it is not solely the volume of their trade that results in their overrepresentation in the detentions data base. For example, the rate of detentions for seafood imports was much higher for Thailand than for Canada, even though both export similar volumes to the U.S. (Allshouse et al., 2003).

The E.C. 2004 Rapid Alert report shows that mycotoxins, chemical contaminants (e.g., prohibited food dyes), microbial pathogens, and veterinary drug residues are the most important hazards appearing in alerts related to products from third countries. Nuts (the primary source of violative mycotoxins), seafood and fish, meats and poultry, and fruits are the most important products implicated in alerts. Third countries of origin that were most common in alerts included three exporters of nuts to the European Union: Iran, Turkey,

Table 2
Food safety management failures in global supply chains

	U.S. FDA Import Detentions, 2001	E.C. Rapid Alert Notifications, 2004
Most important hazards	Microbial contamination (e.g., salmonella in seafood)	Mycotoxins
	Pesticide residues (e.g., violative residues on vegetables)	Other chemical contaminants (e.g., additives and food dyes)
	Other sanitary violations (e.g., "filthy" fruit)	Microbiological contamination
		Veterinary drug residues
Most important products	Vegetables	Nuts
	Seafood	Fish
	Fruits and nuts	Meat and poultry
	Spices	Fruits and vegetables
	Dairy	Spices
Most important countries of origin	Vietnam, Thailand, and Indonesia (seafood)	Iran (nuts)
	China, Guatemala, and Mexico (vegetables)	Turkey (nuts, fruits and vegetables, spices)
		China (nuts, fruits and vegetables)
		India (seafood, spices)
		Brazil (poultry, meat, seafood)

Sources: European Commission, 2004; Allshouse et al., 2003; and Buzby et al., 2003.

and China; as well as two exporters of fish and/or meat: Brazil and India.

For both the European Union and U.S., it is middle-income exporting countries that are most often implicated in food safety alerts or detentions. Microbial pathogens in seafood and fish are a common and recurring problem. Other issues of importance differ between these two importers, reflecting differences in standards and regulation. In the European Union, mycotoxins and chemical contaminants are more important. This reflects, at least in part, the very high standards for mycotoxins imposed by the European Union in 2001. These standards were controversial, and elicited considerable comment from trading partners (Otsuki et al., 2001). The 2004 alert data show that these standards are indeed a source of continuing difficulty for exporters of nuts to the European Union. For the U.S., mycotoxins and food additives are not as important in detention data, but pesticide residues are at issue. Zepp et al. (1998) found that most pesticide residue violations in U.S. imports are for unregistered chemicals, rather than for residues that exceed Maximum Residue Limits (MRLs).

5. Addressing food safety failures as global public goods

The type of market failure differs among these food safety hazards, but in all cases, international trade has made the local or national public good into a global public good. For each hazard, the global public good questions raised above are considered. These include the type of trade capacity building needed, whether international standard setting could mitigate failures, and whether there would be spillover benefits for consumers in the exporting country.

5.1. Microbial hazards

Microbial hazards are naturally occurring and increasingly regulated in high-income countries. Their importance in seafood trade reflects the difficulties of enforcing sanitation and cold chain control over a longer supply chain, as well as in countries with minimal public sanitation infrastructure (e.g., Cato and Subasinge, 2003). Microbial pathogens can enter the food supply at any point during processing and transit,

multiply once present, and spread more widely as a result of commingled supply sources. Thus, incentives for control may be difficult to enforce or internalize. Capacity building investment for this hazard would ideally address the "weakest link," by focusing on sanitation infrastructure and on implementation of the Hazard Analysis Critical Control Point (HACCP) system. Standards and equivalence are difficult to define for this hazard, as it is costly to test (Unnevehr and Jensen, 1999). Verification focuses on assessment of processes more often than products. This makes it difficult to determine equivalence in internationally traded products. There are likely large spillover benefits for consumers within the exporting country from improvements in microbial pathogen control, as this is such an important source of health risk in developing countries.

5.2. Pesticides

Pesticides are regulated so as to minimize risks to human health and the environment. In the U.S., pesticides are registered for use only on particular crops. Some violations in international trade arise from an "orphan goods" problem. There are insufficient incentives to undertake the costs of registration for minor uses outside of the U.S., leading to the violations that arise from unregistered uses. For registered uses that exceed Maximum Residue Limits, research and extension are needed for integrated pest management in tropical horticulture (as illegal pesticide use is rarely economic). The knowledge base for pest management in tropical horticultural crops is an area of underinvestment (Norton et al., 2003), and thus, needed capacity building. Problems with unregistered chemicals might be overcome by use of internationally recognized Maximum Residue Limit standards set by the Codex Alimentarius. The spillover benefits of better pesticide management for developing country producers, through reduced exposure in the farm environment, are likely larger than the benefits from reduced residues for high-income consumers.

5.3. Mycotoxins

Mycotoxins, produced by fungi on crops, are a naturally occurring hazard, which is more likely to be present in certain production conditions, especially in the humid tropics. Management in crop production and marketing can reduce the incidence of mycotoxins, but they are sometimes impossible to eliminate in the food supply, except through diversion of supply to alternative uses, such as animal feeds. Capacity building investment could foster innovation in management, and inspection and certification to internalize incentives. This is a hazard that might be mitigated by trade, if supply from areas with lower incidence can replace supply from areas with higher incidence. The differences in standards among high-income countries provide a likely opportunity for gains from harmonization. The spillover benefits for developing country consumers might be substantial, especially for control of mycotoxins in staples.

5.4. Veterinary drug residues

Veterinary drug use is regulated to reduce risks to human and animal health. Illegal veterinary drug residues arise from use of banned drugs or illegal use of drugs, and these pose various kinds of risks to consumers, including possible allergic reactions, chronic health risks from exposure, or the development of antibiotic-resistant organisms. Capacity-building investments might include inspection and monitoring, or research on improved management. It is possible that subsidies to reduce antibiotic use would have global public health benefits in preventing the development of resistance. Standards differ among countries, and harmonization to the Codex standard would enhance trade (Wilson et al., 2003), although it is not clear how it might alter consumer risks. Spillover benefits might be large for consumers everywhere, if retention of antibiotic effectiveness results from more effective regulation.

The hazards identified as issues in data from these two major markets are not the only food safety issues in international trade, but they do represent issues of recurring concern. Moreover, they represent long-standing hazards that have been controversial in regulation and are costly to manage in any country. Fortunately, with the possible exception of microbial pathogens, the likely risks to high-income consumers from the identified "failures" in food safety are small. And, trade in most of the commodities highlighted in Table 2 has been expanding, notwithstanding food safety issues.

There do seem to be opportunities for improved global management of food safety. First, capacity-building investments might include research to support management and control of hazards, improved infrastructure for sanitation and preservation, and inspection or monitoring to support certification. Second, greater efforts towards equivalence recognition or even harmonization of international standards would mitigate difficulties for all of the above hazards. These two areas have been identified as the least successful elements of the SPS Agreement implementation (Unnevehr and Roberts, 2005), suggesting the need for greater investment in these facilitating mechanisms. Such investments have been subsidized by efforts since 2001 to support developing country participation in the international standard-setting bodies. However, the political will to adopt and utilize internationally recognized standards is still lacking in many cases. Third, the existence of stringent standards in high-income countries may provide the motivation for investments in food safety in developing countries that have large spillover benefits for developing country consumers and producers.

6. Trade capacity building to address food safety

In 2001, WTO members agreed on steps to improve implementation of the current agreements at the Doha Ministerial (WTO, 2001). These initiatives included, among others, increased technical and financial assistance to enable developing countries to increase their participation in the international standards organizations and to fulfill their obligations (such as the creation of enquiry points) under these agreements; and increased technical assistance to help developing countries to comply with new standards if they pose significant impediments to trade.

The WTO and the Organization for Economic Cooperation and Development (OECD) jointly maintain the Doha Development Agenda Trade Capacity Building Database, which provides information on bilateral and multilateral efforts to build trade capacity in less-developed countries. Projects specifically addressing Sanitary and Phytosanitary (SPS) Measures were downloaded for analysis on May 30, 2006. These data reflect efforts from a total of 695 SPS projects, with total expenditures of $270 million.

Table 3
Technical assistance for sanitary and phytosanitary issues, 2001 to May 2006

	United States		European Union Members[a]	
	Number	Million $	Number	Million $
All projects	237	$30.76	117	$176.0
Most important individual country recipients (number projects)	Mexico (24) Serbia and Montenegro (9) Egypt (7)		Guatemala (5) Iran (3) Colombia (3)	
Capacity building projects[b]	142	$24.8	41	$47.8
Risk-specific projects[c]	48	$2.1	47	$51.2
Most important risks (number projects)	General food safety (14) Pesticides (8) Microbial pathogens (5)		General Food Safety (27) Phytosanitary (9) Animal Health (5)	
Method-specific projects[d]	29	$2.3	15	$68.1
Most important methods (number projects)	GAP/GMP (12) HACCP (7)		Inspection (8) Testing (5)	
Commodity-specific projects[e]	18	$1.4	13	$8.9
Most important commodities (number projects)	Fish (9) Fruits and vegetables (5)		Fruits and vegetables (3) Meats and poultry (3)	

[a] EU projects include those administered by the European Commission, as well as bilateral projects originating from EU members: France, Germany, Spain, Belgium, Netherlands, United Kingdom, Portugal, and Sweden.

[b] General investments in capacity building, such as training on SPS issues, workshops, or consultations.

[c] Risks include pesticides, grain standards, mycotoxins, veterinary drug residues, animal health, bioterrorism, biotechnology, bioengineering, microbial pathogens, general food risks (e.g., acrylamide, food additives) and phytosanitary (i.e., plant health).

[d] Methods include Hazard Analysis Critical Control Point systems (HACCP), process control, sanitation, Good Agricultural Practices (GAP), Good Manufacturing Practices (GMP), inspection, testing and laboratories, and traceability.

[e] Commodities includes fish, fruits and vegetables, grains, meats, herbs/medicines, cocoa/coffee, animal feeds, animal by-products, and forestry products.
Source: World Trade Organization Trade Capacity Building Database (WTO, 2006).

Table 3 reports information about the projects funded by the U.S. and the European Union (including member countries). The U.S. funded $31 million in 237 projects; and the European Union countries invested $176 million in 117 projects. These two major donor sources account for half of the projects and three-quarters of the funding represented in the database on SPS projects. Project descriptions available in the database were used to classify projects according to whether they are general investments in capacity building (e.g., training on SPS issues, workshops, consultations) or whether they address specific risks, management methods, or commodities (Table 3). Most projects funded by the U.S. and the European Union countries fell into the category of general capacity building, and many of those had multilateral recipients (e.g., a training workshop is held with participation from several developing countries or the same workshop repeated in several countries).

Projects focused on specific risks or countries tend to line up with the sources of risk identified in Table 3. U.S. projects addressed commodities and risks identified as issues in the FDA data, i.e., fish, fruits and vegetables, food safety and pesticides. The methods that were the focus of capacity building would largely translate into better food safety control. One of the countries identified in Table 3, Mexico, was also the recipient of the largest number of country-specific projects. The EU projects with a specific focus primarily addressed general food safety, or were focused on inspection and testing methods which can address all SPS risks. Commodities specifically addressed by projects included those with greater problems, with the exceptions of nuts and fish. Of the countries receiving assistance, Iran stands out as also appearing in Table 2, and two of the three projects for Iran address mycotoxins (these were the only projects specifically addressing that risk). Thus, EU efforts in the more focused projects were more general in nature, while the U.S. efforts in focused projects relate more closely to problems shown in Table 2.

Trade facilitation, particularly focused on SPS measures, is a relatively new activity. The emphasis on general capacity building can be seen as a sensible first step that sets the stage for more specific activities in particular sectors or to address particular risks. The focus on inspection, testing, and food safety management in some projects is also a way to address multiple risks, with potential positive spillovers for recipient country consumers. However, it seems clear that more could be done to address the persistent problems that appear in Table 2.

7. Conclusions and implications for future global investments

The global public goods framework is appropriate for food safety, given the increased international sharing of risks, costs, and benefits from food safety improvement. Sharing of control costs, coordination of risk management, and capturing international spillovers from investments would enhance the net benefits from global food safety management, particularly in the growing food export trade from developing countries to developed countries.

Three food safety problems present continuing challenges—microbial pathogens in seafood, fish, and meat; pesticide residues on horticultural products; and mycotoxins in nuts. All of these challenges might be mitigated through greater attention to harmonization and equivalence in setting standards, reinforcing the finding of Unnevehr and Roberts (2005) that these were areas of relative weakness in implementation of the SPS Agreement. Although higher standards in developed countries impose costs and barriers to trade, they also motivate foreign aid for trade capacity building. Such capacity building could address these challenges through investments in research to support management and control of hazards, improved infrastructure for sanitation and preservation, and inspection or monitoring to support certification. Recent trade capacity building efforts are largely very general in nature, and likely represent only the first step towards meaningful efforts to reduce hazards.

Because it is increasingly a global public good, there is likely underinvestment in food safety. Directing global public good investments for greatest global benefit will require understanding of the incidence of benefits and costs both within and across borders, of the potential benefits from coordination in standard setting and control, and of the potential positive spillovers for low-income consumers. Motivation for such investments may come about through high-income consumers' growing demand for higher standards, but there could be large positive spillovers for developing country consumers as well.

Acknowledgments

This article draws upon work supported by cooperative agreements with the U.S. Department of Agriculture's Economic Research Service. Thanks are due to my cooperators, Jean Buzby, Anita Regmi, and Donna Roberts, for their guidance and comments, and to Sean Peters and Hiroyuki Takeshima for research assistance. All interpretations and any errors are the responsibility of the author.

References

Aksoy, M. A., "The Evolution of Agricultural Trade Flows," in M. A. Aksoy and J. C. Beghin, eds., *Global Agricultural Trade and Developing Countries* (World Bank: Washington, DC, 2005).

Allshouse, J., J. Buzby, D. Harvey, and D. Zorn, "International Trade and Seafood Safety," in J. Buzby, ed., *International Trade and Food Safety: Economic Theory and Case Studies*, AER-828, U.S. (Department of Agriculture, Economic Research Service: Washington, DC, 2003). Available at http://www.ers.usda.gov/publications/aer828/.

Bennett, M. K., "Wheat in National Diets," *Wheat Studies* 18 (1941), 37–76.

Birdsall, N., and R. Z. Lawrence, "Deep Integration and Trade Agreements: Good for Developing Countries?" in I. Kaul, I. Grunberg, and M. A. Stern, eds., *Global Public Goods: International Cooperation in the 21st Century* (UNDP and Oxford University Press: New York, 1999).

Blayney, D., J. Dyck, and D. Harvey, "Economic Effects of Animal Diseases Linked to Trade Dependency," *Amber Waves* 4 (2006), 23–29.

Buzby, J., L. J. Unnevehr, and J. Allshouse, "Analysis of FDA Detention Data by Product, Violation, and Country Source," unpublished working paper (2003).

Caswell, J. A., M. Bredahl, and N. Hooker, "How Quality Management Metasystems are Affecting the Food Industry," *Review of Agricultural Economics* 20 (1998), 547–557.

Caswell, J. A., and J. Wang, "Quantifying Regulatory Barriers to

Asian-U.S. Food Trade," *Journal of Agribusiness* 19 (2001), 121–128.

Cato, J. C., and S. Subasinge, "Case Study: The Shrimp Export Industry in Bangladesh," in L. J. Unnevehr, ed., *Food Safety in Food Security and Food Trade*, Vision 2020 Focus Brief 10 (International Food Policy Research Institute: Washington, DC, 2003).

Coyle, W., "A Revolution in Food Retailing Underway in the Asia-Pacific Region," *Amber Waves* 3 (2006), 22–29.

Dyck, J., and K. Nelson, *Structure of the Global Markets for Meat* AIB-785 (U.S. Department of Agriculture, Economic Research Service: Washington, DC, 2003).

European Commission, "Annual Report on the Functioning of the Rapid Alert System for Food and Feed (RASFF), Health and Consumer Protection Directorate General," (2004), accessed May 5, 2006, http://ec.europa.eu/food/food/rapidalert/report2004_en.pdf.

Ferroni, M., and A. Mody, *International Public Goods: Incentives, Measurement, and Financing* (World Bank and Kluwer Academic Publishers: Washington, DC, 2002).

Henson, S., and T. Reardon, "Private Agri-Food Standards: Implications for Food Policy and the Agri-Food System," *Food Policy* 30 (2005), 241–53.

Jaffee, S., and S. Henson, "Standards and Agro-Food Exports from Developing Countries: Rebalancing the Debate," in M. A. Aksoy, and J. C. Beghin, eds., *Global Agricultural Trade and Developing Countries* (World Bank: Washington, DC, 2005).

Josling, T., D. Roberts, and D. Orden, *Food Regulation and Trade: Toward a Safe and Open Global System* (Institute for International Economics: Washington, DC, 2004).

Kaul, I., I. Grunberg, and M. A. Stern, eds., *Global Public Goods: International Cooperation in the 21st Century* (United Nations Development Program and Oxford University Press: New York, 1999).

Norton, G. W., G. E. Sanchez, D. Clarke-Harris, and H. K. Traore, "Case Study: Reducing Pesticide Residues on Horticultural Crops," in L. J. Unnevehr, ed., *Food Safety in Food Security and Food Trade*, Vision 2020 Focus Brief 10 (International Food Policy Research Institute: Washington, DC, 2003).

Otsuki, T., J. Wilson, and M. Sewadeh, "Saving Two in a Billion: Quantifying the Trade Effect of European Food Safety Standards on African Exports," *Food Policy* 26 (2002), 495–514.

Reardon, T., C. P. Timmer, C. B. Barrett, and J. Berdegue, "The Rise of Supermarkets in Africa, Asia, and Latin America," *American Journal of Agricultural Economics* 85 (2003), 1140–1146.

Regmi, A., and M. Gelhar, eds., *New Directions in Global Food Markets.* AIB-794 (U.S. Deptartment of Agriculture, Economic Research Service: Washington, DC, 2005).

Unnevehr, L. J., "Food Safety Issues and Fresh Food Product Exports from LDCs," *Agricultural Economics* 23 (2000), 231–240.

Unnevehr, L. J., "Mad Cows and Bt Potatoes: Global Public Goods in the Food System," *American Journal of Agricultural Economics* 86 (2004), 1159–1166.

Unnevehr, L. J., and H. H. Jensen, "The Economic Implications of Using HACCP as a Food Safety Regulatory Standard," *Food Policy* 24 (1999), 625–635.

Unnevehr, L. J., and D. Roberts, "Resolving Trade Disputes Arising from Trends in Food Safety Regulation: The Role of the Multilateral Governance Framework," *World Trade Review* 4 (2005), 469–497.

Unnevehr, L., T. Roberts, and C. Custer, "New Pathogen Testing Technologies and the Market for Food Safety Information," *AgBioForum* 7 (2004), 212–218.

U.S. Department of Agriculture, Economic Research Service, "Food Safety Briefing Room," (2005) accessed July 2, 2006, http://www.ers.usda.gov/Briefing/FoodborneDisease/foodandpathogens.htm.

Wilson, J. S., T. Otsuki, and B. Majumdsar," Balancing Food Safety and Risk: Do Drug Residue Limits Affect International Trade in Beef?" *Journal of International Trade and Economic Development* 12 (2003), 377–402.

World Trade Organization, "Implementation-Related Issues and Concerns—Decision of 14 November," WT/MIN(01)/17, November 20 (2001).

World Trade Organization, "Trade Capacity Building Database," (2006), accessed May 20, 2006, http://tcbdb.wto.org/index.asp?lang=ENG.

Zepp, G., F. Kuchler, and G. Lucier, "Food Safety and Fresh Fruits and Vegetables: Is there a Difference between Imported and Domestically Produced Products?" in VGS-274, 23-28 (U.S. Deptartment of Agriculture, Economic Research Service: Washington, DC, 1998).

Plenary 4

Plenary A

Technological progress for sustaining food-population balance: achievement and challenges

Mahabub Hossain*

Abstract

The growth in land productivity in rice cultivation has slowed down substantially since the early 1990s due to technological progress reaching its limit in the irrigated ecosystem and nonavailability of suitable technologies for the unfavorable rainfed environments. This development raises concern regarding the world's ability to meet the food-population balance in the coming decades. Rice research must deal with a number of difficult problems to meet the challenge: raising the yield ceilings of the current available rice varieties; protecting the past yield gains in the irrigated ecosystem; and using biotechnology tools to develop high yielding varieties for the rainfed systems that are tolerant to drought, submergence, and problem soils. The speed and extent of meeting these challenges depends on the level of resources that can be mobilized to support crop improvement research in the public sector.

JEL classification: 033, 013, 019

Keywords: rice economy; induced innovation; technological progress; growth trends; yield gaps; unfavorable ecosystems

1. Introduction

Population growth is the dominant determinant of the demand for staple food. The world population has more than doubled since the 1950s and has already reached 6.4 billion. It may increase another three billion before stabilizing in 2100 (UN, 2006). Over the next quarter century, the world population is projected to increase by 1.95 billion, mostly in the developing countries and in the regions where poverty and hunger is widespread, such as in South Asia and Sub-Saharan Africa.

Developed countries may not need further increase in the production of staple food, as most of them have reached a stationary population and some have started experiencing an absolute decline.[1] Population,

however, continues to increase at a high rate in the developing countries. It is projected that the total cereal consumption will continue to increase, despite a moderate decline in the per capita consumption of cereals as human food, due to population growth and the growing demand for livestock products (Rosegrant et al., 2001; Sombilla et al., 2002).

The potential for increasing the supply of food through expanding the land frontier has long been exhausted, particularly in the densely settled countries in Asia where 60% of the world's population live. With the increase in the pressure of the population on limited natural resources, land prices have continued to increase relative to prices of other factors of production. The land-saving technical change that increases the crop yield (productivity per unit of land per season) has been the dominant source for maintaining the food-population balance. However, the potential for increased land productivity created by the dramatic technological breakthroughs in the late 1960s for the irrigated and favorable rainfed environments have almost been exhausted (Barker and Herdt, 1985; David and Otsuka, 1994; Pingali et al., 1997; Barker and Dawe,

---

Bangladesh Rural Advancement Committee (BRAC), Dhaka.

[1] The situation may change if petroleum prices continue to increase. The demand for maize may increase rapidly as it is used as raw materials in the production of ethanol—a substitute for petroleum. Brown (2006) reports that the use of grain for fuel is growing by over 20% per year compared to 1% per year growth for use as food and feed.

Table 1
Sources of cereal production growth in developing countries: 1970–1990 and 1990–2005

Cereals	1970–1990			1990–2005		
	Yield	Area	Production	Yield	Area	Production
Rice	2.35	0.49	2.84	0.92	0.31	1.23
Wheat	3.75	0.88	4.62	1.27	−0.35	0.91
Maize	2.65	0.97	3.61	1.64	0.66	2.3
All cereals	2.68	0.73	3.41	1.2	0.21	1.41

Source: Analysis of trend with FAO time series data.

2002; Huang et al., 2002). Since the late 1980s, there has been a drastic slowdown of yield growth for all cereal crops (Table 1). The growth in yield has decelerated from 2.4% to 0.9% per year for rice, from 3.8% to 1.3% for wheat, and from 2.7% to 1.3% for maize. After reaching the bottom in 2001, the prices of rice, wheat, and maize have been rising consistently, and the stocks of cereals have reached below the critical level. Again, concerns are raised regarding the world's ability to maintain the food-population balance, as during the 1960s and the early 1990s (Paddock and Paddock, 1967; Brown, 1995, 2006; Huang et al., 2002).

Against the backdrop of this development, this article reviews the induced innovation that shifted the technology frontier, analyzes its contribution to increases in crop production through adoption of land-saving technologies, and outlines the challenge ahead for research to sustain the food-population balance. The discussion is limited to the rice crop, which is the dominant food staple in the developing countries.

2. Institutional innovation for land-saving technologies

The theory of induced innovation (Hicks, 1932; Hayami and Ruttan, 1985; Hayami, 1997) states that changes in resource endowments induce innovation and technological progress. As the endowment of one factor becomes abundant relative to other factors, a change in technology is induced towards using the abundant factors for saving the scarce factor. The green revolution is considered an innovation in agricultural production technology induced by population pressure on limited land resources. Owing to the availability to developing economies of scientific knowledge accumulated in industrialized countries, an institutional innovation was

induced in the form of a public-supported agricultural research system to develop technologies that helped save the increasingly scarce land with higher use of the relatively more abundant labor and chemical fertilizers.

In the developed countries, technological innovations are usually carried out mainly by large farms that have research and development capacities. The objective was to reduce the cost of production by substituting relatively more abundant resources for expensive resources. The crop breeding programs that are supported by farmers by purchasing improved seeds at higher prices had produced several generations of modern crop varieties in developed countries by the early 1950s, whose adoption led to rapid increase in land productivity.

When the population pressure on limited land resources accelerated in the developing countries, the need for development of such land-saving technological progress was felt. But, it became clear that private sector farms were unlikely to make significant investments in crop improvement research targeted at the major crops grown in the developing countries. Since there was no effective intellectual property protection in crop varieties at that time, there was no incentive for private sector to invest in such research. As agriculture was strongly constrained by environmental conditions, it was difficult to transfer improved technologies developed for the temperate zone in the industrialized countries to the tropical and subtropical zone in the developing countries. It was felt that with appropriate adaptive research in the developing countries, agricultural technology transfers from developed to developing countries would be possible.

The institutional response to these realities was to establish international agricultural research centers (IARCs) supported by international donors. This system eventually led to development of a formal structure known as the Consultative Group for International Agricultural Research (CGIAR) that has a mandate among others to develop improved technologies for the major food crops in the developing countries (Evenson and Gollin, 2003; Hayami and Ruttan, 1985). The IARCs that the CGIAR system supports work with national agricultural research systems (NARS) in developing countries to undertake and support crop breeding and genetic improvement research, and to develop options for efficient and sustainable management of crops and natural resources (soil, water, and biotic resources).

The International Rice Research Institute (IRRI) established in 1960 in the Philippines made the first breakthrough in 1966 in developing a semidwarf rice variety (IR8) that saves land by using additional chemical fertilizers and labor, provided that farmers have good water control in their fields (the "seed-fertilizer-water" technology). The new variety gave two to three times higher yield (output per unit of land per season) compared with traditional varieties grown by farmers (Barker and Herdt, 1985). Built on that success, successive generations of improved varieties and breeding materials (germplasm) were developed to address other concerns such as resistance to pest pressures, reducing the duration of crop maturity, and improving grain quality (Khush, 1995). As national programs grew in strength, IRRI abandoned the practice of releasing varieties directly. It adopted the strategy of supplying germplasm and elite breeding lines to national programs for evaluation, selection, and use (Evenson and Gollin, 1997). This role was facilitated by an international network for germplasm exchange that provides NARS breeders ready access to breeding materials.

Almost 90% of the rice area is located in Asia, with 133 million ha out of 155 million ha of rice land. Rice is also a significant crop in a number of countries in Africa and Latin America. The non-Asian countries received improved rice varieties from IRRI through INGER, which channeled advance elite lines developed at IRRI and other research organizations in the public sector in Asia. But, the Asian rice varieties were not particularly well adapted to Latin America or Africa. Later, the *International Center for Tropical Agriculture (CIAT)* located in Colombia established a rice breeding program that undertook adaptive breeding to develop varieties combining improved germplasm from Asia with in-

digenous varieties grown in Latin America. Brazil also developed an advanced rice breeding program for the uplands and for the temperate climate in South America. These institutions have made progress in developing appropriate rice varieties for South America reducing the dependence on IRRI for improved germplasm.

Although many improved germplasm from Asia were evaluated under African conditions, only a few are adopted by farmers due to difficult growing environments. *The West Africa Rice Development Association (WARDA)* established for adaptive research on rice in Africa was not effective until it was established as a center capable of doing its own breeding in the 1980s. By mid 1990s, WARDA produced a range of improved germplasm by crossing improved Asian varieties with locally adapted and multiple stress-resistant African landraces. The improved germplasm is labeled as *New Rice for Africa* (NERICA). The NERICA appears to offer a rich source of genetic resistance to drought, weed competition, blast, virus diseases, soil acidity, and iron toxicity (Dingkuhn et al., 1998; Diagne, 2006). The NERICA materials promised to be particularly well-suited to low-input conditions of rainfed rice farming in Africa.

A recent study conducted under the leadership of Evenson and Gollin (2003) reveals that in Asia, production of improved varieties by NARS with support from IARCs increased substantially in the 1980s compared to the 1970s, but declined in the 1990s. For Latin America, the production of improved varieties was low in the early period, but has accelerated in the 1990s. For Africa, the production has remained negligible throughout the period. The adoption of modern varieties has reached over 70% for Asia, 55% for Latin America, but only about 20% for Africa.

The estimate of the net gains from the adoption of modern rice varieties for selected Asian countries can be seen from Table 2. The yield gain from the adoption of modern varieties is about 2.1 t/ha. But, the adoption entails additional cost on account of fertilizers, irrigation charges, labor, and pesticides. This additional cost is estimated at 1.16 t/ha in rice equivalents. The net yield gain is estimated at 0.94 t/ha, about 41% over the yield of traditional varieties.

Evenson and Gollin (2003) estimate that the total factor productivity growth for the 1965–1995 period was 1.2% per year; 1.5% per year for the first two decades (the Green Revolution period) but has decelerated to

Table 2
Estimates of the net gains from the adoption of modern rice varieties

Country	Rice yield (kg/ha)		Cost in rice equivalent (kg/ha)		Net gain from the adoption of MV (kg/ha)
	MV	TV	MV	TV	
Bangladesh	3,980	1,970	2,614	1,600	996
West Bengal, India	4,174	1,921	2,631	1,475	1,097
Vietnam	4,805	2,297	4,044	2,419	883
Philippines	3,780	2,100	2,363	1,579	896
Indonesia	5,176	3,093	1,759	521	845
Average	4,383	2,276	2,683	1,519	943

Note: For Indonesia, the figures for modern varieties (MV) are for Java, where adoption rate is almost complete, while the figures for traditional varieties (TV) are for Kalimantan, where most of the area is grown with traditional varieties. The traditional varieties fetch a higher price in the market because of better quality. The yields for traditional varieties are adjusted for the price premium over the modern varieties.
Source: Hossain et al. (2003).

0.6% during 1985–1995. Several other studies have indicated a decline in total factor productivity growth in rice cultivation at the country level. A recent review of the productivity impact of the modern rice varieties (Otsuka and Kalirajan, 2006) shows that the new generations of modern rice varieties developed in the public sector research systems in Asia had limited contribution to further increase in technical efficiency over and above the gains made from the replacement of traditional varieties by the first generation of modern varieties (Estudillo and Otsuka, 2006; Hossain et al., 2006; Ut and Kajisa, 2006). The later generations incorporated resistance of rice plants to pest pressures and/or reduced the crop maturity period for facilitating crop intensification and diversification.

3. Achievements in technological progress

This section assesses the achievement in technological progress in rice farming at the individual country level by generating information on growth in rice yield and area, by estimating trend equations with time series data for the period 1970–2005. The analysis has been conducted for all countries with a rice area of over 20,000 ha. For India, the analysis has been conducted at the state level, since the country has diverse agroecological condition across states with large variations in yield.

To assess whether technological progress has decelerated in the recent period, the growth in rice yield has been compared for two periods, 1970–1990 (the Green Revolution period) and 1990–2005 (the post-Green Revolution period). The following trend

equation was fitted to estimate the growth rates:

$$LnY = a + bD + cT + d(D*T) + u;$$

where Ln = natural logarithm, Y = yield and rice area for which the rate of growth is estimated, D = dummy variable (1 = 1990–2005 period and 0 otherwise) and, T = time trend (takes the value of 1 starting from 1970).

The rate of growth for 1970–1990 is given by the value of the estimated parameter c and that for 1990–2005 is given by $c + d$. The negative value of the parameter d indicates that the growth has decelerated during 1990–2005 compared with 1970–1990. The trend equation has been estimated both for yield as well for the rice area, to assess the contribution of expansion of both area and yield to the growth in output.[2]

3.1. Performance in the post-1990 period

Out of 43 countries under study, the growth in yield decelerated in 19 countries as indicated by the negative coefficient of the interaction variable in the trend equations. Among nine of them, the value of the coefficient is significantly negative at 5% level. The three giant economies of Asia, i.e., India, China, and Indonesia, that account for 60% of the global rice area are among them. For China, the yield growth has decelerated from 3.1% during 1970–1990 to only 0.7% during 1990–2005; for Indonesia the growth has declined even faster from 3.3% to 0.3%. In these countries, rice

---

[2] The estimation results of the trend equation are available upon request.

Table 3
Sources of growth in rice production in different regions: 1970–1990 and 1990–2005

Regions	1970–1990			1990–2005		
	Yield	Area	Production	Yield	Area	Production
Asia	2.32	0.37	2.69	0.89	0.19	1.07
East Asia	2.72	−0.37	2.35	0.58	−1.07	−0.49
Southeast Asia	2.51	0.91	3.42	1.46	1.18	2.64
South Asia	2.14	0.57	2.71	1.4	0.25	1.65
Sub-Saharan Africa	0.94	2.22	3.17	−0.73	2.62	1.89
Latin America	1.94	0.78	2.72	3.04	−0.56	2.48

Source: Analysis of trend with FAO time series data.

is grown mostly under irrigated conditions, the adoption of modern varieties is almost complete, and the yield has reached high levels. For India, the decline in yield growth has also been quite severe, from 2.3 per year during 1970–1990 to 1.0% during 1990–2004. The drastic slowdown in the growth in rice yield and production in the world during 1990–2005 was mainly on account of these three giant countries in Asia.

The other countries experiencing deceleration in yield growth are Myanmar, Philippines, Iran, Dominican Republic, and Nigeria. In Iran and Dominican Republic, rice is grown under irrigated conditions and the decline in growth may indicate reaching plateau in the adoption of existing technologies. Myanmar, Philippines, and Nigeria have substantially expanded the area under rice in the later period. The decline in yield growth may indicate that such expansion has taken place on marginal lands.

Nine countries experienced significant acceleration in yield growth during the recent period. These countries are Bangladesh, Brazil, Cambodia, Egypt, Guinea, Madagascar, Mozambique, Nepal, Pakistan, Peru, Spain, and Thailand. In all these countries (except in Peru and Brazil), rice is grown under predominantly rainfed conditions and the growth in yield was low in the earlier period. The increase in yield growth in these countries is a reflection of the expansion in the coverage of irrigation during the later period.

3.2. Performance across regions

The growth in rice yield and its contribution to production at the broad regional levels can be seen from Table 3. The growth in rice production was respectable

during 1970–1990 at more than 2.2% per year for all the regions, which eased the pressure of expansion of cultivation to marginal areas due to population growth. There was very little increase in the expansion of rice area during this period.[3] The yield growth during 1990–2005 has decelerated in all regions, except in Latin America.

The decline in the yield growth has been fast in East Asia, from 2.7% per year during 1970–1990 to only 0.6% during 1990–2005. The growth in yield has declined in all four countries in the region. The deceleration is presumably in response to both a downward trend in per capita rice consumption and of population in the region (except in North Korea). This development started much earlier in Japan and South Korea. China has experienced the same trend since the early 1990s. Along with the deceleration in yield growth, the region has also experienced reduction in the area under rice cultivation. During 1990–2005, rice harvested area declined by 2.1% per year in Japan, 1.1% in South Korea, and 1.0% in China.

Southeast Asia is the home of the two major rice exporters—Thailand and Vietnam—as well as two major rice importing countries in the world—Indonesia and the Philippines. The yield growth was relatively fast in Indonesia and the Philippines in the early period, as irrigation infrastructure was already developed that facilitated rapid technological progress. With no further investment in the expansion of irrigation in the later

---

[3] In many countries the small growth in rice area was mainly due to expansion of irrigation which allowed farmers a dry season rice crop after harvesting the monsoon season rice. The expansion of rice harvested area is the result of the increase in cropping intensity with rice.

period and the degradation of the existing irrigation system, the yield growth has tapered off. With continuing population growth, both have reverted from self-sufficiency in rice production to import dependence. Only Vietnam was able to maintain the growth in both the rice harvested area and yield through development and diffusion of high-yielding shorter-maturity rice varieties. Vietnam has almost exhausted its capacity for increasing rice production and has started adopting a policy of agricultural diversification to boost farmers' incomes. Thailand, Myanmar, and Cambodia have considerable potential capacity for increasing rice production. The rice yield remains at a low level and additional land could be brought under cultivation with expansion of irrigation, particularly through increasing the area under the second rice crop in the dry season. Thailand has continued to increase exports even when rice prices remained low in the world market. Farmers have maintained a low cost of production despite increasing wage rates through consolidation of farm holdings and mechanization of agricultural operations.

For South Asia, India and Bangladesh account for a third of the global rice area with 53 million ha of rice land. In Eastern India, Nepal, and Bangladesh, the dominant rice production system is rainfed, while in the northern and southern India and in Sri Lanka and Pakistan, rice is grown mostly under irrigated conditions. In Pakistan, rice is a commercial crop, and the technological progress responds to favorable prices in the world market. India continues to expand rice production through subsidies in irrigation and chemical fertilizers and a minimum support price provided to farmers. The trend analysis at the state level, however, shows that out of 14 states (rice area of over 100,000 ha), the yield growth has declined in the recent period in 12 states. The decline in growth is statistically significant in Punjab, Haryana, Tamil Nadu, Andra Pradesh, and Uttar Pradesh. In these states, rice is cultivated mainly under irrigated conditions, and the yield has reached high levels. With technological progress approaching the plateau, the stagnation in yield is setting off. In the rainfed system in Eastern India and Nepal, the technological progress has been continuing, but occasional droughts and floods due to erratic monsoons disrupts the productivity growth.

Bangladesh has substantially reduced the yield gap in the irrigated ecosystem over the last decade with rapid private sector investment in shallow tube wells

for pumping ground water. The productivity growth may slow down in the future because of the plateau in yield for the dry season rice crop (boro) and slow technological progress in the large flood-prone and salinity-prone coastal areas. Sri Lanka made yield gains through technological progress in the earlier period, but recent progress has been hampered by labor scarcity and high wage rates compared to other South Asian countries.

In Sub-Saharan Africa, the growth in yield was only marginal during the earlier period, and turned negative during the later period. The production growth was more than 3.0% to meet the rapid growth in demand emanating from population growth and the increase in per capita consumption. The demand was met mainly through the expansion of rice area and imports from Asia.[4] During 1990–2005, rice area has expanded at over 2.0% per year in Ghana, Liberia, Mozambique, and Nigeria. With continued expansion of rice area to marginal land, the yield started to decline in absolute terms.

In Latin America, Brazil is the dominant rice producer accounting for over 80% of the total rice area in the region. The growth in rice yield was low in most countries of the region during the early period indicating a late start in technological progress. The yield growth has accelerated in the later period from the initial low base for all countries in the region from 1.6% per year during 1970–1990 to 3.5% per year during 1990–2005 for Brazil, 1.1–2.0% for Peru, 1.3–2.5% for Uruguay, 1.5–2.2% for Columbia, and 3.2–3.3% for Cuba. Only in Dominican Republic, the yield growth has slackened, as it expanded the growth in rice area from 1.8% per year during 1970–1990 to 2.7% during 1990–2005. In Brazil, the increase in the growth in yield reflects the reduction in area under upland rice in the central Amazon region, and the expansion of area under irrigated ecosystem in the South. Rice area increased by 0.3% per year during 1970–1990 but drastically reduced to a negative 1.9% during 1990–2005.

3.3. *Performance in irrigated versus rainfed systems*

We have classified the countries and states of India into three groups: predominantly irrigated (with more that 70% of the rice area irrigated); partially irrigated

---

[4] About half of the total rice consumption in Africa is met through imports. Africa now accounts for a third of the global rice market.

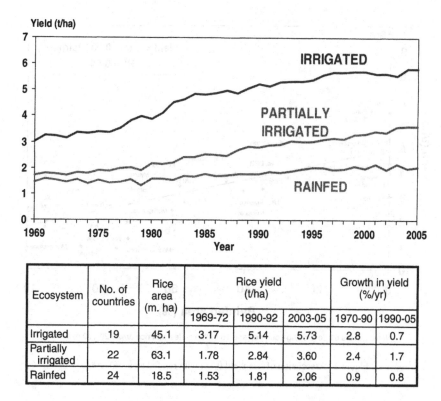

Figure 1. Trend in rice yield, irrigated and rainfed environments, 1969–2005.

(with 20 to 70% irrigated area); and predominantly rainfed (with less that 20% irrigated area), and assessed the trend in rice yield for these groups. The growth performance and yield gaps among the three groups can be seen in Figure 1. It can be noted that the first group has the highest growth (2.8% per year) in rice yield in the earlier period, but has almost stagnated in the later period after reaching a high level. The second group continues to have respectable growth in yield (1.7%) even in the later period, presumably through continuous technological progress supported by expansion of irrigation coverage. The predominantly rainfed group (mostly in Africa) had the worst performance: a growth of yield of 0.9% per year during 1970–1990 and 0.8% during 1990–2005. The gap in yield between the irrigated system and the rainfed ecosystem remains large. The data indicate that appropriate land-saving technologies for the rainfed system have not yet been developed.

The negative association between the rainfed ecosystem and the level of rice yield at the cross-country level is clearly shown in Figure 2. The correlation coefficient for the association is large and highly significant. The countries that have low rice yields are also those having high levels of poverty (Figure 3). Although there are many reasons behind poverty, the low productivity of the staple food crop is a significant factor. The increase in productivity in the production of staple food, which is a dominant economic activity at the low income level, helps generate surplus for capital accumulation for other economic activities and for human capital development that triggers economic development and poverty reduction.

The above review of the growth in rice area and yield at the country level supports the following major points: (a) the technological progress proceeded early in countries that already had a well-developed irrigation infrastructure; (b) the countries with rainfed ecologies adopted technologies (developed for the irrigated ecologies) in the later period with gradual expansion of irrigation through government or private sector investment; (c) attempts to increase rice production through area expansion in countries that failed to adopt improved technologies have led to further decline in rice

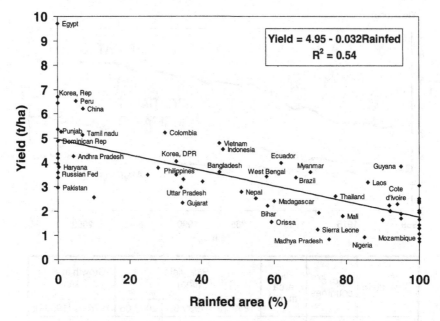

Note: Covers 61 developing countries and 16 Indian states with rice area >20,000 has

Figure 2. Association of rice yield (t/ha) with rainfed area (%), 2002.

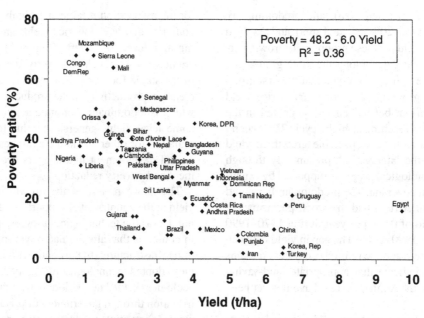

Note: Covers 61 developing countries and 16 Indian states with rice area >20,000 has

Figure 3. Association of poverty (%) with rice yield (t/ha), 2000–2004.

yield from already low level; and (d) the yield stagnation sets in as the technological progress reaches the plateau (at a level of about 6.0 t/ha). This suggests that there has been no further land-saving technological change after the first innovation.

The low yield in the rainfed system, limited scope for further expansion of irrigated area due to growing water scarcity (Rosegrant and Pingali, 1994: Seckler et al., 1998; Barker et al., 1999), and the exhaustion of technological progress in the irrigated ecosystem raise concern regarding our ability to maintain food-population balance in future.

4. Challenges ahead

The community of rice scientists continue to face the following challenges in sustaining the food population balance: (a) raising the yield frontier of rice that has remained almost unchanged since the first generation of rice varieties were released; (b) sustaining the current high yields in the intensively cultivated irrigated systems; and (c) closing the yield gap between the irrigated and rainfed systems (Scobie et al., 1993; Hossain and Fisher, 1995).

4.1. Shifting the yield potential for the irrigated system

The yield potential of current high-yielding varieties developed for the tropics is 10 t/ha for the dry season and 6.5 t/ha for the wet season. Since the release of IR8 in 1966, only marginal increases have occurred in the yield potential of rice. Since then, scientists have largely focused on incorporating insect and disease resistance into improved varieties, shortening the growth duration of the crop, and on improvements in grain quality (Khush, 1995; Peng and Senadhira, 1998).

IRRI scientists proposed modifications to present high-yielding semidwarf plant architecture and developed a "new plant type" for direct seeded crop establishment. Compared with current modern varieties, the new plant type will have fewer tillers, but those tillers will have longer panicles bearing more grains, thick and erect leaves for higher photosynthesis efficiency, and sturdier stems and deeper roots to support the increased grain weight. The grain-biomass ratio for the new plant type will be increased from 50% for the present improved varieties to 55–60% in the new plant type. The

new plant type will shift the yield potential by another 25%. The new plant types have already been developed and shared with NARS, who are currently using them in their breeding programs. Two improved varieties (super rice) have already been released in China, which contain the new plant type material.

A relatively more mature technology that shifts the yield frontier is hybrid rice. Hybrids, the progeny of distinct parents, create increased vigor and yield through heterosis. Hybrid rice has been grown in China since 1976 and on average has a yield advantage of 15–20% over conventional high-yielding varieties (Virmani, 1994). New experimental evidence indicates the possibility of further enhancing the level of heterosis by crossing indica with tropical japonica rice varieties. Several hybrid rice varieties have already been released by NARS in the tropics, but the expansion of area has been slow because of limited profitability gains emanating from high seed costs and lower quality grains (Janaiah and Hossain, 2003). These problems are expected to be overcome with further breeding, as similar problems were experienced in China during the initial period of extension of hybrid rice (Lin, 1994).

Rice is a plant with C3 photosynthesis, which has lower photosynthetic rate than the C4 plants, such as maize and sorghum. Scientists have been examining the possibility of converting rice into a C4 plant. Recently, several genes for C4 pathway have been isolated, and efforts are underway to introduce these genes into rice through transformation.

4.2. Sustaining the current yields in irrigated systems

The irrigated systems now contribute to over 70% of rice production. Maintaining this contribution through achieving yield stability is a major challenge (Cassman and Pingali, 1995; Cohen et al., 1998). The stability of rice production is constantly threatened by chronic pest infestations and epidemic outbreaks. Major genes conferring resistance against diseases and insect pests have been widely used in rice improvement programs. Useful genes have been transferred from wild species to rice through the wide hybridization program. The successful isolation of many resistance genes and insecticidal proteins has further enhanced the ability of the rice breeders to incorporate these genes into rice varieties. Recent advances in dissection of defense pathways in plants have revealed novel genes that may lead to a rational design of broad-spectrum resistance. However, rapid erosion of host resistance due to adaptation by pathogens and insects remains a primary concern in sustaining high yields. Future challenges will require not only the accumulation of effective resistant genes, but also an understanding of the consequences of the deployment of the genes in the field.

Rice is a heavy water-using crop. As water becomes an increasingly scarce resource, action will have to be taken to make better use of existing water supplies, if wetland rice cultivation is to be sustained. Options for more efficient management of water in rice farming and appropriate water pricing policies will have to be developed to induce farmers to adopt these technologies. IRRI scientists are also working to develop improved varieties (aerobic rice) that can be grown with less water, without much yield penalty (Bouman and Tuong, 2001; Tuong and Bouman, 2003).

Traditionally, farmers keep the field inundated with water to reduce weed competition. Research on increasing water use efficiency, therefore, will have to take into account weed control. The traditional practice of flooding the field for paddling and transplanting is being replaced by direct seeding of rice in response to growing shortage of agricultural labor (Zeigler and Puckridge, 1995). New ways of controlling weeds are required because of changes in weed flora, herbicide resistance, and growing public concern about the harmful effects of agrochemicals on human health and environment.

4.3. Reducing yield gaps for unfavorable rainfed environments

Almost half of the global rice area is dependent on rainfall and is subjected to both droughts and submergence, sometimes during the same season. Even if sufficient moisture is received over the growing season to support the physiological needs of the crops, the precipitation may not be evenly distributed to satisfy water requirement at various stages of plant growth. The uneven distribution of rainfall may result in temporary flooding and water logging from heavy rains particularly in areas with poor drainage and dry spells in between leading to drought conditions.

Many traditional varieties have developed traits through centuries of evolution that enable them to withstand the submergence and drought stresses. Rice scientists have so far had limited success in identifying these traits and incorporating them into high-yielding varieties. The currently available modern varieties may do well in normal years, but perform poorly compared to traditional varieties, if there is prolonged drought and sudden submergence due to an erratic monsoon. So, where the rainfall is unreliable, the farmer either grows traditional varieties or use inputs into suboptimal amounts when adopting an improved variety, which results in low yields.

Biotechnology, and the use of gene mapping and marker-aided selection have much to offer for the development of varieties tolerant to submergence, drought, and problem soils (Bennett, 1995). A gene for submergence tolerance (Sub1) has already been incorporated into *Swarna*, a widely grown variety in South Asia (Xu et al., 2006; Neeraja et al., 2007). The improved germplasm can withstand submergence for 10–12 days. Another gene for salt-tolerance (Saltol) has been fine mapped, and has been introgressed with maker-assisted breeding to develop improved lines. Despite substantial efforts, developing tolerance to droughts in high-yielding varieties has remained elusive. However, minor genes for various subcomponent traits of drought tolerance in rice have been mapped, and this information is being utilized to develop improved varieties with drought tolerance.

With intellectual property rights guaranteed under World Trade Organization, it was expected that the private sector would come forward to make investments in biotechnology research for rice improvements in rainfed environments. Initially, there was a positive response from a few large multinational companies. But, it is now realized that the market for private sector rice biotech will be limited due to poor economic conditions of millions of small and marginal rice farmers, the tradition of getting improved rice technologies free of charge from international and national public sector research organizations, the problem of enforcing intellectual property rights in developing countries, and negative perceptions of civil society organizations regarding the genetically modified food. So, the high expectation of private sector research organizations taking the lead in this area may not be realized. The realization of the potential for developing appropriate technologies for the unfavorable rice environments will depend on investments in rice biotech research made by international research centers and advanced research institutions in the public sector in developing countries.

5. Conclusion

The most promising avenue to sustaining the food security in the face of growing pressure of population on limited land resources is continuous growth in land productivity through development and diffusion of land-saving technologies. Since agricultural technologies are difficult to transfer from developed to developing countries due to different agroecological situations, an institutional innovation was induced in the 1960s to develop such technologies through establishment of international and national research institutes in the public sector. For rice, the dominant food staple in developing countries, successive generations of improved varieties were developed that substantially increased the rice yield with additional use of chemical fertilizers, labor, and irrigation. The yield gain net of additional cost of inputs was about 1.0 t/ha, about 40% of the yield of traditional varieties. The progress in the adoption of the technology contributed to a yield growth to meet the growing demand for food.

The growth in yield has, however, slowed down substantially since the early 1990s due to technological progress reaching its limit in the irrigated ecosystem, limited expansion of irrigated area due to growing scarcity of water, and a large yield gap in the rainfed system due to nonavailability of technologies suitable for the unfavorable environments. The development raises concern regarding the world's ability to meet the food-population balance in the coming decades. Rice research must deal with a number of difficult problems to meet the challenge: raising the yield ceilings of the current available rice varieties, protecting the past yield gains in the irrigated ecosystem, and using biotechnology tools to develop high-yielding varieties for the rainfed systems that are tolerant to drought, submergence, and problem soils. The speed and extent of meeting these challenges depends on the level of resources that can be mobilized to support crop improvement research in the public sector.

References

Barker, R., and R. W. Herdt, *The Rice Economy of Asia* (Resources for the Future: Washington, DC, 1985).

Barker, R., and D. Dawe, "The Transformation of the Asian Rice Economy and the Directions for Future Research," in M. Sombilla, M. Hossain, and B. Hardy, eds., *Developments in the Asian Rice Economy* (International Rice Research Institute: Manila, Philippines, 2002).

Barker, R., D. Seckler, and U. Amarasinghe, "The World's Water: Emerging Issues in the Era of Growing Scarcity," *Choices* 14 (1999), 28–31.

Bennett, J., "Biotechnology and the Future of Rice Production," *GeoJournal* 35 (1995), 333–336.

Bouman, B. A. M., and T. P. Tuong, "Field Water Management to Save Water and Increase in Productivity in Irrigated Lowland Rice," *Agricultural Water Management* 49(2001), 11–30.

Brown, L. R., *Who Will Feed China?* (W.W. Norton: New York, 1995).

Brown, L. R., "World Grain Stocks Fall to 57 days of Consumption: Grain Prices Starting to Rise," Earth Policy Institute, 2006. http://www.earth-policy.org/Indicators/Grain/2006.htm

Cassman, K. G., and P. L. Pingali, "Intensification of Irrigated Rice Systems: Learning from the Past to Meet Future Challenges," *GeoJournal* 35 (1995), 299–306.

Cohen, M. B., S. Savary, N. Huang, O. Azzam, and S. K. Datta "Importance of Rice Pests and Challenges for their Management," in N. G. Dowling, S. M. Greenfield, and K. S. Fischer, eds., *Sustainability of Rice in Global Food System* (International Rice Research Institute: Davis, CA, 1998).

David, C. C., and K. Otsuka, *Modern Rice Technology and Income Distribution in Asia* (Lynne Reiner Publishers: Boulder and London, 1994).

Diagne, A., "Diffusion and Adoption of NERICA Rice Varieties in Cote Ivorie," *Developing Economies* 44 (2006), 208–231.

Dingkuhn, M., M. P. Jones, D. E. Johnson, and A. Sow, "Growth and Yield Potential of Oryza Sativa and O. Glaberrima Upland Rice Cultivars and their Interspecific Progenies," *Field Crops Research* 57 (1998), 57–69.

Estudillo, J. P., and K. Otsuka, "Lessons of Three Decades of Green Revolution in the Philippines," *Developing Economies* 44 (2006), 123–144.

Evenson, R. E., and D. Gollin, "Genetic Resources, International Organizations and Improvement in Rice Varieties," *Economic Development and Cultural Change* 45 (1997), 471–500.

Evenson, R. E, and D. Gollin, *Crop Variety Improvement and Its Effect on Productivity: The Impact of International Agricultural Research* (CABI Publishing: Wallingford, UK, 2003).

Hayami, Y., *Development Economics: From the Poverty to the Wealth of Nations* (Clarendron Press: Oxford, 1997).

Hayami, Y., and R. W. Ruttan, *Agricultural Development: An International Perspective* (Johns Hopkins University Press: Baltimore, 1985).

Hicks, J. R., *The Theory of Wages* (Macmillan: London, 1932).

Hossain, M., and K. S. Fischer, "Rice Research for Food Security and Sustainable Development in Asia: Achievements and Future Challenges," *GeoJeornal* 35 (1995), 286–298.

Hossain, M., D. Gollin, V. Cabanilla, E. Cabrera, N. Johnson, G. S. Khush, and G. McLaren, "International Research and Genetic Improvement in Rice: Evidence from Asia and Latin America," in R. E. Evenson, and D. Gollin, eds., *Crop Variety*

Improvement and Its Effect on Productivity (CABI Publishing: Wallinford, 2003).

Hossain, M., M. L. Bose, and B. A. A. Mustafi, "Adoption and Productivity Impact of Modern Rice Varieties in Bangladesh," *Developing Economies* 44 (2006), 149–166.

Huang, J., C. Pray, and S. Rozelle, "Enhancing the Crops to Feed the Poor," *Nature* 148 (2002), 678–684.

Janaiah, A., and M. Hossain, "Can Hybrid Rice Technology Help Productivity Growth in Asian Tropics Farmers' Experiences," *Economic and Political Weekly* 38(2003), 2492–2500.

Khush, G. S., "Breaking the Yield Frontier for Rice," *GeoJournal* 35 (1995), 325–328.

Lin, Y. J., "The Nature and Impact of Hybrid Rice in China," in C. C. David, and K. Otsuka, eds., *Modern Rice Technology and Income Distribution in Asia* (Lynne Reinner Publishers: Boulder and London, 1994).

Neeraja, C. N., R. Mahirang-Rodriguez, A. Pamlona, S. Huer, B. C. Y. Collard, E. M. Septiningshi, G. Vergara, D. Sanchez, K. Xu, A. M. Ismail, and D. J. Mackill, "A Marker-Assisted Backcross Approach for Developing Submergence-Tolerant Rice Cultivars," *Theor Appl Genet* (2007).

Otsuka, K., and K. P. Kalirajan, "Rice Green Revolution in Asia and its Transferability to Africa: An Introduction," *Developing Economies* 44 (2006), 107–121.

Paddock, W., and P. Paddock, *Times of Famine* (Little, Brown and Company: Toronto, 1967).

Peng, S., and D. Senadhira, "Genetic Enhancement of Rice Yields," in N. G. Dowling, S. M. Greenfield, and K. S. Fischer, eds., *Sustainability of Rice in Global Food System* (International Rice Research Institute: Davis, CA, 1998).

Pingali, P. L., M. Hossain, and R. V. Gerpacio, *Asian Rice Bowls: The Returning Crisis?* (CAB International: Wallingford, UK, 1997).

Rosegrant, M. W., and P. L. Pingali, "Policy and Technology for Rice Productivity Growth in Asia," *Journal of International Development* 6 (1994), 665–688.

Rosegrant, M. W., M. Paisner, S. Meijer, and J. Witcover, "Global Food Projections to 2020: Emerging Trends and Alternative Futures," (International Food Policy Research Institute: Washington, DC, 2001).

Scobie, B. M., D. McDonald, and R. Willey, *Investment in Rice Research in the CGIAR: A Global Perspective* (TAC Secretariat, FAO: Rome, 1993).

Seckler, D., U. Amarasinghe, D. Molden, R. de Silva, and R. Barker, "World Water Demand and Supply, 1990 to 2025: Scenarios and Issues," *Research Report* 19 (International Water Management Institute: Colombo, 1998).

Sombilla, M. A., M. W. Rosegrant, and S. Meijer, "A Long-Term Outlook of Rice Supply and Demand Balances in South, Southeast and East Asia," in M. Sombilla, M. Hossain, and B. Hardy, eds., *Developments in the Asian Rice Economy* (International Rice Research Institute: Los Baños, Philippines, 2001).

Tuong, T. P., and B. A. M. Bouman, "Rice Production in Water-Scarce Environments," in J. W. Kijne, R. Barker, and D. Molden, eds., *Water Productivity in Agriculture: Limits and Opportunities for Iimprovement* (CABI publishing: Wallingford, UK, 2003).

United Nations, *World Urbanization Prospects: The 2005 Revision* (United Nations: New York, 2006).

Ut, T. T., and K. Kajisa, "The Impact of Green Revolution on Rice Production in Vietnam," *Developing Economies* 44 (2006), 167–189.

Virmani, S. S., *Hybrid Rice Technology: New Developments and Future Prospects* (International Rice Research Institute: Manila, Philippines, 1994).

Xu, K., X. Xia, T. Fukao, P. Canals, R. Mahirang-Rodriguez, S. Huer, A. M. Ismail, J. Baily-Serres, P. C. Ronal, and D. J. Mackill, "*SubIA* Is an Ethylene Response Factor-Like Gene that Confers Submergence Tolerance to Rice," *Nature* 442 (2006), 705–708.

Zeigler, R., and D. Puckridge, "Improving Sustainable Productivity in Rice-Based Rainfed Lowland Systems of South and Southeast Asi," *GeoJournal* 35 (1995), 307–324.

Rural nonfarm employment in developing countries in an era of globalization

Thomas Reardon*, Kostas Stamoulis**, and Prabhu Pingali***

Abstract

Rural nonfarm employment (RNFE) has become a topic of major importance in rural development, as by the mid 2000s, RNFE constituted 35% of rural incomes in Africa and 50% in both Asia and Latin America. The traditional view of RNFE was a sleepy hinterland activity cut off from changes in the national, let alone the global economy. That view was assailed by sweeping changes in rural areas starting with the Green Revolution, then rur-urbanization, and lately, by globalization intervening via both trade and modernization of the national economy including the rise of modern retail and processing. In this article, we hypothesize and offer emerging evidence that the strongest and most positive effects on RNFE of globalization come in the zones that are rur-urbanized, with a tradeables growth-motor induced RNFE sector with clusters of small/medium enterprises for manufactures, and a preponderance of services. Surprisingly, the trade effects are least and the domestic market transformation effects are the strongest. The most challenges are posed for zones that are rur-urbanized and dense zone RNFE with low-moderate local growth motors. The least effects are on hinterland zones. The policy implications are to promote tradeables growth motors (key to creating RNFE in services, the major component of RNFE), and to incorporate "competitiveness"—in a changing urban and global economy—into RNFE promotion.

JEL classification: O17, O33, O54, Q12, Q13

Keywords: globalization; rural nonfarm employment; rural towns; supermarkets

1. Introduction

Rural nonfarm employment (RNFE) is important to rural households in developing countries.[1] By the mid 2000s, RNFE averaged roughly 35% of rural household incomes in Africa, and 50% in Asia and Latin America (Haggblade et al., 2007). Research shows that household income from RNFE generally dwarfs rural

households' migration income, farm wage income, and credit and gifts received. RNFE has grown fast over only the past few decades. Data from the 1970s show that RNFE shares rarely exceeded 20% of rural incomes (Reardon et al., 2007).

The spate of research in the 1980s and 1990s that revealed RNFE's importance contradicted the earlier "conventional wisdom" that farmers only do farming, and spurred various governments, donors, and NGOs to create RNFE promotion programs. Many of the programs were, however, based on an image of RNFE that we call "the historical RNFE," which concerns semi-subsistance rural-hinterland villages producing Z-goods, as termed by Hymer and Resnick (1969), and not reliant on local "growth motor." Further, these programs were undertaken in a "closed economy" format without much exposure to either opportunities in or competition from urban or foreign markets. That meant that the "competitiveness" debate, common in

*Agricultural Economics, Michigan State University, East Lansing, Michigan, MI 48824-1039, USA.

**Agricultural Sectorin Economic Development Service (ESAE), Agricultural and Development Economics Division (ESA), FAO Rome Viale delle Terme di Caracalla, 00100 Rome, Italy.

***FAO, Rome, Viale delle Terme di Caracalla, 00100 Rome, Italy.

[1] It includes employment in rural areas in manufactures such as food processing or clothing manufacture, and services, such as vehicle repair and commerce, whether as an employee or self-employed, whether of products production-linked or not to the primary sector, in any scale, and in any location, whether in the home or outside.

the export promotion domain, did not touch RNFE promotion. To generalize somewhat, the typical program target was micro-enterprises engaged in manufacturing for the local rural market, making traditional cheese, jams, and clothing.

The above traditional view and program approach became increasingly inadequate over the past several decades to deal with a changing RNFE in a rapidly changing context, for several reasons. First, RNFE was revealed to be very heterogeneous in nature and unevenly distributed; resource-poor zones and households most needed but often did not have the capacity to generate RNFE, especially of the kind that would lift them from poverty (Reardon et al., 2000, 2001). The implication was that one needs a highly differentiated, rather than a "one size fits all" program approach.

Second, RNFE growth was revealed to develop most quickly and spread most widely in zones with "growth motors" that generate ripple effects of production linkages, consumption linkages (through the aggregate demand spurred by the motors), and investment linkages, providing surpluses to invest in RNF activity. The growth motors can be tourism (linked to external demand) such as in Cancun (Reardon et al., 2001), intercity transport corridors passing through the rural area such as in India (Bhalla, 1997), or an agricultural boom, such as the Green Revolution.

Third, recent research (reviewed briefly in this article) has emerged to show that RNFE development, especially in the 1990s to present, is taking place in rapid spatial and economic transformation of rural areas. These rural areas had been undergoing "rural opening" from infrastructure investment (in particular in Asia and Latin America, less so in Africa) coupled with "rur-urbanization," which is defined as the rapid development of rural towns and intermediate cities, and thus the segmentation of rural space into two areas, namely, rur-urban and hinterland-rural.

Fourth, we add yet another recent "shock" to the rural context that is hypothesized to affect RNFE—and that is globalization both via trade and via domestic market transformation. In other words, the influence of globalization occurs via an increase in exposure to trade, coupled with the rapid rise of large processors in urban areas sending products to rural areas and modern retail penetrating rur-urban areas.

There has been little systematic analytical stock taken of the third and fourth factors noted above, for the RNF economy. We focus this article on that gap in the literature. For the third point, we briefly review research highlighting rural opening and rur-urbanization, mainly to set the stage for the article's focus on globalization's impacts on RNFE, our contribution. We believe that much of globalization's effects on RNFE is so recent and extremely under-researched that our focus is to introduce the theme to the literature, present testable hypotheses, identify illustrations and emerging scant empirical evidence, and set out a research agenda.

Section 2 focuses on rural opening and rur-urbanization and ends with a taxonomy of RNFE over zone types, on the eve of globalization. Taking that as a starting point, Section 3 hypothesizes impacts of globalization on RNFE in different types of zones. Section 4 concludes with implications for RNFE development strategy and a research agenda.

2. RNFE on the eve of globalization: impacts from rural opening and rur-urbanization

The traditional vision of "RNFE as hinterland enclave" has been progressively undermined by the "rural opening" and "rur-urbanization" starting in the 1980s and 1990s. We discuss those two shocks and emerging evidence of how they differentiate RNFE, presenting a classification of rural zones based on that differentiation that we use in Section 3 to inform our analysis of globalization impacts.

2.1. "Opening" of the rural economy

We hypothesize that transaction costs of rural-urban links have trended downward, broadly speaking, over the past several decades, inducing a "de-protection" and opening of rural economies. This assumption is based on three points. First, official restrictions to movements of goods over rural zones and to urban areas have been largely abolished in many countries during structural adjustment (even though graft and vestigial regulations still plague the flow of goods).

Second, there have been dramatic increases in infrastructure (roads, bus systems, electricity, and telephone in particular), starting in the 1960s and 1970s, and picking up dramatically in the 1980s and 1990s. The gains have been by far the greatest in Asia, moderate in Latin America, but very little in Africa. For example, paved roads from 1980 to 2000: (1) increased 310% in China (Fan and Chan-Kang, 2004); (2) 400% in Bangladesh, India, Indonesia, Pakistan, Philippines, and Vietnam (Rashid et al., forthcoming); (3) 75% in Latin America, (Calderon and Serven, 2003); but (4) only 14% in Sub-Saharan Africa (Wilson and Wasike, 2001). The interregional disparities are sharp. Meager road-building left Africa with a very low road density: India's road density is 100 times that of Africa, but its population density per sq km is only 10 times (www.devdata.worldbank.org). World Bank (2007) shows the share of rural populations that live within two kilometers of an all-season road: Africa (Ghana, 34%, Kenya 44%, Nigeria 47%, Tanzania, 38%), South Asia (India 94%, Pakistan 77%), and Southeast Asia (Indonesia, 94%, Vietnam, 73%).

Third, for infrastructure development to lead to "opening," it must reduce transaction costs. A recent example is that of Escobal (2005) for rural Peru in the mountainous region. He finds the following: (1) stark differences in transaction costs between rural areas that have good road access (which he calls rur-urban) and those with low access; (2) a tendency to asset bundling, with roads correlated with rural population density and with the presence of nonroad infrastructure; and (3) a correlation between road access and agricultural commercialization, as well as price transmission from major food markets to rural areas.

2.2. Rur-urbanization of the rural space

First, there has been explosive growth especially in Latin America and Asia in the past two decades in the populations of rural towns and "intermediate cities." The latter are third- or fourth-tier cities with economies closely linked to surrounding rural areas— "ideally suited to act as an interface between the urban and the rural world" (GRAL/CEDAL, 1994, p. 130; Hardoy and Satterthwaite, 1989; Jordan and Simioni, 1998). Latin American geographers termed the segment of rural towns and intermediate cities the "rururban" areas. The rur-urbanization trend is strikingly evident in much of Latin America (outside the vast forest and pampas zones) and in Asia, in extremely dense rur-urban areas like much of rural India but especially in the "corridor zones" (Bhalla, 1997), or Nepal (Fafchamps and Shilpi, 2003), in Central and Eastern China, and Java in Indonesia.

The rise of the rur-urban segment eliminates the sharp distinction of urban areas versus rural hinterland, and creates a segmented rural space with hinterland-rural and rur-urban segments. This research has recently led to a new vision of the rural space: a continuum from small villages to small, medium, and large rural towns and to intermediate cities; as one moves along the continuum, each new segment has greater population concentration, more public services, less direct participation in agriculture, and less direct production–consumption linkages with agriculture or other rural growth motors. Researchers have argued that this continuum implies an integrated rural territory or space that should be the basis of RNFE analysis (Reardon and Stamoulis, 1998; Schejtman and Berdegue, 2002; Perry et al., 2005).

Escobal (2005) illustrates the above point that the rur-urban segment is an interface in rural space between urban and hinterland rural. He notes that the Andean rur-urban areas (that grew very quickly in the 1980s and 1990s, while the hinterland stagnated) tend to be economically integrated with urban areas (with exchange of goods and transmission of prices) as well as with hinterland-rural areas via marketing of farm products and two-way exchange of RNFE goods and services. Part of this is facilitated by labor commuting daily between villages and rural towns, a trend that rose sharply in the 1980s and 1990s both in Peru and elsewhere such as Chile. Berdegué et al. (2001) note for Chile that half of RNFE income is earned by villagers commuting daily to rural towns, facilitated by the proliferation of van and bus systems in the 1990s.

A variety of authors (Humphrey and Schmitz, 1996; Reardon and Stamoulis, 1998; Renkow, 2007) have hypothesized that RNFE should, for reasons of economies of agglomeration, lower transaction costs, and rising land costs (after von Thünen), concentrate in rururban areas. There have been few empirical tests of this hypothesis, but the scant evidence tends to confirm it. Fafchamps and Shilpi (2003) show for Nepal that RNFE (in particular wage income, implying they are working in small-medium enterprises) is concentrated within four hours of cities, mainly in rural towns and large villages (where horticulture production also is important); as one moves into the intermediate rural area, farm wage employment and self-employment in RNFE increase and commercialized grains, and then in the rural hinterland, one finds subsistence farming and low levels of RNFE.

This is consistent with findings by Bhalla (1997) for India; she finds the development of wage RNFE mainly in services in small/medium firms in "corridors" of interurban transport and in broad swaths circling large cities, but low levels of RNFE, mainly in self-employment micro-enterprise in manufactures, in the rural hinterlands. Elbers and Lanjouw (2001) have similar findings for Ecuador, as does Escobal (2005) for Peru.

3. Taxonomy of RNFE-rural contexts as framework for assessment of globalization impacts

Here we undertake a stylized classification of types of RNFE, economic zone, and segment of rural space. Table 1 presents this classification. For this section, the reader is asked to focus on rows 2, 3, and 4 only (we will look at the other rows in the next section). The classification shows: (1) segment of rural space (degree of openness and rur-urbanization, which we assume for simplicity to be roughly correlated); (2) economic type of zone—proxied by whether there is a tradeables "growth motor" in the rural area (such as commercial horticulture or tourism); and (3) the sectoral composition of RNFE (services versus manufactures). We abstract in the table from wage-labor versus self-employment, and by scale, but discuss those in the text. The table shows permutations of the variables to create a series of clusters of types of areas (for use in the next section as scenarios of globalization impacts). We briefly discuss the six column "clusters" using one example for each.

Column 1, typified by the booming (export-focused) fruit zones of Central Chile, and advanced rur-urbanization. Those two things are linked: the fruit boom drove rapid growth in rural towns at first via production-linkage activities (fruit packing sheds, farm equipment and chemical shops, and so on) and later by consumption-linkage effects, favoring local services. RNFE from services grew quickest and have far outstripped RNFE in manufactures. Villagers commute into town as wage-workers in commerce, construction, restaurants, and transport (Berdegué et al., 2001). This result aligns with the general (and surprising finding given the traditional view that RNFE is mainly self-employment manufactures) finding for developing countries overall that 75% of RNFE is on average in

Table 1
Stylized classification of types of RNFE, economic zone, and segment of rural space

Globalization cum domestic market transformation effect category	1. High	2. High-Medium	3. Medium	4. Low-Medium	5. Low	6. Very low
Classifying variables						
1. Strength of globalization shock to RNFE (mainly domestic market transformation)	High	High	Medium	Low	Low	Low
2. Openness/rur-urbanization	High	High	High	High	Medium	Low
3. Tradeable agricultural growth-motor in zone	High	High	Medium	Low	Low	Low
4. RNFE composition	Services Dominate	Manufactures	Manufactures and services	manufactures	manufactures	manufactures
Example 1	Fruit zones of Chile (Santa Cruz)	Eastern China rural	West Java	Indian hinterland (Bihar)	Central Kenya	Western Kenya
Example 2	Coffee zones of Colombia (Cauca)	Northern Mexico	"Corridor" zones of India like Haryana	Bangladesh rural	Southern Chile	Rural Laos

services, and only 25% in manufactures, and that both the service and the wage share tend to rise as rural development occurs, as time series and cross-section data show (Bhalla, 1997; Reardon et al., 2001; Haggblade et al., 2007).

Column 2, typified by the "maquiladora" rural industrialization zones of Eastern China and Northern Mexico, is again "export-focused" RNFE. The earnings from that RNFE base are linked in two-way causality (virtuous circle) with the growth of rural towns and intermediate cities. Column 3, typified by the "corridor zones" (areas with highways between cities that give rise to economies of agglomeration and low transaction costs to tap urban demand) and rur-urban areas of India (Bhalla, 1997) and Nepal (Fafchamps and Shilpi, 2003), is mainly "urban-market focused."

Columns 4 and 5 (4 is similar to 5 except that it is denser) should be contrasted with the Column 1 type zone. Column 5 is typified by southern Chile, where commodity potatoes and wheat, and low-quality grapes for local wine are produced, and thus there is an absence of a growth motor. That lack meant absence of substantial re-investable surplus or demand-push for nodal points of services to grow into rural towns (in contrast to what happened in the fruit-boom areas). Manufactures (in self-employment microenterprises) are dominant and focused on local hinterland demand—and paradoxically, are much more linked to agriculture than rural manufactures in the fruit zones to the north (Berdegué et al., 2001). This is similar to Elbers and Lanjouw (2001) in the poorer areas of Ecuador, or Bhalla (1997) in rural Bihar in India, or the Nepali hinterland per Fafchamps and Shilpi (2003). Bhalla (1997) offers what is in fact a very rare time series analysis showing how the rural hinterland of Bihar "de-industrialized" while rural manufactures shifted to (or were out-competed by) rur-urban zones around cities and in the corridors. Column 6 shows the "rural hinterland" extreme, typified by many African rural areas bereft of infrastructure or growth motors (Reardon, 1997).

The above taxonomy of rural areas and RNFE can be distilled into three poles:

1. "rur-urbanized dynamic growth-motor" (Columns 1 and 2)—with an open RNFE economy, a local dynamic growth motor such as tourism or commercial horticulture, dominated by services, and open to competition as well as opportunities from urban and foreign markets.

2. "intermediate" (Column 3)—with an open RNFE economy, dependent on urban demand, without a significant local growth motor, dominated by small/medium enterprise manufactures and wage employment and substantial services. These are vulnerable to competition from urban areas, but also benefit from access to urban markets. This pole is typified by the corridor zones in India.

3. "hinterland" (columns 4, 5, and 6), with a semi-closed RNFE economy mainly dependent on local demand from a weak resource base, little or no "growth motor," and dominated by micro enterprises mainly engaged in manufactures for local needs, and some services. Those enterprises are vulnerable to competition from the rapidly developing rur-urban areas. This current hinterland image is in fact the image in the pre-1980s RNFE literature, which should come as little surprise! While every country has some of this kind of area, rural Africa is still typically this.

In the next section, we examine how globalization impacts these areas.

4. RNFE in the era of globalization: the shocks and the hypothesized outcomes

4.1. Globalization comes to the recently opened and rur-urbanized rural markets

While the above "stage-setting" is a review of recent literature, here we present hypotheses new to the literature—concerning how globalization affects RNFE. Before turning to those impacts on RNFE below, we review briefly recent literature (mainly in the 2000s) on how globalization affects developing country agrifood sectors. For this short article, we focus on that vector of impact of globalization on RNFE.

First, in the 1980s (of course, unevenly over countries, and with some undertaking this later), product trade was liberalized through bilateral structural adjustment and in some regions, regional trade agreements. The initial effects have mainly been in increasing "north-south" trade. (This is a well-known story so we do not elaborate.) This reduced the cost to rural areas of imported goods such as farm inputs and machinery and consumer durables such as vehicles. We know of no systematic analysis of how much of the surge in imports went specifically to rural areas versus urban areas.

Second, mainly in the late 1980s and then into the 1990s, food industry foreign direct investment (FDI) was liberalized by many countries, usually as parts of or extensions of the trade and foreign exchange market liberalization provisions of the structural adjustment programs.

Third, the FDI liberalizations led to a massive wave of FDI by U.S. and European processing companies into developing countries, in particular into Latin America, then Asia, then Central and Eastern Europe (CEE) (Wilkinson, 2004), but much less so in Africa. This was followed by liberalization of retail FDI which led to an avalanche of retail FDI again from the U.S. and European multinational retailers, as well as regional multinationals in the developing regions (Reardon et al., 2003). This FDI spurred or was anticipated by large investments by local supermarket chains. Those investments, combined with propitious demand side conditions such as rapid urbanization and income growth, led to the "take-off" of modern retail and retail/wholesale chains (convenience and neighborhood store chains, discounts and cash & carries, supermarkets, and hypermarkets). Modern retail had been a tiny slow-growing niche before the early 1990s, and thereafter took off and grew quickly, diffusing over countries in roughly three waves. The first and second waves were mainly in Latin America and East and Southeast Asia and Central Europe. The third wave was in countries with propitious demand-side conditions (high rates of urbanization and income growth) but that had liberalized late (China, Vietnam, India) or poor-moderate demand side conditions (Eastern/Southern Africa outside South Africa) (Reardon et al., 2003).

Fourth, within a given country, the typical pattern of modern processing diffusion has the tendency to be located in first- and second-tier cities. The pattern of modern retail diffusion has been in first-, second-, then third-tier cities, and then into intermediate cities and rural towns. It is in the latter two that modern retail chains thus spill into (our broadly defined) rural space, in particular, the rur-urban portion of it. The lower-bound of rural town size into which one finds modern retail moving or planning to move varies over countries. There are many recent examples (and most of this is very re-

cent, at earliest since 2000) of which we note a few. The following are chains that have recently, are now, or are planning to soon open many chain stores (convenience stores or small supermarkets) in rural towns: (1) Soriana and Wal-Mart in Mexico; (2) G7 Mart building 10,000 stores throughout Vietnam, even in remote areas (3) Pick-n-Pay, via its franchise "Boxer" in former homeland areas of South Africa; (4) Indomaret and Alfa mini-markets chain with many stores in rural towns and provincial cities on Java, Indonesia; (5) Reliance (of India) is "creating a massive retail commercial infrastructure focused in Punjab's 12,000 odd villages" (Asian Age, 2006); and (6) Lianhua (the largest chain in China with circa 4,500 stores) is opening many stores in townships in eastern China.

The reasons for this spatial diffusion strategy associated with supermarket development in developing countries, as noted in interviews with chain managers, are as follows. First, analogous to what foreign chains see as the attraction of expanding into developing countries in general, competition is relatively weak and initial profit rates are relatively high in rural towns relative to urban centers. Second, the rural towns draw in villagers (including regular commuters) to shop for nonperishables at supermarkets (see below). Thirdly, in the retail 'war' chains are forced to occupy as much territory as fast as possible to forestall the geographical penetration of their competitors; a *pied à terre* in a rural town, given fast rates of urbanization, can become a solid position in a small tertiary city a decade later. Fourthly, in many regions, there are returning migrants seeking the kind of retail experience they had during their time in urban areas, and thus, there is demand-pull for rural retail investment.

The above sequence of globalization (and domestic response) shocks drove the diffusion of modern processing into a range of cities, and modern retail is now diffusing from its initial base in cities into the rur-urban portion of rural markets. The diffusion pattern mirrors the overall patterns of the waves over regions and countries noted above.

But, the diffusion of retail forms that can potentially affect RNFE has one more manifestation: the spread of chain stores selling farm inputs. These of course have for decades been present in the ubiquitous farm chemical store chains (Bayer and others) in rural areas. But the liberalization of FDI, and the domestic investment response, spurred the rapid globalization of farm equipment companies like John Deere and the competitive spread of domestic counterparts in many countries, like Mahindra, or the Hariyali Kisaan Bazaar (www.dscl.com), in India. These "upstream" retailers directly affect production-linkage RNFE.

4.2. Impacts of the globalization shock on RNFE—hypotheses and emerging evidence

The effects of the above "shocks" on RNFE are hypothesized to be conditioned by the three rows of Table 1 discussed in Section 3, plus now the degree of globalization's shock which translates into domestic market (urban and rur-urban) transformation and trade (involving the rural space).

The tripolar classification (mapped to the table's columns) introduced at the end of Section 3 now can be used to present our hypotheses. Recall that the three poles are (1) "rur-urbanized dynamic growth-motor" (Columns 1 and 2), (2) "intermediate" (Column 3), and (3) "hinterland" (Columns 4, 5, and 6).

As the table shows, we simply hypothesize the strength of the effect of globalization drops slowly between 1 and 2 and then fast down to 3—and that the net effect is on-balance positive in pole 1, ambiguous in pole 2, and minor in pole 3. We discuss these below, structuring the discussion first by the two "vectors" of effect, and then an overall assessment by type of rural area.

4.3. Globalization impacts: trade

Trade impacts are the most direct effect of globalization's component, are often the centerpiece of debate—yet, we hypothesize, the *least important* channel of impact except in a few places. First, researchers have for decades noted that rural zones import items that compete with local products. Examples include the ubiquitous "maggi cubes" flavoring sauces in rural areas of West Africa competing with local women producing condiments (Grains du Sel, 1997), metal and plastic buckets and tools in rural West Africa squeezing out local basket and tool making (Ancey, 1974), imported powdered milk in rural Peru (Lajo-Lazo and Morgan, 1983), second-hand clothing into rural Rwanda (Haggblade, 1989), and so on. However, we posit that in general the crowding-out effect was not large in general, with some localized exceptions. Hinterland rural consumption patterns tend to be dominated by food expenditure (at least 60%) and basic services. Basic nonfood goods consumed tend to be made locally (baskets) or bought very infrequently (clothing) or both. This is, however, conjecture, as we have seen no systematic analysis of this, old or recent.

Second, it is probable that such imports increased with trade liberalization. But, again, we have seen no systematic empirical research on the extent of these imports in the 1990s or 2000s. However, we posit that it is unlikely that at least imported food products have increased substantially for the following reasons. While there has been a massive increase in developing countries in the past two decades of purchase of processed foods with brands of foreign companies (such as Nestlé dairy products bought in Brazil), the great majority of these products are produced in-country, via FDI-based firms. Relatively little arrives as imports. Regmi and Regmi and Gehlhar, (2005) note, for example, that U.S. companies export five times less processed food products than is sold by those U.S. companies' FDI ventures in foreign markets, manufactured in those foreign markets. This is similar for Western European companies (such as the largest food company in the world, Nestlé). Wei and Cacho (1999) note that U.S. and European firms, as well as Taiwanese and Thai firms, focused on FDI-based operations manufacturing branded food products inside China, rather than exporting to China from home countries.

Third, there are direct trade impacts where RNFE enterprises export, but that appears to be relatively rare (although, again, we have seen no systematic estimates of this). Cheap labor and low rents in rural areas of developing countries, coupled with trade liberalization, induced a wave of FDI (and domestic investment) in RNFE manufacturing linked to export markets. However, while there is much attention to this phenomenon, it is restricted to the relatively few places where there are "maquiladora" operations such as for consumer light durables (e.g., clothing) in rural Ecuador, El Salvador, northern Mexico, the TVEs in rural China, and shoe operations in Sinos Valley in Brazil. Moreover, these operations are in "South-South" competition, evidenced by the debate in Mexico now about the "China impact" on the maquiladora sector (Moreira, 2007). The global export opportunity can spur RNF exports and formation of clusters, and then competitive pressure from the same global market can cause "de-clustering"—such as illustrated in the series of articles on the Sinos Valley shoe clusters by Schmitz (1995, 1998).

4.4. Globalization impacts: modern food processing industry marketing to rural areas

We hypothesize based on observation (but again, have not seen a systematic empirical analysis of this) that large-scale first-stage food processing (such as flour mills or milk collection and cooling points) are located close to raw materials, hence in rur-urban areas and intermediate cities. Second-stage food processing (such as yoghurt, bread, and noodles) tends to be near main consumer points, hence in intermediate cities and urban areas.

We hypothesize that the impact on RNFE of the rise of the above two types of large-scale processors will be thus mainly through marketing their products into rural areas, rather than being mainly located in rural areas. In the past several decades, many large second-stage food processing companies have built extensive distribution systems into rural areas; the diffusion of these rural systems mirrors, with a lag of a decade or more, the diffusion (itself in waves) of the large-scale processors in the countries. A few of many possible examples include:

- In Mexico, Bimbo and Sabritas, domestic compa-nies (and Bimbo a global multinational now), are the largest baked goods and snacks companies in Mexico; they have extensive distribution systems of trucks and warehouses in rural areas since the 1980s and Central America since the 1990s, delivering to small traditional shops as well as modern conve-nience store chains like OXXO and small supermar-kets in rural areas.
- Indofoods has a similar operation, built mainly since the late 1990s, in rural Indonesia (particularly on Java) for a range of snack foods (Natawidjaja et al., 2007).

Starting in the 1980s, there have been several important technological changes in processing and packaging that have greatly extended shelf life, and thus distribution from large processors to rural areas in developing countries. Perishables like juices and dairy products started to be made in urban factories and shipped throughout rural areas. The Swedish com-pany "Tetrapak" was a key innovator. Starting at a tiny scale in the late 1970s in developing countries, they now have massive FDI in many developing coun-tries. Farina (2002) notes that Tetrapak had revolution-ized the dairy product consumption in rural areas of Brazil, spreading very cheap ultra-high temperature (UHT) vacuum-packed milk into small towns and vil-lages. Another striking example is that of "heat and eat" prepared dishes that have very long shelf life and require no refrigeration, a technology created in India a rapidly developing business (led by medium-large companies such as Kohinoor Foods) in the past 5 years (Financial Express, 2006).

The combination of economies of scale in produc-tion and logistics networks, and cheap, good quality packaging, mean that large processing companies can and do deliver today a wide variety of products to rural towns and villages at a scale, low cost, and variety unimagined in the 1970s. Combine that with improvements in rural infrastructure (at least in Asia and Latin America, where coincidentally the rise of large-scale food processing has been most extensive), and the explanation is already clear for why field researchers observe a ubiquitous presence of branded food products in shops in rural areas. We surmise, but have not yet seen surveys on this, that the penetration of these products is most intense in pole 1 and pole 2 areas, where infrastructure is densest and rural purchasing power highest. This is bound to be a source of competition with traditional RNFE products in similar lines (and processed and prepared foods are a major backbone of RNFE manufactures). (In fact, below we present an illustration of that competition in rural Indonesia.) Again, we present these as "educated guess" hypotheses to test empirically, as we have seen no systematic empirics on this.

4.5. Modern food retailers operating in the rur-urban segment of rural areas

As noted above, modern retailers are pushing recently (mainly in the past 3–4 years) into rur-urban ar-eas. They penetrate with small-format supermarket and convenience store or mini-market chains, emphasizing cheap (often cheaper than in traditional stores) packaged/process goods, grains, pulses, oils, and "fast moving consumer goods" such as home, care, and hygiene products (the line of goods that is usually found in supermarkets in the stage of early penetration, and products that can be brought home to a refrigerator-less house). Consumers on the other hand tend to buy fresh produce, fish, or meat, in wet markets and small shops in their villages, and there is usually no price advantage in fresh products in these small stores.

There has been little work to date on how rural consumers are responding to the emergence of modern retail in their areas. We rely on one study from South Africa and a case from Indonesia to illustrate the potential effects. D'Haese and Van Huylenbroeck (2005) studied several poor villages in rural Transkei Province of South Africa. They found that the majority of villagers bought the majority of their foodstuffs (mainly maize meal, wheat flour, sugar, oil, maize, several other bulk processed products, and "fast moving consumer goods" such as soap) from small chain supermarkets in rural towns and transported the bulk purchases back to their villages using the system of rural mini-buses. These products were cheaper than in the village "spazas" or traditional small shops. The latter also had a much narrower range of brands and package sizes. They noted that the majority of the brands are from large processors in urban areas. Thus, both the retail and processing dimensions of this "penetration of modern" are challenging to local RNFE. This study's results tracks closely with our hypotheses, but of course it is but one study, and many more need to be done to establish a pattern.

A second case is that of rural Indonesia, and the penetration of several large chains of mini-markets. While there has not yet been a survey as in the South African case, the assessment recently made by the Provincial government (of West Java) is that the mini-markets are spreading quickly in rural towns and large villages, carrying very cheap processed foods of major national brands (such as Indofoods), attracting many consumers, and creating a major competitive challenge for small-scale RNFE enterprises, mainly of women making traditional processed and prepared foods (Natawidjaja et al., 2007). It is likely that this is occurring in Latin America as well; Faiguenbaum et al. (2002) note that in a rural town of 25,000 people in Chile, a local supermarket chain put in a small store

and many local shops in the small downtown went out of business.

Finally, there will be indirect effects on RNFE through modern retail's demand for goods and services from traditional RNFE. The tendency of modern retail is to source through national (rather than local) networks, to use preferred supplier arrangements (especially for processed goods), and to apply private standards of quality. The tendency of these procurement trends is to be more demanding than traditional retailers, which in turn implies that suppliers need to have the capacity to produce adequate volumes, with consistent quality, and follow commercial practices. Reardon and Timmer (2007) note that the weight of evidence regarding modern retailer relations with processors is that they tend to prefer modern suppliers with a minimum scale that can fit into the modernized procurement system note above. These supplier selection criteria would then either favor urban (hence "leakages") or medium/large RNFE suppliers or both. (The effects of all this on farmers are beyond the scope of this article.)

4.6. Assessment of overall impacts by "pole" category

Returning to our overall hypothesis in this section, we expect the strength of the globalization impact, aggregated over the above dimensions and several others we add below, will be strongest in the first pole (dynamic, rur-urbanized, with tradeables growth motors), and then decline a bit to the second pole (intermediate, little growth motor but dense and rur-urbanized), and then drop off in the third (hinterland). By contrast, the effect is expected to be positive in the first, ambiguous in the second, and minor in the third pole.

The first pole areas have the greatest chance of having positive impacts of greater exportable RNFE trade, but also greater competition (with local RNFE) from the ingress of modern processed products and retail as a competition in the rural commerce sector and an efficient conveyor of urban processed products. The direct employment impact on rural commerce might not be great because most of the formats used in small towns and intermediate cities are small supermarkets and convenience stores which have relatively high labor/output ratios (compared with hypermarkets used in urban zones).

However, the above competition with local manufactures and part of local commerce may be substantially offset by the boost to the tradeables growth motors induced by urban and trade growth. Moreover, as the majority of RNFE is in nontradeable services, the boost in incomes from the growth motors will tend to lead to more demand for these services.

The second pole areas have little chance of having positive impacts on tradeable growth poles (by our definition of these areas), and instead will tend to bear the greater brunt of the competition from modern processing and retail. The South African poor rural and West Java cases cited above appear to fall into this category. This effect would be greatest in the countries in the first and second "waves."

The third pole, the hinterland, would have least effect from all perspectives. That is, RNFE in those areas, like Bihar, Burkina, or Bolivia, tend to be still "protected" de facto from globalization effects, be they positive or negative.

5. Conclusions and implications

Rural nonfarm employment (RNFE) has become a topic of major importance in rural development—as by the mid 2000s RNFE constituted 35% of rural incomes in Africa and 50% in both Asia and Latin America. The traditional view of RNFE was, even into the mid 1990s, as in Hymer and Resnick (1969), a sleepy hinterland activity cut off from changes in the national let alone the global economy. That view was assailed by sweeping changes in rural areas—starting with the Green Revolution, then rural-opening and rur-urbanization, and lately, by globalization intervening via both trade and via modernization of the national economy (including the rise of modern retail and processing) that, via the rur-urban segment, impacts the rural economy.

We hypothesized, based on educated guesses, illustrations, and emerging studies as we could find, that the combination of the development of rural growth motors like the Green Revolution, plus the rural opening and rur-urbanization, had, by the eve of globalization in the late 1990s (when it "hit" rural areas broadly), created differentiated RNFE situations in several "poles" or classifications for rural areas. We depicted these as (1) rur-urbanized, tradeables growth-motor induced RNFE sector with clusters of small/medium enterprises for manufactures, and a preponderance of services; (2) rur-urbanized and dense zone RNFE with low-moderate

local growth motors; and (3) low density hinterland zones without growth motors. We hypothesized that globalization affects most positively and strongest the first pole, ambiguously (with various challenges) the second, and barely, the third.

If the emerging evidence continues to emerge, and continues in its present pattern of supporting our hypotheses, we recommend several development strategies and policy approaches based on these initial findings. The least specific to this article, but supported by this article, is that it is even more important during globalization to promote tradeables growth motors in rural areas, like commercial horticulture. This induces service RNFE spinoffs that counterpose and possibly outweigh the challenges from modern retail and processed goods flooding into rur-urbanized rural areas. The most specific to this article and most exciting is that "competitiveness"—in a changing urban and global economy—needs to be incorporated as a key theme of RNFE promotion. Surprisingly, the trade effects are least and the domestic market transformation effects are the strongest, so competitiveness of RNFE needs first and foremost to be conceived within the national economy.

Acknowledgments

We are grateful for comments on earlier versions from Ruben Echeverria and Kei Otsuka.

References

Ancey, G., "Relations deVoisinage Ville Campagne: Une Analyse Appliquée en Bouake; Sa Couronne et sa Région (Côte d'Ivoire)," *Mémoires ORSTOM* 70 (ORSTOM: Paris, 1974).

Asian Age, "Corporate India will farm in Punjab," April 10 (2006).

Bell, C., P. B.R. Hazell, and R. Slade, *Project Evaluation in Regional Perspective: A Study of an Irrigation Project in Northwest Malaysia* (Johns Hopkins University Press: Baltimore, MD, 1982).

Berdegué, J., E. Ramírez, T. Reardon, and G. Escobar, "Rural Non-Farm Incomes in Chile," *World Development* 29 (2001), 395–409.

Bhalla, S., "The Rise and Fall of Workforce Diversification Processes in Rural India: A Regional and Sectoral Analysis," *Centre for Economic Studies and Planning, DSA Working Paper* (Jawaharlal Nehru University: New Delhi, 1997).

Calderon, C., and L. Serven, "Macroeconomic Dimensions of Infrastructure in Latin America," http://scid.stanford.edu/events/Past%20Latin%20America/LatinAmerica2003/Serven.pdf (2003).

D'Haese, M., and G. Van Huylenbroeck, "The Rise of Supermarkets and Changing Expenditure Patterns of Poor Rural Households

Case Study in the Transkei Area, South Africa," *Food Policy* 30 (2005), 97–113.

Elbers, C., and P. Lanjouw, "Intersectoral Transfer, Growth and Inequality in Rural Ecuador," *World Development* 29 (2001), 481–496.

Escobal, J., *The Role of Public Infrastructure in Market Development in Rural Peru*, Published doctoral dissertation (Development Economics Group, University of Wageningen, 2005).

Fafchamps, M., and F. Shilpi, "The Spatial Division of Labour in Nepal," *Journal of Development Studies* 39 (2003), 23–66.

Faiguenbaum, S., J. A. Berdegué, and T. Reardon, "The Rise of Supermarkets in Chile: Effects on Producers in the Horticulture, Dairy, and Beef Chains," *Development Policy Review* 20 (2002), 459–471.

Fan, S., and C. Chan-Kang, "Road Development, Economic Growth, and Poverty Reduction in China," *Discussion Paper* no. 12 (IFPRI, Development Strategy and Governance Division: Washington, DC, 2004).

Farina, E. M. M. Q., "Consolidation, Multinationalization, and Competition in Brazil: Impacts on Horticulture and Dairy Product Systems," *Development Policy Review* 20 (2002), 441–457.

Financial Express, "Slices of India in a Pack," http://www.ficci.com/news/viewnews1.asp?news_id=449, accessed April 21, 2007.

Grains du Sel, "Commerce, les Dégâts du Cube Maggi," mimeo, December (1997).

GRAL/CEDAL, *Villes Intermédiaires, Vitalité Economique et Acteurs Sociaux, Problèmes d'Amérique Latine* n° 14, Paris, La documentation française, juillet-septembre (1994).

Haggblade, S., "A Review of Rwanda's Textile Clothing Subsector," *Employment and Enterprise Policy Analysis Discussion Paper* 24 (Harvard Institute for International Development: Cambridge, MA, 1989).

Haggblade, S., P. Hazell, and T. Reardon, "Strategies for Stimulating Equitable Growth in the Rural Nonfarm Economy," in S. Haggblade, P. B. R. Hazell, and T. Reardon, eds., *Transforming the Rural Nonfarm Economy* (Johns Hopkins University Press: Baltimore, MD, 2007).

Hardoy, J. E., and D. Satterthwaite, eds., *Small and Intermediate Centres, their Role in National and Regional Development in the Third World* (Hodder and Stoughton: London, 1989).

Hazell, P. B. R., and C. Ramasamy. *Green Revolution Reconsidered: The Impact of the High Yielding Rice Varieties in South India* (Johns Hopkins University Press: Baltimore, MD, 1991).

Humphrey, J., and H. Schmitz, "The Triple C Approach to Local Industrial Policy," *World Development* 24 (1996), 1859–1877.

Hymer, S., and S. Resnick, "A Model of an Agrarian Economy with Nonagricultural Activities," *American Economic Review* 59 (1969), 493–506.

Jordan, R., and D. Simioni, eds., *Ciudades Intermedias de América Latina y el Caribe: Propuestas para la Gestión Urbana* (CEPAL /Ministero degli Affari Esteri -Cooperazione Italiana: Santiago de, Chile, 1998).

Lajo-Lazo, M., and M. Morgan, "Agroalimentación y Agroindustria," *Realidady Perspectivas* ed., *Fundación F. Ebert. Serie Diagnóstico y Debate*, No 1, July (1983).

Natawidjaja, R., T. Reardon, and S. Shetty, with T. Perdana, E. Rasmikayati, T. Insan Noor, S. Bachri, T. Reardon, and R. Hernandez, *The Impact of the Rise of Supermarkets on Horticulture Markets and Farmers in Indonesia*. UNPAD/MSU Report to the World Bank (2007).

Perry, G. E., W. Foster, D. Lederman, and A. Valdés, *Beyond the City: The Rural Contribution to Development* (World Bank: Washington, DC, 2005).

Pingali, P. L., and M. W. Rosegrant, "Agricultural Commercialization and Diversification: Processes and Policies," *Food Policy* 20 (1995), 171–185.

Rashid, S., R. Cummings, Sr., and A. Gulati, "Grain Marketing Parastatals in Asia: Results from Six Case Studies," *World Development*, forthcoming.

Reardon, T., "Using Evidence of Household Income Diversification to Inform Study of the Rural Nonfarm Labor Market in Africa," *World Development* 25 (1997), 735–748.

Reardon, T., and K. Stamoulis, "Relating Agro-industrialization, Intermediate Cities, and Farm-Nonfarm Linkages: An Investment Perspective with Latin American Examples," *Politica Agricola*, Número Especial (published by Universidad Autonoma-de Mexico) (1998), 201–226.

Reardon, T., and C. P. Timmer, "Transformation of Markets for Agricultural Output in Developing Countries Since 1950: How Has Thinking Changed?" in R. E. Evenson and P. Pingali, eds., *Handbook of Agricultural Economics: Agricultural Development: Farmers, Farm Production and Farm Markets* (Elsevier Press: Amsterdam, 2007).

Reardon, T., J. E. Taylor, K. Stamoulis, P. Lanjouw, A. Balisacan, "Effects of Nonfarm Employment on Rural Income Inequality in Developing Countries: An Investment Perspective," *Journal of Agricultural Economics* 51 (2000), 266–288.

Reardon, T., J. Berdegué, and G. Escobar, "Rural Nonfarm Employment and Incomes in Latin America: Overview of issues, patterns, and determinants," *World Development* 29 (2001), 395–409.

Reardon, T., C. P. Timmer, C. B. Barrett, and J. Berdegué, "The Rise of Supermarkets in Africa, Asia, and Latin America," *American Journal of Agricultural Economics* 85 (2003), 1140–1146.

Reardon, T., J. A. Berdegué, C. B. Barrett, and K. Stamoulis, "Household Income Diversification into Rural Nonfarm Activities," in S. Haggblade, P. Hazell, and T. Reardon, eds., *Transforming the Rural Nonfarm Economy* (Johns Hopkins University Press: Baltimore, MD, 2007).

Regmi, A., and M. Gehlar, eds., *New Directions in Global Food Markets*. USDA Economic Research Service, Agricultural Information Bulletin no. 794, February. Accessed from www.ers.usda.gov on November 3, 2005.

Renkow, M., "Cities, Towns, and the Rural Nonfarm Economy," in S. Haggblade, P. Hazell, and T. Reardon, *Transforming the Rural Nonfarm Economy* (Johns Hopkins University Press, Baltimore, MD, 2007).

Schejtman, A., and J. A. Berdegué, *Desarrollo Territorial Rural* (Center for Latin American Rural Development: Santiago, Chile, Rimisp, 2002).

Schmitz, H., "Small Shoemakers and Fordist Giants: Tale of a Supercluster," *World Development* 23 (1995), 9–28.

Schmitz, H., "Responding to Global Competitive Pressures: Local Cooperation and Upgrading in the Sinos Valley, Brazil," *IDS Working Paper* no 82 (Institute of Development Studies: Sussex, 1998).

Wei, A., and J. Cacho, "Competition among Foreign and Chinese Agro-Food Enterprises in the Process of Globalization," *International Food and Agribusiness Management Review* 2 (1999), 437–451.

Wilkinson, J., "The Food Processing Industry, Globalization, and Developing Countries," *Electronic Journal of Agricultural and Development Economics* 1 (2004), 184–201.

Wilson, S., and K. Wasike, "Road Infrastructure Policies in Kenya: Historical Trends and Current Challenges," *Working Paper* No. 1 (Kenya Institute for Public Policy Research and Analysis: Nairobi, 2001).

World Bank, *World Development Report 2008: Agriculture for Development* (World Bank: Washington, DC, 2007).

Invited Panels

Agricultural research and policy for better health and nutrition in developing countries: a food systems approach

Per Pinstrup-Andersen*

Abstract

This article is about the two-way causal relationships between the global food system and health and nutrition. It argues that the global food system begins and ends with health and that the prioritization and implementation of agricultural research and policy should consider health and nutrition effects. An integrated health and food policy approach is likely to be more effective in achieving both health and economic development goals that the current practice of separate sectorial policies. The article identifies a large number of health and nutrition factors affecting and affected by the food system and suggests research and policies to enhance positive effects and reduce negative ones.

JEL classification: I18, I32

Keywords: health and agriculture; food policy; global food system; agricultural research; nutrition policy; health and the food system

1. Introduction

This article is about one aspect of the interaction between human health and the global food system. It is about how agricultural research and government policy can alter the impact of the health and nutrition status of individuals and societies on the global food system and how it can alter the impact of the global food system on human health and nutrition. The goal of the article is to enhance the understanding of how agricultural research and government policy can best improve the health and nutrition of poor people in developing countries.

The author believes it is reasonable to argue that the global food system begins and ends with health and nutrition. Health influences the food system as an input through its effect on the human resource and through interactions with natural resources used in food production. The health and nutrition status of the labor force occupied in the food system—and that is a large share of the poor in developing countries—will make a significant impact on the degree of efficiency and

effectiveness of the food system and how it ends up serving societies, including the poor. Similarly, health interactions with natural resources such as waterborne diseases in irrigation and other water management systems can influence the food system both through its impact on farm labor and through the use-efficiency of the resource. That is what the author calls the beginning of the global food system. Healthy and well-nourished individuals are critical to a well-functioning global food system. The "end," as visualized here, is the impact of the global food system on people's well-being including their health and nutrition. Since a large share of the people who suffer from poor health and/or poor nutrition is involved directly in the food system, the world is dealing with a self-enforcing vicious cycle in which poor health and nutrition leads to low productivity human resources, which, in turn, contributes to deficiencies in the food system, low incomes, and poor health and nutrition.

The global food system is a means to an end, not an end in itself. A global system that leaves a large share of the global population in a state of poor health and nutrition is not a desirable food system. Neither is a global food system that exploits scarce natural resources in an unsustainable manner. Unfortunately, while being

H.E. Babcock Professor, Food, Nutrition and Public Policy, Division of Nutritional Sciences, College of Agriculture and Life Sciences, Cornell University, 305 Savage Hall, Ithaca, NY, U.S.A. 14853-6301.

very effective in meeting economic demands at falling real prices, the existing global food system is characterized by both of these challenges. Rapidly increasing prevalence of chronic diseases caused, in part, by overweight and obesity, continued widespread prevalence of energy and nutrient deficiencies causing the death of more than 5 million pre-school children annually and poor growth and poor health in many more, as well as hunger in millions of adults, unsustainable use of water, soil degradation, and a variety of other insults on the ecology, all contribute to the conclusion that the global food system could do better. Is it all the fault of the global food system? No, but changes in the global food system brought about by agricultural research and government policy can contribute to improvements.

Efforts to improve human health and nutrition through agricultural research and government policy aimed at the global food system require improved understanding of how health and nutrition influence the global food system, how the food system influences health and nutrition, and where, in the system, interventions such as government policy and research may be effective. The purpose of this article is to contribute to such understanding. The next section will present an overview of the current health and nutrition situation, emphasizing those aspects of particular relevance to developing countries and their poor people in the context of the global food system. The article then proceeds with a schematic overview of the global food system followed by an attempt to identify the most important interactions between health and nutrition, on the one hand, and the global food system, on the other. Potential policy measures and agricultural research that may reduce negative and improve positive interactions between the global food system and human health and nutrition are identified and the article concludes with a brief summary of the suggested priorities for policy and research to improve human health and nutrition through a more appropriate global food system.

2. Human health and nutrition: this is where the global food system begins

The author argues that the global food system begins with the human health and nutrition situation for two reasons. First, a large share of the world's poor is employed in the food system. Their health and nutrition conditions are of critical importance not only for their own well-being but for their productivity and creativity, which, in turn, will influence the efficiency and effectiveness of the global food system. Thus, good health and nutrition is an important input into the food system. Second, while the global food system plays a key role in the generation of economic growth in virtually every developing country, it is at the same time of critical importance as a means to achieve good health and nutrition for all. While economic growth may be necessary to achieve good health and nutrition, it is not sufficient; the nature of the economic growth matters. Because of the importance of both quantity and quality of food in the lives of all and because of the large number of poor, unhealthy, and malnourished people employed within the food system, the critical importance of food in efforts to assure good health and nutrition, and the large differences in the efficiency and effectiveness in the food systems across communities and countries and therefore apparent opportunities for improvements, the author argues that a combined policy focus on that system and the health sector is likely to be more cost-effective to improve human health and nutrition than a focus on other sectors.

3. The current health and nutrition situation

During the last 50 years, increases in life expectancy and reductions in child mortality rates illustrate dramatic improvements in human health at the global level. However, the health status is very low among low-income countries and poor people. Of the total global disease burden, 92% is found in developing countries (Diaz-Bonilla et al., 2002). Furthermore, according to the World Health Organization (2006), pre-school children in poverty face a much higher (2–4 times) probability of death than nonpoor pre-schoolers. Between 10 and 12 million pre-school children die of preventable causes every year—about half of them from hunger and nutrition-related factors. The large majority comes from poor households. The mortality rate among pre-school children from the poorest quintile of the population of 29 countries, for which data were available from surveys conducted since 2000, was found by the World Health Organization (2006) to be 2.5 times that of pre-school children from the richest quintile.[1] That is slightly higher than 10 years earlier. Similarly, the probability of dying is 2–4 times higher among poor adults than nonpoor adults (Diaz-Bonilla et al., 2002).

Stunting among pre-school children is also highly correlated with the wealth of the household. In all of the 47 countries for which data were reported by the World Health Organization (2006), the prevalence of stunting was higher in the poorest quintile of the population than in the richest quintile. A simple unweighted average across the 47 countries showed that the prevalence in the poorest quintile was more than three times (315%) higher than the prevalence in the richest quintile.

Between 70% and 75% of the world's poor people reside in rural areas of developing countries. Their health status is poor. The mortality rate among rural pre-school children in the above-mentioned 29 countries was 50% higher than the mortality rate among pre-schoolers in urban areas during the period since 2000—an increase from 10 years earlier (WHO, 2006). The mortality rate for pre-school children estimated on the basis of the most recent survey in each of 67 developing countries was higher for rural children in all but two countries.[2] A simple average across the 67 countries (without weighing for population size) showed that the mortality rate was 43% higher in rural than in urban areas. In three countries, rural mortality rates were more than twice the urban rates. Data for the prevalence of stunting in pre-school children in rural and urban areas were available for 56 countries. The prevalence was highest in rural areas in all but one country. On the average (unweighted across countries), the rural prevalence of stunting among pre-school children was 63% higher than the prevalence in urban areas. In 10 countries (18% of the sample), the prevalence of stunting in rural areas was more than twice that of urban areas.

The interaction between the environment and human health is important. Thus, in a recent study, Prüss-Ustün and Corvalán (2006) estimated that modifiable environmental factors, including physical, chemical, and

biological hazards, account for 24% of the global health burden (measured in terms of "disability adjusted life years"), 23% of all premature deaths, and more than one-third (36%) of children's health burden. The diseases with the largest burden attributable to modifiable environmental factors were diarrhea, lower respiratory infections, injuries, and malaria. Although the environmental factors included in the analysis are found in both rural and urban areas, other studies have found strong interaction among human health, the natural environment, and the food system, particularly in low-income developing countries where the food system is closely related to natural resources (Diaz-Bonilla et al., 2002). Furthermore, access to improved water sources is less in rural areas. In 2002, 84% of Africa's urban residents had access to improved water sources compared to 45% of the rural residents. In Asia, the estimates were 94% for urban and 79% for rural (World Health Organization, 2006). Thus, it may be hypothesized that the strong causal link between modifiable environmental factors and human health implies a strong causal link between the food system and health.

In addition to poor nutrition and related health problems—which will be discussed below—a large number of diseases and health hazards link human health and the global food system. They include food- and waterborne microbial pathogens causing diarrhea, waterborne diseases such as malaria, zoonotic pathogens such as salmonella, campylobacter, E.coli, Avian flu, BSE, HIV/AIDS, Tuberculosis, poisoning from chemicals, pesticide residues in food, parasites, mycotoxins, antibiotics in food causing the risk of antibiotics resistance in human, and more. Some of the diseases and health hazards influence the food system while others are influenced by it. These causal links will be discussed in a subsequent section.

4. The triple burden of malnutrition

While the above mortality and morbidity rates are influenced by a large number of health factors, malnutrition plays a major role and interacts with many of the diseases mentioned. Existing malnutrition may be classified into three related but distinctly different problems: energy deficiencies, nutrient deficiencies, and excessive net energy intake. This is what the author calls "the triple burden of malnutrition."

---

[1] The data are from 29 countries (16 from Sub-Saharan Africa, 5 from Asia, 5 from Latin America and the Caribbean, and 3 from the Middle East) that have published the results from demographic and health surveys carried out since 2000 and 10 years earlier (WHO, 2006).

[2] The probability of dying within 5 years after birth per 1000 live births. The surveys were carried out during the period 1985–2004, with 55 percent carried out during the period 2000–2004.

Malnutrition interacts with infectious and chronic diseases, and plays an important role in the resistance to, and severity of, various diseases. Thus, the health effects of malnutrition are complex and an exhaustive treatment of the matter is beyond this article. Suffice it to briefly present the magnitudes and nature of the triple burden.

Developing countries are increasingly faced with not just energy and nutrient deficiencies and infectious diseases but also excess net energy intake resulting in overweight, obesity, and chronic diseases such as cardiovascular diseases, diabetes, and certain cancers. Thus, all three burdens are important public health problems in developing countries. Because of their impact on labor productivity, income earning and learning capacity, economic growth, and efforts to alleviate poverty, they are also important development problems. Widespread nutrition problems cause low labor productivity, reduced economic growth, poverty, and large demands for public funds to deal with the resulting health problems. Furthermore, while energy and nutrient deficiencies have traditionally been considered poor people's problems and overweight, obesity, and resulting chronic diseases rich people's problems, such thinking is now outdated. Overweight and obesity are rapidly becoming an integral part of poverty in all but the poorest countries.

About 800 million people suffer from energy deficiencies and between one-third and one-fourth of all pre-school children in developing countries do not grow to their full genetic potential; they suffer from low weight-for-age, low height-for-age, or both. In spite of promises made by virtually all the world's countries at the World Food Summit in 1996 and reaffirmed 6 years later to reduce by half the number of people suffering from energy and nutrient deficiencies between 1990 and 2015, the efforts to do so have been minimal and the results dismal. Only about one-third of the countries have managed to reduce the number at all and about half actually experienced an increase during the first half of the 25-year period. While the number of energy-deficient people dropped slightly during the first half of the 1990s, it has increased since then to the current levels—slightly above 800 million or roughly the same as in 1990. Extrapolations to 2015 show no significant reductions. Thus, with business as usual, there will still be about 800 million energy-deficient people at the end of the 25-year period

during which the number should have been reduced to 400 million.

Some countries, such as China, have made great progress and are expected to exceed the 2015 goal. Because of its population size, China's accomplishments have a great influence on the global data. If China is removed from the global figures, the rest of the world has seen a significant increase in the number of energy-deficient people from 630 million in 1990 to 673 million as an annual average for the 3-year period 2000–2002. Extrapolating to 2015 shows an increase of about 100 million energy-deficient people between 1990 and 2015 instead of the promised reduction from 630 to 315 million—a gap of more than 400 million people. None of the four regions, Sub-Saharan Africa, West Asia and North Africa, Latin America and the Caribbean, and Asia will achieve the World Food Summit goal with business as usual.

The Millennium Development Goal of reducing by half the proportion of the population that suffers from energy deficiencies is easier to achieve because of population growth. While the proportion is falling globally and in all regions except West Asia and North Africa, extrapolation of past performance does not lead to the achievement at the global level. However, Latin America and the Caribbean and Asia are expected to achieve the Goal.

Progress toward achieving the Millennium Development Goal is measured by two indicators: the proportion of the population that suffers from energy deficiencies discussed above and the prevalence of underweight pre-school children. As in the case of energy deficiencies, the prevalence of underweight pre-schoolers is decreasing but the rate of decrease is insufficient to reach the goal by 2015 at the global level (UNICEF, 2006). Two regions—East Asia (dominated by China) and Latin America and the Caribbean—are expected to achieve the goal. South Asia, home to more that one-half of the world's underweight pre-school children and more than half of low-birth-weight babies, Sub-Saharan Africa, where the number of underweight pre-school children is expected to continue to increase at almost the same rate as the population increase, and West Asia and North Africa, where both the number of underweight pre-school children and their proportion of the population are expected to continue to increase, are almost certain not to reduce by half the proportion of their pre-school children that suffer from underweight by 2015.

Micronutrient deficiencies (primarily iron, vitamin A, iodine, and zinc) affect about 40% of the population in developing countries causing severe health problems, particularly among poor women and children. Diets poor in micronutrients can cause, or contribute to, a variety of diseases—blindness, premature death, reduced labor productivity, and impaired mental development (UNICEF, 2004). Sufficient micronutrients in the diet can protect against infectious diseases and reduce mortality (Catelo, 2006). Iron deficiencies are particularly widespread in parts of Asia where 50–75% of pregnant women and pre-school children suffer from iron deficiency anemia. Micronutrient deficiencies are also widespread in Sub-Saharan Africa. In eight out of 36 countries for which data were available (22%), 80–85% of the pre-school children suffered from iron deficiency anemia and more than half of the pre-school children were affected by iron deficiency anemia in all but three of the 36 countries (IFPRI, 2006). UNICEF (2004) estimates that more than a third of Sub-Saharan Africa's population suffer debilitating effects of micronutrient deficiencies and the annual cost to these countries' economies is estimated to exceed $2.3 billion. The Global Alliance for Improved Nutrition (GAIN; 2006) estimates that micronutrient malnutrition will cause one million pre-school children to die within a year of their estimate.

Increases in overweight and obesity, resulting primarily from excessive energy intake relative to energy expenditures, are taking on epidemic proportions in both rich and poor countries. Two-thirds of the United States population and more than half of the populations of several European countries are overweight or obese and the prevalence is increasing fast, particularly among children and adolescents. The high and rapidly increasing levels of overweight, obesity, and related chronic diseases are not limited to high-income countries. The prevalence of overweight and obesity is growing rapidly in many middle-income developing countries and some low-income ones. The growth is particularly noteworthy in China where it is projected that about one-third of the population will be overweight or obese by 2020 (Horton, 1999). In high-income countries, the prevalence of overweight and obesity is highest among low-income population groups, while both high- and low-income individuals are affected in middle-income countries and the prevalence is highest among the relatively well-to-do population groups in low-income countries.

As national income levels increase, it appears that the prevalence of overweight and obesity increases faster among low-income population groups than among the better-off, presumably in part because of a high correlation between income and educational level. On the basis of results from anthropometric surveys in 80 countries carried out in 2000 or later, WHO found that the national prevalence of obesity among women above the age of 15 years increased with increasing national incomes, while the prevalence of stunting in pre-school children decreased (Figure 1). As noted by the World Health Organization (2006), countries at the same level of national income may have very different prevalence of stunting and obesity, respectively, implying that factors other than those closely correlated with national incomes are important determinants of both stunting and obesity. Policy prescriptions are particularly difficult for middle-income countries because they show the coexistence of high prevalence of stunting in pre-school children, high and increasing prevalence of obesity in women, and widespread micronutrient deficiencies.

Evidence of negative economic impact of the triple burden of malnutrition is convincing although incomplete. Estimates by Horton (1999) show productivity losses for both energy and nutrient deficiencies between 5% and 17%. The World Health Organization estimates that 15.9% of the global burden of child disease is due to under-nutrition. In developing countries, the figure is 18% (Gillespie and Haddad, 2003). The World Bank estimates that malnutrition accounts for 20–25% of the global health burden (World Bank, 1993). Pelletier et al. (1994) estimated that malnutrition was associated with 51% of all child deaths in nine Asian countries. Ross and Thomas (1996) estimated that iron deficiency anemia is associated with 23% of all maternal deaths in these nine countries (65,000 deaths). On the basis of findings from a number of studies of the effect of vitamin A supplementation in deficient populations, Beaton et al. (1993) conclude that mortality in pre-school children and pregnant women fell by 27% and 40%, respectively, and malaria attacks decreased by 30%.

While the importance of overweight and obesity in the increasing prevalence of chronic diseases and the related increase in health costs is well documented,

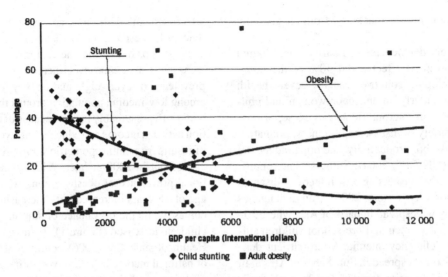

Figure 1. Undernutrition and obesity by the level of GDP per capita. *Source:* WHO, 2006.

estimates of the economic costs of overweight and obesity in developing countries are still to be done.

5. The global food system

Characterizing it as a process or set of processes that converts natural and human-made resources and inputs into food, the food system can be represented by a set of physical activities such as primary production, secondary production or processing, exchange activities such as transfer of ownership, transportation, and storage, and consumption. A food system can also be described as a social and economic system within which these and other physical activities take place. In this article, the author thinks of a food system as one that combines physical activities with economic, social, cultural, and policy factors for the purpose of achieving societal and private goals including improved human health and nutrition. The system is driven by the behavior of a set of actors, including resource owners, farmers, traders, processors, consumers, policymakers, and officials in government and nongovernment organizations, who respond to opportunities, challenges, risks, and constraints imposed by biophysical, socioeconomic, cultural, and policy environments. As such, the global food system is a dynamic behavioral system that can be influenced by public policy through incentives and regulations.

A food system may be local, national, regional, or global. A global food system may be a description of a set of national, regional, or local food systems that may be isolated from one another or they may be connected through exchange, i.e., trade. In this article, the term "global food system" is used to describe a system that connects many national and local systems through trade, information sharing, technology transfer, and other aspects of globalization.

A stylized description of such a system may consist of seven components: health and nutrition, natural (including human) and human-made resources, primary production, secondary production or processing, exchange activities, consumption, and health and nutrition. Except for exchange activities—which operate between any two of the other components—these components are visualized as being carried out in sequence. Hawkes and Ruel (2006) provide a conceptual framework of the linkages between agriculture and health.

6. Interactions between the global food system and human health and nutrition

Energy and nutrient deficiencies, as well as infectious and chronic diseases, may influence the food system through labor productivity, technology adoption, input and credit application, and utilization of land, water, and other resources. The intuition that the health and nutrition status of workers influence their productivity has been affirmed by a large number of studies. Sick and malnourished people generally produce less than healthy and well-nourished people. Low labor productivity translates into lower wages (if hired labor), lower incomes (if self-employed farmers, traders, or processors), and lower efficiency in the food system. Poor health and nutrition among farmers is also likely to reduce the motivation and incentive to adopt new technology, seek credit, and apply appropriate inputs. In addition to energy and nutrient deficiencies, a large number of diseases, such as HIV/AIDS and TB, may contribute to low labor productivity and reduced motivation and incentives. HIV/AIDS may incapacitate or kill working-age members of farming households, leaving the fields unattended and causing all household members to face abject poverty, hunger, and—when all buffers have been exploited—death. A large increase in the number of orphans, falling life expectancy, and high mortality rates among adults in parts of Sub-Saharan Africa and increasingly in parts of Asia are a testimony to the tragedy. While policy interventions specific to each disease, i.e., access to antiviral drugs for people affected by HIV/AIDS, are urgently needed, there is also a need to develop integrated policy measures that address both the diseases and their consequences for people's livelihood. Strategies should be developed jointly by the health and agricultural ministries, the relevant NGOs, and local communities. Policies, aimed at the global food system, that ignore the implications of health and nutrition as inputs into the system will be less efficient than those that take a more comprehensive approach.

Recent developments in science, including the description of genomes for an increasing number of species and the application of molecular biology, in general, and genetic modification in particular, offer tremendous new opportunities for the application of science to improve the global food system for the benefit of better health and nutrition. The most important health and nutrition impact of technological change in the food system is undoubtedly that which comes about through higher incomes among low-income families that depend on incomes coming from the food system and lower prices for poor consumers. However, technological change in the food system can influence human health and nutrition in a number of other ways (Pinstrup-Andersen et al., 1976). First, the relative price

changes among foods will influence the diet composition, which, in turn, will influence the energy and nutrient balance of the diet relative to needs. Priorities in the research that produces new knowledge and technology will influence these relative prices. The most obvious illustration is the tremendous success in research to expand the productivity of rice, wheat, and maize—the so-called Green Revolution. Unit-costs of production of rice and wheat in Asia dropped by around 40%. These cost savings reduced rice and wheat prices to the consumers and increased incomes within the food system. In large measure because research on pulses was not prioritized, the productivity of those food crops did not increase. Asian farmers responded as expected by producing more rice and wheat and relatively less pulses. As mentioned above, rice and wheat prices dropped while the prices for pulses increased. Consumers responded as expected by consuming more rice and wheat and less pulses.

From the point of view of avoiding mass starvation in Asia, which was its overriding objective, the Green Revolution was a thundering success. In addition, it was extremely successful in helping millions of poor farmers and farm workers out of poverty. Having accomplished these goals, the next step from a human health and nutrition point of view would be to emphasize research to reduce unit-costs of production of pulses and other food commodities rich in the micronutrients most deficient in the diets of low-income people—namely iron, vitamin A, and zinc. As already mentioned, the health and economic gains from the reduction of these deficiencies are estimated to be very large.

There are essentially five options that could be pursued: (1) industrial fortification, e.g., adding vitamin A to food commodities as part of the processing activities; (2) distribution of nutrient supplements such as vitamin A pills; (3) launching an educational campaign to change consumer behavior in favor of a diet that would meet the energy and nutrient requirements; (4) change the nutrient composition of the foods poor consumers consume through biofortification, e.g., enhance the content of absorbable iron in foods consumed by populations with a high prevalence of iron deficiency anemia; and (5) creating incentives for consumers to change their diets to meet both energy and nutrient needs, such as research to increase productivity and reduce unit-costs of those foods that could most effectively add the nutrients that are deficient. Price policy, such as commodity or product-specific taxes or subsidies that would change relative prices, would be another potential policy measure.

The choice among the five options will depend on the specific circumstances. While options (1) and (2) may be effective in urban settings and rural areas with good infrastructure, they are likely to be costly and they do not provide a sustainable solution to the problem. They are unlikely to work among the rural poor in most locations because of deficient infrastructure and because most staple foods that could be fortified are not likely to enter into a marketing process where such processing is viable, although small-scale, village-level fortification may be an option in some cases. Distribution of supplements may be a short-term *ad hoc* solution until a sustainable approach is in place. Option (3) may help in cases where the deficiencies are a result of lack of knowledge rather than lack of income. However, in the case of low-income people, it is likely to be useful only in combination with increasing incomes and only by using new innovative communication approaches made possible by the information and communication revolution in developing countries. In this regard, it is useful to keep in mind that the food system is driven by the behavior of the actors in the system, including consumers and retailers, who do not necessarily prioritize improvements of health and nutrition over other goals.

Biofortification (option 4) offers exciting opportunities for helping to solve deficiencies of specific minerals or vitamins in the diets of people with severe income constraints and where the diet is dominated by one or two staples, such as rice or wheat in most of Asia, maize, cassava, or sweet potato in most of Sub-Saharan Africa, and potatoes in most of the Andes of Latin America. Research aimed at the enhancement of the content of absorbable iron and vitamin A in rice and vitamin A in sweet potatoes has shown great promise. Ongoing research within the Consultative Group for International Agricultural Research (CGIAR) is attempting to enhance the content of iron, vitamin A, and zinc in several staple foods. The author believes it is reasonable to expect that these, and related research efforts, will be successful in making biofortified foods of that nature available within a reasonable time frame if the appropriate research and development investments continue to be made. The issue then hinges on economics and behavior. Can the biofortified seed be made available to farmers at costs that are less than the expected benefits to the farmers? Must the price of biofortified food be higher than other food for the farmer to be interested and will consumers pay more for biofortified food? The reason for bringing up these questions is not to try to provide answers but to illustrate the importance of behavioral responses to external influences such as public policy and agricultural research. While the global food system can be described as a set of physical activities, failure to recognize its behavioral aspects is likely to lead to disappointing outcomes of policy and research initiatives.

Option (5) provides the ideal outcome—namely, a diversified diet that meets all energy and nutrient requirements. The principal barrier to such a diet is poverty. Thus, the obvious policy choices are for those that would help poor people out of poverty. However, there are many other policy measures that might help low-income people obtain a better diet, such as investment in the development and dissemination of productivity-increasing, unit-cost reducing knowledge and technologies for the food system with emphasis on foods that are most likely to add the nutrients that are deficient in the diet, reducing the costs of distribution through more efficient marketing and processing, price policy, information campaigns that promote good nutrition, and regulation of promotion and advertising expected to have adverse nutrition effects, such as the promotion of foods high in sugar, sweeteners, saturated and transfat, and low in required nutrients. Policies aimed at dietary changes should take into account the expected impact on both energy deficiency and excess energy intake. Since any one policy measure is unlikely to achieve both reductions in energy and nutrient deficiencies and reductions in excess energy intake, and since both deficiencies and overweight and obesity are prevalent in an increasing number of developing countries—notably middle-income countries—the design and implementation of an appropriate policy package is a serious challenge in those countries.

Another way in which the food system and health interacts is through waterborne diseases and parasites. Waterborne bacteria, viruses, and parasites causing diarrhea, malaria, and other waterborne diseases may influence the food system through reduced labor productivity and the food system may influence the prevalence of malaria through irrigation and poor water management. Because of the two-way causal link between malaria and water management, effective policy measures should include both the health and the food system aspects. Water contaminated with arsenic, cadmium, or other poisonous metals may cause illness through drinking water or the consumption of contaminated fish. Arsenic poisoning is particularly problematic in South Asia.

A large number of other health factors may influence the food system, e.g., microbial and chemical contamination leading to illness among workers and consumers and transfer of zoonotic pathogens, such as salmonella, avian influenza, and mad cow disease from animals to humans. These factors may also be outcomes of the food system, thus providing a feedback loop contributing to a potential vicious circle.

In order to support rural health care systems and make them less costly, there is a need for integrated policies for the food system and health to reduce the health risks generated by the food system. Some of the most important in developing countries include microbial contamination such as foodborne salmonella and campyabacter contamination of drinking water, crops, and the microenvironment where children are, including open sewer systems, by bacteria from animal manure and human feces; chemical risks such as pesticide poisoning of farmers and farm workers; pesticide residues in food and nitrate poisoning from drinking water contaminated with nitrogen fertilizers or manure; contamination with heavy metals from urban wastes; and zoonotic pathogens transferred from livestock such as avian influenza, BSE, and related Cruzfeldt-Jacob's disease in humans, Lyme disease carried by ticks, E.coli, and salmonella in animal products. Occupational hazards, including accidents in the food system, are another important source of poor health which feeds back to labor productivity (ILO, 2000). Toxins and allergens in foods may be natural or introduced through research while research may also remove toxins and allergens.

Negative health effects from the use of chemical pesticides are of particular importance both to poor farmers and farm workers and to consumers. This is a problem where both traditional plant breeding and genetic engineering can be particularly helpful by developing pest resistance in plants. Much progress has already been made in, for example, rice production where the use of chemical pesticides has decreased significantly. The potential of genetic engineering to reduce the need for chemical pesticides to protect plants is illustrated by the Bt-gene introduced in several staple crops such as maize and cotton. For example, when first introduced in China, farmers reduced pesticide use by 80% without yield loss. Price policy may also be important. Large price subsidies on pesticides in several Asian countries during the first phase of the Green Revolution resulted in significant overuse of pesticide. Regulative policies that prohibit the use of pesticides considered of great risk to humans would also help reduce the negative health effects. The above are often included in what is popularly referred to as food safety, although the definition of that term is not unique.

The interaction between the food system and health through drugs can have both positive and negative health effects. On the positive side, plants and animals can be used to produce drugs needed to treat important human health problems. This is a dynamic research area at present. On the negative side, the use of antibiotics in the food system, for example in animal production and in the use of certain marker genes in plant breeding, can contribute to antibiotics resistance in infectious diseases and parasites affecting humans.

Campaigns by some civil society organizations against the use of modern science to improve the food supply, such as irradiation and genetic engineering, along with advertising campaigns by the private sector promoting highly processed foods with high content of fats, sugar, and sweeteners tend to outweigh health and nutrition education programs promoted by the public sector. Developments in science may soon make it possible for individual consumers to design diets that reduce genetically determined health risks on the basis of knowledge about their genomes (Dawson, 2006). While nutrigenomics is still in its infancy, the development of such individual diets is not as far-fetched as it may sound. Widespread dietary modifications in response to the testing for blood cholesterol are a step in that direction. Research to develop functional foods, i.e., foods that have physiological benefits beyond those of basic nutrition (McGill, 2006), is advanced and research is under way to develop food with more desirable nutrient profiles using nanotechnology (Ebbesen, 2006). While many of these science-based dietary changes may be of little relevance to poor consumers, they may be important to low-income farmers and labor in the food system because they open up new opportunities for adding value to agricultural commodities and, in that way, generate income among the poor.

Increasing political consumerism attempts to influence not only the individual consumer's behavior but various aspects of the food system, including production and distribution processes. As argued by Micheletti (2006), political consumerism is a response to globalization and the associated weakening of the ability of national governments to regulate and provide incentives to the market and to the lack of effective international institutions. While these civil society activities tend to focus on justice, fairness, food safety, use of modern science, and responsible behavior by private corporations, the nutrition and health effects may be significant. These effects may come about through changes in incomes, relative prices, food safety, and a variety of health risks to workers in the food system.

Rapidly increasing concentration in the supply chain of the global food system, including the development of large supermarkets and supermarket chains, facilitates the impact of political consumerism. Supermarkets may orient their product choice toward the desires expressed by the political consumer, limiting the choice offered to all consumers. The decision by many European supermarkets to exclude legally labeled genetically modified foods and promotion of higher-priced organic foods is a case in point. In fact, the behavior of the increasingly concentrated food distribution system is gradually replacing the role of national governments in providing regulations and incentives within the food system in both high- and low-income countries. The health and nutrition risk of the private sector replacing the government is that efforts to maximize profits are incompatible with health and nutrition goals. Self-regulation by the private sector raises important ethical questions (Pinstrup-Andersen, 2005).

7. A summary of potential agricultural research and policies

As illustrated above, science and policies aimed at the global food system may contribute to improved human health and nutrition in many ways. In this section of the article, I will mention some of the most important areas where such contributions can be made. No attempt is made to present an exhaustive list of research and policy priorities.

Health, education, and food system policies aimed at the alleviation of poverty through enhanced human capital should be integrated. As illustrated by the various interactions, an integrated approach is likely to be much more effective that separate sectorial policies. Although urban poverty and associated health and nutrition problems is expanding in virtually all developing countries, the large majority of the poor are still in rural areas. The supply of health care, clean water, and improved sanitation in these areas is very limited and should be expanded along with income-generating activities within and outside the food system and primary education. Investments in rural infrastructure, including roads—particularly feeder roads—rural institutions, markets, and agricultural research, as well as policies that give the poor access to productive resources such as land and credit are essential to help the rural poor out of poverty and improve their health, but only if such investments are accompanied by improved access to health care, clean water, and primary education. Policies to eliminate gender discrimination in asset ownership and decision making should be pursued, with due consideration to the impact on time allocation by women and the associated health and nutrition implications.

Public policies may influence health and nutrition through regulations and incentives aimed at both the food and health system. Such policies may span the spectrum from international trade and macroeconomic policies through sectorial and technology policies to food safety and transfer policies, school lunch programs, and health care to individuals. As globalization progresses, national policies in one country may affect health and nutrition in others (Pinstrup-Andersen, 2006). This is particularly problematic since globalization has moved faster than the international institutions required to guide it.

Agricultural research priorities should pay attention to both economic demand for food and agricultural commodities and health and nutrition implications. Commodity priorities should promote enhanced investments of research funds to increase productivity and reduce unit-costs of food commodities with high content of absorbable micronutrients in short supply in the diets of the poor as well as biofortification of basic food staples. Other research priorities include research to reduce the need for chemicals in plant protection through the development of resistant or tolerant plants, research to improve existing knowledge about the transfer of major zoonotic pathogens and how such transfer can be better managed or avoided, research to remove important toxins and allergens from foods, and avoid the development of mycotoxins during production and storage.

Modern science, including molecular biology, offers tremendous opportunities for improving human health both directly through curative and preventive measures and indirectly through improvements in the global food system. Unfortunately, the allocation of research resources is biased toward the development of curative measures for health problems affecting the nonpoor. Although recent investments by the Bill and Melinda Gates Foundation is of great importance, opportunities for improving human health and nutrition and reducing child mortality are being foregone by gross underinvestment in the application of science to solve poor people's health and nutrition problems, including the application of molecular biology to improve the global food system. The new agriculture and health research platform developed by the International Food Policy Research Institute for the Consultative Group for International Agricultural Research is an important step in the right direction.

In conclusion, the main message of this article is that the application of science and public policy to the global food system may offer important opportunities for improving human health and nutrition. At the same time, the health and nutrition status of the population is important for a well-functioning global food system. The message is not that farmers and other actors in the food system should reorganize their activities to meet health goals if they conflict with market signals. The food system is part of the private sector which depends on market demand to thrive. Thus, the role of the public sector is to design and implement policies that bridge the gap between societal goals and market signals. If market signals do not reflect health and nutrition goals of society, there is a need for policy intervention.

References

Beaton, G., R. Martorell, K. J. Aronson, B. Edmonston, G. McCabe, A. C. Ross, and B. Harvey, *Effectiveness of Vitamin A Supplementation in the Control of Young Child Morbidity and Mortality in Developing Countries*, ACC/SCN State-of-the-art Series, Nutrition Policy Discussion Paper 13 (UN: Geneva, 1993).

Catelo, M. A. O., *Understanding the Links Between Agriculture and Health: Livestock and Health*, 2020 Vision Focus 13, Brief 9 (IFPRI: Washington, DC, 2006).

Dawson, A., "Genetics and Tailor-Made Diets: Some Ethical Issues," in M. Kaiser and M. E. Lien, eds., *Ethics and the Politics of Food* 8 (Wageningen Academic Publishers: The Netherlands, 2006).

Diaz-Bonilla, E., J. Babinard, P. Pinstrup-Andersen, and M. Thomas, "Globalizing Health Benefits for Developing Countries," TMD Discussion Paper 108 (IFPRI: Washington, DC, 2002).

Ebbesen, M., "Nanofood: Lessons to be Learnt From the Debate on GM Crops," in M. Kaiser, and M. E. Lien, eds., *Ethics and the Politics of Food* 8 (Wageningen: The Netherlands Academic Publishers, 2006), pp. 314–319.

GAIN, "A New Way of Development: Global Alliance for Improved Nutrition," http://www.gainhealth.org/gain/ch/EN-EN/index.cfm (accessed June 2006).

Gillespie, S., and L. J. Haddad, *The Double Burden of Malnutrition in Asia: Causes, Consequences, and Solutions* (Sage Publications: New Delhi, 2003).

Hawkes, C., and M. T. Ruel, eds., *Understanding the Links Between Agriculture and Health*, 2020 Vision Focus 13 (IFPRI: Washington, DC, 2006).

Horton, S., "Opportunities for Investments in Nutrition in Low-income Asia," *Asian Development Review* 17 (1999), 246–273.

International Food Policy Research Institute (IFPRI), HarvestPlus Fact Sheet on Iron Deficiency Anemia and Vitamin A Deficiency. April 1, 2006. Washington, DC.

International Labor Organization (ILO), "Safety and Health in Agriculture," *88th Session of the International Labour Conference*, Geneva, May-June 2000.

McGill, A. E. J., "Nutrigenomics: A Bridge Too Far, for Now?" in M. Kaiser and M. E. Lien, eds., *Ethics and the Politics of Food 8* (Wageningen Academic Publishers: The Netherlands, 2006).

Micheletti, M., "Political Consumerism: Why the Market is an Arena for Politics," in M. Kaiser and M. E. Lien, eds., *Ethics and the Politics of Food* (Wageningen Academic Publishers: The Netherlands, 2006).

Pelletier, D. L., E. A. Jr. Frongillo, D. G. Schroeder, and J. P. Habicht, "A Methodology for Estimating the Contributions of Malnutrition to Child Mortality in Developing Countries," *Journal of Nutrition* 124 (1994), 2106–2122.

Pinstrup-Andersen, P., "Ethics and Economic Policy for the Food System," *American Journal of Agricultural Economics* 87 (2005), 1097–1112.

Pinstrup-Andersen, P., "Food System Policies in Rich Countries and Consequences in Poor Ones: Ethical Considerations," in M. Kaiser and M. E. Lien, eds., *Ethics and the Politics of Food* 9 (Wageningen Academic Publishers: The Netherlands, 2006).

Pinstrup-Andersen, P., N. R. deLondono, and E. Hoover, "The Impact of Increasing Food Supply on Human Nutrition: Implications for Commodity Priorities in Agricultural Research and Policy," *American Journal of Agricultural Economics* 58 (1976), 131–142.

Prüss-Ustün, A., and C. Corvalán, *Preventing Disease Through Healthy Environments: Towards an Estimate of the Environmental Burden of Disease* (World Health Organization: Geneva, 2006).

Ross, J. S., and E. L. Thomas, *Iron Deficiency Anemia and Maternal Mortality*, PROFILES 3 Working Notes Series 3 (Academy for Educational Development: Washington, DC, 1996).

UNICEF, *Vitamin and Mineral Deficiency*, A Global Progress Report (UNICEF: New York, 2004).

UNICEF, *Progress for Children*, A Report Card on Nutrition 4 (UNICEF: New York, 2006).

World Bank, World Development Report, *Investing in Health* (Oxford University Press: New York, 1993).

World Health Organization (WHO), *World Health Statistics 2006* (WHO: Geneva, 2006).

The nutrition transition in high- and low-income countries: what are the policy lessons?

Barry Popkin* and Shu Wen Ng**

Abstract

This article examines the speed of changes in diets, activity patterns, and body composition, summarizes major dietary changes, and provides some sense of the way the burden of obesity is shifting from the rich to the poor globally. The focus is on the lower- and middle-income world with some examples from higher-income countries. Then macro policy options are examined. A case study of edible oil pricing in China is presented. The challenge is for the agricultural economics profession to focus on this major global issue—one which challenges some of the earlier paradigms of food policy and agricultural development.

JEL classification: I12

Keywords: diet composition; price policy; economic growth; health effects

1. Introduction to the nutrition transition

The world is experiencing rapid shifts in structures of diet and body composition with resultant important changes in health profiles. In many ways these shifts are a continuation of large-scale changes that have occurred repeatedly over time; however, this article shows that the changes facing low- and moderate-income countries are very rapid. Broad shifts have and continue to occur around the world in population size and age composition, disease patterns, and dietary and physical activity patterns. The former two sets of dynamic shifts are termed the demographic and epidemiological transitions. The latter, whose changes are reflected in nutritional outcomes, such as changes in average stature and body composition, is termed the nutrition transition. The developing world is seeing most rapid change in dietary and activity patterns and obesity rates. These changes are reviewed here as a first step toward laying out what is being done and can be done to address them as it relates to the economics field.

Carolina Population Center, University of North Carolina at Chapel Hill, 123 W. Franklin Street, Chapel Hill, NC 27516-3997.

Department of Health Policy and Administration, School of Public Health, University of North Carolina, Chapel Hill, 123 W. Franklin St., Chapel Hill, NC 27516-3997.

Two historic processes of change occur simultaneously with or precede the "nutrition transition." One is the demographic transition—the shift from a pattern of high fertility and mortality to one of low fertility and mortality (typical of modern industrialized countries). The second is the epidemiological transition, first described by Omran (1971): the shift from a pattern of high prevalence of infectious disease, associated with malnutrition, periodic famine, and poor environmental sanitation, to one of high prevalence of chronic and degenerative disease, associated with urban-industrial lifestyles (Olshansky and Ault, 1986).

The three most recent patterns of the nutrition transition are described in more detail elsewhere (Popkin, 2002a, b). The patterns proceed from the earliest man—a pattern of hunter-gather societies often linked with Paleolithic man; the second one coincided with the second agricultural revolution (crop rotation, fertilizer) and the Industrial Revolution when extensive famine occurred concurrently (Popkin, 1993); in Pattern 3, famine begins to recede as income rises; in Pattern 4, changes in diet and activity pattern lead to the emergence of new noncommunicable disease problems and increased disability; and Pattern 5 only emerging in selected subpopulation groupings, behavioral change begins to reverse the negative tendencies and make possible a process of "successful ageing" (Manton and Soldo, 1985; Crimmins et al., 1989). The changes are all driven by a range of factors, including urbanization, economic growth, technical change, and culture. For convenience, the patterns can be thought of as historical developments. However, "earlier" patterns are not restricted to the periods in which they first arose, but continue to characterize certain geographic and socioeconomic subpopulations.

2. Dynamics of the food system and related changes

2.1. Dietary shifts: more fats, more added caloric sweeteners, and more animal source foods

The diets of the developing world are shifting rapidly, particularly with respect to fats, caloric sweeteners, and animal source foods (ASF) (Popkin, 2002a, b; Popkin and Du, 2003).

2.1.1. Edible oil

In the popular mind, the Westernization of the global diet continues to be associated with increased consumption of animal fats. While this has certainly been true during the 1980–1995 period in the higher-income world, edible oil has been a major source of dietary change in the lower- and middle-income countries. The recent shift in the pattern of the nutrition transition in developing countries typically begins with major increases in the domestic production and imports of oilseeds and vegetable oils, rather than meat and milk. Elsewhere, Williams and also this author have both written in more depth about the technology behind this shift and the broader nature of these changes in both oil seed extraction technology as well as breeding of new oil seed varieties containing more oil (Williams, 1984; Drewnowski and Popkin, 1997; Popkin and Drewnowski, 1997). Principal vegetable oils include soybean, sunflower, rapeseed, palm, and groundnut oil. With the exception of groundnut oil, global availability of each has approximately tripled between 1961 and 1990.

Fat intake increases with income, but there have also been dramatic structural changes in the gross national product (GNP)/capita-fat relationship. These have been shown carefully elsewhere (Drewnowski and Popkin,

1997). Most significantly, even poor nations had access to a relatively high-fat diet by 1990, when a diet deriving 20% of energy (kilocalories) from fat was associated with countries having a GNP of only $750 per capita. In 1962, the same energy diet (20% from fat) was associated with countries having a GNP of $1,475 (both GNP values in 1993 dollars). This dramatic change arose principally from a major increase in the consumption of vegetable fats. In 1990, these accounted for a greater proportion of dietary energy than animal fats for countries in the lowest 75% of countries (all of which have incomes below $5,800 per capita) of the per capita income distribution. The change in edible vegetable fat prices, supply, and consumption is unique because it affected rich and poor countries equally, but the net impact is relatively much greater on low-income countries.

The intake of edible oil has increased consistently over the past 15 years. In fact in some developing countries, researchers have documented an upward shift in income elasticity for all groups, and a higher one for the poor (see Du et al. [2004] for the China example).

2.1.2. Caloric sweetener

Sugar is the world's predominant sweetener.[1] For this article, however, the term caloric sweetener is used instead of added sugar, as there is such a range of non-sugar products used today. High fructose corn syrup is a prime example as it is the sweetener used in all U.S. soft drinks and it is increasingly being used on a worldwide basis for sweetened beverages and some baked goods (Bray et al., 2002). There are many items in this category including a wide variety of monosaccharides (glucose and fructose) and disaccharides (sucrose and saccharose), which exist either in a crystallized state as sugar or in thick liquid form as syrups. Included in sweeteners are maple sugar and syrups, caramel, golden syrup, artificial and natural honey, maltose, glucose, dextrose, isoglucose (also known as high fructose corn syrup), other types of fructose, sugar confectionery, and lactose. In the last several decades, larger quantities of cereals (primarily maize) have been used to produce sweeteners derived from starch.

---

[1] It is not clear exactly when sugar became the world's principal sweetener—most likely in the 17th or 18th century, as the New World began producing large quantities of sugar at reduced prices (Mintz, 1977; Galloway, 2000).

Table 1
World trends in caloric sweetener intake for GNP and urbanization quintiles (1962 values)

	Quintile 1	Quintile 2	Quintile 3	Quintile 4	Quintile 5	Total
A. Quintiles of GNP (using 1962 GNP levels for each country)						
Caloric sweetener (kcal/capita/day)						
1962	90	131	257	287	402	232
2000	155	203	362	397	418	306
Total Energy (kcal/capita/day)						
1962	2008	2090	2157	2411	2960	2322
2000	2346	2357	2716	2950	3281	2725
B. Quintiles of % Urban (using the 1962 values for % urban for each country)						
Caloric sweetener (kcal/capita/day)						
1962	79	131	236	335	389	232
2000	151	201	339	403	441	306

Source: Popkin and Nielsen (2003); Food and Agriculture Organization FAOSTAT data set for food balance data.

The overall trends show a large increase in caloric sweetener consumed (see Table 1). In 2000, 306 kcal were consumed per person per day, about a third more than in 1962; caloric sweeteners also accounted for a larger share of both total energy and total carbohydrates consumed (Drewnowski and Popkin, 1997).

Unsurprisingly, it is shown elsewhere that all measures of caloric sweetener increase significantly as GNP per capita of the country and urbanization increase (Popkin and Nielsen, 2003). However, the interaction between income growth and urbanization is important. Elsewhere the relationship between the proportion of energy from different food sources and GNP for two different levels of urbanization is shown (see Drewnowski and Popkin [1997] for a description of the analysis). In the less urbanized case, the share of sweeteners increases sharply with income, from about 5% to about 15%. In the more urbanized case, the share is much higher at lower income (over 15%), and hardly increases with income. The analysis confirms previous observations that people living in urban areas consume diets distinct from those of their rural counterparts (Popkin, 1999).

2.1.3. Animal source foods

The revolution in ASF refers to the increase in demand and production of meat, fish, and milk in low-income developing countries. The International Food Policy Research Institute's Christopher Delgado has studied this issue extensively in a number of seminal reports and papers (Delgado et al., 1999; Delgado et al., 2001; Delgado, 2003). Most of the world's growth in production and consumption of these foods comes from developing countries, which are estimated to produce 63% of meat and 50% of milk in 2020. By 2020, developing countries will consume 107 million metric tons (mmt) more meat and 177 mmt more milk than they did in 1996/1998, dwarfing developed-country increases of 19 mmt for meat and 32 mmt for milk. This will transform the grain markets for animal feed. It also leads to resource degradation, rapid increases in feed grain imports, rapid concentration of production and consumption, and social change.

Delgado (2003) has shown that the share of the world's meat consumed in developing countries rose from 37% to 48%, and their share of the world's milk rose from 34% to 44%. Pork and poultry accounted for 76% of the large net consumption increase of meat in developing countries from 1982/1984 to 1996/1998.

There are different developing countries which dominate consumption for different animal products. China and Brazil play this role in meat consumption while India is the key milk consumer. In the mid 1990s, Indian milk consumption amounted to 13% of the world's total and 31% of milk consumption in all developing countries (Delgado, 2003).

Aggregate meat consumption in developing countries is projected to grow by 106 mmt between the late 1990s and 2020, whereas the corresponding figure for developed countries is 19 mmt. Similarly, additional milk consumption in the developed countries of 32 mmt of liquid milk equivalents will be dwarfed by the additional consumption in developing countries of 177 mmt.

2.2. China example of dietary changes

Data from China are useful for summarizing these changes for a typical fast growing economy. The overall shifts in China is presented in depth elsewhere (Du et al., 2002; Popkin and Du, 2003). Here, only the changes are simply summarized. The shift in the Chinese diet follows a classic Westernization pattern. First, intake of cereals decreased considerably during the past two decades in both urban and rural areas and among all income groups. The relative proportion of refined rice and flour increased and coarse grains such as millet, sorghum, and corn, decreased greatly.

Second, consumption of animal products increased, more so for the rich than the poor, and for urban than rural residents. The amount and growth of intake of animal foods were positively associated with income levels. The intake level and the increase in the high-income group from 1989 to 1997 were almost three times those in the low-income group (Popkin and Du, 2003; Du et al., 2004).

Third, partly as a result of this change, data from the China Health and Nutrition Survey (CHNS) also show a shift in the diet away from carbohydrates to fat. Energy from carbohydrates fell for all residents, and by over 20% for urban residents. Energy from fat more than doubled in the past 15 years. Finally, when the combined effect of these various shifts in the structure of rural and urban Chinese diets are specifically examined, there is an upward shift in the energy density of the foods consumed (Popkin and Du, 2003).

2.3. Higher income country shifts

Most in-depth research on dietary shifts in higher-income countries comes from in-depth studies in the United States. Japan, the U.K., and South Korea actually have more extensive dietary data collection systems—systems that go back to the late 1940s or so. However, very little in-depth research has been carried out by scholars in any country either on national eating patterns or trends. Essentially what is known from nationally representative studies on shifts in either foods consumed or location or timing of meal patterns comes from American research. In the United States, scholars have shown very large shifts in dietary behavior over time. The shifts differ by income, education, and race (Popkin et al., 1996, 2003) but generally show the following: refined food intake continues to increase, led by caloric sweeteners; meal patterning has shifted from three meals a day to an additional two meals of close to equal size that are snacks; away from home intake continues to increase rapidly in all age-race-socioeconomic status (SES) groupings; and energy intake is increasing at a time when energy expenditures are decreasing (Jahns et al., 2001; Zizza et al., 2001; Nielsen et al., 2002). The biggest difference with the developing world is that there is much more heterogeneity related to these patterns in the developed world—e.g., there is little snacking or away from home intake or fast food intake in China whereas the Philippines looks

more similar to the United States (Adair and Popkin, 2005).

2.4. Critical related reductions in physical activity

Clearly, the economics profession is not very involved in activities related to physical activity. However, shifts in physical activity are half of the reason why global obesity is increasing and a minimal understanding of these issues is useful. There are several linked changes in physical activity occurring jointly. As any economist knows, there have been large changes in the structure of employment, primarily from high energy expenditure activities such as farming, mining, and forestry toward lower energy expenditure activities in the service sector, which has had a large effect (Popkin, 1999). Reduced energy expenditures within the same occupation due to technological advancements are a second change. Other major changes relate to mode of transportation and activity patterns during leisure hours.

China again provides interesting illustrations. China has exhibited a major shift away from physical activity even for adults in the same occupation (Popkin, 2006). In rural areas, however, there has been a shift for some toward increased physical activity linked to holding multiple jobs and more intensive effort. For rural women, there is a shift toward a larger proportion engaged in more energy-intensive work, but there are also sections where light effort is increasing. In contrast, for rural men there is a small decrease in the proportion engaged in light work effort. These shifts in occupation have been shown to represent a major cause for the development of obesity in China (Bell et al., 2001, 2002).

In China, 14% of households acquired a motorized vehicle between 1989 and 1997. One study showed that the odds of being obese were 80% higher ($P < 0.05$) for men and women in households which owned a motorized vehicle compared to those which did not own a vehicle (Bell et al., 2002).

A major increasing source of leisure globally is television viewing. In China, ownership of television sets has grown to over 97% of the population and color TVs are now found in close to two-thirds of households. Further, TV advertising has sharply increased during the past 15 years as has Western TV programming.

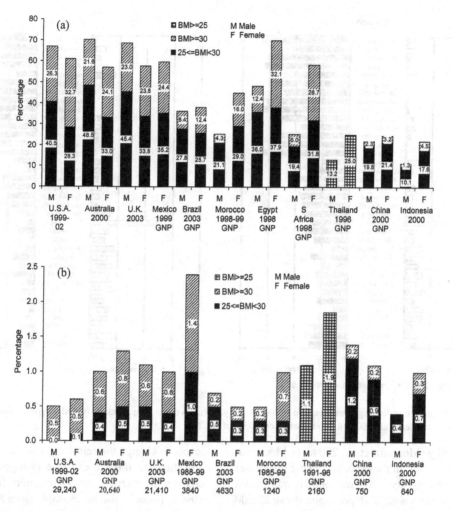

Figure 1. (a) Obesity patterns across the world. (b) Obesity trends among adults in selected countries (the annual percentage point increase in prevalence). *Source:* Popkin, Barry M. (83): Owns copyright. GNP stands for Gross National Product Per Capita.

3. Obesity dynamics: rapid shifts in urban and rural areas, shift from under- to overnutrition and toward the poor

Over the past several years, the obesity story has received global attention. Presented here is a set of figures to provide some sense of these global shifts. Figure 1a highlights the large prevalence of overweight and obesity (measured, respectively, by body mass index [BMI represents kg/m^2] as the standard population-based measure of overweight and obesity status. For adults, the cutoffs used to delineate overweight is a BMI of 25.0–29.99 and obesity is 30.0 and over) in low- and middle-income countries. Figure 1b shows that the rates of change in low- and middle-income countries are often very high (Popkin, 2002a, b).

The urban-rural patterns of over- and underweight are shown in Figure 2 for 38 countries. All of these data come from weighted samples of nationally representative surveys of women of child-bearing age in which the women's weight and height were collected (Mendez et al., 2005). These data show that overweight status is far greater than underweight status in both urban and rural areas of most developing countries. Also it shows that urban levels of overweight are typically above those in rural areas.

A separate set of studies using these same data plus for some countries data for men explored the issues of the relationships between GNP per capita, individual

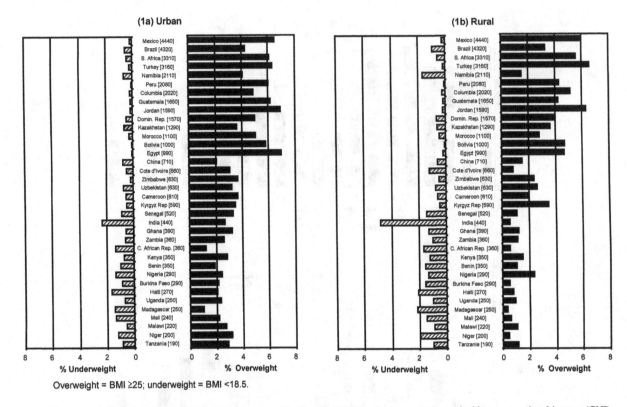

Figure 2. Overweight and underweight prevalence in women 20–49 years in 36 developing countries ranked by gross national income (GNI) per capita. *Source:* Mendez et al. (2005): Reprinted with permission of AJCN.

SES and obesity (Monteiro et al., 2004a, b; Monteiro, Moura, et al., 2004). In these studies, using multilevel techniques with obesity as the outcome, it was shown that for all countries with GNP per capita above $2,500 in 2005 US$ terms, there was greater obesity among women of lower SES groupings than higher ones. This was found for women but the opposite was found for men. In other work done just on trends in Brazil, Monteiro et al. (2004b) have shown these shifts in more depth.

4. Policy experiences

Ideally, a large number of examples from both the developing and developed worlds would provide better guidance for ways to promote healthier diets, thus reducing obesity. Unfortunately, there are no national examples of reductions in obesity related to major push on the food or activity side at the national level. There are from the Scandinavian countries of Finland and Norway some examples of the use of macroeconomic levers to change the relative pricing of selected foods and then the linkage of these changes with positive changes in nutrition-related chronic diseases (Milio, 1990). There is also an example from South Korea of major policy options that allowed South Korea to consume a much healthier diet with major improvements in health linked with that diet (Kim et al., 2000; Lee et al., 2002).

The Scandinavian country that has most systematically merged health and agricultural concerns into an effective nutrition policy is Norway. Norway began to be concerned with reducing dietary fat in the 1960s and developed the Norwegian National Nutrition Policy in 1976, formally linking economic and agricultural policy with nutrition and health (Milio, 1990). The results were impressive: Norway stimulated research on breeding cows for lower-fat milk; denied consumer price subsidies when sugar import prices soared in the mid 1970s; increased consumer subsidies for skim milk more than for whole milk, for poultry more than for pork, and for fish more than for beef; and implemented a set of producer subsidies to favor fish production over beef production. Thus research and price policy were used actively. As noted above, the results were dramatic, including a large change in the proportion of whole and reduced-fat milk, rapid increases in the consumption of poultry, and changes in the amount of edible fat and the proportion of margarine and light margarine. Norway has most markedly reduced the proportion of energy obtained from animal fats, from 29% in 1961 to 23% in 1988. The reductions in total fat of about 6 percentage points (from 41% to 35%) were observed between 1975 and 1989, with equally large declines in saturated fat (Milio, 1991).

Finland also focused on similar issues but its achievements were focused in one region and were much more community-based with minimal attention to macroeconomic factors (Puska et al., 2002). The North Karelia Project was launched in 1972 as a community-based, and later on, national program to influence diet and some other lifestyles that are crucial in the prevention of cardiovascular diseases. The intervention focused on a local community organization strategy and involved local communities in a most active manner. Studies have shown a strong reduction in total fat intake, a shift away from saturated fat, and major reductions in population serum cholesterol and blood pressure levels (Puska et al., 2002). It has also shown how ischemic heart disease mortality in a working-age population has declined by 73% in North Karelia and by 65% in the whole country from 1971 to 1995.

South Korea provides a unique example of the good things a country can do to preserve the healthful elements of its traditional cuisine. A combination of large-scale training of housewives in preparation of the traditional low fat, high vegetable cuisine coupled with strong social marketing have led to very low fat and high vegetable intake levels (Kim et al., 2000; Lee et al., 2002). Obesity is considerably below that expected for a country with its high income level as is the percentage of energy from fat. The relationship between GNP per capita and dietary fat intake was studied for 121 countries. From these studies, it was expected that in 1996 the proportion of energy from fat in the Republic of Korea would be 35.5%. The actual percentage of energy from fat was 16.7 percentage points less than this expected level. Given the fat intake level in 1996, it was calculated that the GNP should be US\$311. From

estimate food disappearance data for the Republic of Korea, based on the data on which this relationship was calculated in both the studies, predictions for the Republic of Korea is that the food disappearance intake of fat as a percentage of energy would be 13.5 percentage points more in 1996 than what was actually found. Further similar analyses for GNP and obesity show that obesity levels were also much lower than may be expected given the Republic of Korea's economic development level compared with other Asian countries, let alone most Western countries (Kim et al., 2000).

A few lower-income countries have made some initial forays into large-scale prevention activities related to obesity and nutrition-related noncommunicable diseases. This includes both China and Brazil; however, in both cases there is little evidence of any impact of these early efforts (Coitinho et al., 2002; Zhai et al., 2002).

5. The role for agricultural economics: price policy

It is argued by many and increasingly being shown that incentives and disincentives built into our food pricing system have distorted consumption patterns more heavily toward ASF, edible oil, caloric sweeteners, and increased inactivity, among others (Tillotson, 2004).

On the other side, opponents of pricing policies argue that there are no classic externalities to obesity in the way there are for smoking or HIV-AIDS. This is not true, however, since obesity has a major effect on medical care costs, insurance rates, government subsidized health-care expenditure (such as Medicare and Medicaid in the United States), and losses in productivity. Hence, the true cost of food energy is not properly reflected in the price and is a form of market failure because those who make poor dietary choices incur costs that are borne by everyone, even those who are healthy. One way to deal with such market failure is to have the price mechanism better reflect the true cost of various foods, which in theory will provide a more economically efficient solution. However, the effectiveness of such a measure depends on how responsive consumers are to price changes.

There are several major issues that directly could involve the agricultural economic sector. One is understanding and measuring the vast array of ways that government spending—be it on research or direct subsidies and other mechanisms—affects the relative prices of healthier and unhealthier foods. Second is to understand how shifts in the relative prices of a vast array of foods will change overall diet. The latter would involve studying the direct and cross-price elasticities and the ways they affect food and nutrient intake patterns. There are many issues that can utilize economic analysis from demand studies to ways to use pricing and regulations to shift portion sizes and other eating behaviors toward more healthful ones.

A central issue affecting the world's public health is the need to shift the relative prices of a range of foods to encourage healthier, less energy-dense, and more nutrient-dense foods. A second key issue is figuring out ways to reduce caloric intake while not adversely affecting the poor's nutritional status. These are quite related issues that this author has examined once for China (Guo et al., 1999; Guo et al., 2000) and will present a brief example here of ongoing research on this topic.

One of the items in the diet that has increased most rapidly in China and many other developing countries is edible oil intake (Drewnowski and Popkin, 1997; Du et al., 2002). A sizable proportion of the total energy increase over the past several decades for Asian, Middle Eastern, and African countries has come from this commodity.

6. China edible oil case study

6.1. Background

Edible oil was strictly controlled as a key commodity during the period up to 1991 by the Chinese government. In May 1991, the price of grain and edible oil on ration was readjusted by a large margin for the first time since the mid 1960s. The price of grain was raised by 70%, and the price of edible oil almost doubled. The government also released supplies previously unseen in China, resulting in demand and consumption increasing significantly during this period (Popkin et al., 1993; Du et al., 2002). By 1992, governmental control over price of edible oil was lifted across the country. To lessen the impact of the rise in costs on the population's living standard, the government provided subsidies on certain nonstaple food to urban residents. In addition,

in 1996, state-owned enterprises were exempted from value-added tax when selling oil (Qian and Wu, 2000).

The most recent development is China's accession into World Trade Organization in 2006. This resulted in the elimination of a quota on sunflower, peanut, and corn oil, in place of a 10% tariff, as well as a phasing out tariff quota for soy oil in January 2006 (Agri-Canada, 2002). In addition, the supply of domestic oil production has been rising, especially for rapeseed and soy, with improved technology (in seed crushing and processing). There has been enormous rationalization of the Chinese production sector—employment is dropping significantly, and larger, more capital-intensive modern production facilities are emerging.

6.2. Data

All of these signal general declines in edible oil prices to approach international market prices, and might have implications on consumer demand. Table 2 presents consumption data for adults aged 20–45 for the 1989–2004 period. These data come from the nine-province CHNS, the source of many China examples in this article. Three days of weighed household edible oil along with daily 24-hour recalls are used for this analysis. The design of the survey, the dietary, and other measurements are presented elsewhere (Zhai et al., 1996; Guo et al., 2000; Popkin et al., 2002; Du et al., 2004). The China Health and Nutrition data, available free on the web, are a longitudinal survey of about 16,000 individuals with data collected from over 200 communities in 1989, 1991, 1993, 1997, 2000, 2004, and 2006. This analysis focuses on adults between 20 and 45 years old surveyed over the 1989–2000 period.

Table 2

Shift in edible oil consumption in the Chinese diet (China Health and Nutrition Study, 1989–2004) for adults, ages 20–45 (Mean intake g/per capita/per day)

Edible oil	Urban	Rural	Low income	Mid income	High income	Total
1989	17.2	14.0	12.9	15.8	16.4	15.0
1991	23.9	22.6	19.1	23.0	26.5	23.0
1993	27.6	23.0	22.3	24.1	26.7	24.3
1997	31.8	27.8	26.4	29.5	31.2	29.0
2000	33.5	31.4	30.9	32.1	33.3	32.0

Prices were collected in a systematic manner from each community surveyed. The key independent variable of interest is the price of edible oil. Two approaches were used to create an oil price. One option used the cheapest edible oil sold in each community. The second created a weighted price linked with the oils consumed in each region. Since there are a variety of edible oils consumed in China, this analysis matched available edible oil prices and regional consumption patterns from the 1992 China Nationwide Nutrition Survey (CMPH, 1994) to create a weighted edible oil price. Other prices included in the modeling were for common food groupings: rice, flour, chicken, eggs, fatty pork, and the cheapest retail coarse grain for each community (among corn, millet, and sorghum).

Household income was approximated from the survey through responses to direct questions about income and through the summation of net receipts from all reported activities. This detailed estimation of income represents a significant advance in the measurement of income in China, allowing the inclusion of nonmonetary government subsidies, such as state-subsidized housing. This study will include all cash and noncash income, except food subsidies.

Price and income variables were deflated by year- and province-specific consumer price indices developed for urban and rural areas (SSB, 1990, 1992, 1994, 1998, 2001, 2005). The use of real deflated values in the analyses will remove the effect of inflation and allow the analysis to focus on the effect of the increase in real price and real income. The 1980 consumer price index was used as the baseline to deflate the nominal values for urban and rural consumers by province.

Other household-level variables include household size, whether the household resides in a community with an urban designation, and region of residence. The measurement of region was developed by the World Bank in collaboration with the State Statistical Bureau (World Bank, 1995), reflecting contiguous groupings with comparable income levels. With respect to agricultural economics and food behavior, samples were regrouped into three regions: the South Hinterland (Guezhou, Guangxi, Hunan); the Central Core (Henan, Hubei, Jingsu); and the North (Liaoning, Heilongjiang, Shangdong).

Individual-level data controlled for in the models include age, gender, and education. Age and number of years of education are continuous variables and gender is a dichotomous variable. In addition, year dummies were included to account for possibly time trends.

6.3. Estimation

Our focus is on the estimation of own-price and cross-price elasticities in a rigorous manner. In our specifications, all models include time, region, household income, food prices, age, gender, education, urban residency, household size, interactions between edible oil price with time dummies, and interactions between edible oil price with income tertiles as control variables. All estimations were also clustered at the household level due to possibility of having multiple adults within each household, and hence related error terms across observations. Alternative specification explored included using income as a continuous variable together with the square of household income, as well as different interaction terms between income, region, prices, and time.

This analysis presents the estimation of only the proportion of energy from fat, protein, and carbohydrate. The analyses used two sets of estimations. The first is based on percent of energy from protein, fats, and carbohydrates and is constrained such that they always sum to 100%. Therefore, the sum of the coefficients across the three dependent variables should always be zero. The second set of estimations looks at elasticities.

For ease of interpretation, the authors derived predictions on macronutrient consumption to estimate the effect of a 10% increase in the price of the cheapest oil in the community on the average consumption decisions of adults. In addition, predictions by income tertiles were derived to see what differences in consumption decisions due to changing oil prices might exist.

6.4. Results

Results from using the two oil prices were generally similar, except for some slight differences in significance for the effects of other food prices on energy from fat and carbohydrates (Table 3). Only the estimation results from using the cheapest oil price available to each community are presented because the results appear more stable. They show that there is a

Table 3
Coefficient estimates from random effects models clustered at household level using cheapest oil price

$N = 21,389$	Proportion of energy			Demand elasticity		
	% Energy from protein	% Energy from fat	% Energy from carbohydrates	Log % energy from protein	Log % energy from fat	Log % energy from carbohydrates
Log real cheapest oil price	0.36	−5.71**	5.35**	0.02	−0.43**	0.08**
Log real cheapest oil price*1991	0.40	−9.26**	8.85**	0.05	−0.52**	0.13**
Log real cheapest oil price*1993	0.84	−3.02	2.18	0.09**	0.02	0.06
Log real cheapest oil price*1997	1.70**	−2.64**	0.95	0.17**	0.09	0.04
Log real cheapest oil price*2000	0.12	−1.46	1.34	0.05*	0.09	0.05
Log real cheapest oil price*medium income	−0.40**	0.88	−0.49	−0.03	0.14**	0.01
Log real cheapest oil price*high income	−0.79**	1.86**	−1.06	−0.06**	0.21**	0.01
1991	−0.13	6.08**	−5.95**	−0.01	0.42**	−0.07
1993	−0.86	2.08	−1.22	−0.10*	−0.11	−0.05
1997	−1.68**	0.48	1.18	−0.17**	−0.23*	−0.01
2000	0.55	1.24	0.69	0.01	−0.23*	−0.002
Medium income tertile	0.71**	2.46**	−3.17*	0.05*	−0.001	−0.07**
High income tertile	1.72**	4.51**	−6.24**	0.13**	0.05	−0.14**
North	0.43**	−5.00**	4.57**	0.04*	−0.21**	0.09**
Central	0.03	−3.34**	3.31**	0.01	−0.15**	0.06**
Log real price rice	0.43**	−1.29*	0.86*	0.04**	−0.08**	0.01
Log real price flour	−2.09**	1.16	0.92	−0.18**	0.04	0.02
Log real price eggs	−0.11**	−0.17	0.27*	−0.01	0.02	0.01*
Log real price fat pork	2.78**	−2.87**	0.10	0.24**	−0.10*	0.01
Log real price cheap grain	−0.01	−0.78	0.80	−0.001	−0.05*	0.01
Age (years)	−0.002	0.04**	−0.04*	−0.0003	0.001	−0.001**
Household size	0.03	−0.78**	0.75**	0.003	−0.04**	0.01**
Education (years)	0.06**	0.42**	−0.48**	0.005**	0.02**	−0.01**
Male	−0.05*	−1.33**	1.38**	−0.004	−0.06**	0.02**
Urban	0.80**	2.24**	−3.03**	0.07**	0.11**	−0.05**
Constant	4.99**	37.91**	57.11**	1.86**	3.81**	4.01**
R-square	0.10	0.22	0.25	0.09	0.23	0.21

*Denotes significance at the 5% level.
**Denotes significance at the 1% level.
Note: Reference categories for year is 1989; for income tertile is poor; and for region is South.

relationship between the real price of the cheapest edible oil, the percentage of energy from fat (strongly negative), and the percentage of energy from carbohydrates (strongly positive). This suggests substitution for fats with carbohydrates as the price of edible oil increases. Meanwhile, there is little change in consumption of proteins.

The results are consistent across the two sets of estimations, and show that there are strong negative elasticities of the demand for energy from protein with respect to the real price of flour and eggs, while there are positive elasticities with respect to the real prices of rice and fatty pork. It also appears consistent across the various macronutrient that flour and rice are substi-

tutes. Moreover, income appears to have a strong effect on macronutrient composition, as do region, education, urban residency, and gender.

To understand the full effect of increasing the price of oil, simulations were run, and shown in Figures 3a and b. Figure 3a shows the predicted change in the composition of energy due to a 10% increase in the real weighted price of edible oils for all observations and also for those in the rich and poor tertiles. The poor are more price responsive in reducing their consumption of fats and possibly substituting by increasing their carbohydrate and protein intake as a proportion of total energy consumed. Figure 3b illustrates the change in demand for percent of energy from protein, fats, and

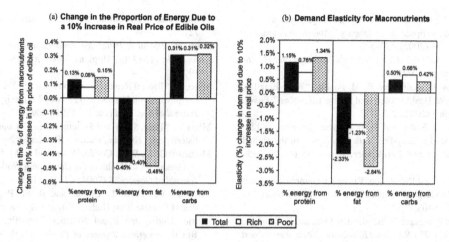

Figure 3. Effects of changes in the price of edible oil on macronutrients. *Source:* China Health and Nutrition Surveys.

carbohydrates due to a 10% increase in the real prices of edible oil. Again, the elasticity is larger and negative for fats and smaller and positive for carbohydrates and proteins.

7. Discussion

The agricultural economics profession has done little to examine policy options as they relate to the remarkable shift in diet, activity, and body composition toward a pattern of the transition linked with noncommunicable diseases. Obesity is the norm globally and undernutrition, while still important in a few countries and in targeted populations in many others, is no longer the dominant disease. While there are great disputes and limited understanding of the full set of economic, technological, and other factors that explain this transition, the reality is that globally far more obesity than undernutrition exists and the rates of change for the former are large and positive while those of the latter are negative. The first part of this article essentially uses a combination of multicountry studies, ecological data plus some case studies from China and a few other countries to layout the nature of the shifts underway.

The issue of policy options is really quite complex. There is little knowledge about the role of major macro mechanisms which must be an element in our arsenal to shift demand and supply toward a healthier food supply and reduced total energy intake. The example from China is an important one. It shows that a situation where price changes are used against one element in the diet which contributes fairly adversely to health can be reduced in intake. By examining total direct and cross elasticities and looking here just at the overall effect on energy from fat, protein, and carbohydrates, insights into this option for China are gained and one can see the potential power embedded in the vast array of subsidies and credit and price shifts currently used in most countries. Essentially if China used taxation or other policies to increase the price of edible oils, one would see a shift away from fat (each gram of which contains 9 cal of energy), a bit away from protein (4 cal/g) and toward carbohydrates (4 cal/g).

The effect of price policies and many other regulations need much more careful exploration prior to our being able to undertake massive shifts of a healthy nature in the structure of diet. Many other mechanisms available to the economic sector must be rigorously explored. This area is really one relatively ignored by the profession but one deserving of much more research.

References

Adair, L. S., and B. M. Popkin, "Are Child Eating Patterns Being Transformed Globally?" *Obesity Research* 13 (2005), 1281–1299.

Agri-Canada, "China's Vegetable Oil Industry," from http://atnriae.agr.ca/asia/e3282.htm, (2002).

Bell, A. C., K. Ge, and B. M. Popkin, "Weight Gain and Its Predictors in Chinese Adults," *International Journal of Obesity* 25 (2001), 1079–1086.

Bell, A. C., K. Ge, and B. M. Popkin, "The Road to Obesity or the Path to Prevention: Motorized Transportation and Obesity in China," *Obesity Research* 10 (2002), 277–283.

Bray, G. A., S. J. Nielsen, and B. M. Popkin, "High Fructose Corn Sweeteners and the Epidemic of Obesity," *American Journal of Clinic Nutrition* 79 (2002), 537–543.

CMPH, *Report of the 1992 (China National Nutrition and Health Survey* (in Chinese), (1994).

Coitinho, D., C. A. Monteiro, and B. M. Popkin, "What Brazil Is doing to Promote Healthy Diets and Active Lifestyles," *Public Health Nutrition* 5 (2002), 263–267.

Crimmins, E. M., Y. Saito, and D. Ingegneri, "Changes in Life Expectancy and Disability-Free Life Expectancy in the United States," *Population and Development Review* 15 (1989), 235–267.

Delgado, C. L., "A Food Revolution: Rising Consumption of Meat and Milk in Developing Countries," *Journal of Nutrition* 133 (2003), 3907S–3910S.

Delgado, C. L., M. Rosegrant, H. Steinfield, S. Ehui, and C. Courbois, *Livestock to 2020: The Next Food Revolution* (International Food Policy Research Institute, 1999).

Delgado, C. L., M. Rosegrant, and S. Meijer, *Livestock to 2020: The Revolution Continues* (Auckland, New Zealand, 2001).

Drewnowski, A., and B. M. Popkin, "The Nutrition Transition: New Trends in the Global Diet," *Nutrition Revolution* 55 (1997), 31–43.

Du, S., B. Lu, F. Zhai, and B. M. Popkin, "The Nutrition Transition in China: A New Stage of the Chinese Diet," in B. Caballero, and B. M. Popkin, eds, *Diet and Disease in the Developing World* (Academic Press: London, 2002), pp. 205–222.

Du, S., T. A. Mroz, F. Zhai, and B. M. Popkin, "Rapid Income Growth Adversely Affects Diet Quality in China–Particularly for the Poor!," *Social Science and Medicine* 59 (2004), 1505–1515.

Galloway, J. H., "Sugar," in K. F. Kiple, and K. C. Ornelas, eds., *The Cambridge World History of Food* I (Cambridge University Press: New York, 2000).

Guo, X., B. M. Popkin, T. A. Mroz, and F. Zhai, "Food Price Policy can Favorably Alter Macronutrient Intake in China," *Journal of Nutrition* 129 (1999), 994–1001.

Guo, X., T. A. Mroz, B. M. Popkin, and F. Zhai, "Structural Changes in the Impact of Income on Food Consumption in China, 1989–93," *Economic Development Cultural Change* 48 (2000), 737–760.

Jahns, L., A. M. Siega-Riz, and B. M. Popkin, "The Increasing Prevalence of Snacking among US Children from 1977 to 1996," *Journal of Pediatrics* 138 (2001), 493–498.

Kim, S., S. Moon, and B. M. Popkin, "The Nutrition Transition in South Korea," *American Journal of Clinical Nutrition* 71 (2000), 44–53.

Lee, M. J., B. M. Popkin, and S. Kim, "The Unique Aspects of the Nutrition Transition in South Korea: The Retention of Healthful Elements in their Traditional Diet," *Public Health Nutrition* 5 (2002), 197–203.

Manton, K. G., and B. J. Soldo, "Dynamics of Health Changes in the Oldest Old: New Perspectives and Evidence," *Milbank Memorial Fund Quarterly Health and Society* 63 (1985), 206–285.

Mendez, M. A., C. A. Monteiro, and B. M. Popkin, "Overweight Exceeds Underweight among Women in Most Developing Countries," *American Journal of Clinical Nutrition* 81 (2005), 714–721.

Milio, N., *Nutrition Policy for Food-Rich Countries: A Strategic Analysis.* (The Johns Hopkins University Press: Baltimore, MD, 1990).

Milio, N., "Toward Health Lessons in Food and Nutrition Policy Development from Finland and Norway Longevity," *Scandinavian Journal of Soc. Medicine* 19 (1991), 209–217.

Mintz, S., "Time, Sugar, and Sweetness," in C. Counihan, and P. Van Esterik, eds., *Food and Culture.* (Routledge, New York, 1977).

Monteiro, C. A., W. L. Conde, B. Lu, and B. M. Popkin, "Obesity and Inequities in Health in the Developing World," *International Journal of Obesity* 28 (2004a), 1181–1186.

Monteiro, C. A., W. L. Conde, and B. M. Popkin, "The Burden of Disease from Undernutrition and Overnutrition in Countries Undergoing Rapid Nutrition Transition: A View from Brazil," *American Journal of Public Health* 94 (2004b), 433–434.

Monteiro, C. A., E. C. Moura, W. L. Conde, and B. M. Popkin, "Socioeconomic Status and Obesity in Adult Populations of Developing Countries: A Review," Bulletin of *World Health Organization* 82 (2004), 940–946.

Nielsen, S. J., A. M. Siega-Riz, and B. M. Popkin, "Trends in Energy Intake in U.S. between 1977 and 1996: Similar Shifts Seen Across Age Groups," *Obesity Research* 10 (2002), 370–378.

Olshansky, S. J., and A. B. Ault, "The Fourth Stage of the Epidemiologic Transition: The Age of Delayed Degenerative Diseases," *Milbank Quarterly* 64 (1986), 355–391.

Omran, A. R., "The Epidemiologic Transition. A Theory of the Epidemiology of Population Change," *Milbank Memorial Fund Quarterly* 49 (1971), 509–538.

Popkin, B. M., "Nutritional Patterns and Transitions," *Population and Development Review* 19 (1993), 138–157.

Popkin, B. M., "Urbanization, Lifestyle Changes and the Nutrition Transition," *World Development* 27 (1999), 1905–1916.

Popkin, B. M., "An Overview on the Nutrition Transition and Its Health Implications: The Bellagio Meeting," *Public Health Nutrition* 5 (2002a), 93–103.

Popkin, B. M., "The Shift in Stages of the Nutrition Transition in the Developing World Differs from Past Experiences!," *Public Health Nutrition* 5 (2002b), 205–214.

Popkin, B. M.,"Global Nutrition Dynamics: The World Is Shifting Rapidly toward a Diet Linked with Noncommunicable Diseases (NCDs)," *American Journal of Clinical Nutrition* (2006), 289–298.

Popkin, B. M., and A. Drewnowski, "Dietary Fats and the Nutrition Transition: New Trends in the Global Diet," *Nutrition Reviews* 55 (1997), 31–43.

Popkin, B. M., and S. Du, "Dynamics of the Nutrition Transition Toward the Animal Foods Sector in China and Its Implications: A Worried Perspective," *Journal of Nutrition* 133 (2003), 3898S–3906S.

Popkin, B. M., and S. J. Nielsen, "The Sweetening of the World's Diet," *Obesity Research* 11 (2003), 1325–1332.

Popkin, B. M., G. Keyou, F. Zhai, X. Guo, H. Ma, and N. Zohoori, "The Nutrition Transition in China: A Cross-Sectional Analysis," *European Journal of Clinical Nutrition* 47 (1993), 333–346.

Popkin, B. M., A. M. Siega-Riz, and P. S. Haines, "A Comparison of Dietary Trends among Racial and Socioeconomic Groups in the United States," *New England Journal of Medicine* 335 (1996), 716–720.

Popkin, B. M., B. Lu, and F. Zhai, "Understanding the Nutrition Transition: Measuring Rapid Dietary Changes in Transitional Countries," *Public Health Nutrition* 5 (2002), 947–953.

Popkin, B. M., C. Zizza, and A. M. Siega-Riz, "Who is Leading the Change? U.S. Dietary Quality Comparison between 1965 and 1996," *American Journal of Preventive Medicine* 25 (2003), 1–8.

Puska, P., P. Pirjo, and U. Uusitalo, "Influencing Public Nutrition for Non-Communicable Disease Prevention: From Community Intervention to National Programme—Experiences from Finland," *Public Health Nutrition* 5 (2002), 245–251.

Qian, Y.-Y., and J.-L. Wu, *China's Transition to a Market Economy: How Far across the River?* (Stanford University: Palo Alto, CA, 2000).

State Statistical Bureau (SSB), *Statistical Yearbook for China.* (State Statistical Bureau of China, 1989, 1991, 1993, 1997, 2000, 2004).

Tillotson, J. E., "America's Obesity: Conflicting Public Policies, Industrial Economic Development, and Unintended Human Consequences," *Annual Review of Nutrition* 24 (2004), 617–643.

Williams, G. W., "Development and Future Direction of the World Soybean Market," *Quarterly Journal of International Agriculture* 23 (1984), 319–337.

World Bank, *China Regional Disparities* (World Bank: Washington, DC, 1995).

Zhai, F., X. Guo, B. Popkin, L. Ma, Q. Wang, W. Yu, S. Jin, and K. Ge, "Evaluation of the 24-Hour Individual Recall Method in China," *Food Nutrition Bulletin* 17 (1996), 154–161.

Zhai, F., D. Fu, S. Du, K. Ge, C. Chen, and B. M. Popkin, "What Is China Doing in Policy-Making to Push Back the Negative Aspects of the Nutrition Transition?," *Public Health Nutrition* 5 (2002), 269–273.

Zizza, C., A. M. Siega-Riz, and B. M. Popkin, "Significant Increase in Young Adults' Snacking between 1977–1978 and 1994–1996 Represents A Cause for Concern!," *Preventive Medicine* 32 (2001), 303–310.

Coping with drought in rice farming in Asia: insights from a cross-country comparative study

Sushil Pandey*, Humnath Bhandari**, Shijun Ding***, Preeda Prapertchob****, Ramesh Sharan*****, Dibakar Naik******, Sudhir K. Taunk*******, and Asras Sastri*******

Abstract

Drought is a major constraint affecting rice production, especially in rainfed areas of Asia. Despite its importance in rice-growing areas, the magnitude of economic losses arising from drought, its impact on farm households, and farmers' drought coping mechanisms are poorly understood. This article provides insights into these aspects of drought based on a cross-country comparative analysis of rainfed rice-growing areas in southern China, eastern India, and northeast Thailand. The economic cost of drought is found to be substantially higher in eastern India than in the other two countries. Higher probability and greater spatial covariance of drought and less diversified farming systems with rice accounting for a larger share of household income are the main reasons for this higher cost of drought in eastern India. Farmers deploy various coping mechanisms but such mechanisms are largely unable to prevent a reduction in income and consumption, especially in eastern India. As a result, welfare consequences on poor farmers are substantial with a large number of people falling back into poverty during drought years. The overall implications for technology design and for policy improvements for drought mitigation and drought relief are discussed in the light of the empirical findings of the study.

JEL classification: D1, I3

Keywords: drought; economic cost; coping mechanisms; poverty

1. Introduction

Climate-related natural disasters (drought, flood, and typhoon) are principal sources of risk and uncertainties in agriculture. These are important constraints affecting the production of rice—the staple crop of Asia. Although the production of rice has increased over time in the wake of the green revolution, major shortfalls caused by climatic aberrations such as drought and flood are frequent. At least 23 million ha of rice area (20% of total rice area) in Asia is estimated to be drought-prone (Pandey et al., 2007).

The economic costs of drought can be enormous. For example, drought has been historically associated with food shortages of varying intensities, including those that have resulted in major famines in different parts of Asia and Africa. In India, major droughts in 1918, 1957–1958, and 1965 resulted in famines during the 20th century (FAO, 2001). The 1987 drought affected almost 60% of the total cropped area and 285 million people across India (Sinha, 1999). Similarly, the average annual drought-affected area in China during 1978–2003 is estimated to have been 14 million ha and the direct economic cost of drought is estimated to have been 0.5–3.3% of the agricultural sector GDP. In Thailand, the drought of 2004 is estimated to have affected

*Social Sciences Division, International Rice Research Institute (IRRI), Los Banos, Laguna, Philippines.

**International Research Center for Agricultural Sciences (JIRCAS), 1-1, Ohwashi, Tsukuba, Ibaraki 305-8686, Japan.

***Zhongnan University of Economics and Law, #1 South Nanhu Road, Wuhan City, Hubei Province, P.R. China 430073.

****Khon Kaen University, 123 Mittraparp Highway, Khon Kaen, Thailand 40002.

*****Department of Economics, Ranchi University, Ranchi, India.

******Orissa University of Agriculture and Technology, Bhubaneswar-751003, Orissa, India.

*******Indira Gandhi Agricultural University, Raipur, India.

2 million ha of cropped area and over 8 million people (Bank of Thailand, 2005).

The effect of drought on human societies can be multidimensional. The effect of drought in terms of production losses and consequent human misery is well publicized during years of crop failure. However, losses to drought of milder intensity, although not so visible, can also be substantial. Production loss, which is often used as a measure of the cost of drought, is only a part of the overall economic cost. Severe droughts can result in starvation and even death of the affected population. However, different types of economic costs arise before such severe consequences occur. Due to market failures, farmers attempt to "self-insure" by making costly adjustments in their production practices and adopting conservative practices to reduce the negative impact during drought years. Although these adjustments reduce the direct production losses, they themselves entail some economic costs in terms of opportunities for income gains lost during good years.

In rural areas where agricultural production is a major source of income and employment, a decrease in agricultural production will set off second-round effects through forward and backward linkages of agriculture with other sectors. A decrease in agricultural income will reduce the demand for products of the agroprocessing industries that cater to the local markets. This will lead to a reduction in income and employment in this sector. Similarly, the income of rural households engaged in providing agricultural inputs will also decrease. This reduction in household incomes will set off further "knock-on" effects. By the time these effects have been fully played out, the overall economic loss from drought may turn out to be several times more than what is indicated by the loss in production of agricultural output alone. The loss in household income can result in a loss in consumption of the poor whose consumption levels are already low. Farmers may attempt to cope with the loss by liquidating productive assets, pulling children out of school, migrating to distant places in search of employment, and going deeper into debt. The economic and social costs of all these consequences can indeed be enormous.

Much of the current knowledge on drought is based mainly on arid and semiarid regions (Jodha, 1978; Campbell, 1999; Hazell et al., 2001; Rathore, 2004; Shivakumar and Kerbart, 2004). Despite reasonably high rainfall, drought occurs frequently in the subhumid regions of Asia (Steyaert et al., 1981). However, the nature and frequency of drought in subhumid regions, its impact on farmer livelihoods, farmers' drought coping strategies, and welfare implication of drought have not been adequately studied. Analyses of drought characteristics, drought impacts, and household coping mechanisms are important for understanding the nature of risk and vulnerability associated with drought and for formulating various interventions for effective drought mitigation.

This article provides a synthesis of findings and recommendations based on a recent cross-country comparative study of the impact of drought and farmers' coping mechanisms (Pandey et al., 2007). The countries included in the study were China, India, and Thailand. These countries vary in climatic conditions, the level of economic development, rice yields, and institutional and policy contexts of rice farming. The specific regions selected for the study were southern China, eastern India, and northeast Thailand. In southern China, the provinces included were Hubei, Guangxi, and Zhejiang. Eastern India was represented by the states of Chattisgarh, Jharkhand, and Orissa. All provinces of northeast Thailand were included. Some of the basic characteristics of rice production systems and economic indicators of the countries/regions in the study are summarized in Table 1.

2. Drought: definition, coping mechanisms and consequences

Conceptually, drought is considered to describe a situation of limited rainfall that is substantially below what has been established to be a "normal" value for the area concerned, leading to adverse consequences on human welfare. Although drought is a climatically induced phenomenon, its impact depends on social and economic context as well. Hence, in addition to climate, economic and social parameters should be also taken into account in defining drought. This makes developing a universally applicable definition of drought impractical. Three generally used definitions of drought are based on meteorological, hydrological, and agricultural perspectives (Wilhite and Glantz, 1985).

Meteorological drought is defined as a situation in which the actual rainfall is significantly below the

Table 1
General characteristics, three countries

Characteristics	China	India	Thailand
Per capita GNI ($)	1290	620	2540
Population below poverty line (%)	10	25	10
Population of study area (million)[a]	155	88	21
Average landholding (ha/hh)	1.48	1.4	2.3
Share of agriculture to total GDP (%)	14	25	9
Share of agriculture to total employment (%)	49	60	49
Irrigated rice area (% of total rice area)	93	50	20
Rice yield (t/ha)[b]	6.2	2.9	2.6
CV of rice production (%)[c]	5	18	10
Share to world rice production (%)	30	21	4
Annual rainfall (mm)	1200–1400	1000–1300	1100–1500

[a] This refers to the total population of the provinces/states included in this study.
[b] Rice yield was estimated using 2002–2004 data, for the whole country.
[c] Coefficients of variation (CV) were estimated using 1970–2003 data for the provinces/states included in this study.

long-term average (LTA) for the area. This definition does not take into account factors other than rainfall. Hydrological drought is defined as the situation of depletion in surface and subsurface water resources due to shortfall in precipitation. The effect on depletion of water resources is the main concern in this definition.

Agricultural drought is said to occur when the soil moisture is insufficient to meet crop water requirements resulting in yield losses. As the effect of rainfall deficiency on crops also depends on soil and crop characteristics, the definition of agricultural drought requires consideration of actual and potential evapotranspiration, soil water deficit, and production losses simultaneously.

Risk-coping strategies can be classified into *ex ante* and *ex post* depending upon whether they help to reduce risk or reduce the impact of risk after the production shortfall has occurred. Due to lack of efficient market-based mechanisms for diffusing the risk, farmers modify their production practices to provide "self-insurance" so that the likely impact of adverse consequences is reduced to an acceptable level. *Ex ante* strategies help reduce the fluctuations in income and are also referred to as income-smoothing strategies. These strategies can, however, be costly in terms of forgone opportunities for income gains as farmers select safer but low-return activities.

Ex ante strategies can be grouped into two categories: those that reduce risk by diversification and those that do so by imparting greater flexibility in decision making. Diversification is simply captured in the principle of not putting "all eggs in one basket." The risk of income shortfall is reduced by growing several crops that have negatively or weakly correlated returns. This principle is used in different types of diversification common in rural societies. The examples include spatial diversification of farms, diversification of agricultural enterprises, and diversification from farm to nonfarm activities.

Maintaining flexibility is an adaptive strategy that allows farmers to switch between activities as the situation demands. Flexibility in decision making permits farmers not only to reduce the chances of low incomes but also to capture income-increasing opportunities when they do arise. Examples are using split doses of fertilizers, temporally adjusting input use to crop conditions, and adjusting the area allocated to a crop depending on the climatic conditions. While postponing agricultural decisions until uncertainties are reduced can help lower the potential losses, such a strategy can also be costly in terms of income forgone if operations are delayed beyond the optimal biological window. Other *ex ante* coping mechanisms include maintaining stocks of food, fodder, and cash.

Ex post strategies are designed to prevent shortfall in consumption when the income drops below what is necessary for maintaining consumption at its normal level. *Ex post* strategies are also referred to as consumption-smoothing strategies as they help reduce the fluctuations in consumption. These include migration, consumption loans, asset liquidation, and charity. Consumption shortfall can occur despite these *ex post* strategies if the drop in income is substantial.

Farmers who are exposed to risk use these strategies in different combinations. Over a long period of time, some of these strategies are incorporated into the nature of the farming system and are often not easily identifiable as risk-coping mechanisms. Others are deployed only under certain risky situations and are easier to identify as responses to risk.

Opportunity costs associated with the deployment of various coping mechanisms can, however, be large. The climatic uncertainties often compel farmers, particularly those who are more risk-averse, to employ conservative risk management strategies that reduce the negative impact in poor years, but often at the expense of reducing the average productivity and profitability. For example, by growing drought-hardy but low-yielding traditional rice varieties, farmers may be able to minimize the drought risk but may end up sacrificing a potentially higher income in normal years. Also, poor farmers in high drought-risk environments may be reluctant to invest in seed-fertilizer technologies that could increase profitability in normal years but lead to a loss of capital investment in poor years. The economic cost of risk aversion in developing countries has been estimated to be in the range of 10–15% (Antle, 1987; Anderson, 1995). Although the inefficiency cost may appear to be small in percentage terms, this involves a substantial reduction in the average income of poor farmers who are on or barely above the poverty line.

In addition to these opportunity costs, poor households who are compelled to sell their productive assets such as bullocks and farm implements will suffer future productivity losses as it can take them several years to reacquire those assets. A cut in medical expenses and children's education will impact future income-earning capacity of the household. Such an impact may linger on to the future generation also. The loss of income and assets can convert transient poverty into chronic poverty, making the possibility of escape from poverty more remote (Morduch, 1994; Barrett, 2005).

3. Analytical approach

Two main types of analyses were conducted to meet the objectives of the study. The first relates to

Table 2
Description of secondary data used in the study, three countries

Country	Province/state/zone[a]	Number of selected county/district/province[b]	Data period covered[c]
China	Guangxi	10	1982–2001
	Hubei	10	1982–2001
	Zhejiang	10	1982–2001
India	Chattisgarh	7	1970–2002
	Jharkhand	6	1970–1999
	Orissa	13	1970–2002
Thailand	Zone 1	6	1970–2002
	Zone 2	8	1970–2002
	Zone 3	2	1970–2002

[a] Province, state, and agroecological zone at the aggregate level and county, district, and province at the disaggregate level were utilized for this study in southern China, eastern India, and northeast Thailand, respectively.

[b] Geographical size of province in northeast Thailand is almost similar to the size of districts in India. Over time old districts/provinces were partitioned into new districts/provinces due to various administrative and/or political needs. This created difficulties in constructing a consistent time series database. The problem was handled by integrating the database of new districts/provinces into old districts/provinces. Thus, all the analyses in this study were based on the old districts/provinces that existed in 1970.

[c] In some cases, recent data were available at the aggregate level only. So, data up to the year 2003 were used at the aggregate level analysis in some cases.

characterization of drought and estimation of the aggregate value of production loss resulting from drought. The second involves an assessment of the impact of drought at the farm household level and an analysis of farmers' coping mechanisms.

The estimation of aggregate production loss involved the analysis of published temporal data on rainfall and crop production. Province (or state) and county (or district) level data were utilized for this (Table 2). These data were also used to estimate the aggregate economic losses from drought by correlating drought events with crop production. Actual crop production over a run of years covering both drought and nondrought years were utilized in this study as opposed to the usual practice of subjectively estimating the production loss using either farmers' or researchers' subjective estimates of yield losses and probability of drought (Widawsky and O'Toole, 1990; Hossain, 1996).

Drought was defined in terms of deficiency of actual rainfall compared to LTA. Following the similar approach used by Indian Meteorological Department

(IMD) and other literature (Pandey et al., 2000; DAC, 2003), drought was considered to occur in a particular year if the annual rainfall was less than 80% of the LTA. The main focus of this study is on rice which is grown mainly during the monsoon season. Hence, in the context of this study, drought was considered to have occurred if rainfall during the monsoon season was less than 80% of the LTA. The frequency of drought was estimated as the ratio of the number of drought years to the total number of years considered. Characterization of the timing, intensity, frequency, and spatial pattern of drought was conducted using the long-term monthly rainfall data. Province (or state) and county (or district) level data were utilized for this.

The rice-growing period was divided into three growing seasons for assessing the incidence of drought during different periods and its impact on production. These were early, medium, and late seasons. The frequency of drought during each season was estimated as the number of years in which rainfall was below 80% of the LTA for that particular season.

A discrete drought dummy variable was specified in a linear trend equation on production (Q). In this specification, drought results in a discrete downward shift in the intercept. The model was specified as

$$Q = a + bT + cD + u, \tag{1}$$

where T refers to the time trend which captures the effect of technological change and D is the drought dummy. The drought dummy variable takes the value of "1" in drought years and "0" otherwise. The coefficient "c" measures the average effect of drought on production when all drought years are considered.

The analysis of the household-level impact of drought and farmers' coping mechanisms was conducted using cross-sectional data from a survey of 1,310 farm households. For this, households were selected from study areas using a stratified random sampling approach. Detailed information of cropping patterns, rice production, household income, employment, and drought coping mechanisms were elicited during the survey using pre-tested survey questionnaires. Farmers were asked to provide information on production practices and farm productivity for "normal" and "drought" years. Information on the overall impact of drought on income and how households attempted to cope with drought was also collected during the survey. The collected information was compared between "normal" and "drought" years to analyze the impact of drought.

The meteorological definition of drought used for the aggregate analysis is inappropriate for estimating the household-level impact. A village may suffer from drought in a particular year even though the meteorological data do not indicate drought at the aggregate (province/state/zone) level. Thus a village-based identification of a "normal" and a "drought" year experienced in the recent past was utilized. These "normal" and "drought" years were identified based on farmer group consensus.

4. Results and discussions

The analysis of monthly rainfall data for the period 1970–2003 indicated that drought is a regular phenomenon in the regions included in the study in all three countries. The probability of drought varied in the range 0.1–0.4, with the probability being higher in eastern India relative to southern China and northeast Thailand (Figure 1). The probability of late-season drought was found to be higher than that of the early-season drought generally. The late-season drought was also found to be spatially more covariate than the early-season drought. As rice yield is more sensitive to drought during flowering/grain fill stages (i.e., during late season, according to the definition used here), the late-season drought is thus likely to have a larger aggregate production impact than the early-season drought.

The temporal instability in rice production as measured by the detrended coefficient of variation of rice yield was found to be high in eastern India relative to the other regions. The corresponding coefficients of variations for southern China and northeast Thailand were much lower (Table 3), indicating that droughts in these regions are not as covariate spatially as in eastern India, with their effects being limited to some pockets. Given the nature of the temporal variability, the aggregate impact of drought on production is also likely to be higher in eastern India relative to the other two regions.

The estimated average loss in rice production during drought years using the dummy variable model described earlier for the three states of eastern India is 5.4 million tons (Table 4). This is much higher than

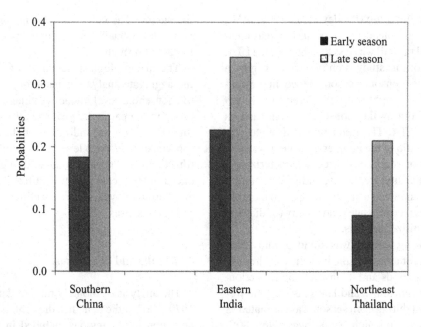

Figure 1. Estimated probabilities of early- and late-season drought, in southern China (1982–2001), eastern India (1970–2000), and northeast Thailand (1970–2002).

Table 3
Coefficient of variation(%) of rice area, yield, and production, three countries, 1970–2003

Rice	Southern China	Eastern India	Northeast Thailand
Area	3	2	7
Yield	4	17	9
Production	5	18	10

Note: Coefficients of variation were estimated based on secondary data of study provinces/states. Coefficients of variation for China were estimated using quadratically detrended data. Coefficients of variation for India and Thailand were estimated using linearly detrended data.

for northeast Thailand (less than 1 million tons) and southern China (around 1 million tons but not statistically significant). The loss (including any nonrice crops included) during drought years is thus 36% of the average value of production in eastern India. This represents indeed a massive loss during drought years (estimated at $856 million).

As droughts do not occur every year, the above estimate of production loss needs to be averaged over a run of drought and nondrought years to get the annual average loss estimate. Again for eastern India, this represents the annual average of loss of $162 million

(or 6.8% of the average value of output). For northeast Thailand and southern China the losses were found to be much smaller and averaged at less than $20 million per year (or less than 1.5% of the value of output).

The estimates thus indicate that, at the aggregate level, the production losses are much higher for eastern India than for the other two regions. Lower probability of drought, smaller magnitude of loss during drought years, and less covariate nature of drought together resulted in a lower production loss at the aggregate level in the other two regions relative to eastern India.

The overall economic cost of drought includes the value of production loss, the costs farmers incur in making adjustments in production systems during drought years, opportunities for gains forgone during good years by adopting *ex ante* coping strategies that reduce losses during drought years, the generally lower productivity of drought-prone areas due to moisture deficiency, and the costs of government programs aimed at long-term drought mitigation. The public-sector provision of relief also involves large financial costs, but these are mainly transfer payments, and hence, do not involve an economic cost. The average annual cost for the three states of eastern India included in this study is in the neighborhood of $400 million (Pandey et al., 2007). Overall, the cost of drought is a substantial

Table 4

Estimated value of crop production loss due to drought using rainfall-based drought year, 1970–2002

Country[a]	Drought years			Annual	
	Quantity of rice production loss (million t)	Value of crop production loss[b] (million US$)	Ratio of loss to average value of production (%)	Value of crop production loss[b] (million $)	Ratio of loss to average value of production (%)
Southern China	1.2	133	3	16	0.4
Eastern India	5.4	856***	36	162	6.8
Northeast Thailand	0.7	85*	10	10	1.2

[a] The values were estimated based on secondary data of study provinces/states.

[b] The value of production loss was estimated using data for both rice and nonrice crops for India while only rice was included for China and Thailand.

*$P < 0.1$ and ***$P < 0.01$.

Table 5

Average income per household (US$) in normal and drought year, three states, eastern India

Income sources	Normal year			Drought year			Change over normal (%)		
	CH[a]	JH	OR	CH	JH	OR	CH	JH	OR
Total income	850	500	620	360	380	460	−58	−24	−26
Agriculture	670	310	420	140	160	240	−79	−48	−43
Crop income	600	210	300	90	70	160	−85	−67	−47
Rice	430	150	130	30	60	60	−93	−60	−54
Nonrice	170	60	170	60	10	100	−65	−83	−41
Farm labor	60	60	90	30	50	40	−50	−17	−56
Small animals[b]	10	10	30	20	10	30	100	0	0
Forest produce	0	30	0	0	30	10		0	100
Nonagriculture	180	190	200	220	220	220	22	16	10
Hired labor	50	120	110	90	150	150	80	25	36
Services	90	60	60	90	60	50	0	0	−17
Business	0	10	30	0	10	20		0	−33
Self-employment	30	0	0	30	0	0	0		
Others[c]	10	0	0	10	0	0	0		
Additional income from asset sale and/or borrowing	30	20	60	70	30	80	133	50	33
Sale of livestock[d]	10	10	10	10	10	20	0	0	100
Sale of major assets[e]	10	0	20	40	0	20	300		0
Sale of minor assets[f]	0	0	10	0	0	10			0
Mortgage/Borrow	10	10	20	10	20	30	0	100	50
Relief operation	0	0	0	10	0	0	100		
Total disposable income	880	520	680	430	410	540	−51	−21	−21

[a] CH-Chattisgarh, JH-Jharkhand, and OR-Orissa.

[b] Small animals include goat, sheep, chicken, ducks, calves, and animal produce like milk, ghee, egg, etc.

[c] Others include sale of fruits, sale of fish, old age pension, small petty business, small artisan work, and so on.

[d] Livestock includes large animals like cattle, buffalo, bullock, and pig.

[e] Major assets include land and building.

[f] Minor assets include farm implements, jewelry, and other small assets.

proportion of the agricultural value added in eastern India.

Drought resulted in an overall income loss in the range of 24–58% (Table 5). The drop in rice income was the main factor contributing to the total income loss. Earnings from farm labor also dropped substantially due to a reduced labor demand. Farmers attempted to reduce the loss in agricultural income during drought

Table 6

Incidence of rural poverty among sample households in normal and drought year, eastern India

States in eastern India	National estimate of rural poverty ratio[a] (%)	Sample estimate of poverty ratio[b]		Percentage point increase (% point)	Number of people falling back into poverty (million)
		Normal year	Drought year		
Chattisgarh	37	43	76	33	5.5
Jharkhand	44	57	69	12	2.5
Orissa	48	54	70	16	5.0

[a] Poverty ratios for Chattisgarh and Jharkhand were based on values for undivided states of Madhya Pradesh and Bihar, respectively. The national poverty ratio is for 1999–2000.

[b] Monthly rural poverty line income of Rs 311.34, 333.07, 323.92 was used to define poverty line for Chattisgarh, Jharkhand, and Orissa, respectively.

years by seeking additional employment in the nonfarm sector. This mainly included employment as wage labor in the construction sector for which farmers often migrated to distant places. The additional earning from nonfarm employment was, however, clearly inadequate to compensate for the loss in agricultural income.

Farmers relied on three main mechanisms to recoup this loss in total income. These were the sale of livestock, sale of other assets, and borrowing. These adjustment mechanisms helped recover only 6–13% of the loss in total income. Compared to the normal years, households still ended up with substantially lower level of income despite all these adjustments. Thus, all the different coping mechanisms farmers deployed were found to be inadequate to prevent a shortfall in income during the drought years.

The incidence of poverty increased substantially during drought years (Table 6). Almost 13 million additional people "fell back" into poverty as a result of drought. This is a substantial increase in the incidence of poverty and translates into the increase in rural poverty at the national level by 1.8 percentage points. Some of the increase in poverty may be transitory with households being able to climb out of poverty on their own. However, other households whose income and assets fall below certain threshold levels may end up joining the ranks of the chronically poor (Barrett, 2005). The data collected, however, did not permit the estimation of the proportion of these two categories of households.

Overall, farmers do not seem to have much flexibility in making management adjustments in rice cropping in relation to drought. Other than delaying the crop establishment if the rains are late, replanting and resowing when suitable opportunities arise, and some reduction

in fertilizer use, farmers mostly follow a standard set of practices irrespective of the occurrence of drought. This could partly be due to the fact that drought mostly occurs during the late season by which time the opportunities for crop management adjustments to reduce losses are no longer available. The timing of drought (mostly late rather than early) and the lack of suitable technological options probably limited the flexibility in making tactical adjustments in crop management practices to reduce the losses.

Since rice is the staple food, a loss in its production can be expected to result in major adjustments in consumption. Such adjustments may range from reduced sale of rice, reduced quantity retained as seeds for the following year, increased amounts purchased, substitution of other crops for rice, supplementation of food deficit by other types of food not normally consumed, and in the worst-case scenario, a reduction in consumption. Farmers made all these types of adjustments to a varying degree. Despite these various adjustments, most farmers were unable to maintain consumption at the pre-drought level. They reduced both the number of meals taken per day as well as the quantity consumed per meal. As a result, the average number of meals taken per day dropped from close to three to close to two, with 10–30% of the households reducing their frequency of food intake to one meal per day. A large proportion (60–70%) of the households also reduced the quantity of food consumed per meal. In addition, households consumed other "inferior" food items that were not normally consumed.

The interruption and/or discontinuation of children's education is a disinvestment in human capital which will most definitely reduce their future earning potentials in most cases. An important pathway for escape

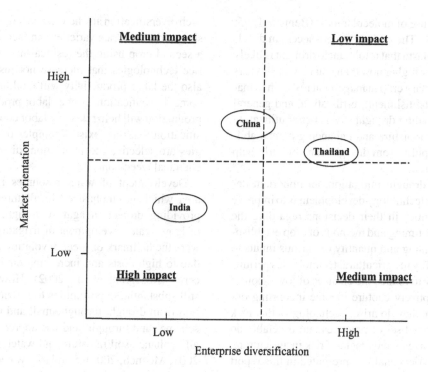

Figure 2. Household-level impact of drought.

from poverty may be foreclosed as a result of drought. More than 50% of the farmers reported curtailing children's education.

Relative to eastern India, the economic costs in southern China and northeast Thailand were found to be small, both in absolute and relative terms. The production losses at the aggregate level in these two regions were relatively small due to a lower frequency and less covariate nature of drought. In addition, rice accounted for a smaller proportion of the household income due to a more diversified income structure. The differences in the rice production systems, the level of income diversification, and the nature of drought in these two latter regions are hence the major factors determining the relative magnitudes of economic losses.

In the case of eastern India, rice accounts for around 40% of the total household income. The share of rice in the total household income in southern China and northeast Thailand is about half that in eastern India. Eastern Indian farmers thus lose proportionately more income during drought years. Due to limited diversification of farm income which is generated mainly from rice, the household level consequences of drought in eastern India are thus more severe relative to the other two regions. In both northeast Thailand and southern China, agricultural income is more diversified. In addition, the share of nonfarm income in the total income is much higher. Thus, a more commercialized agriculture and a greater diversification of farm incomes seem to have contributed to a smaller consumption consequence of drought in southern China and northeast Thailand relative to eastern India by weakening income correlations and improving the effectiveness of coping mechanisms. The effect of these factors on household-level impact is stylized in a summary form in Figure 2.

5. Drought mitigation options

Improved rice technologies that help reduce the losses to drought can play an important role in long-term drought mitigation. Important scientific progress is being made in understanding the physiological mechanisms that impart tolerance to drought (Blum, 2005). Similarly, progress is being made in developing drought-tolerant rice germplasm through conventional breeding and the use of molecular tools (Bennett, 1995; Atlin et al., 2006). The probability of success in developing rice germplasm that is tolerant to drought is likely to be substantially higher now than what it was 10 years ago. Complementary crop management research to manipulate crop establishment, fertilization, and general crop care for avoiding drought stress, better utilization of available soil moisture and enhancing plant's ability to recover rapidly from drought can similarly help reduce the losses.

For effective drought mitigation, an important design criterion for technology development is to improve farmers' flexibilities in their decisions regarding the crop choices, the timing and methods of crop establishment, and the timing and quantity of various inputs to be used. Flexibility in agricultural technologies permits farmers not only to reduce the chances of low incomes but also to adaptively capture income-increasing opportunities when they do arise. Technologies that lock farmers into a fixed set of practices and timetable do not permit effective management of risk in agriculture. In fact, the empirical analyses presented in this report indicate that the current rice-production practices, especially in drought-prone areas of India, are somewhat inflexible and routine. Rice varieties and general crop management practices used are almost the same in normal years and in years with early-season drought. Examples of technologies that provide greater flexibilities are varieties that are not adversely affected by delayed transplanting caused by early-season drought, varieties that perform equally well under both direct seeding and transplanting, and crop-management practices that can be implemented over a wider time window.

The late-season drought is more frequent and tends to have more serious economic consequences for poor farmers than the early-season drought. In addition to having to deal with consequences of low or no harvest, farmers also lose their investments in seeds, fertilizers, and labor if the crop is lost due to late-season drought. Although early-season drought may prevent planting completely, farmers can switch early to other coping strategies such as wage labor and migration to reduce income losses in such years. Thus the poverty impact of technology is likely to be higher if research is focused on developing technologies that help plants better tolerate the late-season drought.

Crop diversification is an important drought coping mechanism of farmers. Rice technologies that promote such diversification are, hence, needed. In rainfed areas, shorter duration rice varieties can facilitate planting of a second crop using the residual moisture. Similarly, rice technologies that increase not just the yield but also the labor productivity will facilitate crop and income diversification. Higher labor productivity in rice production will help relax any labor constraint to diversification that may exist. Examples of such technologies are selective mechanization, direct seeding, and chemical weed control.

Development of water resources is an important area which is emphasized in all three countries for providing protection against drought. Opportunities of large-scale development of irrigation schemes that were the hallmark of green revolution are limited now due to high costs and increasing environmental concerns (Rosegrant et al., 2002). However, there are still substantial opportunities to provide some protection from drought through small and minor irrigation schemes and through land-use approaches that generally enhance soil moisture and water retention (Shah, 2001; Moench, 2002). Similarly, watershed-based approaches that are implemented in drought-prone areas of India provide opportunities for achieving long-term drought proofing by improving the overall moisture retention within the watersheds (Rao, 2000).

In all three countries studied, a major response to drought has been to provide relief to the affected population. India has the most elaborate institutional setup for providing drought relief which mainly takes the form of employment generation through public works. Affected people are also provided with some inputs and credit. While the provision of relief is essential to reduce the incidence of hunger and starvation, the major problems with the relief programs are slow response, poor targeting of beneficiaries, and limited coverage due to budgetary constraints. A "fire-fighting" approach that underlies the provision of drought relief cannot provide a long-term drought proofing despite the large amount spent during the drought years (Rao, 2000; Hirway, 2001). It is important that the provision of relief during drought years is complemented by a long-term strategy of investing in soil and water conservation and utilization, policy support, and infrastructure development to promote crop and income diversification in drought-prone areas (Rao, 2000).

The scientific advances in meteorology and informatics have made it possible now to forecast drought with reasonable degrees of accuracy and reliability. Various indicators such as the Southern Oscillation Index are now routinely used in several countries to make drought forecasts (Wilhite et al., 2000; Meinke and Stone, 2005). Suitable refinements and adaptations of these forecasting systems are needed to enhance drought preparedness at the national level as well as to assist farmers in making more efficient decisions regarding the choice of crops and cropping practices (Abedullah and Pandey, 1998).

Although drought occurs regularly, a detailed scientific characterization of drought, analysis of its impact, and mapping are not being adequately conducted both at the local (province, district, state) and the national levels. Such analyses and mapping are critically important for developing and implementing suitable short- and long-term strategies for drought mitigation.

While technological interventions can be critical in some cases, this is not the only option for improving the management of drought. There is a whole gamut of policy interventions that can improve farmers' capacity to manage drought through more effective income- and consumption-smoothing mechanisms. Improvements in rural infrastructures and marketing that allow farmers to diversify their income sources can play an important role in reducing the overall income risk. Investment in rural education can similarly help diversify income. In addition, such investments contribute directly to income growth that will further increase farmers' capacity to cope with various forms of agricultural risks. Widening and deepening of the rural financial markets will also be a critical factor for reducing fluctuations in both income and consumption over time. Although the conventional forms of crop insurance are unlikely to be successful due to problems such as moral hazard and adverse selection (Hazell et al., 1986), innovative approaches such as rainfall derivatives and international reinsurance of agricultural risks can provide promising opportunities (Skees et al., 2001; Turvey, 2001; Glauber, 2004). However, these alternative schemes have not yet been adequately evaluated. There are important challenges in employing weather risk markets in developing countries (Skees et al., 2001; Varangis, 2002). More work is needed for developing and pilot testing new types of insurance products and schemes suited to hundreds of millions of small farmers of Asia who grow rice primarily for subsistence.

6. Concluding remarks

Even in subhumid rice-growing areas of Asia, drought is clearly an important climatic factor that has large economic costs, both in terms of the actual economic losses during drought years and the losses arising from the opportunities for economic gains forgone. The provision of relief has been the main form of public response to drought. Although important in reducing the hunger and hardship of the affected people, the provision of relief alone is clearly inadequate and may even be an inefficient response for achieving longer-term drought mitigation. Given the clear linkage between drought and poverty as demonstrated in this study, it is critically important to include drought mitigation as an integral part of the rural development strategy. Policies that in general increase income growth and encourage income diversification also serve to protect farmers from the adverse consequences of risk, including that of drought.

The scientific progress made in understanding the physiology of drought and in the development of biotechnology tools have opened up promising opportunities for making a significant impact on drought mitigation through improved technology. However, agricultural research in general remains grossly under-invested in developing countries of Asia. This is a cause for concern, not only for drought mitigation, but for promoting an overall agricultural development.

Acknowledgments

The research team gratefully acknowledges the financial support from the Rockefeller Foundation. Thanks are due to Mahabub Hossain, Head of the Social Sciences Division of IRRI for his valuable suggestions and to research support staff from our respective organizations for their assistance. Comments from J. Brian Hardaker in an earlier version helped improve the clarity of this article. We also thank Keijiro Otsuka and other reviewers who provided valuable suggestions to improve the quality of this article.

References

Abedullah, and S. Pandey, "Risk and the Value of Rainfall Forecast for Rainfed Rice in the Philippines," *Philippine Journal of Crop Sciences* 23 (1998), 159–165.

Anderson, J. R., "Confronting Uncertainty in Rainfed Rice Farming: Research Challenges," in IRRI, *Fragile Lives in Fragile Ecosystems*, Proceedings of the International Rice Research Conference, 13–17 Feb 1995 (International Rice Research Institute: Manila, 1995).

Antle, J. M., "Econometric Estimation of Producers' Risk Attitudes," *American Journal of Agricultural Economics* 69 (1987), 509–522.

Atlin, G. N., H. R. Lafitte, D. Tao, M. Laza, M. Amante, and B. Courtois, "Developing Rice Cultivars for High-Fertility Upland Systems in the Asian Tropics," *Field Crops Research* 97 (2006), 43–52.

Bank of Thailand, *The Inflation Report January 2005* (The Bank of Thailand: Bangkok, Thailand, 2005).

Barrett, C. B., "Rural Poverty Dynamics: Development Policy Implications," *Agricultural Economics* 32 (2005), 45–60.

Bennett, J., "Biotechnology and the Future of Rice Production," *GeoJournal* 35 (1995), 335–337.

Blum, A., "Drought Resistance, Water-Use Efficiency, and Yield Potential—Are They Compatible, Dissonant, or Mutually Exclusive?," *Australian Journal of Agricultural Research* 56 (2005), 1159–1168.

Campbell, D. J., "Response to Drought among Farmers and Herders in Southern Kajiado District, Kenya: A Comparison of 1972–1976 and 1994–96," *Human Ecology* 27 (1999), 377–416.

DAC (Department of Agriculture and Cooperation), "Drought Situation in the Country," in *The Forty-Fifth Report of the Standing Committee on Agriculture Submitted to the Thirteenth Loksabha* (DAC, Ministry of Agriculture: New Delhi, India, 2003).

FAO (Food and Agriculture Organization of the United Nations), "Report of the Asia-Pacific Conference on Early Warning, Prevention, and Preparedness and Management of Disasters in Floods and Agriculture," Chiangmai, Thailand, 12–15 June 2001, FAO regional office for Asia and the Pacific (RAP) publication no. 2001/14. (FAO: Bangkok, Thailand, 2001).

Glauber, J. W., "Crop Insurance Reconsidered," *American Journal of Agricultural Economics* 86 (2004), 1179–1195.

Hazell, P., C. Pomerada, and A. Valdes, *Crop Insurance for Agricultural Development* (Johns Hopkins University Press: Baltimore, MD, 1986).

Hazell, P., P. Oram, and N. Chaherli, "Managing Droughts in Low-Rainfall Areas of Middle East and North Africa," Environment and Production Technology Division (EPTD) Discussion Paper 78 (International Food Policy Research Institute: Washington, DC, 2001).

Hirway, I., "Vicious Circle of Droughts and Scarcity Works: Why not Break It?," *Industrial Journal of Agricultural Economics* 56 (2001), 708–721.

Hossain, M., "Recent Developments in the Asian Rice Economy: Challenges for Rice Research," in R. E. Evenson, R. W. Herdt, and M. Hossain, eds., *Rice Research in Asia: Progress and Priorities* (CAB International: Wallingford, UK, 1996), 17–33.

Jodha, N.S., "Effectiveness of Farmers' Adjustment to Risk," *Economic and Political Weekly* 13 (1978), A38–A48.

Meinke, H., and R. C. Stone, "Seasonal and Inter-Annual Climate Forecasting: The New Tool for Increasing Preparedness to Climate Variability and Change in Agricultural Planning and Operations," *Climatic Change* 70 (2005), 221–253.

Moench, M., "Groundwater and Poverty: Exploring the Connections," in R. Llamas, R. and E. Custodio, eds., *Intensive Use of Groundwater Challenges and Opportunities* (Bulkema Publishing: Abingdon, UK, 2002).

Morduch, J., "Poverty and Vulnerability," *American Economic Review* 84 (1994), 221–225.

Pandey, S., D. D. Behura, R. Villano, and D. Naik, "Economic Costs of Drought and Farmers' Coping Mechanisms: A Study of Rainfed Rice Systems in Eastern India," International Rice Research Institute (IRRI) Discussion Paper Series 39 (IRRI: Los Banos, Philippines, 2000).

Pandey, S., H. N. Bhandari, and B. Hardy, *Economic Costs of Drought and Rice Farmers' Coping Mechanisms: A Cross Country Comparative Analysis from Asia* (International Rice Research Institute [IRRI]: Los Banos, Philippines 2007, forthcoming).

Rao, C. H. H., "Watershed Development in India: Recent Experiences and Emerging Issues," *Economic and Political Weekly* 35 (2000), 3943–3947.

Rathore, J. S., "Drought and Household Coping Strategies: A Case of Rajasthan," *Industrial Journal of Agricultural Economics* 59 (2004), 689–708.

Rosegrant, M. W., X. Cai, and S. Cline, *World Water and Food to 2025: Dealing with Scarcity* (International Food Policy Research Institute [IFPRI]: Washington, DC, and International Water Management Institute [IWMI]: Colombo, Sri Lanka, 2002).

Shah, T., "Wells and Welfare in the Ganga Basin: Public Policy and Private Initiative in Eastern Uttar Pradesh, India," *Research Report* 54 (International Water Management Institute [IWMI]: Colombo, Sri-Lanka, 2001).

Shivakumar, S., and E. Kerbart, "Drought, Sustenance and Livelihoods: "Akal" Survey in Rajasthan," *Economic and Political Weekly* 39 (2004), 285–294.

Sinha, A., *Natural Disaster Management in India*, A Country Report from Member Countries (Asian Disaster Reduction Center [ADRC]: Kobe, Japan, 1999), http://www.adrc.or.jp.

Skees, J. R., S. Gober, P. Varangis, R. Lester, and V. Kalavakonda, "Developing Rainfall-Based Index Insurance in Morocco," World Bank Policy Research Working Paper 2577 (The World Bank: Washington, DC, 2001).

Steyaert, L.T., A. V. Rao, and A. V. Todorov, *Agroclimatic Assessment Methods for Drought Flood Strategies in South and Southeast Asia.* (United States Agency for International Development [USAID]: Washington, DC, 1981).

Turvey, C. G., "Weather Derivatives for Specific Event Risks in Agriculture," *Review of Agricultural Economics* 23 (2001), 333–351.

Varangis, P., "Innovative Approach to Cope with Weather Risk in Developing Countries," *Climate Report* 2 (Climate Risk Solutions, Inc., 2002).

Widawsky, D. A., and J. C. O'Toole, *Prioritizing the Rice Biotechnology Research Agenda for Eastern India* (The Rockefeller Foundation: New York, 1990).

Wilhite, D. A., and M. H. Glantz, "Understanding the Drought Phenomenon: The Role of Definitions," *Water International* 10 (1985), 111–120.

Wilhite, D. A., M. K. V. Shivakumar, and D. A. Wood, eds., *Early Warning Systems for Drought Preparedness and Drought Management.* Proceedings of an expert Group Meeting in Lisbon, Portugal, 5–7 Sept (World Meteorological Organization: Geneva, Switzerland, 2000).

Productivity in Malagasy rice systems: wealth-differentiated constraints and priorities

Bart Minten*, Jean-Claude Randrianarisoa**, and Christopher B. Barrett**

This study explores the constraints on agricultural productivity and priorities in boosting productivity in rice, the main staple in Madagascar, using a range of different data sets and analytical methods, integrating qualitative assessments by farmers and quantitative evidence from panel data production function analysis and willingness-to-pay estimates for chemical fertilizer. Nationwide, farmers seek primarily labor productivity enhancing interventions, e.g., improved access to agricultural equipment, cattle, and irrigation. Shock mitigation measures, land productivity increasing technologies, and improved land tenure are reported to be much less important. Research and interventions aimed at reducing costs and price volatility within the fertilizer supply chain might help at least the more accessible regions to more readily adopt chemical fertilizer.

JEL classification: O1, O3, Q12

Keywords: rice productivity; poverty; technology adoption; Madagascar

1. Introduction

Recent research suggests that improvement in the productivity of staple food crops, especially rice, offers a key lever for alleviating rural, as well as urban, poverty in Madagascar (Minten and Barrett, 2006). The crucial question remains how best to advance that objective. This study explores the constraints on agricultural productivity and priorities in boosting productivity in rice, the main staple in Madagascar, using a range of different data sets and analytical methods. We pay particular attention to differences across regions and the income distribution, and we focus especially on exploring why chemical fertilizer uptake rates appear so low.

The structure of the article is as follows. Section 2 discusses the data and descriptive statistics. In Section 3, we discuss farmers' self-reported constraints that limit agricultural and rice productivity. This qualitative analysis provides preliminary results we then

corroborate in Section 4 using plot-level panel data to estimate the marginal rice productivity and yield elasticities with respect to the primary inputs in Malagasy rice systems, as well as a key indicator of the type of rice production method employed and climatic shocks suffered. Then, in Section 5, we look in more detail at chemical fertilizer use, a crucial driver for increased productivity in other rice economies and an input for which the marginal gains to the poor are substantially greater than to the rich. Section 6 briefly concludes.

2. Data and descriptive statistics

We use several different types of data. First, in Section 3, we exploit data from three nationally representative surveys: the 2001 and 2004 household surveys (the *Enquête Permanente auprès des Ménages*, or EPM) and the 2004 commune survey, fielded at the most local level of government administration in the country. Each of these three surveys includes qualitative assessments of constraints to agricultural and rice productivity.

Those productivity constraint questions from the nationally representative surveys are quite comparable to similarly worded ones in more detailed household

*International Food Policy Research Institute (IFPRI), New Delhi Office, India.
** Cornell University, Ithaca, NY, USA.*

surveys fielded in 2002 and 2003 by the USAID BASIS CRSP project of Cornell University. Both surveys were run three to four months after the main rice harvest in two different highlands regions: the Vakinankaratra region of Antananarivo province and the rural communes surrounding the city of Fianarantsoa in the eponymous province. Farmers in both areas have a long experience in rainfed and irrigated rice production. The 2002 data were gathered through a comprehensive survey collecting information at the plot and household level. The same farmers were visited in 2003 using a very similar questionnaire to facilitate analysis of interannual household- and plot-level dynamics. Comparison with the nationally representative survey data allows us to triangulate to check the robustness of our results across different surveys, methodologies, and samples. The BASIS data also allow us to tie the analysis of productivity constraints to quantitative estimation of production functions and of willingness-to-pay for chemical fertilizers, in Sections 4 and 5, respectively, as those data are only available in the BASIS survey modules.

The depth and breadth of rural poverty in Madagascar is starkly reflected in the BASIS data. Our welfare indicator is 2002 per capita household income, computed as the sum of the consumption and sales of agricultural commodities and livestock and nonagricultural and wage income. 2002 average annual per capita incomes vary significantly across the income distribution (Table 1), from almost 30,000 Ariary (equivalent to $25 US) for the poorest quintile to a bit more than ten times as much for the richest quintile (quintile 5). This difference is driven by both relatively and absolutely more off-farm income—off-farm income represents 54% of the richest quintile versus 30% for the poorest quintile—as well as agricultural income that is almost eight times higher for the richest quintile. Off-farm earnings are strongly related to educational attainment and proximity to town-based employment. Rice production overwhelmingly dominates all other land uses and sources of agricultural income across the income distribution. Hence, the importance of studying rice productivity as a central feature of improving rural livelihoods in Madagascar.

Per capita paddy rice production corresponds to only one third (2002) to one half (2003) of the national average consumption of 110 kg of white rice (170 kg of paddy) per capita per year among the lowest income quintile. These poorest households typically complement own rice production with purchases, especially during the preharvest lean season. The two richest quintiles produce more than average consumption and most of the households in these categories are likely net sellers of rice. However, market participation is not sufficient to smooth consumption over the year, and this is especially so for the poorest households, as the self-reported length of the lean period drops significantly from the poorest to the richest quintile, from almost six months to less than four months.

These descriptive statistics signal how closely food security, income, and rice production are linked in the rural highlands of Madagascar and thus the importance of rice productivity to household welfare in these villages. Differences in agricultural income across the income distribution arise both due to greater productivity among the richer households as well as larger cultivated land area. The poorest households' average rice yields are 22–35% lower than the richest quintile in 2002 and 2003, respectively, while they cultivate roughly half as much land (and land in rice). Variation in other inputs is similarly pronounced, with the ratio of agricultural equipment owned by the richest to poorest quintile equal to roughly 10, and livestock holdings 60–70% higher among the richest quintile. Partly this reflects substitution between labor—used more intensively on poorer farms' plots—and capital. But it likely also reflects binding constraints that limit access to critical agricultural inputs, as we explore further.

As to have a better sense of our yield data, we first look descriptively at paddy yields dynamics over the two years (Table 2). We divided the plots into high- and low-yielding plots for the two years, depending on whether the yields were below or above 2.5 tons per hectare, the national average (Faostat). About three quarters of the plots stayed in the same category in the two years: 22% in the low productivity category and 52% in the high productivity category. One quarter of plots changed categories: 13% of the plots moved from low to high productivity and 12% *vice versa*. We thus note quite some variation over such a short time period.

3. Qualitative analysis on constraints to increased productivity

The 2001 national household survey asked farmers about the biggest constraints they faced to improved

Table 1
Farm characteristics by income level

| | | | Per capita income quintile in 2002 | | | | | | | | | | Overall | |
| | | | Quintile 1 | | Quintile 2 | | Quintile 3 | | Quintile 4 | | Quintile 5 | | | |
			Mean	SD	Mean	SD	Mean	SD	Mean	SD	Mean	SD	Mean	SD
Income – welfare measures														
Per capita annual income	ariary	2002	28,680	10,001	54,695	6,428	86,552	10,610	128,144	19,722	334,275	306,853	116,724	165,111
Per capita agricultural income	ariary	2002	20,212	9,758	36,199	14,079	54,984	22,561	77,234	31,373	155,645	96,184	64,337	63,609
Length of lean season	month	2002	5.95	2.52	5.42	2.50	5.66	2.40	4.58	2.76	3.88	2.86	5.18	2.69
Paddy rice production														
Production per capita	kg	2002	61	39	92	54	142	99	196	113	375	397	163	209
		2003	83	50	108	71	141	115	190	111	352	306	166	176
Average yield	kg/are	2002	21.3	16.9	26.7	17.3	23.5	16.6	29.6	18.5	28.9	21.9	26.4	18.9
		2003	25.8	18.4	26.8	16.4	23.9	17.2	28.2	17.9	31.4	19.8	27.5	18.3
Total cultivated rice area	ares	2002	39.46	27.97	37.35	37.15	50.83	43.47	59.10	62.13	72.26	75.38	48.20	52.29
		2003	31.13	31.48	38.74	39.83	50.44	42.90	59.45	61.92	72.07	75.62	48.83	52.87
Production factors and shifters														
Total agricultural land area	ares	2002	76.49	80.95	82.50	79.99	135.18	107.53	160.28	156.97	161.76	143.92	119.68	119.31
		2003	79.02	82.82	83.93	72.74	134.03	106.58	160.62	156.90	161.57	142.43	120.37	119.01
Value of agricultural equipment	ariary	2002	8,568	27,054	47,916	109,001	27,761	67,720	58,760	108,427	85,990	125,487	42,896	94,556
		2003	11,258	32,566	49,301	108,864	29,132	69,100	59,957	109,567	86,943	126,625	44,484	95,479
Number of cattle and cows	no	2002	1.78	2.13	2.09	2.42	1.54	1.95	2.33	2.34	2.98	3.46	2.10	2.50
		2003	1.64	2.17	2.31	3.46	1.53	1.74	2.17	2.32	2.90	2.93	2.07	2.60
Total labor use	hours/are	2002	23.4	12.4	17.7	10.2	15.5	9.6	15.5	10.1	13.7	9.7	17.2	10.9
		2003	19.0	11.9	15.5	8.9	13.5	9.1	14.8	10.1	11.6	7.1	14.9	9.9
Age of transplanted plants	days	2002	49.25	17.82	49.02	16.92	48.40	14.95	44.20	16.32	38.26	16.55	45.85	17.02
		2003	44.92	14.13	13.93	12.22	42.63	10.51	40.82	12.63	42.02	13.34	42.87	12.68
Mineral fertilizer users	1 = user	2002	0.24	0.42	0.36	0.48	0.32	0.47	0.25	0.43	0.28	0.45	0.29	0.46
		2003	0.23	0.42	0.36	0.48	0.22	0.42	0.25	0.44	0.41	0.49	0.30	0.46
Mineral fertilizer use (for users only)	kg/are	2002	0.86	4.36	0.51	1.52	0.09	0.21	0.11	0.33	0.44	1.54	0.40	2.20
		2003	0.16	0.73	0.16	0.35	0.09	0.30	0.18	0.70	0.48	1.24	0.21	0.76
Drought	1 = yes	2002	0.14	0.35	0.15	0.36	0.18	0.39	0.14	0.35	0.12	0.33	0.15	0.35
		2003	0.15	0.36	0.13	0.33	0.13	0.34	0.12	0.33	0.11	0.31	0.13	0.33
Flooding	1 = yes	2002	0.13	0.33	0.13	0.33	0.11	0.32	0.07	0.26	0.10	0.30	0.11	0.31
		2003	0.07	0.25	0.07	0.26	0.07	0.26	0.07	0.26	0.11	0.31	0.08	0.27

Table 2
Yield transition matrix

| | | | Yield in 2003* | | Overall |
			Low	High	
Yield in 2002*	Low	Number of observations	166	95	261
		% of observations	22%	13%	35%
		Average yield in 2002	14.7	14.8	14.8
		Average yield in 2003	14.5	39.4	19.5
	High	Number of observations	92	389	481
		% of observations	12%	52%	65%
		Average yield in 2002	35.9	46.7	43.9
		Average yield in 2003	17.7	46.2	37.5
Overall		Number of observations	258	484	742
		% of observations	35%	65%	100%
		Average yield in 2002	18.6	36.1	26.3
		Average yield in 2003	15.3	44.5	27.6

* Low yields: less than 2.5 tons/ha; high yields: equal to or more than 2.5 tons/ha.

agricultural productivity. The same question was asked in the 2004 national household survey, based on a different sampling frame and with a bigger sample. Respondents had to rank options from "not important" to "very important." The results are presented in Table 3 ordered in decreasing percentage of households that identified the constraint as "quite" or "very" important.

Answers were strikingly consistent between the two surveys, three years apart and with a different sample. The most and least frequently cited constraints were common to both surveys. Access to agricultural equipment, access to cattle for traction and transport, and access to labor are ranked among the top four constraints in both surveys. Access to land was the second most cited constraint in the 2001 EPM but omitted from the 2004 version, while access to irrigation was second most cited in the 2004 EPM but lacked a direct analog in the 2001 national household survey. The clear pattern in these answers is that inputs that complement labor and boost its productivity are most limiting in farmers' opinion.

The second most important set of constraints in the 2004 EPM relates to shocks associated with plant disease, drought, and flooding. More than half of all households report these constraints to be "quite" or "very important." By contrast, less than 40 percent of households identify land tenure insecurity or the siltation of land as important constraints and these are more commonly identified as not a constraint on agricultural pro-

ductivity. While secure property rights are in general an important determinant for soil investment and thus higher productivity (Feder and Feeny, 1991), tenurial security does not appear to farmers to be a serious impediment to agricultural productivity in rural Madagascar, a finding consistent with results elsewhere in Sub-Saharan Africa (Migot-Adholla et al., 1991) and with recent quantitative analysis in Madagascar (Jacoby and Minten, 2007). This contrasts with renewed emphasis on land titling by the government and some international donors in Madagascar.

The same qualitative questions were used to get at the constraints for increased rice production more specifically. In the 2003 BASIS household survey, one randomly selected rice plot was chosen for each household and respondents were asked to identify the main constraint to increased rice productivity on that particular plot and to rank 12 different potential constraints. The commune survey of 2004 asked focus group in each of the 300 communes the same question and to do the same ranking.

As reported in the top panel of Table 4, the commune survey rankings are broadly consistent with the results of the EPM national household surveys. The biggest constraints were, again, labor productivity boosting factors: access to better irrigation, agricultural equipment, and livestock to work the land. Second came shock mitigation, concerning plant disease and flooding, especially. The least widespread constraints concerned land tenure security and silting of land.

Table 3
Farm households' reported constraints on improved agricultural productivity

Variables	Percentage of households that state this constraint is . . . important			
	Not	A bit	Quite	Very
Constraints to overall agricultural productivity				
EPM 2001, 2,470 agricultural households				
Access to agricultural equipment	19	18	27	35
Access to land	27	19	29	25
Access to cattle for traction and transport	24	23	29	24
Access to labor	22	28	30	20
Access to credit	36	19	23	22
Degradation of irrigation infrastructure due to environmental problems	29	31	22	18
Access to agricultural inputs (e.g., fertilizer)	34	26	19	21
Access to cattle for fertilizer	42	23	19	16
Land tenure insecurity	44	26	22	8
Silting of land	46	29	18	7
EPM 2004, 3,543 agricultural households				
Access to agricultural equipment	11	14	32	43
Access to irrigation	13	21	29	37
Access to cattle for traction and transport	16	20	35	29
Access to labor	17	22	37	24
Avoid droughts	20	19	27	34
Access to agricultural inputs (e.g., fertilizer)	24	20	26	30
Phyto-sanitary diseases	19	25	30	26
Avoid flooding	25	20	26	29
Access to cattle for fertilizer	28	22	25	25
Access to credit	31	23	22	24
Silting of land	33	29	23	15
Land tenure insecurity	38	24	23	15

The BASIS survey responses by rice-growing households in the densely populated highlands differ noticeably from the nationally representative commune and household survey results. In this setting, land intensification technologies play a far more prominent role as a limiting constraint on rice productivity than at the national level. Access to cattle for manure is ranked first and access to agricultural inputs such as fertilizer is ranked fourth, where both of these fell at or below the median rank in the nationally representative surveys. These indicators of demand for land intensification technologies are ranked higher than access to labor, agricultural equipment, or cattle for working the land. Climatic shocks are also considered less important in the highlands of Madagascar, presumably because these areas are less frequently and severely hit by cyclones than coastal areas. However, when we look only at the EPM data for households from Antananarivo province (the highland region in which most of

the BASIS respondents live), the same pattern emerges: access to cattle for manure and to inputs become the top constraints. This underscores the spatial heterogeneity of constraints to improved agricultural productivity, as perceived and reported by farmers, consistent with the Boserupian hypothesis that land intensification is most in demand where population densities are greatest.

4. Production function analysis

Farmers' self-reported productivity constraints are informative, but only up to a point. We supplement those findings with rice production function analysis based on the plot-level BASIS survey panel data. Using a generalized quadratic functional form to allow for a second-order approximation to the true underlying production function and controlling for fixed

Table 4

Farm households' reported constraints on improved rice productivity

Variables	Percentage of households that state this constraint is . . . important			
	Not	A bit	Quite	Very
Constraints to rice productivity				
Commune survey 2004, 290 communal focus groups				
Access to better irrigation systems	3	12	27	58
Access to agricultural equipment	4	19	27	50
Access to livestock for traction and transport	8	22	27	43
Access to credit	16	24	23	37
Avoid losses due to plant diseases	11	31	24	34
Avoid floods	16	26	22	36
Access to improved seeds	13	29	21	37
Access to labor	17	27	26	30
Access to chemical fertilizer	29	29	20	22
Access to livestock for manure	26	32	20	22
Avoid silting	22	36	21	21
Avoid droughts	48	15	12	25
Land tenure	27	37	23	13
Basis Crsp survey, 2003, 316 agricultural household in highlands				
Access to cattle for manure	5	6	13	76
Access to better irrigation	5	14	20	61
Access to credit	11	8	37	44
Access to agricultural inputs (e.g., fertilizer)	4	17	35	44
Access to labor	10	15	40	35
Access to agricultural equipment	20	15	26	39
Access to cattle for transaction and transport	28	11	25	36
Avoid losses due to plant diseases	19	23	42	16
Avoid droughts	22	23	27	28
Avoid floods	24	37	25	14
Insecure property rights	59	11	14	16
Avoid silt	34	38	21	7

effects,[1] we estimate the expected marginal physical productivity of each factor, computed at the mean value for each other input in each quintile of the 2002 income distribution. This enables us to explore the possibility of heterogeneity in marginal response across the income distribution, providing some insight as to how constraints on productivity vary between poorer and richer farmers.

Table 5 summarizes the elasticity and marginal productivity estimates. The results show that rice productivity is relatively sensitive to labor availability, with an average elasticity of 0.35. One additional hour of work would result in an increase of 0.65–1.06 kg of rice yield depending on the income quintile. Evaluated at the average paddy price in 2002, this physical marginal return corresponds to a marginal value product of 1,040 Ariary for the poorest households,[2] about 25% lower than the prevailing wage rate at the site of the surveys, and to 1,700 Ariary for the wealthier households, almost 20% higher than the average agricultural wage rate.[3]

---

[1] A test of the null hypothesis that labor use is exogenous to output is not rejected. Labor use was instrumented by family size and family composition, households' agricultural assets (e.g., plows and ox carts), access to draught oxen, and participation in nonagricultural or off-farm employment activities. A Hausman test favors a fixed effects specification over a random effects model.

[2] These marginal value products were computed based on 8 hours of work per day and a price of paddy rice of 200 Ariary per kg.

[3] By its direct effect of draft power for plowing and transportation and its indirect effect for manure supply, an extra cattle increases expected rice yields by an average of 0.9 kg per are, for an estimated yield elasticity of 0.06. Richer households enjoy a 40% higher expected return than do poorer households. While the richer households might have more cattle in absolute numbers, livestock density

Table 5
Plot-level panel data estimates of marginal returns to rice production inputs

		Per capita income quintile in 2002					Overall	P-value (F-test)
		Quintile 1	Quintile 2	Quintile 3	Quintile 4	Quintile 5		
Total cultivated area	Additional kg of paddy per are	0.02	0.03	0.04	0.05	0.07	0.04	0.04
	Doubling area: Yield increases by	3.8%	6.8%	14.2%	21.8%	34.7%	16.2%	
Labor	kg of paddy per hour	0.65	0.84	0.85	0.89	1.06	0.86	
	Doubling labor: Yield increases by	36.4%	36.9%	34.5%	34.8%	31.8%	34.9%	***
Value of agr. equipment	kg of paddy per hour	−0.01	−0.02	−0.02	−0.02	−0.02	−0.02	
	Doubling agricultiral equipment: Yield increases by	−0.2%	−1.4%	−1.4%	−1.9%	−2.7%	−1.5%	
Number of cattle	kg of paddy per unit of cattle	0.75	0.72	0.79	1.01	1.16	0.89	
	Doubling number of cattle: Yield increases by	3.8%	5.5%	3.8%	6.0%	10.4%	5.9%	
Chemical fertilizer	kg of paddy per kg of fertilizer	4.23	4.12	4.31	4.29	3.74	4.14	***
	Doubling fertilizer use: Yield increase by	5.1%	3.7%	1.0%	1.6%	4.0%	3.2%	
Age of plants (technology)	kg of paddy per day	−0.02	−0.03	0.00	0.00	0.03	0.00	**
	Doubling age: Yield decrease	−2.5%	−4.0%	−0.3%	0.1%	2.9%	−0.7%	
Climatic shocks	Yield changes in kg/are if shocks	−12.94	−8.66	−5.99	−5.2	−4.27	−7.43	***
	% change on yield if shocks	−34.4%	−23.0%	−16.8%	−13.4%	−10.1%	−19.6%	

Notes: F-test is used to check the significance for each variable. If tests jointly, at least one of the coefficient estimates differs from zero.
***, **indicate significance level at the 1% and 10% level.
Source: BASIS CRSP 2002, 2003 surveys.

Total landholdings and the value of agricultural equipment did not have a statistically significant impact on rice productivity, on average. The estimated elasticities with respect to agricultural equipment are consistently low across the income distribution, in contrast to farmers' self-reported constraints to productivity growth. But, the effect of increased cultivated area on yield exhibits an interesting pattern as one moves from poorer to richer households. The long-observed inverse farm size-yield relation (Benjamin, 1995; Barrett, 1996; Lamb, 2003) appears to hold only for the poorest farmers, while for richer farmers, yield is increasing in cultivated area, likely reflecting that among the rich there are both small, part-time farmers who are relatively unproductive as they depend primarily on off-farm earnings and larger, full-time farmers who are relatively productive (Barrett et al., 2005).

We find positive effects of improved rice production technology on yields. We use the age of the rice plant at transplanting as a proxy for use of improved production methods; for example, transplanting seedlings at 7–14 days old is a central part of the promising System of Rice Intensification (SRI) package of techniques.[4] The effect of adopting improved rice production methods is greatest for the poorest two income quintiles.

Rice production appears quite sensitive to climatic shocks. The estimation results indicate that expected yields decrease by 34% and 10% for the poorest and the richest household, respectively, when struck by flooding or drought. The adverse effect of a climatic shock on the poorest (second poorest) income quintile is roughly three (two) times greater than on the richest quintile. While the poor and rich farmers suffer shocks with equal frequency (Table 1), poorer farmers appear more vulnerable to climatic shocks, likely due to less shock mitigation capacity due to their limited ability to invest in risk-avoidance measures (e.g., pumps or irrigation), in hiring labor to replace flooded plants, etc.

---

per hectare is actually lower on richer farms (Table 1), potentially explaining the larger returns per unit land in the highest income quintile. However, the estimated coefficients are not significant at conventional statistical levels.

[4] SRI uses no purchased inputs but relies on a suite of agronomic adjustments: very early transplanting and wide spacing of seedlings, frequent weeding, and controlling the water level to allow for the aeration of the roots during the growth period of the plant, i.e., no standing water on the rice field (Moser and Barrett, 2003; Barrett et al., 2004).

Finally, estimated yield elasticities with respect to chemical fertilizer are statistically significant and nearly 30% greater for the poorest quintile than for the richest quintile. This suggests that the effective cost of fertilizer is higher for the poor than for the rich, whether due to liquidity constraints, volume discounts, or other factors. We return to an analysis of chemical fertilizer use and demand in Section 5.

5. Mineral fertilizer use patterns and willingness to pay

The June 2006 Africa Fertilizer Summit of African heads of state, held in Abuja, Nigeria, underscores the importance currently placed on stimulating fertilizer uptake as a central plank of agricultural development strategies in Sub-Saharan Africa. This is as true in Madagascar as in the rest of the sub-continent. In this section, we therefore look more closely at mineral fertilizer input use patterns, average and estimated marginal productivity effects, and willingness-to-pay estimates based on our survey data.

Mineral fertilizer use is uniformly low in rural Madagascar, with only about 30% of the BASIS farmers applying any fertilizer and average application rates among users amounting to only 0.40 kg per acre in 2002, and 0.21 kg per acre in 2003. These rates fall far below the average for other low-income rice-producing countries such as Vietnam, Nigeria, or Mali. A simple unconditional comparison of plots that received mineral fertilizer and those that did not reveals a 20% difference in average rice yields—an increase of 4.5 kg/acre—suggesting substantial gains to mineral fertilizer application. The production function estimation results from the previous section imply a marginal output of 4.1 kg/acre,[5] with poorer farmers exhibiting a statistically significantly higher estimated marginal return from chemical fertilizer than do richer farmers (Table 4).

So why is fertilizer use so low, especially among the poor who stand to benefit most from increased fertilizer application in Malagasy rice systems? The most likely explanation is the excessive cost of fertilizer.

---

[5] These estimates are consistent with previous work in this area (e.g., Bernier and Dorosh, 1993). The slightly greater estimated marginal effect, relative to average yield effect, reflects the highly skewed nature of the fertilizer application data.

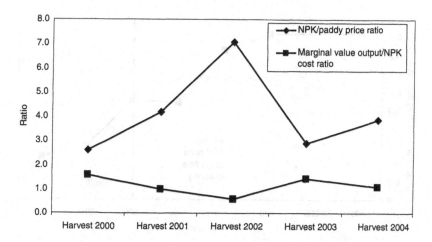

Figure 1. Cost-benefit ratios for chemical fertilizer and paddy.

The chemical fertilizer (NPK) to paddy price ratio in Lac Alaotra region, the rice basket of Madagascar—for which we have data available and where input and output prices are typically quite similar to the highlands— varies considerably across years, between 2.6 and 7.0 from 2000 to 2004 (Figure 1), the high point occurring during the presidential crisis when the country teetered on the brink of civil war. Using the estimated marginal return of 4.1 kg paddy per kg of fertilizer (Table 4), the ratio of the value of marginal output over the cost of fertilizer varied between 1.6 (in 2000) and 0.6 (in 2002). So fertilizer use on rice appears profitable on average.

However, given the greater likelihood of flooding and droughts on rice fields, households may consider the risk of fertilizer application too high on these fields. In an overview of fertilizer incentives facing African farmers, Yanggen et al. (2002) argue that the ratio of the value of marginal output over fertilizer cost must be at least 2, preferably 3, to be attractive to small farmers, given risk, seasonal credit constraints, and other factors limiting uptake and effective profitability. Tellingly, we estimate this ratio to never have reached 2 in these five years. This suggest that highlands and Lac Alaotra rice farmers find chemical fertilizer only marginally profitable, which may explain the limited uptake in rural Madagascar.

These ratios contrast sharply with similar estimates from other rice-producing countries, especially in Asia. For example, the ratio of urea over paddy prices in 2001 (based on the data of Faostat) was below 2 in India and Pakistan, less than half the level observed in

Madagascar at that time. This difference in ratios explains to a large extent why Malagasy farmers less frequently use fertilizers—and apply less fertilizer when they use any—than do their counterparts in other rice economies. The favorable ratio in Asian countries is due in large measure to the much lower prices of fertilizer, which is often locally produced and/or subsidized.[6] Moreover, yield responses vary, often depending on varieties and soil types, and appear to be much higher in Asia too.

We further investigate the demand for chemical fertilizer via willingness-to-pay analysis. In the 2003 BASIS survey, households were asked about their current use and perceived benefits of chemical fertilizer.[7] Then farmers were offered the opportunity to accept, refuse, or remain undecided about fertilizer purchase at one of eight randomly assigned prices, following the dichotomous choice format popularized in environmental economics (Mitchell and Carson, 1989). As is standard in the literature, uncertainty/indecision was included as a refusal in our analysis.

As shown in Figure 2, willingness to pay for fertilizer appears quite responsive to price beyond an atypically

---

[6] For example, retail fertilizer prices (e.g., urea) in India ($0.21/kg) and Pakistan ($0.29/kg) are significantly lower than the prices in rural areas of Madagascar's highlands ($0.50/kg). (Prices for India and Pakistan are out of the Faostat database for the year 2002.)

[7] Only two-thirds of the households thought that the use of chemical fertilizer was beneficial on rice fields. This might underscore the need for extension to communicate more clearly and broadly how to use chemical fertilizer to improve rice output.

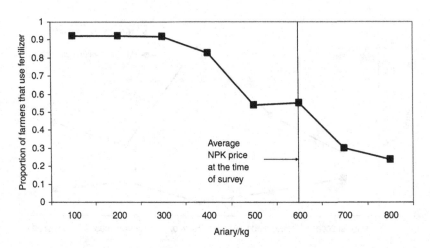

Figure 2. Demand for chemical fertilizer by price level.

low range. For example, a price increase from 400 to 700 Ariary per kg would reduce the estimated percentage of households willing to buy fertilizer from 83% to 30%. Using the results of a parsimonious model where the acceptance dummy was regressed on an intercept and the logarithm of the price, median willingness to pay is estimated at about 575 Ariary per kg or roughly $0.50/kg, the mean price observed in the highlands. Yet only 30% of farmers actually use fertilizers, reflecting some combination of hypothetical bias and spatial variation in prices, since fertilizer prices are lowest in the highlands and Lac Alaotra regions typically. Interestingly, these willingness-to-pay answers suggest that almost all Malagasy farmers would use chemical fertilizers if prices were similar to those in Asian rice economies.[8]

While unfavorable price ratios might explain partly the low chemical fertilizer use, other factors likely play a role as well. Given the deficient or nonexis-

tent extension system,[9] farmers are often not aware of the recommended quantity, timing, or mode of utilization of chemical fertilizer, and therefore opt not to risk fertilizer use. The local varieties that are widely used in Madagascar are also more sensitive to the disease pyriculariose when they are used in combination with fertilizer than in the absence of chemical fertilizer application (Andriatsimialona, 2004). Unless fertilizer is used together with improved varieties, pay-offs might thus be too low to attract farmer interest.

6. Conclusion

Improvement in staple crop, especially rice, productivity appears a powerful way to alleviate rural, as well as urban, poverty in Madagascar (Minten and Barrett, 2006). In this article, we study constraints on increased productivity and variation in marginal input productivity and yield elasticities across the rural income distribution. Integrating qualitative assessments by farmers and quantitative evidence from panel data production function analysis and willingness-to-pay estimates for chemical fertilizer, we find several consistent patterns. Nationwide, farmers seek primarily labor productivity enhancing interventions, e.g., improved access to agricultural equipment, cattle, and irrigation. Shock mitigation measures, land productivity

---

[8] We also estimated a more comprehensive model that included the bid level, household characteristics, proxies for shocks over the last 10 years, beliefs about fertilizer use and constraints on rice productivity, and village dummies. The results illustrate the internal consistency in household responses. Farmers who believe that fertilizer is beneficial for rice production, are more likely to accept the fertilizer purchase bid. Few other variables are significant. The more the household is involved in off-season cash crops, the more likely it will accept the bid, probably as profitability on these crops is typically higher than on rice. Older heads of households are less likely to accept. No other variables proved statistically significant. Results of this regression are available from the authors by request.

[9] In the 2004 national household surveys, it was estimated that about 7% of the farmers had contact with an extension agent prior to the year of the survey.

increasing technologies and improved land tenure are reported to be much less important. These priorities vary by region, however. Farmers in the more densely populated highlands rate access to manure and other land-intensifying agricultural inputs, such as chemical fertilizer and improved irrigation, highest in terms of expected rice productivity improvements. These results are consistent with the induced innovation theory (Hayami and Ruttan, 1985) and caution against a "one size fits all" approach to agricultural development policy for the country as a whole.

Poorer farmers have significantly lower rice yields than richer farmers, as well as significantly less land. Estimated productivity gains are greatest for the poorest with respect to adoption of improved rice production practices, climatic shock mitigation measures, and chemical fertilizer. However, fertilizer use on rice appears only marginally profitable and highly variable across years. Our willingness-to-pay estimates suggest that fertilizer demand is highly price sensitive, suggesting that low fertilizer uptake in rural Madagascar largely reflects prices beyond the reach of most farmers, especially poorer ones. If fertilizer prices were at the levels seen in Asian economies—less than 50% of the price in Madagascar—our estimates suggest that a significantly higher number of farmers would purchase and apply chemical fertilizer. It thus seems that research and interventions aimed at reducing costs and price volatility within the fertilizer supply chain might help at least the more accessible regions to more readily adopt chemical fertilizer. Fertilizer use, shock mitigation, and relieving binding labor constraints faced by Malagasy farmers appear the key elements of a strategy to increase rice productivity, food security, and incomes in rural Madagascar.

Acknowledgments

We thank Luc Christiaensen, Christine Moser, Lalaina Randrianarison, and Eliane Ralison for useful discussions. This work has been made possible by support from the World Bank and from the United States Agency for International Development (USAID), through grant LAG-A-00-96-90016-00 to the BASIS CRSP, the Strategies and Analyses for Growth and Access (SAGA) cooperative agreement, number HFM-A-00-01-00132-00. The views expressed here and any remaining errors are the authors' and do not represent any official agency.

References

Andriatsimialona, D., "Les Mesures de Rendement en Production Rizicole: Vers des Sondages plus Réalistes," *Karoka* 22 (2004), 23–26.

Barrett, C. B., "On Price Risk and the Inverse Farm Size–Productivity Relationship," *Journal of Development Economics* 51 (1996), 193–216.

Barrett, C. B., C. M. Moser, O. V. McHugh, and J. Barison, "Better Technology, Better Plots or Better Farmers? Identifying Changes in Productivity and Risk among Malagasy Rice Farmers," *American Journal of Agricultural Economics* 86 (2004), 869–889.

Barrett, C. B., M. Bezuneh, D. C. Clay, and T. Reardon, "Heterogeneous Constraints, Incentives and Income Diversification Strategies in Rural Africa," *Quarterly Journal of International Agriculture* 44 (2005), 37–60.

Benjamin, D., "Can Unobserved Land Quality Explain the Inverse Productivity Relationship?" *Journal of Development Economics* 46 (1995), 51–84.

Bernier, R., and P. A. Dorosh, "Constraints on Rice Production in Madagascar: The Farmer's Perspective," *CFNPP working paper* 34 (Cornell University, Ithaca, NY, 1993).

Feder, G., and D. Feeny, "Land Tenure and Property Rights: Theory and Implications for Development Policy," *World Bank Economic Review* 5 (1991), 135–153.

Hayami, Y., and V. Ruttan, *Agricultural Development: An International Perspective* (Johns Hopkins University Press: Baltimore, 1985).

Jacoby, H., and B. Minten, "Is Land Titling in Sub-Saharan Africa Cost-Effective? Evidence from Madagascar," *World Bank Economic Review* (2007), forthcoming.

Lamb, R. L., "Inverse Productivity: Land Quality, Labor Markets and Measurement Error," *Journal of Development Economics* 71 (2003), 71–95.

Migot-Adholla, S., P. Hazell, B. Blarel, and F. Place, "Indigenous Land Rights in Sub-Saharan Africa: A Constraint on Productivity," *World Bank Economic Review* 5 (1991), 155–175.

Minten, B., and C. B. Barrett, *Agricultural Technology, Productivity and Poverty in Madagascar* (World Bank mimeo: Washington, DC, 2006)

Mitchell, R. C., and R. T. Carson, *Using Surveys to Value Public Goods: the Contingent Valuation Method* (Resources for the Future: Washington, DC, 1989).

Moser, C., and C. B. Barrett, "The Disappointing Adoption Dynamics of a Yield-increasing, Low External Input Technology: The Case of SRI in Madagascar," *Agricultural Systems* 76 (2003), 1085–1100.

Yanggen, D., V. Kelly, T. Reardon, and A. Naseem, "Incentives for Fertilizer Use in Sub-Saharan Africa: A Review of Empirical Evidence on Fertilizer Yield Response and Profitability," *MSU International Development Working Paper* 70 (Michigan State University: East Lansing, 2002).

Economic statistics and U.S. agricultural policy

Bruce Gardner*, Barry Goodwin**, and Mary Ahearn***

Abstract

Economic statistics can be used to inform policy as it is being designed, avoid policy design mistakes, or implement government programs once they are established into law. Oftentimes, statistics are used for all three purposes. This article considers the relationships between statistics and agricultural policy in the case of the United States. We address first the broad historical picture of U.S. official economic statistics concerning agriculture, and then turn to selected examples that relate policies to economic statistics in more detail. The examples show diversity in the interplay between statistics and policy. Over time, policymakers have asked for more detailed information about the financial situation of individual farm businesses and households, sources of risk in farm returns, and production practices that affect the environment.

JEL classification: C8, N52, Q18

Keywords: agricultural policy; data collection and estimation; economic history of U.S. agriculture

1. Introduction

An important but relatively neglected topic of the political economy of agriculture is the role of economic statistics in the evolution of policy. This article considers the relationships between statistics and policy in the case of the United States. We address first the broad historical picture of U.S. official economic statistics concerning agriculture, and then turn to selected examples that relate policies to economic statistics in more detail: the distribution of government subsidies, the relationships between U.S. agricultural commodity programs and agricultural economic statistics, crop insurance and disaster payments, and conservation policies. The examples illustrate the differing roles that statistics play in the policy arena, from having little effect on policies to being used directly in program implementation.

*Department of Agricultural and Resource Economics, University of Maryland, 20742, U.S.A.

**Department of Agricultural and Resource Economics, North Carolina State University, 27695, U.S.A.

***Economic Research Service, U.S. Department of Agriculture, 20036, U.S.A.

The views expressed are those of the authors and do not necessarily represent the policies or views of the University of Maryland, North Carolina State University, or of the USDA. Senior authorship is not assigned.

2. Overall historical picture

Causal relationships between government statistics and policy run in both directions: policy implementation and legislation have generated demands for statistics, and statistical information has influenced policy debate. Sometimes, the development of specific economic statistics is undertaken at the request of elected officials through appropriations of agency funds. There are also occasional requirements by elected officials to cease producing particular economic statistics, as has been the case for forecasts of cotton prices since 1927. Farmers are often the primary providers of agricultural economic data, and are often viewed as a major beneficiary of agricultural statistics. However, farmers often report that the information they provide and receive back in the form of publicly available reports is of more value to others than to them (Jones et al., 1979). Farmers have even expressed suspicions that statistics are used to manipulate markets against their interests.

When President Lincoln established the U.S. Department of Agriculture (USDA) in 1862, he specified that one of the duties of the Secretary of Agriculture was to provide agricultural statistics to the nation. Estimates of farm acreage and numbers go back to 1850 and commodity production and price data were published starting in 1866. Nationally-representative economic information about farming was first collected by the Census of Agriculture of 1910. The scale and scope of economic information expanded steadily in the 1930s and 1940s as government policies required more information for both the implementation and evaluation of policies, particularly those that were focused on managing surpluses of products and low farm incomes. More recently, policy issues and data needs have added a focus on distributional consequences of farm programs and globalization. The U.S. government expresses its demand for information about the agricultural economy in two main ways: appropriation of funds for statistical purposes and legislation mandating particular data and related information about the rural/farm sector.

In 1895, the Secretary of Agriculture reported that "the annual cost of securing agricultural statistics which are published from time to time by this department is about $100,000" (USDA, 1895, p. 33), which is analogous to $2.4 million today. The actual budget of the National Agricultural Statistics Service (NASS), which covers essentially the same statistical area as the Division of Statistics did, was $128 million in 2005. Thus real federal spending on basic agricultural statistics rose by a factor of 53 during the 110-year interval from 1895 to 2005—an annual rate of increase of 3.6%.

The total 2005 NASS and ERS budgets together accounted for 9% of the $1.9 billion total U.S. federal statistics budget. In 1977 agriculture's share of the statistical budget comparably measured was 19% and as recently as 1995 it was 14%.[1] But even in FY2005, agriculture's share of statistical spending far exceeded its 0.8% share of U.S. gross domestic product (GDP). In short, the long-term demand for agricultural statistics has increased continually, though the demand for nonagricultural statistics has increased even faster.

3. Examples of the role of economic statistics in U.S. agricultural policies and programs

Economic statistics can be used to inform policy as it is being designed, avoid policy design mistakes,

---

[1] The data for these calculations are from publications of the U.S. Office of Management and Budget (1985, 1990, 2005) which are not fully consistent over time. These publications are from OMB's Statistical Policy Branch created under the Paperwork Reduction Act of 1980.

or implement government programs once they are established into law. Oftentimes, economic statistics are used for all three purposes. In most of the remainder of this article, we describe examples of the roles economic statistics have played in informing the larger policy process. Our list excludes some important series. We have selected examples related to major farm policies and programs and show how the role played by statistics has varied. Sometimes, statistics seemingly have had little impact on policies and other times they are used directly to implement programs.

3.1. Government payments

A contentious issue in farm commodity programs from their inception has been the question of who benefits most from them. A key element of this issue is share of benefits accruing to large, financially better-off farmers as compared to small, low-income farm operations. In 1938, the payment limit was $10,000 per producer; the current limit is $360,000 (i.e., in 2000 dollars, $101,937 and $313,152, respectively). The 2002 Farm Bill contained explicit provisions requiring tracking of benefits provided directly or indirectly to individuals and entities. The purpose of this legislation was to improve the transparency of farm program benefits and to allow USDA a means to verify that payment limits were not being exceeded.

Using data on the sum of payments over the 1990–2005 period from USDA and farm acreage statistics from the 2002 *Agricultural Census*, we calculated payments in real dollars per acre. Figure 1 illustrates a large degree of geographical heterogeneity, with payments per acre in the Midwest far exceeding those in other areas. This heterogeneity has served to heighten controversy over the equity of current farm programs.

Three distinct sources of data on government payments have contributed to documenting the facts about the levels and impacts of the major programs.

3.1.1. Administrative data

There are currently approximately 70 different farm programs that make up the $13.3 billion in direct payments reported in the 2004 U.S. farm income

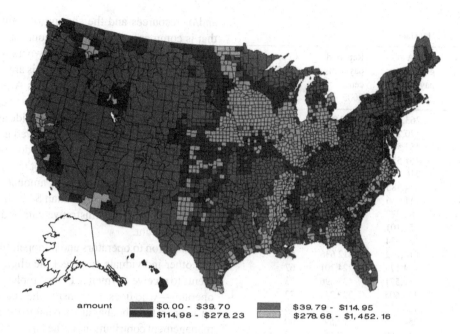

amount $0.00 - $39.70 $39.79 - $114.95
          $114.98 - $278.23 $278.68 - $1,452.16

Figure 1. Total U.S. direct government payments (real 2005 dollars per acre total, 1990–2005).

accounts.[2] This $13.3 billion is the sum of payments made by the program agencies based on their administrative records. Government payment data are available by program for each of the 50 U.S. states. An example of how these administrative data come into play in policy discussions followed the dissemination of payment data by the nonprofit Environmental Working Group (EWG). The EWG posted these data on-line during a period when farm legislation was being debated. The data indicate that the top 20% of the payment recipients received 87% of all payments, and the top 1% received 23% of all payments during the 1995–2004 period.

3.1.2. Census of agriculture

Farmers were asked to report their government payments for the first time in a follow-on survey to the 1964 Census of Agriculture. Since 1987, the question about government payments has been included in the full Census of Agriculture. The Census data are provided in published form as aggregated tables showing the distribution by size of farm (measured as gross sales class). USDA's economic research service (ERS) constructed an annual series using the Census data as a benchmark (along with other sources) which showed the distribution by sales class of farms (USDA, 1988), beginning with data for 1960.

Having data from both the providers of payments, in the USDA administrative data, and the farm recipients of data, from USDA's Agricultural Censuses and surveys, enables further issues to be addressed about where payments go, and possibly the accuracy of reporting. Table 1 shows that for the U.S. as a whole, farmers reported on the Census of Agriculture receiving only 58% as much as USDA reported paying out. For some states the divergence is quite remarkable, notably in the Southeast where Georgia farmers for example reported receiving only 18% of what USDA reported as paid to that state. Besides reporting accuracy, what might account for this difference?

One reason explaining the difference between the administrative and the reported data is that the Census data only include payments going to farm operators. Others, besides farm operators, are eligible to receive payments if they are deemed to be "actively" engaged in farming through contributions of labor, management

---

[2] The farm income accounts are for the calendar year, compared to the original fiscal budget year data. The program count includes multiple types of EQIP and disaster programs. Direct payments exclude programs which provide benefits to exporters and users of commodities, as well as loans and crop insurance indemnities.

Table 1
Government payments by state

State	USDA government payments 2002	Reported payments census 2002	Census as % of USDA reported payments
Alabama	263,866	77,930	30
Arizona	70,211	31,760	45
Arkansas	453,565	238,577	53
California	461,539	168,698	37
Colorado	210,967	125,774	60
Connecticut	4,885	3,681	75
Delaware	11,966	8,643	72
Florida	83,377	21,818	26
Georgia	658,101	118,535	18
Idaho	165,334	93,934	57
Illinois	614,752	412,636	67
Indiana	334,179	224,701	67
Iowa	739,521	538,896	73
Kansas	456,605	328,244	72
Kentucky	138,218	94,053	68
Louisiana	254,355	123,599	49
Maine	13,709	8,664	63
Maryland	48,676	33,131	68
Massachusetts	6,040	4,268	71
Michigan	190,481	144,771	76
Minnesota	476,745	350,709	74
Mississippi	251,908	145,508	58
Missouri	398,354	264,475	66
Montana	261,975	210,749	80
Nebraska	539,264	347,517	64
Nevada	11,287	4,322	38
New Hampshire	3,854	3,823	99
New Jersey	6,428	4,441	69
New Mexico	73,231	50,201	69
New York	159,238	110,234	69
North Carolina	278,454	97,696	35
North Dakota	383,499	293,067	76
Ohio	280,827	197,425	70
Oklahoma	317,217	149,942	47
Oregon	80,489	52,085	65
Pennsylvania	129,405	85,794	66
Rhode Island	652	528	81
South Carolina	65,884	38,384	58
South Dakota	334,750	215,084	64
Tennessee	107,772	59,231	55
Texas	998,543	528,979	53
Utah	54,141	26,669	49
Vermont	36,298	24,377	67
Virginia	181,780	54,677	30
Washington	215,911	133,763	62
West Virginia	5,655	5,180	92
Wisconsin	332,380	247,942	75
Wyoming	66,262	37,913	57
United States	11,236,299	6,545,678	58

Sources: USDA, 2004 and 2006c.

and/or resources and the sharing of returns in a way that is commensurate with their contributions. For example, for some programs, land owners who rent land out to farm operators on a share-basis are eligible to receive direct payments.[3] On USDA's Agricultural and Resource Management Survey (ARMS, described below), farm operators are asked to provide an estimate of what they think their landlords received in government payments. Although many farmers do not know what their landlords receive, or prefer not to report financial data on another individual, that amount of $705 million was far below the more than $4 billion difference between the 2002 administrative data and the reported Census amount.

In addition to operators and nonoperating land owners, other individuals can meet the eligibility requirements to receive payments. For example, a spouse of an operator—who does not consider herself or himself to be an operator—but has an ownership interest or makes management contributions to the farming operation can be eligible to receive payments. ARMS collects information on payments going to farming *operations*, in contrast to farm *operators* of an operation. In 2002, the ARMS-based estimate of federal payments received by *operations* was $9.4 billion, compared to the Census' $6.6 billion received by *operators*.

Another source of the difference in payments between what is known to be paid out and what is reported as received is likely related to the practice among many cooperatives of receiving the payments on behalf of the recipients. The cooperatives then disburse the payments directly to farmers along with other market payments for the sale of their product, and farmers cannot always easily decipher from their statements whether the source of payments is the market or the government.[4] So, while we can account for most of the differences between the *Census of Agriculture* data and the administrative data largely through definitional differences, the census data are widely available and

---

[3] Unfortunately, there are no surveys of nonoperating farmland owners which collect information on the government payments they receive. The last time a survey was conducted of farmland owners who do not operate farms was in 1999, (U.S. Department of Agriculture, 2001), but the government payments data were not collected. It should be noted that landowners may also be effective in receiving payments indirectly through higher rental rates on owners receiving payments.

[4] This explains why the largest payment recipients in the EWG data base are cooperatives.

often form the consensus view of how payments are distributed.

3.1.3. Farm costs and returns survey and agricultural resource management survey

With the establishment of the annual Farm Costs and Returns Survey (FCRS) in 1984 and the ARMS in 1996, economists had ready access to comprehensive individual farm and household data (USDA, 2006a). In the early 1980s, the U.S. farm sector was experiencing and recovering from a financial crisis, which was especially evident in the balance sheet of farm businesses and was dominating policy discussions at every level. This environment provided the impetus for agency administrators to combine survey funds from farm expenditure and costs of production surveys to develop a more comprehensive general farm survey, the FCRS.

The first report based on the FCRS addressed the farm financial crisis at the time, focusing on the income and balance sheet of farm businesses (USDA, 1985). This was followed soon after by articles on the role of government payments, from a business perspective (Baum and Johnson, 1986) and from the farm household perspective (Ahearn et al., 1986). In 1994, the 15th annual family farm report, requested in the 1977 and the 1985 farm acts, was the first based on FCRS data; subsequent reports have continued to rely on FCRS and, more recently, the ARMS.[5]

Since ARMS' beginnings, its data have supported a wide variety of policy-relevant analyses, and continue to be the most comprehensive source of economic data for USDA and university researchers today. The FCRS-ARMS data have allowed ERS to establish basic facts about how many farms receive payments, and other information, such as how payments vary by size of farm, and the financial position of farm households that receive payments relative to other farm households and the average U.S. household. Before the existence of those data, USDA commonly reported the aggregate amount of payments farmers received. For example, using current data from the sector-level estimates, we know that government payments were 16% of net farm income and 5% of gross farm income in 2004 (USDA, 2006a). Using the ARMS data, we know the type of distributional data shown in Table 2. For example, in 2004, approximately 39% of family farms received a

commodity or conservation payment from the government, averaging $12,435 per farm. Of those that participated in government programs, their average household income was $88,194 and their average net worth was $882,186. On average, farm households that participated in government programs had higher incomes and greater net worth than other farm households and the general U.S. population. Of course, similar data can be reported for farm households or farm businesses by any classification scheme, such as by farm size or commodity specialization.

3.2. Commodity programs and the role of economic statistics

The collapse of commodity prices after the end of World War I led to a period of sustained political debate about governmental action. The terms of debate involved the fundamentals of how the U.S. agricultural economy functioned and were also highly quantitative, setting the stage for the use of economic statistics in policy design. A Congressionally mandated Commission of Agricultural Inquiry (U.S. Congress, 1921) gave high priority to improved statistics and economic intelligence in the USDA and implementation followed with the creation in 1922 of the Bureau of Agricultural Economics (BAE), the forerunner to the current ERS. In Congressional legislation of 1924–1928, calls were made for equality for agriculture. These calls for equality were defined as prices that "would bear the same relation to the general price level as the price of the commodity supported had borne to the general price level just prior to the war" (Benedict, 1953, p. 212). This approach was incorporated into the first major farm legislation, as part of the Roosevelt Administration's New Deal program, in 1933.

During the debates of the 1920s and 1930s, economists both in government and outside questioned the theoretical and practical aspects of Congress's approach, and their work contributed to the systematic development of U.S. farm economic statistics. The major roles economic statistics have played in agricultural policies include the following.

3.2.1. Income parity

In the Soil Conservation and Domestic Allotment Act of 1936, Congress declared its purpose as the reestablishment of "the ratio between the purchasing

---

[5] The latest family farm report is Hoppe and Banker (2006).

Table 2

Finances and characteristics of farm operator households by whether or not they participated in government commodity or conservation programs, 2004

Item	Participation status		All
	Not participating	Participating	
Number of farms	1,264,807	796,015	2,060,822
Percent of farms	61.4	38.6	100.0
Total cash farm business income	38,151	163,427	86,540
Livestock income	14,667	59,752	32,081
Crop income	16,282	66,939	35,849
Government payments	0	12,435	4,803
Other farm-related income	7,203	24,300	13,807
Total cash expenses	33,609	117,212	65,902
Net cash farm income of business*	4,542	46,214	20,638
Earnings of the household from farming*	3,599	31,046	14,201
Off-farm income, all household members	73,655	57,148	67,279
Average farm operator household income	77,254	88,194	81,480
Share with nonfarm earnings			
No nonfarm work	26	31	28
Nonfarm work	74	69	72
Share with farm loss/profit			
Farm loss	60	28	48
Farm profit	40	72	52
Average farm net worth	451,669	698,005	546,819
Average nonfarm net worth	210,922	184,181	200,593
Average household net worth	662,592	882,186	747,413
Farm business debt-asset ratio			
<0.10	82	65	75
≥0.10	18	35	25
Educational attainment of operator			
High school or less	54	51	53
Some college or more	46	49	47
Age of operator			
Less than 55	44	43	44
55 or older	56	57	56
Race of operator			
Nonwhite	9	6	8
White	91	94	92

Source: 2004 USDA Agricultural Resource Management Survey.

   * Differences between these two estimates result largely from the senior farm operator household not receiving all of the net income of the farm business. Based on 19,468 observations. SAS data set is BANK, created-18MAY2006:01:02:46.12 PM, last modified-18MAY2006:01:02:46.12 PM, with 99 variables.

power of the net income per person on farms and the income per person not on farms that prevailed during the five-year period August 1909–July 1914" (USDA, 1944, p. 1).[6] The lack of income parity between the

farm and nonfarm population was a central component of the "farm problem" as defined at that time. Although the income parity concept was introduced as a goal, per person farm incomes relative to nonfarm incomes were never directly used as a trigger for implementing particular policy provisions. This may be related to difficulty in measuring and comparing incomes, or perhaps it relates to the incompleteness of income as a measure of welfare. On the other hand, it may be due

---

[6] The term "parity" was used in the Agricultural Adjustment Act of 1938 to refer to both the price parity of the 1933 Act and the purchasing power, i.e., income, parity of the 1936 Act (Rasmussen and Baker, 1979, p. 10).

to the perceived difficulty in implementing a program based on income parity.

There were two early sources of statistics on the income of farmers. The first statistical series compared the disposable personal income per capita for farm residents to that of nonfarm residents for 1910–1943 (USDA, 1944). In the early 1960s, the consensus judgment about these statistics is reflected in the following: "There have been substantial advances in recent years in quality and quantity of data available to make farm-nonfarm income comparisons. However, it appears that the present data fall short of our needs" (Hathaway, 1963, p. 375). The major factor in leading Hathaway to this conclusion was not the quality of the income data, but rather he questioned the income concept as a measure of relative welfare because of the large net worth of farm persons relative to nonfarm persons, which was not considered in an income comparison.[7]

The second historical series on the incomes of farm households begins with 1960. The approach of this series was to build on the widely used sector-level estimate of net farm income and the information on off-farm income available occasionally from the Census of Agriculture. Both of these historical series were based on a variety of primary data sources and were later discontinued. The disposable personal income series was last published for the year 1983 (USDA, 1984) and the second series on total household income of farm operators was last published for the year 1985 (USDA, 1986).

A new series of farm household income estimates was based on primary survey data from USDA. An estimate was first made with 1984 data (Ahearn, 1986), but later refined with the 1988 data in a variety of ways, including recognizing that not all farms are family farms and that not all farm business income went to the farm operator household (Ahearn et al., 1993). This series is the current statistical series on farm operator household income and is compared to the incomes of the average U.S. household and published annually (USDA, 1994).

The longest-running series that compares incomes of farm and nonfarm people, 1910–1983, shows that income of farm people lagged those of nonfarm people by a significant amount in the early years. Over time, this gap was narrowing. The current series described above shows that not only has the gap narrowed between the average incomes of farm and U.S. households, but that the income of the average farm household exceeds that of the average U.S. household. This suggests that goals other than income parity now motivate policies.

3.2.2. Costs of production

In the 1977 Food and Agricultural Act, target prices were adjusted by an index based on production costs for corn, wheat, cotton, and rice (McElroy, 1987). This was not the first time, however, that costs of production were considered as policy instruments. In the late 1920s, legislation based on cost of production statistics was rejected. Although the BAE had a program of developing cost of production, the Secretary of Agriculture argued against policies relying on cost of production estimates because he recognized the difficulty in computing estimates that would be representative of all areas of the country (Rasmussen and Baker, 1979, p. 2). In the 1985 Food Security Act, costs of production were also used to set support levels for peanuts and sugar.

3.2.3. Commodity supply information

During the period 1985 to 1995, USDA, in its administration of farm programs, and Congress, in its legislation, moved decisively away from the tools of supply management. These tools, principal policy management instruments used from 1933 through the early 1980s, consisted of production controls and government-controlled commodity storage. Both kinds of tools were intensively used for purposes of increasing and stabilizing the prices received by farmers for their products. In the mid 1980s almost 80 million acres (about 20% of all U.S. cropland) was idled under government programs.

Yet by the mid 1990s, USDA had sold off almost all of its stocks of the main commodities and had stopped acquiring commodities to support prices even when market prices were low. Further, in the 1996 Farm

---

[7] ERS continues to emphasize the inadequacy of income as a welfare measure because of the significantly greater net worth of farm households compared to nonfarm households (El-Osta et al., 2005). This is even truer for the approximately one-third of farm households that participate in commodity programs. See, for example, Jones, et al. (2006), who note that in 2003 only 5% of U.S. farm households had both income and wealth levels that were less than the U.S. median household income and wealth levels. They also note that farm households with low income and wealth levels were less likely to receive government payments.

Act, Congress mandated that the Secretary of Agriculture not use acreage restrictions as a policy tool. What caused this total turnaround? The key fact is that representatives of farmers came to believe that supply management was counterproductive. Government purchases of commodities when prices were low created surplus supplies that overhung the market for years afterward and on net, the stabilization efforts did nothing for or perhaps even harmed farmers' interests, it came to be believed. In addition, idling acreage created opportunities for foreign producers in countries like Brazil to expand their output, and so had too little price-increasing effect to compensate for the income lost from idled acreage. (For further discussion of these changes of view, see Gardner (2002, Ch. 7).)

It is apparent that the accumulation of information, as opposed to a shift in political power between parties or interest groups or a change in preferences or values of the groups, underlies the policy shift. The sources of the new information that made a difference are less clear. The main possible sources are statistical data, analytical work with those data, or informal (anecdotal) information accumulated by the interested parties from their own experience. While the interest-group representatives who testified before Congress on supply management often spoke of government stocks overhanging the markets or loss of our production to foreign producers as matters they directly observed, this cannot be the full story. These phenomena cannot be directly observed. What the interested citizenry and policy makers saw were the data on public and private commodity stocks, crop acreages, USDA program parameters, and enrollment. So, although the precise mechanism is not observable, it is hard to avoid concluding that this is a case where economic statistics played a major role in the direction of policy decisions.

3.3. Data critical for risk management and conservation program implementation

Many current farm programs have substantial demands for detailed data in order to implement the programs and carry out the intent of policy makers. In some cases, there is a need for farm-level data, often collected over several years. In terms of current policies, this is especially true for crop insurance, disaster aid, and conservation programs. In each case, the programs have extensive data needs which may place significant demands on program administrators and may even shape the policies that are feasible to implement. For example, many crop insurance programs were designed in accordance with the data that happen to be available rather than what would seem more natural—the design of data collection efforts to support desired policies.

The importance of data for the implementation of policy is especially significant in the case of *ad hoc* disaster relief and crop insurance. In both cases, policies are intended to provide immediate (or at least timely) assistance to agricultural producers who have suffered production shortfalls brought about by the randomness of agricultural production and markets. Disaster assistance and insurance programs come in many different forms and thus differ substantially in terms of their data needs. However, all such programs share a common need for timely information regarding the current state of a particular agricultural sector, crop, or economy, such that the extent of a disaster or production shortfall can be estimated and disaster assistance can be appropriately defined.

In the discussion that follows, we outline the disaster assistance process and the mechanisms used to convey such assistance to agricultural interests. We also discuss the data needs of policymakers and program administrators. As we emphasize, crop insurance and disaster assistance are, *by their very nature*, very dependent upon reliable data about *individual* yields and prices. The structure and function of these programs is largely shaped by the data that are available to policymakers. For example, the construction of crop insurance programs, which currently cover almost $50 billion worth of U.S. agricultural crops, is usually driven by the amount of data that is available to define contracts, assign rates, and determine indemnifiable events. Policy makers seek to define the terms of a particular insurance program in a way that offers meaningful coverage to producers while protecting the interests of taxpayers against overpayment, fraud, and abuse. To do so requires careful and comprehensive understanding of the risks associated with the events being insured against. This, in turn, usually requires historical data which can be used to measure risks.

Congressional attention was drawn to crop losses as far back as 1922 when the USDA published extensive information about crop losses from drought, disease, pests, and frost. Congressional interest in a crop insurance program remained strong over the next several years, with individual congressmen and senators focusing on localized losses in their own districts. In 1936, a research project evaluating the viability of crop insurance was initiated at the USDA using data on wheat and cotton yields collected by the Agricultural Adjustment Administration (AAA). With the strong endorsement of agricultural commodity groups and farm organizations, the 1938 Agricultural Adjustment Act included specific provisions for individual yield, multiple peril crop insurance.

Data concerns were pertinent to the early history of the federal crop insurance program. In particular, the program was administered by local committees of the AAA. The hazards associated with such a design are obvious—neighbors were charged with setting rates and assessing losses. Rates were established using county-wide average yields—a practice that has persisted in many situations to this day.

Disaster relief programs are typically of an *ad hoc* nature—meaning that the design and mechanisms of the programs (and their data needs) may adjust from situation to situation. Congress established a formal disaster relief program in 1949 through the Farmers' Home Administration. Disaster payments were also introduced in legislation in the early 1970s. Disaster payments were typically paid on the basis of base acreage (i.e., acres eligible for program participation) and county-average yields.

3.3.1. The agricultural disaster relief process

Disaster assistance has been seen as a responsibility of the federal government over most of the history of the United States. The Congressional Act of 1803, which addressed fire losses in Portsmouth, New Hampshire, was one of the first legislative moves to provide disaster assistance. There are currently four major types of agricultural disaster declarations. These include a Presidential major disaster declaration, a USDA Secretarial disaster designation, a physical loss notification by the farm service agency (FSA) administrator, and the declaration of a plant or animal quarantine.

A Presidential declaration of disaster must be initiated by a request from one or more governors of the affected states. Disaster relief measures which are triggered by Presidential declarations are exercised through the Federal Emergency Management Agency (FEMA). FEMA activities pertaining to agriculture are typically exercised in coordination with the FSA or other agencies of the USDA.

In the case of Secretarial disaster declarations, specific guidelines for what qualifies as a disaster and the process for disaster relief are in place. Specifically, a disaster must involve at least a 30% drop in yields for at least one crop in a county and must be due to a natural event. The county FSA offices are charged with collecting the relevant data needed to document the extent of the disaster in the form of a report. The disaster assessment report submitted to the secretary must contain specific data regarding the disaster. These data must include: (1) the 5-year average production history for the crops and farms described in the report, (2) the average farm price for the affected crops over the preceding 3 years, and (3) the dates and causes of crop or livestock losses. In the event that sufficient data are unavailable to document the disaster, the disaster declaration may be deferred to await future data.

Perhaps the most common event underlying Secretarial disaster declarations is drought. Drought and other production conditions are monitored on a weekly basis throughout the growing season through the "crop progress and condition" reports. These reports are generated by a group of reporters consisting of extension agents and local FSA staff and are typically submitted through a website, making the data available in a timely manner. Disaster relief measures are also supported by data collected through remote sensing methods, including through the use of NOAA satellites.

Recent developments in the livestock and plant industries have given rise to new concerns regarding methods for tracking animal and plant health concerns. Recent concerns regarding bovine spongiform encephalopathy (BSE or "mad cow disease"), Asiatic citrus canker, soybean rust, and the avian influenza A (H5N1) virus are examples of the threats to animal and plant health that have raised concerns. Legislative actions to address these concerns have included quarantines, the closure of borders to imports of suspect products, and extensive inspection programs. For example, Florida has had an active grove inspections program to identify and quarantine areas infected with Asiatic citrus canker and to provide policy makers and regulators with data on the movement of the disease. Similar concerns have been used to argue in favor of an animal identification program that would allow improved traceability and monitoring of BSE threats.

3.3.2. Crop insurance programs

The 1994 Federal Crop Insurance Reform Act and the 2000 Agricultural Risk Protection Act have expanded the depth, scope, and range of crop insurance programs. Premium subsidies have been used to encourage participation and by 2005, 245 million acres were insured with a total liability of over $44 billion (USDA-RMA, 2006). In addition, a number of new insurance products have been developed to provide price risk coverage to livestock producers.

The demands for data by risk management agency (RMA) program administrators are extensive. Crop insurance programs, though marketed and serviced through private insurance providers, are reinsured and regulated by the federal government. Producers are charged premiums for coverage that, according to legislative mandates, must result in the program performing at actuarially sound levels. These premiums are subsidized by taxpayers. However, the underlying premium rates are expected to be actuarially sound.

Crop insurance programs offer protection against yield shortfalls that result from nearly any cause (with exceptions being made for deliberate losses or losses resulting from a failure to follow proper production practices). Two key parameters of the insurance programs are dependent upon historical production data. The first is the premium rate, representing a measure of the risk associated with production. These data are collected at the county level and every producer in a county with the same average yield pays an identical price for their insurance. A second important parameter is the average yield itself, which in addition to being used to adjust premium rates is used to also establish a level of protection.

The need to measure risks, determine premium rates, and assign levels of protection *at the farm unit level* imposes significant data demands. Current procedures use a 4–10-year yield history at the individual farm level. Many issues underlie the use of individual yields, which are often absent for any individual producer. For example, producers unable to produce at least four verifiable years of yields are assigned a proportion of the county average yield.

The RMA has a very extensive data management system that is known as the "data acceptance system" (the system is also known as the M-13 and is described in detail on the RMA's website). Millions of policy records are collected at the subunit level and entered into the system each year by the insurance providers. This system is also used to provide research to policymakers regarding operational issues and proposed changes to the program.

In order to be actuarially sound, an insurance program must have an accurate measure of risk and an adequate means of measuring the value of the asset being insured. Actuarial practices typically depend upon *historical data* to derive such measures. Indeed, the types of programs that are offered are generally constrained by the data that are available to policymakers and to those tasked with constructing and rating the contracts.

3.3.3. Conservation policies

A wide variety of conservation measures exist in current U.S. farm policy and many of these measures have explicit eligibility criteria which, in turn, require detailed data regarding land quality and conservation practices. Surveys of the quality of soil and other natural resources have played an important role in targeting conservation programs toward areas with the greatest need or most significant benefit from conservation.

The 2002 Farm Bill included a significant conservation title, with substantial resources being directed toward conservation programs. These programs require adoption of various conservation measures which must be certified through interviews.

Data requirements for implementation of the Conservation Reserve Program (CRP) have been substantial, since eligibility is limited to those lands that are the most environmentally vulnerable, such as susceptible to erosion, and the most likely to demonstrate benefits from conservation measures. One factor that will qualify a given tract of land for CRP benefits involves its erodibility, which is measured using the "erodibility index" or EI. A field's cropping history is also relevant to its eligibility for land that meets certain other environmental requirements, such as being marginal pastureland, wetlands, subject to scour erosion, and land that is contained in CRP priority areas, may also be eligible for enrollment.

Finally, the likelihood that a given tract will be accepted into the CRP is determined by its "environmental benefits index (EBI)." The EBI is a measure of the benefits that would result from enrollment in the CRP. Land offered for enrollment into the CRP program is ranked according to its EBI. The EBI considers a range of factors including wildlife habitat benefits, water quality benefits, on-farm benefits from reduced erosion, long-term benefits accruing after the CRP contract period, air quality benefits from reduced wind erosion, and cost-efficiency issues (based on local data on the cash rental market) (U.S. Department of Agriculture, 2006b).

A major source of environmental quality and land use data is the National Resources Inventory (NRI). The NRI is a detailed survey that collects information about land use, land quality, and natural resources on nonfederal lands across the U.S. The NRI surveys were originally administered on a 5-year basis, but are now conducted every year. The most recent 5-year survey involved data collection from over 800,000 sampling points. The new annual surveys include about 200,000 points each year.

4. Summary and concluding remarks

Statistical data, both as stand-alone description and as raw material for analysis of economic issues in U.S. agriculture, have played an important role in the political economy of the U.S. agriculture. Policy developments have generated increasing demands for economic statistics relating to farms, and in turn statistical data have influenced policy developments. As policies have become broader in scope, addressing not only farm commodity markets but also differences among farms and a widening set of activities on farms, policy makers have asked for more detailed information about the financial situation of individual farm businesses and households, sources of risk in farm returns, and production practices followed that affect the environment.

It is difficult to imagine how the policies we briefly described could be designed, implemented, or evaluated effectively in the absence of the relevant database. In fact, it is interesting to consider what the environment for agricultural policies would be in the absence of the collection of U.S. economic statistics on agricultural. Plausible scenarios include pleas to help the failing "family farm" would have more support because we would still have the prevailing general sense that all farmers are financially hard-pressed. It is likely that there would be greater regulation of agriculture, with less of a market-based approach incorporated in farm bills. Without cost of production data, there would likely be more expressions of concern that farm labor is being displaced by technology, leading to criticisms of new technologies. This would suggest less support for research. In general, the development of agricultural economic statistics have likely caused the adoption of more growth-oriented policies (with less deadweight losses), evidence for a high rate of return for public investment in statistics.

The interactions among statistics, policy design, and program implementation has meant a steady increase in business for USDA's statistical agencies, and has resulted in new data series describing the agricultural sector and new detail in cross-sectional data for individual farms. It has also meant an increased research capacity to analyze the effectiveness of programs in achieving their stated goals, such as in the design of "decoupled" payments.[8] This capacity is very complementary with the government-wide effort to incorporate more accountability into the management of government programs. The American Agricultural Economics Association's Economic Statistics Committee has often participated in improving the economic statistics for agriculture by identifying current weaknesses and potential future strategies (Kraenzle, 2000).

The data generated constitute an important public good for economists, providing necessary material for a wide range of investigations in agricultural economics, fueling Ph.D. dissertations and journal articles by agricultural economists. Future data collection and analysis challenges in the U.S. will be influenced by the greater industrialization of agricultural production and the demands for greater product traceability and information on production practices. Government-wide, there is currently an interest in relying more on administrative records in order to reduce costs and respondent burden, but as of yet, that has not been a major focus in the development of new economic statistics for agriculture. Increasing globalization will continue

---

[8] For example, see Goodwin and Mishra (2006).

to highlight the importance of greater harmonization in comparative international statistics.

References

Ahearn, M., "The Financial Well-Being of Farm Operators and their Households," USDA, ERS, AER-563, September 1986.

Ahearn, M., J. Johnson, and R. Strickland, "The Distribution of Income and Wealth of Farm Operator Households," *American Journal of Agricultural Economics* 67, no. 5, Dec. (1986), 1087–1094.

Ahearn, M., J. Perry, and H. El-Osta, "The Economic Well-Being of Farm Operator Households, 1988-90," USDA, ERS, AER-666, January 1993.

Baum, K., and J. D. Johnson, "Microeconomic Indicators of the Farm Sector and Policy Implications," *American Journal of Agricultural Economics* 68 (1986), 1121–1129.

Benedict, M., *Farm Policies of the United States: 1790-1950* (Twentieth Century Fund: New York, 1953).

El-Osta, H., A. Mishra, and M. Morehart, "Composite Measure of Well-Being," *Amber Waves*, September (2005), 10–11. Available at http://www.ers.usda.gov/AmberWaves/September05/DataFeature/

Gardner, B., *American Agriculture in the 20th Century* (Harvard University Press: Cambridge, MA, 2002).

Goodwin, B., and A. Mishra, "Are 'Decoupled' Farm Program Payments Really Decoupled? An Empirical Evaluation," *American Journal of Agricultural Economics* 88 (2006), 73–89.

Hathaway, D. E., "Improving and Extending Farm-Nonfarm Income Comparisons," *Journal of Farm Economics* 45 (1963), 367–375.

Hoppe, R., and D. Banker, "Structure and Finances of U.S. Farms: 2005 Family Farm Report," USDA, ERS, *Economic Information Bulletin* 12, May 5 (2006).

Jones, C., P. Sheatsley, and A. Stinchcombe, *Dakota Farmers and Ranchers Evaluate Crop and Livestock Surveys* (NORC Report 128: Chicago, 1979).

Jones, C., H. El-Osta, and R. Green, "Economic Well-Being of Farm Households," Economic Research Service, USDA, EB7, March 2006.

Kraenzle, C., "A Review of the Activities of AAEA's Economic Statistics and Information Resources Committee," Rural Business and Cooperative Service, USDA, Staff Report 93-S3, May 2000.

McElroy, R., "Major Statistical Series of the U.S. Department of Agriculture, Vol. 12: Costs of Production," *Economic Research Service*, USDA, AHN 671, September 1987.

Rasmussen, W. D., and G. L. Baker, "Price-Support and Adjustment Programs from 1933 through 1978: A Short History," Washington, DC: USDA, ESCS, AIB NO. 424, February 1979.

U.S. Congress, *Report of the Joint Commission of Agricultural Inquiry,* House Report No. 408, U.S. Government Printing Office, Washington, DC, October 1921.

U.S. Department of Agriculture, *Yearbook* (Report of the Secretary of Agriculture, Government Printing Office: Washington, DC, 1895).

U.S. Department of Agriculture, *Income Parity for Agriculture,* Part 1 (Bureau of Economic Analysis: Washington, DC, October 1944).

U.S. Department of Agriculture, "Economic Indicators of the Farm Sector: Income and Balance Sheet Statistics, 1983," *Economic Research Service,* ECIFS 3-3, September 1984.

U.S. Department of Agriculture, "Financial Characteristics of U.S. Farms, January 1985," *Economic Research Service,* AIB No. 495, July 1985.

U.S. Department of Agriculture, "Economic Indicators of the Farm Sector: National Financial Summary, 1985," *Economic Research Service,* ECIFS 5-2, November 1986.

U.S. Department of Agriculture, *The Farm Income Handbook,* Vol. 9 (Major Statistical Series of the USDA: Washington, DC, November 1988).

U.S. Department of Agriculture, "Economic Indicators of the Farm Sector: National Financial Summary, 1992," *Economic Research Service,* ECIFS 12-1, January 1994.

U.S. Department of Agriculture, "1997 Census of Agriculture, Vol. 3," Agricultural Economics and Land Ownership Survey, Special Studies, Part IV, AC97-SP-4, National Agricultural Statistics Service, December 2001.

U.S. Department of Agriculture, "2002 Census of Agriculture. United States Summary and State Data," NASS, Vol. 1, Part 51, AC-02-A51, June 2004.

U.S. Department of Agriculture, "Agricultural Resource Management Survey Briefing Room," *Economic Research Service,* http://www.ers.usda.gov/Briefing/ARMS/, 2006a.

U.S. Department of Agriculture, "Conservation Reserve Sign-Up General Sign-Up 33: Environmental Benefits Index," *Farm Service Agency,* April, 2006b, http://www.fsa.usda.gov/pas/publications/facts/crp33ebi06.pdf.

U.S. Department of Agriculture, "Farm Income Data Files," *Economic Research Service,* http://www.ers.usda.gov/Data/FarmIncome/finfidmu.htm. 2006c.

U.S. Department of Agriculture, Risk Management Agency (RMA), "Summary of Business Statistics," http://www.rma.usda.gov/data/sob/html, 2006.

U.S. Office of Management and Budget, "A Special Report on the Statistical Programs and Activities of the U.S. Government," *Statistical Policy Office,* June (1985).

U.S. Office of Management and Budget, "Statistical Programs of the U.S. Government," (1990 and 2005).

Income distributional effects of using market-based instruments for managing common property resources

Siwa Msangi* and Richard E. Howitt**

Abstract

In this article, the authors show the trade-offs between efficiency and equity that arise from the application of market-based instruments to a heterogenous population of agents drawing from a natural resource pool. Using the example of groundwater, they find that there are overall losses in allocative efficiency when the centralized planner is constrained by equity considerations, and that the distribution of gains or losses to management becomes skewed asymmetrically across agents. These results demonstrate the importance of considering both efficiency gains and disparities in distributional inequity, when designing policy instruments that create winners and losers with potentially serious sociopolitical ramifications.

JEL classification: C61, D61, Q25

Keywords: groundwater policy; market-based instruments; economic dynamics

1. Introduction

Policy makers and researchers have faced the challenge of addressing pressing issues of environmental and natural resource management and regulation with policy instruments that are both effective, in terms of achieving the desired outcomes, while striving to improve the economic efficiency, as defined in terms of the resulting change in net benefits of the economic agents involved. The consideration of such problems ranges, in the literature, from that of pollution of air and water, to that of the management of water, soil, and other natural resources. Among the challenges that are faced by environmental managers and policy makers are that of coordinating the behavior of individual economic agents whose actions have direct impacts on the environment and the state of important natural resources, which lie under their stewardship. While direct centralized control and intervention might be called for, resource and personnel limitations necessitate the

application of decentralized policy instruments, which are designed with a view to maximizing overall benefits, and achieving the best possible environmental outcomes. Nonetheless, some form of centralized regulation is often considered due to the difficulty of realizing decentralized Coasian bargaining, either due to the presence of transactions costs and asymmetry in information (Farrell, 1987), scale considerations (Nalebuff, 1997), or other reasons.

Market-based instruments (MBIs) have slowly gained popularity among those environmental managers who seek to improve environmental outcomes within a context in which there are multiple agents, whose heterogeneity might reduce the efficiency of a nondiscriminatory policy instrument. The classical application of market-based policy instruments of environmental regulation has been that of pollution control, in which the costs of abatement might vary across the polluters (Baumol and Oates, 1975). The seminal works of McGartland and Oates (1985) and Tietenberg (1985) were the first to discuss a decentralized system of tradable permits that could be bought and sold within a transparent market structure that could be used to improve the environment. The application of market-based instruments can also be found within the

*International Food Policy Research Institute, 2033 K Street NW, Washington, DC 20006.

**Department of Agricultural & Resource Economics, University of California at Davis, One Shields Ave., Davis, CA 95616.

context of natural resource management, such as in the application of tradeable quotas in fishery management (Anderson, 1995; Hanley et al., 1997). The success of the system of tradable emissions permits to address the acid-rain problem in North America has been noted widely, and is a recognized example of the successful application of economic theory to institutional and market design (Tietenberg, 1985; Joskow et al., 1998).

While achievement of environmentally sound outcomes is important, policy makers must also take into account considerations of equity, which can sometimes have stronger sociopolitical ramifications than the simple achievement of welfare-neutral gains in overall economic efficiency. While some authors have investigated efficiency and equity considerations within the context of water management, these have mostly centered around the issue of surface water pricing (Tsur and Dinar, 1995), but have not directly addressed the context of groundwater usage—which has strong implications for resource dynamics over time and long-run sustainability.

The aim of this article is to contribute to the literature on groundwater management policy by examining the tradeoffs between efficiency and equity, when applying market-based policy instruments aimed at reducing the negative externalities imposed by noncooperative groundwater pumping. Using a stylized model within a specific empirical context, the article examines how the distribution of potential gains to groundwater management changes under the application of alternative policy instruments, in the presence of agent heterogeneity. Through this exercise, one gains useful insights into how policy makers and environmental managers might address issues of equity and efficiency when considering policy intervention in other groundwater basins, as well as in other common-pool problems, more generally. The article also demonstrates the importance of addressing agent heterogeneity when trying to address the issues of equity and efficiency in policy design, especially in a dynamic context.

2. Groundwater management policy and problems

Groundwater is a frequently overexploited common-pool resource for irrigated agriculture, and its depletion, in numerous cases that have been studied, has led to serious conflicts between users (Ostrom, 1990).

Gisser and Sanchez (1980) were among the first to examine the externalities arising from the extraction of groundwater as a common-property problem. In this article, the authors examined the loss of efficiency that occurs when a groundwater aquifer moves from a sole-owner extraction regime to one in which there is competition in pumping. Various other authors within the natural resources literature have also addressed the efficiency problems that arise under competitive in groundwater pumping (Feinerman and Knapp, 1983; Allen and Gisser, 1984; Kim et al., 1989), both theoretically and empirically.

Some of these conflicts arose from disputed third-party impacts attributed to policy-promoted water transfers, such as those made to the California Emergency Drought Water Bank (Hanak, 2003) or from other voluntary market transactions (Murphy et al., 2003). While the State Water Bank was initiated with the understanding that third-party interests would be observed and adequately protected, the majority of the impacts resulting from the water transfers to the Drought Bank were borne by the groundwater basin, causing third-party impacts on the local economies (resulting from sale of surface water rights) to be substituted for third-party impacts on groundwater users (Howitt, 1993a,b). As an illustration of this effect, nearly 37% of the increased depletion of groundwater in the Lower Cache Unit of Yolo County was attributable to transfers made to the Water Bank in 1991 (McBean, 1993).

This article examines, more closely, how the dual criteria of both efficiency enhancement and equity preservation can be evaluated and compared, when addressing the design of market-based instruments of re-allocation applied to the context of groundwater.

3. Assessing efficiency and equity of policy interventions

The analytical framework used in this article examines the trade-offs between the efficiency of water allocations and the implications for equity in the distribution of benefits is a dynamic one, which explicitly takes into account the dynamic nature of the externalities that arise when socially optimal, intertemporal behavior is replaced by noncooperative and myopic behavior of heterogeneous agents.

3.1. Defining the benchmark of efficiency

The problem facing the social planner who takes the intertemporal welfare of all agents into account, when making allocations of the natural resource over time, forms the benchmark for efficiency that economists consider, when comparing the performance of decentralized policy instruments and regimens. Considering the case of i players, who differ according to the marginal benefits that they enjoy in the exploitation of the resource. Denoting the marginal benefit curve as $MB(w_i) = a - b \cdot q_i$, where a and b are the intercept and slope of the agent's demand curve, respectively, for water withdrawals q_i. For i heterogeneous agents, one could consider a distribution of slope parameters, such that we have values ranked as $b_1 < \cdots b_i < \cdots < b_N$ along an interval of length $b_N - b_1$. Taking into account the costs of groundwater pumping, which depend on the depth of the groundwater table below the surface $(s - h)$,[1] the aggregate benefits accrued by all N agents would then be given by

$$\sum_{i=1}^{N} B_i(q_i) = \sum_{i=1}^{N} \left[a \cdot q_i - \frac{1}{2} b_i \cdot q_i^2 - e(s - h) \cdot q_i \right]$$

$$(1)$$

where e is the common energy cost of pumping that is faced by all agents pumping from depth of $(s - h)$. According to the principle of optimality laid out by Bellman (1957), and which is commonly used in the definition of the intertemporal benchmark of allocative efficiency in natural resource economics, the central manager (social planner) of the groundwater resource, would make a centralized distribution of groundwater resources over time according to the solution of the following problem.

$$V^{SP}(h)$$

$$= \max_{\{q_i\}} \left\{ \sum_{i=1}^{N} \left[a \cdot q_i - \frac{1}{2} b_i \cdot q_i^2 - e(s - h) \cdot q_i \right] \right.$$

$$\left. + \beta_{SP} V^{SP} \left(h + \gamma \sum_{i=1}^{N} q_i - \bar{r} \right) \right\},$$

$$(2)$$

[1] Where s and h are, respectively, the heights of the ground surface and groundwater table above a given reference level.

where, in addition to the aggregate benefits captured in Eq. (1), the planner also takes into account the value of groundwater stock that remains in the next period (and by implication, into the future). The "value function" $V^{SP}(h)$ in the Bellman Eq. (2), captures this maximized value, and is a mapping of the allocations accruing to all agents (an N-dimensional vector) onto the real number line—and which is recursively defined for both the current stock of groundwater (captured by h), as well as for that which remains in the following period h^+. The evolution of the state of the groundwater table between one period and the next is governed by the equation of motion

$$h^+ = h + \gamma \sum_{i=1}^{N} q_i - \bar{r}$$

$$(3)$$

which includes the recharge into the aquifer $(\bar{r})$ and a parameter (γ) that translates units of pumping volume into groundwater table height.

Equation (4), below, embodies the trade-off between intertemporal benefits captured by the first-order conditions of the Bellman Eq. (2), which yield the following Euler equation

$$a - b_i \cdot q_i - e(s - h) + \gamma \cdot \beta_{SP} V_q^{SP}(\cdot) = 0. \quad (4)$$

This "policy function" could be contrasted to the much more simplified extraction "rule" implied by an individual agent who pumps myopically and, therefore, ignores the "user cost" embodied in the term $\gamma \cdot \beta_{SP} V_q^{SP}(\cdot)$ of the social planner's Euler equation. The extraction rule of such an agent is simply given by

$$q_i = \frac{a - e(s - h)}{b_i}, \quad (5)$$

which only takes into account the current period's marginal benefits and costs. The divergence in pumping and therefore total net benefits between the solutions given by Eqs. (2) and (5) represent the "gain" that can be realized under centralized (and socially optimal) management of the aquifer, using Eq. (1), they are

$$\text{Gain} = B^{SP}(q_i) - \sum_{i=1}^{N} B^i(q_i), \quad (6)$$

which forms the basis by which water economists measure the efficiency gains to centralized control.

3.2. *Defining distributional equity*

A simple and convenient measure of inequality was defined by Theil (1987) in his seminal treatise of economic applications of information theory. A simple index which he constructed is that based upon the principle of "entropy," which conveys the degree to which a distribution differs from a uniform and uninformative profile—thereby capturing the "surprise" that is embodied in a (random) outcome (Shannon, 1948a,b). In juxtaposition to Shannon's entropy measure $H = \sum_n -p_n \log(p_n)$ for n discrete random events, we can also express the *cross-entropy* of a distribution by the measure, $CE = \sum_n -p_n \log(\frac{p_n}{\bar{p}_n})$, which includes the *prior* distribution of weights (or probabilities) $\{\bar{p}_n\}$ that can be assigned for each random outcome. As shown by Kullback (1959), the maximization of the Shannon criterion with respect to the adding up constraint $\sum_n p_n = 1$ is equivalent to the minimization of the cross-entropy criterion, similarly constrained, if the prior distribution is uniform (i.e., assigns an equal likelihood to each outcome). The divergence of a calculated distribution from prior beliefs, as calculated by the cross-entropy criterion conveys information content in a similar way to that calculated by the Shannon measure of information (Kullback and Liebler, 1951).

The Theil index for inequality has a similar cross-entropy formulation to the Kullback–Leibler criterion, and can be written as

$$T = \sum_{i=1}^{N} \left[\left(\frac{y_i}{Y} \right) \cdot \log \left(\frac{y_i/Y}{1/N} \right) \right], \tag{7}$$

where y_i is the income of the ith individual, and Y is the sum over all N agents. The share of aggregated income held by an individual $\frac{y_i}{Y}$ is contrasted to the share that would be held if the distribution were strictly uniform (i.e., if $\frac{y_i}{Y} = \frac{Y/N}{Y} = \frac{1}{N}$). However, rather than seeking the minimizing distribution, the Theil index simply uses the implied cross-entropy to convey the sense of inequality in existing distribution of incomes among individuals. By this measure, the income distribution of an N-membered population can range from 0 (for complete equality) to $\log(N)$, which conveys a maximal level of inequality.

In the article, the Theil measure is used to convey the inequality in the distribution of net benefits that accrue over time to each heterogeneous agent pumping water

from the aquifer, in order to assess the impact of the alternative policy instruments on equity, and to contrast them to the outcome derived by the social planner's outcome. Given the present value net benefit of each player $PVB_i = \sum_{t=1}^{T} \beta^{t-1} \cdot B_i(q_{i,t})$, one can calculate the Theil measure of intertemporal inequality as

$$T = \sum_{i=1}^{N} \left[\left(\frac{PVB_i}{PVB_T} \right) \cdot \log \left(\frac{PVB_i/PVB_T}{1/N} \right) \right], \tag{8}$$

where $PVB_T = \sum_{i=1}^{N} PVB_i$. By using this criterion of inequality, we are able to compare equity outcomes across various policy instruments and compare them with that of the social planner's outcome.

4. Empirical specification of policy instruments and model

4.1. *Empirical parameterization of the model*

Following Feinerman and Knapp (1983) and Feinerman (1988), the simplified hydrology of this example includes the net recharge into the aquifer ($\bar{r}$) inside an equation of motion with condensed notation for γ and $\bar{r}$, representing the translation of volumetric aquifer recharge and net groundwater withdrawal, into units of lift, according to the following definitions:

$$\gamma = \frac{(1 - \theta)}{As} \quad \bar{r} = \frac{(1 - \xi + \theta\xi)I + \hat{r}}{As}. \tag{9}$$

In these expressions, θ represents the deep percolation into the aquifer, while A represents the areal extent of the aquifer, and s is its specific yield. Recharge is given in terms of total inflow into the aquifer, i, a base annual level of recharge $\hat{r}$, and a calibrating parameter ξ. These parameters γ and $\bar{r}$ are both used in the equation of motion (3), which govern the evolution of the state of the groundwater resource over time.

On the basis of these parameter definitions, one can now proceed to carry out the analysis of alternative market-based instruments for reallocation. The essential hydrological parameters used to characterize groundwater usage in Kern County are summarized in Table 1.

Table 1
Hydrological parameters for aquifer model of Kern county

Parameter	Description	Value
A	Area overlying aquifer	1.26 (million acres)
s	Specific yield of aquifer	0.1
θ	Deep percolation coefficient	0.2
e	Energy cost per unit pumping lift	$0.09 acre-ft/ft
h_1	Initial lift (depth-to-water)	220 ft
$\hat{r}$	Reference level for aquifer recharge	1410 ft
ξ	Calibrating parameter for recharge eqn	0.7
I	Average annual surface water inflow	1.90 (million acre-ft)
a	Demand curve intercept	$92.7/acre-ft
b	Demand curve slope	$0.0000175/(acre-ft)^2
i	Real interest rate	0.05
(β)	(discount factor)	(0.952)

4.2. Groundwater policy instruments

The decentralized policy instruments used to capture the efficiency gains realized under central management controls will be of two types—market-based and nonmarket-based. The market-based instrument that will be considered will be that of a tradable quota on groundwater pumping, which is imposed on each of the agents. The nonmarket counterpart to this is a fixed limit on pumping, which is imposed by a central regulator, and which ignores the heterogeneity of the agents and assign a limit based on the "average" type across all individuals. This is a fairly representative type of mechanism, as informational asymmetries typically prevent regulators from imposing highly differentiated instruments on a heterogeneous population of economic agents. The fixed limit is assigned according to the average pumping solution of the social planner, with respect to both time (t) and the number of agents (i), such that

$$\bar{q} = \frac{\sum_{t=1}^{T} \sum_{i=1}^{N} \hat{q}_{i,t}^{SP}}{T \cdot N}, \tag{10}$$

where $\hat{q}_{i,t}^{SP}$ is the optimal, intertemporal solution of the social planner.

The performance of each of these instruments is contrasted with the imposition of a tax,[2] and that of no intervention at all. The tax is calculated on the basis of the social planner's optimization problem, and takes on the average value, over time, of the socially optimal "user cost" given by the term, $\gamma \cdot \beta_{SP} V_q^{SP}(\cdot)$, which is embedded in the Euler condition (4) of the dynamically optimal solution. This term represents the divergence between the marginal cost imputed to groundwater pumping by the social planner and that imputed by the optimality criterion of the agent who extracts myopically, which is simply

$$a - b_i \cdot q_i - e(s - h) = 0, \tag{11}$$

and which leads to the simple, myopic extraction rule given, earlier, by Eq. (5). By equating the average value of this 'user cost,' over the social planner's extraction horizon, to an optimal per-unit tax on pumping (tx), such that $tx = \sum_{t=1}^{T} \{\gamma \cdot \beta_{SP} V_q^{SP}(\cdot)\}_t$, we can recast the myopic extraction problem as

$$q_i^{opt} = \arg \max \left\{ a \cdot q_i - \frac{1}{2} b_i \cdot q_i^2 \right.$$
$$\left. - e(s - h) \cdot q_i - tx \cdot q_i \right\}, \tag{12}$$

and would expect the behavior of the individual agent to conform closely to that of the social planner.

The efficiency gains of both the market and nonmarket instruments are compared with that of the socially optimal solution imposed by the centralized groundwater manager, and also compared in terms of the equity outcomes. Given the perfect information which the idealized social planner possesses, one would expect that the divergences in outcomes also incorporate the effect of information-deficit that is faced by the regulator when imposing decentralized policy instruments. The market-based instrument, however, is better able to handle this deficit, as it relies on the interactions between individual agents, who each have knowledge of their own preferences and who can act accordingly, and is explored in the next subsection.

---

[2] This is nonmarket-based and its revenue is redistributed in lump-sum.

4.3. Tradable quotas in groundwater allocations

In order to characterize the market-based realloca-tions that are considered in this article, one turns toward a regime in which the (otherwise) fixed allocations on groundwater pumping assigned to each heterogenous agent can be traded between individuals. Starting from the basic idea of assigning a maximum quantity—or a quota—of allowable pumping to each economically behaving (and extracting) agent in an economy, one conjectures that each agent has a preference to receiv-ing greater amounts of quota.

Having now defined the demand for quota for a sin-gle agent, one can now extend the discussion to con-sider the problem facing two agents, so as to motivate a de-centralized system of tradable quota allocations. If each agent is assigned rights to a portion of the to-tal allowable limit on pumping, as individual quota, $\bar{q}_1 + \bar{q}_2 = \bar{Q}$, the central planner would solve the op-timization problem (13) in order to re-allocate quota between the agents efficiently:

$$\max_{z \leq \bar{q}_1} \int_0^{\bar{q}_1 - z} \lambda_1(q_1)dq_1 + \int_0^{\bar{q}_2 + z} \lambda_2(q_2)dq_2. \quad (13)$$

The first-order, necessary conditions which charac-terize the frictionless transfer of rights, under this full information, centralized reallocation can be written as $\lambda_1(\bar{q}_1 - z^*) = \lambda_2(\bar{q}_2 + z^*)$.

The decentralized re-allocation of quota described above, however, corresponds to the case where there are no transactions costs facing the two agents, and is a highly idealized environment in which to study a tradable permit scheme. The more realistic case of nonzero transaction costs (τ) gives rise to the realloca-tion of the initial endowment of quota that corresponds to the equilibrium depicted in Figure 1. In this situ-ation, the equilibrium reallocation of initial quota en-dowment between agents corresponds to the condition, $\lambda_2(\bar{q}_2 + \hat{z}) = \lambda_1(\bar{q}_1 - \hat{z}) + \tau$, which drives the opti-mized re-allocation $\hat{z}$ to fall short of that which would result from a cost-free transfer (z^*). The "wedge" cre-ated by the per-unit transaction cost of transfer would widen if the cost τ were to increase further.

By using the inverse demand relationships for each farmer type, ($p = a - b_i q_i, i = 1, 2$), one can integrate them to obtain the total benefit that each farmer receives for a given allocation of quota q, as $B_i(q) = aq - \frac{1}{2}b_i q^2$ and can use this to specify the following equilibrium model. Following Takayama and Judge's (1964) for-mulation for a spatial equilibrium model, the surplus maximizing, decentralized re-allocation of quota can be obtained by solving the following problem:

$$\max_{z_1, z_2 \geq 0} \sum_{i=1}^{2} \left[a \cdot q_i - \frac{1}{2}b_i (q_i)^2 \right] - \sum_{i=1}^{2} \tau_i z_i$$

$$s.t. \quad (14)$$

$$q_1 = \bar{q}_1 - z_1 + z_2$$
$$q_2 = \bar{q}_2 - z_2 + z_1,$$

where the initial allocations for the types 1 and 2 farm-ers is given as $\bar{q}_{i=1,2}$ and the outgoing transfers from

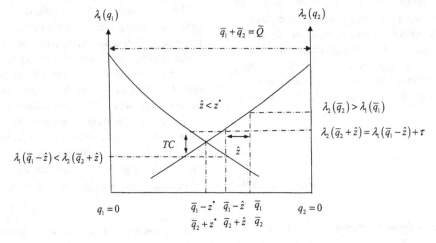

Figure 1. Equilibrium reallocation of quota between two agents.

farmer 1 (z_1) or farmer 2 (z_2) incur a per unit transaction cost of $\tau_{i=1,2}$. The solution to this problem can then be compared with that from an egalitarian redistribution, which would result in a total surplus of $\sum_{i=1}^{2} [a \cdot \hat{q}_i - \frac{1}{2}b_i(\hat{q}_i)^2]$, where $\hat{q}_1 = \hat{q}_2$.

This article applies this to the reallocation of pumping quota, in order to characterize the operation of a market-based policy instrument, so that we can contrast the efficiency gains and equity outcomes with other decentralized policy instruments. In this article one can also ignore the transactions costs, and proceed on the basis of friction-less transfers, for the purpose of simplifying our analysis.

5. Empirical analysis of groundwater policy instruments

5.1. Evaluating the efficiency-equity frontier

By turning back to the benchmark efficiency case, embodied in the social planner's solution, described in Section 3.1, one can evaluate the possible combinations of economic efficiency gains and equity outcomes that are possible in the planner's socially optimized outcome. This can be done by introducing a constraint into the basic formulation of the social planner's optimization problem, described by Eq. (2), such that one obtains the modified problem shown below, which is expressed as an open-loop, finite-horizon problem over T time periods, with an appropriately chosen terminal value function to give the infinite-horizon carry-over value of the level of groundwater stock left in period T (h_T):

$$\max_{\{q_{i,t}\}} \sum_{t=1}^{T} \left[a \cdot q_{i,t} - \frac{1}{2}b_i \cdot q_{i,t}^2 - e(s - h_t) \cdot q_{i,t} \right]$$
$$+ V^{SP}(h_T)$$

$s.t.$

$$h_{t+1} = h_t + \gamma \sum_{i=1}^{N} q_{i,t} - \bar{r} \qquad (15)$$

$$\sum_{i=1}^{N} \left[\left(\frac{PVB_i}{PVB_T} \right) \cdot \log \left(\frac{PVB_i/PVB_T}{1/N} \right) \right] \leq T^{\text{lim}},$$

where T^{lim} is an imposed limit on inequality, and where PVB_i and PVB_T are cumulative measures of the present value of net benefits for each individual i as well as for all agents, as it is measured in each time period of the social planner's horizon.

By "parameterizing" the right hand side value (T^{lim}) of the constraint in Eq. (15), one can observe how the efficiency gains change with the mandated limit on intra-agent inequality. By so doing, a "frontier" can be derived that describes the possible combination of "best" social outcomes that are possible under centralized control, when maximum levels of inequality are defined for a heterogeneous population of economic agents.

The result of this parameterization exercise is shown in Figure 2, which illustrates the trade-off between efficiency and equity—such that higher levels of efficiency gains are possible only when higher levels of inequality are allowed in the solution of the constrained social planner's problem. Figure 2 demonstrates that lower levels of intra-agent inequality, as captured by the Theil cross-entropy measure, come at the expense of efficiency gains, as measured by the calculated quantity in Eq. (6). Underlying this frontier there is also a readjustment in terms of the share of the aggregate net benefits that the individual agents receive, as the upper limit of inequality is lowered successively. As shown in Table 2, the unconstrained socially optimal outcome gives both a higher level of efficiency gains and a higher share of the aggregate net benefits to the first agent, as compared to the last one (the fifth, in the case of this particular numerical experiment with five agents). As the social planner is constrained to adhere to more egalitarian social standards of intertemporal welfare, the share of benefits to the first agent decreases, while that of the last agent increases, as is also shown in Figure 3. By doing this, the percentage of the total gains that are realized under centralized management intervention become more "skewed," as shown in Figure 4, such that they begin to accrue more to that "end" of the spectrum that was the most disadvantaged (in terms of the share of aggregate net benefits received) in the unconstrained case—i.e., the Nth agent. Given that the slope of the demand curve gets steeper for those approaching the Nth agent, the management *gains* (under centralized intervention) get skewed to favor the agents who pump a relatively small amount of groundwater, compared to those toward the "front" of the spectrum, who perceive a larger marginal benefit for a given quantity of pumping, while still allowing the distribution

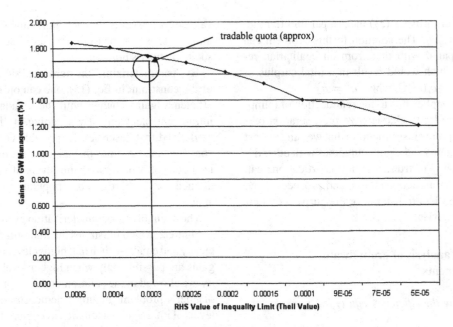

Figure 2. Frontier of efficiency and equity derived from social planner's problem.

of actual aggregate net *benefits* to become more even.

Now in what follows, the reader will see how the social planner's result compares to those under decentralized allocation schemes that employ alternative policy instruments to achieve higher levels of allocative efficiency across all agents.

5.2. Implications for policy

The results in Table 3 describe the outcomes of efficiency and inequality that are achieved under alternative policy instruments within a decentralized

Table 2
Gains in cumulative net benefits to adopting centralized management of groundwater with and without equity constraints

	Total % gain from centralized management	% Share of PV net benefits of first agent	% Share of PV net benefits of Nth agent
Unconstrained social planner problem			
Unconstrained	1.84	20.9	19.1
Constrained social planner problem			
$T \leq 0.0003$	1.74	20.7	19.3
$T \leq 0.0002$	1.62	20.5	19.3
$T \leq 0.0001$	1.4	20.3	19.5

allocation scheme. From these results the reader can see that the gains in efficiency achieved under the policy instruments increases moving towards the market-based instrument, which allows the upper limit (quota) on pumping to be traded across agents. When the tradable instrument is compared to the fixed quota and the pumping tax, one observes that the level of inequality is also much lower, and that nearly all of the gains to centralized groundwater management are captured. By looking at where this result lies in relation to the efficiency-inequality frontier derived from the central planner's solution (Figure 2), one sees that it lies nearly on the "envelope" of equity and efficiency.

Given that the tradable instrument is better able to take into account the individual preferences of each agent in the equilibrium-based allocation resulting from Eq. (14), compared to the nonmarket instruments, it is not surprising that the resulting allocation is both higher in overall allocative efficiency and lower in inequality. Since the nonmarket instruments make no distinction between the agents on the basis of their individual characteristics, there is no overall change in the equity of the allocation, compared to the no-intervention case.

These results illustrate that while the objective of efficiency gain is traded off against equity, within the context of the social planner's problem, there can be

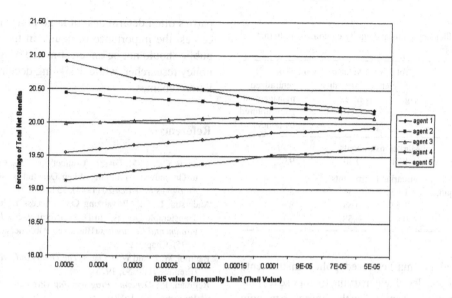

Figure 3. Distribution of net benefits under increasing equality constraints.

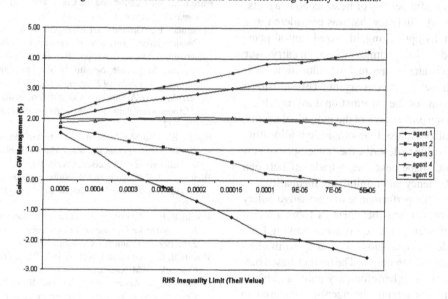

Figure 4. Distribution of efficiency gains under increasing equality constraints.

both efficiency gains and improvements in equity, when one considers decentralized allocations. Since all of the allocations represented by the alternative policy instruments lie "below" the efficiency-equity frontier shown in Figure 2, there is room for improvement in both efficiency and equity—which entails moving in a north-easterly direction toward the envelope of the social planner's problem. The policy maker, who cares about both allocative efficiency and allocative equity

might, therefore, want to consider the instrument that brings them as close as possible to this "frontier."

6. Conclusions

This article made use of a theoretical framework in which to analyze the trade-offs between efficiency and equity, illustrated by an example of groundwater

Table 3

Comparison of efficiency gains and equity outcomes of alternative policy instruments

	Total % efficiency gain	Value of Theil inequality index ($\times 10^{-4}$)	% of centralized management gain captured by policy
Market instruments			
Tradable Pumping Quota	1.71	0.30	93
Nonmarket instruments			
Fixed pumping quota	1.63	0.58	89
Pump tax	1.53	0.58	83
No intervention	0	0.58	0

extraction, and the market-based policy instruments that might be considered, when trying to impose regulation and de-centralized control on the otherwise myopic and mutually harmful actions of heterogenous agents. The benchmark of efficiency that was considered was that of the socially optimizing, idealized central planner, who considers the dynamically optimal carry-over value of groundwater, when making allocation decisions for each heterogeneous agent. This idealized planner faces none of the informational asymmetries, with respect to the preferences of the individual agents, that would confront a less-than-omniscient allocating authority, and is able to describe the "envelope" of best solutions whose shape describes a trade-off between maximizing efficiency and minimizing inequality.

By examining the performance of alternative policy instruments, one can see that there is room for improving both efficiency and equity when moving from the centrally determined quotas and taxes to market-based instruments of regulation. The market-based outcome achieves both higher efficiency gains and lower levels of inequality among the agents, compared to the nonmarket instruments. This result would seem to strengthen the case for market-based instruments, which might otherwise be thought to be prejudicial to less-advantaged groups, due to the commonly held notion that purely market-driven outcomes are hurtful to the poor and more vulnerable groups of society. Policy makers often face politically motivated opposition when making politically sensitive decisions on the adoption of policy measures that may create winners and losers in a heterogeneous (and real) world. While the political influence of the winning or losing

parties often determines, in large part, the policy outcomes, the importance of equity in the minds of the public should not be underestimated or ignored by the policy researcher, while designing decentralized regulation schemes.

References

Allen, R. C., and M. Gisser, "Competition Versus Optimal Control in Groundwater Pumping When Demand is Nonlinear," *Water Resources Research* 20 (1984), 752–756.

Anderson, L. G., "Privatizing Open Access Fisheries: Individual Transferable Quotas," in D. W. Bromley, ed., *Handbook of Environmental Economics* (Blackwell Publishers: Cambridge, MA, 1995). Chapter 20.

Baumol, W. J., and W. E. Oates, *The Theory of Environmental Policy* (Prentice-Hall: NJ, 1975).

Bellman, R., *Dynamic Programming* (Princeton University Press: Princeton, NJ, 1957).

Farrell, J., "Information and the Coase Theorem," *Journal of Economic Perspectives* 1 (1987), 113–129.

Feinerman, E., "Groundwater Management: Efficiency and Equity Considerations," *Agricultural Economics* 2 (1988), 1–8.

Feinerman, E., and K. C. Knapp, "Benefits from Groundwater Management: Magnitude, Sensitivity, and Distribution," *American Journal of Agricultural Economics* 65 (1983), 703–710.

Gisser, M., and D. A. Sanchez, "Competition Versus Optimal Control in Groundwater Pumping," *Water Resources Research* 16 (1980), 638–642.

Hanak, E., *Who Should Be Allowed to Sell Water in California? Third Party Issues and the Water Market* (Public Policy Institute of California: San Francisco, CA, 2003).

Hanley, N., J. F. Shogren, and B. White, *Environmental Economics: In Theory and Practice* (Oxford University Press: New York, 1997).

Howitt, R. E., "The Role of Groundwater in Water Transfers," *Paper Presented at the 13th Biennial Conference on Groundwater, Sept. 21st, 1993* (Sacramento: California, 1993a).

Howitt, R. E., "Economic Effects of 1991 Water Transfers," in R. H. Coppock and M. Kreith, eds., *Proceedings of a Conference Sponsored by the Agricultural Issues and Water Resources Center, California Water Transfers: Gainers and Losers in Two Northern Counties, November 4th, 1992* (University of California: Davis, 1993b).

Joskow, P. L., R. Schmalensee, and E. M. Bailey, "The Market for Sulfur Dioxide Emissions," *American Economic Review* 88 (1998), 669–685.

Kim, C. S., M. R. Moore, J. J. Hanchar, and M. Nieswiadomy, "A Dynamic Model of Adaptation to Resource Depletion: Theory and an Application to Groundwater Mining," *Journal of Environmental Economics and Management* 17 (1989), 66–82.

Kullback, S., *Information Theory and Statistics* (John Wiley: New York, 1959).

Kullback, S., and R. A. Leibler, "On Information and Sufficiency," *Annals of Mathematical Statistics* 22 (1951), 79–86.

McBean, E., "Environmental Effects of 1991 Water Transfers," in R. H. Coppock and M. Kreith, eds., *Proceedings of a Conference Sponsored by the Agricultural Issues and Water Resources Center, California Water Transfers: Gainers and Losers in Two Northern Counties, November 4th, 1992* (University of California: Davis, 1993).

McGartland, A. M., and W. E. Oates, "Marketable Permits for the Prevention of Environmental Deterioration," *Journal of Environmental Economics and Management* 12 (1985), 207–228.

Murphy, J. J., A. Dinar, R. E. Howitt, E. Mastrangelo, S. J. Rassenti, and V. L. Smith, "Mechanisms for Addressing Third Party Impacts Resulting from Voluntary Water Transfers," *Working Paper No. 2003-7* (Department of Resource Economics, University of Massachussetts: Amherst, 2003).

Nalebuff, B., "On a Clear Day, You Can See the Coase Theorem," in P. Dasgupta, and K.-G. Mäler, eds., *The Environment and Emerging Development Issues* 1 (Oxford University Press: Oxford, UK, 1997).

Ostrom, E., *Governing the Commons: The Evolution of Institutions for Collective Action* (Cambridge University Press: Cambridge, UK, 1990).

Shannon, C. E., "A Mathematical Theory of Communication," *Bell System Technical Journal* 27 (1948a), 379–423.

Shannon, C. E., "A Mathematical Theory of Communication," *Bell System Technical Journal* 27 (1948b), 623–656.

Tietenberg, T. H., *Emissions Trading: An Exercise in Reforming Pollution Policy* (Resources for the Future: Washington, DC, 1985).

Takayama, T., and G. C. Judge, "Spatial Equilibrium and Quadratic Programming," *Journal of Farm Economics* 46 (1964), 67–93.

Theil, H., *Economics and Information Theory* (Rand McNally: Chicago, 1987).

Tsur, Y., and A. Dinar, "Efficiency and Equity Considerations in Pricing and Allocating Irrigation Water," *Policy Research Working Paper* 1460 (World Bank: Washington, DC, 1995).

Designing frameworks to deliver unknown information to support market-based instruments

Mark Eigenraam*, Loris Strappazzon**, Nicola Lansdell*,
Craig Beverly*, and Gary Stoneham*

Abstract

This article reports on an Australian auction to procure multiple environmental outcomes: *EcoTender*. EcoTender uses a Catchment Modelling Framework (CMF) to estimate the impact landholder actions have on carbon, terrestrial biodiversity, aquatic function (water quality and quantity), and saline land area. This framework solves the problem of linking paddock-scale land use and management to catchment-scale environmental outcomes. This is the first time a market-based instrument has been fully integrated from desk to field with a biophysical model for the purchase of multiple environmental outcomes. A multiple outcome auction provides several new economic and scientific challenges. This article discusses the EcoTender approach to incorporating agency preferences, modeling the joint production of environmental outcomes and reporting environmental scores. Results indicate that linking EcoTender to the carbon market reduced the cost of procuring the environmental goods by 26%. Further, preliminary estimates show that the environmental gains from scoring the joint production of multiple outcomes are between 30% and 50% to the agency.

JEL classification: Q57, Q58

Keywords: auction; multiple environmental outcomes; carbon; biodiversity; water quality; salinity; EcoTender

1. Introduction

In Australia over the past five years the use of market-based approaches has received considerable attention from both state and federal government agencies. Most notably there has been an allocation of funds to pilot Market Based Instruments (MBI) for the environment by the National Action Plan for Salinity and Water Quality, funded by both the state and federal governments. The National MBI Pilots Program seeks to increase Australia's capacity to use MBIs to manage natural resource issues, in particular to address the problems of salinity and water quality.

MBIs attempt to produce relatively more efficient outcomes than traditional instruments such as grants and fixed price schemes for the provision of environmental services (NMBIWG, 2005). They do this by increasing the environmental outcomes attainable for a given budget or maintaining a given level of pollution at a lower cost.

One of the key reasons that MBIs can obtain more efficient outcomes is their ability to deal with asymmetric information problems. If designed appropriately, MBIs take better account of the type and quality of information held by different players, and how this information is brought to bear in decision making. Auctions and cap and trade programs are examples that illustrate this approach.

However, for MBIs to function effectively they also require a clear definition and measurement of the environmental good(s) in question. The implementation of the national pilot program highlighted the need for new and often unknown information linking actions in

---
Environmental Economics Unit, Department of Sustainability and Environment, Victoria, Australia.
**Economic and Policy Research Branch, Department of Primary Industries, Victoria, Australia.*

the landscape to environmental outcomes (NMBIWG, 2005). For example, an agency may need to determine the impact of a landholder's revegetation on river flows, erosion, and saline land area in the catchment, (watershed). An agency will generally need good biophysical modeling at the farm or paddock level to capture such information, which may be of both a spatial and temporal nature (Grafton, 2005). Sourcing this information is particularly difficult for nonpoint environmental problems, which made up the bulk of the pilots funded under the national MBI program.

The Department of Primary Industries Victoria received funding from the national MBI program to pilot an auction to procure multiple environmental outcomes: The pilot, called EcoTender, procured several environmental goods including saline land, carbon sequestration, terrestrial biodiversity, and aquatic function (Eigenraam et al., 2006). EcoTender was applied to two sub-catchments in Victoria (Figure 1): the Avon Richardson (371,000 ha), and Cornella (47,000 ha).

EcoTender is a multi-outcome extension of the Bush-Tender auction approach, which focused on one environmental outcome, terrestrial biodiversity (Stoneham et al., 2003). The basic rationale for including several goods in the auction is twofold. First, environmental goods may be "jointly supplied." For example, if a land-holder plants trees, this may simultaneously provide carbon sequestration, saline land, and aquatic function benefits. Second, since auctions for environmental goods involve site visits, it may be more economical to visit landholders once in relation to all goods, rather than visiting them separately for each good.

The multiple outcome nature of EcoTender provides several new economic and scientific challenges. EcoTender's predecessor, BushTender, dealt with the asymmetric information problem of revealing land-holders' costs of undertaking actions by using an auction. However, BushTender was a single-good auction, which means that the revelation of agency preferences was relatively straightforward: the budget can be exhausted on the good being procured, as long as there is a sufficient number of competitive bids. The procurement of multiple environmental goods raises the difficult issue of how an agency will order its preferences across several (nonmarket) goods. The agency needs to express the weight (preference) it gives to each good relative to one another in order to choose between bids. Further, there is the interaction between market and nonmarket goods, in this case carbon and other environmental goods, respectively. In EcoTender, there was the potential for landholders to sequester carbon that could be sold to a third party. This had the

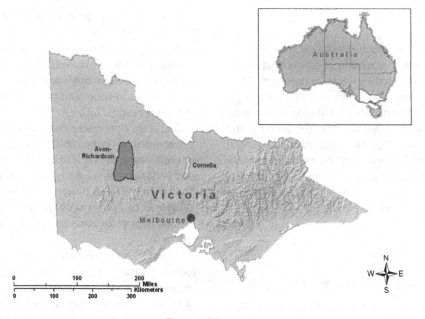

Figure 1. Pilot areas.

potential for reducing the amount a landholder would need to bid in order to provide the other environment outcomes competitively.

Scientifically, EcoTender requires the estimation of an "environmental production function" that can express landholder actions in terms of environmental goods. This raises issues about how to estimate this function and the cost of doing so. The science is further complicated because it needs to connect with the increased economic demands for environmental scoring and expressing preferences for each of the goods in a comparable manner.

In the following section we examine these challenges in more detail. Section 3 provides a description of the EcoTender approach to agency preferences, environmental scoring system, and implementation. In Section 4, we provide results and conclude in Section 5.

2. Multiple outcome design challenges

Auctions for conservation contracts aim to provide private landholders with an incentive to undertake actions that produce environmental outcomes, and truthfully reveal the associated cost. In the past, the Victorian State Government used an auction approach called BushTender to procure one environmental outcome, improvements to terrestrial biodiversity (Stoneham et al., 2003). In it landholders bid to provide additional management of remnant vegetation sites on their farms.

However, there is a growing recognition that many environmental outcomes are jointly produced by the same action(s). For instance, revegetation may jointly produce carbon, improvements to water quality, and wildlife benefits. Wu and Bogess (1999) refer to this as an ecosystem-based approach that recognizes the interaction between alternative environmental benefits and show that an efficient fund allocation must account for both physical production relationships between environmental outcomes and the value of those outcomes. An auction to procure multiple environmental outcomes must take account of all jointly supplied environmental outcomes in order to maximize the benefits of the bids accepted, and to avoid unnecessarily creating negative environmental effects. Wu and Skelton-Groth (2002) developed and applied an empirical model to demonstrate the extent of fund misallocation

when jointly produced environmental benefits are ignored.

If environmental outcomes are jointly supplied, the agency needs to incorporate its demand-side preferences for different environmental outcomes into the bid selection process. Preferences for each of the environmental goods need to be revealed and incorporated into the scoring system in order to determine the quantum of each good to be procured and which bids to accept.

Further complicating the joint production issue and the need for preferences is the production of market goods with public goods. Revegetation for environmental outcomes results in sequestration of carbon, which in some circumstances is a market good. Strappazzon et al. (2003) examined how an agency might deal with jointly supplied environmental goods when one had an associated "market" operating. For example, the case in which both biodiversity maintenance and carbon sequestration are produced from one action, and there is a well-functioning market for carbon sequestration such as an emissions trading system to cut (maintain) greenhouse gases. Strappazzon et al. argue that in such cases an agency should base its scoring and bid choice on the nonmarket (biodiversity) goods, and allow landholders to sell their units of sequestration into the emissions trading system.

2.1. Scientific—environmental production function

The above discussion assumes that the agency can systematically obtain information about the way landholder actions convert to environmental outcomes. In other words, the agency has at its disposal a *production function* for environmental goods. The essential feature of a nonpoint production function is that it allows market-based instruments to be based upon those factors which determine pollution rather that the pollutant itself (Griffin and Bromely, 1982).

The EcoTender pilot required a nonpoint production function that explained landholder actions in terms of environmental outcomes. The environmental outcomes needed to be estimated at the catchment-scale and incorporate both their temporal and spatial characteristics. Equation (1) below shows the general form of a nonpoint production function which can include inputs such as land, water, labour, landuse, soil type, location, slope, rainfall, etc.

$$EBI = \sum_i^N EO\,(a_i, b_i, c_i, \ldots)$$
$$= f\,(land,\ water,\ labour,\ technology,\ SA_i),\quad (1)$$

where EBI is environmental benefit index, for sites $i = 1$ to N; EO, is environmental outcomes $a_i, b_i, c_i, \ldots$ for site i; SA is the site-specific spatial attributes which may include soil type, slope and aspect.

The Catchment Modeling Framework (CMF) was developed to estimate the EBI and present it to potential bidders (landholders) and the purchaser (Victorian Government). The CMF consists of a simulation environment and an interface. The simulation environment operates on a 50-m resolution and incorporates a suite of one-dimensional farming system models into a catchment scale framework with modification to account for lateral flow/recharge partitioning (see Eigenraam et al. [2006] for a detailed description). The farming system models are explicitly linked to a fully distributed three-dimensional groundwater model. The simulation environment has been designed to produce scripts that automate the process of employing MODFLOW for groundwater assessment (McDonald and Harbaugh, 1988; Beverly et al., 2005). The CMF simulates daily soil/water/plant interactions, overland water flow processes, soil loss, carbon sequestration and water contribution to stream flow from both lateral flow (overland flow and interflow) and groundwater discharge (base flow to stream).

Using the interface, outputs from these simulations can be compiled for visualization, interpretation, and interrogation. The interface was also designed to assist in both the pre- and post-processing of spatial and temporal data sets and apply rule-based methods to analyse landscape features. For instance, the extent of current remnant native vegetation is used to assess the spatial significance of alternative revegetation options with respect to connectivity and size. Generally, this type of analysis is rule based—patch size and shape, connectivity of remnant patches, distance from sources of refuge such as river corridors, or sources of replenishment such as large patches of native vegetation. In most cases the rules are developed based on current understanding of the spatial needs of relevant species and incorporated

into the interface for application in different catchments (watersheds). The interface was developed using MATLAB (commercially available software) and was distributed as an executable to nontechnical users and stakeholders.

3. The EcoTender approach

The basic auction design of EcoTender is the same as BushTender, but with a difference in terms of information revelation and, as discussed, the number of goods purchased. In BushTender, very limited information was revealed to landholders in order to prevent collusion. In EcoTender, the agency revealed to the landholders their score for each of the environmental goods (terrestrial biodiversity, aquatic function, saline land) and the distribution of aggregate scores (EBI).

Revealing information about the score indicated to the landholders the relative importance of their site with respect to others. This may provide dynamic benefits when those that are not successful or did not participate recognize that maintaining the quality of remnant sites on their land may have a future benefit, if further auctions were run. Collusion is not thought to be a problem when there are 30 or more bidders and they are a spatially well distributed.

3.1. Estimating environmental outcomes

A key innovation of EcoTender was the application of the CMF to score multiple environmental outcomes. Outputs from the CMF can be characterized based on scale as either specific to the management scale (paddock/farm) or the subcatchment to catchment scale. At the management scale, these include:

- complete water/soil balance (soil moisture, soil evaporation, transpiration, deep drainage, runoff, erosion),
- vegetation dynamics (crop/plantation yield, forest stem diameter, forest density, carbon accumulation).

At the subcatchment to catchment scale outputs include:

- stream dynamics (water quantity and salt loads);

Table 1
Summary of outcomes, service, and significance

Attribute	Change in level of service	Significance
Terrestrial biodiversity	Δ habitat score (maintained or improved)	Biodiversity conservation significance, threatened species conservation status, habitat quality, landscape preference
Aquatic function	Δ water "quality" (erosion t/ha)	(Not applied in pilot)
	Δ water quantity (mm of water / ha)	
Saline land area	Δ saline land (ha groundwater <2m)	Can discriminate, but given equal weighting in pilot
Carbon sequestration	Δ carbon sequestered (tonnes/ha)	N/A

- ground water dynamics (depth to watertable, aquifer interactions, groundwater discharge to land surface and stream).

Modeled outputs from the CMF were needed so purchasers (in this case the Victorian State government) could express their preferences for investment in each of the environmental outcomes. Such investment decisions are often further complicated by the need to compare a range of actions across broad landscapes and different ecosystem types that may produce varying amounts of different outcomes of dissimilar intrinsic value.

The EcoTender pilot uses an information framework that defines each environmental outcome in terms of:

- *service,* the change in the level of service (which includes a sites, ability to provide refuge, diversity, etc.) resulting from the landholder actions and
- *significance,* of the change within the context of the broader landscape.

To estimate the change in level of service, it is necessary to have a standard reference point against which change is measured. Adapting the policy approach applied in Victoria for assessing conservation status of biodiversity assets (NRE, 2002), pre-1750 is used as the "natural benchmark" against which current ecosystem function and change in function arising from landholder management actions in the catchment can be assessed. Under such an approach, the pre-1750 landscape is modelled using the assumed pre-European settlement vegetation types to provide an understanding of native vegetation cover both current and prior to clearing. The current and pre-1750 modeled landscapes can then be used to measure changes in landscape function resulting from landholder interventions based on a progression toward 1750. In this context, the pre-1750 "function" is not a target but simply a reference point

for measuring change. The pre-1750 benchmark approach is also used to estimate the change in native vegetation quality or extent resulting from landholder actions.

Landholder actions in the pilot were limited to *revegetation* and improved *remnant management.* Revegetation requires the establishment of indigenous species in formerly cleared areas to achieve a required target based on the modelled pre-1750 vegetation types for the site. Remnant management involves landholder commitments that improve the native vegetation quality of the site as assessed in comparison to a "benchmark" that represents the average characteristics of a mature and apparently long-undisturbed state for the *same* vegetation type (Parkes et al., 2003; DSE, 2004). In the future other on-farm management actions could be evaluated but further research is required to determine appropriate monitoring and enforcement strategies. Table 1 summarizes the environmental outcomes estimated and scored in the pilot.

3.2. Environmental benefits index (EBI)

A landholder's bid is ranked according to an EBI. The EcoTender EBI ranks a bid based on how much it moves each environmental outcome toward its pre-1750 level[1]. The starting point for calculating the EBI score is to compare the current state of each environmental variable (in aggregate) to its pre-1750 level. These were calculated under steady state conditions for the catchment (Table 2).

Equation (2) was then applied to determine the score for each site assessed in the auction.

$$EBI = \left(\frac{A_i}{D_A} + \frac{S_i}{D_S} + \frac{B_i}{D_B} \right) * 100, \tag{2}$$

---

[1] This pre-dates European settlement of Australia.

Table 2
Pre-1750 and current environment outcome stocks

Environmental outcome	Pre-1750 stock (A)	Current stock (B)	Difference (A-B)
Habitat hectare*	418,140	19,081	−399,059
Saline land area (<2m)	83,702	127,153	+43,451
Aquatic function	27,070	94,320	+67,250

* Applied to both remnant management and revegetation.

where A_i, S_i, and B_i are the aquatic, saline, and biodiversity outcomes, respectively, for site i: and D_A, D_S, and D_B are the respective aquatic, saline, and biodiversity differences from Table 2.

By using this method, the agency is indicating that it is indifferent between a score that reflects a 1% movement toward pre-1750 levels for biodiversity and a score that reflects a 1% movement toward pre-1750 levels of aquatic function. The agency then ranks bids from lowest to highest cost in terms of $/EBI, and chooses successful bids until the budget is exhausted.

Carbon sequestration was not scored as part of the EBI. Instead landholders that sequestered carbon were given two options. A landholder could either:

- Sell carbon sequestration units to a third party for a fixed price ($12 per unit), as if there were a fully functioning market for carbon sequestration services (e.g., an emissions trading system). The third party then assumes rights to such carbon credits.
- Choose to "not sell" the carbon credit, in this case the landholder does not receive $12 per unit, but instead

only receives his or her bid price, and the landholder therefore has the option of selling the carbon credits later.

Table 3 outlines the steps taken to implement the pilot. Each step required a different level and type of communication ranging from very simple to intensive and complex.

3.2. Site assessments and application of CMF

The site assessment step was critical in communicating the "whole of catchment" view to each landholder and providing a relative view of where their property was placed with respect to the various environmental outcomes being sought. This was new information that had not been previously communicated to any landholders in the pilot areas and required the field officers understand the outputs generated by the CMF and be able to communicate this in a simple way.

As such, field officers needed training to understand the principles of the CMF and how to use the purpose-built interface for scoring environmental outcomes. It was important the field officers had a sound appreciation of the CMF in order to address questions posed by landholders about the scoring methodology. The officers needed to feel comfortable with the concept of modeling landscape processes so that during the site visit landholders were left feeling confident in the scoring process and felt the agency was using a reliable methodology. Given the spatial nature of the pilot, a

Table 3
Pilot implementation steps

1. Expressions of interest—landholders located in project areas register an expression of interest through their EcoTender field officer.
2. Site assessments—the EcoTender field officer arranges a site visit with each registered landholder. The field officer assesses the site and advises the landholder on the significance of the site from a range of environmental perspectives, and identifies potential native vegetation management and revegetation options for consideration by the landholder.
3. Development of draft management plans—landholders identify the actions they are prepared to undertake and the field officer prepares a management plan as the basis for a bid.
4. Submission of bids—landholders submit a sealed bid that nominates the amount of payment being sought by them to undertake the agreed management plan.
5. Bid assessment—all bids are assessed objectively on the basis of:
   - the estimated change in the on- and off-site environmental outcomes (the amount of change in environmental outcome);
   - the value of the assets affected by these changes (significance);
   - dollar cost (price determined by the landholder).
   Funds are then be allocated on the basis of 'best-value for money.'
6. Management agreements—successful bidders are able to sign final agreements based on the previously agreed draft management plan (from 3 above).
7. Reporting and payments—periodic payments and reporting occur as specified in the agreement.

system was devised whereby field officers entered GPS data into a hand-held device (IPAQ, similar to a personal organizer with a GPS attachment), which was later down-loaded for use in the CMF.

For each site, field officers used the IPAQ to collect and store GPS coordinates, record current landuse or indigenous vegetation and its current condition (tree density, logs present, weeds, pests, etc.). This was followed by a discussion with the landholders about actions (for inclusion in the management plans) that could be undertaken to provide environmental outcomes. Field officers would indicate to each landholder the type of actions best suited for the site and the minimum standards required.

The field officer then used the interface to down-load the information from the IPAQ to the CMF. They used the interface to validate data already within the model (e.g., ground truth land-use data) and then calculate the environmental outcomes for the site. The field officers also had access to color "maps" that spatially represented the catchment view for each of the four environmental outcomes being sought on a scale from low to high. These catchment views were produced to assist landholders in understanding the idea that environmental outcomes arising from land-use change are spatially variable. They were also designed to provide landholders with a simple relative view of where their property was placed in a catchment environmental outcome context.

4. Results and analysis

The pilot called for expressions of interest from May 2005 and completed site assessments in late October 2005. 84 sites were assessed on a total of 40 farms. Fifty sites were submitted as bids from 21 farms. The total value of these bids was $835,000.

The following notes characterize the bids:

- All bids provided a biodiversity benefit, 46% were for revegetation and the remainder for remnant management.
- 72% provided an aquatic function benefit.
- 8% provided salinity benefits.
- Revegetation bids resulted in an estimated 21,000 tons of sequestered carbon.
- 72% of the bids produced two or more environmental outcomes.

A tender-evaluation panel was appointed to open the bids and enter them into an electronic database. Once all the bids were opened, the cost per environmental benefit was calculated for each bid and the bids were ranked on the basis of "best value for money," lowest cost per unit benefit to highest. Bids were then selected from lowest cost up until the $400,000 budget was exhausted. Figure 2 shows the supply curve for the all submitted bids.

The supply curve shows the rising price of environmental benefits from landholders that bid. The supply curve in Figure 2 does not show the full price range on the y-axis; the price went up to $1,500 per unit environmental benefit. The last bid accepted within the budget ($400,000) cost $14.81 per unit environmental benefit. A total of 360,755 units of EBI were provided by successful bidders.

The following points characterize the accepted bids:

- 31 bids accepted (62% of total) representing 360,755 units of EBI.
- Successful bids covered 259 ha (revegetation 76 ha, native vegetation management 183 ha). This was 70% of the total area offered (353 ha).
- 10,078 tons of carbon of which 8,087 tones were sold by the landholders to a third party, the remaining carbon was retained by landholders.
- Of the bids selected 97% of them had two or more environmental outcomes.

Only a few bids provided a salinity benefit, which can be explained somewhat by the size and location of the sites. The largest site was 45 ha which is sufficient to provide salinity benefits. However, it was located in an area of the catchment that is not amendable to providing salinity benefits. Other smaller sites were located in areas of the catchment amenable to providing salinity benefits, but they were not large enough.

Landholders that undertook revegetation could sell their carbon in the auction to a third party for $12.00/t or retain it. Sixty one percent of those that produced carbon elected to sell it in the auction. In order to investigate the impact of removing the opportunity to sell the carbon, the bids were adjusted upwards and reordered. This was done by adding the full price of the carbon sold to the bids reflecting the cost landholders would have to bear if they could not sell their carbon. This increased the cost of some bids (those selling carbon), which made it possible to purchase only 355,486 units

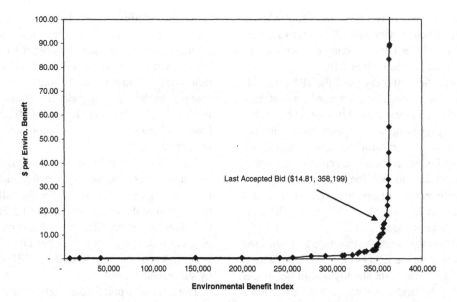

Figure 2. EcoTender supply curve.

of EBI, a fall of 5,269 units. Alternatively if the agency tried to maintain the 360,755 units of EBI and select from the higher cost bids it would cost approximately $544,000, a 26% cost increase.

Assuming the EBI in Eq. (2) above accurately reflects the preferences of the purchaser, it is possible to determine the loss in EBI if only one environmental good were used to select bids. When the bids are re-ordered based on aquatic function alone (A, in Eq. (2) above) and the budget is held constant only 171,635 units of EBI are attained; a fall of 52%. If the same procedure is followed for terrestrial biodiversity only 244,493 units of EBI are attained; a fall of 32%. There are not sufficient saline benefits to exhaust the budget and complete the calculations. The results for aquatic function and terrestrial biodiversity indicate a loss in utility (EBI) where the agency does not take account of joint production. Further, it indicates the importance of accurately determining the preferences and in turn the method for aggregating multiple environmental outcomes.

5. Concluding comments

The EcoTender pilot used an auction to procure multiple environmental outcomes as part of a larger market-based instruments program run by the Australian government. EcoTender represents a significant ad-

vance toward implementing a comprehensive market-based approach to managing environmental problems. The design of a successful auction requires an agency to process two important pieces of information. First, the cost of landholder actions (which is generally private [landholder] information). Second, highly complex information about the effect that each landholder's actions have on environmental outcomes (that we have generally called "unknown information"). Both pieces of information are important to ensure that an agency uses taxpayer funds cost effectively.

Whilst BushTender used an auction mechanism to reveal the cost information, this is the first time a market-based policy has been fully integrated from *desk to field* with a biophysical simulation model to procure multiple outcomes. EcoTender overcomes the problem of unknown information: a nonpoint production function such as the CMF links paddock-scale land use and management to environmental outcomes (that occur at both the paddock and catchment scale).

The CMF takes account of biophysical processes for soil erosion, water, carbon, and saline land to estimate environmental outcomes. Biodiversity algorithms evaluate the current location of native vegetation and biodiversity landscape preference, and they assess the future spatial needs of key mobile fauna species. The CMF is the only framework (the authors are aware of) that has brought together both biophysical and ecosystem information at such a fine level of resolution, and combined it with a procurement mechanism, such as an auction. The framework has demonstrated the importance of joint production in environmental outcomes and the heterogeneous nature of the landscape in terms of environmental outcomes at the farm level. Preliminary estimates show that the gains from considering joint production, as against single environmental goods, could be between 30% and 50% to the agency.

The removal of the opportunity to sell carbon to a third party increased the cost of procuring the environmental outcomes by 26%. This result indicates that an active carbon market makes the cost of procuring public goods lower when they are jointly produced. Further, as the price of carbon increases the cost of those public goods will fall.

Many authors have argued for greater disaggregation of the environmental production function (Shortle and Dunn, 1986; Just and Antle, 1990, Babcock et al., 1997). This enables better targeting and hence improved policy efficiency. However, the costs of highly disaggregated spatial simulation models have been seen as prohibitive. We acknowledge the potentially large upfront investment costs required to build models such as the CMF. However, this cost needs to be amortized over the life of the technology: policy makers can use the information incorporated in the CMF in subsequent applications of EcoTender or in other programs.

The CMF enables the Victorian government to accurately determine the environmental outcomes from landholder actions on any site within the landscape. The CMF can be readily calibrated to any catchment where there is sufficient data. Further, the framework can be readily updated as new data becomes available. Hence, the CMF approach is fully transferable to other regions within Australia and overseas. The CMF requires standard information such as soil type, slope, elevation, and land use, all of which are important for other policy requirements.

References

Babcock, B., P. Lakshminarayan, J. Wu, and D. Zilberman, "Targeting Tools for the Purchase of Environmental Amenities," *Land Economics* 73 (1997), 325–339.

Beverly, C., M. Bari, B. Christy, M. Hocking, and K. Smettem, "Predicted Salinity Impacts from Land Use Change: Comparison between Rapid Assessment Approaches and Detailed Modelling Framework," *Australian Journal of Experimental Agriculture* 45 (2005), 1453–1469.

Department of Sustainability and Envirnment (DSE), *Vegetation Quality Assessment Manual—Guidelines for applying the habitat hectares scoring method. Version 1.3* (Victorian Government:East Melbourne, 2004).

Eigenraam, M., L. Strappazzon, N. Lansdell, A. Ha, C. Beverly, and J. Todd, "EcoTender: Auction for Multiple Environmental Outcomes. National Action Plan for Salinity and Water Quality," *National Market Based Instruments Pilot Program. Project Final Report* (2006).

Grafton, Q., "Evaluation of Round One of the Market Based Instrument Pilot Program," *National Market Based Instruments Working Group* (2005).

Griffin, R., and D. Bromley, "Agricultural Runoff as a Non-point Externality: A Theoretical Development," *American Journal of Agricultural Economics* 68 (1982), 668–677.

Just, R., and J. Antle, "Interactions Between Agricultural and Environmental Policies: A Conceptual Framework," *American Economic Association Papers and Proceedings* 80 (1990), 197–202.

McDonald, M. C., and A. W. Harbaugh, "MODFLOW, A Modular Three-Dimensional Finite Difference Ground-Water Flow Model," *Chapter A1 Open-file report 83-875* (US Geological Survey: Washington, DC, 1988).

Natural Resources and Environment (NRE), *Victoria's Native Vegetation Management: A Framework for Action* (The State of Victoria, Department of NRE: East Melbourne, 2002).

NMBIWG, "National Market-based Instruments Pilot Program: Round 1," *An Interim Report* (National Market Based Instrument Working Group, December, 2005) http://www.napswq.gov.au/mbi/pubs/interim-report.pdf.

Parkes, D., G. Newell, and D. Cheal, "Assessing the Quality of Native Vegetation: The 'Habitat Hectares' Approach," *Ecological Management and Restoration* 4 (2003), S29–S38.

Shortle, J., and J. Dunn, "The Relative Efficiency of Agricultural Source Water Pollution Control Polcies," *American Journal of Agricultural Economics* 68 (1986), 668–677.

Stoneham, G., V. Chaudhri, A. Ha, and L. Strappazzon, "Auctions for Conservation Contracts: An Empirical Examination of Victoria's Bush Tender Trial," *Australian Journal of Agricultural and Resource Economics* 47 (2003), 477–500.

Strappazzon, L., A. Ha, M. Eigenraam, C. Duke, and G. Stoneham, "The Efficiency of Alternative Property Right Allocations When Farmers Produce Multiple Environmental Goods under the Condition of Economies of Scope," *Australian Journal of Agricultural and Resource Economics* 47 (2003), 1–27.

Wu, J., and W. G. Boggess, "The Optimal Allocation of Conservation Funds," *Journal of Environmental Economics and Management* 38 (1999), 302–321.

Wu, J. W., and K. Skelton-Groth, "Targeting Conservation Efforts in the Presence of Threshold Effects and Ecosystem Linkages," *Ecological Economics* 42 (2002), 313–331.

Tariff line analysis of U.S. and international dairy protection

Jason H. Grant*, Thomas W. Hertel**, and Thomas F. Rutherford***

Abstract

General equilibrium (GE) models have been criticized because of policy aggregation issues. Partial equilibrium (PE) models can be more disaggregated but do not account for the economy-wide effects from trade reform. In this article, we illustrate a methodology that combines a fully disaggregated, subsector (PE) model with a standard GE framework permitting us to extend GE analysis to the tariff line. We offer some insight into the aggregation errors implicit in standard GE analyses by comparing our PE/GE approach to that of GE only under a global dairy liberalization experiment. Our PE/GE approach allows for a comprehensive treatment of tariff rate quotas at the sub-sector level across narrowly defined product lines.

JEL classification: F01, F17, Q17, Q18

Keywords: tariff-rate quotas; mixed-complementarity problem; partial equilibrium; general equilibrium; Doha development agenda

1. Introduction

Market access has been at the core of eight trade liberalizing rounds of the General Agreement on Tariffs and Trade (GATT) and its successor, the World Trade Organization (WTO). In the Uruguay Round (UR) of multilateral trade negotiations, agriculture was brought under the disciplines of the GATT for the first time. However, economists tend to agree that the major achievement of the Uruguay Round Agreement on Agriculture (URAA) was in achieving transparency of import protection and in limiting the type and scope of border measures countries could use, rather than creating significant improvements in market access (Josling et al., 1996; Josling and Rae, 1999; Meilke et al., 2001; Tangermann, 2001; Vanzetti and Peters, 2003). It is up to negotiators in the DDA to generate further market access by reducing the levels of bound tariffs established during the UR and providing further market access opportunities in tariff-quota trade.[1]

One of the cornerstones of the URAA was the "tariffication" process.[2] Tariffs achieve transparency of import protection and are generally preferred by exporting nations because they are predictable, are nondiscriminatory when applied on an MFN basis, and are easier to negotiate in future trade rounds. However, many developed countries chose to convert their nontariff barriers into specific tariffs or establish systems tariff-rate-quotas, which made visible the high levels of protection previously hidden by nontariff barriers. TRQs are two-tiered tariffs characterized by a low tariff applied to a fixed amount of imports (the tariff quota) and usually a much higher tariff applied to out-of-quota imports. Forty-three WTO Members have TRQs designated in their tariff schedules for a total of 1,427 individual quotas (de Gorter and Boughner, 1999).

*Department of Agricultural Economics, Purdue University, West Lafayette, IN, USA.

**Department of Agricultural Economics, Purdue University, West Lafayette, IN, USA. Center for Global Trade Analysis, Purdue University, West Lafayette, IN.

***Ann Arbor, MI, USA.

[1] Article 20 of the URAA committed WTO Members to negotiating a new round of negotiations on agriculture.

[2] This process mandated WTO Members to convert their nontariff barriers (NTBs) into bound tariff equivalents to reduce them by an average of 36% over six years for developed countries and 24% over 10 years for developing countries. Least Developed Countries were exempt from tariff reductions but either had to go through the tariffication process or bind their tariffs creating a ceiling which could not be increased in the future.

Furthermore, TRQs are pervasive in international dairy trade and many over-quota tariff rates are complex, combining elements of specific and *ad valorem* duties (Meilke and Lariviére, 1999; Skully, 1999).

Computable general and partial equilibrium (CGE and CPE) models that quantify the global benefits of trade liberalization have become common fixtures in recent trade negotiations. To remain tractable, CGE models require a large degree of aggregation across product lines, across different policy instruments, and across regions. Partial equilibrium (PE) models on the other hand are often more disaggregated but lack internal consistency and have nothing to say about the economy-wide effects of trade reform or how reform in other sectors might interact with those in the target sectors. Such intersectoral trade-offs are the hallmark of successful trade negotiations. It is because of the heterogeneity in protection instruments, the frequent use of specific tariffs, the multitude of tariff-rate quotas (TRQs) and detailed nomenclatures, and the fact that many countries mix different policy tools at very disaggregate levels that most CGE and CPE models face a serious index number problem since an aggregate index of the implied protection rate is needed. Bureau and Salvatici (2003) argue that this is one of the main reasons why policy results are often fundamentally different when analyzing the same set of policy scenarios. These issues are particularly important in the international dairy complex which is the focus of this article.[3]

In this article we illustrate a new methodology that combines partial and general equilibrium modeling, permitting us to extend GE analysis to the tariff line. We call this the PE/GE approach to trade policy modeling. Specifically, we apply a decomposition procedure (sequential recalibration) which involves coordinated solution of both PE and GE models in selected sectors. A mixed-complementarity formulation subsector (PE) model is used to represent trade policy at the tariff line

including tariff-rate quotas and is calibrated to 2001 HS6 policy levels. Equilibrium outcomes in the PE model are iteratively introduced in a modified Global Trade Analysis Project (GTAP [GE]) model tracking liberalization results from global dairy reform. Our analysis offers a means of quantifying approximation errors in conventional GE analyses. Finally, we exploit the tariff line detail in the sub-sector (PE) model and examine TRQ reform options *vis-á-vis* quota expansion.

This article is organized into six sections. Section 2 describes the current policy environment in the U.S. and international dairy markets. Section 3 introduces our model and framework. Section 4 discusses the data. In Section 5, we present the results and in Section 6 we conclude and highlight future research directions.

2. Dairy policy environment

To demonstrate our approach we use the heavily protected U.S. dairy sector as our case study. Dairy imports accounted for the largest share of U.S. agricultural imports in 2001 totaling U.S.$1.5 billion (Nicholson and Bishop, 2004). The U.S. is also the world's largest dairy importer with fresh and specialty cheeses (HS 040690) accounting for over half of U.S. imports in terms of value. The European Union (EU), New Zealand, Australia, Argentina, and Canada are the world's largest dairy exporters. Together, these countries supplied approximately 90% of U.S. dairy imports in 2001 and almost 95% of U.S. fresh cheese imports with EU cheese exports accounting for the largest share. These countries clearly have a lot at stake when it comes to liberalizing U.S. dairy policy.

Dairy protection in the U.S. comes under a variety of different guises. Figure 1 shows the 24 HS6 commodity lines making up the dairy sector. For 15 out of 24 dairy commodities the U.S. has an *ad valorem* tariff policy ranging from 0% to 20%[4]. The U.S. also applies specific tariffs with an *ad valorem* equivalent impact ranging from 0% to 52% for all but one of the 24 tariff lines and underscores the importance of specific tariffs in the analysis of international dairy liberalization. The U.S. has also established a system of tariff-rate-quotas

---

[3] Meilke and Lariviére (1999) document the level of product aggregation for 16 simulation studies of world and/or regional dairy trade. For 12 out of 16 studies, dairy was treated as just a single commodity sector; for two studies, dairy was disaggregated into five commodities; and two studies disaggregated dairy into seven product lines. Thus, while a high degree of product aggregation has been required from a practical standpoint in GE and PE models, to date these models have been limited in their ability to analyze complex policies among several product lines comprising the dairy sector.

---

[4] Figure 1 only shows the mean tariff rate over all partners for a particular HS6 product line.

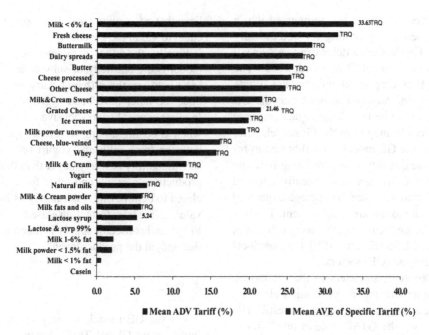

Figure 1. Import protection in the U.S. dairy market. *Source:* CEPII (2001) and author's calculations.

(TRQs) under the URAA for a remarkable 18 out of 24 HS6 product lines (Figure 1). TRQs combine elements of quantitative restrictions (the quota) and tariffs (in- and over-quota tariff rates) which creates a number of modeling difficulties. First, if import demand is relatively weak and less than the quota level, regime one applies where the in-quota tariff is binding. In regime one, the TRQ operates as a simple tariff and quota rents do not accrue. If import demand is stronger such that imports occur just at the quota level, the situation is akin to a pure quota and domestic prices are determined by the intersection of the quota level and the import demand function (regime two). In regime two, quota rents accrue and are equal to the shadow value of the quota multiplied by in-quota imports. Finally, if import demand is strong, imports can enter over-quota with a much higher tariff rate applying (the over-quota tariff) and quota rents accrue on all in-quota imports.[5]

In summary, illustrating the impacts of complex trade policy instruments such as TRQs in a CGE framework presents trade policy analysts with a complex

situation (Elbehri et al., 2003). Preferentially applied tariff rates introduce large dispersions in U.S. tariff rates applied to different exporters; in addition, quotas are allocated bilaterally to preferred exporters (i.e., U.S. dairy TRQs); and both tariffs and TRQs are defined at very disaggregated levels of commodity detail. Thus, modeling efforts must be able to determine bilateral trade, as opposed to net trade typical of many PE models, and such efforts must be sufficiently disaggregated if we want to model trade policy seriously. Our PE/GE approach nests an HS6 disaggregated, source-differentiated sub-sector model in a standard GE framework, thereby representing an important advancement over previous studies using applied GE or PE methods.

3. Methods

We use the framework of Böhringer and Rutherford (2005) in combining a "top-down" model with a "bottom-up" energy modeling and apply it to GE and PE modeling of international trade. The sub-sector (PE) model is implemented as a mixed-complementarity program (MCP) and mirrors the broad structure of the GTAP model (Rutherford, 1995). Products are differentiated by country of origin (Armington, 1969), and

___
[5] Quota rents can accrue to the importer, the exporter, or some combination of the two. Who gets the rents depends on the method of TRQ administration and this can make a big difference in the welfare analysis. See Skully (1999) for more details on the possible administrative choices of TRQs.

imports from different sources are aggregated into a composite good before substituting for domestically produced output. For the GE model, we use version 6.0 of the GTAPinGAMS model (Rutherford, 2005). The basic idea of the PE/GE approach incorporates simple isoelastic demand and supply functions into the GE model representing the industry's aggregate response to aggregated prices coming from the PE model. After each PE solution, the GE model is recalibrated to reflect new aggregate quantity levels emerging from the PE model solution. Convergence is typically achieved after just a few iterations, once the aggregate quantity predictions by both models are in agreement. To illustrate our approach, we focus on global dairy reforms in 14 regions, with 24 HS6 subsector (PE) dairy products and 15 other aggregate (GE) sectors.[6]

There are three key parameters in the PE model. First, we set the import-import substitution elasticity (σ^M) to be twice as large as the import-domestic elasticity (σ^D) following the GTAP "rule of two." In our base case in the PE model, we adopt the values used in GTAP for the import-import ($\sigma^M = 7.3$) and import-domestic ($\sigma^D = 3.65$). These are clearly the most important parameters in this modeling exercise, as they determine the degree to which reductions in the tariffs will affect trade flows within the sector. As a sensitivity exercise, we vary these elasticities by a factor of two in the PE model, in order to assess the impact of greater substitutability in demand.[7]

Aggregate output in the PE model which is determined by the GE model can be transformed amongst 24 different subsector products (Figure 1), based on a constant elasticity of transformation (σ^T). This elasticity governs the ease with which the dairy sector can change its output mix. Because most dairy products share the same basic input—fluid milk—we are inclined to believe that σ^T is quite large, in absolute value and set it equal to 4.0 in the baseline.[8]

Finally, the other parameter required by our PE model is the elasticity of substitution in consumption (σ^C) between the different dairy subsector products, once the latter have been aggregated across sources. In other words: how responsive are consumers to price when choosing among different types of cheeses, or between fresh milk and yogurt products? While this substitutability is surely larger than that between dairy products as a group and other food items, we are inclined to believe this is not nearly as large, in absolute value, as the transformation elasticity. We set σ^C equal to 1.0, and subsector supply is much more elastic than demand, at the product level.[9]

4. Data

For the GE model, we rely on version 6.0 of the widely used Global Trade Analysis Project (GTAP) model detailed in Hertel (1997) and Dimaranan (2006). For the PE model, we draw from a couple of different sources for disaggregated trade and policy information in the year 2001. HS6 tariff data are from the Market Access Maps (MAcMap) database (Bouët et al., 2004).[10] Bilateral trade data at the HS6 level are from CEPII's BACI database. However, GTAP (GE) trade data are provided by Mark Gehlhar (Gehlhar, 2007).[11] For this reason, we reconcile CEPII's trade data with GTAP's bilateral trade flows by (1) eliminating intra-EU trade from the GTAP database since these flows are not available in the CEPII data, and (2) adjusting CEPII's sub-sector dairy trade flows to match GTAP's

---

[6] The regions are: the U.S., Canada (CAN), Australia (AUS), New Zealand (NZL), Argentina (ARG), Japan (JPN), Mexico (MEX), EU-15 (EU), Rest of Europe (ROE), Rest of Asia and Oceania (SAO), South America (SAM), Middle East and North Africa (MNA), Central America and Caribbean (LAM), Rest of Africa (ROA).

[7] The Armington parameter has been estimated with a fair degree of precision on disaggregated dairy import data for the U.S. and several other importers (cf. Hertel et al., 2004). In that study the Armington parameter was constrained to be equal for all product lines in the dairy sector. It is likely that its value varies considerably between relatively homogeneous products such as skim milk powder, and more differentiated products, such as cheese.

[8] In the short run, for very large increases in a given dairy product, capacity may become a constraint, and this can be evaluated *ex post* to see whether it is an issue.

[9] The PE model does not require an elasticity of transformation between domestic sales and exports. We set this to infinity matching our assumption in the GTAP (GE) model.

[10] MAcMap has been developed jointly by the International Trade Center in Geneva (ITC) and Paris-based CEPII. The dataset includes an exhaustive list of applied and bound *ad valorem* and specific tariffs, indicators of TRQs, as well as taking into account an extensive list of tariff preferences. Since this is done for all merchandise trade, MAcMap offers a unique snapshot of world protection and trade flows for 163 countries and 208 partners in 2001.

[11] CEPII stands for the Centre d'Etudes Prospectives et d'Informations Internationales and is France's leading institute for research on the international economy (www.cepii.org).

dairy level bilateral flows at the industry level. At this point both PE and GE models agree on the total amount of dairy industry trade between partner countries in the model.

To incorporate the TRQs into the sub-sector (PE) model, we draw on the more extremely disaggregated, HS8 TRQ information contained in the Agricultural Market Access Database (AMAD, 2002).[12] We focus on a particular U.S. TRQ regime, HS 040690, which includes cheese except fresh, grated, processed, or blue-veined (herein referred to as specialty cheese).[13] Given the limitations imposed by our source data on bilateral trade flows, the PE model is detailed at the HS6 digit level, so we aggregate AMAD's HS8 digit TRQ information to the HS6 digit level. Because the quota level is defined in terms of physical quantities, we collected U.S. bilateral import quantities at the HS8 digit level from the U.S. International Trade Center's (USITC) Interactive Tariff and Trade Data Web for the year 2001 (USITC, 2006). Next, we aggregated import quantities and the quota level across model countries using trade values as weights and calculated a quota fill rate, which vary bilaterally, by dividing the quantity imported by the quota level. Once fill ratios were aggregated to the HS6 digit level, in- and over-quota tariff rates were assigned (bilaterally) using MAcMap tariff data.[14]

Our calculations revealed that, 8 out of our 14 model countries faced a bilateral TRQ policy in the U.S. import market and 6 out of 8 of these countries were over-

quota (i.e., a fill ratio greater than one). For these six countries, quota fill ratios ranged from a high of 2.22 in the case of South American countries to a low of 1.12 for Canada. In-quota tariff rates ranged from a high of 9.5% applied to South American specialty cheese imports to a low of 5% applied to EU trade. Over-quota tariff rates ranged from a high of 47% applied to South America to a low of 28% applied to New Zealand imports.

5. Results

The results are organized in two sets of experiments. In the first experiment, we quantify the size of aggregation errors implicit in current GE analyses of agricultural trade liberalization. We do this by simulating a global dairy liberalization experiment, once with a standard GE-only simulation using the GTAP model and then re-running the same experiment with our extended PE/GE framework which includes dairy trade policy at the tariff line. We compare market variables and welfare results from the standard GTAP model to those from our PE/GE model. In scenario two we focus on the sub-sector (PE) model and discuss the effects of TRQ liberalization in the U.S using one HS6 commodity line (specialty cheese) as our case study. In this scenario, we progressively expand the bilateral tariff quotas until they become nonbinding for all countries, tracking bilateral in- and over-quota imports and tariff quota rents associated with liberalization.

5.1. Experiment 1: Global dairy liberalization

Figure 2 depicts the welfare results defined in terms of equivalent variation as a percentage of total domestic demand, for six representative countries and two parameter combinations ($\sigma^T = 4$; $\sigma^C = 1$; $\sigma^M = 3.65, 7.3$). The first thing to note is how well the standard GTAP (GE) model does in getting aggregate welfare right when the GE and PE parameters are equal ($\sigma^T = 4$; $\sigma^C = 1$; $\sigma^M = 7.3$). For example, in New Zealand's (NZL) case, moving to a free trade situation in dairy results in a 5.4% increase in welfare (measured as a percentage of total dairy consumption) as predicted by the GTAP model. Similarly, our PE/GE model predicts a 4.8% increase in welfare when the parameters are equal and a slightly larger

---

[12] AMAD (2002) is available at: www.amad.org. The AMAD database details an exhaustive list of bilateral quota allocations for US TRQ policy. An interesting element of US TRQ policy is the Most Favored Nation (MFN) quota market which specifies a quota level available for any country including countries with bilateral allocations. We do not incorporate this type of competition or tradable quotas into the current modeling framework, but is a topic addressed in another paper of the authors.

[13] Indeed, imports of specialty cheese (HS 040690) are the most important dairy product imported in the U.S. accounting for over half of the U.S. dairy import bill in 2001.

[14] It should be noted that the over-quota tariff rates for specialty cheese in AMAD (2002) are 20–40% higher than the tariff rates in CEPII's MAcMap dataset. Much of this can be attributed to CEPII's fill ratio calculation which shared out the "total" U.S. cheese quota equally among partners and then calculated filling rates. However, we recognize, as does AMAD (2002), that the cheese quota is allocated bilaterally and can lead to very different tariff rates depending on which TRQ regime is binding (correspondence with David Laborde, 2006). Nevertheless, the results are quite illustrative even with the lower CEPII tariff rates.

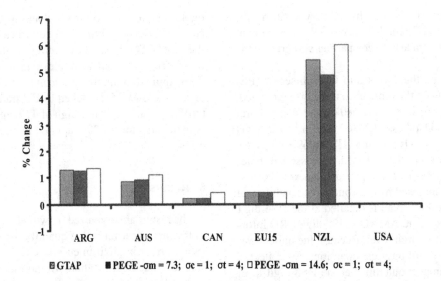

Figure 2. Welfare impacts of global dairy liberalization: percent of national dairy expenditure.

6.1% increase when we double σ^M *($\sigma^M = 14.6$)*. The large welfare increase in New Zealand is no surprise since New Zealand is the world's top dairy exporter with very low rates of protection and subsidies granted to dairy producers, and stands to gain the most from global dairy reform.

Figure 3 shows the output response by both models for the same six countries and parameter settings. Again the GTAP (GE only) model does a remarkably

good job in predicting the aggregate response of aggregate output compared to our PE/GE model for the base case elasticities. However, when we allow for greater import-import substitution in the disaggregated PE/GE model, the GE-only model sharply under-predicts dairy output. For example, the dairy sector output response in Australia (AUS), another large dairy exporter, is 40% using GE only model and slightly larger (47%) in the PE/GE model when the Armington parameters

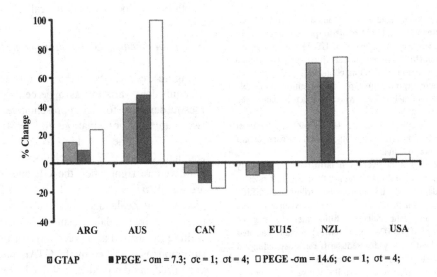

Figure 3. Output impacts of global dairy liberalization: percent of national dairy expenditure.

Table 1
Regression results for bilateral trade comparison—global dairy liberalization

Parameter settings						
	(1)	(2)	(3)	(4)	(5)	(6)
	$\sigma_T = 4$[a]	$\sigma_T = 4$[a]	$\sigma_T = 4$[a]	$\sigma_T = 4$[a]	$\sigma_T = 2$[a]	$\sigma_T = 2$[a]
	$\sigma_C = 1$	$\sigma_C = 1$	$\sigma_C = 2$	$\sigma_C = 2$	$\sigma_C = 1$	$\sigma_C = 2$
	$\sigma_M = 1$	$\sigma_M = 2$	$\sigma_M = 1$	$\sigma_M = 2$	$\sigma_M = 2$	$\sigma_M = 2$
Intercept	13.85	12.57	−3.22	−18.15	51.4	22.84
	(43.79)	(286.9)	(2.00)	(295.1)	(264.9)	(274.8)
Slope[b]	0.90	5.68	1.04	6.04	5.12	5.44
	(0.07)	(0.46)	(0.003)	(0.49)	(0.44)	(0.46)
R^2	0.50	0.48	0.99	0.50	0.47	0.48
No. obs.	157	157	157	157	157	157

[a] σ_T denotes subsector transformation elasticity; σ_C denotes the elasticity of substitution; σ_M denotes the sub-sector Armington elasticity.

[b] In all regressions the slope variable is the GTAP (GE) simulated data as a predictor of the simulated PE/GE trade.

Note: Each regression (1–6) is run separately. Standard errors are in parentheses.

are equal in both models. However, when we double σ^M, our PE/GE model predicts an output response of almost 100% in Australia compared to just 40% predicted by the GE-only model.

Finally, to get an idea of how well the GE-only and PE/GE models agree on the change in bilateral trade flows, Table 1 presents some simple regression results. In each regression, the simulated PE/GE bilateral trade flows are regressed on an intercept and the simulated GTAP (GE only) trade flow response. In this way, we can judge how well the GE-only model predicts our PE/GE trade flow response. Six regressions are reported in Table 1, one for each set of sub-sector parameters. The regression results indicate that when the Armington elasticities (σ^M) are equal (columns 1 and 3), the GE-only model performs quite well as a predictor of PE/GE bilateral trade flows. In parameter setting (1), a significant slope coefficient of 0.90 suggests that GTAP trade flows would have to be scaled down by only 10% on average to match our PE/GE model. The GE and PE/GE models are even closer in parameter setting (3) with a slope coefficient of 1.04. However, when we double σ^M for sub-sector trade in the PE/GE model, the results differ widely. For example, in column 4, a statistically significant slope coefficient of 6.04 suggests that the GE-only model underpredicts PE/GE trade flows and would have to be scaled up by a factor of six. Similar regression results are obtained for other parameter combinations in which σ^M equals 7.3 (columns 2, 5, and 6).

5.2. Experiment 2: Liberalizing bilateral U.S. tariff-quotas

In experiment two we gradually liberalize the U.S. tariff-quota policy on *specialty cheeses only* (HS 040690) by expanding the quota level in increments of 10% until the quota is no longer binding for all countries. We start by tracking over-quota imports depicted in Figure 4. If the DDA were to negotiate a 20% quota expansion, Canada (CAN) would be the only country to move out of regime three, according to our estimates. A 40% expansion in the quota level eliminates over-quota imports from New Zealand (NZL) as well. Figure 5 tracks the level of in-quota imports and includes an additional country, ROE (Rest of Europe) which is not over-quota in the baseline. As expected, in-quota imports increase (linearly up to the point where the quota becomes nonbinding) for all countries. However, there are two points worth emphasizing. First in the baseline, U.S. imports of ROE specialty cheese enter under the quota level. As we expand the quota level, however, ROE in-quota imports are largely displaced as the U.S. substitutes toward CAN and NZL cheese products when these countries move out of regime three and prices fall.

Second, we see immediately the ability of our model to capture the impact of the regime changes inherent in tariff-quota trade. As soon as the exporters fall into regime one (quota no longer binding), in-quota imports begin to be displaced by the more severely constrained

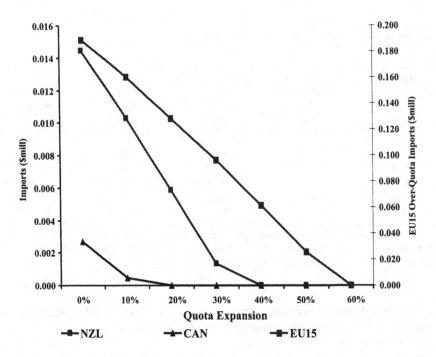

Figure 4. Over-quota imports with progressive bilateral quota liberalization.

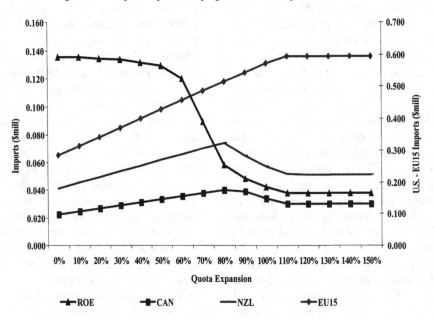

Figure 5. U.S. in-quota imports from selected exporters.

exporters (EU in this case). This is even clearer in Figure 6, which tracks tariff-quota rents on a bilateral basis. For example, tariff quota rents in NZL, an important source for U.S. imports, increase at the same rate as the EU15 when both countries remain over-quota (case 3). However, with sufficient quota expansion (40%), New Zealand enters regime two and tariff quota rents dissipate quickly, falling to zero (regime

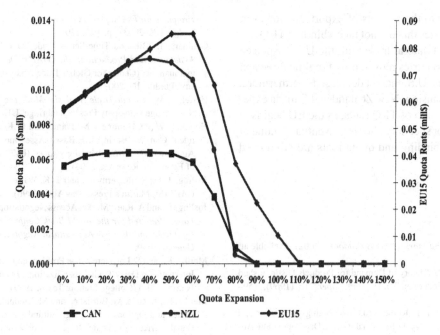

Figure 6. Value of tariff quota rents for selected countries.

one) by the time the quota expansion factor reaches 90%. From New Zealand's perspective in the trade negotiations, it can benefit from increased trade and quota rents as long as the U.S. quota expansion is less than 40%. Larger quota expansions will result in NZL's quota rents falling substantially as they are displaced by EU exports to the U.S. Thus, a modest TRQ liberalization in the DDA is likely to benefit some, but this comes at the expense of other exporters whose quota rents are eroded.

6. Conclusion

Agricultural market access continues to be a contentious issue in the DDA. Many WTO members have made it clear that they are unwilling to negotiate on other topics until a suitable agreement on agriculture exists. Policy analysts interested in the effects of trade liberalization often face a tradeoff: on the one hand, they can use a general equilibrium framework which typically requires a large degree of aggregation (the GTAP database offers a maximum of 57 sectors); or constructing a partial equilibrium model that can be more disaggregated but has nothing to say about the general equilibrium effects and the overall impact of an agreement. We developed a methodology that bridges this gap by combining a fully disaggregated sub-sector (PE) model within a standard GE framework.

The first objective of this article was to provide a measure of the aggregation errors implicit in standard GE analyses of trade liberalization. We found that the aggregate GTAP (GE) model is quite robust in predicting aggregate welfare impacts from global dairy reform compared to our PE/GE approach that disaggregated dairy into 24 product lines. However, when it comes to predicting other market variables such as output responses and bilateral trade flows, standard GE models often understated the impacts especially when we allow for greater product-line substitution in subsector trade, as is likely justified in a product line model. We found that a GE-only analysis understated industry output and bilateral trade compared to reform that was analyzed at the sub-sector level and then aggregated up (our PE/GE approach).

The second objective of this article was to gain insights into TRQ liberalization using complementarity programming methods in the sub-sector model. Reforming U.S. TRQs on the order of 20–40% expansion benefited most exporters through increased trade *and* quota rents—effectively transferring U.S. over-quota tariff revenue into the pockets of exporters. However, exporting countries that did not face a binding TRQ initially saw their bilateral trade with the U.S. displaced as over-quota countries moved out of regime three and their prices in the U.S. market decreased. Furthermore, after a 40% expansion, New Zealand and Canada experience sharp erosion of TRQ rents, as the EU begins to drop its price for specialty cheeses. Eventually, none of the quotas are binding and quota rents are eliminated altogether.

References

AMAD, *Agricultural Market Access Database* (2002). Available at: www.amad.org.

Armington, P. S., "A Theory of Demand for Products Distinguished by Place of Production," *IMF Staff Papers* 16 (1969), 159–178.

Böhringer, C., and T. F. Rutherford, "Combining Top-Down and Bottom-Up in Energy Policy Analysis: A Decomposition Approach," Discussion Paper No. 06-007, Center for European Economic Research, May 8, 2005.

Bouët, A., Y. Decreux, L. Fontagne, S. Jean, and D. Laborde. "A Consistent, Ad-Valorem Equivalent Measure of Applied Protection Across the World: The MAcMap-HS6 Database," *CEPII, Working Paper* No. 2004-22, December (2004).

Bureau, J. C., and L. Salvatici, "WTO Negotiations on Market Access: What We Know, What We Don't and What We Should," *Invited Paper Presented at the International Conference of Agricultural Policy Reform and the WTO: Where Are We Heading?* Capri, Italy, June 23–26, 2003.

de Gorter, H., and D. S. Boughner, "US Dairy Policy and the Agreement on Agriculture in the WTO," *Canadian Journal of Agricultural Economics* 47 (1999), 31–42.

Dimaranan, B. V., ed., *Global Trade, Assistance, and Production: The GTAP 6 Data Base* (Center for Global Trade Analysis, Purdue University, 2006).

Elbehri, A., M. Ingco, T. W. Hertel, and K. Pearson, "Liberalizing Tariff Rate Quotas: Quantifying the Effects of Enhancing Market Access," Chapter 10, in M. Ingco, and A. Winters, eds., *Agriculture and the New Trade Agenda: Creating a Global Trading Environment for Developmentx* (Cambridge University Press: Cambridge, UK, 2003) pp. 194–220.

Gehlhar, M. "Bilateral Time-Series Trade Data," in *Global Trade, Assistance, and Production: The GTAP 6 Data Base*, B. V. Dimaranan, ed. (Center for Global Trade Analysis, Purdue University: Purdue, IN, 2007).

Hertel, T. W., *Global Trade Analysis: Modeling and Applications* (Cambridge University Press: Cambridge, UK, 1997).

Hertel, T. W., D. Hummels, M. Ivanic, and R. Keeney, "How Confident Can We Be in CGE-Based Assessments of Free Trade Agreements?" *NBER Working Papers* 10477 (National Bureau of Economic Research, 2004).

Josling, T. E., S. Tangermann, and T. K. Warley, *Agriculture in the GATT* (St. Martin's Press: New York, 1996).

Josling, T., and A. Rae, "Market Access Negotiations in Agriculture," *Paper Prepared for the World Bank Conference on Developing Countries and the New Agricultural Negotiations,* 1-2 October, Geneva, 1999.

Meilke, K., and S. Larivière, "The Problem and Pitfalls in Modeling International Dairy Trade Liberalization," *IATRC Working Paper Number 99-3* (College Station: Texas, 1999).

Meilke, K., J. Rude, M. Burfisher, and M. Bredahl, "Market Access: Issues and Options in The Agricultural Negotiations," International Agricultural Trade Research Consortium (IATRC) *Commissioned Paper* 14, May 2001.

Nicholson, C. F., and P. M. Bishop, "US Dairy Product Trade: Modeling Approaches and the Impact of New Product Formulations," Final Report for NRI Grant 2001-35400-10249, March 2004.

Rutherford, T. F., "Extensions of GAMS for Complementarity Problems Arising in Applied Economics," *Journal of Economic Dynamics and Control* 19 (1995), 1299–1324.

Rutherford, T. F., "GTAP6 in GAMS: The Dataset and Static Model," *Prepared for Workshop on Applied General Equilibrium Modeling for Trade Policy Analysis in Russia and the CIS,* Moscow, December 1–9, 2005.

Skully, D., "The Economics of TRQ Administration," *IATRC Working Paper* #99–6 (University of Minnesota: St. Paul, 1999).

Tangermann, S., "Has the Uruguay Round Agreement on Agriculture Worked Well?" *International Agricultural Trade Research Consortium (IATRC), Commissioned Paper* #01–1, May, 2001.

United States International Trade Center (USITC) *Interactive Tariff and Trade Database* (2006). Available at: http://dataweb.usitc.gov.

Vanzetti, D., and R. Peters, "An Analysis of the WTO, US and EU Proposals on Agricultural Reform," United Nations Conference on Trade and Development (UNCTAD), Geneva, April 2003.

Meta-analysis of general and partial equilibrium simulations of Doha Round outcomes

Sebastian Hess* and Stephan von Cramon-Taubadel

Abstract

Quantification of welfare changes due to trade liberalization plays a crucial role for political decision making. However, significant differences in simulated gains from liberalization do not serve to increase confidence in quantitative assessments based on trade models. A meta-analysis of trade simulations under the WTO Doha Round is employed to identify model characteristics that influence the magnitude of simulation results. Findings from a simple regression model are plausible and show that each simulation experiment represents a complex interaction of model characteristics and experimental settings that may not easily be communicated to nonexperts. Meta-analysis proves to be useful for empirically assessing this complexity.

JEL classification: C00, C23, C68, F10

Keywords: meta-analysis; CGE; partial equilibrium; trade liberalization; WTO

1. Introduction

Ongoing debates about the pros and cons of further agricultural trade liberalization often hinge on empirical estimates of the gains and losses that would accrue to specific interest groups, countries, and regions. Applied trade models provide such estimates and have become an important part of the political decision-making process (Devarajan and Robinson, 2002). However, applied trade models are frequently criticized as having weak empirical foundations (Alston et al., 1990; McKitrick, 1998; Anderson and Wincoop, 2001) and as being insufficiently transparent (Ackerman, 2005; Piermartini and Teh, 2005). In addition, different models often produce trade simulation results that " . . . differ

quite widely even across similar experiments" (Charlton and Stiglitz, 2005), and convincing explanations for these differences are, due to the complexity of most models, difficult to provide. These problems complicate an already controversial debate on agricultural trade liberalization, and are water on the mills of those who question the benefits of liberalization and the ability of economists to provide objective measures of these benefits.

In this article, a meta-analysis of partial and general equilibrium results on the Doha Development Round of WTO negotiations is employed. The aim of this analysis is to identify model characteristics (e.g., partial vs. general equilibrium, level of disaggregation) and other factors (e.g., the database employed) that influence simulation results in a systematic manner, and to derive quantitative estimates of these influences.

Department of Agricultural Economics and Rural Development University of Göttingen, Germany.

The authors are grateful to Yves Surry, Bernhard Brümmer, Martin Banse, and Frank van Tongeren for many useful suggestions, and to Tinoush Jamali and Inken Köhler for valuable research assistance. This project has been supported by the German Research Council (DFG). Sebastian Hess has partly been supported by the Friedrich-Naumann-Foundation, and Stephan von Cramon gratefully acknowledges support from the Fulbright Commission.

2. Meta-analysis

Meta-analysis is a comparatively recent inductive empirical method that seeks to find similarities and explain differences between scientific findings on similar research questions across publications (Stanley,

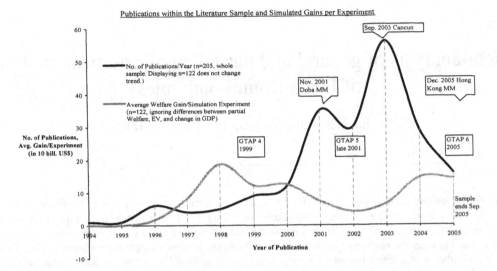

Figure 1. Number of publications in our literature sample, and average reported welfare gain (1994–2005). *Source:* Own calculations based on literature search. MM = ministerial meeting.

2001). The meta-analysis in this article is based on the following general model:

$$I_i = f(MC_i, LE_i, DB_i, SC_i, u_i), \qquad (1)$$

where *I* is the simulated impact of a trade liberalization experiment, *MC* is a vector of model characteristics (such as partial or general equilibrium, level of disaggregation), *LE* describes the liberalization experiment (the magnitude of the simulated tariff reductions), *DB* is the database underlying the simulation (e.g., GTAP 4 or 5), *SC* is a vector of study characteristics (for example affiliation of the authors, whether the study has been published), *u* is an error term, and *i* subscripts are individual simulations.

3. The literature sample

3.1. Data collection

The aim of this analysis is to sample publications on applied general and partial equilibrium simulations of the Doha Round agricultural trade liberalization in refereed journals but also in the so-called "grey literature," where an important share of the relevant simulations is published. The literature sample is derived according to the following sampling strategy:

From a recent review of trade models (van Tongeren, et al., 2001), a vector of keywords that describe the type

of applied models in question is derived. In addition, the set of applications is furthermore restricted using a second vector of keywords taken from section 13 of the Doha Ministerial Declaration (the section on agricultural markets). The combination of both vectors yields a matrix of search words that is applied to the most important literature databases (e.g., Econlit, Repec, etc.).[1] In addition, the internet is searched in order to sample "grey" literature that might not be listed in scientific literature databases. Figure 1 presents information on the year of publication of the sampled studies and the average reported welfare change over all sampled studies in each year from 1994 to 2005.

The number of publications peaks twice, in conjunction with the Doha and Cancun ministerial meetings. Since the Cancun ministerial meetings, the number of published simulations has fallen as expectations have been lowered and completely new proposals have not been forthcoming. Some authors have pointed to the "shrinking gains from Doha" (Achterbosch et al., 2004, p. 53; Ackerman, 2005), addressing the fact that over time the reported findings from trade models have declined. The literature sample supports this view, but only up to the Cancun ministerial meetings (Figure 1). After Cancun, the average simulated

---

[1] The keyword matrix and the literature databases employed are described in detail under http://memo-agecon.uni-goettingen.de/memo/searchstrategy.html.

gains from trade liberalization increase again. These movements in average simulated welfare changes are primarily due to the different proposals that were being considered in each phase of the Doha Round.

3.2. Data processing and variable definitions

To estimate Eq. (1), the variables in it must be defined precisely. Within the literature sample, the quality of documentation with regard to the variables in (1) varies widely. Studies that have been subject to a scientific review process tend to be more transparent and thoroughly documented than others. In some instances, documentation of even very fundamental characteristics of a liberalization experiment and/or the model used to produce simulation results is missing, and as a result some studies in the literature sample could not be employed in the empirical meta-analysis.[2]

The dependent variable (I) is defined as the simulated change in economic well-being (welfare) in a particular country/region due to a liberalization step for a particular product/product aggregate. Most studies report, among other findings, some measure of welfare change, making this a natural choice to measure the impact of a liberalization experiment. These publications report different welfare measures (equivalent variation, compensating variation, change in GDP, etc. See Mas-Colell et al. (1995) for a discussion of the relations between these measures). All different measures are transformed into million U.S.$, and dummy variables on the RHS of (1) are used to account for any effects of the measures used.

Quantifying the liberalization experiments (LE) in a consistent and comparable manner is difficult. Much confusion about differences in simulation results arises because important differences in what appear to be identical liberalization experiments are not adequately considered. While two experiments that both simulate, for instance, a 50% cut in OECD agricultural tariffs may appear to be identical, they can differ considerably depending on the type of tariff (bound versus applied, treatment of preferences, and mixed tariffs, etc.) and

the aggregation of sectors and regions used. The domestic price of good i in region r following a change in import tariffs can be given as

$$p_{ri}^{\text{domestic}} = p_{ri}^{\text{border}} * (1 + t_{ri} + t_{ri} * s), \qquad (2)$$

where p_{ri} = the price of good i in region r, t_{ri} = the *ad valorem* tariff levied on imports of i, and s = the simulated proportional change in t_{ri}, which will in most instances be negative. Clearly, even moderate differences in t_{ri} paired with different levels of p_{ri}^{border}, due for example to different aggregations and treatments of tariffs, will lead to different impacts of a given s. Comparing simulation experiments is therefore not possible without controlling for the level of protection that has effectively been reduced in an experiment, and the economic size of the sector to which a tariff reduction s is applied.

To deal with this problem, a reference database is constructed which includes information on tariffs, production volumes, and trade flows. Key sources for this reference database are GTAP-5, FAO, and MacMap. With this reference database, it is possible to re-aggregate the regional and sectoral settings of each simulation experiment, and thus to calculate comparable initial *ad valorem* tariffs for each combination of country/region and products/product aggregates in a given study. This *ad valorem* tariff is then multiplied with the proportional tariff change s and the average production value of the product in question (in million U.S.$). The result is a standardized measure of the size of the liberalization step underlying a particular simulation result.

This approach to operationalize the variable LE works for experiments that involve unilateral liberalization for a given product/product aggregate and for a given country/region *vis-à-vis* the rest of the world; it is not (yet) well suited to adequately quantify the effectively removed protection in simulated regional preferential/free trade agreements.

To capture study characteristics (SC), many meta-analyses use descriptive bibliographical information about studies (year of publication, number of authors) as well as information about the contexts in which the studies have been conducted (institution of origin, subject to peer review, etc.). However, these variables have not been included in the final estimation of Eq. (1) because they fail to have a significant impact after the variables MC, DB, and LE have been controlled for.

---

[2] An internet questionnaire is being employed to collect missing information from the authors of studies in our sample. However, in a pre-test the response rate was very low. This is partly because some authors were not involved in the practical modelling underlying their studies and are therefore not able to answer our questions, while the actual "modellers" (e.g., research assistants and grad students) can no longer be reached.

3.3. Special cases

Publications using the Michigan Model of World Production and Trade (Brown et al., 2004) for some liberalization scenarios report simulated welfare gains for specific countries (as well as for the sum of certain experiments) that are 50% to 100% larger than the average gains of all other studies. Initial estimates of Eq. (1) attributes these large gains to the fact that the Michigan model uses the Johansen macro closure, keeps trade balances for all countries fixed, explicitly models flows of foreign direct investment (FDI) as a result of liberalization, uses own estimates of firm level markups (for imperfect competition), and partly includes own estimates of nontariff barriers (NTBs) that are removed along with tariffs. The reference database for calculating standardized liberalization experiments (*LE*) cannot deal with publication-specific estimates of NTBs. The leverage (Cook's distance) of these features (proxied with dummy variables) on the estimation of Eq. (1) is extraordinarily large. Such studies have therefore been omitted from the final dataset.

The exclusion of these studies, as well as other exclusions due to inadequate documentation, etc., reduces the number of studies used to produce the estimates of Eq. (1) reported below to 53. These 53 studies contain a total of roughly 1,600 individual observations, each representing the impact of a particular liberalization of specific products/product aggregates summed for a specific country/region. Almost all publications report results at the country level and therefore this aggregation level has been chosen for the dependent variable, although an analysis at the sectoral level would potentially yield more detailed insights into the distributional effects of trade policies within a country, as simulated throughout our literature sample.

4. Estimation and results

Equation (1) is estimated using OLS. Econometric difficulties arise from the complex, nonconstant variance structure of the dataset employed. The selection of independent variables and interaction terms in the linear model is accomplished according to a stepwise regression algorithm so as not to exclude effects that are unanticipated *a priori*. Results of the estimation of Eq. (1) are presented in Table 1.

The independent variables that are included in the estimation results in Table 1 are not the only ones that have significant influences on the dependent variable (simulated impact of liberalization). However, many of the variables in the *MC* vector are correlated with one another. It is therefore important to choose variables that are as independent of each other as possible (Florax, 2002), and at the same time are not by definition restricted to only a subset of the models in focus. The estimated coefficients can be interpreted in the following way:

Policy shocks: For each percent of effective reduction in tariff protection (including export subsidies and amber box support approximated through the tariff level), welfare gains amount to U.S.$21,000 per million U.S.$ of production value. Gains from production-related blue and green box reductions are also statistically significant but much smaller, partly because some partial experiments model the EU's recent decoupling reforms as reductions of direct payments and a simultaneous increase in decoupled payments.

Shocks to technical change parameters: In a few studies, simulations provide insight into the effect of shocks to technical change, e.g., when genetically modified plants are adopted by farmers. The variable is expressed relative to the production value of a sector. The estimated coefficient states that a 1% increase in production value due to technical change yields on average 1.6 million of welfare gains. This huge average gain from technical change is not implausible relative to observed and estimated gains from trade liberalization alone. In their meta-analysis, Alston et al. (2000) find an average 100% rate of return to agricultural research and development.

Databases: The coefficients for databases prior to 1997 and for GTAP 5 are significant and negative, suggesting that the use of these databases leads *ceteris paribus* to lower simulated welfare gains than the reference GTAP 3 database.

Dynamic model: This dummy must be interpreted in conjunction with the "fixed capital stock" dummy. The latter captures the difference between standard comparative static GE models with fixed stocks of capital and labor, and dynamic models that are mostly GE models in which capital is permitted to grow during a simulation run. Controlling for the capital accumulation effect, dynamic models predict larger welfare gains to liberalization than static models, but this effect is not

Table 1

OLS regression results for the restricted literature sample (weighted by number of observations from each publication)

Variables	Mean	Min Max	β (Std. err.)	Prob. ($> \lvert t \rvert$)
Intercept			2034.6 (917.3)	0.026
Database GTAP-4 (=1 if yes)	0.24	0 1	−1068.2 (933.3)	0.252
Database GTAP-5 (=1 if yes)	0.33	0 1	−1549.8 (912.6)	0.089
Other database after 1997 (includes GTAP-6) (=1 if yes)	0.30	0 1	327.1 (1043.1)	0.753
Other database before 1997 (=1 if yes)	0.07	0 1	−3299.4 (960.5)	0.000
Number of regions (count)	55.5	1 161	−7.4 (5. 9)	0.206
Number of agricultural sectors (count)	16.47	1 40	−72.1 (24.2)	0.002
Trade volume of country (million U.S.$)	175912	2.247 2928459	0.015 (0.0004)	0.000
Shocks to technical change or related variables in percent (million U.S.$/1% shock)	28.4	0 22807	1.6 (0.25)	0.000
Changes in tariffs, export subsidies and amber box measures (million U.S.$/1% reduction in protection)	−39260	−4503000 35270	−0.021 (0.0008)	0.000
Changes in blue/green box policies (million U.S.$/1% policy shock)	−128400	−30930000 31660	−0.0002 (0.00008)	0.025
Armington with high elasticities (=1 for twice GTAP standard or higher)	0.18	0 1	2282.4 (484.3)	0.000
Increasing returns to scale (=1 if IRTS in some sectors)	0.12	0 1	403.4 (901.0)	0.654
Trade volume * increasing returns to scale (interaction term)			−0.01 (0.002)	0.000
Dynamic model (=1 if yes)	0.21	0 1	506.7 (457.4)	0.268
Fixed capital stock (=1 if yes)	0.44	0 1	−1378.3 (460.4)	0.002
Partial equilibrium model (= 1 if yes)	0.33	0 1	2263.3 (678.1)	0.000

Residual standard error: 1,150 with 1,587 degrees of freedom.
Multiple $R^2 = 0.773$, adjusted $R^2 = 0.771$. F-statistic: 338 with 16 and 1587 degrees of freedom, P-value $= 0.000$.
Source: Own

significant. This is similar to qualitative findings reported by Brown et al. (2004), who also cite Harrison et al. (2003).

Disaggregation of the agricultural sector: Increased disaggregation of the agricultural sector is associated with smaller welfare gains, which can be explained by the fact that some aggregations in CGE models are vertical rather than horizontal combinations of agricultural sectors across all levels of processing. Thus, comparatively large artificial sectors such as "livestock and livestock products" are created in some models, and this seems to be associated with much larger gains than more "natural" aggregations for similar levels of processing.

Armington elasticities: Large Armington elasticities (values that are twice those in the standard GTAP model or higher) lead to significantly higher simulated welfare gains. Note that some partial models (such as the ATPSM model) also employ the Armington assumption, but not always through a CES specification.

Partial vs. general equilibrium: Controlling for the size of the liberalization step and all other explanatory factors included in Table 1, welfare changes simulated using PE models are on average 2.3 billion U.S.$ higher than the changes simulated using GE models (excluding BDS). Among the GE models, the impact of modelling increasing returns to scale in some sectors (typically not primary agriculture) appears to be insignificant. However, the interaction between "increasing returns to scale" and "trade volume" reveals that large traders tend to lose under such scenarios. This is in line with findings in the literature according to which increasing returns to scale are most important in developing countries and particularly increase their competitive advantage in trade if they can be captured.

5. Discussion and conclusions

The results presented above suggest that a simple linear regression using variables that describe the liberalization experiment, the characteristics of the model, and the database employed can identify important causal relationships that are plausible and explain a major share of the variance in the dependent variable "welfare change" in a sample of Doha Round trade liberalization studies. The results may yield few new insights for modelling experts. However, for policy makers and all others on the demand side of applied trade modelling the following can be concluded.

Trade simulation models can generate quantitative insights into real world policies and are comparable with each other if the combination of assumptions behind a simulation experiment is carefully controlled for and understood. A comparatively small set of fundamental model characteristics can explain the majority of the variation in simulation results across studies of the Doha Round agricultural liberalization. The causality behind applied trade models is complex. A variety of model and database characteristics interact to determine the results of a liberalization experiment, and general conclusions about the influence of individual components cannot readily be drawn without detailed empirical investigation. The analysis presented in this article also highlights the vital importance of rigorous standards of documentation, so that users are fully aware of the assumptions that underlie specific liberalization simulations. We have found that a signif-

icant subset of the available literature does not fulfill such standards.

References[3]

Achterbosch, T. J., H. B. Hammouda, P. N. Osakwe, and F. W. van-Tongeren, "Trade Liberalization under the Doha Development Agenda," *The Hague, Agricultural Economics Research Institute (LEI) Report* 6.04.09 (2004).

Ackerman, F., *The Shrinking Gains from Trade: A Critical Assessment of Doha Round Projections* (Global Development and Environment Institute: Medford, MA, 2005).

Alston, J. M., C. A. Carter, R. Green, and D. Pick, "Whither Armington Trade Models," *American Journal of Agricultural Economics* 72 (1990), 455–467.

Alston, J. M., C. Chang-Kang, M. C. Marra, P. G. Pardey, and T. Wyatt, *A Meta-Analysis of Rates of Return to Agricultural R&D – Ex Pede Herculem?* (IFPRI: Washington, DC, 2000).

Anderson, J. E., and E. V. Wincoop, "Borders, Trade and Welfare," *NBER Working Paper Series* 8515 (2001).

Brown, D. K., K. Kiyota, and R. M. Stern, "Computational Analysis of the U.S. Bilateral Free Trade Agreement with Central America, Australia, and Morocco, Ford School of Public Policy, University of Michigan, Ann Arbor, Michigan 48109–1220," *Discussion Paper No.* 527 (2004).

Charlton, A. H., and J. E. Stiglitz, "A Development-friendly Priorisation of Doha Round Proposals," *The World Economy* 28 (2005), 293–312.

Devarajan, S., and S. Robinson, *The Influence of Computable General Equilibrium Models on Policy* (IFPRI: Washington, DC, 2002).

Florax, R. J. C. M., "Accounting for Dependence among Study Results in Meta-Analysis: Methodology and Applications to the Valuation and Use of Natural Resources," *Research Memorandum* 2002-5 (Vrije Universiteit: Amsterdam, 2002).

Harrison, G. W., T. F. Rutherford, and D. G. Tarr, "Rules of Thumb for Evaluating Preferential Trading Arrangements: Evidence from Computable General Equilibrium Assessments," *Working Paper* WPS 3149 October (2003).

Mas-Colell, A., M. D. Whinston, and J. R. Green, *Microeconomic Theory* (Oxford University Press: New York, 1995).

McKitrick, R. R., "The Econometric Critique of Computable General Equilibrium Modeling: The Role of Parameter Estimation," *Economic Modeling* 15 (1998), 543–573.

Piermartini, R., and R. Teh, "Demystifying Modelling Methods for Trade Policy," *World Trade Organization Discussion Paper No.* 10 (2005).

Stanley, T. D., "Wheat from Chaff: Meta-Analysis As Quantitative Literature Review," *Journal of Economic Perspectives* 15 (2001), 131–150.

van Tongeren, F., H. van Meijl, and Y. Surry, "Global Models Applied to Agricultural and Trade Policies: A Review and Assessment," *Agricultural Economics* 26 (2001), 149–172.

---

[3] A list of the publications included in our literature sample is available under http://memo-agecon.uni-goettingen.de/memo/literature sample.html.

The Doha development round and Africa: partial and general equilibrium analyses of tariff preference erosion

Mohamed Hedi Bchir, Stephen N. Karingi, Andrew Mold, Patrick N. Osakwe,
and Mustapha Sadni Jallab*

Abstract

Erosion of trade preferences currently being enjoyed by the least developed countries (LDCs) and some developing countries remains an important area in the ongoing trade negotiations. The different positions regarding the preference erosion question besides being informed by political economy considerations are also founded on empirical results of this particular question. But does the methodology used for the empirical analysis matter? In this article, the importance of preference erosion due to MFN liberalization on agriculture is analyzed. Drawing from the potential complementary strengths in triangulation, the article uses both partial and general equilibrium analyses. The article shows that the ranking of preference erosion as an issue of policy concern is influenced by the empirical methodology adopted. However, irrespective of the rank, the article concludes that preference erosion is an important issue not only in terms of welfare, but also as it has impacts on incomes for preference-receiving countries.

JEL classification: C15, F17

Keywords: Doha round; African economies; global models; preference effects

1. Introduction

The market access question has remained one of the critical areas in the multilateral trade talks. This is a question that has been relevant to not only the trade in agricultural goods but also the trade in industrial goods, especially with respect to the role the latter can play in the diversification of African countries' economies. However, the liberalization of agricultural trade in the ongoing Doha Round negotiations has attained something akin to the pole position. This prominence is not in any way by accident but is a reflection of the sig-

nificance of liberalizing market access for agricultural exports from developing countries, especially African countries. Enhancement of market access in agricultural trade, particularly in the developed countries' markets, is supposed to bolster exports and economic activity in developing countries.

This liberalization, however, is expected to favor countries whose exports are currently impeded by multilateral protection through tariffs and nontariff measures. At the same time, the liberalization is expected to be a challenge to the least developed countries (LDCs) and some developing countries, especially those from Africa, which currently enjoy preferential market access through different schemes set up by the developed countries. Therefore, for Africa, a key issue has been whether MFN liberalization under the Doha Round will adversely affect their market access to developed countries, through erosion of the preference margins that they currently enjoy. The question of preference erosion has almost attained a deal-breaker status in the current negotiations. For the African countries, preference

*Trade and Regional Integration Division, United Nations Economic Commission for Africa, P.O. Box 3005, Addis Ababa, Ethiopia.

*The authors are staff members of the Trade and Regional Integration Division of the United Nations Economic Commission for Africa. This article should be attributed to the authors. It is not meant to represent the position or opinions of the United Nations or its Members, nor the official position of any UN staff member.

erosion from any multilateral liberalization needs to be treated not just as a market access issue, but as a development issue.

The link of the preferences to the development dimensions of the trade negotiations has been a key factor in the incorporation of the preference erosion question to the aid-for-trade discussions. Yet for the nonpreference-receiving developing countries, especially those from Latin America and some parts of Asia, either the preferences are extended to them, or they will not support any agreement that continues to provide asymmetrical preferences. They are a market access issue from their point of view and there is no justification whatsoever for their continuation as development support to the LDCs and some of the developing countries especially those from Africa. Even as the developing countries from Africa and Latin America continue to take different positions on the treatment of preferences in the negotiations, for the developed countries, compensation for preference erosion can only be contemplated if the magnitude of this erosion is appropriately measured.

As discussed in Section 2 of this article, several studies have been carried out, using different methodologies to address the question of preferences in different contexts, ranging from their relevance to the implication of multilateral liberalization to the existing schemes. Indeed, in the context of the ongoing negotiations, two key questions have come out clearly. First, do preferences matter to those countries receiving them? And second, what is the magnitude of preference erosion that is likely to result from global trade liberalization? The answers to these two questions have been addressed in several studies. Yet, review of existing literature presents no single study that sought to answer the two questions, while at the same time using different methodologies. That the political significance of the preference erosion question is dictated upon by the methodology used is not in doubt. Thus, it would be useful using the triangulation framework to address the question of preferences in a unified way in order to seek consensus and consistency in the conclusions and recommendations with regard to the preference erosion question. And that is the task that this article has set upon itself, to use the triangulation framework to see whether a consistent result on the relevance of the preference erosion question can be obtained.

The article provides an evaluation of the current trade preferences granted to African countries and of their potential erosion due to MFN liberalization on agriculture. Drawing from the potential complementary strengths in triangulation, the article uses both partial and general equilibrium analyses. The article shows the importance of taking account of preferences in trade liberalization scenarios using the two methodologies. In particular, it aims to assess the effects of Doha Round MFN liberalization on trade flows and macroeconomic variables. The focus of the article on agriculture trade liberalization does not mean that preference erosion is not important for the industrial goods trade, but is more informed by the availability of a well-tested partial equilibrium model that is used for agriculture trade policy analysis.

The article is organized as follows. Section 2 provides a summary of the studies that have been carried out on the preference erosion question in the context of trade liberalization. That all the studies have used one particular methodology to answer this question comes out clearly in this review. Section 3 briefly describes the modeling frameworks and methodologies employed in order to capture the triangulation element of the study. In particular, two different general equilibrium models are highlighted to compare the results obtained from the two models, before comparing them with the partial equilibrium model. In Section 4, the aggregation of the database and the scenarios are described. In order to be able to apportion the differences in the results to the modeling frameworks, it was important that the regional and sectoral aggregations for the general equilibrium models are similar. Section 5 discusses the results of the simulations while Section 6 concludes.

2. Literature review

In the empirical literature, there are several ways in which preferential schemes have been evaluated. Some articles provide purely descriptive measures of the effectiveness of preferences, based on utility and utilization rates (e.g., UNCTAD, 2003), whereas others are based on econometric techniques which attempt to analyze their impact on trade volumes and aggregate welfare. For example, Romalis (2003) reports a growth dividend over a period of 15 years of 10% for the average African country resulting from preferential market access.[1] Haveman and Shatz (2003) estimate an expansion of LDC export volumes by as much as US$7.6 billion if duty-free access is granted *simultaneously* by the European Union (EU), Japan, and the United States. Cline (2004) also reports a substantial increase in export volumes due to the Lome/Cotonou Agreements, but pointedly his SSA dummy is negative, implying that the SSA countries have not taken advantage of preferential access in the same way as other beneficiary countries. Other things being equal, preferential regime membership has boosted real export growth by 7.2% annually for Caribbean Basin Initiative (CBI) countries and 8.8% for Lomé countries. But he also suggests that the model confirms the poor performance of SSA (despite preferential market access), and indicates that "a SSA country typically had a 10.7% lower real export annually than would otherwise be expected" (Cline, 2004, p. 97).

Simulation techniques have also been employed to examine the impact of multilateral trade reforms on preference-receiving countries. Some of these studies adopt a partial equilibrium approach while others are based on a general equilibrium framework. For example, IMF (2003) used a partial equilibrium model to examine the impact of a 40% cut in tariffs by the QUAD on LDCs. They found that, due to preference erosion, the reform would result in a loss equivalent to about 1.7% of total exports. Using a partial equilibrium framework and data for middle-income countries, Alexandraki and Lankes (2004) evaluated the effect of a 40% cut in aggregate preference margins received by beneficiary countries. They conclude that it would result in a loss of between 0.5% and 1.2% of total exports of the middle-income countries considered. In a related study, Limao and Orreaga (2005) undertake a partial equilibrium analysis of the welfare costs of switching from a unilateral preference to an import subsidy scheme. They found that the three preference-granting countries considered (U.S., EU, and Japan) would gain US$2,934 million. Furthermore, the 49 LDCs would gain US$520 million.

General equilibrium studies of the costs of preference erosion per se are relatively few and far between (for a recent review of these, see Hoekman et al. [2006]), essentially because until quite recently preferential margins were not included in the GTAP database as well as other key databases used for analyses of the impact of global trade reform. That said, in recent years several authors have provided estimates of the welfare effect of multilateral trade liberalization resulting from preference erosion using CGE models. For example, Francois et al. (2005) examined the scope for preference erosion resulting from full elimination of EU and OECD tariffs. Their results suggest that trade liberalization by the EU would lead to income losses of around $460 million for African LDCs.[2] They argue that if preference erosion is viewed in the broader context of potential tariff reduction by all OECD, not just EU members, the magnitude of the total losses is reduced to $110 million. They explain that this is in part because the EU has been the most aggressive in using preferences as a tool for development assistance. Thus the gains associated with non-EU MFN tariff reductions could partially offset losses due to the erosion of EU preferences. In a related study, Lippoldt and Kowalski (2005) examined the welfare consequences of preference erosion resulting from a 50% linear cut in the *ad-valorem* equivalent measure of protection. They show that such multilateral trade reform would lead to modest welfare losses for some non-OECD countries, most of which are in Sub-Saharan Africa.

A key finding of the results from CGE models is that the estimated welfare effects associated with preference erosion is relatively small (see Table 1). This is due in part to the fact that CGE models assume that domestic goods are differentiated from imported goods and so are imperfect substitutes. This assumption, which follows from Armington (1969), implies that exporters of goods receiving preferences will not face stiff competition as a result of liberalization and so reduces the potential welfare losses that could arise from preference erosion.

----

[1] These results should however be treated with some caution. Romalis's model could be criticized on the grounds that it is underspecified, using as it does only a measure of the value of preferences and a variable representing the structural characteristics of exports to explain GDP growth.

[2] Francois, Hoekman, and Manchin also recalculate the effects of preference erosion taking into account the costs of compliance (due to rules of origin and other administrative costs), estimated at around 4% of the value of the goods traded. This reduces the value of preferences, and implies losses of only $342 million, instead of $460 million, as per the baseline unadjusted estimate.

Table 1
Impact of preference erosion

Study	Preference-receiving countries	Preference-granting countries	Type of reform and framework	Remarks and results
Limao and Orreaga (2005)	LDCs	U.S., EU, and Japan	Considers cost of replacing unilateral preferences by a fixed import subsidy. Used a partial equilibrium framework.	Switching from unilateral preferences to an import subsidy scheme produces an annual welfare gain of US$2,934 for the US, EU and Japan. It also produces welfare gain of US$520 million and US$900 million for LDCs and the rest of the world respectively.
IMF (2003)	LDCs	Quad	40% cut in tariffs. Used a partial equilibrium framework.	Focuses on trade effects. Finds that reform will result in a loss of about 1.7% of total LDC exports. In value terms the loss of exports is US$530 million.
Alexandraki and Lankes (2004)	Middle-income	Quad	40% cut in preference margin. Used a partial equilibrium framework.	The objective of the study is to identify middle-income countries that are potentially vulnerable to export losses from preference erosion. Finds that the impact of preference erosion is between 0.5% and 1.2% of total exports. Study suggests that vulnerable countries are small island states dependent on sugar, bananas and textiles.
Lippoldt and Kowalski (2005)	Developing countries	Quad and Australia	50% linear reduction in *ad valorem* equivalent measure of protection	The study finds that certain economies are at risk of experiencing negative welfare effects from preference erosion (Tanzania, Uganda, Mozambique, etc.). However, the impact tends to be relatively modest. For example, for African countries the change in per capita welfare is less than 0.3%.
Francois et al., (2005)	African LDCs	EU and OECD	Full MFN liberalization. Used a general equilibrium framework.	Finds that the real income loss to African LDCs from liberalization by the EU is US$458 million. For liberalization by the OECD the figure is US$110 million.

3. Modelling framework and methodology

To examine the consequences of agricultural trade liberalization for African economies, three well-known models of trade policy analyses that take account of trade preferences are used: the Global Trade Analysis Project (GTAP) model; the MIRAGE model; and the Agricultural Trade Policy Simulation Model (ATPSM). The first two are computable general equilibrium models while the third is a partial equilibrium methodology and so it would be interesting to compare and contrast the results from these different but complementary models.

The GTAP model was developed by the Center for Global Trade Analysis at Purdue University in the United States. The standard GTAP model used in our analysis and its key features are described in Hertel (1997). It is a static multi-country and multi-sector general equilibrium model which assumes perfect competition as well as full employment of factors. Since we are focusing on the role of preferences, we use version 6 of the model, which includes trade preferences. The MIRAGE model was developed by CEPII and has been widely used to analyze agricultural and multilateral trade issues. For a full description of the standard MIRAGE model, see Bchir et al. (2002). To make the results of the MIRAGE model as comparable as possible to those of GTAP, we use a static version of the

MIRAGE model that also assumes perfect competition as well as full employment of factors of production. The ATPSM is a deterministic, static, partial equilibrium model developed by UNCTAD and FAO. It is multi-country, multi-commodity model that takes account of the distribution of quota rents as well as differences between bound and applied tariffs. A full description of the model can be found in Vanzetti and Graham (2002).

4. Aggregation and scenarios

Since the focus of our study is Africa and agricultural trade liberalization, the 87 GTAP regions in version 6 of the database were aggregated into nine regions; namely, Sub-Saharan Africa (SSA), North Africa, U.S., EU25, Japan, Rest of the World Developed (ROWD), China, India, and Rest of the Developing World (ROW). The composition of these groups and their mapping to the GTAP 6 sectors are presented in Table 2.

Turning to the sectors, the 57 GTAP sectors in version 6 were aggregated into 18 sectors in our analysis. Eleven of the eighteen sectors deal with agricultural goods. This sectoral aggregation allows us to focus on the commodities and sectors of interest to African countries in the negotiations. Table 3 contains the exact composition of the sectors used in our analysis as well as their relation to the GTAP 6 regions and sectors.

Table 2
Regional aggregation

Group	GTAP region
USA	United States
EU25	Austria, Belgium, Denmark, Finland, France, Germany, United Kingdom, Greece, Ireland, Italy, Luxembourg, Netherlands, Portugal, Spain, Sweden, Cyprus, Czech Republic, Hungary, Malta, Poland, Slovakia, Slovenia, Estonia, Latvia, Lithuania
Japan	Japan
Rest of the World Developed (ROWD)	Australia, New Zealand, Canada
North Africa	Tunisia, Morocco, Rest of North Africa
Sub-Saharan Africa (SSA)	South Africa, Botswana, Malawi, Mozambique, Tanzania, Zambia, Zimbabwe, Rest of SADC, Rest of South African Customs Union, Madagascar, Uganda, Rest of Sub-Saharan Africa
China	China
India	India
Rest of the Developing World (ROW)	Rest of Oceania, Hong Kong, Korea, Taiwan, Rest of East Asia, Singapore, Vietnam, Rest of Southeast Asia, Bangladesh, Sri Lanka, Rest of South Asia, Mexico, Rest of North America, Colombia, Peru, Venezuela, Rest of Andean Pact, Rest of FTAA, Rest of Europe, Albania, Bulgaria, Croatia, Romania, Russian Federation, Rest of Former Soviet Union, Turkey, Rest of Middle East, Indonesia, Malaysia, Philippines, Thailand, Argentina, Brazil, Chile, Uruguay, Rest of South America, Central America

Table 3
Sectoral aggregation

Sector	GTAP category
Cereals	Paddy rice, wheat, cereal grains nec, crops nec
Veg_fruit	Vegetables, fruits, nuts
Oil_seeds	Oil seeds
Sugar	Sugar cane, sugar beet, sugar
Cot_bev	Plant-based fibers, beverages, and tobacco products
Meat	Cattle, sheep, goats, horses, animal products nec
Dairy	Raw milk, dairy products
Wol	Wool, silk-worm cocoons
Frs	Forestry
Fsh	Fishing
Res_nat	Coal, oil, gas, minerals nec
Agro_ind	Vegetable oils and fat, processed rice, food products nec
Tex_vet	Textiles, wearing apparel
Heavy Industry	Motor vehicles and parts, transport equipment nec, electronic equipment, machinery, and equipment nec
Medium Industry	Petroleum, coal products; chemical, rubber, plastic prods; mineral products nec; ferrous metals; metals nec; metal products; manufactures nec
Light Industry	Leather products, wood products, paper products, publishing
Services	Electricity; gas manufacture, distribution; water; construction; communication; financial services nec; insurance; business services nec; recreation and other services; pubAdmin/defence/health/educat; dwellings
Transport	Trade, transport nec, sea transport, air transport

As indicated earlier, the focus of the study is on agricultural trade liberalization. However, within this sector, there is also focus on the market access pillar. This means that the liberalization experiments performed will not involve the domestic support and export competition pillars of the agricultural negotiations. In the simulations, three trade policy scenarios are considered. Scenario 0 is the full liberalization scenario in which all tariff barriers to agricultural trade for all products and all regions are eliminated. Although this scenario is a good benchmark for comparison of the results of the different models, it is not a realistic scenario, because it is unlikely to happen in the current Doha Round negotiations. Consequently, we also consider two scenarios designed to reflect the range of

proposals that are being considered in the modalities phase of the Doha negotiations. Scenario 1 involves deep cuts for developed countries and minor cuts for developing countries. It is a version of the proposal contained in the "draft possible modalities for agriculture" issued by the Chair of the Committee on Agriculture (Special Session) on 22 June 2006. It is interesting because it involves aggressive cuts in trade barriers by developed countries but contains elements for Special and Differential Treatment for developing countries. Scenario 2 is basically the G20 proposal and is less ambitious than the cuts in scenarios 0 and 1. More details on the scenarios are provided below.

Scenario 0: This scenario is considered as a benchmark as it implements a full liberalization for the entire product and all the regions.

Scenario 1: This scenario considers the deepest cuts for developed countries and conservative cuts for developing countries that are one third of those for developed countries as suggested by the ACP countries. It is an ambitious liberalization scenario for developed countries both in terms of thresholds and depth of liberalization.

Tariff band (%)	Cuts by developed countries (%)	Cuts by developing countries (%)	LDC
0–20	65	20	No liberalization
20–40	75	25	
40–60	85	28	
Above 60	90	30	

Scenario 2: This scenario, which is less ambitious than the previous two, captures the G-20 proposal and is therefore interesting given the influence that this group has in the negotiations.

Tariff band (%)	Cuts by developed countries (%)	Cuts by developing countries (%)	LDC
0–20	20	15	No liberalization
20–40	30	20	
40–60	35	25	
Above 60	42	30	

Table 4
MIRAGE results

Variable	Sub-Saharan Africa						North Africa					
	With preferences			Without preferences			With preferences			Without preferences		
Scenarios	S0	S1	S2	S0	S1	S2	S0	S1	S2	S0	S1	S2
Welfare[a]	357	174	315	1651	441	914	3197	−362	−316	4267	371	475
Terms of Trade[b]	−0.48	−0.11	0.15	−0.77	−0.11	0.27	−7.81	−0.71	−0.52	−7.34	−0.41	−0.33
GDP[b]	0.72	0.05	0.07	1.13	0.12	0.19	4.21	−0.13	−0.12	4.68	0.16	0.19
Exports[b]	21.96	0.66	1.03	28.69	1.22	2.32	45.39	−0.6	−0.37	60.09	1.63	1.85
Imports[b]	22.39	0.7	1.09	29.27	1.26	2.43	43.07	−0.5	−0.23	57.02	1.60	1.93

[a] U.S. million $.

[b] % variation.

5. Simulation results

In this section, results of the key simulation experiments performed are reported. For the general equilibrium models, the focus will be on five key variables: welfare, output, term of trade, import, and exports.

For the MIRAGE model, simulation results for the three scenarios considered are presented in Table 4. In the full liberalization scenario (S0), the welfare gain to SSA in the model with preferences is $357 million. For North Africa the figure is $3,197 million. However, when preferences are not taken into account the welfare gains are $1,651 million and $4,267 million for SSA and North Africa, respectively. The key implication of this finding is that preferences have serious consequences for welfare in recipient countries. The results also suggest that relative to SSA, North Africa has more to gain from agricultural liberalization. This has to do with the fact that countries in North Africa tend to have better infrastructure and also better capacity to take advantage of trading opportunities created in the multilateral trading system. With respect to the terms of trade, full liberalization leads to a deterioration in the terms of trade for both SSA and North Africa. But the deterioration is more pronounced for North Africa in the models with and without preferences.

In terms of output (GDP), the results suggest that full liberalization increases output in both SSA and North Africa but, again, the impact is much higher for North Africa than SSA. For example, in the model with preferences, output increases by 0.72% in SSA and by 4.21% in North Africa. As for exports and imports, the results are qualitatively similar to those of the other

variables. The increase in exports and imports resulting from liberalization is higher in the model without preferences. They are also higher for North Africa.

Looking at the Doha Scenarios (1 and 2) considered, the welfare results suggest that for both SSA and North Africa, the gains are higher without preferences. In addition, unlike SSA, North Africa incurs welfare losses in both scenarios when preferences are taken into account. For example, while SSA derives welfare benefit of $174 million in Scenario 1, North Africa incurs losses of $362 million.

How do these results compare to those from the GTAP model? Table 5 presents results of the simulations using the GTAP model. The results of the version of the model? with preferences suggest that full liberalization of agricultural trade would yield welfare gains of $542 million for SSA and a welfare loss of $62 million for North Africa. When preferences are not taken into account both SSA and North Africa derive gains from full liberalization but the gains are larger for North Africa ($977 million for SSA and $2,903 for North Africa).

As in the MIRAGE model, the results from the GTAP simulations suggest that preferences matter. However, for SSA in the full liberalization scenario the difference between the results with and without preferences is larger when we use the MIRAGE model. In terms of output, the result suggests that full liberalization increases output and this result is true for both SSA and North Africa. It is also noticed in the versions of the model with and without preferences. However, as expected the changes are larger in the model without preferences. Interestingly, for SSA, the terms of trade changes associated with full liberalization are positive

Table 5
GTAP results

Variable	Sub-Saharan Africa						North Africa					
	With preferences			Without preferences			With preferences			Without preferences		
Scenarios	S0	S1	S2	S0	S1	S2	S0	S1	S2	S0	S1	S2
Welfare[a]	542	418	121	977	538	137	−62	179	82	2903	727	423
Terms of Trade[b]	0.19	0.2	0.03	0.19	0.25	−0.03	−0.86	0.01	−0.12	−0.74	0.1	−0.08
GDP[b]	0.1	0.06	0.03	0.23	0.09	0.05	0.21	0.07	0.07	1.62	0.33	0.23
Exports[b]	2.34	0.65	0.36	4.45	1.01	0.49	6.17	1.13	0.8	6.49	1.16	0.80
Imports[b]	0.5	−0.03	0.19	7.3	5.53	0.52	4.38	0.78	0.54	10.35	5.22	0.82

[a] U.S. million $.

[b] % variation.

Table 6
ATPSM results

Variable	With preferences	
	Sub-Saharan Africa	North Africa
Scenarios	Full liberalization of agricultural product (S0)	Full liberalization of agricultural product (S0)
Change in welfare[a]	−375	551
Consumer surplus	3438	6046
Producer surplus	−1199	−4652
Change in government Revenue	−2614	−843
GDP[b]	2.87	−15.44

[a] U.S. million $, only in the agricultural sector (no interaction with the NAMA one), Version 3, January 2005.

[b] Percent variation.

while they are negative for North Africa. This explains why the welfare changes for North Africa in the model with preferences are negative in this scenario. For exports and imports, in general, the results suggest that liberalization would lead to an increase in these variables and this result holds for both SSA and North Africa. They also hold for versions of the model with and without preferences.

Simulation results for the ATPSM model are presented in Table 6. It suggests that full liberalization of agricultural trade would lead to a welfare loss of $375 million for SSA but would yield welfare gains of $551 million for North Africa. The welfare loss for SSA arises from the fact that the changes in producer surplus and government revenue resulting from

full liberalization are negative in SSA and these dominate the positive changes from consumer surplus. Unlike in SSA, the change in consumer surplus in North Africa is large enough to offset the negative welfare effects from changes in producer surplus and government revenue. When the results from the ATPSM model are compared to those of the two general equilibrium models, it is found that there are significant differences in the welfare results. For example, for SSA the MIRAGE and GTAP models suggest that full liberalization would yield positive welfare gains while the ATPSM model suggests a welfare loss. There are also wide differences in the magnitude of the changes in output between the partial equilibrium and the general equilibrium models considered. For example, for SSA the change in output resulting from full liberalization is 2.87% while it is only 0.72% and 0.10%, respectively, for MIRAGE and GTAP.

6. Conclusion

Does the modeling methodology matter to the question of the relevance of preferences within the context of multilateral liberalization? This is the question that this article sought to answer by seeking to establish using a triangulation framework whether there are contradictions in the results and recommendations one arrives at in trade liberalization analysis. Using three different models and a database that takes account of preferences and one that doesn't, it is clear that in terms of magnitudes, modeling framework matters. And to the extent that policy recommendations and ranking in terms of policy importance is determined by the magnitude, then the modeling methodology is critical. And even where one has two different models using the general equilibrium framework, policy ranking in terms of magnitudes is an important issue. This article has clearly indicated that the use of static CGE and partial equilibrium models lead to different results in terms of magnitudes and could lead to different policy ranking. Thus, different levels of importance can be attributed to the preference erosion issue depending on the framework used. However, the general direction of the changes in the economic impacts is the same irrespective of the modeling framework. Barring the differences in magnitudes and by extension the rank in terms of importance in the negotiations, it is clearly evident that preferences matter for Sub-Saharan Africa.

References

Alexandraki, K., and H.-P. Lankes, "The Impact of Preference Erosion on Middle-Income Developing Countries," *IMF Working Paper 04/169* (2004).

Armington, P., "A Theory of Demand for Products Distinguished by Place of Production," *IMF Staff papers* 16 (1969), 179–201.

Bchir, M., Y. Decreux, J. Guerin, and S. Jean, "MIRAGE, un Modèle D'équilibre Général Calculable pour L'évaluation des Politiques Commerciales," *Economie Internationale* 89–90 (2002), 109–153.

Cline, W., *Trade Policy and Global Poverty* (Institute of International Economics: Washington, DC, 2004).

Francois, J., B. Hoekman, and M. Manchin, "Preference Erosion and Multilateral Trade Liberalisation," *World Bank Research Working Paper* 3730, October (2005).

Haveman, J. H., and H. J. Shatz, "Developed Country Trade Barriers and the Least Developed Countries—The Economic Results of Freeing Trade," *Discussion Paper No. 2003/46* (2003).

Hertel, T., *Global Trade Analysis: Modeling and Applications* (Cambridge University Press: Cambridge, UK, 1997).

Hoekman, B., W. Martin, and P. Braga, "Preference Erosion: The Terms of the Debate," In *Trade, Doha, and Development: A Window into the Issues,* R. Newfarmer, ed. (World Bank: Washington, DC, 2006).

International Monetary Fund, "Financing of Losses from Preference Erosion, Notes on Issues Raised by Developing Countries in the Doha Round," communication to the WTO from the IMF, WT/TF/COH/14. 14 February (2003).

Limao, N., and M. Orreaga, "Trade Preferences to Small Countries and the Welfare Costs of Lost Multilateral Liberalisation," *World Bank Policy Research Working Paper* 3565 (2005).

Lippoldt, D., and P. Kowalski, "Trade Preference Erosion: Expanded Assessment," *OECD Trade Policy Working Paper* 20 (2005).

Romalis, J., "Would Rich Country Trade Preferences Help Poor Countries Grow? Evidence from the Generalized System of Preferences," mimeo (GSB: Chicago, 2003).

UNCTAD, *Trade Preferences for LDCs: An Early Assessment of Benefits and Possible Improvements* (UNCTAD: Geneva and New York, 2003).

Vanzetti, D., and B. Graham, "Simulating Agricultural Policy Reform with ATPSM," paper presented at the Fourth Annual Conference of the European Study Group, September 2002.

IAAE Synopsis: contributions of agricultural economics to critical policy issues

The IAAE Conferences can be seen as a triennial professional stock-take. It is a time when agricultural economists from many countries come together to share their theories, ideas, and views and to showcase their latest research endeavors. The 2006 Conference, in particular, has given participants a chance to "catch-up" in a professional sense on:

- What's new?
- What's fashionable?
- What do we know?
- What do we *think* we know?

1. What's new?

There is a lot happening in the world of immense interest to agricultural economists these days. As the IAAE Secretary Treasurer, Walt Armbruster, indicated in his *Cowbell* article on Wednesday, the topics given attention in the IAAE Conferences have changed steadily over time to reflect the new challenges facing the profession.

The depth of coverage given to agribusiness and food chain issues at the 2006 Conference has been one new emphasis that caught my attention. In particular, there were many articles that dealt with various aspects of trade in higher-value food items such as seafoods, fruits, and vegetables.

Trade in these often very perishable and highly specialized agricultural products requires a great deal more sophistication in the terms of transport infrastructure, communications between buyers and sellers, quality assurance, and other marketing services than the traditional trade in bulk commodities such as grains.

Although a significant amount of this new trade is between the old Eastern block countries of Europe and the wealthier countries of Western Europe, this so-called "north-south" trade in these higher-value products clearly represents a most attractive new opportunity

for some farmers in some poorer countries. How the farmers should organize themselves to take full advantage of these new market opportunities remains an open question in many instances.

Sanitary and phytosanitary (SPS) and other aspects of food safety and food standards along with grading and specification of the produce are also emerging as critical new issues. This is especially the case since much of the new trade is controlled by the oligopolistic food retailing chains in the wealthy countries. International SPS agreements, etc. are being replaced by private arrangements that are potentially better suited to the needs of the specific parties trading. However, the farmers in the poor countries are also subject to the potential threat of exploitation as a result of the market power of the importers/buyer in the wealthy countries.

2. What's fashionable?

Independent of the discussions surrounding the possibility of the next triennial conference of IAAE being held in China, the most fashionable topic at the 2006 conference was without doubt "China." There were few sessions at this conference in which there were no references made to the "implications of (or for) China" of whatever it was that was being discussed. China is now so important for so many topics of interest to the profession that it is entirely appropriate that the 2009 triennial meeting of the IAAE will take place in China.

In relation to China, as someone who has undertaken fieldwork-based research in China for more than 20 years, I would like to draw attention to the growing connection between macroeconomic policies (in particular, fiscal policy) and rural development in China.

In his Elmhirst lecture on the first day of this conference, Hans Binswanger emphasized the positive payoff to encouraging decentralized local-government-based approaches to rural development. But in China today perhaps up to 1,000 of the 2,100 counties are fiscally bankrupt! Many poor counties cannot pay the full salaries of their teachers, health workers, agricultural extension officials, even police. Off-budget/illegal revenue collection by local government officials is at the heart of rural discontent. Local government units and officials are encouraged, indeed forced, to try to earn some of their income from "private" activities. With the "loosening up" of constraints to labor mobility, there is a major "brain drain" since government employees (cadres) have enormous incentives to move away from the poor areas. How the Beijing government addresses the fiscal problems of local governments will play a major part in the future political stability of the Chinese countryside.

Apart from China, which is destined to be much more than just a fashion for the profession, the conference also gave considerable space to some other "fashionable" topics, some of which may turn out to be of lesser importance to the profession in the longer term. Four of these topics are: bio-fuels, obesity issues, GM plants, and technical barriers to trade (TBTs).

The emphasis at present is on the technical and economic merits of bio-fuels as replacements for fossil fuels (ie., sustainability issues). However, in the future the questions raised by the impact on food prices of the increasing use of agricultural resources and outputs for the production of fuel rather than food are likely to become of major interest.

The cost to individuals and societies of "avoidable/preventable" health problems exacerbated by obesity has long been of concern in developed countries. However, obesity is no longer a "disease" confined to the wealthy countries. The lack of dietary knowledge as well as cultural values has created an epidemic of obesity-related diseases in the developing world. Clearly, the attack on obesity needs to be multi-disciplinary. Consequently, as the jointly authored articles at this conference demonstrated, agricultural economists interested in obesity issues find themselves working collaboratively with a whole new range of professional colleagues (such as medical scientists, nutritionists, psychologists, etc.).

In time, the current political negativity towards GM plants is likely to dissipate. However, in the meantime, agricultural economists are playing an important role in demonstrating the costs and benefits of GM technology. The "new" fashion or interest in issues raised by

GM organisms demonstrated at this conference calls for the creative application of "old" fashioned benefit/cost analysis. For example, as demonstrated in one of the most interesting sessions at this conference, there is an urgent need for the profession to publicize the economic arguments (not to mention the moral and ethic arguments) in favor of releasing "Golden Rice" varieties in areas where tens of millions of children suffer from blindness or partial blindness due to dietary deficiencies that can be eliminated by "Golden Rice."

Some would argue that technical barriers to trade (TBTs) are hardly a new fashion for the profession. Agricultural economists interested in trade matters have always dealt with Nontariff Barriers (which are mostly technical in nature). What makes me suggest that the articles on TBT in this conference represent a "new fashion" is the emphasis in these articles on the problems (and advantages) of private arrangements between importers and exporters outside (and often in addition to) the international agreements governing such TBTs. I have alluded to these issues earlier in connection with the growing trade in higher-value agricultural products.

3. What do we know?

The IAAE has traditionally placed great emphasis on working to improve the lot of farm families, especially in poorer countries. Whilst there has often been "a healthy level of disagreement" between participants at the IAAE triennial conferences about the most appropriate ways to foster this objective, and this conference has been no exception in this regard, there are some widely accepted old "truisms" that underlie many of the conference sessions. However, at this conference I have noticed that some of these basic tenants have been given a new twist or two.

One of these "truisms" or what might be termed "settled policies" of the agricultural economics profession is that barriers to agricultural trade are a major cause of rural poverty in many poor countries. As a consequence, a significant number of agricultural economists have devoted their professional careers to research that demonstrated the gains from freeing-up international trade in agricultural commodities on a multilateral basis. Some have gone further and become heavily involved in advocating and negotiation toward freer world trade in agricultural commodities. The presentation by Geoff Miller in the "Australia and New Zealand Session" on Wednesday morning vigorously presented the traditional approach to this topic.

Yet, in other sessions, I heard people arguing that whilst it was necessary to continue the fight for freer trade, other things were now more important. Indeed, some commentators felt that traditional trade barriers were increasingly irrelevant to the growing trade in higher-value specialty products referred to earlier. Other participants pointed to the unworkability of the new enlarged World Trade Organization (with a membership of more than 160 countries) and the virtual impossibility of achieving a successful outcome for agriculture from the Doha Round. The failure, despite decades of effort, to free-up significantly multilateral trade in agricultural commodities, seems to have persuaded many agricultural economists to accept bilateral trade deals as second best but achievable alternatives.

Another strongly held belief among IAAE members is that quantitative models lend rigor to economic analyses. Whilst the careful use of such models and the associated statistical analyses was evident in many articles at this conference, there were also some articles that applied these quantitative techniques inappropriately.

There were two major problems. The most common problem was that the analyst(s) used data without understanding the limitations of that data. One major advantage of presenting one's work at conferences such as this IAAE meeting is that peers get a chance to share their knowledge. I participated in several sessions where the author(s) of one or more articles were gently reminded of the "garbage in—garbage out" or GIGO principle.

The other common problem—which is often much harder to detect—is what I call the "black box" syndrome. Nowadays, with the advent of modern computing technology and the proliferation of software packages, it is too easy for researchers to feed data into a package/model (or "black box") without fully understanding the assumptions that underlie that package/model. Under these circumstances, the use of sophisticated statistical techniques may actually be detrimental to rigorous analysis.

Another "truism" that I think we have continued to modify at this conference is that rural development is a matter of "getting agriculture moving." At this

conference, articles reporting studies in countries as different as Macedonia and China stressed the crucial role of nonfarm rural employment (NFRE) in rural areas for broadly based rural development. Given the role of the Township and Village Enterprises (TVEs) in the development of China, no doubt we shall hear a great deal more about the importance of NFRE when we meet in Beijing in 2009. "Getting agriculture moving" is now seen as only part of the rural development story.

4. What do we *think* we know?

The more one learns about "something" the more one realizes how much one does not know about that "something."

Consequently, many younger (and some not so young) participants will leave this conference feeling they know less about their special topic than they did before they came to the Gold Coast. They have learnt more about their "something" and now realize they have even more to learn.

Whilst this is good conference outcome in an intellectual sense, it can be a little daunting for an analyst/researcher to be reminded that there is still a lot to do before they are really "an expert" in their chosen field.

Consequently, many of the participants in this conference will have added a great deal to their intellectual capital. They will return to their place of employment with new knowledge and an enhanced capacity to identify and analyze problems. However, it would be a pity if they allowed their professional contributions to stop at that level.

As Geoff Miller said on Wednesday morning:

- The identification and analysis of problems are a modestly demanding intellectual task.
- The designing of a *real world solution* is a more challenging task.
- And ensuring the implementation of the solution is often a monumental task.

As in most sciences, there has always been a division in the ranks of agricultural economists between those who feel their role stops well short of designing real world solutions and ensuring that these solutions are implemented; and those who feel the duty of the analyst can, under appropriate circumstances, be reasonably extended to include taking on the role of advocate and seeing the solution developed and implemented.

Once one does achieve a sufficient level of expertise and confidence in relation to a given field, the personal satisfaction of being able to participate in designing and implementing solutions to major problems far exceeds the "buzz" one can get from identifying and analyzing the problems in the first place.

We need more "old fashioned" advocates in the profession. In many cases agricultural economists have a great deal to contribute to the policy formulating and implementing process. Of course, the role of the analyst and the role of the advocate are different and require different skills. But good analysts usually make good advocates.

So let me wrap up this summary with some advice to IAAE members. "Don't hang back! If you think you know the solution to a problem, go for it!" You will not always carry the day but when you do there will be a lot of professional satisfaction and you'll have made a meaningful contribution to your society.

John W. Longworth

Every three years members of IAAE who are professionally active in international organizations meet with other agricultural economists, who work in universities and national organizations, to refocus their interests and concerns relating to international agenda. There are updates and new debates about the abiding issue of rural poverty and agriculture's role in combating it, particularly in the most disadvantaged areas. At this conference there was heightened attention to the environmental issues relating to climate change, and to the increase in natural disasters which devastate agricultural communities and are associated with that process. This conference again focused a plenary topic upon food safety, but whereas in the preceding 25th conference the safety issues focused on diet, malnutrition, and safety, on this occasion the principle concerns were problems arising in trade from the existence of differential national food safety standards and testing procedures. One of the perennial lead issues for IAAE conferences is trade and trade reform, and on this occasion it was linked with globalization of markets in a plenary session which marked strong progress in modeling the

potential welfare impacts of further trade reform. The fourth plenary theme was on tackling the development problems of "unfavorable" or disadvantaged rural areas. The difficulty in addressing their persistence stimulates diverse ideas on which forms of public policy intervention to prioritize. However, as priorities appear to be case specific, different solutions are given priority depending on where exactly researchers have engaged in the problem.

The above brief summary of the principal pillars of the 26th conference agenda underlines that contemporary and anticipated human and societal problems relating to agriculture, food, and the farmed environment are the things which draw IAAE's membership together in commonly shared concern and a wish to find solutions. The plenary sessions are designed to engage the interests of all members, to provide common discussion issues, and to establish links with all the other elements of the conference. These other elements include articles and workshops on theoretical and quantitative developments which propel agricultural economics forward and enable our profession to engage so effectively with policy makers and opinion formers.

1. Agricultural growth and economic development

Prabhu Pingali's Presidential Address revisited the issue of agriculture's role in development and the extent to which it will still be the driver of development in rural areas where development is stalled. A strong argument is presented for establishing food security as a prerequisite of economic growth, and that, in areas made remote by poor infrastructure and high transport costs, local agricultural growth will be a necessity for achieving such security. Realistically this assumes that it may be a long time before infrastructure investment removes the handicaps of economic isolation. One of the incentives for constructing new roads or rail links to an area is that it has progressed to a level of economic activity which can justify such investment.

However, even in the most disadvantaged areas globalization of information and tastes will have an impact on the possibilities. While the President sets out a long list of actions and policies which can help put more energy into agriculture as an engine of growth, his article recognizes that globalization is creating circumstances where the smallest farmers find it difficult to engage with the developing markets. More stringent product quality and supply volume requirements are impinging in all areas, and these favor medium and large-scale enterprises. Our Association has on many occasions addressed the future of small farmers, and has become progressively less optimistic about their prospects of playing a large role in anything other than the most local of markets.

In applying the lens of globalization to examine the contemporary role of agriculture in disadvantaged areas, the President effectively established globalization as the unofficial theme of the conference. Many subsequent conference issues, such as the impact of increasingly stringent food safety standards on both international trade and new food chain models (i.e., supermarket-dominated ones), referred frequently to globalization.

In his Elmhirst Lecture, Hans Binswanger also asserts strongly the link between agricultural growth and the reduction of poverty and in kick-starting economic growth generally. In the areas that are still underperforming, he argues "farmers and other rural people in Africa and many other parts of the developing world are still blocked or hindered in doing this by poor institutions, policies, technology and insufficient human and physical capital," and that this is the result of "deliberate policies and institutions which tend to reduce agricultural profitability and disempower rural people, especially the poor and women." Binswanger's thesis is that what is needed to overcome these obstacles is to empower local communities to design and control the implementation of policies. That empowerment he sees as devolving both planning and financial control over public funds earmarked for the various linked purposes of development at the local level. This he sees as necessary if the most disadvantaged areas are to develop profitable agriculture and other rural enterprises, which are necessary for attracting investment in infrastructure and outside capital. This view on local empowerment stimulated debate around the conference, mainly from those who expressed concern about local elites capturing control of devolved resources for their own benefit, a point which had already been anticipated by Binswanger when he states "local governments can become an instrument for elite capture and corruption." To overcome this, he argues, requires "strong communities, and civil society, and a strong local private

sector...," and he cites evidence for successes of this type. There were doubts at the conference of the ability to achieve this in all the most disadvantaged areas, but the Elmhirst Lecture's emphasis on institutional issues was one which carried over into many symposia and into the plenary on "Transformation of Unfavorable Areas."

2. Trade and agricultural policy reform

For the last two decades members of IAAE working in various capacities have made very significant contributions to the processes of agricultural and trade policy reform in the Uruguay and Doha Rounds of multilateral trade negotiations. These contributions have included framing the concepts around which the political negotiations have become organized in the key area of agriculture, and providing quantitative measures of policy distortion and estimates of the trade and welfare effects of reducing these distortions. Inevitably the reform agenda had a major place in this conference. During 2005 and 2006, a question hanging over the conference preparations was "would the agricultural trade negotiations in the Doha Round have been concluded by the time of this conference, and would the analysis be of what had been achieved, and what might be the agenda for the next multilateral trade round." Instead the negotiations were suspended only three weeks before our conference began, a rather surprising outcome which offered a dramatic source of discussion amongst those attending, many of whom in one way or another had been involved in advising governments and agencies on the reforms.

One strong insight into the contributions that IAAE members make to the negotiations was provided by the plenary article presented by Will Martin and Kym Anderson. They argue that the power of computable general equilibrium models (GTAP specifically) to analyze the potential impacts of policy reform scenarios has been greatly increased since comparable work performed during the Uruguay Round negotiations. "Part of this is due to improvements in the basic data on production, consumption and trade associated with the development of the GTAP database and part due to the greater availability of disaggregated data on not only applied but also bound rates of protection." It is also due to the greater sophistication of the model itself facilitated by the ever-rising processing capacities of computers. Furthermore they argue that there is considerable potential for further improvements "in at least six areas: measurement of protection for goods; incorporation of barriers to foreign trade and investment in services; representation of the counterfactual; disaggregation of products and regions; incorporation of new products; and inclusion of the productivity enhancement associated with trade reform."

Australia, as the lead country in the Cairns group, has been one of, if not the most forceful country in both the Uruguay and Doha Rounds in putting the economic case for reduced agricultural protection in Europe, the U.S., and Japan. Having the 26th IAAE Conference in Australia provided the opportunity for Australia to put its case directly to a large number of agricultural economists involved in the politics of trade reform. This was reflected in the generous support of AUSAID, ABARE, and other Australian sponsors for the conference, but also in the Wednesday morning conference session organized by the host country. On this occasion this was a serious academic session, in which ABARE officials presented a strong case for reducing agricultural protection, with a focus on how reducing Australia's own trade barriers was proving a motor for economic growth. The conference also provided an opportunity for sharing of views on reform between IAAE members and senior Australian civil servants in both private and formal meetings—one of a number of very valuable side-products of IAAE conferences.

3. Climate change

The increase in natural disasters, associated with increased population density and climate change, prompted the conference organizers to create a plenary session on the economics of natural disasters. This set out a scene not only of their increased frequency, but also increased economic severity (both in urban and rural areas), as well as the need for more *ex ante* planning of safety nets for victims and risk sharing mechanisms. As ever the plenary provided a focal point, but the conference program as a whole reveals a substantial body of presentations on related issues. There were no less than 29 presentations relating to drought, which is a substantial problem in the host country, Australia. Among the 164 presentations which mentioned risk,

a substantial number was specifically related to risk mitigation for natural disasters, and these were both empirical and theoretical. Carbon trading featured in 3 articles, floods in 11, and greenhouse gas emissions in 3.

It was, in fact, an article on "Costs and Mitigation Potential for Agricultural Greenhouse Gas Emissions around the Globe" that won the competition for the T.W. Schultz prize for the best article by a young professional. Robert Beach is the lead author of an article that exemplifies the developments in large-scale modeling of the global economic and environmental implications of potential changes in agricultural practice. The submodels and their linkages are so large and disaggregated that only limited detail could be presented in the article, but some fascinating estimates are distilled from them in the form of global marginal abatement costs. This is the sort of work we can anticipate seeing much more of as the model, and others like it, are tested and developed. It reflects one of the many important future directions of research into which agricultural economists will be drawn.

4. Food safety, quality, and security

The extent to which IAAE conferences have moved a significant part of their focus away from the farm is exemplified by the large body of presentations on food safety (55), food quality (105), food security (86), and food chains (24). There is some overlap with some articles appearing in more than one of the above categories. Nevertheless, the coverage of these related topic areas was very extensive at the conference, and the diversity of issues and approaches too wide to permit a simple summary. At the one end there is criminological-economic modeling of white collar crime in the food sector (Hirschauer and Musshoff) and at the other "Food Safety as a Global Public Good: Is there Underinvestment" (Laurian Unnevehr). The latter article relates to issues of who pays for, or benefits from, investments in food safety in the context of rapid growth in international trade in perishable products. The increasingly stringent standards of food safety, on say pesticide revenues, in one country imposes costs on potential overseas suppliers, and may entail costly interventions by the public sector in the supplying country. These higher safety standards constitute barriers to trade, which, unlike the nontarriff barriers eliminated in the Uruguay Round, are permissible under the rules of the WTO. However, as Nicole Ballinger said in responding to the article, these phytosanitary trade barriers might now become as trade restricting as the forms of protection resisting reform in the Doha Round negotiations. There were in fact many other articles on the trade restricting aspects of food standards presented at the conference.

5. Methodological and theoretical advances

A substantial payoff of the conference is the opportunity it gives to participants to be introduced to new methods and theories. The six days of the main conference, plus the preceding day of four workshops (attended by 319 registrants), provides time for participants to follow-up on innovations relevant to their research with innovators, and even to suggest further improvements. On the day before the main conference the joint sessions of the China and Water workshops focused on water trading and pricing, which were topics which carried over into several sessions of the main conference, reflecting the high profile of drought and water management topics. Simultaneously, under the leadership of Kym Anderson and Will Martin the Trade workshop entailed exposure to developments in general equilibrium modeling for trade policy reform. The Learning workshop on the same day contained sessions on biophysical modeling, supply response modeling, and on game-based PES experiments. It also contained a training session on a spatially specific agricultural production model.

That training option was carried over into the main body of the conference with two computer program sessions introducing new applied software packages to participants.

Many of the articles with theoretical and methodological advances involved relatively young authors, and one of the striking successes of the conference was that it attracted large numbers of new, younger participants from all regions, many of them being women. This was driven home at the plenary presentation of the three articles and three posters in competition for the T. W. Schultz and Nils Westermarck prizes for young authors. Four of the six selected articles and posters and all the presenters were women. These reflected the wealth of talent still engaging with agricultural economics,

which augurs well for the future of the profession and of IAAE.

David Colman

Since time allocated to my remark is so severely limited, I should better concentrate on challenging President Prabhu Pingali's theme expressed in the final sentence of his presidential address, which was quoted many times throughout the conference. That is, "For low income countries with a high share of rural populations and few opportunities outside the agriculture sector, if agriculture cannot be the 'engine of growth,' then what can?" In contrast, my hypothesis postulates that agriculture might not be a chief engine for developing economies under the current wave of globalization, although it will continue to be a critically important supporting engine.

In my view developing economies have been integrated into the world economy over the three globalization waves under the hegemony of Western nations. The first wave was provoked by "merchant capitalism" in the 15th–18th centuries aimed at plundering treasures, such as precious metals, spices, and humans (slaves), from tropical economies by means of monopoly trade and superior military/navigation technologies under the support of absolute monarchs. The second wave was generated by "industrial capitalism" á la Marx from the 19th to the early 20th century. Unlike merchant-adventurers in the first wave, industrial capitalists who could command modern industrial technology emanating from the Industrial Revolution, which were far superior to those of traditional cottage industries, found it advantageous to amass wealth through the promotion of exchange between their manufactures and primary commodities in topical economies. The free trade and the open capital account imposed on colonized/semi-colonized economies for this purpose resulted in their de-industrialization and thereby established the vertically integrated world trading system under the dictate of comparative advantage.

In contrast, the third wave of globalization currently in progress after the Second World War, especially since the demise of central-panning and import-substitution industrialization paradigms, has been characterized by the shift of comparative advantage in advanced economies from the industrial production of standardized commodities based on tangible capital to the production of services based on knowledge and information. Under the present structure of comparative advantage, the integration of domestic with international markets stimulates the growth of manufacturing activities in developing economies, which is contrary to the case of the second globalization wave. The balance of trade in manufactured commodities is rapidly improving for developing economies. The so-called "East Asian Miracle" represents the cases that have best exploited the industrialization opportunities created by the second wave, which low-income economies in other regions are now likely to follow. Thus, the current globalization wave is promoting industrialization in developing economies and de-industrialization in developed economies under competitive global markets.

An apparent anomaly is that this shift of comparative advantage in manufacturing from developed to developing economies is associated with the reverse shift of comparative advantage in agriculture from the latter to the former, as evident from the declining balance of trade in agricultural commodities in recent years. On this observation, President Pingali in his address expressed a concern on declining competitiveness in agriculture in developing economies. However, the observed decline in comparative advantage in agriculture resulted not so much from the slowdown in the growth of agricultural productivity as from the spurt of industrial productivity in developing relative to developed economies. Likely underlying these changes is the greater difficulty of technology transfer from developed to developing countries in agriculture than in manufacturing. That is, because agricultural production is a biological process, it is critically influenced by natural environments which are difficult to control artificially. Therefore, superior farming methods and plant varieties developed in advanced countries located in the temperate zone cannot readily be applied in developing countries under tropical environments. In contrast, manufacturing production is largely a mechanical process conducted in the controlled environments inside factories, so its technology is much easier to transfer from developed to developing countries. In this way, agriculture's comparative advantage tends to decline in developing countries achieving rapid industrialization through technological borrowing, with a

few exceptions, such as Brazil, that are endowed with especially favorable conditions for agricultural technology transfer from developed countries.

Considering the mechanism underlying the third wave of globalization, I would dare to present a counter-hypothesis to President Pingali's, which argues that manufacturing, not agriculture, is likely to be the engine of economic growth even in low-income economies. The enormous capacity of absorbing labor in the production of standardized labor-intensive manufactures geared for global markets that resulted in dramatic poverty reduction has been amply demonstrated in the process of the East Asian Miracle, especially in the recent development in China. The problem is how to channel such employment opportunities to rural areas where the majority of poor people are living. Many labor-intensive manufactures, such as cloth, garments, and standard electric/electronic parts, are characterized by weak scale economies and modest transportation costs. Therefore, their production need not be located in metropolitan cities. For these activities to be located in the hinterlands, however, there must be a domestic trade network appropriately linking foreign demands and rural producers. In the absence of such a network, emerging demands for labor-intensive manufactures in developing economies, for example, tend to be met exclusively by factories located in a metropolis with ready access to foreign buyers and immigrant labor from the hinterlands. This fails to stimulate cottage industries in rural areas, even though their manufacturing costs could be lower. The result would be the widening of rural-urban disparities to such a magnitude as to endanger sustainability of the development process, which is typically faced by China today. Therefore, it should be a central task of our profession to identify ways and means to support rural-based industrialization in response to opportunities emerging under the current wave of globalization.

No doubt, the healthy development of agriculture provides indispensable support for industrial development. The success of labor-intensive industrialization critically hinges on the supply of food staples as basic wage goods at modest costs. The Ricardian solution to this problem relying on food imports from abroad will not be possible for developing economies today, considering their share of world population. For land resource as given, increases in domestic food supply through innovations in crop production are necessary for sustaining industrial development, as attested by the high correlation between the success of industrialization and the success in the Green Revolution in Asia. Thus, investments in research and infrastructure for upgrading agricultural production technology will continue to be as important as ever, especially with respect to harmonization between food production and environmental quality, as discussed extensively throughout the conference.

Moreover, even though agriculture as a whole is likely to be losing comparative advantage in developing economies, there is a new set of agricultural commodities of which production and export are expanding rapidly corresponding to emerging demands from high-income economies, such as flowers, fruits, and vegetables. They are characterized by intensive use of labor for crop care and many are exotic niche products grown exclusively in tropical environments. These new agricultural commodities of rising global demand are mostly perishable, so fast delivery from producers to consumers or processing plants is critically important. Yet, it is not easy to assemble a sufficiently large bulk of standardized commodities adequate for marketing and processing to meet large urban or foreign demands. Quality standardization of these commodities is also difficult, especially for the assurance of "organic cultivation" with low use of chemicals due to severe information asymmetry. For this purpose, farm-level production from planting to harvesting must be much more closely coordinated with the needs of marketing and processing over the whole value chain up to the retail and export levels.

This characteristic of the new agricultural commodities is reflected in many presentations at this conference employing the value chain analysis, which is a good theoretical basis for policy making in this area. In contrast, presentations were very scanty on the marketing chain for industrial commodities channeling global demands to rural producers as the basis of rural-based industrialization. Was this because of agricultural economists' propensity to concentrate on problems within agriculture? If so, I hope a proper balance will be achieved by the next conference at Beijing, considering the fact that our ultimate target is not agriculture itself but the well-being of rural people.

Yujiro Hayami

Good afternoon. It's a great pleasure to be here

I was given the task of synthesizing in 5 minutes! I will try but will have for read my remarks for you.

I would like to start by saying there are many great things about this workshop, especially the very warm and kind hospitality of Australians for which we are very grateful. But unfortunately my focus will be on gaps as I have only 5 minutes for this.

My remarks will focus on the issue of agriculture and achieving poverty reduction in all its dimensions and how well we have done in this respect at this conference and generally in what we are doing. In making a contribution to those goals, I believe our profession remains constrained by the way we think about and deal with poverty as an income phenomenon. I strongly believe that poverty is wealth connected and primarily determined by the state of and change in wealth. We certainly need to reorient our thinking and approach to dealing with poverty in the direction of measuring change in wealth if we are concerned with the welfare of current and future generations.

One crucial task here is to understand how much wealth are we taking out of rural areas and how much wealth is ploughed back there and what determines that? By wealth I mean wealth inclusive of all forms of capital. Among the components of wealth that are of high significance to the role of agriculture in poverty reduction are the following:

1. Human capital. There is a general observation at this conference and elsewhere that the share of public and private investment in building rural human capital is negligible but more important there is lack of direction and rationality about where the priorities are.
   - One important constituent of this is human health. What is more important than the burden of HIV/AIDS (and other diseases) on rural Africa for example? How much have we done and are doing in understanding this and in informing investment priorities and public policy on that? And how much are we investing in enhancing the health and nutrition of the more vulnerable segments of the rural population (women, children, and the very poor).
   - Education and access to information. For one thing we know that we failed to make agricultural extension work and we do not know what to

do with that. But how much are we investing in farmers' education and access to information in rural areas?

Will private investment do it and what are the optimal levels of public investments to provide the required structure of incentives for attracting and facilitating private investment in building rural human capital? Currently the bulk of public and private investment in human capital concentrates in urban areas. Maybe that is because poverty in many places in the developing world concentrates in urban areas. But there are very powerful linkages between who are the poor in urban areas and the exodus and migration from rural areas. Unfortunately understanding the dynamics of rural labor markets is another area where our efforts seem to have recently ceased.

2. Natural capital. There is ample evidence that there is steady depletion of the natural resource base on which the livelihoods of millions of rural people are dependent. Many examples of high rates of liquidation, extraction, and flight out of rural areas of natural wealth. How much of the resource rents generated from liquidation of these assets is recovered and reinvested in sustaining the capacity of the natural ecosystems to continue providing the critical services on which millions of the poor in rural areas depend for livelihood? How much of that is reinvested in maintaining the forests, the land, the fisheries, and the wetlands in rural areas? How much do we know about that and how much have we done?

3. Social capital. There is also evidence of serious erosion of social capital especially in developing countries' rural areas and more to come with globalization. How much do we know about and have done to understand the critical role and contributions of social capital to agricultural growth and poverty reduction? How much do we invest in promoting and enhancing the role of social institutions in rural areas? Most of the emphasis and investment in agricultural research continued to be in agricultural technology. Will technology alone do it? A big question.

4. Another last related observation is the fact that our profession has done quite a bit on the returns to agricultural research but mainly agricultural technology research. I would like to have seen some efforts in better understanding the contributions of agricultural economics and policy research. I know it is

much harder with attribution of policy impacts but that will be very useful in defining priorities and informing and guiding investment in policy research. I look forward to seeing few PhDs and plenaries on these in the future.

Assalamu alaikum

Rashid Hassan

Thank you very much. I will have to be highly selective and arbitrary in my coverage given the brief time available, but let me get right to it.

1. Water

This is the year of Water Policy at IAAE.

In addition to a preconference workshop on water policy, there were seven contributed article sessions on water policy. I'm not sure whether this is a trend that is peaking or whether the relevance of the issue to Australia makes this an outlier year. There was a strong focus in the water sessions on economic incentives for water management, including an exploration of alternative mechanisms for achieving more efficient water management. A number of articles pointed out that while market-based instruments for water allocation have demonstrable efficiency-enhancing qualities, they might not serve the best interests of equity in all cases. As such, market-based instruments for reallocation of water should be designed properly, or accompanied by the appropriate policies in order to ensure that inequality is not deepened among the agents involved. There was a lively debate over how much equity should matter.

Relatively few articles addressed the difficult political economy of the introduction of water markets, particularly in developing countries. I have the sense from the articles presented here that these difficulties are underestimated in the profession. Equity issues must be addressed when considering water pricing. The concept of water pricing may conflict with the idea that the provision of water services is a basic right to all individuals if water prices rise to a level that low-income households cannot afford. The high costs of measuring and monitoring water use where infrastructure and institutions are weak can also be a major constraint to implementation of water pricing. Adding to the difficulty of pricing reform, both long-standing practice and cultural and religious beliefs have treated water as a free good, and entrenched interests benefit from the existing system of subsidies and administered allocations of water.

Although there were some excellent articles on water salinity and policies to address salinity, other water quality issues seemed underrepresented relative to the growing importance of the issue. To address growing water quality issues, investments in and capacity of water quality monitoring need to be enhanced; measurable and feasible water quality standards for different uses established; water quality connotations incorporated into water rights systems, and the awareness and status of water quality and environmental water uses raised with developing-country policy makers. Enforcement of water quality standards will be the greatest challenge—making those who pollute water pay for the consequences, and changing habits of using and discharging low-quality water.

2. Land

By contrast, only three contributed article sessions were on land management, and these only partially addressed sustainable land management. Interesting case studies showed significant direct profits and external benefits from various sustainable land management practices. For example, an article about Kenya showed that sustainable land management (SLM) practices such as leguminous hedgerows have robust profits for farmers raising dairy cows since the leguminous trees control erosion and are used to feed dairy cows. But there are often high initial investment costs to SLM at the farm level that are not compensated by direct returns to farmers.

More broadly, there seems to be no strong general case made regarding the applicability of input use and land management practices that are productive and profitable, but that also protect longer term land quality. Given the critical importance of soil fertility issues in Africa, it seems essential to derive broader understanding and appropriate policy prescriptions for land

and input management. Two broad questions need to be better answered, including (1) why should governments intervene to address land degradation or promote SLM? This is often a normative case not clearly made and for which empirical basis is lacking; (2) when intervention is appropriate, how should governments and others intervene and how can policies and programs be more effective? To answer these questions, key knowledge gaps on adoption and impacts of land management should be addressed on a comparative cross-regional basis. These are (a) impacts of land management practices and programs on profitability, risk, household income, and externalities; (b) dynamic relationships between land management, degradation, and poverty; (c) mechanisms of impact of specific factors such as household endowments, technical assistance, collective action, and social capital—combining qualitative and quantitative approaches needed; factors affecting collective more ambiguous and context-dependent; (d) implementation issues (incentives, information constraints, transaction costs, etc.) within government and NGO programs.

3. Payment for environmental services (PES)

An increasingly prominent area of policy and research interest to promote sustainable natural resource management is payment for environmental services, and a number of articles at these meetings addressed this topic. PES provides a mechanism for those who manage the natural resources to generate external benefits to potentially receive *transfer payments* from those who benefit from these services. In addition to potentially providing incentives to protect natural resources, PES are attractive because they provide a stream of income for often poor farmers and provide a market-oriented alternative to traditional "regulatory" approaches of adopting costly technological solutions to achieving environmental standards. But a number of articles here also pointed out the difficulties in developing systems for implementing PES. Most fundamentally, creating markets in services, designing payment mechanism, and finding nongovernmental purchasers for environmental services are extremely difficult. Adverse incentives and impacts can also be created depending on the design of payment systems.

1. Incentive payments could lead to increased land rents with negative impacts on poor tenants;
2. Encourage destructive behavior in anticipation of payments to be implemented—for example, increase in deforestation now since people expect future payment will be offered for reforestation;
3. Payments can distort incentives like excessive promotion of whatever is being paid for relative to other less easily monitored environmental services, possibly at the expense of those services. For example, payments for carbon sequestration will encourage monocrop planting of the fastest growing trees (like eucalyptus) at the expense of biodiversity and negative impacts on water availability, etc.;
4. Lack of information on resource-rights by the indigenous people may lead to social conflicts (cultural sensitivity); and
5. High transaction costs.

This remains an important area for research and like land management, one that needs to derive more generalizable lessons on what works and what doesn't and how to implement effective systems.

4. Emerging topics

Finally, let me just address more briefly some issues that have—or should have—increasing prominence in research, including biotechnology, biofuels, and climate change and variability.

A number of articles addressed the impact of current biotechnology and GMO such as Bt cotton on farm income, input use, pest infestation, and environmental impacts. There seems to be a wide range of outcomes on this, often depending on the season and specific region studied. But it is hard to understand why farmers would be paying high prices for technology that isn't profitable. In the future, research on GMO may turn increasingly to the *ex ante* impacts of the next generation of crop traits, such as drought and salt tolerance, and nitrogen use efficiency, that may have much more profound income effects and positive environmental impacts for farmers in less favored areas. In addition, valuable work remains to be done to assess consumer acceptance of transgenics, to understand the impact of transgenics on the environment, and to examine the impacts of domestic biosafety systems, international trade regulations and the regulations of major

importing countries on the rate of discovery, adoption and benefits of transgenic varieties.

Biofuels have become a hot topic, and important research remains to be done on the food security and poverty implications of rapid expansion of the use of food and feed crops for the production of biofuels, in addition to the direct technology and energy issues. There were relatively few articles on this topic at the meetings, perhaps because the rapid increase in oil prices was largely felt after the submission deadline of the conference. Valuable research can be done on the potential of the agricultural sector for providing renewable energy for its own needs, as well as that of other key economic activities, such as transport (which represents a majority of fossil-fuel-based consumption). How do the constraints on land and water resources limit the potential for biofuel feedstock production from agriculture, in emerging and developing agricultural economies? How could the investments in agricultural research, productivity-boosting technologies and extension services for farmers be complementary to both food security goals and the needs of agriculturally based biofuel production processes?

Research on the impact of climate change research on agriculture, water, and natural resources is still in its relative infancy. New developments in GIS and remote sensing make policy-relevant work in this area more feasible, but much work needs to be done to address impacts, and the role of agriculture and other policies in adapting to climate change at appropriate scales of analysis. Over the coming decades, global change will have significant, yet highly uncertain impacts on food and water security. Appropriate adaptation strategies and accompanying policy response options to global change, including options for infrastructure investment, reform of water allocation, land use patterns, and food trade, are needed and will be vital to improve the living conditions of farmers and rural men and women in the developing world. Responses to climate change need to encompass several levels, including crop and farm-level adaptations, national-level agricultural and supporting policies and investments, and regional and global policies and investments. Research is needed to understand the impacts of global change on agriculture and water resources at the global, national, and river basin, and local levels, to assess the effects of climate variability and change on water and food security in vulnerable rural areas of developing countries, and to identify adaptation measures that reduce the impacts of global change on these communities. The research results developed should provide policy makers and stakeholders in these countries with tools to better understand, analyze, and inform policy decisions for adaptation to climate change.

Mark W. Rosegrant

Conference Program

POSTER SESSIONS

Adejobi, A., "Enhancing the Access of Rural Households to Output Markets for Increased Farm Incomes"

Ahlheim, M., "The Role of Participation in CVM Survey Design: Evidence from A Tap Water Improvement Program in Northern Thailand"

Ajibefun, I. A., "Linking Socio-Economic and Policy Variables to Technical Efficiency of Traditional Agriculture: Empirical Evidence from Nigeria"

Aldas, J., "Is Green Revolution Vanishing? Emperical Evidence from TFP Analysis for Rice"

Ali, M., "Analysis of the Impact of Urbanization and Enhanced Incomes on Demand for Food Quality in Hanoi"

Amaza, P. S., "Determinants and Measurement of Food Insecurity in Nigeria: Some Empirical Policy Guide"

Arriaza, M., "Andalusian Demand for Non-Market Goods from Olive Groves"

Ater, P. I., "Comparative Analysis of the Impact of Root and Tuber Expansion Programme on Poverty Alleviation of Peri-Urban and Rural Communities in Benue State—Nigeria"

Ayoola, G. B., "Analysis of Budget Policy on Agriculture Under Different Governance Regimes"

Bahta, Y. T., "Rural Credit for Resource Poor Entrepreneurs: Lessons from the Eritrean Experience"

Bakhshoodeh, M., "Adoption of Technology Under Production Risk: Evidence from Rice in Iran"

Baltenweck, I., "Dynamic Changes in Dairy Technologies Uptake in the Kenya Highlands"

Barnes, A., "A Total Social Factor Productivity Index for the UK Post-Farm Gate Food Chain"

Bashaasha, B., "Determinants of Well-being Among Smallholders in Adjumani District, Uganda"

Basu, J. P., "Cointegration and Market Integration: An Application to the Potato Markets in Rural West Bengal, India"

Berges, M., "Quality Warranties and Food Products in Argentina. What Do Consumers Believe in?"

Bertuglia, A., "Factors Related to the Adoption of Good Agrarian Practices (Gap) in Plastic Covered Horticulture of Southeastern Spain"

Beyene, F., "Examining Collective Action Among Mieso Agropastoralists of Eastern Ethiopia"

Bhattarai, M., "Direct and Total Benefits of Irrigation in India and Its Implications to Irrigation Financing and Cost Recovery"

Bhullar, A. S., "Reformulating Policies for Integrated Land and Water Use for Sustainable Agricultural Development: A Case of Indian Punjab"

Breustedt, G. B., "Measurement and Comparison of Risk Reduction by Means of Farm Yield, Area Yield, and Weather Index Crop Insurance Schemes: The Case of Kazakhstani Wheat Farms"

Brink, L., "Constraining U.S. and EU Domestic Support in Agriculture: The October 2005 WTO Proposals"

Brown, C., "Improving the Economic Decision-Making Capability and Viability of Chinese Wool Textile Mills"

Brunke, H., "Demand Enhancement Through Food-Safety Regulation: Benefit-Cost Analysis of Collective Action in the California Pistachio Industry"

Burnett, K., "Environmental Policy Issues for Sustainable Economic Development in China"

Cáceres-Hernández, J. J., "Heterogeneous Seasonal Pattern in Agricultural Data and Evolving Splines"

Calatrava-Leyva, J., "Adoption of Soil Erosion Control Practices in Southern Spain Olive Groves"

Carew, R., "Hedonic Pricing of Australian Wines in the British Columbia Wine Market: The Importance of Wine Brands and Reputation"

Casellas, K., "What Determines the Economic Links Among Organic Farmers? Empirical Evidence from Argentina"

Chang, T., "The Physical, Social and Cultural Determinants of Obesity: An Empirical Study of the U.S."

Colyer, D., "Environmental Issues in Free Trade Agreements"

Comerford, E., "Using Auctions for Conservation Contracts to Protect Queensland's Vegetation: Lessons from the Vegetation Incentives Program"

Corsi, A., "Which Italian Family Farms will have a Successor?"

Costa, E. F., "An Interactive Decision Model Integrating Broiler Production and Processing Responsiveness to Consumer and Producer Prices"

Cramb, R. A., "The 'Landcare' Approach to Soil Conservation in the Philippines: An Assessment of Farm-Level Impacts"

Delve, R. J., "Evaluation of Resource Management Options for Smallholder Farms Using an Integrated Economic Modelling Approach"

Dhehibi, B., "Productivity and Economic Growth in Tunisian Agriculture: An Empirical Evidence"

Dieu Ne Dort, N. W., "Socio-Economic Impact of a Cocoa Integrated Crop and Pest Management Diffusion Knowledge through a Farmer Field School Approach in Southern Cameroon"

Dillon, E., "A Cost-Effectiveness Study of Animal Disease Eradication Strategies: Foot-and-Mouth Disease in Ireland"

Dixon, J., "The 2003 Mid Term Review of the Common Agricultural Policy: A Computable General Equilibrium Analysis for Ireland"

Dorosh, P. A., "Rice Price Stabilization in Madagasccar: Price and Welfare Implications of Variable Tariffs"

Dutta, M. K., "Institutional Factors Behind Effectiveness of Irrigation: A Study in the Brahmaputra Valley in Eastern India"

Ehui, S., "Modelling the Impact of Credit on Intensification in Mixed Crop-Livestock Systems: A Case Study from Ethiopia"

Eigenraam, M., "A Producer's Propensity to Conserve Framework: Application to a U.S. and Australian Conservation Program"

Ellatifi, M., "Importance of Agricultural Economics and Watershed Protection in the Forest Total Economic Value Towards a Sustainable Development: The Case of Morocco"

Escobal, J., "Access to Dynamic Markets for Small Commercial Farmers: The Case of Potato Production in the Peruvian Andes"

Ferto, I., "Marginal Intra-Industry Trade and Adjustment Costs in the Hungarian Food Industry"

Fletcher, S., "Strategic Behavior and Trade in Agricultural Commodities—Competition in World Peanut Markets"

Fok Ah Chuen, M., "Liberalization and Globalization: Trojan Horse for the Cotton Traders' Domination in Francophone Africa"

Forgacs, C., "Leadership May Have Decisive Influence on Successful Transition of Production Cooperative"

Fritz, M., "Trust and Control Dynamics in Agrifood Supply Networks: Communication Strategies for Electronic Transaction Environments"

Fuller, F. H., "The Impact of the European Enlargement and Cap Reforms on Agricultural Markets. Much Ado about Nothing?"

Furuya, J., "Impacts of Water Supply Changes on the Rice Market of Lao PDR: Stochastic Analysis of Supply and Demand Model"

Ganewatta, G., "An Economics Analysis of Bushfire Management Programs"

Gavrilescu, C., "The Accession of Romania to the European Union—Scenario Analysis for Key Agricultural Crop Markets Using Agmemod Model"

Gibson, J., "Natural Experiment Evidence on Whether Selection Bias Overstates the Gains from Migration"

Glukhikh, R., "Vulnerability and Risk Management Among Turkmen Leaseholders"

Godo, Y., "Financial Liberalization and Japan's Agricultural Cooperatives"

Goetz, L., "The EU's Import Regime for Oranges—Much Ado About Nothing?"

Goldberg, I., "Parental Response to Health Risk Information: A Lab Experiment on Evaluating Willingness-to-Pay for Safer Infant Milk Formula"

Gollin, D., "Changes in Yield Stability: Wheat and Maize in Developing Countries"

Goncharova, N., "Investment Spikes in Dutch Horticulture: An Analysis at Firm and Aggregate Firm Level over the Period 1975–1999"

Grethe, H., "Using the Logistic Functional Form for Modelling International Price Transmission in Net Trade Simulation Models"

Grover, D. K., "Enhancing and Use-Efficiency Through Appropriate Land Policies in Ethiopia"

Haering, A. M., "Agricultural Policy Assessment and Development by Stakeholders: A Cross-Country Analysis of National Organic Farming Policy in 11 European Countries"

Hansen, H., "Destabilizing Farmers' Revenues by Shifting to Direct Payments? The Case of EU's Common Agricultural Policy"

Hattam, C., "Adopting Organic Agriculture: An Investigation Using the Theory of Planned Behaviour"

Headey, D., "Something of a Paradox: The Neglect of Agriculture in Economic Development"

Heidelbach, O., "Efficiency of Selected Risk Management Instruments—An Empirical Analysis of Risk Reduction in Kazakhstani Crop Production"

Hendriks, S. L., "The Impact of Smallholder Commercialisation of Organic Crops on Food Consumption Patterns in Kwazulu-Natal, South Africa"

Hendrikse, G., "Organization and Strategy of Farmer Specialized Cooperatives in China"

Henke, R., "Agri-Food Trade Between Italy and China: Integration, Similarity and Competition"

Henseler, M., "An Agro-Economic Production Model for a Middle European River Basin—First Results of Cap Reform Scenario Calculations"

Herath, A., "Flexible Trade Policies in Agriculture Sectors of Developing Countries: Proposing a Technical Approach for Sri Lanka"

Herath, G., "Reconciling Value Conflicts in Regional Forest Planning in Australia: A Decision Theoretic Approach"

Hockmann, H., "Factors Constraining Efficiency of Russian Corporate Farms: The Case of the Moscow Region"

Holloway, G., "New Results on Censored Regression with Applications to Transactions Costs, Household Decisions and Food Purchases"

Honda, M., "Increase of Residential Electricity Consumption in Urban and Rural China by Province"

Huang, C. L., "A Hedonic Analysis on the Implicit Values of Fresh Tomatoes"

Huang, C. L., "Willingness to Pay for Irradiated Meat Products: A Comparison Between Poultry and Pork"

Huang, K. S., "A Look at Food Price Elasticities and Flexibilities"

Huang, S. W., "On Measuring Consumer Welfare Effects of Trade Reform"

Jabbar, M. A., "Trader Behaviour and Performance in Live Animal Marketing in Rural Ethiopian Markets"

Jackson, E., "Farmer-to-Farmer Advice: What's the Best Way to Sell Raw Wool in Australia?"

Jessup, E., "Transportation Optimization Modeling for Washington State Hay Shipments: Mode and Cost Implications Due to Loss of Container Services at the Port of Portland"

Juana, J. S., "Marginal Productivity Analysis of Global Industrial Water Demand"

Jyotishi, A., "Institutional Analysis of Swidden: The Case of Swiddners in Orissa"

Kageyama, M., "An Empirical Analysis of Agglomeration Effect in the Japanese Food Industry-Panel Analysis Using Flexible Translog Production Function"

Kareemulla, K., "Wastelands Afforestation in Northern India by Cooperatives: A Socio-Economic Evaluation"

Kariuki, I. M., "Export Market Linkage Via Gentleman's Agreement: Evidence from French Bean Marketing in Kenya"

Kaur, K., "Total Value Assessment of Tree Clearing for Developing Grazing Systems in Central Queensland"

Kaye-Blake, W., "Current Contribution of Four Biotechnologies to New Zealand's Primary Sector"

Kijima, Y., "Emerging Markets After Liberalization: Evidence from the Raw Milk Market in Rural Kenya"

Koffi-Tessio, E. M., "Assessing Environment in Agriculture in Sub-Saharan Africa: A Time Series Estimation"

Kolawole, O., "Determinant of Profit Efficiency of Small Scale Rice Farmers in Nigeria: A Profit Function Approach"

Kotu, X., "Farmers' Post-Harvest Grain Management Choices Under Liquidity Constraints and Impending Risks: Implications for Achieving Food Security Objectives in Ethiopia"

Krieger, S., "Quality Systems in the Agri-Food Industry—Implementation, Cost/Benefit and Strategies"

Kurkalova, L., "Empirical Assessment of Baseline Conservation Tillage Adoption Rates and Soilcarbon Sequestration in the Upper Mississippi River Basin"

La Rovere, R., "Targeting Research for Enhanced Impact on Poverty in Marginal Dry Areas of Syria"

Laurenceson, J., "NGO Microfinance in Vietnam: Stakeholder Perceptions of Effectiveness"

Lee, D., "Estimating Global Environmental Implications of Agricultural Trade Liberalization: A Dynamic Computable General Equilibrium Analysis"

Lema, D., "Contracts, Transaction Costs and Agricultural Production in the Pampas"

Li, L., "Grocery Retailer Pricing Behavior for California Avocados with Implications for Industry Promotion Strategies"

Lien, G., "Simulating Multivariate Distributions with Sparse Data: A Kernel Density Smoothing Procedure"

Lin, B. H., "Consumer Knowledge and Meat Consumption in the U.S."

Lissitsa, A., "Agricultural Productivity Growth in the European Union and Transition Countries"

Lu, W., "Modeling Risk Behavior of Agricultural Production in Chinese Small Households"

Lu, W., "Prospects of Grain Supply and Demand in China: A Regionalized Multimarket Model Simulation"

Macharia, J. M., "Economic Evaluation of Organic and Inorganic Fertilizer Resources in Recapitalizing Soil Fertility in Maize-Based Farming Systems in Central Kenya"

Maertens, M., "Trade, Food Standards and Poverty: The Case of High-Value Vegetable Exports from Senegal"

Maharjan, K. L., "Role of Cooperatives in Improving Accessibility to Production Resources and Household Economy of Backyard Pig Raisers in Batangas, Philippines"

Maharjan, K. L., "Household Food Security in Rural Areas of Nepal: Relationship Between Socio-Economic Characteristics and Food Security Status"

Malcolm, S. A., "Land Quality and International Agricultural Productivity: A Distance Function Approach"

Manaloor, V., "CO_2 Emissions from Central Canadian Agriculture: Meeting Kyoto Targets and Its Implications"

Marchant, M. A., "China's Biotech Policies and Their Impacts on U.S. Agricultural Exports to China"

Marinda, P., "Technical Efficiency Analysis in Male and Female-Managed Farms: A Study of Maize Production in West Pokot District, Kenya"

Marsh, S. P., "Social Costs of Herbicide Resistance: The Case of Resistance to Glyphosate"

Mashinini, N. N., "Deregulation of the Maize Marketing System of Swaziland and Implications for Food Security"

Maytsetseg, B., "Changes and Actual State of Mongolian Meat Market and Distribution System: A Case Study of Ulaanbaatar City's Khuchit Shonhor Food Market"

Medicamento, U., "Socal Networks and Supply Chain Management in Rural Areas: A Case Study Focusing on Organic Olive Oil"

Melo, O., "The Effect of Genetics and Infrastructure Investments in Dairy and Beef Producers' Profit in Chile"

Meyer, F., "Model Closure and Price Formation Under Switching Grain Market Regimes in South Africa"

Meyer-Aurich, A., "Cost Efficient Tillage and Rotation Options for Mitigating GHG Emissions from Agriculture in Eastern Canada"

Mithofer, D., "The Role of Food from Natural Resources in Reducing Vulnerability to Poverty: A Case Study from Zimbabwe"

Miyata, S., "Credit Accessibility, Risk Attitude, and Social Learning: Investment Decisions of Aquaculture in Rural Indonesia"

Moellers, J., "A Synthesis of Theoretical Concepts for Analysing Non-Farm Rural Employment"

Moellers, J., "Systematic Policy Decisions on Direct Income Payments in Agricultural Policies"

Moura, A. D., "The Assessment of the Production Outsourcing Strategy in the Wood Furniture Industry of the Ubá Region (Brazil), Through the Development of a Dynamic Model"

Mousavi, S. N., "The Relationship Between Rice Market Liberalization and Food Security"

Murray, C., "Social Capital and Cooperation in Central and Eastern Europe—Toward An Analytical Framework"

Nankhuni, F. J., "HIV/AIDS and Adolescent's School-Work Choices in Malawi"

Neal, M., "The Potential Cost to New Zealand Dairy Farmers from the Introduction of Nitrate-Based Stocking Rate Restrictions"

Nillesen, E., "BT and HT Maize Versus Conventional Pesticide and Herbicide Use. Do Environmental Impacts Differ?"

Obi, A., "Recent Trends in Agricultural Land Prices in South Africa: A Preliminary Investigation Using Cointegration Analysis"

Odhiambo, M. O., "Analysis of the Structure and Performance of the Beans Marketing System in Nairobi"

Ohe, Y., "Evaluating Multifunctional Activities As Rural Institution in Japan"

Okoruwa, V. O., "Efficiency and Productivity of Farmers in Nigeria: A Study of Rice Farmers in North Central Nigeria"

Olson, K. D., "The Value of Crop Borders for Management of Potato Virus Y (PVY) in Seed Potatoes"

Olubode-Awosola, F., "Mentorship Alliance Between South African Farmers: Implication for Sustainable Agriculture Sector Reform"

Omiti, J., "Decentralization and Access to Agricultural Extension Services in Kenya"

Omitsu, M., "The Importance of Controlling for Pre-Disaster Conditions in Evaluating Natural Disasters: Evidence from Nicaragua"

Onyuma, S. O., "Testing Market Integration for Fresh Pineapples in Kenya"

Owuor, G., "Does Land Use Patterns Matter for BT-Maize: The Case of Maize Farming System in Kenya"

Owuor, G., "Milk Handling in the Supply Chains: The Case of Smallholder Retail Outlets in Nakuru, Kenya"

Oyewumi, O. A., "Implications of Tariff Rate Quotas Liberalization in the South African Livestock Industry"

Padinjaranda, C., "Impact of Research Investment on Technology Development and Total Factor Productivity in Major Field Crops of Peninsular India"

Pal, S., "Delivering Seeds of 'Orphan' Crops: The Case Studies of Potato and Groundnut in India"

Pemmanda, R., "Livelihood Dependence on Non-Timber Forest Products (NTFPS): A Study of Jenukuruba Tribes in South India"

Peroni, M., "Long Term Structural Changes in the EU Countries (1970–2000): Convergence or Divergence in the Agri-Food System?"

Pieniadz, A., "Explaining Quality Differences at the Procurement Stage in the Polish Milk Sector"

Prahadeeswaran, M., "Food Security and Efficacy of the Intervention Mechanism in India"

Pushkarskaya, H., "Schemes to Regulate Non-Point Water Pollution: Making Sense of Experimental Results"

Puskur, R., "Investing in Livestock Development in Water-Scarce Semi-Arid Watersheds: Technological, Institutional and Policy Dimensions"

Quaddus, M., "An Investigation of Significant Factors Influencing Western Australian Woolproducers to Produce Wool: A Structural Equation Modelling Approach"

Quiroga, J., "A Framework for Estimating U.S. WTO Domestic Support to 2015"

Reddy, G. P., "Assessment Strategic Research Extension Plan (SREP) Methodology for Upscaling and Institutionalisation of R-E-F Linkages"

Rezende, G. C., "The Recent Outburst of Soybeans and Livestock in Brazil and Its Impact on the Environment"

Rodríguez, E., "Consumers' Perceptions about Food Quality Attributes and Their Incidence in Argentinian Organic Choices"

Roeder, N., "Impact of the Cap Reform on Southern German Grassland Regions"

Sakurai, S., "Rural Diversification and Social Capital in Rural Japan"

Sampaio, Y., "Social-Economic Impacts of the Marine Shrimp Culture in Selected Brazilian Cities"

Schleyer, C., "Institutional Change in East German Water Management Systems"

Segarra, E., "Aquifer Depletion and the Cost of Water Conservation: The Southern High Plains of Texas Case"

Sharma, K. L., "High-Value Agricultural Products of Fiji Islands—Performance and Prospects"

Simtowe, F., "Determinants of Moral Hazard in Microfinance: Empirical Evidence from Joint Liability Lending Schemes in Malawi"

Singh, J., "Wheat Diversity and Productivity in Indian Punjab After the Green Revolution"

Sini, M. P., "Social Opportunities and Private Convenience of Choices at Farm Level: An Approach to the Links Between Farm Income and Sustainable GDP"

Soliman, M., "The Regional and Multilateral Dilemma: Institutions Do Matter"

Somwaru, A., "Multilateral or Regional Agreement: The Case of Mediterranean Non-EU Countries"

Speelman, S., "Productive Water Uses at Household Level in Rural Kenya: Case Study of the Ukambani District"

Stauder, M., "Concentration in Hungarian Food Retailing and Supplier-Retailer Relationships"

Stricker, S., "Marketing Wine on the Web"

Subbaraman, S., "Determinants of Wages and Returns to Education in Rural India"

Szabo, Z., "Analysing Wine Buying Behaviour in Hungarian Hypermarkets"

Szonyi, J. A., "Poverty Mapping in Rural Syria for Enhanced Targeting"

Teweldemedhin, M., "International Trade Performance of the South African Fish Industry"

Thomson, K. J., "The Promotion of Rural Tourism in Korea and Other East Asia Countries: Policies and Implementation"

Tiffin, R., "Dynamic Strategic Behaviour in the Deregulated England and Wales Liquid Milk Market"

Tobgay, S., "Agriculture Diversification in Bhutan"

Tollens, E. F., "Market Information Systems in Sub-Saharan Africa—Challenges and Opportunities"

Umeh, J. C., "Technical Efficiency Analysis of Nigerian Cassava Farmers: A Guide for Food Security Policy"

Urutyan, V., "The Role of Specialized Agricultural Credit Institutions in the Development of the Rural Finance Sector of Armenia: Case of Credit Clubs"

Van Tilburg, A., "Market Performance of Potato Auctions in Bhutan"

Vandermeulen, V., "Decentralized Rural Development Policies: Does it Make Sense: The Example of Diversification in Flanders"

Von Witzke, H., "The Economics of Consumer Protection in Developing Countries' Food Economy: The Case of Diarrhea Prevention and Treatment in Rwanda"

Vranken, L., "The Impact of Property Rights Imperfections on Resource Alocation and Welfare: Co-Ownership of Land in Bulgaria"

Waithaka, M., "Rationalization and Harmonization of Seed Policies and Regulations in Eastern and Central Africa: Effecting Policy Change Through Private Public Partnerships"

Wegener, S., "Distortions in a Multi-Level Co-Financing System: The Case of the Agri-Environmental Program of Saxony-Anhalt"

Weingarten, P., "Agricultural Employment Trends in an Enlarged European Union: Does the Cap Reform/Introduction Matter?"

Wheeler, S. A., "The Influence of Market and Agricultural Policy Signals on the Level of Organic Farming"

Wolz, A., "The Impact of Social Capital on Economic Performance of Agricultural Producers in the Czech Republic"

Wubeneh, N., "Technical Efficiency of Smallholder Dairy Farmers in the Central Ethiopian Highlands"

Yaguchi, Y., "Evolution of Crop-Dairy Production Systems in South India from 1971 to 2002"

Yahshilikov, Y., "Spatial Price Transmission in Kazakh Wheat Markets"

Yokoyama, S., "Social Capital and Farmer Welfare in Malaysia"

Yunez-Naude, A., "Productive Efficiency in Agriculture: Corn Production in Mexico"

Zalewski, R., "Food Safety. Commodity Science Point of View"

Zhang, L., "Insuring Rural China's Health? An Empirical Analysis of China's New Collective Medical System"

Ziolkowska, J., "Financing Agri-Environmental Programs in Poland: The Importance of Regional Preferences"

SYMPOSIA

Symposia 1

The Anticommons in Biotechnology: How Serious is the Problem and What Can/Needs to be Done About It?
Eran Binenbaum, Carl Pray, Carol Nottenburg, and Brian Wright

Strengthening the Linkages Between Policy Research and Policy Practice in Sub-Saharan Africa.
Duncan Boughton, Thom Jayne, and Mike Weber

Current Status and Challenges of Applied Policy Research Using the Example of Current Policy Debates on Export Crop Sectors and Interlocking Credit and Output Market Arrangements.
John Young, Rui Benfica, and Colin Poulton

Contributions of Agricultural Economics to Research Policy in Developing Countries: A Perspective from Latin America.
Greg Traxler, Ruben G. Echeverria, Flavio Ávila, John Dixon, Greg Traxler, Maria Jose da Silveira, Maria da Graça D. Fonseca, and Eduardo Trigo

Risk, Vulnerability and Poverty in Asia and the Pacific: Problems, Prospects and Priorities.
Ganesh Thapa, Raghav Gaiha, C. Leigh Anderson, and Raghbendra Jha

Assessing the Contribution of Agricultural Research to Achieving the Millennium Development Goals: A Framework and Examples.
Meredith J. Soule, Stanley Wood, George W. Norton, and Sergio R. Francisco

The "New" Agriculture in Asia: Smallholders and Contract Farming of High Value Commodities.
Clare Narrod, Nicholas Minot, and Marites Tiongco

Role of Contract Farming and Other Institutional Arrangements in Increasing Production and Sales of High-Value Perishable Foods by Small-Scale, Poor Producers.
Nipon Poapongsakorn, Nicholas Minot, Marites Tiongco, Spencer Henson, Karl Rich, Chris Delgado, and Laurian Unnevehr

Governance and Agricultural Development in Sub-Saharan Africa.
Regina Birner, Xiaobo Zhang, Klaus Deininger, Robert E. Evenson, Jonathan Kydd, and Carl Pray

Wheat Marketing Efficiency: Country Comparisons, Wheat Quality Issues and Future Trends.
Bryan T. Lohmar, Bu Yibiao, Vasant Gandhi, Vince Smith, and Erika Meng

Poverty Reduction and Economic Reforms in South Asia.
Aldas Janaiah, Suresh Babu, N. Raghuveera Reddy, D. K. Panwar, Ramesh Chand, R. R. Prasad, C. Ramaswamy, S. Mahendra Dev, Jeevika Weerahewa, Sonam Tobgay, Mahabub Hossain, and Farzana Noshab

The Economics of Natural Resource Management Research in the CGIAR.
Hermann Waibel, David Zilberman, Madan M. Dey, Timothy J. Dalton, and Olu Ajayi

How to Advance NRM Research Impact Assessment in International Agricultural Research.
David Zilberman, Jim Ryan, Prabhu Pingali, and Olaf Erenstein

Media and Consumer Response to New Technology.
Johan F. M. Swinnen, N. Kalaitzandonakes, and Jill J. McCluskey

IPRs and the Plant Breeding Industry: Policy and Methodological Issues.
Derek Eaton, Suresh Pal, Ruifa Hu, Dermot J. Hayes, Sergio H. Lence, and Chittur Srinivasan

New Technology Development to Reduce Hunger in Sub-Saharan Africa.
Aliou Diagne, Hugo De Groote, Frank Place, Yoko Kijima, and Mulugetta Mekuria

Exploring the Linkages between Public Transfers, Private Transfers and Rural Development.
Benjamin Davis, Gero Carletto, Kostas Stamoulis, Paul Winters, Tom Hertz, and Nancy McCarthy

Global Trends in Farm Structure.
Mary Bohman, Janet Perry, Krijn Poppe, and Ignez Lopes

Symposia 2

Risk and Uncertainty in Agricultural Economics and Agricultural Policy.
John Quiggin, Alistair Watson, and Chris O'Donnell

Strengthening the Linkages Between Policy Research and Policy Practice in Sub-Saharan Africa.
Duncan Boughton, Thom Jayne, and Mike Weber

Current Status and Challenges of Applied Policy Research Using the Example of Domestic Food Staple Production and Marketing Policy Debates in Southern and Eastern Africa.
Lindiwe Sibanda, Anthony Mwanaumo, Gem Argwings-Kodhek, Steve Wiggins, and Thom Jayne

Towards Operational Methods in Measuring Absolute Income Poverty: New Methodological Approaches with Empirical Findings from Household Surveys in Asia, Africa, and Latin America.
Manfred Zeller, Bunasor Sanim, Manohar Sharma, and Stefan Schwarze

Global Agricultural Productivity Slowdown—Measurement, Trends and Forces.
Robbin Shoemaker

Are Fast Growing Countries Slowing Down?
Julian Alston, P. Kumar, Scott Rozelle, Robert Evenson, and Eldon Ball

Making Rural Households' Livelihoods More Resilient—The Importance of Social Capital and the Underlying Social Networks.
Gertrud Buchenrieder, Vladislav Valentinov, Tom Dufhues, Tina Beuchelt, Isabel Fischer, Rüdiger Korff, Milada Kasarjyan, Axel Wolz, Jana Fritzsch, and Klaus Reinsberg

The "New" Agriculture in Asia: Smallholders and Contract Farming of High Value Commodities.
Clare Narrod, Nicholas Minot, and Marites Tiongco

Cross-Country Case Studies.
Clare Narrod, Archie Costales, Nipon Poagongsakorn, Lucy Lapar, Mohammad Jabbar, Fakrul Islam, P. G. Chengappa, Vinod Ahuja, Steven Staal, Katinka Weinberger, Nick Minot, Jo Swinnen, and Miet Maertens

Governance and Agricultural Development in Sub-Saharan Africa.
Regina Birner

Reform Strategies to Meet the Governance Challenges of Agricultural Development.
Jock Anderson, Daniel Bromley, Peter Hazell, Eleni Gabre-Madhin, Colin Thirtle, Ousmane Badiane, and Samuel Benin

Sustainable Development of Aquaculture and Fisheries—Challenges for Economists.
Madan Mohan Dey, Clement A. Tisdell, Elisabeth Petersen, and Diemuth E. Pemsl

Poverty Reduction and Economic Reforms in South Asia.

Aldas Janaiah, Suresh Babu, N. Raghuveera Reddy, Anjani Kumar, Ramesh Chand, R. R. Prasad, C. Ramaswamy, S. Mahendra Dev, Jeevika Weerahewa, Sonam Tobgay, Mahabub Hossain, and Farzana Noshab

The Millennium Ecosystem Assessment (MA) and the International Assessment of Agricultural Science and Technology for Development (IAASTD)—Implications for the Future of Agriculture.
Mark W. Rosegrant, Gerald Nelson, Stanley Wood, Monika Zurek, Prabhu Pingali, Brian Fisher, Helal Ahammad, Siwa Msangi, Claudia Ringler, and Mark W. Rosegrant

Integrating Participatory Approaches into Economic Modeling, Assessment and Valuation for Agricultural Development and Natural Resource Management.
Andreas Neef, Thomas Berger, Michael Ahlheim, Nicolas Becu, and Rebecca Letcher

Agrobiotechnology in China: Impacts on U.S. Competitiveness in the World Soybean Market.
William Lin, Francis Tuan, Mary A. Marchant, Nicholas Kalaitzandonakes, and Wen S. Chern

Assessing University Technology Transfer Offices.
Leslie J. Butler, Richard S. Gray, Mike Adcock, Derek Eaton, and Paul J. Thomassin

Assessing the Impact of Agricultural Research on Rural Livelihoods in Developing Countries: Approaches, Challenges, and Results.
Arega D. Alene, V. Manyong, G. Norton, C. Legg, A. Diagne, and O. Coulibaly

The Demand and Feasibility for Market Based Minimum Price and Weather Insurance for Low Income Agricultural Producers in Commodity Dependent Developing Countries.
Alexander Sarris, Barry Goodwin, and Xavier Gine

Symposia 3

Dealing with Agricultural Risk in Developing Countries.
Shiva S. Makki, Peter Hazelle, Barry Goodwin, Shiva S. Makki, Agapi Somwaru, Hyunok Lee, and Olivier Mahul

Towards More Policy-Relevant Empirical Analysis in Agricultural Economics.
Lars Brink, Soren Frandsen, Eugenio Serova, and Eugenio Cap

Seed-Fertilizer Technology, Cereal Productivity and Pro-Poor Growth in Africa: Time for New Thinking?
Derek Byerlee

Thematic Papers.
X. Diao, T. Jayne, S. Ehui, and V. Kelly

Global Agricultural Productivity Slowdown—Measurement, Trends and Forces.
Robbin Shoemaker

Measures and Methods for Estimating Developing Country Productivity.
Keith Wiebe, Lilyan Fulginiti, Colin Thirtle, and Jung-Keun Park

Issues in Measuring Developing Country Productivity.
Robbin Shoemaker and Keith Wiebe

The Future of Agricultural Economics Research (AER) in the International and National Agricultural Research Systems.
Jock R. Anderson, S.Were Omamo, and G. E. Schuh

Prevailing Capacity and Quality (National Systems in Developing Countries).
J. K. Huang, S. Pal, D. Byerlee, J. Kirsten, M. Obwona, C. Csaki, A. Balisacan, S. Offutt, B. Fisher, and V. Smith

Prevailing Capacity and Quality (International Systems).
Ade Janvry and E. Sadoulet

Future Needs: Opportunities and Threats.
P. Hazell, R. Birner, W. Omamo, and J. VonBraun

Valuing Seasonal Climate Forecasts.
John Mullen, John Freebairn, Jim Hansen, Jason Crean, and Canesio Predo

Climate Change Impacts on African Agriculture and Adaptation Options: Methodologies and Preliminary Results.
James K. A. Benhin, Rashid Hassan, Pradeep Kurukulasuriya, Robert Mendelson, Niggol Seo, David Maddison, Claudia Ringler, and Siwa Msangi

Sustainable Development of Aquaculture and Fisheries—Challenges for Economists.
R. Quentin Grafton, Akhmad Fauzi, R. K. Talukder, Madan Mohan Dey, and Roehlano Briones

Factors Affecting Poverty Dynamics in Rural Asia: Analysis of Panel Data from Repeat Household Surveys.
Mahabub Hossain, Nigar Nargis, Jonna P. Estudillo, Supatra Cherdchuchai, and Luping Li

Market Access, Market Integration, Remoteness & Agricultural Development: A Review of Cutting-Edge Spatial Approaches and Applications.
Stanley Wood, Gerald Nelson, Steve Staal, John Dixon, Chris Legg, and Uwe Deichmann

Changing Landscape of Global Food Regulations and Standards and Implications for Trade and Competitiveness: Lessons from Empirical Economic Analyses.
Aziz Elbehri, Donna Roberts, John Wilson, John Beghin, Spencer Hansen, and Roldan Muradian

The First Decade of Adoption of Biotech Crops—A Worldwide View.
Jorge Fernandez-Cornejo, Utpal Vasavada, Bryan Lohmar, Matin Qaim, Richard Gray, Carl Pray, and Vasant P. Gandhi

IPM Technology Transfer in Developing Countries: Slow Diffusion, What's the Bug?
George W. Norton, Jeffrey Alwangm, Gershon Feder, and Geoff Norton

Markets, Crop Diversity and Farm Welfare: Comparative Empirical Evidence.
Leslie Lipper, Erika Meng, Aslihan Arslan, Paul Winters, and Leigh Anderson

Symposia 4

Agricultural Productivity, Sustainability, Poverty and Democracy: Linkages and Measurement Issues.
Timothy J. Coelli, M. Alauddin, D. S. P. Rao, Lilyan E. Fulginiti, Richard K. Perrin, Terrence S. Veeman, Colin Thirtle, and Jennifer Piesse

Seed-Fertilizer Technology, Cereal Productivity and Pro-Poor Growth in Africa: Time for New Thinking?
Derek Byerlee

Country Case Studies.
M. Blackie, D. Byerlee, J. Nyoro, B. Gebremdhin, and A. Adesina

Is There A Future for Small Farms?
Steve Wiggins, Colin Poulton, Peter Hazell, and Jonathan Kydd

Rural Income-Generating Activities in Developing Countries.
Kostas Stamoulis, Paul Winters, Benjamin Davis, Kostas Stamoulis, Gero Carletto, Paul Winters, and Alberto Zezza

Climate Change Impacts on African Agriculture and Adaptation Options: Methodologies and Preliminary Results.
James K. A. Benhin, Rashid Hassan, James Benhin, Rashid Hassan, Pradeep Kurukulasuriya, Robert Mendelson, Niggol Seo, David Maddison, Claudia Ringler, and Siwa Msangi

The Future of Agricultural Economics Research (AER) in the International and National Agricultural Research Systems.
Jock R. Anderson, S.Were Omamo, and G. E. Schuh

Prevailing Capacity and Quality (National Systems in Developing Countries).
J. K. Huang, S. Rozelle, C. Pray, S. Pal, D. Byerlee, J. Kirsten, M. Obwona, C. Csaki, A. Balisacan, S. Offutt, B. Fisher, and V. Smith

Prevailing Capacity and Quality (International Systems).
Ade Janvry, and E. Sadoulet

Future Needs: Opportunities and Threats.
P. Hazell, R. Birner, and Joachim von Braun

Invasive Species: Trade, Management and Biosecurity Policy.
Rob Fraser, Bill Fisher, Dave Cook, Daniel Sumner, Annemarie Breukers, Barry Goodwin, and Zishun Zhau

The Future of M.Sc. Agricultural Economics Curriculum—A Discussion through the Global Open Food and Agriculture University.
Joachim von Braun and Suresh Babu

Regional Perspectives: GO-FAU Curriculum and Its Implication for Development.
Willis Oluoch-Kosura, Kwadao Asenso-Okyere, Jeevika Weerahewa, Funing Zhong, and Chris Barrett

CONTRIBUTED PAPERS

Water Policy Facing Salinity

John, Michele, "Climate Change and the Economics of Farm Management in the Face of Land Degradation: Dryland Salinity in Western Australia"

Ancev, Tihomir, "Offsetting with Salinity Credits: An Alternative to Irrigation Zoning"

Connor, Jeff, "Complex Adaptive System Modelling of River Murray Salinity Policy Options"

Grové, Bennie, "A Dynamic Risk Optimization Model for Evaluating Profitable and Feasible Water Management Plans"

Schmid, Erwin, "On the Choice of Cost and Effectiveness Indicators—In the Context of the European Water Policy"

Policies to Preserve Biodiversity

Meng, Erika, "Wheat Landrace Cultivation in Turkey: Household Land-Use Determinants and Implications for On-Farm Conservation of Crop Genetic Resources"

Russell, Noel, "Economics and Biodiversity in Intensively Managed Agro-Ecosystems"

Greenville, Jared, "Marine Protected Areas in Fisheries Management"

Wale, Edilegnaw, "Computing Opportunity Costs of Growing Local Varieties for On-Farm Conservation: The Case of Sorghum in Ethiopia"

Joshi Ganesh, Raj, "Determinants of Rice Variety Diversity on Household Farms in the Terai Region of Nepal"

Adoption of Biotechnology

Wesseler, Justus, "Did the Economic Conditions for Bt-Maize in the EU Improve from 1995 to 2004? A MISTICs Perspective"

Thirtle, Colin, "Monsanto's Adventures in ZuluLand: Output and Labour Effects of GM Maize and Minimum Tillage"

Diagne, Aliou, "Taking a New Look at Empirical Models of Adoption: Average Treatment Effect Estimation of Adoption Rates and Their Determinants"

Krishna Vijesh, Vijaya, "Estimating the Adoption of Bt Eggplant in India: Who Benefits from Public-Private Partnership?"

Piggott, Nicholas, "Measuring Part-Whole Bias: Some Evidence from Crop Biotechnology"

Determinants of Farmers' Adoption of Crops and Techniques

Zavale, Helder, "Smallholders' Cost Efficiency in Mozambique: Implications for Improved Maize Seed Adoption"

Matuschke, Ira, "Adoption and Impact of Hybrid Wheat in India"

Holden, Stein, "Sharecropping Efficiency in Ethiopa: Threat of Eviction and Kinship"

Solis, Daniel, "Technical Efficiency and Adoption of Soil Conservation in El Salvador and Honduras"

Rahim, Afaf, "Economic Incentives for Entry and Exit in Gum Arabic Agroforestry System in Sudan"

Introduction of Weather-Based Index Insurance

Musshoff, Oliver, "Modeling and Pricing Rain Risk"

Breustedt, Gunnar, "Mutual Crop Insurance and Moral Hazard: The Case of Mexican Fondos"

Schmitz, Bernhard, "Weather Derivatives as an Instrument to Hedge Against the Risk of High Energy Cost in Greenhouse Production"

Wang, Holly, "Weather-Based Crop Insurance Contracts for African Countries"

Kurosaki, Takashi, "Weather Risk and Off-Farm Labor Supply of Agricultural Households in India"

Recent Changes in Transition Countries

Curtiss, Jarmila, "Less Discussed Dynamics in the Czech Farm Structure Development"

Bakucs, Lajos Zoltan, "Monetary Impacts and Overshooting of Agricultural Prices in a Transition Economy: The Case of Slovenia "

Bojnec, Stefan, "Competition and Dynamics in Trade Patterns: Hungarian and Slovenian Agri-Food Trade with the European Unions' Trading Partners"

Zanni, Alberto, "Analysis of Vocational and Residential Preferences of Rural Population: Application of an Experimental Technique to Rural Slovenia"

Agriculture Under Decoupled Support

Latruffe, Laure, "CAP Direct Payments and Distributional Conflicts over Rented Land within Corporate Farms in the New Member States"

Rehman, Tahir, "Modelling the Impact of Decoupling Structural Change in Farming: Integrating Econometric Estimation and Optimisation"

Shrestha, Shailesh, "Analysing the Impact of Decoupling at a Regional Level: A Farm Level Dynamic Linear Programming Approach"

Elekes, Andrea, "How Decoupled is the European Union's Single Farm Payment"

Arriaza, Manuel, "Viability of the Raw Cotton Production in Spain After the Decoupling of the Subsidies"

New Findings on Consumer Demand Models

Gibson, John, "Household Energy Demand and the Equity and Efficiency Aspects of Subsidy Reform in Indonesia"

Beghin, John, "Japanese Consumer Demand for Dairy Products"

Zhao, Xueyan, "Heterogeneity in Alcohol Consumption: The Case of Beer, Wine and Spirits in Australia"

Piggott, Nicholas, "Consumer Price Formation With Demographic Translating"

Tan, Andrew, "Determinants of Malaysian Household Expenditures on Food-Away-From-Home "

Policy and Poverty Levels

Zeller, Manfred, "How Accurate Is Participatory Wealth Ranking (PWR) in Targeting the Poor? A Case Study from Bangladesh"

Julia, Johannsen, "Operational Poverty Targeting by Means of Proxy Indicators—The Example of Peru"

Simler, Kenneth, "Poverty Comparisons with Endogenous Absolute Poverty Lines"

Jansen, Hans, "Public Investment Targeting in Central America"

Agricultural Policies and the Economics of Obesity

Clark, J. Stephen, "Will Fat Taxes Cause Americans to Become Fatter? Some Evidence from U.S. Meats"

Vosti, Stephen A., "Are Agricultural Policies Making Us Fat? Likely Links Between Agricultural Policies and Human Nutrition and Obesity, and their Policy Implications"

Wallace, Huffman, "The Economics of Obesity-Related Mortality Among High Income Countries "

Jolliffe, Dean, "The Income Gradient and Distribution-Sensitive Measures of Overweight in the U.S."

Mann, Stefan, "Framing Obesity in Economic Theory and Policy"

Recent Results of Value Chain Analysis

Canavari, Maurizio, "Traceability as Part of Competitive Strategy in the Fruit Supply Chain"

Lu, Hualiang, "A Two-Stage Value Chain Model for Vegetable Marketing Chain Efficiency Evaluation: A Transaction Cost Approach"

Saenz-Segura, Fernando, "Seasoning a Monopsonic Processor for Collective Action amongst Pepper Producers in Costa Rica"

Yanrong, Zhang, "Supply Chain Management of Fresh Produce: Melons in Western China"

Jefferson-Moore, Kenrett, "The Distribution of Rents in Supply Chain Industries: The Case of High Oil Corn"

Local and Global Competition in the Dairy Market

Soregaroli, Claudio, "Dairy Policy Modelling under Imperfect Competition"

Staal, Steven, "Smallholder Dairy Farmer Access to Alternative Milk Market Channels in Gujarat, India"

Hockmann, Heinrich, "Price Developments on the World Markets for Milk Products: The Case of Butter"

Vavra, Pavel, "Milk Quota Systems: Considerations of Market and Welfare Effects"

Agriculture and Growth and Vice Versa

Barros, Geraldo, "Supply and Demand Shocks and the Growth of the Brazilian Agriculture"

Ruben, Ruerd, "Land Inequality and Economic Growth: A Dynamic Panel Data Approach"

Vosti, Stephen A., "Agricultural Change and Population Growth: District-Level Evidence From India"

Fleming, Pauline, "A Reappraisal of the Role of Agriculture in Economic Growth in Melanesian Countries"

Rambaldi, Alicia, "Re-Testing the Resource Curse Hypothesis Using Panel Data and an Improved Measure of Resource Intensity"

Farmers and the Determinants of Their Access to the Market

Langyintuo, Augustine, "The Effect of Household Wealth on Input Market Participation in Southern Africa"

Benfica, Rui, "Interlinked Transactions in Cash Cropping Economies: The Determinants of Farmer Participation and Performance in the Zambezi River Valley of Mozambique"

Thiele, Rainer, "The Impact of Coffee Price Changes on Rural Households in Uganda"

Edmeades, Svetlana, "Varieties, Attributes and Marketed Surplus of a Subsistence Crop: Bananas in Uganda"

The Role of Research & Development

Crowe Bronwyn, Claire, "The Benefits and Beneficiaries of Public Investment in Herbicide Use R&D"

Erenstein, Olaf, "Assessing the Impact of International Natural Resource Management Research: The Case of Zero Tillage in India's Rice-Wheat Systems"

Abele, Steffen, "The Niger Food Crisis: Causes and Implications for Research and Development from an Integrated Agricultural Economics Perspective"

Alene Arega, Demelash, "The Efficiency-Equity Tradeoffs in Agricultural Research Priority Setting: The Potential Impacts of Agricultural Research on Economic Surplus and Poverty Reduction in Nigeria"

The Design of Water Markets

Legras, Sophie, "Designing Water Markets to Manage Coupled Externalities: An Application to Irrigation-Induced Salinity"

Carmona-Torres, M. Carmen, "Bid Design and its Influence on the Stated Willingness to Pay in a Contingent Valuation Study"

Juana James, Sharka, "Inter-Sectoral Water Use in South Africa: Efficiency Versus Equity"

Smith, Rodney, "Water Markets and Third Party Effects"

Fang, Lan, "Application of a Spatial Water Model in a Chinese Watershed"

Agricultural Policy and Multifunctionality

Hayashi, Takashi, "Developing an Indicator for Environment Improvement Potential in the Agricultural Sector "

Boisvert, Richard, "Implications of Geographic Heterogeneity for Multifunctional Rice Policy in Taiwan"

Parra-López, Carlos, "A Multifunctional Comparison of Conventional Versus Alternative Olive Systems in Spain by Using AHP"

Kallas, Zein, "Are Citizens Willing to Pay for Agricultural Multifunctionality?"

Colombo, Sergio, "Transferring the Benefits of Water Quality Enhancements in Small Catchments"

The Challenge of New Crops

Abdula, Rahimaisa, "A Computable General Equilibrium Analysis of the Economic and Land-Use Interfaces of Bio-Energy Development"

Eaton, Derek, "The Effects of Strengthened IPR Regimes on the Plant Breeding Sector in Developing Countries"

Krishna, Vijesh V., "Bioprospection Beyond Intellectual Property Rights"

Léger, Andréanne, "Intellectual Property Rights and Innovation in Developing Countries: Evidence from Panel Data"

Chern, Wen, "Genetically Modified Organisms (GMOs) and Sustainability in Agriculture"

Village Effects of China's Policy

Rozelle, Scott, "Marketing Channel and Technology Adoption; Chinese Villages in the Local Horticulture Market"

Xing, Li, "Village Inequality in Western China"

Yao, Yi, "Evolution of Income and Fiscal Disparity in Rural China"

Heerink, Nico, "China's New Rural Income Support Policy: Impact on Grain Production and Rural Income Inequality"

Herzfeld, Thomas, "The Persistence of Poverty in Rural China: Applying an Ordered Probit and a Hazard Approach"

Berg, Ernst, "Farm Level Risk Assessment Using Downside Risk Measures"

Otieno, David Jakinda, "Risk Management in Smallholder Cattle Farming: A Hypothetical Insurance Approach in Western Kenya"

Boerner, Jan, "Rainfall or Price Variability: What Determines Rangeland Management Decisions? A Simulation-Optimization Approach to South African Savannas"

Thorne, Fiona, "The Role of Risk in the Decision to Produce Post-Decoupling—Stochastic Budgeting Example"

Communities and Collective Action

Cullen, Ross, "Poverty Alleviation or Aggravation? The Impacts of Community Forestry Policies in Nepal"

Arifin, Bustanul, "Transaction Cost Analysis of Upstream-Downstream Relations in Watershed Services: Lessons from Community-Based Forestry Management in Sumatra, Indonesia"

Subramanian, Arjunan, "Competition, Kinship or Reciprocity? Village Experiments in Alternative Modes of Exchange"

Shiferaw, Bekele, "Collective Action for Integrated Community Watershed Management in Semi-Arid India: Analysis of Multiple Livelihood Impacts and the Drivers of Change"

Bogale, Ayalneh, "Peaceful Co-Existence? What Role for Personal Wealth and Entitlement in Conflict Mitigation in Unfavourable Areas of Eastern Ethiopia"

Local Effects of Global Changes

Minten, Bart, "Spillovers from Globalization on Land Use: Evidence from Madagascar"

Katranidis, Stelios, "The Effects of Trade Liberalization in Textiles and Clothing on the Greek Market for Cotton Yarn: A Multi-Market Analysis"

Sattaphon, Weerapong, "Do Japanese Foreign Direct Investment and Trade Stimulate Agricultural Growth in East Asia? Panel Cointegration Analysis"

Consumer Behaviour vis-à-vis New Products

Burton, Michael, "Non-Participation in Choice Models: Hurdle and Latent Class Models"

Veeman, Michele, "Consumers' Preferences for GM Food and Voluntary Information Acquisition: A Simultaneous Choice Analysis"

Lin, William, "Are Urban Consumers in China Ready to Accept Biotech Foods?"

Qiu, Huanguang, "Consumers' Trust in Government and Their Attitudes Towards Genetically Modified Food: Empirical Evidence from China"

Smith, Aaron, "Estimating the Market Effect of a Food Scare: The Case of Genetically Modified Starlink Corn"

Determinants and Consequences of Rural Poverty

Gebreegzianher, Zenebe, "Land Degradation in Ethiopia: What Do Stoves Have to Do With It?"

Minot, Nicholas, "Market Access and Rural Poverty in Tanzania"

Soloaga, Isidro, "Agricultural Growth and Poverty Reduction. The Case of Mexico"

Nkonya, Ephraim, "The Influence of Asset and Access Poverty on Crop Production and Land Degradation in Uganda"

Kuyiah, Joanne Wasswa, "Agriculture, Income Risks and Rural Poverty Dynamics: Strategies of Smallholder Producers in Kenya"

The Spatial Integration of Agricultural Markets

Lee, David, "Spatial Price Integration in U.S. and Mexican Rice Markets"

Gopinath, Munisamy, "Productivity, Geography and the Export Decision of Chilean Farms"

Salhofer, Klaus, "Spatial Competition of Milk Processing Cooperatives in Northern Germany"

Sakurai, Takeshi, "Rice Miller Cluster in Ghana and Its Effects on Efficiency and Quality Improvement"

Alemu, Zerihun Gudeta, "Measuring Market Integration in Mozambican Maize Markets in the Presence of Transaction Costs: A Threshold Vector Error Correction Approach"

Management and Policies of Food Industries

Roebeling, Peter Cornelis, "Exploring Environmental-Economic Benefits from Agri-Industrial Diversification in the Sugar Industry: An Integrated Land Use and Value Chain Approach"

Merel, Pierre Romain, "About the Efficiency of Input vs. Output Quotas"

Hirschauer, Norbert, "An Interdisciplinary Approach to White-Collar Crime in the Food Sector"

Dubois, Pierre, "Optimal Incentives under Moral Hazard and Heterogeneous Agents: Evidence from Production Contracts Data"

Nguyen, Nam, "Decision Support Systems in Australian Agriculture: State of the Art and Future Development"

Farm Households and Livestock Prices

Williams, Timothy, "A Hedonic Analysis of Cattle Prices in the Central Corridor of West Africa: Implications for Production and Marketing Decisions"

Doss, Cheryl, "Milk Money and Intra-Household Bargaining: Evidence on Pastoral Migration and Milk Sales from Northern Kenya"

Adugna, Teressa, "Determinants of Market Prices of Cattle in Eastern Ethiopia"

Waldron, Scott, "The Integration of Rural Households into Ruminant Livestock Industries in China"

New Evidence on Price Transmission

von Cramon-Taubadel, Stephan, "Vertical Price Transmission between Wheat and Flour in Ukraine: A Markov-Switching Vector Error Correction Approach"

Loy, Jens-Peter, "The Impact of Cross Sectional Data Aggregation on the Measurement of Vertical Price Transmission: An Experiment with German Food Prices"

Liefert, William, "Decomposing Changes in Agricultural Producer Prices"

Gil, José M., "Local Polynomial Fitting and Spatial Price Relationships: Price Transmission in the EU Markets for Pigmeat"

After Liberalization: The Maize Market in Kenya

Ouma, James Okuro, "Determinants of Improved Maize Seed and Fertilizer Use in Kenya: Policy Implications"

Mghenyi, Elliot, "Food Pricing Policy and Rural Poverty: Insight from Maize in Kenya"

Mose, Lawrence Obae, "Firm Size Distribution and Performance of Maize and Fertilizer Traders after Market Liberalisation: Evidence from Kenya"

Jayne, Thomas, "The Effects of Government Maize Marketing Policies on Maize Market Prices in Kenya"

Research and Development, Researching the Farmer

Ehui, Simeon, "Identifying Agricultural Research and Development Investment Opportunities in Sub-Saharan Africa: A Global, Economy-Wide Analysis"

Labarta, Ricardo, "Multi-Institutional Implementation of Farmer Field Schools among Nicaraguan Bean Growers, Do Different NGOs Perform Differently?"

Horna, Julia Daniela, "Supporting Agricultural Extension: Could Farmers Contribute?"

Yamazaki, Satoshi, "Does Sending Farmers to School Have Some Impact? A Spatial Econometrics Approach"

Recreation and Environmental Goods

Kragt, Marit Ellen, "Effects of Great Barrier Reef Degradation on Recreational Demand: A Contingent Behaviour Approach"

Glebe, Thilo, "National Differences in the Uptake of EU Agri-Environmental Schemes: An Explanation"

Pannell, David, "Using Incentives to Buy Land—Use Change in Agriculture for Environmental Benefits"

Concu, Giovanni, "Investigating Distance Effects on Environmental Values. A Choice Modelling Approach"

Christie, Michael, "An Economic Assessment of the Amenity Benefits Associated with Alternative Coastal Protection Options"

IPM & Organic Farming

Rutto, Esther, "Participatory Evaluation of Integrated Pest and Soil Fertility Management Options Using Ordered Categorical Data Analysis"

Irawan, Evi, "The Effect of Farm Labor Organization on IPM Adoption: Empirical Evidence from Thailand"

Nuppenau, Ernst, "Bargaining on Ecological Main Structures for Natural Pest Control: Modelling Land Use Regulations as Common Property Management"

Tutkun, Aysel, "Explaining the Conversion to Organic Farming of Farmers of the Obwalden Canton, Switzerland—Extension of the Theory of Planned Behavior within a Structural Equation Modeling Approach"

Schmid, Erwin, "Modelling Organic Farming at Sector Level—An Application to the Reformed CAP in Austria"

Measuring Productivity Changes

Latruffe, Laure, "The Use of Bootstrapped Malmquist Indices to Reassess Productivity Change Findings: An Application to a Sample of Polish Farms"

Villano, Renato, "Productivity Change in the Australian Sheep Industry Revisited"

Coelli, Tim, "CAP Reforms and Total Factor Productivity Growth in Belgian Agriculture: A Malmquist Index Approach"

Torres, Marcelo, "Measuring Productivity Change and Its Components for Fisheries: The Case of the Alaskan Pollock Fishery, 1994–2003"

Rahman, Sanzidur, "Farm Productivity and Efficiency in Rural Bangladesh: The Role of Education Revisited"

Policies Towards Rural Credit Provision

Hartarska, Valentina, "Rating in Microfinance: Cross-Country Evidence"

Chang, Ching-Cheng, "Productivity Change in Taiwan's Farmers' Credit Unions: A Nonparametric Risk-Adjusted Malmquist Approach"

Wiboonpongse, Aree, "The Demand for Loans for Major Rice in the Upper North of Thailand"

Petrick, Martin, "How to Make Institutional Economics Policy-Relevant: Theoretical Considerations and an Application to Rural Credit Markets in Developing Countries"

Teixeira, Erly, "Agricultural Credit Interest Rate Equalization Policy: A Growth Subsidy?"

Policies, Institutions and Farm Land

Thuc Vien, Ha, "Land Privatization and Livelihood Diversification: An Examination from the Southern Uplands of Vietnam"

Mwakubo, Samuel Mazera, "The Influence of Social Capital on Natural Resource Management in Marginal Areas of Kenya"

Lankoski, Jussi, "Impacts of Agri-Environmental Policies on Land Allocation and Land Prices"

Akter, Shaheen, "Land Rental Markets in India: Efficiency and Equity Considerations"

Gandhi, Vasant P., "Economic Liberalization and Rural Land and Labour Markets in India: A Study"

Trade Policies and Trade Patterns

Olper, Alessandro, "Explaining National Border Effects in the Quad Food Trade"

Lee, Hyunok, "Effects of the WTO and Free Trade Agreements on Japonica Rice Markets"

Jones, Keithly, "The Effect of Relative Prices and Exchange Rates on Domestic Market Share of U.S. Red-Meat Utilization"

Glebe, Thilo, "Enlargement of Trade Blocs: National Welfare Effects if Trade Is Liberalized"

Cheng, Fuzhi, "Exchange Exchange Rate Misalignment and Its Effects on Agricultural Producer Support Estimates (PSEs) in India"

Consumer Food Consumption and Health Aspects

Liu, Yi, "A Panel Data Study of the Determinants of Micronutrient Intake in China"

Shimokawa, Satoru, "Economic Growth, Lifestyle Changes, and the Coexistence of Under and Overweight in China: A Semiparametric Approach"

Stein, Alexander J., "Potential Impacts of Golden Rice on Public Health in India"

New Approaches to Poverty Assessment

Kuiper, Marijke, "Poverty Targeting, Resource Degradation and Heterogeneous Endowments—A Micro-Simulation Analysis of a Less Favored Ethiopian Village"

Zeller, Manfred, "Developing Poverty Assessment Tools Based on Principal Component Analysis: Results from Bangladesh, Kazakhstan, Uganda, and Peru"

Glenk, Klaus, "Differential Influence of Relative Poverty on Preferences for Ecosystem Services: Evidence from Rural Indonesia"

Schreinemachers, Pepijn, "Simulating Farm Household Poverty: From Passive Victims to Adaptive Agents"

Measuring Consumer Preferences

Kimenju, Simon Chege, "Comparing Accuracy and Costs of Revealed and Stated Preferences: The Case of Consumer Acceptance of Yellow Maize in East Africa"

Thiene, Mara, "Consumer's WTP for Environment-Friendly Production Methods and Collective Reputation for Place of Origin: The Case of Val di Gresta's Carrots"

Drescher, Larissa Sabrina, "The Taste for Variety: A Hedonic Analysis for Food Products"

Steen, Marie, "Flower Power at the Dutch Flower Auctions? Application of an Inverse Almost Ideal Demand System"

From Farm to Fork, via the Retailer

Reardon, Thomas, "Kenyan Supermarkets and Horticultural Farm Sector Development"

Dong, Xiaoxia, "Producing and Procuring Horticultural Crops with Chinese Characteristics: Why Small Farmers Are Thriving and Supermarkets Are Absent in Rural China "

Lloyd, Tim, "Market Power in UK Food Retailing: Theory and Evidence from Seven Product Groups"

Bonnet, Céline, "Two-Part Tariffs versus Linear Pricing Between Manufacturers and Retailers: Empirical Tests on Differentiated Products Markets"

Invasive Species and Breeding Programs

Makokha, Stella, "Valuation of Cow Attributes by Conjoint Analysis: A Case Study in Western Kenya"

Wahl, Thomas, "Invasive Species Management: Foot-and-Mouth Disease in the U.S. Beef Industry"

Mehta, Shefali, "Optimal Detection and Management Strategies for Non-Native Invasive Species"

Abdulai, Awudu, "Contribution of Economics to Design of Sustainable Cattle Breeding Programs in Eastern Africa: A Choice Experiment Approach "

International Markets for Grains and Other Crops

Ferris, John, "Forecasting World Crop Yields as Probability Distributions"

Scoppola, Margherita, "Economies of Scale and Endogenous Market Structures in International Grain Trade"

You, Liangzhi, "Generating Global Crop Distribution Maps: From Census to Grid"

Vachal, Kimberly, "Differential Effects of Rail Deregulation in the U.S Grain Industry"

Testing the Effects of Liberalization in South and East Africa

De Groote, Hugo, "Market Liberalization and Agricultural Intensification in Kenya (1992–2002)"

Ndibongo, Traub Lulama, "The Effects of Market Deregulation on Maize Marketing Margins in South Africa"

Langyintuo, Augustine, "A Unified Approach to the Estimation of Demand for Improved Seed in Developing Agriculture"

Nzuma, Jonathan, "Testing for Oligopoly Power in the Kenyan Seed Maize Processing Industry"

Performance of Farmers' Organizations

Maitre D'Hotel, Elodie, "Do Ideas Matter in Strategic Choices Made by Organizations? An Empirical Work on the Participation of Agricultural Organizations to the Political Making Process in Costa Rica "

Mude, Andrew, "Weaknesses in Institutional Organization: Explaining the Dismal Performance of Kenya's Coffee Cooperatives"

Bavorova, Miroslava, "What Motivates Farms to Associate? The Case of Two Competing Czech Agricultural Associations"

Rebelo, João, "Governance Control Mechanisms in Portuguese Agricultural Credit Cooperatives"

Galdeano-Gomez, Emilio, "Productivity and Environmental Performance in Marketing Cooperatives: Incentive Schemes on the Horticultural Sector"

Irrigation Policy and Management

Yilma, Tsegaye, "Complementarity between Irrigation and Fertilizer Technologies—A Justification for Increased Irrigation Investment in the Less-Favored Areas of SSA"

Magingxa, Litha, "Factors Influencing the Success Potential in Smallholder Irrigation Projects of South Africa: A Principal Component Regression"

Rasphone, Arounyadeth, "The Irrigation Service Fees and Affordability after the Management Transfer: Empirical Evidence from Ban Vuen-Tonhen WUA in Savannakhet Province, Lao PDR"

Roe, Terry, "Understanding the Direct and Indirect Effects of Water Policy for Better Policy Decision Making: An Application to Irrigation Water Management in Morocco"

Lee, David, "Payments for Watershed Services: An Application to Irrigation Pricing in the El Angel Watershed, Carchi, Ecuador"

New Approaches to Valuation

Tisdell, John, "Bringing Biophysical Models into the Economic Laboratory: An Experimental Analysis of Sediment Trading in Australia"

Vukina, Tomislav, "Do Farmers Value the Environment? Evidence from the Conservation Reserve Program Auctions"

Bullock, David, "On Measuring the Value of a Nonmarket Good Using Market Data"

Cattaneo, Andrea, "Auctioning Conservation Payments using Environmental Indices"

Thomassin, Paul, "Canada's Domestic Carbon Emission Trading Institution: Rules, Workability and the Role of Offsets"

Policies and the Use of Forests

Jumbe Charles Blessings, Laurence, "Household's Choice of Fuelwood Source in Malawi: A Multinomial Probit Analysis"

Schwarze, Stefan, "Income Sources, Poverty, and Forest Encroachment: Implications for Rural Development Policies in Central Sulawesi, Indonesia"

Birner, Regina, "Need, Greed or Customary Rights—Which Factors Explain the Encroachment of Protected Areas? Empirical Evidence from a Protected Area in Sulawesi, Indonesia"

Ninan, Karachepone, "Non Timber Forest Products and Biodiversity Conservation—A Study of Tribals in a Protected Area in India"

Lopez-Feldman, Alejandro, "Does Natural Resource Extraction Mitigate Poverty and Inequality? Evidence from Rural Mexico"

The Importance of Scale in Farming

Weersink, Alfons, "Structural Changes in the Sri Lankan Tea Industry: Family Farms vs. Plantations"

Xu, Zhiying, "Maize Yield Response to Fertilizer and Profitability of Fertilizer Use among Small-Scale Maize Producers in Zambia"

Staal, Steven, "Will Small-Scale Dairy Producers in Kenya Disappear Due to Economies of Scale in Production?"

Thirtle, Colin, "Efficiency and Pooling in Western Cape Wine Grape Production"

Institutional Aspects of Risk Mitigation

Bardhan, Dwaipayan, "An Assessment of Risk Attitude of Dairy Farmers in Uttaranchal (India)"

Skees, Jerry, "Innovations in Government Responses to Catastrophic Risk Sharing for Agriculture in Developing Countries"

Santos, Paulo, "Informal Insurance in the Presence of Poverty Traps: Evidence from Southern Ethiopia"

Keil, Alwin, "Determinants of Farmers' Resilience Towards ENSO-Related Drought: Evidence from Central Sulawesi, Indonesia"

Bielza, Maria, "Evaluating the Potential of Whole-Farm Insurance over Crop-Specific Insurance Policies"

Labor Market and the Role of Migration

Dalton, Timothy J., "Transient Health Shocks and Agricultural Labor Demand in Rice-Producing Households in Mali"

Zezza, Alberto, "Choosing to Migrate or Migrating to Choose: Migration and Labor Choice in Albania"

Wouterse, Fleur, "Migration and Income Diversification: Evidence from Burkina Faso"

Napasintuwong, Orachos, "Immigrant Workers and Technological Change in U.S. Agriculture: A Profit Maximization Approach of Induced Innovation"

Herzfeld, Thomas, "The Dynamics of Chinese Rural Houssholds' Participation in Labor Markets"

Trade Policy and Agriculture

Conforti, Piero, "Preferences Erosion and Trade Costs in the Sugar Market: The Impact of the Everything but Arms Initiative and the Reform of the EU Policy"

Pelikan, Janine, "Agricultural Market Access: A Moving Target in the WTO Negotiations?"

Elbehri, Aziz, "Preferential Tariffs, WTO and Developing Countries: Do the Gains from Multilateral Market Access Outweigh Preferential Access?"

Mutambatsere, Emelly, "Trade Policy Reforms in the Cereals Sector of the SADC Region: Implications on Food Security"

Yu, Wusheng, "Improving Agricultural Market Access for African LCDs: Deepening, Widening, Broadening and Strengthening Trade Preferences"

Consumer Food Safety Issues

Lobb, Alexandra, "Food Scares and Consumer Behaviour: A European Perspective"

Hanf, Claus-Hennig, "Trust as a Relevant Determinant of Consumer Behaviour in Food Safety Crises"

Tanner, Mariah, "The Relative Importance of Preference for County-of-Origin in China, France, Niger and the United States"

Saghaian, Sayed, "The Effects of E. Coli 0157:H7, Fmd and Bse on Japanese Retail Beef Prices: A Historical Decomposition"

Determinants and Consequences of Poverty in Sub-Saharan Africa

Yamano, Takashi, "The Long-Term Impacts of Orphanhood on Education Attainment and Land Inheritance among Adults in Rural Kenya"

Boughton, Duncan, "Using Rural Household Income Survey Data to Inform Poverty Analysis: An Example from Mozambique "

Karugia, Joseph, "Access to Land, Income Diversification and Poverty Reduction in Rural Kenya"

Van Den Berg, Marrit, "Poverty and the Rural Non-Farm Economy in Oromia, Ethiopia"

Policies for Ground Water

Managi, Shunsuke, "Testing Increasing Returns to Pollution Abatement in Pesticides"

Msangi, Siwa, "Third Party Effects and Asymmetric Externalities in Groundwater Extraction: The Case of Cherokee Strip in Butte County"

Zhang, Lijuan, "Groundwater Entrepreneurs in China: Selling Water to Meet the Demand for Water"

Kajisa, Kei, "The Dissemination of Private Wells and Double Tragedies: The Overexploitation of Groundwater among Well Users and Increased Poverty among Non-Well Users in Tamil Nadu, India"

Wilson, Paul N., "Groundwater Conservation Policy in Agriculture"

Sustainable Farming

Ajayi Oluyede, Clifford, "Environmental Conservation and Food Security in Developing Countries: Bridging the Disconnect"

Escalante, Cesar, "Farm-Level Evidence on the Sustainable Growth Paradigm from Grain and Livestock Farms"

Bashaasha, Bernard, "Determinants of Land Use in Kigezi Highlands of Southwestern Uganda"

Van Passel, Steven, "Explaining Differences in Farm Sustainability: Evidence from Flemish Dairy Farms"

Rethinking the Profession

Roumasset, James, "The Economics of Agricultural Development: What Have We Learned"

Noell, Chris, "Self-Organisation in Agricultural Sectors and the Relevance of Complex Systems Approaches for Applied Economics"

Van Huylenbroeck, Guido, "New Developments in Agricultural Policy Modelling and Consequences for Managing the Policy Analysis Systems"

Berger, Thomas, "From Bioeconomic Farm Models to Multi-Agent Systems: Challenges for Parameterization and Validation"

Effects and Sources of Efficiency

Rejesus, Roderick, "Economics of Management Zone Delineation in Cotton Precision Agriculture"

Oude Lansink, Alfons, "Dynamic Efficiency Analysis Using a Directional Distance Function"

Jansen, Hans, "Land Management Decisions and Agricultural Productivity in the Hillsides of Honduras"

Farquharson, Robert, "Changes in Management Can Improve Returns from Cambodian Upland Crops"

Paulos, Zeleka, "Measuring Male-Female Productivity Differentials in Ethiopian Agriculture: Policy Implications for Improving the Livelihood of Female Farmers"

Family Economics: Education, Orphans and Gender

Woldehanna, Tassew, "Children's Educational Completion Rates and Dropouts in the Context of Ethiopia's National Poverty Reduction Strategy"

Sharma, Manohar P., "Orphanhood and Schooling Outcomes in Malawi"

Ayoola, Josephine Bosede, "Gender Policies in Entrepreneurship Development—An Intra-Household Market Analysis"

Factors Affecting the Land Rental Market

Wu, Ziping, "Land Distributional and Income Effects of the Chinese Land Rental Market"

Kellermann, Konrad, "How Smart Should Farms be Modeled? Behavioral Foundation of Bidding Strategies in Agent-Based Land Market Models"

Tu, Qin, "Factors Affecting the Development of Land Rental Markets in China—A Case Study for Puding County, Guizhou Province"

Hung, Pham-Van, "Land Transactions in the North of Vietnam: A Modelling Approach"

Trade Policy and WTO Issues

Rigby, Dan, "Precaution and Protectionism: 'Likeness' and GM Food at the WTO"

McCarney, Geoff, "The Effects of Trade Liberalization on the Environment: An Empirical Study"

MacLaren, Donald, "The Economic Effects of State Trading Enterprises: Market Access and Market Failure"

Hsu, Shih-Hsun, "An Economy-Wide Analysis of Impacts of WTO Tiered Formula for Tariff Reduction on Taiwan"

Liu, Xue, "The Initial Impact of WTO Membership on China's Trade Performance in Primary Agricultural and Processed Food Products"

Grades and Standards and Their Effects on Trade

Rau, Marie-Luise, "Food Quality Standards in Equilibrium Models: A Discussion of Current Modeling Approaches"

Vermeulen, Hester, "Private Standards, Handling and Hygiene in Fruit Export Supply Chains: A Preliminary Evaluation of the Economic Impact of Parallel Standards"

Van Tongeren, Frank, "Modeling Differentiated Quality Standards in the Agri-Food Sector: The Case of Meat Trade in the EU"

Fletcher, Stanley, "Quality Premiums and the Post-Harvest Spot Market Thinness: The Case of U.S. Peanuts"

Kleinwechter, Uli, "The Adoption of the Eureogap Standard by Mango Exporters in Piura, Peru"

Input Use, Farmer's Health and Poverty

Easter, K. William, "What are the Economic Health Costs of Non-Action in Controlling Toxic Water Pollution?"

Okello, Julius, "The Effect of Developed-Country Pesticide Standards on Health and Pesticide-Induced Morbidity of Kenya's Green Bean Family Farmers"

Dorosh, Paul, "Transitions Out of Poverty: Drivers of Real Income Growth for the Poor in Rural Pakistan"

Gruere, Guillaume, "Marketing Underutilized Plant Species for the Poor"

Kristjanson, Patricia, "Pathways into and out of Poverty and the Role of Livestock in the Peruvian Andes"

Assessing the Impacts of Technology and Management Practices in Asia

Wise, Russell Montgomery, "Optimal Land-Use Decisions in the Presence of Carbon Payments and Fertilizer Subsidies: An Indonesian Case Study"

Azad Md. Abdus, Samad, "Double Transplanting: Economic Assessment of an Indigenous Technology for Submergence Avoidance in the Flood-Prone Rice Environment in Bangladesh"

MacLeod, Neil, "An Exploratory Assessment of the Economic Impact of Forage Options for Beef Production on Smallholder Farms in the Red Soils Region of China"

Praneetvatakul, Suwanna, "Impact Assessment of Farmer Field School Using A Multi-Period Panel Data Model"

Policies Toward More Intensive Land Use

Kim, Chang-Gil, "Economic Effects of Environmental Taxation on Chemical Fertilizers"

Pender, John, "Impacts of Inventory Credit, Input Supply Shops and Fertilizer Micro-Dosing in the Drylands of Niger"

Casado, José María, "Introducing Different Land Uses (Irrigated and Non-Irrigated) in Policy Analysis Modelling for Mediterranean Countries"

Barmon Basanta, Kumar, "Economic Evaluation of Rice-Prawn Gher Farming Technology on Soil Fertility for Modern Variety (MV) Paddy Production in Bangladesh"

Global Convergence

Brasili, Cristina, "Convergence in the Agricultural Incomes: A Comparison between the U.S. and EU"

Ludena, Carlos, "Productivity Growth and Convergence in Crop, Ruminant and Non-Ruminant Production: Measurement and Forecasts"

Jin, Shaosheng, "Agglomeration Effects and Japanese Food Industry Investment in China: Evidence from the Cities"

Sassi, Maria, "Agricultural Convergence and Competitiveness in the EU-15 Regions"

The Market for Regional Foods

Schamel, Guenter, "Auction Markets for Specialty Food Products with Geographical Indications"

Fanfani, Roberto, "A Mosaic Type of Development: The Agri-Food Districts Experience in Italy"

Fischer, Christian, "The Nature of the Relationship between International Tourism and International Trade: The Case of German Imports of Spanish Wine"

Herrmann, Roland, "Markets Segmented by Regional-Origin Labeling with Quality Control"

The Perspectives of the Non-Farm Economy for Poverty Reduction

Kuiper, Marijke, "Rural Livelihoods: Interplay Between Farm Activities, Non-Farm Activities and the Resource Base"

Yunez-Naude, Antonio, "Regional Growth Linkages between Villages and Towns in Mexico: A Village-Wide Modeling Perspective"

Torero, Maximo, "Does Privatization Deliver? Access to Telephone Services and Household Income in Poor Rural Areas Using a Quasi-Natural Experiment for Perú"

Moellers, Judith, "Non-Farm Diversification Decisions of Rural Households in Macedonia"

Prize Winners (Prelim)

Wollni, Meike, "Do Farmers Benefit from Participating in Specialty Markets and Cooperatives? The Case of Coffee Marketing in Costa Rica"

Beach, Robert, "Costs and Mitigation Potential for Agricultural Greenhouse Gas Emissions around the Globe"

Pemsl, Diemuth, "Ecosystem Disruption and the Economics of Biotechnology"

PLENARY SESSIONS

Presidential Address

Prabhu Pingali, "Agricultural Growth and Economic Development: A View through the Globalization Lens"

Elmhirst Lecture

Hans Binswanger, "Empowering Rural People for their Own Development"

1. Economics of Natural Disasters

Hartwig de Haen and Günter Hemrich, "The Economics of Natural Disasters: Implications and Challenges for Food Security"

Stephen Devereux, "The Impact of Droughts and Floods on Food Security and Policy Options to Alleviate Negative Effects"

Yasuyuki Sawada, "The Impact of Natural and Manmade Disasters on Household Welfare"

2. Trade and Marketing of Agricultural Commodities in a Globalizing World

Will Martin and Kym Anderson, "The Doha Agenda and Agricultural Trade Reform: The Role of Economic Analysis"

Johan F. M. Swinnen and Miet Maertens, "Globalization, Privatization, and Vertical Coordination in Food Value Chains in Developing and Transition Countries"

David Orden and Donna Roberts, "Food Regulation and Trade Under the WTO: Ten Years in Perspective"

3. Risk, Food Safety, and Health

Matin Qaim, Alexander J. Stein, and J. V. Meenakshi, "Economics of Biofortification"

Dina Umali-Deininger and Mona Sur, "Food Safety in a Globalizing World: Opportunities and Challenges for India"

Laurian Unnevehr, "Food Safety as a Global Public Good"

4. Transformation of Unfavorable Areas: Technologies, Institutions, and Market Access

Mahabub Hossain, "The Technology Issues for Unfavorable Areas"

Thomas Reardon, Kostas Stamoulis, and Prabhu Pingali, "Rural Nonfarm Employment in Developing Countries in an Era of Globalization"

Eleni Gabre-Madhin, "Marketing Issues in Sub-Saharan Africa"

COMPUTER SESSIONS

James W. Richardson, "Simetar (Simulation & Econometrics to Analyze Risk)"

Ram Ranjan, "TSTAR—Invasive Species Decision Support System"

INVITED PANEL SESSIONS

1. Food Safety Standards and Agri-Food Exports from Developing Countries

Clare Narrod, "Sanitary and Phytosanitary Measures as Barriers to Trade for the Poor in Developing Countries: How Much Do We Know?"

Spencer Henson, "Strategic Perspective on the Impact of Food Safety Standards on Developing Country Exports"

Johan Swinnen, "Standards as Barriers and Catalysts for Trade and Poverty Reduction"

2. Advances in Spatial Economic Analysis for Agricultural Economists: Tools and Topics

Gerald C. Nelson, "Spatial Economic Analysis: An Introduction to Concepts, Methodologies and Data"

Garth Holloway, James LeSage, Donald Lacombe, "Spatial Econometrics Issues for Bio-Economic and Land Use Modeling"

Kathleen Bell, Timothy Dalton, "Spatial Economic Analysis in Data-Rich Environments"

Alex De Pinto, Gerald C. Nelson, "Modeling Deforestation and Land Use Change: Sparse Data Environments"

David S. Bullock, James Lowenburg-DeBoer, "Using Spatial Analysis to Study the Values of Variable Rate Technology and Information"

3. Agriculture, Nutrition, and Health in High and Low-Income Countries: Policy Issues

Per Pinstrup-Andersen, "Agricultural Research and Policy for Better Health and Nutrition"

Barry Popkin, "The Nutrition Transition in High and Low-Income Countries: What are the Policy Lessons?"

Ben Senauer, Masahiko Gemma, "Is Obesity a Result of Faulty Economics Policies? The Case of the United States and Japan"

Hans Binswanger, "Food and Agricultural Policy to Mitigate the Negative Consequences of HIV/AIDS"

4. Drought: Economic Consequences and Policies for Mitigation

Sushil Pandey, H. N. Bhandari, S. Ding, P. Prapertchob, R. Sharan, D. Naik, S. K. Taunk, Asras Sastri, "Coping with Drought in Asia: Insights from a Comparative Study"

Greg Hertzler, Ross Kingwell, Jason Crean, Chris Carter, "Managing and Sharing the Risks of Drought in Australia"

Madhur Gautam, "Managing Drought in Africa: Policy Perspectives"

Jock R. Anderson, "Global Overview"

5. Rural Industrial Clusters in Developing Countries

Yuichi Kimura, Tetsushi Sonobe, "Cluster-Based Rural Industrialization: The Case of Northern Vietnam"

Zuhui Huang, Xiaobo Zhang, Yunwei Zhu, "The Formation of Wenzhou Shoe Clusters: How the Entry Barriers Were Overcome"

Qiuqiong Huang, Scott Rozelle, Jikun Huang, Jinxia Wang, Dinghuan Hu, "Pump Clusters in China: Explaining the Organization of the Industry that Revolutionized Asian Agriculture"

Jianqing Ruan, Longbao Wei, Xiaobo Zhang, "Clusters as a Way to Lower Credit Barriers: The Case of Cashmere Sweater Industry in Tongxing, Zhejiang"

6. Land Productivity, Land Markets and Poverty Reduction in Africa

Sam Benin, Ephraim Nkonya, John Pender, Frank Place, "How Do Land Rental Markets Affect Efficiency and Sustainability of Land Use?"

Mintewab Bezabih, Stein Holden, "Tenure Insecurity, Transaction Costs in the Land Lease Market and their Implications for Gendered Productivity Differentials"

Klaus Deininger, Takashi Yamano, "Legal Knowledge and Economic Development: The Case of Land Rights in Uganda"

Alexander Sarris, Sara Savastano, Luc Christiaensen, "The Role of Agricultural Land Productivity in Reducing Poverty in Tanzania: A Household Perspective from Rural Kilimanjaro and Ruvuma"

Bart Minten, Claude Randrianarisoa, Chris Barrett, "Productivity in Malagasy Rice Systems: Wealth-differentiated Constraints and Priorities"

7. Access of African Farmers to Domestic and International Markets: Opportunities and Constraints

Marwan Soliman, "Access of Northern African Farmers to Domestic and International Markets: Opportunities and Constraints"

Kofi Yerfi Fosu, "Access of Western African Farmers to Domestic and International Markets: Opportunities and Constraints"

Godfrey Bahiigwa, "Access of Eastern African Farmers to Domestic and International Markets: Opportunities and Constraints"

Mohammad Karaan, "Access of Southern African Farmers to Domestic and International Markets: Opportunities and Constraints"

8. The Role of Economic Statistics in Agricultural Policy Shifts

Naman Keita, "A Developing Economy Perspective: Selected African Countries"

Eugenia Serova, "A Transition Economy Perspective: Russia"

Bruce Gardner, Barry Goodwin, Mary Ahearn, "A Developed Country Perspective: The U.S."

9. Market-Based Instruments: Policy and Information Issues

Nicola Lansdell, Gary Stoneham, "The Australian Market Based Instruments Program: Experience and Learning"

Richard Howitt, Siwa Msangi, "Income Distributional Effects of Using Market Based Instruments for Water Reallocation"

Mark Eigenraam, Craig Beverly, Loris Strappazzon, Nicola Lansdell, "Designing Frameworks to Deliver Unknown Information to Support Market Based Instruments"

Charlotte Duke, "Policy Applications of Experimental Economics: Asking the Right Questions"

10. Economics of Biofuels

Graham Love, "Meeting the Australian Government's Target of 350 Million Litres of Biofuels Produced from Renewable Resources by 2010"

Oliver Henniges, "Economics of Bioethanol Production—A View from Europe"

Vernon Eidman, "U.S. Agriculture's Role in Energy Production: Current Levels and Future Prospects"

Miguel Dabdoub, "Brazil's Fuel Ethanol Program: Reasons for Its Success"

11. Agricultural Trade Liberalization and Developing Countries: What Do We Really Know?

Hans van Meijl, Frank van Tongeren, "Multilateral Trade Liberalization and Developing Countries: A North-South Perspective on Agriculture and Processing Sector"

Jean-Christophe Bureau, Sebastian Jean, Alan Matthews, "The Consequences of Agricultural Trade Liberalization for Developing Countries"

Herve Guyomard, Chantal Le Mouel, "The Tariff-Only Import Regime for Bananas in the European Union: Setting the Tariff at Right Level Is Impossible Mission"

Klaus Frohberg, Ulrike Grote, Etti Winter, "EU Food Safety Standards, Traceability and Other Regulations: A Growing Trade Barrier to Developing Countries' Exports"

12. WTO and Asian Agriculture

Jin kyo Suh, "Agricultural Negotiation of DDA and Its Implications for East Asian Agricultural Trade"

Siming Wang, "China's Entry into WTO: Opportunity, Challenge and Strategy"

Masayoshi Honma, "WTO, FTA and Seeking Common Agricultural Policy in Asia"

Kaliappa Kalirajan, "WTO's Agreement on Agriculture (AA) and India's Agricultural Trade"

13. Using both Partial and General Equilibrium Analyses to Gain Insights into the Agricultural Trade Impacts of the Doha Development Agenda

Sebastien Hess, Stephan von Cramon, "General and Partial Equilibrium Simulations of Agricultural Trade: A Meta-Analysis"

Jason Grant, Thomas Hertel, Thomas Rutherford, "Extending General Equilibrium Analysis to the Tariff Line: U.S. Dairy in the Doha Development Agenda"

Jean-Christophe Bureau, Alexander Gohin, "Bridging Micro- and Macro-Analyses of the EU Sugar Program: Methods and Insights"

Hedi Bchir, Mustapha Sadni Jallab, Patrick Osakwe, Stephen N. Karingi, "The Doha Development Round and Africa: Partial and General Equilibrium Analyses of Tariff Preference Erosion"

Name Index

Subject Index